A map of the world

Name Dependent territories of Commonwealth states (in brackets) SCALE 1 : 88,000,000

Christina Nostitz 10F

Orange **Line**

Erweiterungskurs 6

Herausgeber: Frank Haß

Ernst Klett Verlag
Stuttgart • Leipzig

Orange Line 6 Erweiterungskurs

für Klasse 10 an allen differenzierenden Schulen

Im Auftrag des Verlags herausgegeben von:
Frank Haß, Kirchberg

Unter besonderer Mitwirkung von:
Harald Weisshaar, Bisingen

Erarbeitet von:
Holly De Marco, Cambridge; Elizabeth Rutledge, München

Unter besonderer Mitwirkung von:
Hamida Aziz, Tübingen; Sheila McBride, Stuttgart

Beratung:
Anette Christiani, Dortmund; Ulf Degen, Braunschweig; Ingrid Hartmann-Scheer, Kaarst; Margitta Kuty, Greifswald; Monika Teichmann, Wuppertal; Annegret Preker-Franke, Bielefeld

1. Auflage ISBN 978-547561-8 (fester Einband) 1 11 10 9 8 7 | 2021 20 19 18 17

1. Auflage ISBN 978-547661-5 (flexibler Einband) 1 11 10 9 8 7 | 2021 20 19 18 17

Alle Drucke dieser Auflage sind unverändert und können im Unterricht nebeneinander verwendet werden. Die letzte Zahl bezeichnet das Jahr des Druckes.

Internetadresse: www.klett.de

Redaktion: Claudia Handwerker; Cornelia Schaller, Lektorat editoria, Fellbach

Gestaltung: Sabine Kittel; Ulrike Wursthorn, Stuttgart
Illustrationen: Sylvia Wolf, Wiesbaden; Scivos/Klett Perthes (Karte Vorsatz vorne); Perthes World Atlas, 2nd Printing 2009, Revised, p. 78–79, Gotha 2006 (Karte Vorsatz hinten)
Umschlaggestaltung: Koma Amok, Stuttgart
Umschlagfoto: Avenue Images GmbH RF (Digital Vision), Hamburg
Reproduktion: Meyle + Müller, Medien-Management, Pforzheim
Druck: W.B. Druckerei GmbH, Hochheim am Main

Printed in Germany
ISBN 978-3-12-547561-8 (fester Einband)
ISBN 978-3-12-547661-5 (flexibler Einband)

9 783125 475618 9 783125 476615

Welcome back to Orange Line!

In Band 6 findet ihr viel Neues. Hier ein kurzer Überblick:

Die vier **Topics** (Kapitel) können in beliebiger Reihenfolge bearbeitet werden. Innerhalb jedes Topics gibt es obligatorische Teile und 3–4 **Options** (Themen zur Auswahl). Zu jeder Option gibt es **Tasks** (Aufgaben). Diese werden in einer Gruppe bearbeitet und schließen immer mit einer **Presentation** in der Klasse ab.
Ein Topic besteht aus:

Check-in	Einstimmung auf das Hauptthema anhand von Fotos
Aspects	Kurze Texte und Verständnisübungen
Options (x3 oder x4)	Texte, Übungen und Aufgaben
Check-out	Selbstüberprüfung
Test yourself!	Probeklassenarbeit

Zu dem **Topic**-Teil gehören vier Projektteile (E), die nicht obligatorisch sind. Das erste Projekt findest du nach Topic 2 (*An extract from a novel*). Weitere drei Projekte findest du nach Topic 4 (*People, pictures and images*; *The European Union*; *A short story*).

Nach den Topics und Projekten findest du folgende Teile:
Skills (Arbeitstechniken und Fertigkeiten), **Mediation and communication** (Sprachmittlung) und **Grammar** (Grammatik).
Der **Skills**-Teil beinhaltet Tipps zu Lern- und Arbeitstechniken und nützliche Ausdrücke. Bei manchen Übungen und Aufgaben innerhalb der Topics findest du Verweise auf diesen Teil. Weitere Übungen findest du in dem Teil **Mediation and communication**.
Im **Grammar**-Teil kannst du nachschlagen, wenn du dir unsicher bist, z. B. beim Verfassen von eigenen Texten.
In dem Teil **Overview** (Überblick) kannst du z. B. Aktiv und Passiv zusammengefasst anschauen.
Der Teil **Grammar practice** bietet darüber hinaus Übungen zu den Punkten im **Overview** an.

Am Ende des Buches findest du den Teil **Vocabulary** (Vokabelliste). Hier findest du nicht nur alle neuen Vokabeln, sondern auch Wortfeld- und Wortbildungsübungen sowie Kästen zu *Everyday English*. Das **Dictionary** (Wörterbuch) listet die Vokabeln alphabetisch auf. Es ist zum Nachschlagen gedacht.

Erläuterungen:

Let's talk	Lasst uns reden
Let's listen	Lasst uns zuhören
Work with a picture	Vorbereitung auf mündliche Prüfung
Task	Hauptaufgabe bei einer Option
Presentation/ Choose a presentation	Arbeitsergebnisse in der Klasse auswählen bzw. präsentieren

(CD-Symbol)	Übung auf CD
(1 Person)	Einzelarbeit
(2 Personen)	Partnerarbeit
(3 Personen)	Gruppenarbeit

Skills	1, 3, 6	Overview	Ov 3
Online-Link	⇨ 547561-0001	Skills aus Band 5	5

4 Topics

Maybe these photos and comments can help you to choose.

Topic 1 – A 'global' language

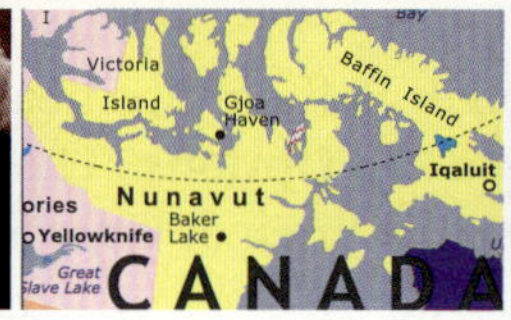

Is English the same all over the world?
What exactly is Hinglish?
How important is English, for example, in finding a job?

▶ If you choose Topic 1, you'll learn all about English.

Topic 2 – Living democracy – human rights

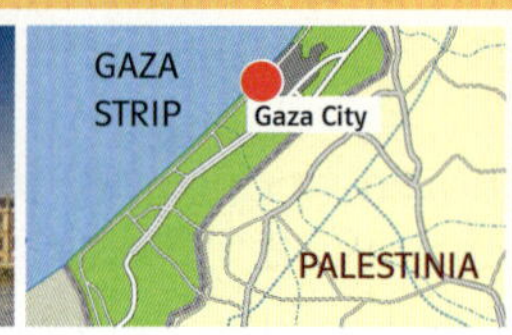

We all have rights, but where did they come from and how are they protected?

▶ In Topic 2 you can find out more about democracy in the past and today.

Topic 3 – Our world in our hands

There are lots of problems in the world but we can't expect others to solve them for us.

▶ Read more about these problems and how we can all help in Topic 3.

Topic 4 – Choices and decisions

At sixteen everyone has more rights but also more responsibilities.

▶ Topic 4 tells you more about 'life' decisions and how to make them.

Topic 1 A 'global' language

1 *International backpackers in the Canadian Rockies*

1. Work with a picture: Look at photo 1 and read the caption. What could the young people be saying? (→ p. 2/ex. 1)
2. Look at photos 2–5 and read the captions. Try to work out which language(s) the people might be speaking and say why you think this.
3. 1,1 Listen and match each dialogue with a photo.
4. Continue one dialogue. Share it with the class and vote to find the most interesting one.
5. Use the map at the front of your book and find where the five photos were taken. Find out more about one of these countries on the Internet (official languages, population, capital city …). Prepare a two-minute talk on it.

2

3

4

5

2 *Angela Merkel and China's Deputy Prime Minister, Zeng Peiyan, in China*

3 *Philipp Lahm joins a football game at an international school in South Africa*

4 *Shark alarm in Australia*

5 *A meeting of two media stars, 50 Cent and Thomas Gottschalk, in Germany*

A The common language

Eurofoot Summer Camps for girls and boys

in the UK, Canada, Germany, Asia, the Gulf States & South Africa

Eurofoot wants to give professional coaching to young football players (8–18) from all parts of the world. You won't share a mother tongue but you must share a passion for the game and the wish to improve your skills. Thanks to our sponsors we are able to offer three free places to talented young people who normally wouldn't be able to take part. Our fully-qualified coaches all used to be international players.

Although they're also multi-lingual, training sessions will be held in English. Each coach will train a group of up to twelve players and the groups will rotate. During coaching they will be assessed. Promising young players may be invited to go to trials for admission to an international football college!

For more information or to apply for a place at one of our camps, please click here: CAMP-INFO

→ Option 1

B Another sort of English

There are hundreds of books on the market today about English – its history, idioms and variations. Some will tell you how long it has been used as a lingua franca or that it is still the most important language in business, on the Internet and in technology. You can read that Japanese pilots speak to the tower at Tokyo airport in English. You will learn that most people who learn English as a second or foreign language make mistakes when they speak it or translate into it. And you can discover how they add their own words to create new forms of English. You may even use Denglisch (Deutsch – Englisch) e.g. *gemailt*, *chillen* yourself, but have you ever heard of Spanglish? It's spoken in many of the Spanish-speaking parts of the US. And what about Hinglish? This mixture of English with Hindi (e.g. a *pukka* meal), Punjabi and Urdu is spreading rapidly. At one time only people in Britain with an Asian background used to speak it but it is common now on the Indian sub-continent. If you want to find out more, we're sure you'll enjoy an interesting and fun book called **The Queen's Hinglish**, by B.K. Mahal.

→ Option 3

1 The language of sports 10, 14

a) *Imagine you have a cousin who is 15 and is crazy about football. Read the website page. Would this camp be interesting for him/her? Give reasons.*

b) *Read it again. What do you find out about the coaches and the training sessions?*

c) *You decide to find out more before you tell your cousin. You phone Eurofoot and ask 4–5 questions. Your partner answers the phone.*

2 New trends in English (→ p. 3/ex. 2)

a) *Before you read: List areas of life where English is important.*

b) *Read text B and add more areas.*

c) *Use the book cover and the text. Say where Hinglish is spoken and by whom.*

d) *Think of three more Denglisch words.*

e) *Think of two other 'languages' like Denglisch of which English is a part.*

 To do Topic 1 you'll need: Reported speech → Ov 4 • Modal substitutes → Ov 8 • 'used to' → Ov 7

C Languages in Canada

FACT BOX
- Canada has two official languages, English and French.
- 67.5% of Canadians speak only English.
- 85% of French speakers live in Quebec which is unilingual.
- New Brunswick is bilingual.
- In Northwest Territories 9 Aboriginal languages are official.
- The majority (and official) language in Nunavut is Inuktitut, spoken by the Inuit people*.
- Non-official languages (< 5 million) are Chinese, Italian, German and Punjabi.

1 *At Vancouver airport*
2 *In Winnipeg, Manitoba*
3 *In Nunavut*

*The term 'Eskimo' is no longer correct.

➜ Option 2

D Views on outsourcing

In recent years, to reduce costs many companies have 'outsourced' parts of their business. This means they have transferred them to a country where workers earn less. Some banks and public transport services have, for example, outsourced their call centres to India.
In a recent interview one critic said that call-centre customers had problems with foreign accents and that outsourcing led to local unemployment. Others felt it made products cheaper and provided more jobs for people worldwide. One manager even suggested that young people should 'outsource themselves' and look for work abroad.

➜ Option 4

3 Let's talk: Official languages

a) *You are doing a project on languages and find the fact box and the signs on the Net. Read the fact box and say which languages are used in the signs.*

b) *Use the map of Canada at the back of your book and choose one state or territory from the fact box. Compare its language policy with the policy in your country. Use the Internet.*

4 Let's listen: Wrong messages 12 7 (→ p. 3/ex. 3)

1, 2

a) *Before you listen: Read text D. Find arguments for and against outsourcing.*

b) *Now explain the cartoon. What do you think the girl wants to do and why? Explain her dad's answer.*

c) *Listen. Which service is each customer calling? Which do you think is outsourced? Why?*

A world language

A

EUROFOOT WEBZINE

Coach's Report – From our camp in Germany

No. 7

Some parents used to worry about their kids' English. They thought that it wasn't good enough. They wouldn't be able to understand us or talk to the other kids. But you don't get that impression these days. As coaches we must all be able to speak a couple of foreign languages but we hardly ever need to use them now. The kids all seem to use English. Maybe they don't want to be different. Whatever the reason, English certainly does help to bring us all together. We decided to give future participants and their parents an idea of how this works. So we talked to some kids from this year's camp. We asked them about English in their lives, both in their home country and during their stay with us.

Get more information here!

Hi, there. I'm Andrea Ziebarth from Vancouver, Canada. English and French are official languages there. I'm at a 'French immersion' school (we mostly speak French there), so I'm sort of bilingual. That makes life easier for me here! It must be hard for kids who find languages difficult ... German?! No, I'm hopeless at German – even though my dad's parents were from Hamburg! In fact, that's where my cousin Ina is from. She's here, too. Her English is sort of OK, but her football is awesome! I think she'll be on the German women's team one day. ...

Hi, my name is John Dhlomo and I'm from Cape Town, South Africa. I grew up speaking Zulu and English. I was really lucky: I got a scholarship to come here! When I arrived, I was worried because I couldn't speak a word of German. But everyone at camp speaks English – even though we all sound very different! Jakob Veit, my new mate, is teaching me some German: That's 'echt toll'! ...

Get more information here!

Get more information here!

Hi, my name is Jakob Veit. I'm German so I usually speak that when I play football. I was really surprised when the coaches spoke English to us. English is my worst subject. I know this is an international camp but we're in Germany!! But I think I'm managing OK. Well, words like 'foul', 'offside' or a 'header' are no problem, they're international now, I guess. But in the first week, when I wanted to make friends, it was hard. Maybe I should spend more time on my English and less on football! ...

Hello, I'm Faye Jiayi from Hong Kong. Chinese (Cantonese) and English are our official languages. I think both are really important today, especially for big companies. Andrea is from Vancouver, Canada. We were talking last week about world languages and she said that signs at the airport there weren't just in French and English – they were in Chinese, too! I just couldn't believe it! Nobody here speaks Chinese, so I'm glad I can speak English as well. ...

Get more information here!

B English: Facts and figures

Did you know?

- English is the most widespread (spoken and written) language in the world.
- English was brought to every corner of the world by explorers like Captain Cook, traders like the East India Company and settlers like those on the First Fleet.
- In former British colonies like Australia, the US, Canada and India English has remained the official language.
- It is the language of communication in all 54 countries of the Commonwealth (former colonies).
- English is the official language in more than 55 countries including the UK and Ireland.
- English is an official language in many African countries. In South Africa, for example, English is one of its 11 official languages.
- Over 340 million people have English as their mother tongue (Chinese: 1,210 million; Hindi: 366 million; Spanish: 358 million).
- Over 700 million people speak English as a foreign language.
- Of all the world's languages, English is the richest in vocabulary (*Oxford English Dictionary*: > 600,000 words).
- The longest word in the English language is a lung disease called pneumonoultramicroscopicsilicovolcanokoniosis.
- The shortest full sentence in English is: Go.
- Pilots on international flights must use English. (*See the map at the front of your book for more information.*)

Task: To learn about the role of English in different countries

1 An international camp

a) *Before you read: In which situations could English be useful to you in your country? Make a list and compare it with your partner's ideas.*

b) *Read lines 1–7 of text A. Where is the camp? What language do the coaches there speak? What about the kids?*

1,3 2 Let's listen: Eurofoot kids 12 (→ p. 4/ex. 4–6)

a) *Before you listen: Read what Andrea, John, Jakob and Faye say and write notes on where they're from, what language(s) they're able to speak and who their friends are.*

b) *Listen to the podcast. What else do you find out about the four young people?*

c) *Write a short text about a situation in which you had to use English (e.g. on holiday, at the airport, etc.).*

3 A list of facts (→ p. 5/ex. 7, 8)

a) *Read text B and agree on the most interesting fact.*

b) *Write it on a card with the number 1. Write the other facts on cards and agree how to number them (2–12).*

c) *Write multiple-choice questions about each fact.*

4 Choose a presentation 2, 9 20 (→ p. 5/ex. 9)

1. *A talk: Use part A to make a poster showing the four footballers. You can draw them or use photos. Add their names, countries and the languages they speak. You can invent some facts about their coach and add them, too. Use your poster to give a talk on how English helps international communication.*
   OR
2. *Display your cards from Ex. 3 and use your questions to do a quiz. The others do a gallery walk and read the cards. Then you ask your questions.*

Student of the month!

A An interview

Every month Seaview Secondary in Vancouver chooses a 'student of the month'. One of their website team is interviewing this month's winner, Sean Martin (16). Like many Canadians he has moved around a lot, but that isn't why he was chosen. Sean has an interesting hobby. Read Wai King's interview to learn about his background and his special talent:

Wai Hi, Sean. Or should I say Jean?

Sean Erm! I don't mind. Sean's my real name. It's Irish. But my mum prefers 'Jean' – she thinks it sounds better, but that's 'cause she's half-French.

Wai Oh, so it's the same name in both languages – how neat! French-Irish? Does that mean you're from Quebec?

Sean No, Mum is actually directly from France and my dad is Irish. We emigrated when I was six.

Wai So you must be bilingual, right? Have you been able to use both languages in Canada?

Sean Yeah! In Ireland we usually spoke English at home, but I had to speak French at school in Montreal. Then we had to move again when I was ten because Dad got a job in Medicine Hat, Alberta. My elementary school and my junior high school in Medicine Hat were both 'French immersion', so all lessons were in French.

Wai Did you like living in Medicine Hat?

Sean No, not really. Small town life is boring, I guess, when you've lived in a big city like Montreal. And I sort of missed my friends there.

Wai But you started your hobby in Medicine Hat, didn't you? How did that happen?

Sean Well, I've always loved mangas. And I like drawing. I used to copy the pictures when I was younger. But that got boring, so I started to do my own manga characters and storyboards.

Wai Did you join the school Art Club there?

Sean No, it was for indigenous art, but I was only interested in animé. So I joined an Internet forum.

Wai Did that give you the idea for an animé club?

Sean No. It was the Vancouver artist Mei Yu – I worked with one of her animé art instruction books. That gave me the 'club' idea.

Wai And did you set one up in Medicine Hat, then?

Sean No! We moved again before I was able to do anything – to British Columbia. I hoped there'd be an animé club here at Seaview Secondary. But, as you know, there wasn't.

Wai So you decided to start one! Tell us about that.

Sean Well, I designed a poster for the club, scanned it for our school website and added a link to my old art forum. I was amazed how many kids were interested. We've now got 120 members.

Wai And you all go to the school club?!

Sean No, most of us exchange our work and ideas online. But I would say about 15–20 come to the club session each week. That way we learn new techniques from each other. ...

Wai Well, thanks for the interview, Sean – and keep up the good work!

 To do Topic 1 you'll need: Reported speech → Ov 4 • Modal substitutes → Ov 8 • 'used to' → Ov 7

⇨ 547561-0001

B A 'KRAZY' exhibition

A Day in the Delirious World of Animé …

by Sean Martin (founded Animé Club)

Many kids read comics and watch animé on TV or DVDs. But they never stop to think how they are made. 'THE KRAZY! THE DELIRIOUS WORLD OF ANIMÉ + COMICS + VIDEO GAMES + ART' is your chance to find out! It's the first exhibition of its kind. You can learn how this art has developed since the last century. It shows examples of first drawings and notes through to final production, including 3D models. What is really fascinating is to see how computer technology has changed animé. And to learn how Japanese works have influenced Western animation. This exhibition in Vancouver shows you how famous artists of this style and technique think and work today. A real must for all comic and animé lovers (and future artists!). Even if you're not into animé, it's still an exciting experience with lots to see, to think about – and to watch!

Task: To do an interesting interview

1 Preparing an interview 14

a) *Read the introduction to text A and think of 5–6 questions which you could ask Sean.*

b) *How should you conduct an interview? Start a list. Write down 3 or 4 important points.*

2 Wai's interview (→ p. 6/ex. 10, 11)

a) *Read lines 8–16 and complete these sentences:*
1. First Wai wanted to know if … .
2. Sean told her that … .
3. Then she asked if … .
4. Sean said that … .

b) *What else did Sean tell her in the interview?* He told her that … .

c) *Check Wai's interview techniques (beginning, ending, way of asking, …). Add any new techniques to your list from 1 b).*

3 Let's listen: All about 'Krazy' 12 (→ p. 7/ex. 12, 13)

1, 4

a) *Before you listen: Look at the poster in part B. Say why you would/n't like to visit the exhibition.*

b) *Look at Wai's notes and read the review (text B). Write Wai's last questions and Sean's answers.*

Went to see exhibition where? • Good or bad? • Saw what? • Most fascinating things?

c) *Listen. Compare your version with the recorded interview and improve your version.*

d) *Write a profile for Sean on the computer.*

4 Presentation: An interview 19 (→ p. 7/ex. 14)

a) *Write a list of good interview techniques and give it to the others in the class.*

b) *Each couple in your option group uses their profile from Ex. 3, prepares an interview with Sean and conducts it in class.*

c) *The class uses the list of techniques to decide which interview was best and why.*

d) *The class votes for the best interview.*

The changing face of English

A A magazine for learners of English

Time to get yourself a pukka English dictionary?

If you'd overheard these two kids in England, you'd probably have thought they were speaking a strange foreign language. But it's English, slang of course, and an example of 'language fusion'.
OK, it's a bit exaggerated. But, it's not unlike some of the English spoken in parts of London today.
So let's take a closer look at it. We immediately realise that they don't think much of **mouse potatoes**! But still, this phrase itself is perhaps a good point to begin with:
Couch potato is a fairly new English (and also German!) expression which clearly didn't exist before television was invented. And for you computer-age kids, who use terms such as blog and e-mail daily, the meaning of mouse potato won't be too difficult to guess. But soon even this word will become 'uncool' and with a **doubleclick** the term mouse potato will be replaced by the even newer word **screenager**.

There are other words in the teenagers' exchange which may offer clues to further language influences – words like **whaassuuup**, **thug** and **bling**. These, as some may realise, are words borrowed from the music and lifestyle of hip hop. Along with words like **homie**, **hood**, **wannabe** and **gangsta** they belong to a long list of hip hopper expressions that are now common in everyday English.
Whaassuuup is just a slang form of 'What's up?' which today doesn't usually mean 'What's new?', but just 'Hello!'.
And the word thug (BE = someone who beats people up) came into English from Hindi. It was the word for members of a religious organisation of assassins in India! It is also used to insult young Blacks, especially in the US. Now, among hip hoppers, it means someone who is streetwise, tough and 'the real thing'. Some bits in the dialogue above are just shorter words (like **ya** for 'you' or 'your') or they're spoken differently (e.g. **dat** for 'that'). But what about **pukka** and **chuddies?**
These and many other words such as **achha**, **desi**, **mela**, **masala**, **balti** and **bhangra** are in fact examples of 'Hinglish': They come from Hindi, Urdu or Punjabi and are spreading across Britain via television, (multi)cultural events, Bollywood films and an interest in Indian food.
So, you can pick out three main influences on the young people's choice of words: computer language, hip hop culture and popular Hinglish expressions. The next time you catch bits of colourful conversation which you don't understand, remember: It could be English. And it might just be time for you to get yourself a pukka English dictionary, innit?!

Hello! Have you been at your computer all day, or something? – No, I'm a first class person who is streetwise: showing my pants and jewellery and so on, aren't I? – Oh, really?

 To do Topic 1 you'll need: Reported speech → Ov 4 • Modal substitutes → Ov 8 • 'used to' → Ov 7

B Word box

Hinglish

balti ['bɔ:lti] curry served in a special pot
bhangra ['bæŋgrə] Punjabi folk music/dance
chutney ['tʃʌtni] spicy, sweet and sour mixture, e.g. made with fruit, tomatoes; a bit like 'salsa'
desi ['desɪ] local, real Asian
masala [mə'sɑ:lʌ] spices *(Gewürze)*
mela ['mi:lʌ] traditional festival; also in big cities in UK (1) + (2)
thali ['θɑ:li] rice, curry, naan (bread), chutney, yoghurt, etc. served in little metal bowls on a tray *(Tablett)*
tikka ['tikʌ] meat in spicy mixture

A 'traditional' mela in India

A 'mela' in London

Task: To find out about new words in English

1 Teenage chat

a) *Before you read: Guess what language the kids in the photo are speaking. Look for words you already know.*

b) *Skim text A and translate their dialogue into English. Check at the bottom of the page. Did you get everything right?*

2 All about words 1, 2 (→ p. 8/ex. 15, 16)

a) *Read the text again: Explain the term 'language fusion'.*

b) *Collect new English words from the article under the headings Computer and Hip hop. Add any meanings that you know.*

1,5 3 Let's listen: Yoghurt versus masala? 12
(→ p. 9/ex. 17)

a) *Before you listen: With the help of text B collect the Hinglish words in text A and explain them to your partner.*

b) *Listen. One of the teenagers, Raj, goes to the Indian snack bar 'Masala House' with his friend, Drew, from the US. What does the American decide to eat? Why?*

4 Presentation: A 'dictionary' quiz 1, 2
(→ p. 9/ex. 18, 19)

a) *The option group (experts) makes three posters (computer, Hinglish or hip hop) with words, phonetics and meanings.*

b) *The class does a gallery walk. Each student tries to remember 3 or 4 words.*

c) *The 'experts' challenge the class. One of them reads out a new word. Someone from the class has to decide if it's a Hinglish, computer or hip hop word and then has to explain its meaning.*

Widen your horizons

When David MacDonald was asked to give a talk on his career to some pupils from his old school, he started thinking about what had helped him.

One thing was clear: Outside the UK his biggest asset had been having English as his native language. But other things like his colleagues were important, too. He showed his own and their profiles during his presentation.

Ali Hassan

Education: 6 GCSEs (English, Maths, Science, Computers, French, Art) + 2 A-levels (Computers, Maths)

Job experience: 4 years in customer services department of insurance company

Present position: Section leader

Special skills: Selling, computers, English

Personality: Reliable, trustworthy, independent

Strengths: I can sell things (even my ideas), computer skills, good English, I'm mobile, teaching qualification

Weaknesses: I'm scared of spiders, I can't speak Chinese

Family: Parents in Manchester, three younger brothers and two older sisters

My dream: To spend a few years in Asia

In the next 12 months: I see myself in my own business

One more thing I would like people to know about me: I teach disabled kids to swim

Mia Wang

Education: 6 GCSEs (Maths, English, Music, Chinese, Geography, Computers) + 3 A-levels (Maths, Chinese, English)

Job experience: 2 years in insurance company

Present position: Personal assistant

Special skills: Computers, languages, organizing

Personality: Outgoing, conscientious, creative

Strengths: I stay calm in most situations, I'm a good organizer, good Chinese, I'm mobile

Weaknesses: I have no teaching qualification, chocolate ice-cream, I hate lifts

Family: Parents divorced, I'm an only child

My dream: To be the first woman on Mars

In the next 12 months: I would like to change my career and move abroad

One more thing I would like people to know about me: I like driving fast cars

➪ 547561-0002

David MacDonald

Education: 5 GCSEs (English, Maths, Computers, French, Geography)

Job experience: 6 years in customer services department of insurance company

Present position: Insurance consultant

Special skills: Computers, communicating, selling

Strengths: I'm not afraid of hard work, I can explain things, good at languages, mobile

Weaknesses: I have no teaching qualification, I can't speak Chinese, I'm a bit chaotic

Family: Parents in Salisbury, one older brother

My dream: To have my own office with a leather sofa

In the next 12 months: I would like to find a really exciting job

One more thing I would like people to know about me: I love Chinese opera

Guess why my nickname was 'Curly'!

Task: To look at how you can present yourself to an employer

1 Before you read: Strengths and weaknesses

a) *Think: What strengths and weaknesses do you have? Write a short list for each.*

b) *Pair: What does your partner think? Ask him/her to check your lists.*

c) *Share: Who has a special strength or talent? What is it? In which job could it be useful?*

2 Let's listen: We outsourced ourselves! (→ p. 10/ex. 20)

1, 6–8

a) *Listen to the first part of David's talk. What did he ask the kids to do? (2 things)*

b) *Listen to the second part. What was his idea and what role did English play in it?*

c) *Listen to the third part. Name three things that he said he did to become successful.*

d) *Listen to the third part again. What did he advise the kids to do?*

3 Who am I? 15 (→ p. 10/ex. 21, 22)

a) *Read the three profiles and then write your own profile on the computer. Exchange it with a partner.*

b) *Give feedback but don't be hurtful.*

c) *Name one thing your partner could improve in the next 12 months.*

4 Presentation: A discussion 11, 13 (→ p. 11/ex. 23, 24)

Split the group:

a) *One half uses their answers to Ex. 2 and writes a report (100–120 words) on David's talk. Give the others in the class a copy to read.*

b) *The other half uses David's profile to tell the class more about him.*

c) *Hold a discussion: The class compares the two sources of information from a) and b) and says which they think would be more useful to an employer and why.*

OPTION 1

✔ … explain the role of English in the world.

a) *Explain these language terms:* multi-lingual • mother tongue • official language • bilingual • foreign language • world language

b) *Name three situations in your country in which you might have to use English.*

✔ … talk about what you used to do. Ov7

Matt, a famous footballer, is talking about what he used to do. Use the phrases and try to reconstruct what he says. Example: My friends and I **used to** play in a field.

friends/field • stay there/get dark • kick ball/river • jump in/get wet • parents/go crazy, lock/bedroom • take away/ball • hide/football • climb out/window • play/street

✔ … present facts and figures about the English language.

a) *Correct these statements about English.*
1. Over 700 people speak it as a foreign language.
2. Captain Cook was a settler on the First Fleet.
3. Its shortest sentence is: Grow!
4. It's the official language in 55 countries.
5. Its longest word has 43 letters.
6. International pilots sometimes use it.

b) *Name five countries where English is the or an official language. Explain why.*

OPTION 2

✔ … talk about the languages spoken in Canada.

a) *Which two languages are official everywhere in Canada? Make one sentence about each.*

b) *What do you know about Inuktitut?*

c) *What are Canada's four non-official languages?*

✔ … talk about past experiences in Canada. Ov2, Ov3, Ov7

Use 'simple past' or 'used to' and complete the text about Sean.

Sean … *(to live)* in Ireland but now he lives in Canada. He … *(to emigrate)* with his parents when he … *(to be)* six. They … *(to live)* in Montreal but now they live in Vancouver. Sean … *(to go)* to a French school when he was six and he … *(to speak)* French there most of the time. When he … *(to be)* ten, the family … *(to move)* to Alberta. In Medicine Hat he … *(to moan)* that he … *(to find)* town life boring. He often … *(to read)* comics and he … *(to spend)* time at weekends drawing. Later he … *(to get)* the idea for a club from art books that he … *(to read)* after school.

✔ … discuss mangas.

Describe a manga which you know. Say why you like or don't like it.

✔ … write a profile.

Collect ideas in a mind map and then write a profile for someone you know.

✔ … prepare for an interview.

Name four good interview techniques.

OPTION 3

✔ … describe new trends in English.

a) *Where are these forms of English spoken: Spanglish? Denglisch? Hinglish?*

b) *What Denglisch words do you and your friends use? (5–6 words)*

✔ … understand teenage chat.

a) *What would these words be in the Queen's English?*
mela • mouse potato • pukka • chuddies • innit • bling • desi • Na • homie • thug • bhangra

b) *Choose the right answer. What should you reply if someone asks:*

1. Whaassuuup, man?	a. Nothing's up.	b. Fine!	c. Hi!
2. Dat ya homie?	a. Yes, that's my home.	b. No, he's my brother.	c. No, I'm at school.
3. Ya bina desi?	a. No. I'm German.	b. Yes. I'm late.	c. No. I'm Paul.

✔ … explain a Hinglish menu.

You and your parents are in an Indian restaurant. You can have thali with chutney or balti with lots of masala and naan or tikka. Explain each of the Hinglish words so that your parents can understand.

OPTION 4

✔ … talk about rules at work. Ov 8

Imagine you talked to these people about their jobs. What did they say that they had to/weren't allowed to do?

1

2

3

4

✔ … report on what different people said about their jobs. Ov 4, Ov 8

Imagine the four people in the photos visited your school. Who said/asked what?
1. I have to work a lot in the holidays and at weekends but I love my job.
2. Would anyone like to put on my helmet? OK, why do you think I call it my "life saver"?
3. My job is always interesting but night shifts can be hard.
4. Can you imagine what a big fire is really like? I was really scared the first time.

Start like this: 1. I think the teachter said that she had to … .

✔ … present yourself at a job interview.

a) *Imagine you are in an interview for a job. Talk about yourself (education, experience, family, …).*

b) *Say why you think you should get the job (skills, strengths, personality, …).*

(→ p. 12/ex. 25; p. 13/ex. 26)

The latest[2] fashion in sunglasses in Nunavut

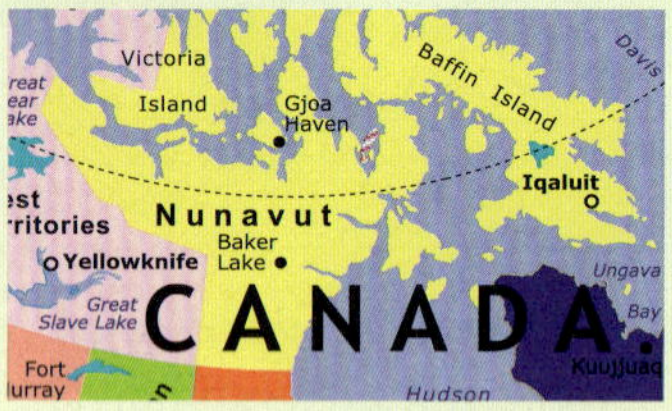

OUR LANGUAGE, OUR SELVES[1] (→ pp. 14–16)

Speaking a foreign language means more than translating words: You need to know something about the culture behind the foreign language. Just as an example, try to find an English word for the German word 'Kehrwoche'. The idea of sweeping[3] the street in front of your house is totally unknown in Britain. You would have to explain the word instead of translating it. If problems like this exist between two neighbouring countries in Europe, imagine what it's like trying to translate something from a language like Inuktitut (the language of the Inuit) into English.

In English, and in most other European languages, a sentence is a string of beads[4]. Each bead is a tiny little word, and the beads in a row have a meaning: I am happy to be here. – *Je suis content d'être ici.* – Yo estoy contento de estar aquí. But in Inuktitut the words are like Lego™ blocks, pieces locked together to produce a bigger block of meaning:
quviasuktunga tamaaniinnama (= *happy + I here + in + be + because I*)
Pariliarumaniralauqsimanngittunga (= *I never said I wanted to go to Paris*).
The following text is adapted from an article about this problem.

The Inuit have a word inuusiq. It comes from the word for person, inuk, and means something like 'the way of being a person'. An English speaker would say 'way of life'. We Inuits say the same thing in a different way, so does this mean that we are different? To put it another way: Is there a link between the language I speak and the person I am?
Some years ago Alexina Kublu applied for a job with an Inuit organization. After she had written her profile in English, she thought, "But this is an Inuit organization. If the person who reads this is an Inuk, what will he think of it, and of me?" So she translated it into Inuktitut, but then it sounded arrogant and cold. So she wrote it again, this time in Inuktitut and it came out fine. When she translated it back into English, the English version was strange and inexact!
Studies have suggested that many bilingual people swap their personalities (or, shall we say, their cultures?) as they swap their language.
So there **is** a link. …
But languages change, so, do the people who speak Inuktitut change with it?
Inuktitut has changed very little in the last century. It is alive and well – not only in Canada but in a good part of the Arctic world. Alexina Kublu can talk quite easily with Greenlanders, for example, and if she found herself in northern Alaska, which is much further away, she'd be able to do the same after about a week.
Kublu says, "I consider myself closer to my parents. Nobody has the same lifestyle that my parents had; like me, all Inuit of my generation hold the same values[5] that their parents had, though they don't always see life around them the same way. I will always be closer to my parents than to my white colleagues because a parent/child relationship[6] is a fixed and permanent part of one's personality while one's professional relationship with colleagues can be adjusted[7] and is temporary."

LANGUAGES IN NUNAVUT

- The Inuit, the indigenous[8] people of the region – which is over 2 million km² in size – have been there for thousands of years. Today they form about 80% of the population.
- Inuktitut is the largest language group in the region. It is spoken by about 70% of the 26,000 people there. The language has different dialects.
- English is spoken by just over 20% of the population.
- Nunavut's capital, Iqaluit, also has a big French-speaking community.

[1]self [self] – *hier: Identität,* [2]latest ['leɪtɪst] – *neueste/r/s,* [3]to sweep [swi:p] – *kehren,* [4]bead [bi:d] – *Perle,* [5]value ['vælju:] – *Wert,* [6]relationship [rɪ'leɪʃnʃɪp] – *Beziehung,* [7]to adjust [ə'dʒʌst] – *anpassen,* [8]indigenous [ɪn'dɪdʒɪnəs] – *einheimisch, eingeboren*

A Reading

1 Before you read: Find these words in the text and make sure that you understand what they mean in it.

block (l. 12) • arrogant (l. 30) • version (l. 32) • inexact (l. 33) • personality (l. 35) • generation (l. 49) • colleague (l. 53) • fixed (l. 54) • dialect (info box)

2 Skim the text and find out about …

a. … the main difference between Inuktitut and most European languages.
b. … Alexina Kublu: the languages she speaks and the problem she had.
c. … changes in the Inuit language.
d. … languages in Nunavut. *(3 things)*

3 Read the text again and complete the sentences.

a. Kublu wrote her profile because she … .
b. When she translated it into Inuktitut, it sounded … .
c. When she translated it back into English, her profile then sounded … .
d. Studies on bilingual people suggest that there is a link between … .
e. With her language 'Inuktitut' Alexina Kublu can easily or quickly speak to … .

B Language

Copy the grid and use the text to complete it.

Place/Country	Capital	People	Language
		Inuit	
			German
Britain			
	Paris		

C Listening

1,9

1 Listen. Kirima, a young Inuit woman, is giving a talk. Does she tell her audience about …

a. … an Inuit monster from space? b. … Inuit myths? c. … an Inuit language?

2 Listen again to part A. Find the right words to complete these sentences.

a. Traditional stories warn about …
1 … living in Canada. 2 … Inuit traditions. 3 … dangers to the environment.

b. In the past the stories helped …
1 … the whole world. 2 … the Inuit people. 3 … Canada.

c. If an animal was killed they believed …
1 … it could hunt[1] its killer. 2 … its spirit died. 3 … it became a person.

3 Listen again to part B.

a. What did other bad spirits do? *(2 things)*
b. How could some people help if the spirits were angry? *(2 things)*

[1]to hunt [hʌnt] – *jagen*

D Speaking

A dog race

A skidoo

A modern house in Iqaluit

An igloo

1 Describing

a. What are the people doing in photos 1 and 2? Which activity would you prefer to do? Why?

b. Compare the two houses in photos 3 and 4. Which would you rather live in and why?

2 Discussing

One of you thinks of some disadvantages of living in an Arctic region. The other collects some advantages (and examples of how modern technology could make life easier there). Discuss them.

3 Role play

You find a link to the website of a youth club in Iqaluit, Nunavut. You'd like to find out about young people's activities there. You call the number on the website via the Internet.

You: *(Sage deinen Namen, wo du lebst und dass du auch Zeit im Jugendzentrum verbringst. Erzähle, warum du anrufst.)*

Doug: Hi there! I'm Doug. Well, our most popular activity is our disco every Saturday evening. But after school we play table-tennis and soccer or use the computers. What about your club?

You: *(Sage, dass du auch ins Jugendzentrum gehst, um Freunde zu treffen und manchmal zur Kinonacht.)*

Doug: Oh, yes, we show films, too – but not in the summer because there's summer camp then.

You: *(Sage, dass es bei euch kein Sommercamp gibt. Erkläre, dass aber viele Jugendzentren besondere Sommerevents veranstalten – zum Beispiel Musikfestivals oder Workshops.)*

Doug: Our community festival is in spring. My friends and I help to organize it.

You: *(Frage, was für eine Veranstaltung das ist und wie lang sie dauert.)*

Doug: We celebrate[1] the start of spring for a whole week with igloo building competitions, skidoo or dog team races and Inuit games.

You: *(Frage, ob man heute noch in Iglus lebt. Du würdest gerne lernen, wie man ein Iglu baut!)*

Doug: Yes, people still use them on hunting trips. I can't build an igloo, but I came third in the skidoo race last year!

You: *(Drücke dein Erstaunen aus und frage, ob es Fotos vom Rennen gibt. Biete einen Austausch per E-Mail an.)* …

Doug: Yes. Lots! That's a great idea! Then you can send us photos, too. Our e-mail address is …

[1]to celebrate ['seləbreɪt] – *feiern*

E Mediation and communication

Your older cousin is very interested in Inuit culture but her English isn't very good. So she sends you an e-mail with this article from the Internet. Read the text and answer her questions.

An Inuit myth: Mother-god of the underworld

There are many different names for the Inuit mother-god and many different stories of how she became Sanna, goddess[1] of the sea. Here is one version:

Down at the bottom of the cold, dark sea lived Anguta, 'God of the Dead'. He had a huge daughter called Avilayoq. She was so huge that she looked a bit like an overwhelming mermaid[2]. But she was also very beautiful. Her Inuktitut name was Sanna and she was always hungry. She ate and ate until there was nothing left in their home and her parents were always out looking for more food.

When she was older, her father wanted her to marry. But she didn't think that any of the men he had suggested were good enough for her.

One day Avilayoq said 'no' to Anguta once again. He was absolutely furious by now, but he showed no response. Instead, he took his daughter out in his kayak with him. When they were out at sea, he threw her into the water. However[3], Avilayoq held on to the side of the kayak.

Anguta got even angrier. He took out his knife and cut off his daughter's fingers, one by one. As they fell into the sea, they became different kinds of fish, or seals and swam away. Finally Avilayoq couldn't hold on any more. Down, down, down she went – down into Adlivun, the underworld. There Avilayoq became Sanna, the great mother-god of all sea creatures.

Now, it was said that if anyone broke society's or nature's laws, it made Sanna very angry. She would lock away all her sea creatures as punishment. Then, of course, the Inuit would return from hunting, hungry and empty-handed. And without food people would start to die. When this happened to the Inuit, it came like a dark cloud of death, they offered prayers and dance to her and promised to improve. As a result Sanna was kind to them: She forgave them and brought back the balance in nature.

a. Sanna war doch eine Göttin, aber was für eine?
b. Wie lebte sie, bevor sie Göttin wurde?
c. Wie sah sie aus?
d. Wie wurde sie zur Göttin?
e. Was für eine Macht hatte sie als Göttin?
f. Wie wirkte sich das bei den Inuit aus?

F Writing

1 Skills

Imagine you have to write an article for the Iqaluit Youth Club webzine about activities in your area/school/club. Collect ideas about how students with different cultural backgrounds spend their free-time. Think, too, about differences between boys and girls. Is there a link between culture and activities?

2 Writing

Use your ideas and write a short article (70 – 80 words).

[1]goddess ['gɒdes] – *Göttin,* [2]mermaid ['mɜːmeɪd] – *Meerjungfrau,* [3]however [haʊ'evə] – *jedoch*

Topic 2 Living democracy – human rights

1 *South Africa: One woman, one vote*

1. Work with the picture: Think of situations where you can or can't vote for something or someone. Use the caption to talk about what the woman in photo 1 is doing. (→ p. 17/ex. 1, 2)

2. Match each of the small pictures a – e with one of these sentences.

All member states promise to allow freedom of the press. • The Bill of Rights gives every citizen the right to carry arms. • The new constitution allows any citizen who is 18 or over to vote in public elections. • This charter was the first to give citizens the right to a fair trial in a court of law. • One of the jobs of the police is to protect people's rights e. g. to express an opinion in public.

a *King John signs Magna Carta*
b *British policeman's helmet*
c *Text from the Bill of Rights*
d *Nelson Mandela*
e *UN symbol*

3. Look at photos 2 – 5. Say what strikes you and decide which right they are using.

4. One of these rights is not a basic human right: Say which you think it is and why. Check the list of rights on online page 0003. (→ p. 17/ex. 3)

2 *Speaker at Speaker's Corner in London*
3 *TV journalists on the Israel-Lebanon border*
4 *Child with gun in Texas*
5 *Inside a court of law in Australia*

⇨ 547561-0003

A Some strange laws

Many laws are made to protect us and our rights, but did you know that …

- § … women in Vermont must get permission from their husbands to wear false teeth?
- § … in Alabama it is illegal for a driver to be blindfolded while driving?
- § … in England no Member of Parliament (MP) may enter the House of Commons in a full suit of armour?
- § … all Englishmen over the age of 14 must do two hours of long bow practice a day?
- § … in London, it is illegal to get into a taxi if you have the plague?
- § … it is legal to murder a Scottish person inside the ancient city walls of York, but only if he is carrying a bow and arrow?
- § … you are breaking the law if you die in the Houses of Parliament?
- § … it is treason to use a stamp showing the British monarch upside down?

These are very old laws, of course. It's difficult to say whose rights they were trying to protect. We no longer need them, but it would take a lot of time and money to get rid of them.

➔ Option 2

B The Middle Ages in England (1066–1485)

The Middle Ages probably mean knights on horses and beautiful ladies in castles to many of you. But most people at this time weren't either of these. If you had lived then, most probably you wouldn't have been a knight or a lady. You would probably have been a serf – the lowest class of all. As a serf you would have lived in a hut and you wouldn't have had much to eat. You certainly wouldn't have owned a horse! Even servants had a higher social position. Just above them came soldiers and freemen. Then came knights who were below barons and bishops. The king was at the top. Most of the land in England was owned by him. He gave parts of it to loyal barons or knights who then became richer and more powerful. Serfs belonged with the land. They had to work on it and give their land owner everything they produced on it. They were given a small field so that they could feed themselves and their family. The only right they had was to be protected by their owner.

➔ Option 1

1 Old laws for old rights 7

a) *Read text A. Choose the law which you find strangest. Put the laws in order with the strangest one at the top.*

b) *Whose rights do you think the strangest law was trying to protect? Invent a story behind it.*

c) *Tell your story to the group. The group then votes to find the best story.*

2 Let's talk: The lowest class (→ p. 18/ex. 4)

a) *Read text B. Make a pyramid of society in the Middle Ages. Which group would you probably have belonged to?*

b) *What do you think you would have missed most if you had lived then? Think especially about the rights that you have today. Discuss with a partner.*

C Freedom of the press

British journalist kidnapped in Gaza City

BBC "seriously worried"
Yesterday a British journalist was kidnapped by members of a militant group in the Gaza Strip. The Palestinian police say armed men followed Alan Johnston from his office and took him hostage just outside his apartment. They found his car and papers later at the scene.
The BBC report that they have been trying since then to contact Mr Johnston but without success. Alan Johnston (44) has been in Gaza for more than three years and he knows the situation there. When other foreign journalists left a few weeks ago, he decided to stay on. If he had gone then, he would have been back safe in London by now.

Kidnappings of this kind are becoming more and more common in Gaza, which is the reason why most international organisations have flown their staff out of the area. The kidnappings are not usually a protest against foreigners or their countries; most often they are used in the violent struggle for power between different militant groups. The last foreign hostage held there was a South American photographer, who was kidnapped on 1st January and set free a week later.

Alan Johnston, BBC journalist

➔ Option 4

D Rights at work

"If you're wondering why you've been chosen 'Employee of the Week,' it's because your work load is about to increase, while your pay remains the same."

"We look for people who can quickly adapt to changes in the workplace."

➔ Option 3

3 A dangerous job! (→ p. 18/ex. 5)

a) *Find Gaza City and the Gaza Strip on a map and start a mind map about it.*

b) *Read the report (text C). What happened to Alan Johnston? Who or what is behind the kidnappings?*

c) *Add more ideas to your mind map from a).*

4 Let's listen: Employees' rights 12 7 (→ p. 18/ex. 6)

1, 10

a) *Before you listen: Look at the cartoons (part D) and describe them. Say what rights you think the employees have.*

b) *Listen and match one talk with each cartoon and explain your choice.*

c) *Listen again. Say which manager you would like to work for. Give reasons.*

From serf to citizen

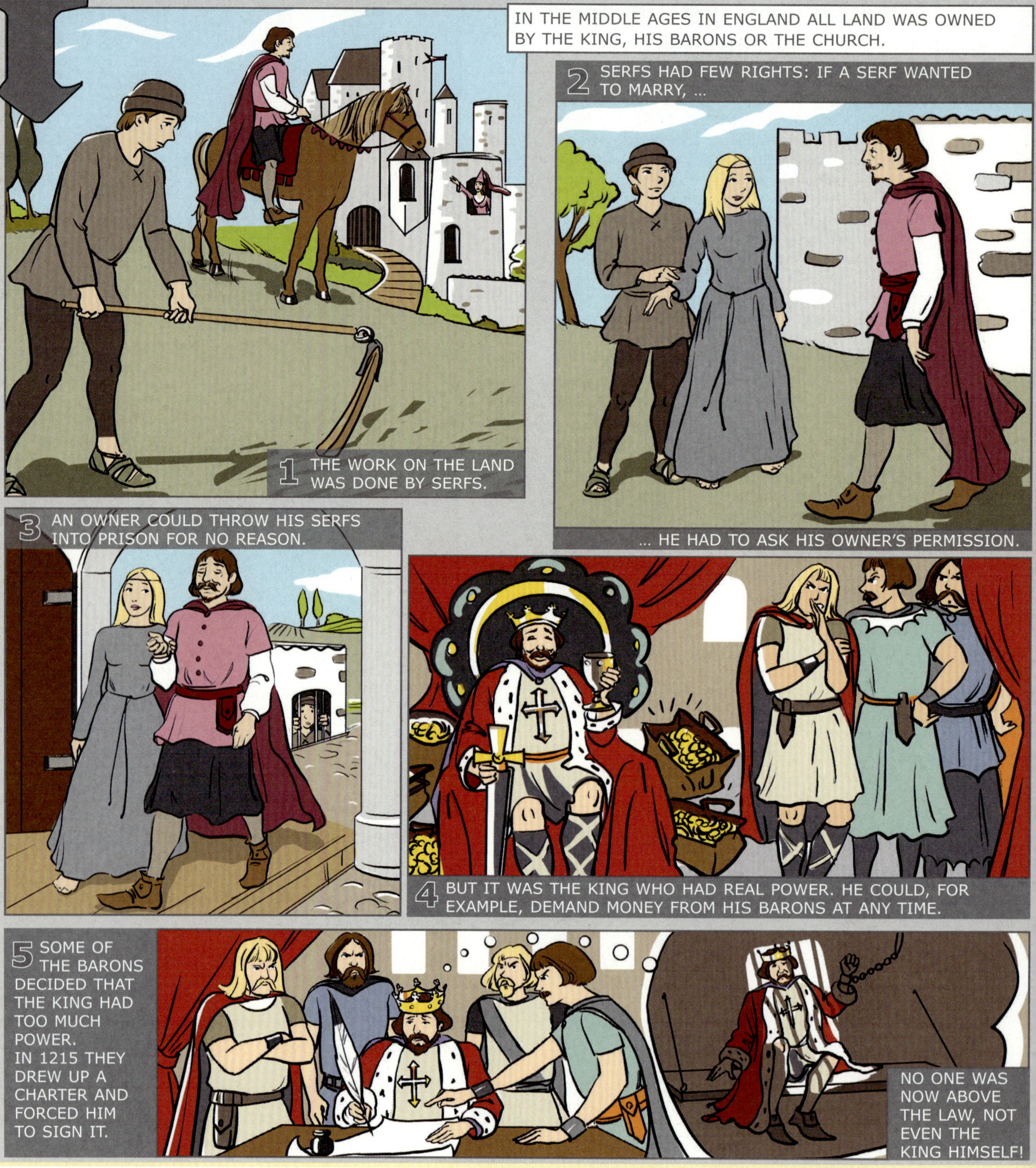

 To do Topic 2 you'll need: The conditional → Ov 11 • The passive → Ov 9

Task: To understand the importance of Magna Carta

1 The Middle Ages

a) *Before you read: Sum up what you already know about the Middle Ages.*

b) *Exchange information with a partner.*

2 A brief history (→ p. 19/ex. 7, 8)

Read the comic strip and then:

a) *Describe the life of a serf in 2–3 sentences.*

b) *Explain why the barons drew up Magna Carta in 1215.*

c) *Say why the charter is still important for people today.*

3 Let's listen: A 'real' copy 12 (→ p. 19/ex. 9)

1, 11

a) *Before you listen: Read the comic strip again. Make a mind map on Magna Carta.*

b) *Now listen to an interview in Lincoln, England.*

1. How old is the copy of Magna Carta there?
2. Where did the Japanese kids see another copy?
3. Why do they go away happy?

c) *Listen again. Add to your mind map.*

4 Presentation: A gallery walk 15 (→ p. 20/ex. 10, 11)

a) *Use your mind map to make three posters:*

- Rights before Magna Carta
- Two Magna Cartas
- Important human rights today

b) *Display the posters in class and let the others do a gallery walk and write notes.*

c) *Discuss the posters. Think about eye-catching features, information, pictures, etc.*

d) *Vote for the best poster.*

Two very different Heads of State

A A job for life!

Every year in November the Queen opens Parliament at Westminster. She reads out the 'Queen's Speech' from her throne in the House of Lords to tell the people about her government's policy and plans for the coming year.

But why the Queen and why the House of Lords, you may ask. Well, we need both of them. On the one hand Britain is a democracy with a parliament elected by the people and the Government sits in the House of Commons. On the other hand the Queen isn't allowed to enter the House of Commons and it isn't her speech at all. It is written by the Government. But she opens Parliament and reads out the Government's speech because she is Head of State. Further duties include dissolving Parliament before a General Election and signing new laws which Parliament has passed.

1

The Queen opens Parliament

All of these duties sound very important: If, for example, the Queen refused to open Parliament then the UK wouldn't have a government! And if she refused to sign a law, she could stop the Government's plans! Officially she is Head of the Armed Forces and can declare war on another state! But she does this only if Parliament tells her to. She can't make treaties with other nations but she has to sign them. In fact she has to remain strictly neutral in political matters. She can't for example support one political party, or add her own opinion to the Queen's Speech.

But she still plays an important role, receiving new ambassadors, visiting hospitals and presenting awards (387,700 since she became Queen in 1952). She has hundreds of social duties, too: Supporting more than 620 organisations and charities and welcoming guests at her famous summer garden parties.

And she is not without influence. She can still refuse to appoint someone as Prime Minister (PM). And she is well-informed. Every Tuesday at 6:30 p.m. she meets the PM (Head of Government) who comes to discuss state matters. She studies government papers which are brought to her every day.

Being queen is not all bad! It's a job for life and she cannot be brought to court, or put in prison for driving too fast or murdering her husband! Unlike King John who lost immunity when he signed Magna Carta, the Queen is not equal to other citizens before the law. But she makes sure that she never breaks the law, so no one has the problem of how to punish her.

2

The Palace of Westminster in London

 To do Topic 2 you'll need: The conditional → Ov 11 • The passive → Ov 9

⇨ 547561-0004

B Limited power

The US federal government has three parts: Congress (The Senate and the House of Representatives), the President and the Supreme Court. The Constitution limits the powers of each branch: The Supreme Court, for example, can suggest changes in the law but Congress has to agree to them. The President can suggest a new bill but he can't write bills himself.
Congress can pass bills but the President has to agree to them before they can become law. The Supreme Court then checks if the new law follows the Constitution. If the President doesn't like a bill, he can use his veto and refuse to sign it. Only if two-thirds of the Members of Congress vote against the President's veto, can the bill still become law. The President also serves as the US Head of State: he meets with the leaders of other countries, for example to make treaties. But the Senate must approve any treaty before it becomes official. He must tell Congress and the country about the 'state of the union'. He may also use this speech to win support for his ideas.
The President is the Chief of Government so he is the boss of every government worker. As the official head of the U.S. military he can send troops overseas. But he needs Congress's permission to declare war.
The US is a democracy but not everybody can become president: You must be at least 35, a natural-born US citizen and have lived there for at least 14 years. After 8 years you'll need a new job: A president is elected for four years and he can't be elected more than twice.

Abraham Lincoln (1861–1865) | John F. Kennedy (1961–1963) | Barack Obama (since 2009)

Task: To explain the systems of government in the US and the UK

1 Before you read: Heads of State

a) *Name your Head of State. Say what his/her title is.*

b) *What are his/her duties? Use the Internet.*

2 The Queen's job 1, 6 (→ p. 21/ex. 12, 13)

a) *Does the Queen have the same duties as your Head of State? What do you think?*

b) *Read text A. Find out what her duties are. Use the diagram at the back of the book to help you (Political systems: UK–US).*

c) *Say who you think has more power in the UK than the Queen. Give reasons.*

3 The President's powers 1, 6 (→ p. 22/ex. 14)

a) *Collect powers which the US President has from text B and say who or what limits these powers.*

b) *Compare his powers with those of the Queen. Say who you think is more powerful and why.*

4 Presentation: A discussion 9 (→ p. 22/ex. 15, 16)

a) *Split the group into three. Each third makes a leaflet:*
- about the system in the US *OR*
- about the system in the UK *OR*
- about the system in another country which they know.

b) *Each group then uses their leaflet to explain the system they have chosen and to give information about the role of the head of state (king, queen, president, …).*

c) *The others in the class say which system they think is best and give reasons.*

Young apprentices (YAs) at work

A Problems

CARD A

Someone you work with makes comments you do not like about your religion and family background. When you ask them to stop, they say that you can't take a joke. Next time you see them the same thing happens.

CARD E

A colleague of the opposite sex starts to show interest in you and asks you to meet them after work to go for a drink

CARD B

The company rules about using the phone and e-mail for personal use have been explained to you. But, in fact, most of your colleagues use the phone to call their friends or play 'Solitaire' and surf the Net when things are quiet at work and tell you that you can do the same.

CARD F

A colleague often puts their face very close to yours when they are talking to you. They also come up behind you and put their hand on your shoulders when they start a conversation.

CARD G

A young apprentice of the opposite sex to you has a placement in your department, too. After a while it is clear that they are given more opportunities than you. When you ask about this, you are told that they have developed better skills than you and so can try more ambitious projects.

CARD C

In school your class had one lesson on health and safety on work experience, but you visited the dentist on that day and missed it. On your first day at work you had a session on health and safety but some of the language was hard to understand and you felt too nervous to ask questions.

CARD D

The health and safety session stressed how important it is to wear personal protective clothing and equipment for special tasks. However, some of your colleagues take these off or do not use the equipment when the supervisor is away as it slows them down.

CARD H

You find that your colleagues use a lot of bad language at work and also read out articles from tabloid newspapers which you find hurtful. They also tell rude and sexist jokes.

B Tips

ADVICE SHEET

✔ ❶ The school should make sure that YAs are well-informed especially if they missed an important lesson. YAs must ask if they do not understand something.

✔ ❷ If you aren't interested, tell the person firmly. A YA should never agree to meet people alone in a private place. A group social event may be different. Follow the law on drinking alcohol.

✔ ❸ Everyone has the right to be treated with respect. If the harassment becomes workplace bullying, the YA should inform their supervisor and teacher.

✔ ❹ YAs have a duty to themselves and others to wear personal protective clothing and equipment. YAs should speak to their supervisor or teacher about this.

✔ ❺ Workplaces with a lot of men often have a culture of sexist jokes, horseplay and bad language. It is not realistic to expect this to stop. The firm should offer placements suitable for 14 – 16 year-olds and with role models.

✔ ❻ All YAs should be given equal opportunities to learn and develop their skills during their placement. YA should discuss problems with their supervisor and the teacher.

✔ ❼ YAs should explain that they don't like people to stand too close or touch them from behind. If the person doesn't stop, they should inform their supervisor and their teacher.

✔ ❽ YAs should ask their supervisor about rules on personal use of the Internet and phone and should follow those rules. YA should not 'shop' work colleagues. YA has the right to ask if personal use is allowed.

Task: To find out about rights and duties at work

1 Before you read: A work placement

a) *What rights and duties do you have on a work placement? Collect ideas.*

b) *Think of a problem you had on your work placement. What happened? How was it solved?*

2 Problems at work (→ p. 23/ex. 17)

a) *Read the cards (A – H) in part A. Think of a heading for each card.*

b) *What advice would you give the YA in each of the situations? Write a list.*

3 Advice for YAs 1, 6 (→ p. 23/ex. 18, 19; p. 24/ex. 20)

a) *Read the eight tips in part B and match each one to a problem in part A.*

b) *Check your list from Ex. 2 b) and try to add your own ideas to the official suggestions.*

c) *What rights and duties do you have as a YA? Use part B and start a list of key words.*

d) *Add more ideas of your own.*

4 A diary entry

Imagine you had the problem described on card G. Write a diary entry about what happened and how you felt.

5 Presentation: A panel of experts 13 21 (→ p. 24/ex. 21)

a) *Write each of the situations in part A on a card and distribute the cards among the 'audience'. Give them time to check new words.*

b) *Your group forms the panel and chooses a chairperson.*

c) *The audience reads out each card and an 'expert' uses his/her notes from Ex. 3 and gives advice.*

d) *The audience argues for or against the advice.*

e) *The audience can ask for advice on other problems at work.*

My kidnap ordeal by Alan Johnston

GAZA CITY. As he reached the end of his time working in Gaza, the BBC's Alan Johnston was kidnapped by a militant group. Here he tells the full story of his 114 days as a hostage.

A The kidnappers had forced me to lie face down on the floor. But after they left, and the small, empty room had become quiet again, I turned over and pulled myself slowly into a sitting position. My hands were tied behind my back, and a black hood had been pulled down over my head. And as I sat there – in danger, and frightened – I had a great sense of being at the very lowest point of my life. It had begun out in the spring sunshine, on the streets of Gaza City. A big car had suddenly driven past mine, and had then stopped in front of us, forcing me to stop, too. A young man climbed from the passenger side and pointed a gun at me.

B I had reported many times on the kidnapping of foreigners in Gaza. Now, as I was always afraid it might, my turn had come. The figure with the gun and another man forced me to get into their car, and as we drove off I was forced to lie on the back seat. A hood had been pulled over my face, but through it I could see the sun flickering between the high buildings. I could tell that we were going south and east, towards the city's more dangerous neighbourhoods. Most kidnappings in Gaza used to be done by angry militant groups trying to get the attention of the authorities in some unimportant argument. And always the foreigner was set free within a week or so, shocked but unharmed. But the game had changed last summer. A much more dangerous group had kidnapped two members of a team from the American Fox News Network. They were set free, but only after making a video in which they attacked the West, and converted to Islam.

BACKGROUND

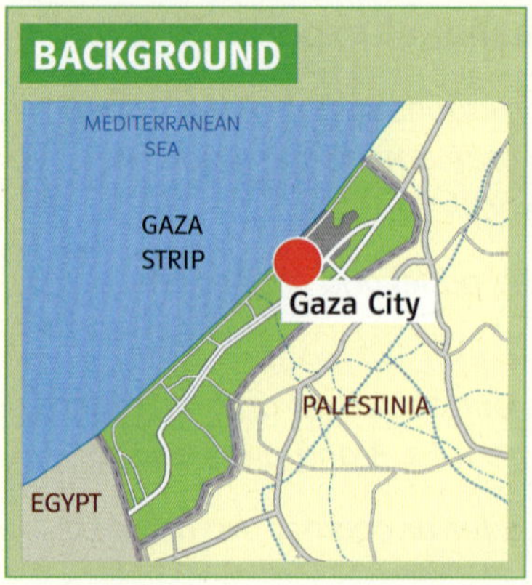

C I knew I was in danger. In Gaza there was now an organisation that wanted to wage a holy war on the West. There were still a few foreigners in Gaza and they were certain to be targets. So I did everything I could to reduce the risks: I moved to a safer apartment, I filmed less in the streets and I used different cars. I felt that Gaza's story was important: It is at the centre of the Palestinian drama which is at the heart of the rising tensions between the East and the West. This has become the most important story of our time. So I decided that the risks were worth taking, and I stayed in Gaza. If I had left three weeks earlier, the kidnapping would never have happened. When the man with the gun appeared from the white car, I had just 16 days left until I was due to leave.

1 Alan Johnston wearing a bullet-proof vest in Gaza

D As I lay on the floor, late on the first night as a hostage, the door opened. A tall figure in a long white robe stood for a moment, looking down at me. A red scarf completely hid his face. The leader had arrived. He stepped into the room and sat down. "Alan Johnston," he said in English. "We know everything." He said that I would not be killed. That I would be treated well, following Islamic codes of behaviour towards prisoners, and that I would eventually be allowed to leave. I asked when, but he just said, "When the time is right." Did he mean weeks, or months, or longer? It wasn't possible to say. But I was left with a strange feeling that what was about to happen would be long and would change my life.

 To do Topic 2 you'll need: The conditional → Ov 11 • The passive → Ov 9

E But how far could I trust this man? Did his word really count for anything? Could he simply change his mind? And I wondered if he really was a leader of the group. Perhaps, in the end, others would decide what happened to me. I fell asleep and was woken by two men coming into the room. They tied my hands together, put the black hood back over my head, and led me slowly out into the cold night. No one explained anything. I tried to understand what was happening. I was frightened, as I walked out into the dark that I might be going to my death – that I was being taken somewhere to be shot and would be found later with a bullet in my brain.

F But soon I began to realise that the men were only moving me to another building. This would, for a time, become my cell. In that room, on the roof of an apartment block, there was just a narrow bed and two chairs. I began to think about what had happened. I knew that if I hadn't decided to stay in Gaza, this would never have happened. I walked across the cell. Five steps, then I turned and walked five steps back, – mile, after mile, after mile! Imagine yourself in that room. One of my lowest moments came during a power cut. I had asked for a radio and on the night of the power cut a guard brought one into my room. Suddenly I had a link with the outside world! But the radio also brought terrible news. In those calm, measured tones of the BBC, I heard reports that claimed that I had been executed.

2

Alan, his Arabic friend Fayed and Hamas fighters

Task: To discuss what risks journalists should/n't take

1 News can be dangerous

a) *Think: Which political 'hot spots' have you seen on TV or read about recently? What do you think life is like for reporters there?*

b) *Pair: Find evidence from the introduction and photo 1 that Alan's job is dangerous.*

c) *Share: Find reasons why you would/wouldn't like to do his job.*

2 Taking risks 1, 15 9 (→ p. 25/ex. 22, 23; p. 26/ex. 24)

a) *Read the story. Find titles for each part.*

b) *You write a short summary of parts A – C, your partner of parts D – F on the computer.*

c) *Exchange your texts by e-mail and check that nothing important is missing.*

3 Let's listen: A dangerous decision 12 (→ p. 26/ex. 25)

1, 12

a) *Look at photo 2. Listen and then describe what is happening in the photo.*

b) *Listen again. Write 1 – 2 sentences about how Alan met his Arabic friend, Fayed, just before this.*

c) *Collect key words from part C and say what you think of Alan's decision.*

4 A meeting

Write a dialogue between Alan and a friend after his return home.

5 Choose a presentation 13 21 (→ p. 26/ex. 26)

1. *A talk: Use your summaries from Ex. 2 to tell Alan's story. Ask the class how they think the story ended. Then tell what really happened. Find out how many think Alan was right to stay on in Gaza.*
   OR
2. *A debate: Choose a chairperson and speakers for and against the motion 'Journalists should never risk their lives to bring us news'. The speakers should use the story to support their arguments.*

OPTION 1

✔ … talk about the Middle Ages in England.

a) *Choose the right dates for the Middle Ages:* 700–1100 • 1485–1800 • 1066–1485

b) *Put these people in order from top to bottom:*
bishops • knights • servants • the King • soldiers • barons • serfs • freemen

✔ … imagine situations that probably won't happen. Ov11

Imagine what you would/n't have done, if you had lived then. Complete the text.
If I … *(live)* in the Middle Ages, I … *(not/be)* a knight or a lady. Probably I … *(be)* a serf. That means I … *(belong)* to the land where I lived, and I … *(not/travel)* around the country. If I … *(want)* to marry, I … *(need)* to ask my owner for permission. If I … *(marry)* without his permission, he probably … *(throw)* me into prison. If he … *(do)* this, I … *(not/have)* a right to a fair trial before a judge. If I … *(escape)* from the owner, and … *(be able)* to hide for one year and a day, I would … *(be)* a freeman. I don't think I … *(like)* life as a serf. I … *(try)* to escape.

✔ … explain the beginnings of rights for citizens.

Complete the following sentences about the Great Charter.

1. Most people call the Great Charter … .
2. Before it was signed, owners of serfs could … .
3. The barons drew it up because … .
4. It said that not even the king … .
5. Common Law in England still has … .
6. It inspired … .

OPTION 2

✔ … recognize two different democratic systems.

a) *US or UK? Sort the words and define them.*
monarch • Senate • president • PM • state of the union • Armed Forces • House of Lords • veto • Supreme Court

b) *Say which members of the two systems are elected and which are appointed.*

✔ … talk about government in the UK and the US. Ov9

Match up the people with their duties and write sentences. Start like this: Treaties are drawn up by … .

draw up treaties • pass laws • choose Ministers • check laws • make policy • declare war • lead meetings	Parliament • the Supreme Court • the Prime Minister • the Ministers • Congress

✔ … describe the Queen's role as Head of State.

Name five of the Queen's duties. What special right does she have as Queen?

✔ … explain the US President's powers.

Which of these statements are true? Correct the false ones.
He can refuse to sign a bill. He can write new bills. If he refuses to sign a bill, it can never become law. He can declare war. He can make treaties with other countries without the permission of the Senate. He is not allowed to use his state of the union speech to explain his policy. All American citizens can become US President.

OPTION 3

✔ … talk about a work placement.

a) *Find the odd one out in these lists.*

apprentice	religion	dentist	rude	harassment
teacher	placement	health	sexist	respect
sex	job	safety	hurtful	interest
colleague	project	protective	well-informed	bullying
boss	task	law	hard	joke
supervisor	work	conversation	bad	horseplay

b) *Give each topic a heading and use 2–3 of the words in each list to write a sentence about each topic.*

✔ … give advice on problems at work. Ov11

Use full sentences and say what you would have done in these situations:

1. A colleague got too close to me and put his hand on my shoulders. – If a colleague had got … .
2. Some colleagues took off their protective clothing when the supervisor was away.
3. Someone made hurtful comments about my religion.
4. Our supervisor gave another young apprentice more ambitious projects than me.
5. A lot of my colleagues told rude and sexist jokes in the cafeteria.

✔ … identify rights and duties at work.

a) *Name five rights which you have as a YA.*

b) *Name three duties.*

OPTION 4

✔ … talk about the risks journalists take.

Look at these situations and say why they could be dangerous for a journalist.
Start like this: 1. A journalist could fall into the river and … .

1

2

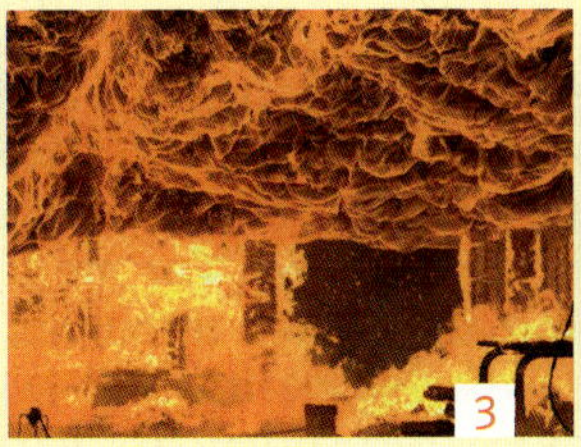
3

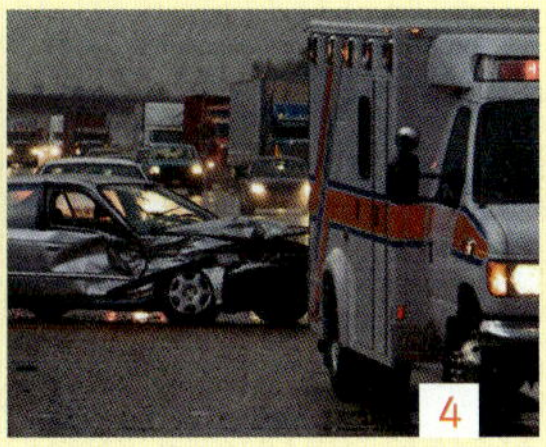
4

✔ … imagine what you would have done in a dangerous situation. Ov11

What would you have done if you had been a journalist at the scenes above?
Start like this: If I had been …, I would/n't have … .

✔ … decide how far journalists should go.

Give your opinion on these statements and add a reason why you think this.

1. Journalists are like soldiers: they are paid to take risks, even if their life is in danger.
2. We have a right to be given information about what is happening in the world.
3. No news is so important that a journalist should risk his life to report it.

(→ p. 27/ex. 27; p. 28/ex. 28)

COMMONWEALTH DAY, 2008: A democratic institution celebrates[1] (→ pp. 29–31)

This year 'The environment – our future' was the subject of the Queen's message to all Commonwealth countries around the world. The message marks the beginning of worldwide events that will continue all through this week. They include a service for people of all religions, parades, concerts, talks and competitions. Some countries have planned drama and dance events and projects and sports activities in schools. But does anyone stop to think about what the 'Commonwealth' is? How did it actually start? What has it become? Why is it celebrated today in far away places like Africa, Asia, the Caribbean[2] and the Pacific?

We asked some young people at Commonwealth Day events:
Many said that they enjoyed the 'multicultural', international feeling of the festivities[3]. Most of them knew that 'Commonwealth' countries had once been colonies of the 'British Empire[4]', which had increased its own wealth by taking their natural resources. But they didn't know that at first only 'white' colonies had belonged to the Commonwealth and it was only after India was admitted to[5] it that it became multiracial[6]. They were aware that the official language was English and that Queen Elizabeth II was their Head but few of them knew that the Commonwealth has 53 independent states (almost a third of the world's population!). And even fewer could list the basic goals of the Commonwealth.

Vasanti Sharma – an 18-year-old student from Chandigarh, India – was at first sceptical about this institution: "When I was younger I couldn't understand why we Indian school kids celebrated something which was once called 'Empire Day'! After all[7], at school we were taught that India had a hard time under British rule[8] before its independence from Britain!" But through discussions with her peers at college, Ms Sharma has changed her opinion. Today she is active in the Commonwealth Youth Programme in her country.
"The idea of 'Empire' has long since changed to 'Commonwealth'," she says. "For me this word means all the resources, values[9], cultural wealth etc. which we have 'in common' – which we all share. So I think this year's environmental theme is really important: In the end, we all share the Earth, don't we? The air that we breathe and the water in our rivers have no boundaries[10]!" Ms Sharma, who recently became a 'Commonwealth Young Ambassador' (CYA), explains why: "Today the Commonwealth of Nations stands for democracy and human rights. Its members pledge to fight poverty, intolerance and injustice. One way is for countries to build bridges between their peoples[11], and also between individual people – which is what we're trying to do in our local programme. And what better and more fun way to build bridges than to get together to celebrate Commonwealth Day!"

HIV street theatre in India

For more about Vasanti Sharma's work as CYA, go to our website and listen to our podcast in which Vasanti Sharma talks to Raj Milton. She tells him about her work in Chandigarh, India, and about her contact with other CYAs some as far away as Jamaica.

[1]to celebrate ['seləbreɪt] – *feiern*, [2]Caribbean [ˌkærɪ'bi:ən] – *Karibik*, [3]festivities [fes'tɪvətiz] – *Feierlichkeiten*, [4]empire ['empaɪə] – *Reich*, [5]to admit to [əd'mɪt tə] – *aufnehmen in*, [6]multiracial [ˌmʌltɪ'reɪʃl] – *viele Rassen umfassend*, [7]after all [ˌɑ:ftər‿'ɔ:l] – *schließlich*, [8]rule [ru:l] – *Herrschaft*, [9]value ['vælju:] – *Wert*, [10]boundary ['baʊndri] – *Grenze*, [11]peoples ['pi:plz] – *Völker*

A Reading

1 Read the text. Find six different parts and match a heading (A–F) with each one.

A What young people know about the Commonwealth
B One person's experience of Commonwealth Day
C Commonwealth Day topic 2008 and events
D Commonwealth goals today
E More information
F Our common wealth

2 Read the text again and find the following information.

a. Commonwealth Day topic for 2008
b. five activities/events in 2008
c. four things the states share
d. number of Commonwealth states today
e. the idea of the Commonwealth today (*2 things*)
f. what its members fight against and one way they do this

B Language

1 Choose the correct meaning for these words from the text.

a. subject (line 2):	1 Fach	2 Thema	3 Person
b. message (line 3):	1 Nachricht	2 Botschaft	3 Meldung
c. marks (line 5):	1 befleckt	2 korrigiert	3 kennzeichnet
d. service (line 9):	1 Bedienung	2 Gottesdienst	3 Aufschlag
e. list (line 43):	1 überlisten	2 auflisten	3 erfinden
f. goals (line 44):	1 Ziele	2 Tore	3 Pfosten
g. resources (line 64):	1 Mittel	2 Bodenschätze	3 Geldmittel

2 Find the words or phrases from the text which mean the same:

a. topic
b. international
c. the total number of people in a country
d. friends of the same age
e. use or have together
f. not very long ago

1,13 C Listening

1 Listen to a podcast interview. Choose an ending to complete each sentence.

a. The programme started with the idea that young people are …
b. In the Youth Programme they are …
c. One right is to develop through things like …
d. Youth Ambassadors perform …
e. Their goal is to inform young people …
f. Members of the audience can ask questions or get …
g. Via the Internet they are in contact with …
h. They're trying to get rid of crime and violence by …

1 about HIV and AIDS.
2 other Youth Ambassadors.
3 responsible.
4 opening a training centre.
5 professional help.
6 society's future.
7 street plays and concerts.
8 good jobs and education.

2 Listen again and correct the sentences.

a. The CYAs are quite young: between 16 and 30.
b. They're involved at every level – even in markets.
c. The group is involved in a 'Possible Living Programme' in Chandigarh.
d. Vasanti and the others in her group are checked by a team of doctors.
e. Then the doctors write the scripts or songs.

D Speaking

1

2

1 Describing

a. Say where you think the volunteers in the photos could be and what kind of project they might be doing. What skills do you think they need?

b. Imagine you are planning to work as a volunteer in a project. Say where you would like to work, what you would like to do and what skills you could offer.

c. Think about problems which you might have and discuss your ideas with your partner.

2 Role play

You're interested in working as a volunteer. You call the Emergency Volunteer Service. What do you say?

EVS: Hello, Emergency Volunteer Service. This is Sandy Law, speaking. How can I help you?
You: *(Sage deinen Namen. Erzähle, dass du an einem Projekt im Ausland interessiert bist.)*
Sandy: Is there a special country or kind of project which you're interested in?
You: *(Erkläre, dass du schon mal bei einem Bauprojekt geholfen hast, dass du die notwendigen Fähigkeiten und Fertigkeiten hast und dass du dir so etwas wieder vorstellen könntest.)*
Sandy: OK, that sounds great! We urgently need helpers in Thailand.
You: *(Frage, was du genau machen würdest, wenn du bei dem Projekt arbeiten würdest.)*
Sandy: Well, the volunteers would help to rebuild a whole village.
You: *(Drücke dein Entsetzen aus und frage, was passiert ist.)*
Sandy: Oh, there was a terrible storm there last week. They need people to clean up, transport building materials, cook for the workers, build new houses …
You: *(Sage, dass du gern mit Holz arbeitest, aber dass du da helfen wirst, wo du gebraucht wirst.)*
Sandy: Good. So … you'll have to come into the office and fill in some forms. And a doctor must check you, too.
You: *(Frage, ob sie dir die Formulare und Infos per E-Mail schicken könnte. Sage auch, dass du sofort zum Arzt gehen wirst.)*
Sandy: Fine. Well, you'll find the form on our website. You can just fill it in and send it to us.
You: *(Sage, dass du versuchen wirst, alles so schnell wie möglich zu erledigen. Vergiss nicht, dich höflich zu verabschieden.)*

E Mediation and communication

You are on holiday in England. At the tourist office you find a brochure on a special museum.

BRITISH EMPIRE & COMMONWEALTH MUSEUM

Visit this fantastic museum in England and experience the wealth we have in common!

The Main Galleries

THERE ARE 16 PERMANENT GALLERIES, WHICH ARE DIVIDED[1] INTO 3 SECTIONS ON BRITISH EMPIRE HISTORY:

1 Britain builds an empire

THIS SECTION SHOWS YOU HOW THE EMPIRE STARTED (1840) WITH THE BUILDING UP OF TRADE ACROSS THE WORLD. WHO BECAME RICH AND WHO SUFFERED AS THE EMPIRE GREW IN NORTH & SOUTH AMERICA? THE GALLERIES INCLUDE THEMES LIKE EXPLORING V. PLUNDERING[2], PLANTATIONS[3] IN THE AMERICAS, ETC.

2 The rise of Queen Victoria's empire (1800 – 1900)

HERE YOU'LL FIND OUT ALL ABOUT HOW THE EMPIRE EXPANDED[4], HOW IT WAS CONTROLLED (E.G. WHO EXACTLY WENT TO THE COLONIES TO DO THIS WORK), WHAT IT WAS LIKE TO LIVE UNDER BRITISH RULE AND WHAT CONFLICTS THERE WERE AT THIS TIME.

3 End of empire (1900 – today)

THIS LAST SECTION TELLS YOU ALL ABOUT HOW THE BRITISH EMPIRE FINALLY ENDED AND HOW THE NEW 'COMMONWEALTH' WAS BORN. HERE YOU WILL ALSO LEARN HOW TWO TERRIBLE WARS CHANGED THE WORLD – AND CHANGED PEOPLE'S ATTITUDES TOWARDS THE IDEA OF HAVING COLONIES. FIND OUT HOW THE EMPIRE OF THE PAST HAS AFFECTED SOCIETY, CULTURE, LANGUAGE AND IDEAS IN BRITAIN AND IS STILL DOING SO TODAY.

THE MUSEUM OFFERS A GREAT NUMBER OF INTERACTIVE DISPLAYS:

- LEARN ABOUT THE BIGGEST EMPIRE IN WORLD HISTORY.
- SEE FANTASTIC RARE[5] OBJECTS AND INTERESTING PHOTOS.
- WATCH EXCITING FILMS.
- PLAY COMPUTER GAMES AND DO PUZZLES.
- LISTEN TO TRUE-LIFE STORIES.

a. Was ist das für ein Museum?
b. Warum wird das Jahr 1840 erwähnt?
c. Geht es nur um die Zeit von Königin Victoria?
d. Was können wir über das Commonwealth lernen?
e. Worum geht es in dem Kasten unten rechts?

F Writing

1 Skills

Collect important ideas about the Commonwealth in a mind map (how it developed, who belongs to it, what it stands for, …).

2 A magazine article

Write a report (80 – 100 words) about the Commonwealth for an international youth magazine.

[1]to divide [dɪ'vaɪd] – *aufteilen*, [2]to plunder ['plʌndə] – *plündern*, [3]plantation [plæn'teɪʃn] – *Plantage*, [4]to expand [ɪk'spænd] – *(sich) ausweiten*, [5]rare [reə] – *selten*

On the rocks (adapted from 'Snakehead' by A. Horowitz)

1,14–18

1 Before you read

a) *Read the title and the introduction and look at the two pictures. What do you think the story is about:*

1. Australian animals in danger? 2. a criminal organization? 3. a boys' gang?

Alex is a British teenager whose father, John Rider, and uncle, Ian, used to work as agents for the British Secret Service MI6. Alex has been doing some work as an agent for them himself. Now he is waiting in Sydney to get his exit visa so that he can go back to school in England.

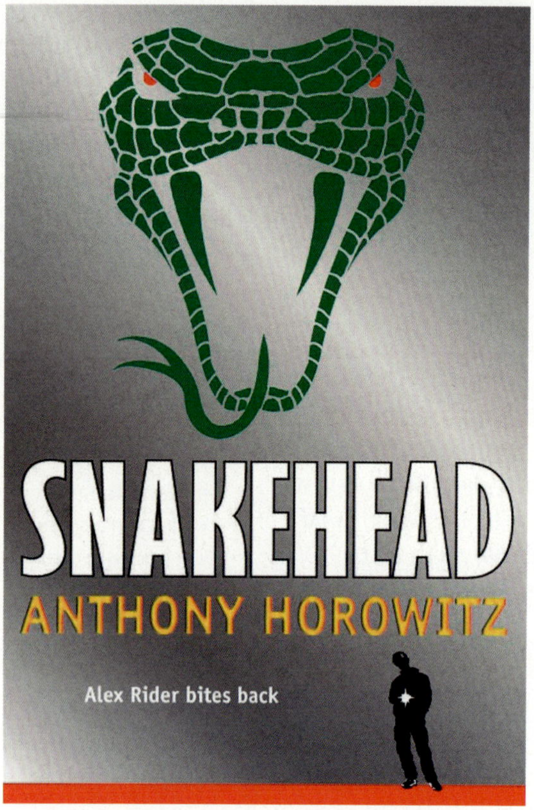

A Alex was sitting outside a café in Sydney, the Opera House on one side, the Harbour Bridge on the other. It was the world's favourite picture postcard view and he had seen it many times. But now he was actually in it, eating strawberry ice cream and watching as the Manly ferry came into the quay[1], scattering[2] the smaller boats. The sun was beating down[3] and the sky was a brilliant blue. It was hard to believe that he was really here.

And he wasn't alone. Jack had joined him the day before. She still had jet lag[4] but she was full of excitement[5] the moment she saw him. It had taken her twenty-six hours to get here and Alex knew she would have been worrying all the way. Jack was meant to look after him. She hated it when he was away – and this time he had never been further. As soon as she'd arrived, she had made it clear that all she wanted was to get him on a plane and take him back to London. Yes, it was cold and raining there, the English winter had already arrived. Yes, they both deserved a holiday. But it was time to go home.

Jack was also eating ice cream, and although she was twenty-eight she suddenly looked younger with her untidy[6] red hair, cheeky smile and her brightly coloured kangaroo T-shirt. More a big sister than a housekeeper[7]. And above all a friend.

"I don't know why it's taking so long," she was saying. "It's crazy. By the time you get back, you'll have missed half the term."

"They said they'd have it this afternoon."

"They should have had it two days ago."

b) *What is worrying Jack and why?*

[1]quay [kiː] – *Kai,* [2]to scatter ['skætə] – *auseinanderjagen,* [3]to beat down [biːt 'daʊn] – *hier: herunterbrennen,* [4]jet lag ['dʒet ˌlæg] – *Schwierigkeiten durch die Zeitumstellung,* [5]excitement [ɪk'saɪtmənt] – *Aufregung,* [6]untidy [ʌn'taɪdi] – *unordentlich,* [7]housekeeper['haʊsˌkiːpə] – *Haushälterin*

B They were talking about Alex's visa. That morning, Jack had received a call at the hotel where they were staying. They had been given an address, a government office in Macquarie Street, just past the old parliament building. The visa would be ready at four o'clock. Alex could pick it up then.

"Could we stay here a couple more days?" Alex asked.

Jack looked at him. She was surprised. "Don't you want to go home?"

"Yes," Alex said. "I do. But at the same time I'm not quite sure I'm ready to go back to school. I've been thinking about it. I'm worried I'm not going to be able to fit in[1]."

"Of course you'll fit in, Alex. You've got lots of friends. They've all been missing you. Once you're back, you'll forget any of this stuff ever happened."

"I don't know, Jack."

Alex looked at the ice cream on his spoon. He wished he could explain how he felt. He didn't want to work for MI6 again. He was sure of that. But at the same time …

"It's half past three," Jack said. "We should get going."

The address they had been given was a modern glass block that was probably filled with less important government offices. The receptionist already had visitor passes waiting for them and told them to go to the fourth floor[2] and a room at the end of a corridor.

"I don't know why they couldn't have just put you on a plane and sent you out of here," Jack said as they left the lift[3]. "It seems a lot of fuss about nothing." There was a door in front of them. They walked through without knocking and stopped. There must have been some sort of mistake. Wherever[4] they were, it certainly wasn't a visa office.

Two men were talking to each other in what looked like a library[5] with old, expensive furniture and a beautiful carpet on a wooden floor. Alex's impression was that the room didn't belong to the building it was in.

"Oh … I'm sorry," Jack began.

"Not at all, Miss Starbright," the man behind the desk replied. "Please come in."

"We're looking for the visa office," Jack said.

"Sit down. I take it[6] Alex is with you? The question may seem strange, but I'm blind."

"I'm here," Alex said.

"Who are you?" Jack asked. She and Alex had moved further into the room. The younger man came over and closed the door behind them.

"My name is Ethan Brooke. And this is Marc Damon. Thank you very much for coming in, Miss Starbright. May I call you Jack? Please – take a seat."

There were two heavy chairs in front of the desk. Feeling more and more uncomfortable[7], Jack and Alex sat down.

"I know you're in a hurry to get back to London," Brooke began. "But let me explain why the two of you are here. The fact is we need a little help."

"You want our help?" Jack looked around her. Suddenly it all made sense. "You want Alex." She spoke the words heavily. She knew now who the men were – or at least who they worked for. She had met their type before.

"We'd like to put a proposition[8] to Alex," Brooke agreed.

"Forget it. He's not interested."

"Won't you at least listen to what we have to say?" Brooke put his hands on the desk. He looked reasonable[9].

"We want the visa."

"You'll have it. As soon as I've finished."

Alex had said nothing. Jack looked at him then turned to Brooke and Damon. She was really angry now. "Why can't you people leave him alone?" she asked.

"Because he's special. In fact, I'd say he's unique. And right now we need him, just for a week or two. But I promise you, Jack. If he's not interested, he can walk out of here. We can have him on a plane tonight. Just give me a minute to explain."

c) *Who do you think the two men are and why do they need Alex?*

[1]to fit in [fɪt‿ˈɪn] – *hier: sich eingewöhnen,* [2]floor [flɔː] – *Stockwerk,* [3]lift [lɪft] – *Fahrstuhl,* [4]wherever [weərˈevə] – *wo auch immer,* [5]library [ˈlaɪbrri] – *Bibliothek,* [6]I take it [ˌaɪ‿ˈteɪk ɪt] – *Ich nehme an,* [5]proposition [ˌprɒpəˈzɪʃn] – *Angebot,* [9]reasonable [ˈriːznəbl] – *vernünftig*

C "Who are you?" Alex asked.

Brooke turned towards Damon. "We work for ASIS," the younger man replied. "The Australian Secret Intelligence Service[1]."

"I've read all about you, Alex," Brooke added. "I have to say, I'm impressed[2]."

"What do you want me for?" Alex asked angrily.

"I'll tell you. Have you ever heard the word 'snakehead', or 'shetou'?" Brooke began. There was silence, so he went on. "All right, let me start by saying that the snakehead groups are definitely the biggest and most dangerous criminal organizations in the world. Compared to them, the Mafia are amateurs. They have more influence – and they're doing more damage – than even al-Qaeda, but they're not interested in religion. All they want is money. That's the bottom line. They're gangsters, but they're a huge organization. Have you ever bought an illegal DVD? The chances are that it was made and sold by a snakehead. And the money they'll have made out of it will have gone straight into one of their other areas of business, which you may not find so funny. Maybe it's drugs or slavery or body parts. You need a new heart? The snakeheads operate the biggest market in illegal organs, and they're not worried about where they get them. Or weapons[3]! Where do you think terrorists go if they want a bomb or a gun or something horrible that comes in a bottle? Think of it as an international supermarket, Alex. But everything it sells is bad.

But what makes the most money for the snakeheads is smuggling[4] people. You probably have no idea how many people here are being smuggled from one country to another all around the world. These are some of the poorest families in the world, desperate to build themselves a new life in the West. Some of them are hungry or are trying to escape from a life with no hope; others live under threat of prison or worse in their own countries." Brooke stopped speaking and looked directly at Alex. "Half of them are under the age of eighteen," he said. "About five per cent are younger than you – and they're travelling on their own[5]. The lucky ones get picked up by the authorities[6]. What happens to the rest of them ... you don't want to know.

There's one snakehead that operates all over Indonesia, and it's more powerful and more dangerous than the rest. We actually know the name of the boss. Major Yu. But that's all we've been able to find out. We don't know what he looks like or where he lives. Twice now we've tried to get into the organization. That is, we put agents inside, pretending to be customers."

"What happened to them?" Jack asked.

"They both died." It was Damon who had answered the question.

"And so now I take it you're thinking about using Alex."

"We have no idea how our agents were discovered," Brooke went on. We need to get inside the snakehead in a way that is unique and also above suspicion[7]."

"A man and a boy," Damon said.

"We have an agent in Bangkok now. We're going to set him up as a refugee[8] from Afghanistan planning to be smuggled into Australia. He'll meet with the snakehead and collect names, faces, phone numbers, addresses – anything he can. But he won't be on his own. He'll be travelling with his son."

"We'll fly you to Bangkok," Damon continued, speaking directly to Alex. "Bangkok is an important centre for false documents[9]."

There was a short silence. Then Jack Starbright shook her head.

"All right," she said. "We've listened to your proposition, Mr Brooke. Now you can listen to my answer. And it's no. Forget it! You said it yourself. These people are dangerous. Two of your agents have already been killed. There's no way I'm going to let Alex get involved in that."

[1]secret intelligence service [si:krət͜ ɪnˌtelɪdʒns 'sɜ:vɪs] – *Geheimdienst*, [2]impressed [ɪm'prest] – *beeindruckt*, [3]weapon ['wepən] – *Waffe*, [4]to smuggle ['smʌgl] – *schmuggeln*, [5]on their own [ˌɒn ðeər͜ 'əʊn] – *allein*, [6]authority [ɔ:'θɒrəti] – *Behörde*, [7]above suspicion [əˌbʌv ˌsə'spɪʃn] – *über jeden Verdacht erhaben*, [8]refugee [ˌrefjʊ'dʒi:] – *Flüchtling*, [9]false documents [ˌfɔ:ls 'dɒkjəmənts] – *falsche Papiere*

d) *Do you think Brooke will persuade[1] Alex to help them? How?*

D "I'd have thought after all Alex has been through, he could decide for himself," Brooke answered.

"He can. I'm just telling you what he's going to say. The answer's no!"

"There is one thing we haven't told you." Brooke rested[2] his hands on the desk. His face gave nothing away but Damon knew what was coming next. His boss was like a card player, only now preparing to show his hand[3]. "I didn't tell you the name of our agent in Bangkok."

"And who is that?" Jack asked.

"You know him, I think. His name is Ash."

Jack sat back, unable to hide the fact that she was shocked. "Ash?" she said.

"That's right."

Alex had seen the effect the name had had on her. "Who's Ash?" he asked.

"You don't know him?" Brooke was enjoying himself now, though only Damon knew it. He turned to Jack. "Maybe you'd like to explain?"

"Ash was someone who knew your dad," Jack said.

"He was rather[4] more than that," Brooke corrected her. "Ash was John Rider's closest friend. He was the best man[5] when your parents married, Alex. He's also your godfather[6]."

"My …" Alex couldn't believe what he was hearing. He didn't even know he had a godfather.

"And he was the last person to see your parents alive," Brooke went on. "He was with them, the morning they died. He was at the airport when they got on the plane for the South of France."

"Ash was an agent with MI6," Brooke explained. "That was how he and your father met. They worked together as a team. Your dad even saved his life once – in Malta. You can ask him about that … if you meet. I'd have thought the two of you would have a lot to talk about."

"How can you do this?" Jack whispered. She was looking at Brooke full of contempt[7].

"Ash left MI6 a few months after your parents died, and emigrated here," Brooke continued. "He came with great references so we were happy to take him on at ASIS. He's been with us ever since[8]. Right now he's in Bangkok, waiting to go undercover. But there's nobody who can pretend better to be your father, Alex. I mean, he's almost that already. He'll look after you. And I think you'll find him interesting. What do you say?"

"I need time," he said after a few minutes.

"Sure. Why don't you and Jack go and talk about it?" Brooke nodded[9] and Damon took out a white card. He must have had it ready in his pocket from the very start. "Here's a number where you can reach me. We'll need to fly you into Bangkok tomorrow. So maybe you could call me this evening?"

e) *How would you feel if you were in Alex's situation? What would you do?*

E "I know what you're thinking, but you can't possibly go," Jack said. "It's wrong."

Alex and Jack had walked over to the Rocks, the little group of shops and cafés on the edge of the harbour, right[10] under the bridge. Jack had brought them here. She wanted to be with the crowds somewhere bright and normal, a world away from the hidden truths and half-lies of the Australian secret service.

"I think I have to," Alex said.

And it was true. Earlier that afternoon, he had promised himself that he would never work for MI6 again. But this was different – and not just because it was the Australians that were asking him this time. It was Ash. Ash made all the difference, even though[11] the two of them had never met and it was a name he had only just heard of for the first time.

[1]to persuade [pə'sweɪd] – *überzeugen,* [2]to rest [rest] – *hier: legen,* [3]hand [hænd] – *hier: Blatt (Karten),* [4]rather ['rɑːðə] – *eher,* [5]best man [ˌbest 'mæn] – *Trauzeuge,* [6]godfather ['gɒdfɑːðə] – *Pate,* [7]contempt [kən'temt] – *Verachtung,* [8]ever since [ˌevə 'sɪnts] – *seither,* [9]to nod [nɒd] – *nicken,* [10]right [raɪt] – *direkt,* [11]even though [ˌiːvn 'ðəʊ] – *obwohl*

"Ash can tell me who I am," he said.

"Don't you know who you are?"

"Not really, Jack. I thought I knew. When Ian was alive, everything seemed so simple. But then, when I found out the truth about him, it all went wrong. All my life he was training me to be something I never wanted to be. … When did you meet him?" he asked.

"It was about a month after I started working for your uncle," she said. "At the time, it was just a vacation job, to support myself while I was studying. I didn't know anything about spies[1] and I certainly didn't know I'd be staying with you forever! You were about seven years old. Do you really not remember him?"

Alex shook his head.

"He was in London for a few weeks, staying in a hotel. But he came over to the house two or three times. He never did talk to you very much. Maybe he felt uncomfortable with kids. But I got to know him a bit."

"What was he like?"

Jack thought back. "I liked him," she admitted[2]. "In fact, if you want the truth, I even went out with him a couple of times, though he was quite a lot older than me. He was very good-looking. And there was something dangerous about him. He told me he was a deep-sea diver. He was fun to have around."

"Is Ash his real name?"

"It's what he calls himself. A–S–H are his initials[3] – but he never told me what they stood for."

"And he's really my godfather?"

Jack nodded. I've seen photos of him at your christening[4]. And Ian knew him, too. The two of them were friends. I never knew what he was doing in London but he wanted to check up on you. He wanted to be sure you were OK."

Alex took a deep breath. "You don't know what it's like, not having parents," he began. "It's never bothered me, because I never knew them. I was so small when they died. But I've often wondered about them. And it sometimes feels like there's a hole[5] in my life. I look back but there's nothing there. Maybe if I spend a bit of time with this man – even if I do have to dress up like a refugee – it'll fill something in for me."

"But, Alex …" Jack looked at him and he could see she was afraid. "You heard what Brooke said. This could be terribly dangerous. You've been lucky so far, but your luck can't last forever. These people – the snakehead – they sound horrible. You shouldn't get involved."

"I have to, Jack. Ash worked with my dad. He saw my parents the day they died. I didn't know he existed until today, but now I do, I've got to meet him." Alex tried to smile. "My dad was a spy. My uncle was a spy. And now I find out I've got a godfather who's a spy. You have to admit, it certainly runs in the family[6]."

Jack rested her hands on Alex's shoulders. Behind them the sun was already going down, leaving a blood red path on the water. The shops were beginning to empty[7]. The bridge hung[8] over them, throwing a dark shadow.

"Is there anything I can say to stop you?" she asked.

"Yes," Alex looked her straight in the eye. "But please don't!"

"All right." She nodded. "But I'll be worried sick about you. You know that. Just make sure you look after yourself. And tell Ash from me that I want you home by Christmas. And maybe this time, just for once, he'll remember to send a card."

Quickly she turned round and continued walking. Alex waited a minute then followed. Bangkok – The snakehead – Another mission[9]! The truth was that Alex had always thought it might happen – but even he hadn't thought it would come so soon.

[1]spy [spaɪ] – *Spion*, [2]to admit [əd'mɪt] – *zugeben*, [3]initial [ɪ'nɪʃl] – *Anfangsbuchstabe*, [4]christening ['krɪsnɪŋ] – *Taufe*, [5]hole [həʊl] – *Loch*, [6]to run in the family [rʌn] – *in der Familie liegen*, [7]to empty ['empti] – *(sich) leeren*, [8]to hang, hung, hung [hæŋ, hʌŋ, hʌŋ] – *hängen*, [9]mission ['mɪʃn] – *Mission*

2 Spy stories

What spy stories do you know? Think of films, TV programmes/comics/ … . Why did/didn't you like them?

3 The storyline[1]

a) *Read each part (A – E) and write one sentence about what happens in each.*

b) *Use the sentences to make a flow chart. Start like this:*

Two young people meet in a café in Sydney. → They go to … . → There they meet … . →

c) *Join up the sentences to give a short summary of the story.*

4 The characters

a) *Who is the main character? Write the name in the middle of a large piece of paper and draw a wide circle round the name.*

b) *Identify the following characters and describe the role which they play in the extract: Miss Jack Starbright, Ethan Brooke, Marc Damon, Major Yu, Ash, John Rider, Ian Rider.*

c) *How close is their connection to the main character? Put the names in circles round the main character – a close circle if they are closely connected – a far circle if they aren't closely connected.*

d) *Write the name of each of the characters in the story on a card. Each person in your group takes on the identity[2] of one of the characters and introduces himself/herself to the rest of your group, without saying any names. The others have to guess the name from the information they are given.*

5 The setting[3]

a) *Which three cities are mentioned in the story? Describe the events in each.*

b) *Find out three or four facts about them (country, population, famous sights, …) on the Internet.*

c) *Say which city you would prefer to be in and explain your choice.*

6 The turning point[4]

a) *Find the turning point in the story and give reasons why you think so.*

b) *Give a title to the parts before and after the turning point.*

7 The next day

a) *Collect ideas about what could happen next. Think about the storyline, the characters and the setting and write about 100 words of text about how you think the story continues.*

b) *Imagine you are Alex. You have to send an e-mail to your school, explaining why you can't come back yet. Write 80 – 100 words.*

[1]storyline ['stɔ:rilaɪn] – *Handlung,* [2]identity [aɪ'dentəti] – *Identität,* [3]setting ['setɪŋ] – *Schauplatz,* [4]turning point ['tɜ:nɪŋ ˌpɔɪnt] – *Wendepunkt*

Topic 3 Our world in our hands

1 *Food flown into the UK from abroad*

2 *Local, organic products in England*

1. Work with a picture: Choose one photo (1–6). Say why you think the photographer took the photo. (article/leaflet/newspaper report/advert/…)
2. Compare your photo from Ex. 1 with the photo beside it. Say something about where they were taken and what they show. Explain the contrast between the two pictures.
3. (2, 1) Listen and match each of the radio ads to a picture. Say which ad you like best and why.
4. Look at all the photos and link each of them to the title of this topic. Think about buildings, natural resources, food production, … . (→ p. 32/ex. 1, 2)

3

4

5

6

3 *Young men using water in New York City*
4 *Women carrying water in Ethiopia, East Africa*
5 *Lots of lights at Christmas time in Seattle*
6 *Building eco houses in Wales*

A A job agent's article

Global warming brings new jobs

If you have been following environmental changes, you'll know that today everything has to be eco: Green, low energy, environmentally friendly, all mean the same – reducing CO_2 emissions.

But global warming has its good side: more jobs. Eco technology, which is trying to provide 'safe' progress, is big business. People like rangers, zookeepers and biologists for example, who work directly for the environment, are needed everywhere. Eco products mean jobs for millions of people, too: Designers, food experts, shop assistants, engineers, … .

At the same time people who have been doing traditional jobs have had to change: Textile workers, heating engineers, farmers and builders to name just a few.

→ Option 4

B A cartoon: Ways to reduce your carbon footprint

"Isn't it nice to see children walking to school?"

→ Option 3

1 Working for the environment 6

a) *Before you read: You have been considering eco jobs and find this article (text A). What do you think the title means? Read the text. Were you right?*

b) *Think of more jobs which have been changed or created by global warming. Use the Internet for ideas. Find one which interests you and tell your partner about it.*

2 CO_2 emissions 7

a) *You find this cartoon in an eco magazine. Look at it and read the title. What do you think a 'carbon footprint' is?*
   1. The footprint you leave when you walk on a dirty road.
   2. The amount of carbon emissions you produce.
   3. The amount of petrol you use in your car.

b) *Read the caption and explain the cartoon. Say why you like/don't like it.*

c) *Do a class survey: Find out how people get to school. Which way of getting there do you think produces the most/least carbon emissions?*

 To do Topic 3 you'll need: Pronouns → Ov 1 • Relative clauses → Ov 10 • Present perfect → Ov 5

C In a supermarket

➜ Option 1

D Think before you drink!

Why bottled water?

- It's cool and modern!
- It's healthier than soft drinks like coke.
- It's a huge industry which creates wealth and jobs, e.g. on Fiji and Hawaii.
- It tastes better than tap water.
- The bottles make you think you are drinking something exotic.
- Fizzy, bottled water is more refreshing.
- One billion people round the world don't have safe tap water. Bottled water could help them.

Why tap water?

- Tap water is safe – it is tested daily.
- It is cheaper: Bottled water in the US is 500 times more expensive.
- 60 million plastic bottles a day are thrown away in the US alone.
- A filter for around $9 or a slice of lemon will improve the taste of your tap water.
- Hundreds of times more greenhouse gases are emitted in producing one litre of bottled water.
- Clean water projects are much cheaper than bottled water.

➜ Option 2

2, 2 ◎ **3 Let's listen: Food miles** 5 17 (→ p. 33/ex. 4)

a) *Before you listen: Name the products in C. Say which are British and which came from abroad.*

b) *Listen to a message in a supermarket in Britain. Were you right?*

c) *Find the rhetorical devices in the poster. Why are they used?*

d) *Make a grid. Think of alternative sources for your food.*

Food	Country	Distance	Alternative
bread	Germany	local	…
coffee	Brazil	… km	…

4 A global problem 21 (→ p. 33/ex. 3)

a) *Describe the poster. What does it want you to do/not to do? Explain how it tries to put its message across to you.*

b) *What water do kids in your class drink? Only bottled? Only tap? Both? Do a survey.*

c) *What do you think is meant by 'clean water' projects? Use the Internet and find two or three examples.*

d) *Read the texts again and hold a class debate: 'We believe that they shouldn't sell bottled water in Europe.' Vote on the motion.*

So what’s <u>your</u> excuse?

A

ALIVE Magazine Special

Healthy for yourself and for the environment

by Jude Keenan

We all find excuses, not to do what we know we should do! Let’s take what we eat for example. There are thousands of diets on the Internet, books about healthy eating and leaflets on how to lose weight. You all probably know what you should eat to keep yourself healthy.

You are aware that fruit and vegetables are good for you and that too much sugar and fat lead to all sorts of health problems, like heart disease or diabetes. You know that doing sport is better than being a couch potato. But ‘knowing’ is usually easier than ‘doing’, so what do we do? We find excuses.

If we look at how we treat the environment, we find that things are no different. We find excuses here, too. Our food is a good example. If we have been doing all those healthy things like buying fruit and vegetables and cycling to school, things may be better for us.

But will all then be well with the world? If we start eating apples instead of chocolate bars, shouldn’t we maybe look at where the apples were grown? Is that apple that is so healthy for us healthy for the environment, too?

In fact have you ever stopped to think where the food you have been eating all your life comes from? No, the right answer isn’t the supermarket! We mean what is its country of origin – 10 miles, 100 miles or even 1,000 miles from where you live? What does this mean not just for you but also for the environment?

Think about it – what’s the difference if you eat an apple from a tree on a farm 10 miles away and if you eat one from New Zealand? You may say that the New Zealand apple tastes better but does it still taste better if you know that transporting it all that way adds to greenhouse gases and global warming?

Some of you may, of course, live in the middle of a huge city like London or Liverpool or in a vast industrial area where pollution is very high. We all know that most of the poisons we take into our bodies come through our food.

So if you live near a waste incinerator your locally grown apples may not be exactly healthy. This could be a good excuse for eating food which comes from farther away and which is transported to your local shops. But how far do you need to go?

And what about exotic foods like seaweed from Japan or pineapples from South Africa? Do we really need them to be healthy? Some people think so. Their excuse is ‘Because the world is so polluted.’

A famous pop star who was staying in one of the most expensive hotels in the Middle East had a special request: Every morning she drank a fruit cocktail which was made from the juice of every fruit in the world. It was difficult to find them all but the hotel was able to produce the juice.

Imagine the pollution if we all made ourselves such exotic, ‘healthy drinks’ every day!

Exotic fruit cocktail

B A poem

Give and Take

by Roger McGough

I give you clean air
You give me poisonous gas
I give you mountains
You give me quarries

I give you pure snow
You give me acid rain
I give you spring fountains
You give me toxic canals

I give you a butterfly
You give me a plastic bottle
I give you a blackbird
You give me a stealth bomber

I give you abundance
You give me waste
I give you one last chance
You give me excuse
after excuse
after excuse.

www.britishcouncil.org/switzerland-climate-change-anthology.htm

Task: To reconsider how you live

1 What's healthy? 6, 15 9 (→ p. 34/ex. 5, 6)

a) *We all find excuses for doing certain things. Find examples in text A.*

b) *Use the skill on page 95 and write a summary (100 – 120 words) of text A on the computer.*

c) *Compare your summaries and choose the best one.*

d) *Write a list of all the fruit you know. Whose list is longest?*

2, 3 2 Let's listen: A 'healthy' family? 12 (→ p. 35/ex. 8)

a) *Before you listen: What excuses do you/your family/your friends give for not doing 'healthy' things. (feel tired/too far/...)*

b) *Listen to Kate and her family. What excuses do they give? Compare what they say with your answers in part a).*

3 Excuses 5, 8 (→ p. 35/ex. 7)

a) *Read the poem and decide who is talking and to whom.*

b) *Say how you think the poet feels and why?*

c) *Find the contrasts and repetitions in the poem and describe the effect they have on you.*

d) *Think about excuses which people in the poem could make for doing the negative things.*

e) *Check the skill on page 97 and write your own stanza on the topic 'healthy food'. Use pictures to illustrate it.*

4 Presentation: A poetry reading 15 (→ p. 35/ex. 9)

a) *Use the best summary of text A and tell the class what the title means.*

b) *Read out the poem to the class and use your answers from Ex. 3 a) – d) to explain it.*

c) *Present your stanzas from Ex. 3 e) and ask the class to choose the one they like best. They should explain their choice.*

Planet water?

A

MYANMAR: Cyclone survivors need water

GWAY CHAUNG,
29 December 2008 (IRIN)

Thousands of survivors of Cyclone Nargis in the West Asian country, Myanmar, face water shortages, as the dry season begins. Communities in country areas get their water from ponds which were badly polluted with sea water in the May 2008 cyclone.

UNICEF and its partners are digging wells, delivering clean water by boat, as well as setting up several water treatment plants. But water shortages in the area are far from new. Even before Nargis, residents faced water shortages during the dry season, but usually much later, between February and April. Then residents bought water from other villages. But this year people have lost everything and have no money to buy the water.

B

Ghana's daily struggle for water

Children pull along yellow plastic bottles. Young men carry old paint tins. But the hardest work is done by women, walking long distances, with huge metal buckets and bowls on their heads. They are collecting water from roadside pumps and tanks or from rivers because the pipes that should deliver it to their homes are dry. In a country which has lots of natural water reserves a large part of the population still doesn't have access to clean water and some of the poorest people pay a quarter of their income on buying it. People are angry and frustrated. And many blame privatisation three years ago for their problems. A private company, Aqua Vitens Rand Limited (AVRL), was given a contract to manage the existing system, while the government promised to improve things like pipes. Andrew Barber, the boss at AVRL, feels his firm is being blamed for problems caused by a lack of investment.

C

Sea water greenhouses to bring life to desert

Huge greenhouses that grow crops could be combined with solar power plants to make food, fresh water and clean energy in deserts, say the members of a team of architects and engineers, who have been working on the Sahara Forest project. The planned project would use solar power to evaporate salt water, creating cool air and pure water, so that food could be grown.

There are already small plants like this in Tenerife, Oman and the UAE*, where they grow things like tomatoes and lettuce. The solar plants produce more than five times the water needed for the greenhouses, so the rest could be used by people in the area. An energy expert told our reporter that instead of supporting dangerous nuclear-powered treatment plants, governments should invest money in projects like this which are good for the environment.

*United Arab Emirates

D Blue planet, blue gold!

Our non-fiction 'Book of the month'

Introduction:

Our Earth is often called the 'blue planet' because it has lots of water. But most is salt water, which we cannot drink. Fresh water supplies (0,5 %) are shrinking: Climate changes, pollution and increasing world population mean less drinking water for everyone.

Water may soon be more valuable than gold! Large companies around the world are already involved in the 'water trade'. Their goal is to own and control global water resources.

• • • • • • • • • •

Blue Gold, by Maude Barlow and Tony Clarke looks at different aspects of this important topic. The book tells us that powerful governments and big businesses see water supplies as goods, to be bought and sold – a dangerous attitude that points to a lot of questions about water. They ask, for example: *"Who owns it? Should anyone own it? After privatisation, who will buy water for Nature? Will poor people have access to it?"*

The authors believe that fresh water is not just a need: It is a human right – a right which everyone should protect. If we don't, we will have a high price to pay.

Jamilla Khan

Task: To inform others about global water

1 Our daily water

a) *Think: What do you yourself use water for? Where does it come from (a drinks company, a reservoir, ...)? Write some notes.*

b) *Pair: Compare your notes and mark any differences. Try to explain them, e.g.* I only drink water from ... but my partner drinks ... .

c) *Share: Imagine there is a water shortage in your country. Think about how it will affect you. Consider other ways to get water and ways to save it. Write a plan.*

2 Water problems

a) *Split the group into 3 mini groups. Each reads one text (A–C) and writes down key words (country, problems, solutions, ...).*

b) *Each mini group tells the others about its text.*

c) *Collect ideas in the group on how to solve global water problems.*

3 The 'gold' of our generation (→ p. 36/ex. 10, 11; p. 37/ex. 12)

a) *Use the photo and text D to explain its title: 'Blue planet, blue gold!'.*

b) *Which information here is also in texts A–C?*

c) *Collect reasons why we shouldn't waste water.*

4 Let's listen: The Murray-Darling 11 (→ p. 37/ex. 13)

2, 4

a) *Listen. Which country is the report about?*

b) *Listen again. List the problems mentioned and say how the government is trying to solve them.*

5 Presentation: A discussion 13 (→ p. 37/ex. 14)

a) *Use the information and facts you have collected and inform the class about 'global water'.*

b) *'Water is a human right.' Discuss different opinions about this statement.*

Steps in the right direction?

A Changing ourselves

Almost everything we do in life adds to our carbon footprint. This footprint is made by all the greenhouse gases that we produce. It comes from all our activities: products we buy, our leisure activities, our travel and the way we live at home and at work. According to the Carbon Trust, each person in the UK has an annual carbon footprint of around 7 tons of carbon dioxide. That's a lot! So how can we reduce it?

Well, changing what we have been doing every day up till now could make a dramatic difference.

The carbon footprint of your car, for example, is made by the distance you drive, how much fuel it has been using per mile and the number of passengers on each trip. One of the best ways to reduce your footprint is to avoid air travel.

Changing to low energy light bulbs and turning down your heating thermostat are two simple steps that will reduce it and also save you money. You can also turn off equipment left on standby.

Think about what you eat and drink, too. Imagine the carbon footprint made by transporting bottled water! And that's before you add the emissions created by making the bottle and recycling it. Look at the packaging on your food: You can reduce your carbon footprint by buying food that isn't in a packet.

http://www.bbc.co.uk

B Working out the footprint

By Justin Rowlatt BBC Newsnight

So how much of an impact does one - pretty ordinary family - have on the environment?

I [Justin Rowlatt] went to see Professor Tim Jackson of the University of Surrey. He's an expert on the impact people like me have on the environment and has agreed to work out my 'carbon footprint'.

Tim asked lots of questions. It was clear why he wanted to know some things: my gas and electricity use for the last year; what sort of car we've got and how far we've driven it; how I get to and from work; how big our house is and what sort of windows and insulation we have (or do not!). But he also wanted some pretty personal information - asking about the holidays we've had, our shopping, and my income.

And the result? Well, not quite what I'd imagined. I thought that we would be well below the national average: we use the car very little and have been careful about how much energy we use in the home. In fact we are well above it - three tons of carbon above the average, to be exact. The question now is - what can I do to reduce that figure …?

 To do Topic 3 you'll need: Pronouns → Ov1 • Relative clauses → Ov10 • Present perfect → Ov5

547561-0005

C The Rowlatts' carbon footprint

Total = 10 tons of carbon

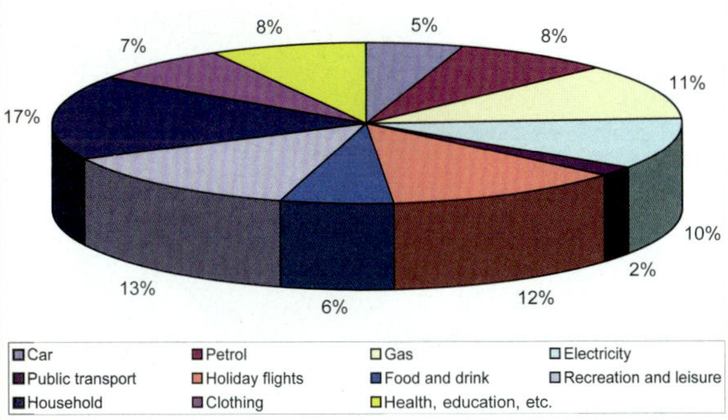

Source: ESRC Research Group on Lifestyles, Values and Environment (RESOLVE), University of Surrey

D Trying to 'go green'

This BBC reporter spent a year trying to go green, so how did he get on?

MAILOnline

By Justin Rowlatt
Last updated at 17:13 07 April 2007

In this age of environmental action, we are all supposed to be aware of our own 'carbon footprint'. But what does going green really involve, and what difference does it make for an ordinary family? To find out, BBC reporter Justin Rowlatt (40), his wife, Bee (35) and daughters Eva (5), Zola (4) and Elsa (9 months), lived ethically for a whole year.

Task: To discuss ways to reduce your carbon footprint

1 Our environment 1, 6

a) *Before you read: Choose the right answers.*
1. … is dangerous for our environment. (Oxygen/Hydrogen/Carbon dioxide)
2. My carbon footprint is rising when I … (buy local food/use low energy light bulbs/drink bottled water)

b) *Read text A. Were you right?*

c) *Collect examples from the text of high emissions and ways to reduce them.*

2 First steps (→ p. 38/ex. 15, 16; p. 39/ex. 17)

a) *Read text B. What did Tim Jackson do for Justin? What was the result?*

b) *Look at the pie diagram (C). How could the family reduce their emissions?*

3 Let's listen: An ordinary family 12 (→ p. 39/ex. 18)

2, 5

a) *Before you listen, read text D. Write notes about Justin, Bee and their children.*

b) *Listen and find out what problems they had when they 'went green'.*

c) *Listen and find out what happened when Bee went into labour. Add more information about the people in her family.*

d) *Who do you think found the year most difficult and why?*

e) *What about you? What would you have found most difficult?*

4 Presentation: A panel discussion 13 (→ p. 39/ex. 19)

a) *Use the information from texts A–D and your results from Ex. 3 and inform the other groups about the Rowlatts. Say who they are, what they did and why. The class can ask questions.*

b) *'We should/n't all try to go green.' The panel members give their opinion and reasons for it.*

c) *The class discusses the statement and votes for or against it.*

The best job in the world?

A A ranger for the Great Barrier Reef

If you have been trying to find an eco job, this might interest you:

Wanted: Island Caretaker

About the job

Tourism Queensland is looking for applicants for the best job in the world! The island caretaker gets a six-month contract on Hamilton Island in the Great Barrier Reef. It's a live-in job with flexible hours, and key duties include exploring the islands of the Great Barrier Reef to discover what the area has to offer.
You'll have to report back on your adventures to Tourism Queensland headquarters in Brisbane (and the rest of the world) via weekly blogs, photo diary, video updates and media interviews. We offer a unique opportunity to help promote the spectacular islands of the Great Barrier Reef.
Other duties may include:

- Feed the fish – There are over 1,500 species of fish living in the Great Barrier Reef. Don't worry – you won't need to feed them all. Most feed themselves.
- Clean the pool – The pool has a filter, but if you see a leaf on the surface it's a great excuse to dive in and enjoy it.
- Collect the mail – During your trips, why not join the flying postal service for a day? It's a great opportunity to see the reef and islands from the air.

About the conditions

AU $150,000 for the six-month contract.
Flights, accommodation and transport on Hamilton Island, travel insurance for the contract period, computer, Internet, digital video and stills cameras access, plus travel to a number of the other islands of the Great Barrier Reef.

Education/Experience

The successful applicant should have excellent communication skills, good written and spoken English, a love for the outdoors, swimming, snorkelling and/or diving skills and one year's job experience in this area of work.

How to apply

Step 1: Create a video application (60 seconds in English) telling us why you're the best person for the job and showing your knowledge of the islands of the Great Barrier Reef.
Step 2: Fill out an application form and send it with your video to www.islandreefjob.com.

Eleven candidates will be invited for an interview. We at Tourism Queensland will choose ten candidates ourselves. Visitors to www.islandreefjob.com will have the chance to choose one 'wild card' candidate.

For more information and to apply please visit www.islandreefjob.com.

⇨ 547561-0006

B Give us an eco job, mate!

The Guardian, Saturday 23 September

That's it, you've been working in this dirty grey office from 9 to 5 for long enough. You're walking out, off to the mountains, off to save the planet. Only problem is ... what do you do?

Perhaps you should try Environment Job first (environmentjob.co.uk): their motto is "If you want to save the planet, make it your job", and they try to connect people with positions. There are several different parts so ask yourself about your skills, and browse through the site to find out what's really out there.

❶ Conservation: fund raising in an office or working in the field, looking after animals, birds, etc. Experience is more important than qualifications.

❷ Campaigning: working to stop clothes companies which use child workers, or on projects to improve cities.

❸ Education: organizing workshops, or communicating with young people and informing them about the environment. You may need teaching qualifications.

❹ Energy: building solar power generators for villages in Africa or looking after wind turbines in Scotland, or you could be in an office in London giving people advice on how to save energy in their homes. A scientific or engineering background will probably be useful.

❺ Recycling: driving trucks or working as a communications officer. They don't usually ask for high qualification levels.

❻ Selling eco products: working on an organic farm, for an organic shop or a food co-operative are all interesting opportunities.

Just remember environmental jobs really don't pay very well, so you may have to prepare yourself for a lower income job. But hey, who needs money when you're saving the world?

Task: To find out about eco careers

1 Jobs you know

a) *Before you read: Brainstorm on jobs. Think about jobs you have read about, people you know, … . Start a list.*

b) *Mark any which could be eco jobs, too.*

2 A job advert 10 (→ p. 40/ex. 20)

a) *Look at the photos in text A. What sort of job do you think the ad is about? Read the text. Were you right?*

b) *Decide why you would/wouldn't like to do this job. Think about the place, duties, the money, experience, skills, … . Write at least six sentences.*

3 More eco jobs 1, 2, 7 (→ p. 40/ex. 21; p. 41/ex. 22)

a) *Skim text B. Match the job in part A with an area of work (1–6) and say why you think they go together.*

b) *The reporter thinks some people might not want to work for the environment. Find his reason and add your own ideas.*

c) *Choose your dream eco job and write an ad for it. You can use the website* environmentjob.co.uk *(job profiles) for ideas. Compare your ad with text A.*

4 Presentation: A job market 15 (→ p. 41/ex. 23)

a) *Display your job ads from Ex. 3 c), let the class do a gallery walk and let them write notes on each job.*

b) *Each member of the class then decides to apply for one of the jobs offered.*

c) *You are the 'employers'. Each applicant is interviewed by one member of your group. Think of five questions for the interview first (education, experience, skills, …).*

d) *Each employer then chooses their best applicant and explains their choice to the class.*

OPTION 1

✔ … discuss living healthily.

a) *Name three things you can do to stay healthy.*

b) *Think of three excuses which you use when you eat or do things which are unhealthy.*

✔ … summarize a text.

Summarize text A on page 52.

✔ … talk about yourself, your friends and the environment.

Choose the correct pronouns to complete the text. Ov1

My mum always makes … *(her/herself)* a sandwich for breakfast and she tells … *(me/myself)* I should at least eat some fruit. But I never make … *(me/myself)* breakfast. I often buy … *(me/myself)* a bagel on the way to school. My friends and I don't always eat things that are healthy for *(us/ourselves)*. After school we sometimes buy … *(us/ourselves)* some chocolate. But we try to keep … *(us/ourselves)* fit. One of my friends doesn't do anything to keep … *(him/himself)* fit. We call … *(him/himself)* 'fossil'. He never comes swimming or skateboarding with … *(us/ourselves)*. And we try to help the environment, too. We all walk or cycle to school. We can't enjoy … *(us/ourselves)* if we know that we are adding to greenhouse gases … *(us/ourselves)*.

✔ … write a stanza of a poem.

Write two new stanzas for the poem on page 55.

OPTION 2

✔ … consider how important water is for you.

a) *Name five things that you use water for and five alternatives that you could use instead.*

b) *Name the places in the picture where people get water. Add more places to your list.*

1

2

3

4

✔ … recognize global water problems.

a) *Sort the words/phrases in the box into problems and solutions.*

pollution • dig wells • shortages • tanks • increasing population • growing need • old pipes • pesticides • treatment plants • salt water • buy water • cyclone • solar power • bottled water • dry periods

b) *Name three countries with water problems and say what their problems are.*

✔ … connect phrases using relative pronouns. Ov10

Explain the meaning of these words. Start like this: ***Salt water*** *is water which … .*

salt water • residents • AVRL • authors • goods • survivors • an expert

OPTION 3

✔ … talk about carbon emissions.

a) *Match the words/phrases in box A with their opposites in box B.*

A	B
to destroy • tap water • to add to • to throw away • high energy • to waste • ordinary • below • very little	a lot • bottled water • above • to save • low energy • to recycle • to reduce • special • to create

b) *Write a short sentence using each word or phrase.*

✔ … describe your activities over a length of time. Ov5

Answer these questions about yourself?

1. What sort of footprint have you been learning about in English this week?
2. Who have you been reading about?
3. Which of your own activities have been adding to your carbon footprint?
4. Have you been trying to reduce your carbon footprint? How?

✔ … understand the problems people have in 'going green'.

a) *Name five problems which you would have if you and your family went green.*

b) *Give three reasons for going green.*

OPTION 4

✔ … understand an ad for a job.

a) *List six important pieces of information that should be given in a job ad.*

b) *How can you apply for a job? Think of 4–5 different ways. Say which you think is best and why.*

✔ … give details about eco jobs.

a) *Which job area (energy/recycling/conservation/education/campaigning/selling eco products) do you think the people in the pictures work in?*

1

2

3

4

b) *Why do you think this? Explain what the people are doing in the photos. What else do they do in their jobs?*

✔ … describe your 'dream' job.

a) *Which of these things are important to you in a job? Explain why.*

a permanent contract • good pay • working outdoors • a friendly boss • flexible hours • being with people

b) *Name three more things that are important to you in a job and say why.*

(→ p. 42/ex. 24; p. 43/ex. 25)

Making water safe to drink (→ pp. 44–46)

Have you ever been thirsty[1]? I don't mean just on a hot day, after running or doing sport. I mean really thirsty, so that you are desperate for a drink! What did you do? You probably turned on a tap or opened a bottle. Well, imagine living somewhere where there are no taps or bottles – in fact, there is hardly any water to drink. And the water that exists is full of highly dangerous bacteria. You're thirsty – but if you dare to drink the water, you'll probably become very sick and even die! Sadly, this is what it's like for over a billion people in the world today.

There are several effective ways that can be used to make water safe for drinking (e.g. filters) but they are often expensive. Scientists, voluntary[2] organisations, some companies and governments have been working together to try to find cheaper alternatives. Here are two which have been developed within the last decade or so:

1 *A straw that kills bacteria as you drink*

This special life-saving equipment was invented by an international company which produces different life-saving products. It is a kind of 'personal water filter' in the form of a big, fat straw which you can wear on a string around your neck[3]. There are no moving parts and the method of use is simple: Just sip the water up through the straw! It has filters, iodine[4] and charcoal[5], inside which remove or kill 99% of the bacteria, viruses etc. in the water as you drink. Then, to keep the straw clean, you blow air back through it after use.

One personal filter lasts for about 700 litres, which is enough for an adult for a year (and up to two years for a child). And it costs about $3.00 – which is one disadvantage: Three dollars may sound cheap (about the price of a coffee in Europe), but in countries where people only earn a dollar a day, it's very expensive!

Another invention for water purification[6] is SODIS (solar water disinfection). As it uses sunlight, it is a relatively[7] cheap way, for example, of getting larger amounts of clean household water supplies.

Scientists have known for a long time that the UV light from the sun kills off bacteria. They then discovered that by leaving water in transparent[8] plastic or glass bottles in the sun, the dangerous bacteria in the water were destroyed!

The use of transparent bottles and the length of time the bottles are kept in the sun are important factors in this method – the cloudier the weather is, the longer it takes! Six hours of sunlight are the minimum needed for safe results. WHO (World Health Organisation) suggests SODIS as a safe method for household water purification. It was successfully used in the 2004 tsunami disaster in Southeast Asia in areas where water supplies were contaminated.

2 *A different kind of 'solar panel' – SODIS in Indonesia*

[1]thirsty ['θɜːsti] – *durstig,* [2]voluntary ['vɒləntri] – *freiwillig,* [3]neck [nek] – *Hals,* [4]iodine ['aɪədiːn] – *Jod,* [5]charcoal ['tʃɑːkəʊl] – *Holzkohle,* [6]purification [ˌpjʊərɪfɪ'keɪʃn] – *Reinigung,* [7]relatively ['relətɪvli] – *relativ,* [8]transparent [træn'spærnt] – *durchsichtig, Licht durchlässig*

A Reading

1 Before you read: Look at the words in the box which are new but similar to German words (or other English words) you know. Try to translate them.

bacteria (l. 4) • filter (l. 7) • method (l. 15) • disinfection (l. 25) • plastic (l. 30) • factor (l. 34) • contaminated (l. 41)

2 Read the text and check your answers.

3 Skim the text and find the best answer.

The text is about a campaign …
a. … for using bottled water in poor countries and against getting water from the ground.
b. … informing people about the importance of clean water and ways to make it safe to drink.
c. … to teach people traditional methods of getting water out of the ground in hot countries.
d. … against methods of water purification which cause environmental disasters.

4 Read the text again carefully and find …

a. … two problems with water that over a billion people in the world have.
b. … a method of water purification which you can carry with you.
c. … a reason why this method may not be suitable in poorer countries.
d. … two advantages of the SODIS technology.
e. … two things you need for the solar disinfection method.

B Language

Find the word or phrase in the text with the same or a similar meaning.

a. other possible ways b. something which keeps you alive c. terrible event

C Listening

2,6

1 A volunteer scientist is talking about drilling[1] wells and using rigs[2] for water. Listen and find the right answers.

a. Jean Pitt is from …	1 Canada.	2 Ghana.	3 a village.
b. She now works in …	1 Canada.	2 Ghana.	3 a national park.
c. She has been there for …	1 three weeks.	2 a few days.	3 many years.
d. Jean's organisation has already built …	1 800 wells.	2 many new villages.	3 88 wells.
e. The price for one well was …	1 $ 30.	2 $ 800.	3 $ 7,000.

2 Look at the grid with a list of reasons why Jean is working as a volunteer and the problems she has in her job. Listen and choose the correct reasons and problems.

Reasons for volunteering	Problems in the job
a. feels she can help people	a. can't buy bottled water
b. likes the climate and nature	b. staying healthy
c. the money she earns	c. the money she earns
d. to give girls there the chance to go to school	d. the old equipment there
e. has skills/experience needed on the project	e. the heat and the climate

[1]to drill [drɪl] – *bohren*, [2]rig [rɪg] – *Bohrvorrichtung*

D Speaking

"Bad water kills more children than war."

"The water with all the answers"

1 Describing

a. Describe the two pictures.

b. What is each poster advertising[1] or campaigning for/against? What makes you think this?

c. Choose a poster. Think about its caption, picture, target[2] group and layout. Collect key words for your ideas.

d. Use your key words and discuss what is (not so) good about the poster you chose. Would you support the campaign/buy the product/...? Explain why/why not.

2 Role play

Someone stops you in the street and asks you to give some money to a charity.

You: (*Frage höflich, für welche Organisation er das Geld sammelt.*)
Man: The organisation is called 'WaterAid'. Here's one of our leaflets for you.
You: (*Bedanke dich. Sage, dass du den Namen schon irgendwo gehört hast und dass du gerne mehr darüber erfahren möchtest.*)
Man: Well, you know, it's 'World Water Day' today. And we're a big charity organisation which helps people in poorer countries to get access to clean drinking water.
You: (*Frage, ob sie das Geld verwenden, um diese Menschen mit Wasser in Flaschen zu versorgen, oder ob sie dort Wasseraufbereitungsanlagen bauen.*)
Man: Well, sending water in bottles is not the answer! We want to help the people to help themselves: We give them technical training so they can improve the quality of the water there.
You: (*Frage, was 'WaterAid' in Gebieten macht, in denen es wenig Wasser gibt.*)
Man: Some of the money we collect goes to pay for drilling wells in places like that. But they still need a method to kill any bacteria in the well water.
You: (*Erkläre, dass du 'WaterAid' etwas/kein Geld geben möchtest. Sage, warum du das (nicht) tust. Sage, dass du vorhast, das Flugblatt zu lesen. Frage, ob sie auch Praktikanten benötigen.*)
Man: Yes, but not abroad. Just check on the Internet – there's an e-mail address in the leaflet.
You: (*Bedanke dich für die vielen Informationen. Sage, dass du hoffst, dass er für 'WaterAid' viel Geld sammeln wird. Verabschiede dich.*)

[1]to advertise [ˈædvətaɪz] – *werben*, [2]target [ˈtɑːgɪt] – *Ziel*

E Mediation and communication

You find some information in German for a school project on SODIS. Your English exchange partner is interested in how the method works but his/her German isn't very good. Answer his/her questions.

Was bedeutet „**Solar-Desinfektion**"?

Solare Trinkwasser Desinfektion (SODIS) ist eines von vielen unterschiedlichen Wasseraufbereitungsverfahren. Einmalig ist aber, dass diese Methode sowohl die UV-Strahlung der Sonne als auch ihre Wärme verwendet, um Keime bzw. für Menschen gefährliche Bakterien im Wasser zu töten. Eine sichere Wasserquelle durch SODIS kann Leben retten, vorausgesetzt ist allerdings die korrekte Anwendung.

❶ Nur saubere, nicht beschädigte (speziell hierfür geeignete) PET-Flaschen benutzen.
❷ Flaschen mit dem kontaminierten Wasser füllen und fest zuschließen.
❸ Flaschen sollen mindestens 6 Stunden in der Sonne (z.B. auf einem Metalldach) liegen. Bei sehr wolkigem Wetter kann es bis zu 2 Tage dauern bis alle Keime getötet sind.
❹ Das saubere Wasser soll immer nur in PET- oder Glasflaschen gelagert werden.
❺ Nur aus sauberen Tassen bzw. direkt aus der Flasche trinken.

Vorteile dieser Methode sind, dass sie relativ leicht aufzustellen und durchzuführen ist: Sie benötigt weder kostspielige Geräte noch teuere Arbeitskräfte.
Vor allem in Ländern mit heißem Klima und viel Sonne funktioniert SODIS hervorragend. In Gebieten, in denen umgekehrte Wetterverhältnisse herrschen, ist dieses Verfahren jedoch nicht zu empfehlen. Die Methode ist nicht für die chemische Reinigung und auch nicht für **sehr** trübes Wasser geeignet. Nicht ganz durchsichtige Flaschen könnten für die UV-Strahlung der Sonne nicht durchlässig genug sein, was eine nicht ausreichende Desinfizierung zur Folge hätte. Darüber hinaus besteht bei nicht geeigneten Flaschen (z.B. PVC-Flaschen) die Gefahr, dass Plastik in winzigen Mengen ins Wasser gelangt, was für Menschen bedenklich sein könnte.

a. So, what's so special about the SODIS method?
b. When can SODIS be dangerous?
c How do you get clean water with this method?
d. Are there any advantages in using SODIS?
e. What about problems with this method

F Writing

1 Skills

Why should we in Europe take care of our water? Think about what we use water for, where it's wasted, how we can save or protect it. What problems could we and others have in the future? Collect your ideas in a mind map.

2 A leaflet

You want to help with a campaign to make people think about how valuable water is. Use your ideas from part 1 and write a text (80–100 words) for a leaflet. Think of a good heading that would attract attention.

Topic 4 Choices and decisions

1. Work with a picture: Look at photo 1. Sum up the situation. Try to imagine what decisions the young people have to make, e.g. (whether or not to tell their parents, how serious the relationship is, when to …). Think about who or what could help them.
2. What decisions do you have to make at the moment? Put them in order of importance.
3. Look at the other photos and try to imagine how the young people feel. What advice would you give them in each situation?
4. Look at the choices in the box and the young people in the photos. Choose one choice and match it with a photo. Talk for about two minutes on this topic in your country. What's different? Do they have the same choices? At what age? (→ p. 47/ex. 1, 2)

Choices at sixteen
- a college course
- a job abroad/away from home
- a partner
- a car
- a way of life

2

3

4

5

⇨ 547561-0007

A Legal ages

This table lists different countries around the world, and shows the ages at which people can legally do things.

	USA	UK	Germany	Poland	Turkey
Leaving school	16–18*	16	16–18*	18	14
Employment	14	13	13	15	12
Age of consent (AOC)	14–18*	16	14	15	18
Marriage	18	16 (with parental consent	18	16 female 18 male	17
Driving a car	14–17*	17	17–18*	17	17
Buying alcohol (MPA)	21	18	16, 18**	18	18
Smoking	18–19*	18	18	18	18
Voting in an election	18	18	18	18	18
Criminal responsibility	6–10*	10	14	17	11

*http://www.chartsbin.com http://eu.wikipedia.org http://www.2pass.co.uk *varies from state to state **18 for spirits*

➔ Option 1

B A teenage tragedy

Tessa was simply a normal teenager: She looked at the world around her and wanted to experience it. She would go to discos with her friend, Zoey, and would daydream about having sex for the very first time. Then she got ill. Doctors told her that she would get better and she did get better. But just as she was starting to enjoy life again, she got ill again. Now she was facing a decision: Should she become bitter and let her illness control her or should she use the time left to her to fulfil as many of her dreams as possible? The choice was hers.

➔ Option 3

1 Let's talk: Different laws (→ p. 48/ex. 3)

a) *Read the table in A and explain the title.*

b) *Put the countries in order with the most restrictive at the top.*

c) *Say which law(s) you agree/don't agree with and give reasons. Start like this:*
I think it's right that males in … because … .
I don't agree with the legal age for … in because … .

2,7 2 Let's listen: Book reviews (→ p. 48/ex. 4)

a) *Read the text on the book cover. What do you find out about Tessa/her problem/ her choices? Start three lists.*

b) *Listen and add to your lists from a).*

c) *What makes you think that you would/wouldn't like to read this novel?*

C Decisions at 16

→ Option 2

This year you are going to have to decide about your future. You have two main choices. You can continue in education to do your A-levels or move into training and work.

1. Choices in education may include:

- → a school sixth form where you'll probably know everyone – unless you join a sixth form in a different school
- → a sixth form college where you'll meet students from other local schools
- → a further education college where you won't just meet students of your own age, but also adults
- → a specialist college offering courses in subject areas such as horticulture, creative arts, music and agriculture, as well as courses for students with additional needs or disabilities.

Specialist colleges are often some distance from home and you could have to do a lot of travelling. You might even have to live in or near the college during the week in term time.
Find out more at www.natspec.org.uk

Get information about financial support for residential courses at www.direct.gov.uk/extrahelp

2. If you aren't continuing in education, choices may include:

- → an apprenticeship, with on-the-job training and study to gain the qualifications you need for a specific job
- → a job with training, where the employer organizes the training
- → a job with time off for study and training, where you organize training that will help you to gain the qualifications you need and improve your employment prospects
- → a training programme to prepare you for work
- → self-employment – very few people do this at the end of Year 11, so if this is your goal, get expert advice as soon as possible.

www.direct.gov.uk/en/EducationAndLearning/14to19/OptionsAt16.index.htm

3 Different directions (→ p. 48/ex. 5)

a) *Before you read: Do a survey and find out what all the kids in your class are going to do next year.*

b) *Read text C and complete this flow chart on choices in the UK at 16.*

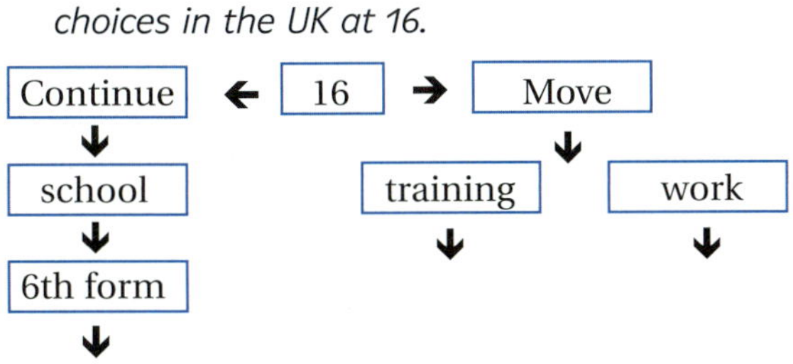

c) *Use the flow chart to talk about the choices which UK kids have at 16.*

d) *Check one of the two Internet sites in the text and find out more about specialist colleges or financial support for students in the UK.*

e) *What about the situation in Germany? Do kids in the UK have any choices which are different from the choices you can make?*

f) *What are you going to do when you're 16. Why?*

Just for parents?

A Important decisions

The US author, Sean Covey, wrote a book for parents of teenagers. It was extremely popular both with the adults and with their kids; many of these young people even wrote to Sean about their problems.

... Life is about choices, and the decisions your teen makes today can affect his or her life in years to come, ... Here are six key decisions you should discuss with your child:

School: How does your teen plan to spend the years in school? Does he/she take studies seriously? Talk openly with your teen about school.

Friends: How does your child choose friends: surround himself/herself with people that support him/her, worry that he/she is "supposed to be" friends with a certain crowd of people? Make sure to have an open dialogue with your teen about all the different aspects of choosing friends.

Parents: How is your relationship with your teen? As he/she begins to want more freedom and fewer restrictions, you must make him/her understand that freedoms come with additional responsibilities.

Addictions: Does your teen recognize the serious dangers that go with alcohol and drugs? Listen to what your teen has to say about them, and encourage him/her to be truthful about any experiments he/she, or even friends, have been involved in.

Dating & Sex: How does your teen feel about dating, and what does he/she know about sex? Let your teen talk openly about feelings, desires and fears, but make sure he/she is clear on the serious risks that come with any serious romantic relationship.

Self-Worth: Of all the 6 decisions, this can be the one that determines how your child will face the other 5. If your teen learns to see himself/herself in the best light possible, learns to love himself/herself – flaws and all – drugs, drinking, dropping out of school, and sex before he/she is ready won't seem so tempting.

Sure, talking to your teen can be difficult. But caring for your teen through a drug or alcohol addiction, an unwanted pregnancy, or failing grades can be a lot worse. The more you share, and the more you listen to your teen, the easier it will be to communicate in the future.

B Help!

Monday, November 5th
OK, so I'm 15 in 10th grade. But I don't know what to do. I understand the classes and they are quite simple but I just can't seem to focus. Last year I was getting good grades until the summer. My grades have been slipping since then. In my last progress report I only had 2 As out of 7 classes, the rest were 1 B and 4 Cs. My parents say I should stop staying after school: I'm in the Spanish club and others. But I like them. The only problem I see is that I can't concentrate – I can't get organized. I just can't seem to make myself sit down and focus.
D.

Monday, November 5th
My mom and I aren't really getting along right now and I don't really know why. Maybe because she really hurt me over the summer. I cry all the time (in private of course) and have talked to my guidance teacher. Although I didn't go to a doctor, I was feeling depressed for about a month but I have finally gotten over it. I get so angry sometimes for no reason and I want to hit something or someone so hard, just to let it out. Then I shut people close to me out and it's not right. I need comments and advice. I'm ready to listen.
B.

Monday, November 5th
In the summer I met this girl in the class above me. She was hanging out with my older sister. They would sometimes take me with them when they went to a disco. I know she likes me because she told my sister that I'm 'real cool'. But a friend of her brother's is crazy about her, too. She says he's too old for her. He's 21. She's not sure what to do. I think we should just go for it and forget that I'm a year younger. What do you think, Sean? By the way, I'm a huge fan of your books.
J.

Task: To consider how to make 'life' decisions

1 Advice for parents 1, 6 (→ p. 49/ex. 6, 7)

a) *Read the text by Sean Covey and explain the pictures.*

b) *Complete the sentences:* He advises parents to … . He advises them not to … .

c) *The advice given is for Americans. Would it be 'good' advice for you/your friends/your parents?*

d) *What is the author's conclusion? Do you agree with him? Give reasons.*

2 Just for kids 1, 6

a) *Do you think parents really need advice like this? Say why/why not.*

b) *If you had a problem with your parents and were given a guide like this, would you read it? Say why/why not in 2–3 sentences.*

3 Advice for teenagers 1, 15 10 (→ p. 50/ex. 8)

a) *Read the three e-mails to Sean (part B) and decide what each writer's problem is.*

b) *Make three mini groups. Each uses Sean's advice and writes a short e-mail answer (50–60 words).*

c) *One member of each mini group reads out their group's answer and the others give feedback.*

d) *Improve your group's answer.*

4 Presentation: A gallery walk 11, 15 (→ p. 50/ex. 9)

a) *Which of Sean's 'areas' is most important? Draw a mind map with this area in the middle. Write one piece of Sean's advice for each area.*

b) *Each mini group says which problem their e-mail writer has and explains what Sean would advise them to do.*

c) *Display the e-mails in class and let the others do a gallery walk.*

d) *Vote on the best advice on each problem.*

Jobs in the car industry

A An American company

Automotive companies

> The US > Detroit > Companies > **Longbow's**

PROFILE

LONGBOW's Motor Co.

Headquarters: 1599 Boulder Way, Michigan 48905, USA
Chief Executive Officer (CEO): Cavendish Homer Longbow Junior

HOME
NEWS
PROFILE
CAREERS
INTERNSHIPS
DEPARTMENTS
> Manufacturing
> Human Resources
> Product Development
> Marketing & Sales
> IT
> Environment & Safety
> Finance
> PR

Longbow's started as far back as 1910 when James Cavendish Longbow developed one of the first EVs or electric vehicles. They were very popular then and you would often see people driving them but they quickly went out of fashion. Over 50 years later James's great-grandson, Cavendish, was looking at some old photos of James's car when he decided to bring back electric vehicles. He started a small business, which produced one of the first modern electric cars. In the late 1990s interest in electric vehicles was still growing, so they moved into truck production. Longbow's is now one of the biggest manufacturers of electric vehicles in the US. We have 12,000 full-time employees.
Our company is based in Detroit, Michigan, USA. We have two main sectors, Automotive and Financial.

The automotive sector:
We design, develop, manufacture, sell and service cars and trucks for a worldwide market. We sell cars with the names 'Swallow' and 'Eagle' and trucks with the name 'Greenroad'.

We market cars, trucks and vehicle parts directly through our retailers throughout the US and Canada. All models and car parts are also sold through dealers in many other countries.
We supply vehicles to fleet customers, rental companies, leasing companies and governments. We also offer customers a wide range of after-sales services, including vehicle parts and repairs.

The financial sector:
We offer financial products to fleet customers and rental companies. We also offer loans to dealers wishing to set up a salesroom, buy vehicles or to improve their facilities. Further products include insurance services for dealers and customers.

⇨ 547561-0008

B Student opportunities

Summer internships at Longbow's
You've spent more than ten years learning about the world in your classroom, so now it's time to find out about the 'real' world. No better way to do that than to spend the summer as an intern in our company. Here are just a few ideas to get you started.

Manufacturing

Mechanic
Mechanics are employed in the Manufacturing Department. Their duties range from damage assessment of accident vehicles to prototype construction. They have to make body shells and vehicle frames or restore old cars. Good grades in Math and Physics are important. They need to be interested in machines and must be able to think in three dimensions. They also need to be reliable and flexible and should enjoy team work.

IT department

Computer specialist
Employees in the IT department are not only expected to design systems for colleagues in other departments. They must also be able to offer advice and support to them. They are the link between what a department needs and the planning of a new system. They must have computer skills and a good grade in Math. They also must be able to communicate well both orally and in writing.

Human resources

Office specialist
This position is based in the Human Resources Department. From there you could move on to the Finance Department or PR (Public Relations). You will need good team working skills. You must be able to use modern communication equipment and explain the equipment to others. Good English and organizational skills are essential.

Task: To choose an internship

1 Car companies

a) *Collect brand names of cars and choose two of your favourites. Say what you like about them.*

b) *Find out more about them on the Internet: CEO? Headquarters? Number of workers? ... ?*

2 Jobs in the auto industry 1 (→ p. 51/ex. 10)

a) *Read text A and look at the 3 photos. Use the text to explain the photos and to give information about them.*

b) *Collect activities that employees at Longbow's do. Sort them into departments. The list in the scroll down menu can help you.*

c) *Read text B and add to your list from b).*

3 A summer job (→ p. 51/ex. 11)

a) *Read text B again and split the group into three mini groups. Each mini group chooses one job.*

b) *Find out more about your 'job' on the Internet and explain to the others why you are going to apply for it. Are there any negative aspects about the job?*

2,8

4 Let's listen: Three interns 12 (→ p. 52/ex. 12)

a) *Three young people, Carl Pinovski, Mel Bradshaw and Abdur Badawi, did internships at Longbow's. Listen and say who did which job.*

b) *Listen again: What did or didn't they like about the job?*

5 Presentation: A job panel 9 (→ p. 52/ex. 13)

a) *One half of the group uses the information in text A to present Longbow's to the class.*

b) *The other half uses text B to encourage the class to apply for internships there.*

c) *All members of the class decide which job they would most like to do and give reasons for their choice.*

An extract from a novel: 'Before I die' *by Jenny Downham (adapted)*

1 Before you read: Describe the pictures on pages 76/77. Say who and what you think they show. The title and text B on page 70 can help you.

2 Read the introduction below and the extract (p. 76–78) and improve your answers. Read for fun! Don't look up new words. Try to guess new words from the context or from words you already know in English and German. Use an English/German dictionary only for important new words.

Introduction:

Tessa, 16, has been fighting leukaemia for four years. She was getting better but she has realised that she is going to die and has written a list of things she still wants to do. She borrowed a dress from her friend, Zoey, and tried to be like her so that she could lose her virginity but now she feels bitter.

A The boy looks surprised when I stick my head over the fence and call him. He's older than I thought, perhaps eighteen, with dark hair and the shadow of a beard.

"Yeah?"

"Can I burn some things on your fire?"

He shambles up the path towards me, wiping a hand across his forehead as if he's hot. His fingernails are dirty and he has bits of leaf in his hair. He doesn't smile.

I lift up the two shoeboxes so he can see them. Zoey's dress is draped across my shoulder like a flag.

"What's in them?"

"Paper mostly. Can I bring them round?"

He shrugs as if he doesn't care either way, so I walk through our side gate and step over the low wall that separates the two houses, across his front garden and down the side of his house. He's already there, holding the gate open for me. I hesitate.

"I'm Tessa."

"Adam."

We walk in silence down his garden path. I bet he thinks I've just been chucked by my boyfriend, that these are love letters. I bet he thinks, 'No wonder she got dumped, with that skeleton face and bald head.' The fire is disappointing when we get there, just a smouldering pile of leaves and twigs, with a few hopeful flames licking at the edges.

"The leaves were damp," he says. "Paper'll get it going again."

I open one of the boxes and tip it upside down.

 To do Topic 4 you'll need: Future forms → Ov6 • Past progressive → Ov3 • Adverbs → Ov12

B From the day I noticed the first bruise on my spine, to the day two months ago when the hospital officially gave up on me, I kept a diary. Four years of pathetic optimism burns well – look at it flare! All the get-well cards I ever received curl at the edges, crisp right up and flake to nothing. Over four long years you forget people's names.

There was a nurse who used to draw cartoons of the doctors and put them by the bed to make me laugh. I can't remember her name either. Was it Louise? She was quite prolific. The fire spits, embers spark away into the trees.

"I'm unburdening myself," I tell Adam.

But I don't think he's listening. He's dragging a clump of bramble across the grass towards the fire. It's the next box I hate the most. Me and Dad used to trawl through it together, scattering photos over the hospital bed.

'You will get well again,' he'd tell me as he ran a finger over my eleven-year-old image, self-conscious in my school uniform, first day at secondary school.

'Here's one of you in Spain,' he'd say. 'Do you remember?'

I looked thin and brown and hopeful. I was in remission for the first time. A boy whistled at me on the beach. My dad took a picture, said I'd never want to forget my first whistle. But I do.

I have a sudden desire to rush back home and get more stuff. My clothes, my books.

I say, "Next time you have a fire, can I come round again?"

Adam stands on one end of the bramble with his boot and folds the other end into the fire.

He says, "Why do you want to get rid of everything?"

I squash Zoey's dress into a tight ball; it feels small in my fist. I throw it at the fire and it seems to catch light before it even reaches the flames. Airborne and still, melting into plastic.

"Dangerous dress," Adam says, and he looks right at me, as if he knows something. All matter is comprised of particles. The more solid something is, the closer the particles are held together. People are solid, but inside is liquid. I think perhaps standing too close to a fire can alter the particles of your body, because I feel strangely dizzy and light.

I'm not quite sure what's wrong with me – maybe it's not eating properly – but I seem to not be grounded inside my body. The garden turns suddenly bright. Like the sparks from the fire, which drift down onto my hair and clothes, the law of gravity says that all falling bodies must fall to the ground.

C It surprises me to find myself lying on the grass, to be looking up at Adam's pale face haloed by clouds. I can't work it out for a minute.

"Don't move," he says. "I think you fainted."

I try and speak but my tongue feels slow and it's so much easier to lie here.

"Are you diabetic? Do you need sugar? I've got a can of Coke here if you want some."

He sits down next to me, waits for me to lean up, then hands me the drink. My head buzzes as the sugar hits my brain. How light I feel, more ghostly than before, but so much better. We both look at the fire. The stuff from my boxes has all burned away; even the boxes themselves are just charred remains. The dress has turned to air. The ashes are still hot though, bright enough to attract a moth, a stupid moth dancing towards them. It crackles as its wings fizz and turn to dust. We both watch the space where it was.

I say, "You do a lot of gardening, don't you?"

"I like it."

"I watch you. Through my window, when you're digging and stuff."

He looks startled. "Do you? Why?"

"I like watching you."

He frowns, as if he's trying to work that out, seems about to speak for a moment, but looks away instead, his eyes travelling the garden.

"I'm planning a vegetable patch in that corner," he says. "Peas, cabbage, lettuce, runner beans. Everything really. It's for my mum more than me."

"Why?"

He shrugs, looks up at the house as if mentioning her might bring her to the window. "She likes gardens."

"What about your dad?"

"No. It's just me and my mum."

I notice a thin trickle of blood on the back of his hand. He sees me looking and wipes it away on his jeans.

"I should probably get on," he says. "Will you be all right? You can keep the Coke if you want."

He walks next to me as I make my way slowly up the path.

I'm very happy that my photos and diary are burned, that Zoey's dress has gone. It feels as if different things will happen.

I turn to Adam at the gate.

I say, "Thank you for helping."

He says, "Any time."

He has his hands in his pockets. He smiles, then looks away, down at his boots. But I know he sees me.

3 These new words are like words you already know in English or German or you know them already with a slightly different meaning. Try to guess their meaning here.

leukaemia • shoebox • to drape • to dump • skeleton • hopeful • to lick • pathetic • optimism • clump • secondary school • to whistle • particle • diabetic • ash • moth

Task: To analyse an extract from a novel

1 The setting 3

a) *Look at the photos and choose the one which best matches the place where the story is set.*

1

2

3

b) *Explain your choice and say whether or not you would like to be in this garden.*

2 Characters 1, 3

a) *Who are the main characters in the story? Say what sort of people you think they are. Think about the way they look, what they say, how they react to others and what they do.*

b) *What other characters appear in the story? How are they connected to the main characters?*

3 The storyline 3, 7 (→ p. 53/ex. 14)

a) *Split the group into three mini groups. Each chooses one part of the extract (A, B or C) and prepares its storyline. You can act it out, write it as a film script or as a radio play.*

b) *Decide which answers are given in the story and which questions are still open. Give your own ideas for answers, e.g. try to answer any open questions.*

c) *How is the relationship between the two main characters going to develop? Write a short text (50–60 words).*

4 The point of view 3 (→ p. 53/ex. 15; p. 54/ex. 16)

Who tells us the story? Say why you think the author chose this point of view.

5 Presentation: A review 3, 15 (→ p. 54/ex. 17)

a) *Split the group into three mini groups. Each chooses a certain aspect (setting, characters, storyline) of the story and collects information about it. You can use Ex. 1–3 to help you.*

b) *Try to visualize basic elements of the aspect you have chosen, e.g. arrange the names and information about the characters in a flow chart or on a poster, so that you can show how close to or far from each other they are. Does this change or develop?*

c) *Use your flow chart or poster to inform the class about your aspect of the story.*

d) *The class discusses if the book could be turned into a film and gives five reasons why or why not.*

OPTION 1

✔ … discuss legal ages.

a) *Name three things which you can't legally do in your country until you are 16.*

b) *Compare them with the legal ages for these things in the US.*

✔ … recognize the 'age of consent' in different countries.

a) *Explain the term 'age of consent' in one sentence.*

b) *Name one country where …*
1. … the 'age of consent' is lower than 16.
2. … sex is legal from the age of 18.
3. … it varies from 14 to 18.

✔ … talk about decisions you have to make at 16. Ov12

absolutely · largely · openly · extremely · normally · carefully · always

Sean writes about six key decisions that teenagers … have to make. The first is about staying or not staying at school. He says parents should talk … to their kids about this. Choosing the right friends can also be … important. It is … vital that parents don't give their kids more freedom without more responsibilities. Decisions about dating, sex and drugs should also be made … . Parents should … discuss risks and dangers with their kids. The most difficult decision is about self-worth. Parents can avoid problems here … by listening and talking.

OPTION 2

✔ … talk about choices in the UK at 16.

a) *What are the two choices which British students have to make at 16?*

b) *Name two further choices for each main choice.*

✔ … describe what happens in an automotive company.

a) *Find the odd word out in these four lists:*

design	market	headquarters	loans
drive	retailers	governments	insurance
manufacture	dealers	rental company	internships
develop	grandson	fleet customers	financial products

b) *Write a heading for each of the lists.*

c) *Use each of the three correct words in each list in one sentence. Write four sentences.*

✔ … talk about people in a company.

a) *Say in 1–2 sentences what these employees do:*

office specialist • mechanic • computer specialist

b) *What qualifications do you need to do the jobs in a)?*

c) *Give three reasons why it might be a good idea to do an internship in a company.*

OPTION 3

✔ … understand how some ill people feel.

a) *Think of someone who is seriously ill. Describe their situation. How did they change?*

b) *What advice would you give to people who know them: ask/don't ask about what's wrong, act normally, be …? (2 things)*

✔ … decide what you are going to do in life. Ov6

a) *Think of 3–4 things that you're doing at the weekend. Say why you are doing them.*

b) *Write a list of five things which you are going to do before you are twenty-one. Put them in order of importance. Who or what could help you to do these things?*

c) *What problems might you have? Start like this: It might be difficult to find… / get to … /… , because … .*

✔ … use an English/German dictionary.

a) *Look up the word 'tip' and find at least four different meanings for it.*

b) *Match the meanings from a) to the word 'tip' in these sentences.*

1. She gave the young man a tip for burning the papers.
2. Her room was a real tip. There were clothes and books everywhere.
3. She decided to tip all the books into a box and burn them.
4. Adam gave her lots of tips about gardening.

✔ … analyse an extract from a novel. Ov3

a) *Which of these pictures shows a scene from 'Before I die'? What was happening at this point in the story?*

1

2

3

b) *Think back to the story. Who was doing what when …*

1. … Tessa spoke to him?
2. … the garden turned suddenly bright?
3. … a stupid moth danced towards the ashes?

c) *Write one sentence each about the point of view and the storyline in 'Before I die'.*

d) *What did/didn't you like about the story? Write a short e-mail (30–40 words) on the computer.*

(→ p. 55/ex. 18, 19; p. 56/ex. 20)

teen magazine

CAREERS *Advice*

DRESS FOR THE JOB (→ pp. 57–59)

In some jobs there may be a dress code. This is a set of rules about what you are expected to wear, for example a dark suit for accountants[1] or bank employees. But in most jobs you don't need to wear a formal uniform, so you may think how you dress is your decision. But is it?
Well, in fact, there are usually (often unspoken) dress codes no matter where you work. A good tip is to dress to match the job you're doing, and to 'fit in' with the other members of staff. The trick is to keep some of your own style, but at the same time, not draw[2] too much attention to yourself. Our checklist on the right will be useful for most jobs.

But what about dressing for a job interview[3]? Well, the rules are almost the same. However, for an interview you'll need to dress just a bit better than you would as an employee. So it's important to find out before your interview if your potential employer has a dress code, for example formal – suit and tie[4], or not quite so formal. A good way to find out (if you don't live far away) is to watch employees arriving for work!

You're not sure about tattoos or body jewellery? Well, to be on the safe side, don't show the tattoos and take off the jewellery for the interview!

DRESS CODE CHECKLIST

- The clothes you wear should match the job that you do.
- Your clothes should always be clean and neat (that also means ironed!).
- Your shoes should be sensible, clean and in good condition[5].
- Any make-up shouldn't be overdone.
- Nails[6] should be clean and not too long.
- Your hair should be neat and clean. In some jobs you may need to put it under a cap (e.g. lab or technical assistant, catering, etc.).
- Hats, headscarves or caps are usually not worn in office jobs (except for religious traditions).

As a teleworker Colin sometimes found it difficult to adjust to[8] normal office life.

Let's say that you get the job and things go well till near the end of your first week. But then on Thursday a colleague tells you Fridays are always 'dress down' days in the company. So what exactly does dress down mean, you wonder. You'd like to ask, but you don't want people to think you're stupid.

Well, in some offices this day is called 'casual[7] Friday'. And casual means the opposite of formal. But it doesn't mean you can just get out of bed and come into work! And it definitely doesn't mean you can arrive in beach clothes and flip flops!

Even if it's dress down day, you may perhaps be asked to bring in a less casual jacket – which you can put on if you get an unexpected visit from a business partner or customer!
No matter where you are, if it's important to you, then think carefully about what the clothes you wear may say to others. Remember: You never get a second chance to make a first impression!

[1]accountant [ə'kaʊntənt] – *Buchhalter/-in,* [2]to draw [drɔː] – *lenken,* [3]job interview ['dʒɒb ˌɪntəvjuː] – *Bewerbungsgespräch,* [4]tie [taɪ] – *Krawatte,* [5]condition [kən'dɪʃn] – *Zustand,* [6]nail [neɪl] – *Nagel,* [7]casual ['kæʒuəl] – *zwanglos, lässig,* [8]to adjust to [ə'dʒʌst tə] – *sich gewöhnen an*

A Reading

1 Before you read: Look at the title of the text. What do you think a 'dress code' is?
a. … a secret way of dressing b. … rules about how to dress c. … clothes sizes in numbers

2 Before you read: Explain the meaning of the words in the box. They are new but are similar to German or other English words you know.

unspoken (l. 6) • fit in (l. 8) • potential (l. 16) • flip flops (l. 31) • unexpected (l. 34) • teleworker (cartoon)

3 Read the text and check that you have understood them.

4 Read the text again carefully and complete the sentences. Use your own words.

a. Even in jobs without written dress codes you can't just … .
b. If there is no written code, it's a good idea to … .
c. You should try to keep your own … .
d. The difference between dressing for work and dressing for an interview is … .
e. On dress down day you can … .

5 Explain in 1–2 sentences what the text is about.

B Language

Find a word or phrase in the text to match each definition.

a. to make sure you don't do anything wrong
b. neat and flat through heat
c. less formal
d. another opportunity

2,9 C Listening

1 Listen to four interviews at a tube station. Match each person (A–D) with the right workplace (1–9).

1) London Underground • 2) legal department • 3) hotel reception • 4) technical design firm • 5) sales department • 6) broadcasting company • 7) radio assistant • 8) job agency • 9) clothes department

2 What does the interviewer ask the interviewees[1] about?

3 Listen again carefully and find out each person's opinion.

a. Interviewee A …
1 is all for suits. 2 is for light suits in summer. 3 only loves dark suits.

b. Interviewee B …
1 is all for uniform at work. 2 is glad there's no dress code. 3 doesn't like the atmosphere at work.

c. Interviewee C …
1 thinks clothes rules are OK. 2 gets clothes dirty at work. 3 loves outrageous clothes.

d. Interviewee D …
1 loves his new job. 2 never wears a tie to work. 3 says you need a tie for an interview.

[1]interviewee [ˌɪntəvjuːˈiː] – *Kandidat/in*

D Speaking

1

2

3

4

1 Describing

a. Describe the people in each picture. Say what they are wearing and what sort of job you think they might have. Give reasons.

b. What sort of people do you think they are? What gives you this impression?

c. Imagine that you have just watched each one in an interview for a job. They are all excellent (equal in their qualifications, answers to questions, experience and personality). Say which one you would choose if you were the interviewer. Give reasons and discuss your ideas.

2 Role play

You are at a job interview in a big company. Answer the interviewer's questions.

Interviewer: So, please tell me: Why are you interested in this job?

You: (*Sage z.B, dass du immer an … interessiert warst/ im Schulfach … gut warst/ ein Praktikum bei … gemacht hast.*)

Interviewer: That's great. I've had a look at your portfolio[1], of course. But tell me briefly about your work placement, voluntary[2] or holiday jobs and some of the tasks you were given there.

You: (*Erzähle, was du im Praktikum/Ferienjob/bei Auslandsaufenthalten gemacht hast.*)

Interviewer: Our company may offer jobs abroad in future. How do you feel about travelling?

You: (*Sage, dass du gerne verreist, und erwähne, welche anderen Sprachen du sprichst.*)

Interviewer: That's fine. So, let's look at the business itself: Some people here say that the quality of our goods is more important than how we present ourselves. What's your opinion on that?

You: (*Sage deine Meinung dazu.*)

Interviewer: OK. It's important that you use our dress code. And that you know how to behave[3] when you meet international clients[4]. Would you be interested in a training course on this?

You: (*Sage, dass du die Kleiderordnung wichtig findest. Zeige dich am Coaching interessiert und gib ein Beispiel dafür, wie man sich falsch verhalten könnte.*)

Interviewer: Fine! Now, do you have any questions you would like to ask?

You: (*Frage, wann du anfangen könntest, wenn sie dir den Job geben würden.*)

Interviewer: We would expect you to start in four weeks. Would that be OK for you?

You: (*Sage, dass es kein Problem wäre.*)

Interviewer: Well, thank you for coming. We'll contact you in a few days.

You: (*Bedanke dich und verabschiede dich formell.*)

[1]portfolio [ˌpɔːtˈfəʊliəʊ] – *Portfolio,* [2]voluntary [ˈvɒləntri] – *freiwillig,* [3]to behave [bɪˈheɪv] – *sich benehmen,* [4]client [ˈklaɪənt] – *Kunde/Ku*

E Mediation and communication

You are going to spend a month abroad as a trainee[1]. Your parents are interested in the company's tips on how to behave while you are in the foreign country, but their English isn't good.
Answer their questions.

Notes on business trips abroad
Business travel is now a normal part of everyday working life for many of us. And this means that cross cultural[2] communication skills have become especially important for managers and employees in international companies. Remember: What we know about cultural aspects before travelling, and the respect we show our business partners while we are there, may make a big difference to the success of the business trip!

Meeting & shaking hands
In many countries shaking hands is normal (e.g. in Australia, the UK, South Africa and the US). In India, with its different religious customs[3], it is better for a man to wait for a woman to offer her hand. One Indian greeting is to say 'Namasté' (= the spirit in me respects the spirit in you), put your hands together as in prayer and bow[4] your head. But if you are not sure about this, shake hands! In Egypt[5] or Arabic[6] countries you shake hands with people of the same sex, or kiss each side of the face, if you know the person better. In Japan they bow formally. The deeper you bow, the more respect you show. However, foreign visitors may just shake hands. At the same time you can bow your head a little as a sign of respect. But don't forget: In contrast to most Western countries, in Japan you do not introduce yourself – so, if possible, wait to be introduced! And wear shoes that are easy to put on and take off, as you may be doing this quite often! In Arabic countries and in India, you need to take your shoes off before entering someone's home or a religious building.

Gift giving
Giving gifts is not usually a part of doing business in Britain, Australia, South Africa or the US. Be careful about giving a business partner an expensive present (especially in America) – you don't want it to look like you're trying to 'buy' good business! In Arabic countries gifts aren't necessary but they give a good impression. If you're a man and you need to give a gift to a woman, be sure to say it is from your mother, sister or wife. Never give pictures of dogs or toy dogs, or any products to do with pigs (not even wallets or handbags) or alcohol (avoid perfume[7], to be on the safe side). In India, cows are often highly respected, so your gift should not be made of anything that comes from a cow. And put your present in yellow, green or red paper as these are lucky colours there. In Japan and China meat, chocolates and alcohol are popular presents. But don't give them in white paper or with white flower decoration – as this means death! Use both hands to give your gift.

a. Man gibt die Hand in allen Ländern, oder?
b. Und was ist dann anders in Indien und Japan?
c. Und wann muss man die Schuhe ausziehen?
d. Was darf man in Amerika nicht tun?
e. Was ist in Indien kein gutes Geschenk?
f. Was kann man Chinesen schenken?

F Writing

1 Skills

Think about meeting someone for the first time. What could be important? Make a list of all your points. Add an example for each point. (face – smiling, clothes – not dirty, …).

2 An article in a school magazine

Use your ideas from part 1 and write an article for young school leavers on preparing for an interview for a job abroad (80–100 words). Find a suitable heading for your article.

[1]trainee [treɪn'iː] – *Praktikant/in,* [2]cross cultural [ˌkrɒs 'kʌltʃərl] – *interkulturell,* [3]customs (*pl*) ['kʌstəmz] – *Bräuche,* [4]to bow (one's head) [baʊ] – *sich verneigen,* [5]Egypt ['iːdʒɪpt] – *Ägypten,* [6]Arabic ['ærəbɪk] – *arabisch,* [7]perfume ['pɜːfjuːm] – *Parfüm*

How we see and are seen

1 Different images

a) *Say which European country/countries you think these people are from. Give reasons.*

*The answers are below

b) *The pictures in a) each present us with an image which we link to certain countries. Where do you think these images come from? Think about films, TV, your family, … .*

c) *Think of 4–5 more images that you have of people from other countries. Test them on your partner. Can he/she say which country they represent[1]?*

2 What we expect

a) *Read what some 10th Graders from a US high school wrote about what they expect to find on their first visit to Germany. Is this image of Germany correct? Say why/why not.*

People	All Germans speak English. They are very friendly but they are a bit old-fashioned[2]!
Language	Bad language is common. Kids swear[3] in school even when teachers are around. Parents don't seem to worry if their kids use bad language either.
Getting around	Germany is tiny. You can drive round it in a few days. You can't drive a car in Germany until you are 18, but there is no speed limit on highways there.
Clothes	You needn't wear smart[4] clothes to go out. All Germans wear traditional clothes at town festivals: Dirndls for girls and leather trousers for boys.
Food	Fridges in houses are small! In restaurants you pay for every extra cup of coffee. But you can get a beer here as soon as you're 16!!
Shopping	Germans don't really like shopping. They do have malls but most shops are closed on Saturday afternoons and on Sundays.
Nudity[5]	Germany is full of adverts, even in the street, showing people with few or no clothes! The really surprising thing is that everyone just walks past them. Germans take all their clothes off in the sauna. Some people may dislike[6] this idea but for others it could be a reason to visit Germany in the first place[7]!

b) *What is your image of the US? Write a similar list.*

c) *Discuss your lists from b). Where do you think your image of the US comes from?*

[1]to represent [ˌreprɪˈzent] – *repräsentieren,* [2]old-fashioned [ˌəʊldˈfæʃnd] – *altmodisch,* [3]to swear [sweə] – *fluchen,* [4]smart [smɑːt] – *schick,* [5]nudity [ˈnjuːdəti] – *Nacktheit;,* [6]to dislike [dɪˈslaɪk] – *nicht mögen,* [7]in the first place [ɪn ðə ˈfɜːst pleɪs] – *überhaupt erst*

*1 England; 2 Italy; 3 Germany; 4 The Netherlands

The EU today

1 Our European family

Read the text and write five facts about the EU.

TOGETHER® SINCE 1957

On 25 March 1957 six countries signed the Treaty of Rome which created the European Economic[1] Community or EEC. In 2007 27 members celebrated[2] the 50th Anniversary[3] of that treaty. Today all the member states have different cultures, languages and traditions, but they have the same values[4]: freedom, democracy, the rule of law, respect for human rights and equality[5].

2 EU countries

a) *Find the names of all the countries in the EU today. You can get help on the Internet. Put the names in a grid like this and complete it.*

Country	Capital city	Language(s)	Money	Member since
Austria	Vienna	German	euro	1995
Belgium	Brussels	…	…	…

b) *Choose one EU country and find out more about it. Why did they become members? What happened or changed after they had become members?*

3 Britain and the EU

a) *Did you know that there have always been people in Britain who do not want to be in the EU? Here are some of the arguments they have used (and still use) against Britain's membership[6]. Do you agree with them? Why/Why not?*

Britain was not allowed to be one of the first six member states.

We have stronger links with Commonwealth countries than with the Continent.

We don't need a strong euro – we have a strong pound.

Britain can't open her borders as easily as other countries in Europe.

We don't want the metric[7] system. We have used inches and miles for hundreds of years.

b) *Use your ideas from a) and make a poster to persuade[8] the people of Britain to stay in the EU.*

[1]economic [ˌiːkəˈnɒmɪk] – *wirtschaftlich*, [2]to celebrate [ˈseləbreɪt] – *feiern*, [3]anniversary [ˌænɪˈvɜːsri] – *Jahrestag*, [4]value [ˈvæljuː] – *Wert*, [5]equality [ɪˈkwɒləti] – *Gleichheit*, [6]membership [ˈmembəʃɪp] – *Mitgliedschaft*, [7]metric [ˈmetrɪk] – *metrisch (System mit Metern, Kilometern usw.)*, [8]to persuade [pəˈsweɪd] – *überreden*

2,10–13

Deportation[1] at breakfast

▶ You can use a dictionary if you don't understand some of the words.

1 Before you read

a) *Partner A looks at the pictures and collects 4–5 words that have to do with 'breakfast' and partner B collects 4–5 words that have to do with 'deportation'. Use your words to say what the story could be about.*

The signs on the windows lured[2] me inside. For a dollar I could get two eggs, toast, and potatoes. The place looked better than most – family run[3] and clean. The signs were hand-lettered and neat[4]. The paper had yellowed some, but the black letters were clear. A green-and-white awning[5] was over the door, where the name 'Clara's' was written. Inside, the place looked old but friendly. The air smelled fresh and homey[6], not of burnt oil. The menu was printed on a board. It was short and clear. It listed the kinds of toast you could choose from. Because I was alone, I sat at the counter[7], leaving the empty tables free for other customers that might come in. At the time business was quiet. Only two tables had customers at them, and I was alone at the counter. But it was still early – not yet seven-thirty.

Behind the counter was a short man with dark black hair, and a youthful beard. He was dressed all in chef's white – but he had no hat. He had a strong accent. The name 'Javier' was written on his shirt.

I ordered coffee, and asked for a minute to choose between the breakfast special for a dollar and the cheese omelette for $1.59. I selected[8] the omelette. The coffee was hot, strong, and fresh. I opened my newspaper on the counter and sipped at the mug[9] as Javier went to cook my meal.

The beaten eggs were spread out on the grill, the bread was inside the toaster, when the authorities[10] came in.

They grabbed Javier quickly and without a word, pushing his hands behind his back. He, too, said nothing. He did not protest, and they pushed him out the door and into their waiting car.

b) *Were your ideas from a) correct? Explain.*
c) *Why do you think Javier gets arrested?*
d) *Do you think this is fair? Say why/why not.*

On the grill, my eggs were cooking. I looked around for another employee – maybe out back somewhere, or in the bathroom. I leaned over the counter and called for someone. No one answered. I looked behind me toward the tables. Two old men sat at one; two old women at the other. The two women were talking. The men were reading the paper. They seemed not to have noticed Javier's exit.

I could smell my eggs starting to burn. I wasn't quite sure what to do about it. I thought about Javier and looked at my eggs. After a few minutes, I got up from where I was sitting and went behind the counter.

I grabbed an apron[11], then picked up a flat spoon and turned my eggs. My toast had popped up, but it was not browned, so I put it down again. While I was cooking, the two old women came to the counter and asked to pay. I asked what they had had. They seemed surprised that I didn't remember. I checked the prices on the chalkboard[12] and added up their order.

They paid slowly and went out, leaving me a dollar tip. I took my eggs off the grill and put them onto a clean plate. My toast had come up. I buttered[13] it and put it on my plate beside my eggs.
I put the plate at my place at the counter, right next to my newspaper.

[1]deportation [ˌdi:pɔ:'teɪʃn] – *Abschiebung, Abtransport,* [2]to lure [lʊə] – *locken,* [3]family-run ['fæmli ˌrʌn] – *familiengeführt,* [4]neat [ni:t] – *ordentlich,* [5]awning ['ɔ:nɪŋ] – *Markise,* [6]homey ['həʊmi] – *heimelig,* [7]counter ['kaʊntə] – *Theke, Tresen,* [8]to select [sɪ'lekt] – *wählen,* [9]mug [mʌg] – *Becher,* [10]authorities [ɔ:'θɒrətiz] – *Grenzpolizei,* [11]apron ['eɪprən] – *Schürze,* [12]chalkboard ['tʃɔ:kbɔ:d] – *Kreidetafel,* [13]to butter ['bʌtə] – *mit Butter bestreichen*

As I began to come back from behind the counter to my seat, six new customers came through the door.

"Can we pull some tables together?" they asked. "We're all one group." I told them yes. Then they ordered six coffees. I thought of telling them I didn't work there.

But perhaps they were hungry. I gave them their coffee. Their order was simple: six breakfast specials, all with eggs and toast.

I got busy. Then the old men came to pay. More new customers began arriving.
By eight-thirty, I had my hands full. With this kind of business, I couldn't understand why Javier hadn't some help. Maybe I'd put a 'help-wanted' ad in the paper tomorrow.
I had never been in the restaurant business. There was no way I could run[1] this place alone.

[adapted from ***Deportation at breakfast*** by Larry Fondation]

2 Two parts 4

a) *Find the turning point in this story.*
Give a title to the part before and the part after it.
b) *Make a flow chart about each part and say what happens in it.*

Flow chart part 1:

Man goes into diner.
→ He reads the menu.
→ He smells … . | He sees … .

3 The setting 4

Collect the adjectives the narrator uses to describe the place. What kind of atmosphere is created? Draw a simple picture of the diner. Add adjectives to the things in it.

4 The story

a) *Why does the narrator take the waiter's job?*
b) *What could the narrator have done differently?*
c) *How could the story go on? Write 5–6 sentences.*

5 Short stories 4

Short stories often start right in the middle of the action and end with a surprise. Look at 'Deportation at breakfast' again. Find these elements and say why they are important here.

6 Illegal immigration 13

In groups of four find as much information as you can on illegal immigration in the US (from books, newspapers, the Internet …). Why do people immigrate illegally? Start a discussion about the positive and negative aspects of immigration.

[1]to run [rʌn] – *führen*

Arbeitstechniken und Fertigkeiten

Inhaltsverzeichnis

Den *Skills*-Anhang aus Band 5 findest du online unter ⇨ 547551-0009. Folgende Techniken und Fertigkeiten trainierst du in Band 6 besonders:

Wörterbücher benutzen	1 2	Ein zweisprachiges Wörterbuch benutzen Ein einsprachiges Wörterbuch benutzen
Lesen	3 4 5 6	Einen Romanauszug analysieren Eine Kurzgeschichte analysieren Ein Gedicht interpretieren Argumentationsketten in Sachtexten auffinden
Schreiben	7 8 9	Texte mit bestimmten Merkmalen produzieren Über eigene Erfahrungen, Erlebnisse oder Gefühle schreiben Einen argumentativen Text verfassen
Hören	10 11 12 13	Gesprächsnotizen anfertigen Ein Protokoll schreiben Gesprächen und Interviews folgen Einer Diskussion folgen
Sprechen	14 15 16	Umgangsformen beachten Feedback geben Sich persönlich äußern
	17 18	Internetrecherche Sprachenlernen

1 Ein zweisprachiges Wörterbuch benutzen

Beim Lesen kannst du manchmal die Bedeutung eines Wortes nicht erraten. Ein zweisprachiges Wörterbuch hilft dir dann weiter. Nehmen wir als Beispiel das Wort *„free"*. Du kennst schon die Bedeutung „frei", aber hier sind drei Sätze, in denen „frei" als Übersetzung nicht passt.

1. *Look these apples are* ***free****. We can take as many as we like.*
2. *Feel* ***free*** *to ask if you have any questions.*
3. *They decided to* ***free*** *him after two weeks.*

Folgende Tipps können dir beim Nachschlagen helfen:

Kategorie	Tipps	Beispiele *
Wortart *Part of speech*	Überlege, zu welcher Wortart das gesuchte Wort gehört. Die Wörter sind nach Wortarten geordnet.	*Adjective: free* [friː] *Verb: to free>freed>freed* *Noun: freedom*
Bedeutung *Meaning*	Viele englische Wörter haben mehrere deutsche Bedeutungen. Falls verschiedene Bedeutungen angegeben sind, wähle die aus, die am besten passt. Jede neue Bedeutung hat eine Nummer.	❶ *frei* ❷ *frei lassen* ❸ *ungehindert, zwanglos* ❹ *kostenlos, gratis, umsonst*
Überprüfung *Check*	Wenn du dich für eine Übersetzung entschieden hast, solltest du im deutsch-englischen Wörterbuch prüfen, ob sie richtig ist.	1. free = ❹ get something free: *etwas umsonst bekommen* umsonst = ❸ (*ohne Bezahlung*) for nothing, free of charge

**Alle PONS Wörterbücher findest du online unter: http://pons.eu/dict/search*

2 Ein einsprachiges Wörterbuch benutzen

Wenn du einen Text auf Englisch schreibst oder eine Präsentation vorbereitest, kann ein zweisprachiges Wörterbuch (siehe *Skill* 1) sehr nützlich sein. Aber auch ein einsprachiges Wörterbuch kann dir beim Verfassen eigener englischer Texte helfen. Hier eine Checkliste:

Kategorie	Tipps	Beispiele
Rechtschreibung *Spelling*	Die Wörter sind alphabetisch in der Reihenfolge Verb, Nomen, Adjektiv, Adverb aufgelistet. Falls das Wort eine ganz andere Bedeutung hat, findest du diese Bedeutung bei den entsprechenden Wortklassen direkt dahinter.	1 *mean* = to express or represent an idea What does rough *mean*? 2 *meaning* = What is the *meaning* of rough? 3 *mean* = to have importance Does it *mean* a lot to you? 4 *meaning* = importance It has no *meaning* for me. 5 *meaningful* = important It was a *meaningful* question.
Wortfallen *False friends*	Viele deutsche Wörter sehen wie englische Wörter aus. Aber Vorsicht! Manche haben eine ganz andere Bedeutung.	**opinion or meaning?** *Meinung* looks like meaning, but this is a 'false friend' (*Meinung* = opinion). Look up the words *meaning* and *opinion* to help you to decide**.
Wortart *Part of speech*	Wähle die richtige Wortart des englischen Wortes aus. Entscheide also, ob du das Wort als Adjektiv, Adverb, Verb usw. verwenden willst.	to write *careful* or to write *carefully*
Aussprache/ Betonung *Pronunciation/ Stress*	Finde die richtige Aussprache. Viele Wörter im *BE* und *AE* werden gleich geschrieben, sie werden aber anders ausgesprochen. Benutze die richtige Betonung. Überprüfe die Wortart: Verschiedene Wortarten haben manchmal eine andere Betonung.	*advertisement* (əd'vɜːtɪsmənt BE or ˌædvə'taɪzmənt AE) record ['rəkɔ:d] to record ['rɪkɔ:d]
Sprachebene *Register*	Formelle Sprache und Umgangssprache sind oft sehr unterschiedlich. Entscheide, welche Ebene und welche Sprache (z. B. *BE* oder *AE*) am besten zu deinem Text passen.	*formal* = young man *informal* = guy *AE* = bloke *BE*

** **o•pin•i•on** /ə'pɪn·jən/ *n* [one of] the ideas that a person or a group of people have about something or someone, which are based mainly on their feelings and beliefs

mean•ing /'miː·nɪŋ/ *n* [U] • (*disapproving*) *What's the meaning of this?*

3 Einen Romanauszug analysieren

Bei einem Roman (*novel*) handelt es sich zumeist um eine fiktive (erfundene) Geschichte. Der Autor/die Autorin denkt sich die Handlung und die Figuren aus oder empfindet sie einem historischen Ereignis/einer tatsächlichen Begebenheit nach. Die Geschichte kann an einem echten oder fiktiven Ort und in einem echten oder fiktiven Zeitraum spielen. Als Beispiel nehmen wir den Auszug aus dem Roman *Before I die* von Jenny Downham (Seiten 76–79).

Kategorie	Besonderheiten	Beispiele
Thema *Theme*	Das Hauptthema oder die Hauptidee der Geschichte ist oft auf dem Umschlag zu finden.	*young girl trying to cope with the fact that she is dying*
Nebenthemen *Secondary themes*	Diese zeigen sich oft erst beim Lesen.	*relationships with friends and family, communicating*
Handlung *Storyline*	Die Handlung enthält immer einen Konflikt (*conflict*), z. B. zwischen einzelnen Figuren. Der Wendepunkt (*turning point*) weist darauf hin, dass sich etwas ändern wird. Oft gibt es einen Höhepunkt (*climax*), nach dem sich vieles, aber nicht immer alles, aufklärt oder löst.	*A girl (Tessa) learns that she has cancer and is going to die. She writes a list of things she still wants to do before she dies.*
Figuren *Characters*	Am wichtigsten ist die Hauptfigur (*protagonist*), die immer mit der Handlung zu tun hat. Oft gibt es einen Gegenspieler, der mit der Hauptfigur in Konflikt steht. Aussagen, Beschreibungen und Aktionen der Figuren helfen uns, uns diese vorzustellen (Aussehen, Eigenschaften, …) und uns mit ihnen zu identifizieren.	*Tessa, Adam, nurse Louise, dad, Zoey, mum*
Handlungsort und -zeit *Setting*	Im Laufe der Geschichte können sich diese ändern.	*garden behind the house where Adam lives*
Perspektive *Point of view*	Der Erzähler (*narrator*) kann aus der Sicht einer oder mehrerer Figuren erzählen. Figuren können detailliert über ihre Gefühle reden, so dass wir uns leicht mit ihnen identifizieren können. Der Erzähler kann aber auch aus der Sicht eines Außenstehenden berichten. Ein solcher Erzähler kann überall sein und über alles berichten. Seine Sicht ist aber distanzierter.	*The story is told by the main female character. We can identify with her problems and feel more intensely for her.*
Sprache *Language*	Der Autor/Erzähler ‚malt' oft Bilder (*images, metaphors*) des Handlungsortes und der Figuren oder fügt Kommentare ein, die für den Fortlauf der Handlung nicht unbedingt notwendig sind.	*The ashes are still hot, bright enough to attract a moth, a stupid moth dancing towards them.*

4 Eine Kurzgeschichte analysieren

Kurzgeschichten (*short stories*) sind fiktiv (erfunden) und haben auch sonst vieles mit Romanen gemeinsam. Sie sind aber viel kürzer und weniger komplex. Als Beispiel nehmen wir *Deportation at breakfast* von Larry Fondation (Seiten 88–89).

Kategorie	Besonderheiten	Beispiele
Thema *Theme*	Das Thema der Geschichte wird oft im Titel erwähnt bzw. erläutert.	*A man is deported while the narrator waits for his breakfast.*
Figuren *Characters*	Meistens gibt es nur eine Hauptfigur (*protagonist*). Kurze Äußerungen und Aktionen der Figur helfen uns dabei, uns diese vorzustellen und uns mit ihr identifizieren zu können. Wir stellen uns z. B. vor, wie er/sie aussieht, was für ein Mensch er/sie ist, und entscheiden, ob wir die Figur mögen oder nicht.	*the traveller, Javier, the officials, two men, two women, customers*
Handlungsort und -zeit *Setting*	Ort und Zeit der Handlung ändern sich kaum. Die Leser werden in die Situation ‚hineingeworfen' ohne jegliche oder mit nur einer kurzen Vorbereitung.	*inside a diner*
Zeitspanne *Time span*	Die Zeit, in der sich alles abspielt, ist begrenzt, z. B. auf eine Stunde, einen Vormittag, einen Tag.	*7:00 to 8:30 in the morning*
Handlung *Storyline*	Die Handlung konzentriert sich auf einen Vorfall. Sie enthält oft einen Konflikt (*conflict*) und einen Wendepunkt (*turning point*), der zu einer Änderung führt usw.	*A traveller in the US stops at a diner to get something to eat. While he is waiting, some officials come in and arrest the man behind the counter. The traveller takes over his job.*
Perspektive *Point of view*	Der Erzähler (*narrator*) kann aus der Sicht einer oder mehrerer Figuren erzählen. Figuren können detailliert über ihre Gefühle reden, so dass wir uns leicht mit ihnen identifizieren können. Der Erzähler kann aber auch aus der Sicht eines Außenstehenden berichten. Ein solcher Erzähler kann überall sein und über alles berichten. Seine Sicht ist aber distanzierter.	*The traveller tells the story. We see everything through his eyes.*
Sprache *Language*	Der Autor konzentriert sich auf die Beschreibung dessen, was für die Handlung notwendig ist.	*First sentence:* *The signs on the windows lured me inside.*

5 Ein Gedicht interpretieren

In Gedichten werden Erfahrungen, Erlebnisse und Gefühle beschrieben. Ziel ist oft, Gefühle zu vermitteln bzw. die Leser zum Nachdenken oder Andersdenken zu ermuntern. Als Beispiel nehmen wir *Give and take* von Roger McGough (S. 55).

Kategorie	Besonderheiten	Beispiele
Thema *Theme*	Was der Dichter ausdrücken will, wird oft im Titel angedeutet, wird aber häufig erst in der letzten Zeile klar.	*The poem is about what the earth gives us and what we, humans, take away from it or destroy.*
Sprache *Language*	In Gedichten werden oft Änderungen in der Wortwahl, ungewöhnliche Wortstellungen oder Kurzformen verwendet. Die normale Satzstellung wird ebenfalls häufig geändert, um die Aussage zu verstärken und die Leser zum Nachdenken zu bringen.	*For example 'toxic canals': This makes us think about waterways which man has made to transport goods. They are often too dirty to have fish in them and are full of rubbish and waste.* *McGough rejects all techniques which could make his poem sound more beautiful. He uses short, simple lines to express his anger.*
Klang *Sound*	Der Dichter benutzt Klänge wie z. B. Alliteration (*alliteration*) und Wiederholung (*repetition*), um mit wenigen Worten ein bestimmtes Gefühl bei den Lesern zu wecken oder um eine bestimmte Vorstellung hervorzurufen.	*The poet uses 'toxic' instead of 'poisonous' because it ends in an 'ic' which sounds more horrible next to the word 'canals' than the 'ous' in 'poisonous' would.* *The word 'abundance' has softer sounds and is longer than 'waste', so they are good words to show a contrast.*
Reime *Rhymes*	Wörter, die sich reimen oder sich ähnlich anhören, verdeutlichen die Aussage des Gedichts (unterhalten, überraschen, …)	*McGough doesn't use rhyme in this poem. The effect is that we feel uncomfortable about what he says and recognise his anger.*
Struktur *Form*	Verse können kurz oder lang sein. Mit Parallelismen (gleicher Satzbau/Satzlänge) und Kontrasten (Änderung des Baumusters/der Satzlänge) hebt der Dichter bestimmte Sachen hervor – ihre Wirkung wird dadurch verstärkt.	*The first stanzas have the same pattern with the same number of lines and syllables. The last line in the last stanza is much longer. In this way McGough produces a strong contrast with the other stanzas.*
Rhythmus *Rhythm*	Der Rhythmus (wie das Gedicht fließt, wenn du es laut sprichst) soll den Inhalt unterstützen bzw. die Gefühle nachahmen: Kurze Sätze wirken flott, frech, aber auch streng und aggressiv, lange Sätze erzeugen oft Harmonie, Zufriedenheit und Langeweile.	*The first stanzas are similar in rhythm but the lines don't flow smoothly because the poet isn't comfortable. In the last line the rhythm falls apart and shows the poet's anger and despair.*
Wirkung *Effect*	Der Dichter versucht bestimmte Emotionen bzw. Gedanken und Erinnerungen bei den Lesern zu wecken.	*We feel challenged to react to his anger and to think about our role in what is happening.*

6 Argumentationsketten in Sachtexten auffinden

In einem argumentativen Text wird eine Aussage (*statement*) von vielen Seiten betrachtet, um am Ende zu einer Schlussfolgerung (*conclusion*) zu kommen. Diese Art von Sachtext findet man z. B. in einer Zeitung oder Zeitschrift. Ziel ist üblicherweise, die Leser für eine bestimmte Meinung zu gewinnen.
Als Beispiel nehmen wir den Text *A job for life!* (S. 32).

Kategorie	Besonderheiten	Beispiele
Überschrift *Title*	Die Überschrift soll das Hauptanliegen des Textes verdeutlichen. Diese kann ein Zitat aus dem Text sein. Sie ist kurz und manchmal zweideutig, um die Aufmerksamkeit der Leser zu gewinnen.	*A job for life!* *This has two meanings: Normally it means a job for all your working life. The Queen's job is a job until she dies.*
Bilder *Pictures*	Bilder von Personen bzw. Orten im Artikel unterstützen oft die Einstellung des Autors, z.B. werden Figuren/Szenen kontrastiv oder als Cartoon dargestellt.	*A picture of the Queen as Head of State is contrasted with Westminster which is a symbol for the Government.*
Grafiken *Other visuals*	Diagramme oder Tabellen werden vor allem bei wissenschaftlichen Texten zur Veranschaulichung eines Sachverhaltes verwendet. Sie sollen spezielle Informationen kurz und übersichtlich darstellen.	*At the back of Orange Line 6: A flow chart shows the British political system and the position of the Queen.*
These/Aussage *Statement*	Die These, über die diskutiert werden soll, steht im ersten oder zweiten Absatz des Textes.	*Well, we need both of them.*
Argumente *Arguments*	Die Argumente für oder gegen die These können in unterschiedlichen Formen dargestellt sein: • in einer Kette, mit dem schwächsten Argument am Anfang, • 1–2 Argumente jeweils mit Gegenargumenten, • alle Argumente aus einer Perspektive, dann alle Gegenargumente, • einfache Darstellung einer Situation, dann Gegenargumente, die hier eventuell gelten könnten.	*Every year in November the Queen opens Parliament at Westminster.* *On the one hand Britain is a democracy … On the other hand the Queen isn't allowed to enter the House of Commons and it isn't her speech at all.* *All these duties sound very important: …* *But she does this only if Parliament tells her to.* *She can't for example support one political party, … .* *… she is not without influence.*
Schlussfolgerung *Conclusion*	Die Meinung des/der Autors/in steht meistens im letzten Absatz.	*Being queen is not all bad.*

7 Texte mit bestimmten Merkmalen produzieren

Diese *Skill* brauchst du, wenn du z. B. einen Text zu Ende schreiben oder Texte umwandeln möchtest. Bearbeite zuerst den Originaltext. In den *Skills* 3–6 (S. 92–95) finden sich Hinweise über die Besonderheiten verschiedener Textsorten. Falls du Hilfe brauchst, kannst du die folgende Checkliste verwenden. Als Beispiel nehmen wir *Before I die* von Jenny Downham.

Kategorie	Tipps	Beispiele
Vorbereitung *Preparation*	Um deinen Text gut an den Originaltext anzupassen, überlege zunächst: Welche Merkmale hat der Originaltext, die du übernehmen musst (Perspektive, Form, …)? In welcher Zeit musst du schreiben (Gegenwart, Vergangenheit, …)? Wie lang soll dein Text werden (Kurzgeschichte, Gedichtstrophe, …)?	Written in the first person: *I, me, my, … .* Written in the present tense: *The boy looks surprised … . He's already there, holding the gate open for me.*
Ideen *Ideas*	Entscheide, was du in deinem Text oder in deiner Strophe ausdrücken möchtest. Sammle Ideen dazu in Notizform oder in einer Mindmap.	*What happens later? Do they get to know each other better? How and when? How does the relationship develop?*
Sprache/Stil *Language/Style*	Überprüfe den Stil des Originaltextes. Was ist daran besonders oder merkwürdig, z. B. gibt es viele altertümliche Vokabeln, kurze oder lange Sätze, direkte Rede, Vergleiche, … ?	A lot of dialogue: *Dangerous dress, I like it, What about your dad? – No. It's just me and Mum.* Short sentences: *I looked thin and brown and hopeful. I was in remission for the first time.* Detailed description of certain things: *His fingernails are dirty and he has bits of leaf in his hair.*
Dialog in Erzähltext *Dialogue*	Verwende indirekte Rede, um direkte Rede in einem Erzähltext wiederzugeben. Überprüfe die Zeit, Pronomen, … , die du verwendest.	*He said that* ***her*** *dress* ***was*** *dangerous.* *He asked about* ***her*** *dad.* *He said it* ***was*** *just* ***him*** *and* ***his*** *mum.*
Erzähltext in Dialog *Narrative*	Verwende direkte Rede, um aus einem Erzähltext einen Dialog zu schreiben. Versuche, dir den Dialog zwischen den Charakteren vorzustellen. Was hätten sie in der Situation sagen können?	*Nurse: Look, Tessa! I've got something for you.* *Tessa: Oh, it's some cartoons.* *Nurse: Can you see who they are of?* *Tessa: Wait! That's Doctor …, isn't it?*
Entwurf *Rough copy*	Schreibe deine Ideen in ganzen Sätzen auf. Versuche dabei, den Stil des Originaltextes zu imitieren.	*I'm sitting in the garden when he comes round later. I'm reading. I hear the gate. It's getting cold. I pull the blanket up over my shoulders. "Like a hot chocolate?" he asks. "Hot and healthy."*
Überprüfung *Check*	Prüfe den Inhalt (ob du alle Ideen berücksichtigt hast) und die Korrektheit (ob du alles, z. B. Zeiten, Rechtschreibung, …, richtig gemacht hast).	Ideas: *The boy visits her. They get to know each other better and he starts to like her.* Verbs: *All present tense.* Spelling: *shoulder, chocolate, …*

8 Gedichte über eigene Erfahrungen, Erlebnisse oder Gefühle schreiben

Gedichte schildern Erfahrungen, Erlebnisse und Gefühle, die jemand mit Menschen, Tieren oder Begebenheiten gemacht hat. Häufig erzählen sie auch kleine Geschichten. Schaue dir die *Skill* 5 auf Seite 94 an. Dort findest du Hinweise über die Besonderheiten von Gedichten. Folgende Checkliste kannst du verwenden, wenn du selber Gedichte schreiben willst.

Kategorie	Tipps	Beispiele
Idee *Idea*	Entscheide, worüber du schreiben willst: ein Erlebnis, das dich bewegt, z. B. ein Urlaub, in dem etwas passiert ist. Fotos und Bilder können eine gute Quelle für ein Gedicht sein.	*last year's holiday at the coast* *found a bird on the beach covered in oil*
Entwicklung *Development*	Lass deinen Gedanken freien Lauf und schreibe über die Situation.	*It was a warm afternoon last summer. I was on the beach, just sitting there watching the waves, when I saw something black … .*
Gefühle *Feelings*	Füge Gefühle hinzu. Beschreibe, wie du dich in der Situation gefühlt hast. Hattest du Angst oder war es überraschend oder eklig? Wie war das Wetter? Was hast du gehört? ‚Male' ein Bild des Vorfalls, wie du ihn erlebt hast.	*It was lying by the edge of the water. I couldn't see it very well. Then the sun came out suddenly from behind a cloud and I looked again. It was covered in oil. I saw its eye.*
Reduktion *Reduction*	Versuche diese Sätze auf das Wesentliche zu reduzieren. Denke dabei an die Stichwörter.	*On the beach, sitting watching waves* *Something black by the water's edge* *Sun came out from behind a cloud* *Its eye was watching me.*
Überprüfung *Check*	Lies dein Gedicht durch. Drückt es noch alles aus, was du sagen wolltest? Möchtest du einen Satz hinzufügen oder ein Wort ändern?	*Something black by the water's edge* *Black as oil by the water's edge …* *Above it white birds screamed a warning.*
Endversion *Final draft*	Schreibe eine Endversion. Lies dein Gedicht einem Partner vor. Vielleicht kann er/sie dir helfen, es noch besser zu machen, z. B. könnte er/sie dir raten, dass du mehr über deine Gefühle sagen solltest.	*The wind was cold around my head* *I saw fear in its eye, in my eye.*

9 Einen argumentativen Text verfassen

Ein argumentativer Text ist ein Sachtext, wie z. B. ein Artikel, in dem mit Argumenten versucht wird, die Leser von etwas zu überzeugen bzw. für eine bestimmte Meinung zu gewinnen. Schaue dir *Skill* 6 auf Seite 95 an. Dort findest du wichtige Hinweise über die Besonderheiten von argumentativen Texten. Wenn du einen solchen Text schreiben willst, kannst du die folgende Checkliste verwenden.

Kategorie	Tipps	Beispiele
Thema *Topic*	Wähle als Thema etwas Kontroverses, z. B. etwas, worüber du gelesen hast oder was du selbst erlebt hast.	*extreme sports*
Recherche *Research*	Recherchiere im Internet und finde ein paar interessante Informationen zum Thema.	*sky diving, mountain boarding, … called action sport or adventure sport*
Aussage *Statement*	Formuliere eine klare Aussage zu dem Thema.	*I think/don't think that people should risk their lives just to have fun. Ordinary sports can be fun, too.*
Argumente *Arguments*	Sammle Argumente für/gegen deine Aussage: • eine Kette mit dem schwächsten am Anfang, • 1–2 Argumente jeweils mit Gegenargumenten, • alle Argumente aus einer Perspektive, dann alle Gegenargumente, • einfache Darstellung einer Situation, dann Gegenargumente, die hier eventuell gelten könnten.	Arguments for: 1. *People who do extreme sports say that these sports are safer than driving a car.* 2. *OK, so they are dangerous but they are only risking their own lives, not those of other people.* Arguments against: *But rescue teams who have to help climbers or snowboarders who get into difficulties tell a different story.*
Einleitung *Introduction*	Überlege, wie du deinen Text einleiten möchtest. Schreibe nicht mehr als zwei bis drei Sätze. Das Interesse der Leser soll geweckt werden.	*Today I'd like to talk about … .* *Many people say that … .* *But have you ever thought about …?*
Bildelemente *Visuals*	Suche geeignete Bildelemente. Wähle Bilder, Statistiken usw., die deine Argumente unterstützen.	*Pictures of people enjoying sports and of accidents or rescue teams.*
Schlussfolgerung *Conclusion*	Schreibe eine Schlussfolgerung. Sage kurz deine Meinung zu dem Thema und begründe sie.	*I think that … ./In my opinion … ./ I believe that … .*
Titel *Title*	Finde einen Titel, etwas Kurzes, was die Aufmerksamkeit der Leser wecken könnte.	*Sports gone crazy!* *Death by sports!*

10 Gesprächsnotizen anfertigen

Wenn du Notizen zu einem Telefongespräch auf Englisch anfertigen sollst, kann die folgende Checkliste dir helfen.

	Checkliste	**Beispiele**
1	Bereite dich vor. Sorge dafür, dass du neben dem Telefon etwas zum Schreiben hast. Schreibe dann wichtige Rubriken auf.	*Date: …* *Private: Yes/No* *Business (Name of company): …*
2	Frage nach dem Namen und der Rufnummer des Anrufers. Schreibe sie auf. Bitte die Person, den Namen zu wiederholen bzw. zu buchstabieren.	*Name of caller: …* *Number:*
3	Notiere, wann und woher die Person anruft.	*Time of call: … Calling from: …*
4	Schreibe auf, was der Gegenstand des Gesprächs ist. Was genau will dein Gesprächspartner wissen bzw. als Nachricht hinterlassen? Achte auf wichtige Informationen, z. B. Termine, Uhrzeiten, Eigennamen, … .	*Reason for call: …* *Questions: …*
5	Wenn du etwas nicht verstehst, bitte um Wiederholung.	*Could you repeat that, please?*
6	Wiederhole wichtige Infos, wie z. B. Name, Telefonnummern, Termine, Zahlen.	*OK, so your name is … . You are calling from … . You would like to know if … /ask about … /suggest that … .*

11 Ein Protokoll schreiben

Es kann besonders schwer sein, alles in einem Gespräch zu verstehen, an dem mehrere Personen teilnehmen. Die folgende Checkliste kann dir helfen, wenn du ein Protokoll eines Gesprächs oder einer Diskussion anfertigen willst.

	Checkliste	**Tipps**
1	Bereite dich vor *Prepare yourself*	Schreibe das Thema des Gesprächs auf. Überlege, was du schon über die Gesprächspartner/innen weißt, z. B. ihre Meinungen.
2	Arbeite mit einem Partner *Work with a partner*	Bitte einen Partner, gleichzeitig Notizen anzufertigen.
3	Schreibe eine Liste *Write a list*	Schreibe die Namen der Gesprächspartner/innen auf. Füge jeweils ein Kürzel hinzu, z. B. Karl Braun (KB).
4	Benutze Kurzformen *Use short forms*	Schreibe auf, wer spricht und was sie sagen. Benutze Kürzel, Kurzformen und Stichwörter. Schreibe Zahlen als Ziffern.
5	Überprüfe *Check*	Vergleiche deine Notizen mit denen deines Partners. Vergewissere dich, dass du keine wichtigen Aussagen, Fakten oder Wörter vergessen hast.
6	Schreibe *Write*	Benutze deine Notizen. Berichte im *simple present* über alles, was gesagt wurde und von wem. Hast du etwas Wichtiges vergessen? Dein Partner sollte den Text auch prüfen.

12 Gesprächen und Interviews folgen

Es kann besonders schwer sein, alles in einem Gespräch zu verstehen, an dem mehrere Personen teilnehmen. Die folgende Checkliste kann dir helfen, wenn du ein Gespräch oder ein Interview verstehen willst.

	Checkliste	Tipps
1	Bereite dich vor *Prepare yourself*	Überlege, um was für ein Gespräch es sich handelt, wo es stattfindet; wer dabei sein könnte, was du schon über die Personen weißt: Was haben sie gemacht, wo kommen sie her, welche Meinungen vertreten sie?
2	Schreibe eine Liste *Write a list*	Schreibe die Namen der Gesprächspartner auf. Lasse Platz für Notizen.
3	Notiere Stichwörter *Note key words*	Schreibe beim Hören neben jeden Namen Stichwörter über das, was gesagt wird, bzw. über das, was passiert.
4	Überprüfe *Check*	Höre den Text noch einmal an. Prüfe dabei, ob du wichtige Aussagen, Fakten oder Wörter vergessen hast.
5	Verbessere *Improve*	Bitte einen Partner, deine Notizen zu lesen bzw. zu verbessern.
6	Fasse zusammen *Summarise*	Fasse das Gespräch/das Interview für einen Partner zusammen: Wer dabei war, was sie gesagt haben, was passiert ist. Hast du etwas Wichtiges vergessen?

13 Einer Diskussion folgen

Folgende Tipps können dir helfen, wenn du im Unterricht an einer Diskussion auf Englisch teilnimmst. Nehmen wir als Beispiel eine Klassendiskussion über das Thema „Trinkwasser".

	Checkliste	Tipps	Beispiele
1	Bereite dich vor *Prepare yourself*	Kläre wer teilnimmt, wie lange es dauert und über was diskutiert wird. Frage, ob du deine eigene Meinung äußern oder eine andere vertreten sollst.	*Group: Paul, Ali; Miriam, … .* *Topic: Tap water or bottled water?* *Opinion: Supporting tap water* *Time: …*
2	Sammle Ideen *Collect ideas*	Schreibe deine Ideen stichwortartig und nach Wichtigkeit geordnet auf ein Blatt.	*Tap water is cheaper.* *Tap water is … .*
3	Schreibe eine Liste *Write a list*	Liste alle Gesprächspartner auf einem Blatt auf und lasse Platz für Notizen.	1. *Paul* 2. …
4	Schreibe Notizen *Write notes*	Notiere wer deiner (✓) und wer anderer (X) Meinung ist. Schreibe Stichwörter dazu. Vielleicht wird eine andere gute (✓✓)/schlechte (X X) Meinung erwähnt, die du übernehmen/entkräften möchtest. Du kannst dabei deine eigenen Symbole verwenden.	1. *Paul: (XX) tap water is bad* 2. *Ali: (✓) tap water is cheaper* 3. …
5	Setze Notizen ein *Use your notes*	Bevor du dich meldest, solltest du deine Ideenliste überprüfen. Markiere Punkte, die schon erwähnt wurden. Diese solltest du nicht wiederholen. Unterstütze andere Meinungen bzw. lehne sie ab.	*tap water is cheaper* *I think … is right/wrong when he/she says … .* *I agree/can't agree with … .*

14 Umgangsformen beachten

1 Begrüßungen

Wenn du mit englischen Muttersprachlern redest, kannst du damit rechnen, dass sie dir Fehler nicht übelnehmen. Folgende Tipps können dir in solchen Situationen behilflich sein.

Land	Du hörst	Tipps	Du kannst antworten
Alle	*Hi!/Hello!*	Die meisten Völker verstehen „*Hi*"/„*Hello*" oder einen Händedruck. Achte darauf, wie die Menschen sich in dem anderen Land begrüßen: Was sagen Menschen, die sich zum ersten Mal sehen? Wie begrüßen sich Freunde?	*Hi, … .* *Hello, Mr/Mrs … .* *Hi! My name is/I'm … .* *I'm from … .*
US	*Hi, there! How are you doing?*	In den USA ist es üblich, sich beim Vornamen zu nennen – auch bei der Arbeit. Man fragt: „*How are you doing?*"	*Good, thanks. And you?*
UK	*Good morning/ afternoon/ evening. How are you?*	Benutze immer *Mr/Ms* plus Nachnamen bei Erwachsenen. Wenn jemand „*How are you?*" sagt, solltest du die Floskel nicht wiederholen, sondern „*Fine, thanks.*" oder „*Pleased to meet you.*" sagen.	*Good morning/afternoon/ evening Mr/Ms/Mrs … .* *Fine, thanks. Pleased to meet you.*
South Africa	*Howzit!*	Die Antwort darauf, „*Sharp-sharp!*", wird auch als Begrüßung, zum Abschied oder als Zustimmung verwendet.	*Sharp-sharp.*
Australia	*G'day, …!*	Sei nie zu formell in Australien, das wird als hochnäsig betrachtet. Vornamen sind üblich, auch zwischen Jugendlichen und Erwachsenen.	*G'day!*

2 Telefonieren

In englischsprachigen Ländern melden sich die Menschen am Telefon sehr unterschiedlich. Manche sagen ihren Namen (mit oder ohne Telefonnummer), manche sagen nur „*Hello*". Es ist besonders bei formellen Gesprächen wichtig, angemessen zu reagieren. Unten findest du Beispiele.

Wenn jemand sich meldet, hörst du z. B.:	**So kannst du darauf antworten:**
Good morning, Burnt Hill Secondary School. *Sandie Bradshaw speaking.* *How can I help you?*	*Good morning, Ms Bradshaw. I'm ringing from Germany.* *My name is … . I wonder if you could help me.* *I just wanted to ask about … . / I need to speak to someone about/find out about … .*
Dann hörst du vielleicht folgenden Satz:	**Dann kannst du folgende Antwort geben:**
Hang, on! I'll see if I can find Mr/Ms … . *I'm putting you through now.*	*OK. I'll hang on.* *Thank you.*

15 Feedback geben

Bei einem Kommentar geht es um eine sachliche Wertung, die, auch wenn ein Text dir nicht gefällt, nicht beleidigend, sondern klar begründet sein muss. Diese Checkliste kann dir helfen, wenn du Feedback zu einem Text oder zu einer mündlichen Präsentation geben willst.

	Checkliste	Tipps	Was du sagen kannst
1	Führe ein *Introduce*	Sage, worüber du schreiben/reden willst.	*I would like to say a few words about an article/… written by/a presentation given by … . Its headline/title/subject is/was … .*
2	Skizziere *Outline*	Erzähle kurz, worum es geht.	*The article is/presentation was about … .* *It tells/The presenter told us in detail/briefly about … .*
3	Lege dar *Explain*	Schildere und bewerte die Struktur des Textes. Bleibe sachlich.	*The article/presentation has/had two/three … parts/paragraphs/… .* *In my opinion it is/was possibly too long/short/… because … .* *I really liked the introduction/photos/the fact that it is/was … .*
4	Bewerte *Assess*	Betrachte den ganzen Text. Erwähne nicht nur das Negative.	*My impression/opinion is that the … is/was informative/… .* *I must say that I found the … a bit boring/very entertaining.* *The … has/had a good/well-written introduction/… .* *But it doesn't/didn't mention …/answer the questions that were asked/give any information on … .*
5	Kritisiere *Criticize*	Bewerte die Sprache und den Stil.	*The language is suitable/too formal/informal for this type of text.* *The tense used in the text/the introduction/the … sentence is correct/not correct. It should be written in the present/past/ … .*
6	Rege an *Suggest*	Überlege, was man ändern könnte und wie. Schlage Verbesserungen vor.	*I think that it would be good to mention/explain/describe/… .* *It might be better if the author didn't repeat the same word so often/changed the ending/added something about … .* *The text might be better if the author explained/added/removed/… .*

Bei einem Kommentar zu einem Film/Video sollten auch visuelle Aspekte und Ton bewertet werden. Diese zusätzliche Checkliste kann dir helfen.

	Checkliste	Tipps	Was du sagen kannst
1	Skizziere *Outline*	Sage, worum es geht und wo der Film spielt.	*It is about … . It is set in … . /The story takes place in … .* *It tells the story of/shows pictures of … .*
2	Bewerte *Assess*	Bewerte visuelle Techniken und Musik. Benutze *simple past* für deine Meinungen.	*I liked the first/ … scene where …/shots of … .* *I thought the music/language … was a bit/very/ … .* *I felt that the film/extract was too slow/violent/… .*
3	Beschreibe *Describe*	Beschreibe die Figuren. Benutze *simple present.*	*The main character(s) is (are) … .* *… is played really well/ … by … .*
4	Empfehle *Recommend*	Spreche eine Empfehlung aus. Nenne Gründe.	*If you like/don't like thrillers/horror stories/love stories/…, I would/wouldn't recommend that you go to see this film.* *It was really scary/exciting/… in the scene where … .*

16 Sich persönlich äußern

In manchen Aufgaben sollst du über dich selbst sprechen. Diese Wendungen können dafür nützlich sein.

Über deine Meinung sprechen	Absichten äußern
In my opinion … • The way I see it, … • I (don't) think … • I have the feeling/impression that … • I find it hard to believe that … • I (don't) agree with … • I couldn't agree more. • To be honest, I can't/don't … • I share the view that … • I am of exactly the same opinion as … • I would support the view that …	*I suggest that we/you … • I'm going to talk about … • Shall I/we …? • Let's … • Let me … • I'd like to begin with/end with/finish … • First of all … / Secondly …*
Über Gefühle sprechen	**Hoffnungen und Wünsche äußern**
I'm excited/bored/sad/happy/… about …/ because … • I'm sick of … • I (don't) feel sorry for … • I'm enjoying this. • I'm so pleased. • I'm looking foward to it.	*I (really) hope … • I wish … • I'd like to … • It would be great if …*

17 Internetrecherche

1. Suche nach Themen oder Stichwörtern

- Durchsuche vorhandene Themenangebote, z.B. bei Yahoo oder Web, nach dem gewünschten Thema, wähle dann ein Teilthema usw., z.B. Reise > Reisetipps > Klimatabellen > Las Vegas
- Verwende eine Suchmaschine, z.B. Google, um mit Stichwörtern zum Thema Informationen zu finden, z.B. Sehenswürdigkeit London.
- Die meisten Suchmaschinen verwenden ODER bei der Suche mit Stichwörtern. Das bedeutet, dass du alle Seiten angezeigt bekommst, die auch nur eines deiner Stichwörter enthalten. Wenn du also z.B. *new south wales* eingibst, bekommst du Seiten für Wales und South Wales in Großbritannien und für New South Wales in Australien.

Bei den meisten Suchmaschinen kann man zusätzlich ein + oder ein - vor einem Stichwort eingeben, um es ein- oder auszuschließen, z.B. *+martin +luther -king*.

Wenn du nach einer zusammenhängenden Wortfolge, z.B. einem Buchtitel, suchst, verwende Anführungszeichen, z.B. „Herr der Ringe".

- Um bessere Ergebnisse zu bekommen, hilft es meist, das ungewöhnlichste oder wichtigste Wort zuerst einzugeben.
- Wenn du zu wenige Treffer erhältst, überprüfe die Rechtschreibung oder verwende andere oder weniger Stichwörter.
- Wenn du zu viele Treffer erhältst, verwende mehr oder genauere Stichwörter.

2. Favoriten *(bookmarks)*

- Um leichter zu einer Seite zurückzukehren, die dir gefällt, kannst du ein *bookmark* setzen, indem du auf Favoriten im Menü klickst, indem du Strg-D drückst oder mit einem Klick der rechten Maustaste.
- Wenn du vergessen hast, ein *bookmark* zu setzen, kannst du mit Pfeil vorwärts oder rückwärts oder mit Strg-H auf alle Seiten zurückkehren, auf denen du während deiner Internetsitzung warst.

3. Auswertung der Ergebnisse/Treffer

- Glaube nicht alles, was du im Internet liest. Bedenke, dass dort jeder alles veröffentlichen kann. Bilde dir ein Urteil über die Vetrauenswürdigkeit einer Webseite, bevor du daraus Informationen verwendest. Ähnelt die Seite etwa eher www.spiegel.de oder eher www.nullachtfuenfzehn-blog.de?
- Bist du auf einer kommerziellenWebseite gelandet? Dann ist diese wahrscheinlich eher daran interessiert, dir etwas zu verkaufen als dir objektive Informationen zu geben.
- Enthält die Seite Fakten oder nur persönliche Meinungen?
- Könnte sich der/die Autor/in wirklich mit dem Thema auskennen, ist er/sie z.B. ein/e Uniprofessor/in oder ein/e Journalist/in?
- Überprüfe auch die Aktualität der Webseite, vor allem wenn du nach dem Neuesten zu einem Thema suchst.

18 Sprachenlernen

Verschiedene Sprachen haben zwar unterschiedliche Wörter für die Dinge, aber sie funktioneren manchmal ganz ähnlich. Es kann dir beim Lernen einer Fremdsprache daher helfen, wenn du dir darüber bewusst bist, wie deine Muttersprache funktioniert.

Hier sind ein paar Beispiele:

	Deutsch	Englisch	Italienisch	Russisch	Türkisch
Artikel	3 bestimmte (der, die, das) und 2 unbestimmte (ein, eine)	1 bestimmter (the), zwei unbestimmte (a, an)	zwei bestimmte (il, la), drei unbestimmte (una, uno, un)	keine	keine
Satzstellung	Subjekt-Verb-Objekt Fragen: Fragewort an Position 1	Subjekt-Verb-Objekt Fragen: Fragewort an Position 1	Subjekt-Verb-Objekt (Subjekt kann fehlen, wenn es ein Personal-pronomen ist)	freie Satzstellung Fragen: Fragewort an Position 1	Subjekt-Objekt-Verb Fragen: Fragewort an der Position, an der das Erfragte stehen würde
Zeiten: Gegenwart	eine: einfache Form	zwei: einfache (simple) und Verlaufsform (progressive)	eine: einfache Form	eine: einfache Form (das Verb "sein" hat keine Gegenwarts-form)	zwei: einfache und Verlaufsform
Zeiten: Vergangenheit	mehrere	mehrere (simple past, present per-fect, past perfect)	mehrere	eine	zwei
Zeiten: Zukunft	eine	zwei (will-future, going-to-future)	eine	eine	eine
Zählung	145 = einhundert-fünfundvierzig (Einerzahl wird vor Zehnerzahl genannt)	145 = one hundred and forty-five (Reihenfolge wie in der Zahl)	wie im Englischen	wie im Englischen	wie im Englischen

Beispielsätze:

Aussage:

Englisch:	I go to school.
Deutsch:	Ich gehe zur Schule.
Italienisch:	(Io) Vado a scuola.
Russisch:	Я иду в школу.
Türkisch:	(Ben) Okula giderim.

Frage mit Fragewort:

Englisch:	Which languages do you speak?
Deutsch:	Welche Sprachen sprichst du?
Italienisch:	Quale lingue parli?
Russisch:	На каких языках ты говоришь?
Türkisch:	Hangi dileri konuşuyorsun?

Mediation and communication

Mediating

Sinn entnehmen: Der Schwerpunkt im Bereich Mediation liegt darauf, Originaltexte mit mehr unbekanntem Wortschatz zu verstehen. Achte beim Hören oder Lesen immer darauf, dass du nichts wörtlich übertragen musst und konzentriere dich darauf, dass du dem Gehörten oder Gelesenen einen logischen Sinn geben kannst.

Gezielt hören/lesen: Lies vor dem Hören oder Lesen immer die Aufgabe genau durch. Oft sind es nur bestimmte Informationen, die du benötigst und auf die du gezielt achten musst.

Zahlen und Internationalismen: Beim Hören musst du dich sehr konzentrieren und dem normalen Redefluss der Sprecher folgen. Je nach Aufgabenstellung helfen dir hier besonders Zahlenangaben, englische oder internationale Wörter, die wir im Deutschen übernommen haben, und natürlich auch dein Allgemeinwissen zu den gehörten Sachverhalten, um Verstehenslücken zu überbrücken.

Bedeutung ableiten: Dies trifft auch für das Lesen zu. Außerdem solltest du hier besonders auf Wörter achten, deren Schriftbild dem deutscher Wörter entspricht oder ähnelt und so die Bedeutung eines Wortes ableiten.

Logik: Denke daran: Wenn der Satz keinen Sinn ergibt, hast du irgendwo etwas nicht richtig übertragen.

Topic 1

Situation 1

2,14

Du und dein/e Cousin/e machen gerade ein Praktikum in London. Er/Sie hat sich dort ein englisches Handy gekauft und möchte gerne seine/ihre Eltern anrufen. Er/Sie benötigt jedoch zuerst Hilfe seines/ihres Telefonanbieters.
Er/Sie hört 5 kurze Informationen des Telefonanbieters Blueline. Dein/e Cousin/e versteht leider nicht alles vom Telefonat. Hilf ihm/ihr, indem du seine/ihre Fragen beantwortest.

1. Was mache ich, wenn mein Guthaben aufgebraucht ist?
2. Zu welchen Dingen bekomme ich Hilfe, wenn ich Taste 3 drücke?
3. Mit wem wollen sie mich verbinden?
4. Was muss ich tun, wenn ich mich über die Kosten meines Ferngesprächs informieren möchte?
5. Wie kann ich meinen aktuellen Kontostand abfragen?

Situation 2

1. Deine Klasse plant einen gemeinsamen Kinobesuch. Du liest diese Filmkritik im Internet. Prüfe, ob dieser Film für eure Klasse geeignet ist.
   Was erzählst du deinen Klassenkamerad/innen über

   1. die Handlung,
   2. das Besondere des Films,
   3. den bisherigen Erfolg des Films?

UK 2008 • Opening: 19 March • Directed by: Danny Boyle
Principal actors: Dev Patel, Anil Kapoor, Saurabh Shukla, Freida Pinto, Rajendranath Zutshi

... In the slums of Bombay two little boys have to watch how their mother is killed during a religious riot. They make friends with another slum child, Latika, and this friendship will continue throughout their lives.
You can watch how India's technological boom starts to bring prosperity to its citizens. Bombay becomes Mumbai as the children grow up, and the slums are transformed into high-rise flats. Jamal (Dev Patel) is the younger brother who takes part in the television quiz show "Who Wants To Be a Millionaire?" His childhood is seen in flashbacks as he answers the questions put to him by the unpleasant Prem Kumar (Anil Kapoor). Mr Kumar believes that a "slumdog" can only answer his questions by cheating, and hands Jamal over to the police, hoping that they can discover how he does it. Is Jamal telling the truth? Will he reach the finals and win twenty million rupees? Most importantly, will he finally find the love of his life?

This Bollywood movie shows how good people triumph over evil, and the ending is certain to be happy. Jamal is a good, honest boy, his older brother Salim (Madhur Mittal) is a victim of his background – he chooses a life of crime. Latika (Freida Pinto) is beautiful and loyal. This impressive movie, with its happy, energetic music, has been spoken about everywhere. It won the Audience Choice Award at the Chicago International Film Festival and was in the Best Film Category at the British Independent Film Awards in 2008, where Londoner, Dev Patel, was awarded the prize for Best Newcomer. It also won eight Academy Awards, including Best Director and Best Picture. *(Peggy Richardson)*

2. Dein/e Brieffreund/in ist zu Besuch. Er/Sie findet diese deutschsprachige Filmkritik, kann aber nicht alles verstehen. Lies die Kritik und beantworte seine/ihre Fragen.

   1. What is everybody asking themselves?
   2. How does the quizmaster answer this question?
   3. What is the real answer?

... Für Jamal Malik (Dev Patel) ist es der größte Tag seines Lebens. Er nimmt an der indischen Version der TV-Show „Wer wird Millionär" teil und nur eine Frage trennt ihn vom 20-Millionen-Rupien-Hauptgewinn. Er, der ehemalige Straßenjunge Jamal Malik aus Mumbai! Alle Welt fragt sich, was ein mittelloser Jugendlicher aus den Slums von Mumbai in dieser Sendung verloren hat und wie es kommt, dass er auf alle Fragen eine Antwort weiß. Für den unsympathischen Quizmaster ist die Antwort auf diese Frage längst klar: Jemand, der aus der Armut der Slums von Mumbai kommt, kann nur ein Betrüger sein. Deshalb übergibt er ihn der Polizei, die ihn des Betrugs überführen soll. Wie aber konnte dieser Junge, der nie eine Schule besucht hat, die Antworten auf die Fülle von komplizierten Fragen wissen. Die Antwort darauf ist verblüffend einfach: Das Leben in den Slums, die Erfahrungen, die er dort in 18 Jahren machen musste, haben ihn die Antworten gelehrt.
Der Film wurde mit einem kleinen Budget und wenig Spezialeffekten gedreht, ohne große Stars aber mit großartigen Laienschauspielern. Ein sehr beeindruckender Film!

Topic 2

Situation 1

Du liest folgenden Artikel im Internet über Obamas berühmte ‚Victory[1] Speech'. Dein Cousin kann nicht sehr gut Englisch und stellt dir ein paar Fragen. Lies den Text und beantworte sie.

1. Ging es dabei um eine triumphierende Rede?
2. Wie will er die riesigen Probleme der USA angehen?
3. Hat er nur den Amerikanern etwas zu sagen gehabt?

Barack Obama's election victory brings a new dawn of leadership[2]

Jonathan Freedland in Chicago

… Obama himself seemed to understand how serious the moment was. Save for a few thank-yous to his team — and a message to his daughters that they had earned the new dog that the Obamas will take with them to the White House — he did not deliver a cheery victory speech. Instead he used the opportunity to give his first speech as president.

He declared that "Change has come to America," but left no doubt that his election marked only the first step along a road that will prove[3] long and hard. "We may not get there in one year or in one term," he cautioned[4]. "But we will get there." …

He called on all Americans – including those who had not voted for him – to join him in the tough work ahead: "I hear your voices, I need your help and I will be your president, too."

It was one of several calls for unity[5]. He had already asked America in 2004 to remember that it is not made up of blue states or red states, but must always be the United States. He seemed to be trying to form a government which could cope with[6] the great challenges of the age. …

"America, we have come so far," he said, as if the whole nation were gathered[7] before him. "We have seen so much. But there is so much more to do."

He also had a message to the rest of the world, one that will be welcomed almost everywhere. "To all those watching tonight from beyond our shores[8], from parliaments and palaces to those who are huddled[9] around radios in the forgotten corners of our world … a new dawn of American leadership is at hand[10]."

In this speech, and with his victory, Barack Obama has drawn a line under the last eight years, ending an American age that few will miss. For today marked nothing less than the first day of the Obama presidency.

2,15 **Situation 2**

Dein amerikanischer Freund ist ein besonderer Barack-Obama-Fan. Er hört sich deshalb gern die Reden von ihm im Original an. Nach der berühmten ‚Victory Speech', die er im Original verfolgt hat, ruft er dich gleich an und berichtet dir über seine Eindrücke. Du berichtest deiner Familie, was der Freund dir erzählt hat.

1. Was waren einige Schwerpunkte in der Rede von Obama?
2. Gibt es etwas besonders Beeindruckendes in der Rede?
3. Was empfand dein amerikanischer Freund als etwas Neues?
4. Welche Aufgabe hat sich Obama unter anderem gestellt?
5. Was sagt er
   – denen, die Krieg wollen,
   – den friedliebenden Menschen der Welt,
   – denen, die an Amerika zweifeln?

[1]victory ['vɪktri] – *Sieges-,* [2]leadership ['li:dəʃɪp] – *Führung,* [3]to prove [pru:v] – *hier: sich erweisen,* [4]to caution ['kɔ:ʃn] – *warnen,* [5]unity ['ju:nəti] – *Einheit,* [6]to cope with ['kəʊp wɪð] – *zurechtkommen,* [7]gathered ['gæðəd] – *versammelt,* [8]shores [ʃɔ:z] – *hier: Land,* [9]huddled ['hʌdld] – *zusammengedrängt,* [10]at hand [ət 'hænd] – *bevorstehend*

Topic 3

Situation 1

2,16 Du machst mit deiner Familie Urlaub an der Westküste der USA: Die anderen schlafen noch, als in eurem Hotel-Apartment das Telefon klingelt. Du hörst eine Tsunami-Warnung als Telefondurchsage. Was erzählst du später deiner Familie?

1. Wo darf deine Familie heute auf keinen Fall hingehen?
2. Erkläre genau, was ein Tsunami ist.
3. Dein Bruder will auf großen Wellen surfen. Was solltest du ihm unbedingt sagen?
4. Warum wäre ein Ausflug auf dem Pacific Coast Highway keine Alternative für heute?

Situation 2

Du hast Besuch aus den USA. Dein/e Partner/in sieht dieses Umweltposter. Beantworte seine/ihre Fragen.

1. Wozu ruft das Poster auf?
2. Was genau tun die Teilnehmer?
3. Wann findet die Aktion statt?
4. Kann man da auch mitmachen?

Rette unseren Wald!

Was wir wollen:
- Urlaub machen und dabei die Umwelt schützen.
- Bergwälder in den Alpen erhalten oder wieder aufforsten.

Wann?
Von April bis Oktober (eine Woche lang).

Wer?
Alle, die der Natur helfen wollen – vom Schüler bis zum Rentner!

Was erwartet dich dort?
- Kostenlose Unterkunft und Verpflegung in Holzhütten – mit großem Abenteuer!
- Aufregende Arbeitstage im Wald!
- Arbeit in kleinen Gruppen mit Fachleuten!
- Viel Unterhaltung und Spaß!

Was tun wir konkret?
- Bäume pflanzen
- Zäune bauen
- Wege anlegen

Komm einfach mit!

Topic 4

Situation 1

2,17 Du und einige andere Schüler besuchen eine amerikanische Schule. Am ersten Tag ist euch alles ziemlich fremd und ihr versteht nicht viel. Deshalb habt ihr abgesprochen, immer alle genau zuzuhören und euch hinterher auszutauschen, damit keine wichtige Information verloren geht.
Deine Klassenkameraden haben einer Lautsprecherdurchsage die folgenden Informationen entnommen. Sind sie korrekt? Wenn nicht, korrigiere oder vervollständige sie.

1. Die erste Deutschstunde fällt aus und ihr sollt euch dafür in der Cafeteria melden.
2. TABU ist ein Anti-Raucher-Klub.
3. Lehrer und Schüler können Brettspiele spielen. Kannst du mit deinen Klassenkameraden/innen da einfach hingehen?
4. Am Donnerstag gibt es kein Mittagessen. Dafür werden Mützen verkauft. Jeder muss mindestens eine für 22 $ kaufen.

Situation 2

Dein/e Freund/in ist 17 und hat noch keine richtigen beruflichen Vorstellungen. Er/Sie kann sehr gut auf Menschen zugehen, absolviert gegenwärtig verschiedene Praktika in unterschiedlichen Handelsketten, um Erfahrungen zu sammeln und verbessert sein/ihr Englisch. Danach möchte er/sie erst einmal gern irgendwo im Ausland arbeiten. Dafür ist er/sie schon jetzt ständig auf der Suche nach interessanten Arbeitsmöglichkeiten.
Du hast diese Anzeige gefunden. Erkläre deinem Freund/deiner Freundin, warum diese Stelle gut für ihn/sie geeignet ist.

"FIT for SPORT", Australia's leading sports shop centres have jobs available for Casual Sales Assistants in the Clothes and Consumer Goods Departments at the Sunshine store in SA.

The successful applicants:
- need exemplary motivation.
- need excellent customer service skills.
- don't need previous retail experience as training will be provided, however, experience is an advantage.

The last two points are musts for this position.

We offer a great career, extensive training and payment above average.
This is a fantastic opportunity to join a successful, fast growing retailer.

Contact: Lucy Capp
LU197, MNO4, South Mall, Sunshine Shopping Centre 50 Park Way
Elizabeth, S Australia 501253
Phone: 18 8252 8011 22

Grammatical terms
Hier findest du eine Zusammenfassung aller wichtigen Grammatikbegriffe, die du brauchst: Links steht der Begriff auf Deutsch, in der Mitte auf Englisch und rechts stehen Beispiele. Die Nummern neben den Begriffen (z.B. Ov 1) verweisen auf die Pensen im Grammatikanhang.

Overviews (Ov 1 – Ov 13)
Die Regeln zur Grammatik sind in systematischen Übersichten *(Overviews)* zusammengestellt. Der Schwerpunkt liegt in diesem Jahr darauf, neu Gelerntes mit bekanntem Wissen gut zu vernetzen.

Grammar practice
Übungen zu jedem Pensum der *Overviews*.

Grammatical terms

Lateinisch / Deutsch	Englisch	Englisches Beispiel
Adjektiv / Eigenschaftswort	adjective	quick, small, nice, old
Adverb / Umstandswort Ov 12	adverb	always, often, quickly, loudly
Adverbialbestimmung der Art und Weise Ov 13	adverbial phrase of manner	easily, busily, wonderfully, fast, hard
Adverbialbestimmung des Ortes Ov 13	adverbial phrase of place	to Stonehenge
Adverbialbestimmung der Zeit Ov 4, 13	adverbial phrase of time	last week, around 600 years later
Aktiv Ov 9	active voice	Parliament makes these laws to protect us.
Bedingungssatz Typ 1 Ov 11	conditional clause type I	The Queen will declare war if Parliament tells her to do so.
Bedingungssatz Typ 2 Ov 11	conditional clause type II	The Queen would stop the government's plans if she refused to sign a law.
Bedingungssatz Typ 3 Ov 11	conditional clause type III	If you had lived in the Middle Ages, you would probably have lived in a hut.
Demonstrativpronomen / Hinweisendes Fürwort	demonstrative pronoun	this, that, these, those
Ersatzformen für Modalverben Ov 8	modal substitutes	(not) be able to, (not) be allowed to, (not) have to
Futur II / Die vollendete Zukunft Ov 6	future perfect	I will have finished this work by the end of the week.
Gerundium	gerund	We enjoy going to parties.
Going to-Futur Ov 6	future with 'going to'	I'm going to sell my computer.
Gradadverb Ov 12	adverb of degree	very, almost, really, quite
Häufigkeitsadverb Ov 12	adverb of frequency	always, often, sometimes, never
Hauptsatz Ov 11	main clause	She wants to buy a comic.
Hilfsverb Ov 2	auxiliary	be, have got, do
Indirekte Rede mit Zeitverschiebung Ov 4	reported speech (later)	He said that he wasn't jealous.
Indirekte Rede ohne Zeitverschiebung	reported speech (immediate)	She says she's ill.
Interrogativpronomen / Fragewort	question word	who, where, what, whom, which, why
Modales Hilfsverb / Modalverb Ov 7	modal verb	must/n't, need/n't, should/n't
Nebensatz Ov 11	sub-clause	If she arrives late, …
Objektpronomen Ov 1	object pronoun	me, you, him, her, it, us, them

Lateinisch / Deutsch	Englisch	Englisches Beispiel
Passiv in der einfachen Gegenwart **Ov 9**	passive voice: simple present	These laws are made to protect us.
Passiv in der einfachen Vergangenheit **Ov 9**	passive voice: simple past	Yesterday a British journalist was kidnapped … .
Passiv im Futur **Ov 9**	passive voice: will-future	If you break a law, you will be arrested.
Passiv im Perfekt **Ov 9**	passive voice: present perfect	Since 1215 many people have been inspired by Magna Carta.
Passiv im Plusquamperfekt **Ov 9**	passive voice: past perfect	A black hood had been pulled down over my head.
Passiv in der Vergangenheit, Verlaufsform **Ov 9**	passive voice: past progressive	I understood that I was being taken somewhere.
Perfekt **Ov 5**	present perfect	Tom has painted the walls.
Personalpronomen / Persönliches Fürwort **Ov 1**	personal pronoun	I, you, she, he, it, we, you, they
Plusquamperfekt / Vollendete Vergangenheit **Ov 3**	past perfect	After they had explained their idea, the reporters wrote articles.
Plusquamperfekt / Vollendete Vergangenheit: Verlaufsform **Ov 3**	past perfect progressive	He had been driving for just three months when the accident happened.
Possessivbegleiter / Besitzanzeigendes Fürwort **Ov 1**	possessive pronoun	my, your, his, her, its, our, their
Präsens / Einfache Gegenwart **Ov 5**	simple present	I live in South Africa.
Präteritum / Einfache Vergangenheit **Ov 3**	simple past	I watched TV yesterday.
Reflexivpronomen / Rückbezügliches Fürwort **Ov 1**	reflexive pronoun	myself, ourselves
Relativpronomen **Ov 10**	relative pronoun	This is the camp that I want to go to.
Relativsatz **Ov 10**	relative clause	People who had been doing traditional jobs had to change.
Signalwort **Ov 9**	signal word	last, ago, yesterday, ever, yet
2. Stammform/3. Stammform **Ov 9**	perfect participle/past participle	ate/eaten, did/done, went/gone
Steigerung von Adverbien	comparison of adjectives	old – older – the oldest, good – better – the best
Verb / Tätigkeitswort	verb	to be, to go, to do, to write
Verlaufsform der Gegenwart **Ov 5**	present progressive	We're listening to our new CD.
Verlaufsform der Vergangenheit **Ov 3**	past progressive	I understood that they were taking me somewhere to shoot me.
Vollverb **Ov 2**	verb	to go, to do, to write
Will-Futur **Ov 6**	'will'-future	I hope it will be warm tomorrow.
Wortstellung **Ov 13**	word order	I never drink alcohol.

Ov 1 Pronomen *Pronouns*

Pronomen werden auch FÜRwörter genannt, weil sie für Personen, Tiere oder Gegenstände stehen, um z. B. ein bestimmtes Wort nicht dauernd zu wiederholen. **Personalpronomen** ersetzen das **Subjekt** im Satz. (*Emma is from Bristol. – **She**'s from Bristol.*) Soll das **Objekt des Satzes** ersetzt werden, verwendest du dafür die **Objektform** der Personalpronomen. (*My friends like my pets. – They often feed **them**.*) **Possessivpronomen** drücken aus, **wem etwas gehört**. (*This is **my** book.*) **Reflexivpronomen** beziehen sich zurück auf das Subjekt und können mit **selbst** übersetzt werden. (*I can do this **myself**.*)

Personalpronomen *Personal pronouns*		**Objektform** *Object pronouns*		**Possessivpronomen** *Possessive pronouns*		**Reflexivpronomen** *Reflexive pronouns*	
I	*ich*	me	*mir/mich*	my	*mein*	I – myself	*ich selbst*
you	*du*	you	*dir/dich/Ihnen/Sie*	your	*dein/Ihr*	you – yourself	*du/Sie selbst*
he	*er*	him	*ihm/ihn*	his	*sein*	he – himself	*er selbst*
she	*sie*	her	*ihr/sie*	her	*ihr*	she – herself	*sie selbst*
it	*es*	it	*ihm/es*	its	*sein*	it – itself	*es selbst*
we	*wir*	us	*uns*	our	*unser*	we – ourselves	*wir selbst*
you	*ihr*	you	*euch/Ihnen/Sie*	your	*euer/Ihr*	you – yourselves	*ihr/Sie selbst*
they	*sie*	them	*ihnen/sie*	their	*ihre*	they – themselves	*sie selbst*

Beispiele:

I like my cat and my cat loves me. *Ich liebe meine Katze und meine Katze liebt mich.*

I'll teach myself cooking. *Ich werde mir Kochen selbst beibringen.*

If you help Mr Brown in his garden, he'll give you five pounds. *Wenn du Mr Brown in seinem Garten hilfst, wird er dir fünf Pfund geben.*

If she hasn't got time, I'll do the shopping for her. *Wenn sie keine Zeit hat, mache ich den Einkauf für sie.*

She told us that she had won a competition at her school and in the town where she lived. *Sie erzählte uns, dass sie an ihrer Schule und in der Stadt, wo sie lebt, einen Wettbewerb gewonnen hat.*

Beachte!
Manchmal verwendet man im Englischen kein Pronomen oder ein anderes:
I bought **myself** a new computer. *Ich habe **mir** einen neuen Computer gekauft.*
I **washed** before I went out. *Ich **wusch mich**, bevor ich ausging.*

Ov 2 Formen von *be* in den einzelnen Zeiten

'be' in different tenses

Das Verb *„to be"* wird sowohl als **Vollverb** als auch als **Hilfsverb** in zusammengesetzten Zeiten benutzt. Für diese Zeitformen benötigst du jeweils die entsprechende gebeugte Form, die du in der Tabelle finden kannst.

Aussagen – Langformen/Kurzformen

	past perfect	present perfect	simple past	simple present	will-future
I	had been / 'd been	have been / 've been	was	am / 'm	will be / 'll be
You	had been / 'd been	have been / 've been	were	are / 're	will be / 'll be
He/She/It	had been / 'd been	has been / 's been	was	is / 's	will be / 'll be
We	had been / 'd been	have been / 've been	were	are / 're	will be / 'll be
You	had been / 'd been	have been / 've been	were	are / 're	will be / 'll be
They	had been / 'd been	have been / 've been	were	are / 're	will be / 'll be

Verneinungen – Kurzformen

	past perfect	present perfect	simple past	simple present	will-future
I	hadn't been	haven't been	wasn't	am not/ 'm not	won't be
You	hadn't been	haven't been	weren't	aren't	won't be
He/She/It	hadn't been	hasn't been	wasn't	isn't	won't be
We	hadn't been	haven't been	weren't	aren't	won't be
You	hadn't been	haven't been	weren't	aren't	won't be
They	hadn't been	haven't been	weren't	aren't	won't be

Beachte!

Nach Personalpronomen verwendet man in der Regel die Kurzform von *be*. Die Langform benötigst du aber nach Substantiven und bei Fragen: *She's **been** to Oz.* **but** *The Queen **has been** to Oz.* • *I'm late.* **but** ***Am I** late?* • *You'**ll be** back.* **but** *When **will you** be back?*

Ov 3 Vollverben in den Zeiten der Vergangenheit — *Verbs in past tenses*

Die Zeiten der Vergangenheit sind ***simple past*** (einfache Vergangenheit), ***past progressive*** (Verlaufsform der Vergangenheit), ***past perfect*** (vollendete Vergangenheit), ***past perfect progressive*** (Verlaufsform der vollendeten Vergangenheit). Sie beziehen sich auf Handlungen in der Vergangenheit. Das *past perfect progressive* und das *past progressive* unterstreichen dabei die Dauer der Handlung (Beispiele 1, 2, 7, 8). Das *past perfect* wird häufig verwendet, wenn eine Handlung vor einer anderen in der Vergangenheit stattfand (Beispiele 3, 4).

	past perfect progressive	past perfect	simple past	past progressive
	had been + verb + ing	***had + verb + ed***	***verb + ed***	***was/were + verb + ing***
I				was playing wasn't playing
You				were playing weren't playing
He/She/It	had been playing hadn't been playing	had played hadn't played	played didn't play	was playing wasn't playing
We				were playing weren't playing
You				were playing weren't playing
They				were playing weren't playing

Beispiele:

1. We **had been playing** for only ten minutes when I heard the whistle. — *Wir spielten gerade mal zehn Minuten, als ich die Pfeife hörte.*
2. We **hadn't been looking** at the sky. — *Wir hatten den Himmel nicht beobachtet.*
3. Our team **had** already **scored** two goals. — *Unsere Mannschaft hatte schon zwei Tore geschossen.*
4. Our goalkeeper **hadn't** even **touched** the ball. — *Unser Torwart hatte den Ball nicht einmal berührt.*
5. Suddenly it **started** to rain. — *Plötzlich fing es an zu regnen.*
6. I **didn't want** to stop. — *Ich wollte nicht aufhören.*
7. The others **were running** into the club house. — *Die anderen liefen in das Vereinsgebäude.*
8. But it **wasn't raining** very hard. — *Aber es regnete nicht sehr stark.*

Beachte!
In Deutschland wird oft *present perfect* verwendet, wo im Englischen *simple past* steht:
Es hat plötzlich angefangen zu regnen.

Ov 4 Indirekte Rede (später berichtet) *Reported speech*

Wenn direkte Rede im Englischen erst später berichtet wird, steht das **einleitende Verb in der Vergangenheit** (*said, asked, wanted to know, answered*). In dem Folgesatz gibt es dann eine **Zeitverschiebung**. Solche Erzählformen findest du auch oft in der Literatur, z.B. in Erzählungen, Romanen, aber auch in Berichten usw.

Direkte Rede simple present	Einleitungssatz simple past		Indirekte Rede simple past
"Most of us **know** about the environmental changes in the world."	They wrote	(that)	most of them **knew** about the environmental changes in the world.
"I **don't like** walking to school."	He said		he **didn't like** walking to school.
"**Are** greenhouse gases bad for our world?"	They wanted to know	if	greenhouse gases **were** bad for their world.
"How much water **do** you **use** to wash your clothes?"	They asked	how much	water we **used** to wash our clothes.
Direkte Rede simple past	**Einleitungssatz simple past**		**Indirekte Rede past perfect**
"Why **didn't** you **buy** local apples?"	She asked	why	I **hadn't bought** local apples.

Beachte!

- Bei den Pronomen wechselt die erste Person zur dritten Person:

I – ich		***he/she*** – er/sie
we – wir	wird zu →	***they*** – sie
my – mein		***his/her*** – sein/ihr
our – unser		***their*** – ihr (Pl.)

Die zweite Person wechselt zur ersten Person:

you – du		***I*** – ich
you – ihr/Sie	wird zu →	***we*** – wir
your – dein		***my*** – mein
your – euer/Ihr		***our*** – unser

- Einige Adverbialbestimmungen der Zeit aus der direkten Rede ändern sich in der indirekten Rede:
  this morning → **that morning**
  today → **that day**
  yesterday → **the day before**
  tomorrow → **the next day**
  next week → **the following week**
  In der umgangssprachlichen deutschen Übersetzung wird diese Zeitverschiebung manchmal nicht übernommen sondern die Gegenwart aus der wörtlichen Rede beibehalten.

- Vorsicht, manche Verben ändern ihre Form nicht.
  "It **should** be OK!" → He **told** me it **should** be OK.

- Bei Fragen entfällt das „do" als Umschreibung und das Vollverb steht dann in der entsprechenden Zeitform.
  "Do you play tennis?" → He **asked** me if I played tennis.

Ov 5 Vollverben in den Zeiten der Gegenwart *Verbs in present tenses*

Die Zeiten der Gegenwart sind ***simple present*** (einfache Gegenwart), ***present progressive*** (Verlaufsform der Gegenwart), ***present perfect*** (Perfekt) und ***present perfect progressive*** (Verlaufsform des Perfekts). Sie beziehen sich auf eine Handlung in der Gegenwart oder auf eine Handlung, die in der Vergangenheit begann und noch bis in die Gegenwart hineinreicht bzw. Auswirkungen auf die Gegenwart hat. Die Verlaufsformen drücken dabei jeweils aus, dass die Handlungen andauern.

	present perfect progressive	**present perfect**	**simple present**	**present progressive**
	have/has been + verb + ing	***have/has + verb + ed***	***verb***	***am/is/are + verb + ing***
I	have been living haven't been living	have lived haven't lived	live don't live	am living 'm not living
You	have been living haven't been living	have lived haven't lived	live don't live	are living aren't living
He/She/It	has been living hasn't been living	has lived hasn't lived	live doesn't live	is living isn't living
We	have been living haven't been living	have lived haven't lived	live don't live	are living aren't living
You	have been living haven't been living	have lived haven't lived	live don't live	are living aren't living
They	have been living haven't been living	have lived haven't lived	live don't live	are living aren't living

Beispiele:

1. I **have been living** here since I was born. — *Ich lebe seit meiner Geburt hier.*
2. I **haven't been learning** English for very long. — *Ich lerne noch nicht sehr lange Englisch.*
3. I **have been** to London several times. — *Ich war mehrmals in London.*
4. But I **haven't been** to New York yet. — *Aber ich war noch nicht in New York.*
5. My aunt **lives** in America. — *Meine Tante wohnt in Amerika.*
6. Unfortunately **she doesn't live** in New York. — *Sie wohnt leider nicht in New York.*
7. **I'm saving** my pocket money, so that I can visit her next year. — *Ich spare mein Taschengeld, damit ich sie nächstes Jahr besuchen kann.*
8. My parents **aren't** just **giving** me the money. I have to earn it. — *Meine Eltern schenken mir nicht einfach das Geld. Ich muss es verdienen.*

Beachte!
Das *present perfect progressive* wird im Deutschen auch manchmal mit der einfachen Gegenwart (Beispiele 1, 2), das *present perfect* mit der einfachen Vergangenheit übersetzt (Beispiele 3, 4).

Ov 6 Formen des Futurs *Future forms*

Wenn du eine **zukünftige Handlung** ausdrücken willst, musst du eine Futur-Form verwenden. Du verwendest das ***will-future*** wenn du dich **spontan für etwas entscheidest**, etwas **versprichst** oder jemandem **Hilfe anbietest**. Signalwörter sind: *probably, maybe, I'm sure, I think, I promise, I hope, I know*. Oft verwendest du in der deutschen Übersetzung das Präsens (Beispiele 1, 2).
Mit dem *future perfect* kannst du auf Geschehnisse in der Zukunft Bezug nehmen, die noch vor der zukünftigen Handlung liegen, die du gerade beschreibst (Beispiele 3, 4).
Mit der Verlaufsform des *will-future* betonst du die Dauer der Handlung (Beispiele 5, 6).

	future	future perfect	future progressive
	will + verb	***will + have + verb***	***will + be + verb + ing***
I/You/He/She/It/We/You/They	will get/'ll get won't get	will have got won't have got	will be getting won't be getting

Beispiele:

1. I hope I will get that job in Australia. — *Ich hoffe, ich bekomme den Job in Australien.*
2. I know it won't be easy. — *Ich weiß, es wird nicht leicht sein.*
3. They will probably have had lots of applications. — *Sie werden wahrscheinlich viele Bewerbungen erhalten haben.*
4. But I'm sure they won't have had time to read them all yet. — *Aber sie werden sicherlich noch nicht alle haben lesen können.*
5. People will probably be writing from all over the world. — *Leute aus der ganzen Welt werden wohl schreiben.*
6. They'll all be hoping to get the job. — *Sie werden alle darauf hoffen, den Job zu bekommen.*

going to-future und das **Futur mit dem *present progressive*** bieten weitere Möglichkeiten, zukünftige Handlungen zu beschreiben. Mit jeder dieser Futurformen kann der/die Sprecher/in ganz spezielle Absichten ausdrücken.

	going to-future	future with the present progressive
Verwendung	Einen **Plan**, eine **Idee** zu einem Ereignis oder einer Handlung in der Zukunft ausdrücken.	**Feste Vereinbarungen** in der Zukunft oder **persönliche feste Vorhaben** ausdrücken.
Bildung	***am/is/are + going to + verb***	***am/is/are + verb + ing***
Struktur	***am/is/are going to play***	***am/is/are playing***

Beispiele:

1. My friends and I are going to visit the South of France this summer.
2. We aren't going to lie in the sun all day.
3. We are taking part in a cycling race.
4. But we aren't taking part in the Tour de France.

Ov 7 Modalverben und Hilfsverben *Modals and auxiliaries*

Mit den modalen Hilfsverben kannst du sagen, was jemand tun sollte (*should*), tun muss (*must*), tun darf (*may*), nicht tun darf (*must not*), tun kann (*can*). Du kannst also **Regeln**, **Empfehlungen**, **Verbote** ausdrücken, indem du ein solches Modalverb vor ein Vollverb stellst. Dabei musst du folgendes beachten:

- *Modals* stehen nur im *simple present*, bilden also keine andere Zeit. (Ausnahme: *can* → *could)*
- Sie erhalten kein *-s* nach *he/she/it*.
- Bei Verneinungen kannst du einfach *not* an das *modal* anhängen. (Beachte! *Must not/mustn't* heißt ‚nicht dürfen'.)
- Bei Fragen steht das *modal* am Satzanfang.

Die Hilfsverben *used to* und *would* werden nur zum Ausdruck von Handlungen in der Vergangenheit verwendet. *Do* verstärkt die Bedeutung des nachfolgenden Verbs in Handlungen der Gegenwart. Für vergangene Handlungen heißt es *did*.

Modalverben	Beispiele	Übersetzung
can *(können)*	I **can** play the drums.	*Ich kann Schlagzeug spielen.*
can't *(nicht können)*	He **can't** swim.	*Er kann nicht schwimmen.*
must *(müssen)*	You **must** learn the new words!	*Ihr müsst die neuen Wörter lernen.*
needn't *(nicht müssen/ brauchen)*	You **needn't** do this task.	*Ihr braucht diese Aufgabe nicht zu machen.*
mustn't *(nicht dürfen)*	You **mustn't** drink alcohol!	*Ihr dürft keinen Alkohol trinken.*
may *(dürfen)*	You **may** use a dictionary.	*Ihr dürft ein Wörterbuch benutzen.*
should *(sollte/t/st)*	You **should** see a doctor.	*Ihr solltet zum Arzt gehen.*
shouldn't *(sollte/t/st nicht)*	You **shouldn't** forget your homework.	*Ihr solltet eure Hausaufgaben nicht vergessen.*
shall *(soll/en)*	**Shall** we wave?	*Sollen/wollen wir winken?*

Hilfsverben	Beispiele	Übersetzung
used to *(üblicherweise)*	Only people with an Asian background **used to** speak Hinglish.	*Nur Menschen asiatischer Herkunft sprachen üblicherweise Hinglish.*
would *(gewohnheitsmäßig)*	When he was younger he **would** buy a comic on Saturdays.	*Als er jünger war, kaufte er samstags immer einen Comic.*
do *(auf jeden Fall)*	English certainly **does** help to bring people of different nationalities together.	*Englisch hilft auf jeden Fall, Menschen unterschiedlicher Nationalitäten zusammenzubringen.*

Ov 8 Modale Ersatzformen *Modal substitutes*

Weil die Modalverben (bis auf *can*) nur im *simple present* vorkommen, braucht man für sie **Ersatzformen**, wenn man mit ihnen **Sätze im *simple past*** oder im ***will-future*** bilden möchte.
Das jeweilige Modalverb und seine Ersatzform kann man bedeutungsgleich im *simple present* benutzen. Meistens wird aber das kürzere Modalverb bevorzugt.

Wenn du sagst, ...	... weißt du	Formen von *be* und *have*
„du hast das zu machen" you **have to** (do it)	*du musst es machen.* you must (do it).	simple present – am, is, are simple past – was, were, na klar!
„du bist in der Lage (etwas zu tun)" you **are able to** (do something)	*du kannst es machen.* you can (do it).	simple present – have/has *je nach* Person simple past – *nur* had! Das war's auch schon!
„dir ist erlaubt, etwas zu tun" you **are allowed to** (do something)	*du darfst es tun.* you may (do it).	

Beispiele:

1. The BBC report that they **aren't able to** contact the journalist. — *Die BBC gibt bekannt, dass sie nicht in der Lage sind, Kontakt zu dem Journalisten herzustellen.*
2. **Is** the Queen **allowed to** make treaties? — *Darf die Königin Verträge schließen?*
3. The Queen **has to** sign treaties with other nations. — *Die Königin muss Verträge mit anderen Staaten unterzeichnen.*
4. The Queen **isn't allowed to** make treaties. — *Die Königin darf keine Verträge schließen.*

Auf einen Blick

Modalverb	Übersetzung	Ersatzformen		
		simple present	**simple past**	**future**
can	*können*	am/is/are able to	was/were able to	will be able to
may	*dürfen*	am/is/are allowed to	was/were allowed to	will be allowed to
must	*müssen*	have/has to	had to	will have to
needn't	*nicht brauchen* *nicht müssen*	don't/doesn't have to	didn't have to	won't have to
mustn't	*nicht dürfen*	am not/aren't/isn't allowed to	wasn't/weren't allowed to	won't be allowed to

Ov 9 Aktiv und Passiv — *Active and passive voice*

Ob ein Satz im Aktiv oder Passiv verwendet wird, hängt von der Absicht des Sprechers ab. Will er ausdrücken, **wer etwas getan hat**, verwendet er das **Aktiv**, soll aber mehr betont werden, **was mit wem geschieht**, verwendet er eine **Passivkonstruktion**. Hier sind also andere Dinge wichtig. Deshalb kann man auch nicht einfach einen Satz aus dem Aktiv ins Passiv umformen. In der Übersicht wurden solche Beispiele deshalb gegenübergestellt, um die Bildungsmerkmale zu verdeutlichen.

Zeitform	past perfect	past progressive	simple past	present perfect	simple present	will-future	modals
Signal-wörter	before that, in the past		yesterday, … ago, last …, in … (year)	just, already, never, for ever, yet, since	always, often, sometimes, every	in … (year), tomorrow, next … (day of the week)	
Bildung Aktiv	***had*** **+ verb+*ed*/ 3. Stammform**	***was/were*** **+ verb+*ing***	**verb-*ed*/ 2. Stammform**	***have/has*** **+ verb-*ed*/ 3. Stammform**	**verb(+s)**	***will*** **+ verb**	***modal*** **+ verb**
Beispiel Aktiv	(Someone) had pulled a black hood over my head …	I understood that they were taking me …	Members of a militant group kidnapped a British journalist yesterday.	Since 1215 Magna Carta has inspired many people.	(Parliament) makes these laws to protect us and our rights.	(The police) will arrest you if you break a law.	(They) cannot bring the Queen to court.
Bildung Passiv	***had been*** **+ verb+*ed*/ 3. Stammform**	***was/were*** **+ *being* + verb+*ed*/ 3. Stammform**	***was/were*** **+ verb-*ed*/ 3. Stammform**	***have been/has been*** **+ verb-*ed*/ 3. Stammform**	***is/are*** **+ verb-*ed*/ 3. Stammform**	***will be*** **+ verb-*ed*/ 3. Stammform**	***modal*** **+ *be* + verb+*ed* / 3. Stammform**
Beispiel Passiv	A black hood had been pulled over my head …	I understood that I was being taken …	Yesterday a British journalist was kidnapped by members of a militant group.	Since 1215 many people have been inspired by Magna Carta.	These laws are made to protect us and our rights.	If you break a law you will be arrested.	The Queen cannot be brought to court.

Beachte!
Das Passiv wird oft verwendet, wenn nicht gesagt werden kann oder soll, wer etwas gemacht hat. Falls bekannt, wird die Person/… mit *by* angegeben!

Ov 10 Relativsätze *Relative clauses*

Relativsätze **erklären ein Substantiv** im Hauptsatz. Sie werden von einem **Relativpronomen** eingeleitet, das sich auf das Substantiv (im Singular oder Plural) bezieht. Sie werden nicht durch Kommas abgetrennt, wenn sie für den Sinn des Satzes notwendig sind.
Relativsätze stehen in Kommas, wenn sie für den Sinn des Satzes nicht unbedingt notwendig, d.h. nur eine Ergänzung sind. (z.B. *People like rangers, zookeepers and biologists, for example, who work directly for the environment, are needed everywhere.* – Menschen wie Ranger, Tierpfleger und Biologen, z.B., die direkt für die Umwelt arbeiten, werden überall gebraucht.)

Erklärung für	Relativpronomen
(ein) Ding/e	**which**
(eine) Person/en	**who**
(ein) Ding/e oder (eine) Person/en	**that**
Zugehörigkeit zu Person/en oder Tier/en	**whose**
das Akkusativobjekt im Satz	**that**

Beispiele:

Communities … get their water from ponds which are badly polluted. — *Gemeinden … bekommen ihr Wasser aus Teichen, **die** stark verseucht sind.*

People who had been doing traditional jobs had to change. — *Menschen, **die** traditionelle Berufe ausgeübt hatten, mussten sich umstellen.*

Our carbon footprint is made by all the greenhouse gases that we produce. — *Unsere CO_2-Bilanz setzt sich zusammen aus allen Treibgasen, **die** wir produzieren.*

The family whose carbon footprint is much too high is now trying to reduce it. — *Die Familie, **deren** CO_2-Bilanz viel zu hoch ist, versucht nun, sie zu reduzieren.*

We all know that most of the poisons (that) we take into our bodies come through our food. — *Wir wissen alle, dass die meisten Gifte, **die** in unseren Körper gelangen, durch das Essen aufgenommen werden.*

Beachte!
Manchmal ist „that“ kein Relativpronomen, sondern eine Konjunktion. Dann übersetzt man mit „dass“.
“We all know **that** most of the poison …” — *Wir wissen alle, **dass** die meisten Gifte …*

Ov 11 Bedingungssätze *Conditional clauses*

Bedingungssätze bestehen aus zwei Teilen, dem **Nebensatz mit *if***, der die **Bedingung** ausdrückt, und dem **Hauptsatz**, der sagt, **was passiert**, wenn diese Bedingung erfüllt wird. Es gibt unterschiedliche Arten von Bedingungen. Aus der folgenden Übersicht kannst du entnehmen, was für Bedingungen das sind und welche Regeln du bei der Bildung solcher Sätze beachten musst.

Typ I: erfüllbare Bedingung

Hauptsatz *will ('ll)* **or** ***can/may*** **+ verb**	*Nebensatz mit* **if** **verb(+s)**
The Queen **will declare** war *Die Königin wird den Krieg erklären,*	if Parliament **tells** her to do so. *wenn das Parlament sie damit beauftragt.*
The President **can use** his veto *Der Präsident kann sein Veto einlegen,*	if he **doesn't like** a bill. *wenn ihm ein Gesetzentwurf nicht gefällt.*

Typ II: offene Bedingung

Hauptsatz *would ('d)* **or** *could/might* **+ verb**	*Nebensatz mit* **if** **verb +** *ed***/2. Stammform**
The Queen **would stop** the government's plans *Die Königin würde die Pläne der Regierung stoppen,*	if she **refused** to pass a law. *wenn sie es ablehnen würde, ein Gesetz zu unterzeichnen.*
The UK **couldn't have** a government *Das UK könnte keine Regierung haben,*	if the Queen **refused** to open Parliament. *wenn die Königin sich weigern würde, das Parlament zu eröffnen.*

Typ III: nicht erfüllbare Bedingung

Hauptsatz *would ('d)/could/might have* **+ verb +** *ed***/3. Stammform**	*Nebensatz mit* **if** *had* **+ verb +** *ed***/3. Stammform**
You **would** probably **have lived** in a hut *Ihr hättet wahrscheinlich in einer Hütte gewohnt,*	if you **had lived** in the Middle Ages. *wenn ihr im Mittelalter gelebt hättet.*
This **could** never **have happened** *Das hätte nie passieren können,*	if I **hadn't decided** to stay in Gaza. *wenn ich nicht beschlossen hätte, in Gaza zu bleiben.*

Beachte!

- Der *if*-Satz kann vor oder nach dem Hauptsatz stehen. Steht er am Anfang, wird er durch Komma abgetrennt: *If he doesn't like a bill, the President can use his veto.*
- In der Verneinung wird *will* zu *won't*, *would* zu *wouldn't* und *had* zu *hadn't*. Ein Vollverb wird mit *don't/doesn't* oder *didn't* verneint.
- Um eine zusätzliche Bedeutung hinzuzufügen, kann *will* durch *can/may* und *would* durch *could/might* ersetzt werden.

Ov 12 Adverbien: Zusammenfassung — *Adverbs: Summary*

Adverbien sind Wörter, die ein **Verb im Satz näher erklären** (wie/wie oft/wann/wo man etwas tut) oder ein anderes **Adverb oder Adjektiv näher erklären** (wie genau, man etwas tut/etwas ist).

Art des Adverbs	Auf die Frage ...	Adverbien	Bildung	Stellung im Satz	Beispiele
*Adverbien des **Ortes** (O)*	Where?	anywhere, downstairs, everywhere, here, over there, outside, …	*Wörter lernen*	*am Satzende/am Satzanfang zur besonderen Betonung*	My grandad has driven his car **everywhere**. *Mein Opa ist überall mit seinem Auto gefahren.*
*Adverbien der **Zeit** (Z)*	When?	tomorrow, now, yesterday, later, yet, not yet, soon, late, …	*Wörter lernen*	*am Satzanfang oder -ende, Beachte: Ort vor Zeit!*	**Yesterday** we wanted to go to the cinema. *Wir wollten gestern ins Kino gehen.*
*Adverbien der **Art und Weise** (A)*	How?	badly, busily, early, easily, helpfully, normally, openly, … far, fast, hard, high, simply, … well, …	*Adjektiv + -ly/* *Adjektiv = Adverb/* *Wörter lernen*	*am Satzende/nach dem Verb Beachte: A – O – Z*	We left **early**. *Wir fuhren früh ab.* We hadn't gone **far** when he stopped. *Wir waren nicht weit gefahren, als er anhielt.*
***Häufigkeits-**adverbien*	How often?	always, never, often sometimes, still, …	*Wörter lernen*	*vor dem Vollverb/ nach Hilfsverb, Modal oder „be"*	He **sometimes** forgets things, so I waited. *Er vergisst manchmal Dinge, daher wartete ich.*
***Grad**adverbien*	How much/ + *Adj/Adv?*	a bit, absolutely, almost, extremely, much, quite, really, super, very, …	*Adjektiv + -ly/ Wörter lernen*	*vor dem Wort, das sie näher erklären*	He said he was **very** sorry, but he had forgotten his glasses. *Er sagte, dass es ihm sehr leid tue, aber er hatte seine Brille vergessen.*

Ov 13 Die Wortstellung im Satz *The position of words in a sentence*

1. Aussagesatz und Verneinung

Im Aussagesatz ist die Wortstellung
- Subjekt -Verb - Objekt (S - V - O) oder
- Subjekt - Hilfsverb + Vollverb - Objekt (S - HV+V - O)
- Diese Grundstellung bleibt immer erhalten.
- Bei Verneinungen wird das HV mit *not* verneint. Ist kein HV im Satz vorhanden, wird eine Form von *do* + *not* (*don't, doesn't, didn't*) vor die Grundform des Verbs gesetzt.

S	(HV) + V	O	Rest des Satzes
I	(don't) like	alcohol.	
My friend	is (isn't)		in trouble with her parents (the police).
She	has (hasn't) been drinking	alcohol	at parties.

2. Fragen

In Fragen wandert das HV (bzw. Fragewort + HV) an den Satzanfang vor das Subjekt.
Ist kein HV vorhanden wird *do/does* oder *did* eingefügt.

Fragewort	HV	S	V	O	Rest des Satzes
	Does	your teen	recognize	the serious dangers	that go with alcohol and drugs?
	Was	it		Louise?	
How	does	your child	choose	friends?	
What	do	you	think,		Sean?
What	should	I	do?		

3. Adverbialbestimmungen des Ortes (O), der Zeit (Z), der Art und Weise (A)

- Am Satzende gilt die Reihenfolge A - O - Z oder O - Z.
- Am Satzanfang steht meist nur eine Adverbialbestimmung - des Ortes oder der Zeit.
- Häufigkeitsadverbien als Adverbialbestimmung der Art und Weise stehen vor dem Vollverb oder nach dem Hilfsverb.
- Gradadverbien als Adverbialbestimmung der Art und Weise stehen vor dem Wort, das sie näher erklären.

Adverbial-bestimmung O/Z	S	V	O	Adverbialbestimmung A	O	Z
When I stick my head over the fence,	the boy	sees	me.			
	We	walk		in silence	down his garden path.	
	I	make	my way	slowly	up the path.	
	She	<u>really</u> hurt	me			over the summer.

S	HV	Häufigkeitsadverb	V	O
Teenagers	are	**often**		some distance from home.
Their family		**still**	plays	an important role.

Ov 1 Pronouns

1 A report about summer camp

Read one girl's report and choose the correct reflexive pronoun for each sentence.

1. I hated my first few days at camp but I told … it would not be forever.
2. In the mornings, for example, we all had to make our beds … .
3. There are always people to help you, of course, but you have to do so much … .
4. They made our breakfast but then the kids …. had to wash up.
5. But camp is also fun. We even learnt to make a fire and cook for … on it.
6. Of course, our leader Mary-Lou checked the fire … each time.
7. The best thing was rock climbing! I really surprised … because I hate heights.
8. Rock climbing … isn't dangerous but you have to follow the safety rules!
9. One of the kids took off his helmet and hurt … badly when he fell.
10. But the rest of us really enjoyed … at the camp.
11. We all want to register … for the same camp next year.

2 A report

Carsten and his sister Nicole are spending four weeks at a football camp. He tries to send an e-mail to some of his mates in English but he isn't sure of some words. Fill in the gaps with the correct pronouns from the boxes to complete his e-mail.

Hi, you guys! Prepare … for my first report on the camp! I'm not going to tell … everything – that would just take … too long. The first thing you need to know is that we're enjoying … . Really! This place is fun. Nicole thinks so, too. Remember when you warned … about the other kids – that we would have to speak English with …? Well, you were right! At first I was really mad at … because … hadn't tried harder in English class. But after a week I surprised … and the coaches! One of the girls hurt …, when a ball hit … in the face. The coaches were on the other side of the field and I had to get help from one of … . I had to speak English with … because he didn't speak German. I was quite proud of …, because he seemed to understand … . But I made a real idiot of … when I told … what was wrong with … . "She has hurt her *nose leg*," I said. He thought she had broken … leg! In English, you see, they say 'bridge of the nose'.

ourselves | them (2x) | him (2x) | herself | her (3x) | us | yourselves | myself (4x) | I | you | me (2x)

Ov 2 '*be*' in different tenses

1 Get it right, Ronaldo!

One of the kids at the camp wasn't very good at English. He often used the wrong words in his sentences. Tell him which word is correct in these sentences.

1. These *(are/aren't/is)* my boots. And this *(is/isn't/wasn't)* my T-shirt.
2. *(Are/were/is)* these my new T-shirts? I thought they *(was/have been/were)* yours.
3. What *(are/is/were)* the name of that French player? His boots *(have been/was/were)* gold.
4. I *(haven't been/has been/wasn't)* very good today. My game *(has been/was/were)* terrible.
5. I think it *(had been/has been/was)* a good idea to come to the camp.
6. I *(have been/had been/was)* frightened at first that I wouldn't find any friends.
7. But this *(were/is/had been)* the best camp that I *(was ever/has ever been/have ever been)* at.

Ov 3 Verbs in past tenses

1 A chain of events

a) *Write six sentences about what Nick did on Saturday morning.*
Start like this: 1. First he **woke up at** … . Then he … . Finally … .

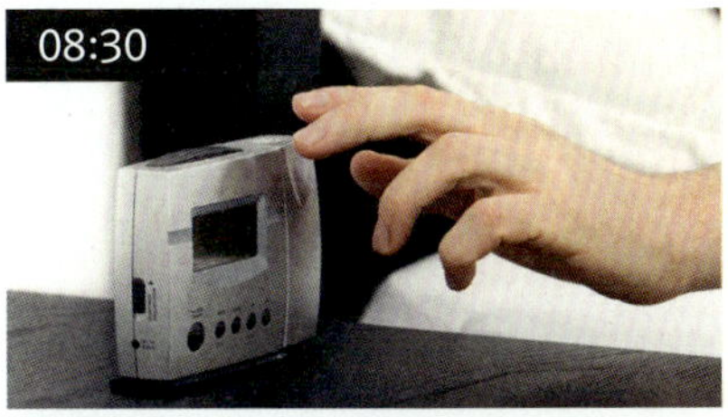

b) *Write sentences about the events in a chain. Start like this:* 1. Nick woke up at … .
2. **After he had woken up**, he … .

2 Before and after

a) *Look at Tom and Bob's list of things to do. What had/hadn't they done before they left on holiday? Write sentences.*
Start like this: They **had fed their** … .
They **had** … . But they **hadn't** … .

feed cat ✓ • pack maps ✓ • throw rubbish in the bins • give keys to the neighbour ✓ • leave a message on the answerphone ✓ • lock flat • post letters • take bottles back to the shop

b) *After they had left, they remembered the other things on their list! They called the neighbour. Imagine you are the neighbour and you did all the things that Tom and Bob had forgotten to do.*
Start like this: After I **had thrown your**…, I **locked** …!/After I **had locked** …, I … ./… .

Ov 4 Reported speech

1 Jane's quiet evening

Jane wants a quiet evening at home but something happens. She writes an e-mail to Adam. He tells her story to a friend. What does he say? Start like this: Jane **was sitting** at home … .

Hi! Adam. I'm sitting at home checking my e-mails. I'm a bit worried. I can hear funny noises from the flat upstairs. Someone is running around the flat. It started at about eight o'clock. First they were running around the kitchen. Now they are throwing things around the living-room. They have just broken a window! I don't know what to do! The Wilsons aren't at home. I saw them leaving the flat. They have been away now for about two hours. Maybe their son came back while I was in the bathroom. I don't know. I didn't see him. I think maybe it's a burglar. But I don't want to bother the police. So I'm wondering what I should do. Please write back quickly. Bye, Jane

2 Mack's accident

a) *Mack had an accident on his skateboard. The police officer took notes. Read his questions and Mack's answers.*

What's your name? – My name is Mack Simpson.
Where do you live? – I live around the corner, number 51 Green Street.
How old are you? – I'm 16 years old.
Do your parents know about the accident? – No, they aren't at home.
Have you got a number to ring to let them know? – I have a number here, in my mobile.

b) *The police officer talked to a colleague a few days later and told her what Mack said. Start like this:* The teenager **said** that … . He also **told** me that … .

3 How the accident happened

a) *In hospital they asked Mack about his accident. Read what he said.*

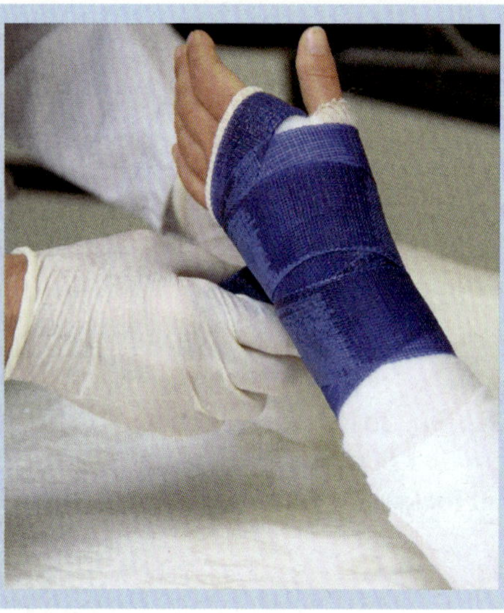

What happened to you?
I hit a streetlamp.

Were you riding your bike?
No, I was riding on my skateboard.

Where were you going?
I was going to my mate's house.

Why were you in such a hurry?
I needed some snacks for a DVD evening.

Why didn't you see the streetlamp?
A guy shouted my name. I turned my head to look.

Was it someone you knew?
No, I didn't recognize the guy.

b) *Complete the sentences and find out what the night nurse told the day nurse about Mack's accident the next morning. Start like this:* The patient said that he **had hit** … . He told me that he **had been** … .

1. The patient said that he … a streetlamp. *(to hit)*
2. He told me that he … on his skateboard. *(to ride)*
3. He said that he … to his mate's house. *(to go)*
4. He explained that he … some snacks for a DVD evening. *(to need)*
5. When I asked about the streetlamp, he said that a guy … his name. *(to shout)*
6. He explained that he … his head to look. *(to turn)*
7. He said that he … the guy. *(to recognize)*

Ov 5 Verbs in present tenses

Choose the correct present tense and complete the text.

A group of young people from Berlin (*to visit*) South England on a language exchange. They (*to be*) here for a week already. They (*to stay*) with local families and (*to see*) lots of interesting things so far. In their language school they (*not just/to improve*) their spoken English. They also (*to find out*) about the people and the culture. It's Tuesday afternoon and Hussein and his girlfriend, Alina, (*to wait*) at a bus stop. Suddenly they (*to hear*) some young British people. They (*to speak*) a strange language. It (*to sound*) like a muddle between Turkish and English. Hussein (*to tell*) Alina that it's just like back home: He and his mates often (*to mix*) German and Turkish. Then they (*to get*) on the bus and (*to go*) home.
A few hours later the same thing (*to happen*) again. Alina (*to hear*) a couple in a shop – and this time the people (*to speak*) English and Russian. When she (*to eat*) supper, Alina (*to tell*) her guest family. They all (*to laugh*). "That's pukka English!" (*to explain*) the daughter, Nasreen. "Mix and match – anything you like!"

Ov 6 Future forms

Look at the pictures and imagine what the people might be saying. Use different future forms.
Start like this: Unfortunately tomorrow **will be** … .

tomorrow/be cloudy/rain

meet/stranger/happy

train/leave/in 2 minutes

I/miss/very much

we/come back/tomorrow

she/not come/this evening

Ov 7+8 Modals, auxiliaries and modal substitutes

1 Some hotel rules

a) *Choose the right beginning and complete the rules.*

☺ ☺	You must …
☹ ☹ ☹	You mustn't …
😐	You can (may) …
☹ ☹	You can't …
😐	You needn't …

→ carry your passport with you at all times.
→ buy train tickets from people in the street.
→ use the lift after 10 p.m. or if there is a fire.
→ have breakfast after 7 a.m.
→ leave your keys at the reception desk when you leave the hotel.
→ get another blanket, if you are cold.
→ make your bed every day – we will do it for you.
→ always turn off the lights when you leave your room.
→ smoke in your room. This is a no-smoking hotel!
→ borrow a bike if you want to cycle round the island.

b) *Imagine you are planning a holiday at the hotel in part a). What will/won't you be able/allowed to or have to do? Start like this:* I **will have to** carry **my** passport … . I **won't be allowed to** … .

c) *Imagine you stayed at this hotel. Use the rules in part a) and choose one thing that you*
- *had to do or didn't have to do.*
- *were able to do or weren't able to do.*
- *were allowed to do or weren't allowed to do.*

Example: I **had to** turn off the lights. I **didn't have to** make my own breakfast.

2 A holiday by the sea

Use 'used to', 'would' *or* 'do' *and rewrite the sentences.*

1. When I was really young my mum and I **lived** in Birmingham.
2. I **dreamt** every summer about spending a holiday near the sea in Devon.
3. I **told** her this but my mum always **said**, "That **sounds** like a good idea."
4. But then she just **went** back to what she was doing.
5. I **went** to our travel agent every summer holidays.
6. The girl there always **gave** me catalogues and leaflets about holidays in Devon.
7. I **took** them home and my bedroom **was** full of them for the next few weeks.
8. There **were** competitions in them. I don't really like them but one year I **did** one and I won!
9. When I showed my mum the prize, she was amazed. "Oh," she said, "it **looks** quite nice there".

Ov 9 Active and passive voice

1 Talking about television

a) *Use the 'simple past passive' to complete these sentences. Start like this:* 1. Television **wasn't invented** by a woman, it **was invented** by … .

1. Television … by a woman, it … by two men called Zworykin and Farnsworth. *(to invent)*
2. It … that because they liked the name, it … that because the word means 'far sight'. *(to call)*
3. The first programmes … in colour, they … in black and white only. *(to show)*
4. In fact colour TV … into Europe in the early 60s, it … much later in 1967. *(to introduce)*
5. TV satellites … into space in the 1950s, they … in the 1960s. *(to launch)*
6. The biggest choice of channels … in Germany, it … in the US. *(to offer)*
7. Bigger screens … immediately, they … many years later. *(to develop)*
8. In the 1980s television … to the Internet, it … in the 1990s. *(to link)*

b) *What do you think television will be like in the future? Will we use screens instead of TVs? Use the 'future passive' of one of the verbs in the box to complete each question. Start like this:* 1. Do you think a touch screen **will be invented**?

1. Do you think a touch screen …?
2. What do you think it …?
3. Do you think the first programmes … in colour?
4. When do you think the first colour screens …?
5. How many channels do you think …?
6. When … bigger screens …?
7. … the screens … to other forms of communication?

to offer | to invent | to introduce | to link | to call | to develop | to show

c) *Answer your questions from b).*

2 Nico's dream

What does he tell his mates? Use the correct form of the passive to complete his story.

In the first scene I was sitting in a spaceship with you and Ted. I knew that we *(to transport)* to some distant planet. My hands *(not/to tie)* behind my back. But I *(not/to allow)* to see anything. A kind of hood *(to pull)* down over my head before I had entered the spaceship. When we landed the hood (to remove) and we *(to take)* to a strange building. It was really huge and it *(to cover)* in silver and gold. Then we *(to leave)* alone. We *(not/to tell)* what to do. Suddenly a door *(to open)* by two green creatures and we *(to push)* through it. Then the scene changed: I was in a dark room alone and I *(to speak)* to by someone. I couldn't see his face because it *(to hide)* behind a curtain. Suddenly I *(to wake)* up by my dad. He was knocking on my door, saying, "Time to get up, Nico!"

Ov 10 Relative clauses

1 The only film that made me …

a) *Use the correct relative pronoun to find out what Danny said about a film that he saw.*

1.	The Pink Panther 2 is the only DVD	+		made me laugh till I cried.
2.	The main character is a detective		whose	is called Clouseau.
3.	He tries to find a burglar		which	name is 'the Tornado'.
4.	He works with a team of detectives		that	come from different countries.
5.	They all think 'the Tornado' is the man		who	they need to find.
6.	It's only Clouseau			believes he was not the burglar.

b) *Read what Danny's friend Sara wrote about a different film and use the correct relative words to complete the text.*

家

'Dragon Tears' is the only film (1) made me cry last month. And I know someone (2) dad acted in the film! Yes, his name's Danny and it was he (3) lent me the DVD. His dad is the character in the film (4) attacks the dragon. It's really exciting but I think the best scene is one (5) is near the end. Lyreena, the young girl (6) is the heroine, becomes the dragon's friend.

The story tells us that dragons can look terrible and make fire but they are really sad creatures (7) are very lonely. It's only the dragon (8) tears can put out its own fire. And it's these tears (9) flood the village where Lyreena lives near the end of the story. It's a great story (10) was taken from an old Chinese myth and it's a film (11) everyone should see!

c) *Use the phrases in the box and write 4–5 sentences about a film that made you laugh/cry/… .*

the character whose • the best thing that • the person who • the scene which

2 Talking about films

Sara is telling Danny about films that she has seen. Where must she use 'that' and where can she leave it out?

'Star Wars' was the first science fiction film that I ever watched. It was also the first film that ever really scared me. I knew that it was very popular. My older brother said that it was the funniest film that he had ever seen. So one afternoon I borrowed his DVD and watched in on the TV that was in my bedroom. But after an hour I suddenly decided that it was too frightening for me. I ran out of my room and fell into an empty box that was outside my door. My brother saw me and he laughed and said 'I told you that it was a funny film!' But only he was laughing.

Ov 11 Conditional clauses

1 If I met the US President, I'd ...

a) *What would you do if ...*

1. ... you met the US President? – If I met ..., I'd ask him about ... .
2. ... you won a lot of money in a TV quiz show?
3. ... Superman flew through your window?
4. ... a friend was angry with you?
5. ... your mobile phone was stolen?
6. ... a firm offered you a job abroad for a year?
7. ... you saw a pickpocket on the job?

b) *What would you certainly **not** do? Example:* If I met ..., I certainly **wouldn't** ... German.

2 Historical events

a) *Look at the people in the pictures. What might you have done/said/asked/... if you had lived then? Start like this:* If I **had lived** in 1492, I **might have crossed** ... .

b) *What would you never have done/said/asked/...? Start like this:* If I had ... , I never would have ... .

3 Just imagine

Answer the questions about what could have happened in your life?

1. If you hadn't lived in this century, when in the past would you have liked to have lived?
2. Where would you probably have lived?
3. Which language(s) would you have spoken?
4. What would you have done and seen?
5. Who would you have liked to meet? What would you have said to them?

Ov 12 Adverbs of degree

1 Very important words

a) *Use these adjectives to make adverbs of degree.*

complete • terrible • extreme • real • special • equal

b) *Think of more adverbs of degree.*

c) *Find the right English word for each German adverb in these sentences.*

1. The trip up the mountain was *(wirklich)* exciting.
2. The view from the top of mountain was *(sehr)* beautiful.
3. But the climbers had to be *(ziemlich)* careful when they climbed down again.
4. This was because they were *(sehr)* high up.
5. They were all *(besonders)* proud of their long climb they had just done.
6. But they were all thirsty – and their water bottles were *(komplett/vollständig)* empty!
7. So they were all *(gleich)* happy when they reached their camp.
8. By evening they were *(schrecklich)* tired and *(extrem)* hungry!

Ov 13 Word order

1 When and where

Choose the right place in the sentences for the words/phrases. Sometimes two answers are correct.

1. last week:	There was a trade fair in West London.
2. to the fair:	On Saturday a group of us went in the afternoon after school
3. at two o'clock:	We took the train to London.
4. at the station:	The train arrived at three o'clock.
5. by 3:20 p.m.:	We were in Hall 2.
6. in Hall 2:	At three o'clock there was a product presentation.
7. a moment later:	A man walked onto a stage in the middle of the hall.
8. suddenly:	He called out some numbers, but I didn't hear them.
9. on the stage:	I was more interested in the box. But one of my mates checked my ticket.
10. in the end:	I was surprised to find out that I had won the box!
11. at five o'clock:	It was huge! So I rang my dad where he worked in London.

2 How often?

Put the words or phrases in the right order and make sensible sentences.

1. **often** – too many products – got – have – shops
2. I – what I need – can – so – find – **never**
3. on the other hand – all OK – I – **sometimes** – three products – which are – see
4. **always** – if that happens – buy – the cheapest product – then I
5. quite – **usually** – expensive – but then – they're

VOCABULARY

SKILLS

Diese Checkliste kann dir helfen, Fehler zu vermeiden und deine Rechtschreibung zu verbessern. Prüfe alle deine Texte damit.

- Schreibung:
  - ☑ ‚gh' wird meist nicht gesprochen. Vergiss es beim Schreiben nicht.
  - ☑ ‚k' kommt vor ‚t' so gut wie nie vor, z.B. action – Ak**t**ion, Oc**t**ober – O**kt**ober
- Gleiche Aussprache, unterschiedliche Schreibung:
  - ☑ [iː] z.B. t**ea**cher, m**ee**ting, m**e**dia, magaz**i**ne, p**eo**ple, f**ie**ld
  - ☑ [uː] z.B. f**oo**d, r**ou**te, to d**o**, swims**ui**t, s**u**permarket, tr**ue**, cr**ew**
- Gleiche Aussprache, unterschiedliche Schreibung und Bedeutung:
  - ☑ [iː] z.B. **see** – sehen, **sea** – Meer; **meet** – treffen, **meat** – Fleisch
  - ☑ [uː] z.B. **two** – zwei, **too** – auch
- Verdoppelung der Endkonsonanten:
  - ☑ to sto**p** – sto**pp**ing, sto**pp**ed
  - ☑ to pla**n** – pla**nn**ing, pla**nn**ed
- ‚y' wird zu ‚ie':
  - ☑ in der 3. Person Singular: z.B. to carr**y** – he carr**ies**; to cr**y** – she cr**ies**; **aber**: to bu**y** – she bu**ys**
  - ☑ im Plural: z.B. cit**y** – cit**ies**, part**y** – part**ies**; **aber**: bo**y** – bo**ys**
  - ☑ bei der Steigerung von Adjektiven: z.B. happ**y** – happ**ier** – (the) happ**iest**; eas**y** – eas**ier** – (the) eas**iest**
- Ähnlich und doch anders:
  - ☑ Wortendung ‚le': z.B. *engl.* simp**le** – *dt.* simp**el**; *engl.* tit**le** – *dt.* Tit**el**; *engl.* midd**le** – *dt.* Mitt**el**
  - ☑ ‚ph' statt ‚f': z.B. *engl.* **ph**one – *dt.* Tele**f**on; *engl.* **ph**oto – *dt.* **F**oto
- Großschreibung:
  - ☑ Monatsnamen: z.B. January, July, December
  - ☑ Wochentage: z.B. Monday, Wednesday, Saturday
  - ☑ Eigennamen: z.B. Tom, Lisa, the Brooks, the London Eye, the Thames
  - ☑ geografische Namen: Bristol, Greenwich, Germany, Italy
- Plural:
  - ☑ Der Plural bekommt normalerweise ein -s: z.B. friend – friend**s**, chair – chair**s**, film – film**s**
  - ☑ Endet ein Wort auf s oder x, wird -es angehängt: z.B. bus – bus**es**, box – box**es**
  - ☑ Manche Wörter haben einen unregelmäßigen Plural: z.B. man – men, child – children, shelf – shelves, mouse – mice
- Apostroph:
  - ☑ bei Kurzformen: z.B. she is → she's; they are → they're
  - ☑ beim Genitiv-s: z.B. Sam's bike, Emma's family, the Jacksons' house, the children's games
- Wörterbuch:
  - ☑ Prüfe die Schreibung aller Wörter, bei denen du dir nicht ganz sicher bist, indem du sie im Wörterbuch nachschlägst.

Vocabulary

Auf den folgenden Seiten findest du alle neuen englischen Wörter und Ausdrücke. Sie stehen in der Reihenfolge, wie sie im Buch vorkommen.
Diese Wortliste ist in drei Spalten aufgeteilt:
- Links stehen die englischen Wörter und Sätze.
- In der Mitte werden sie übersetzt.
- Rechts findest du Beispiele, Erklärungen und Tipps, die dir beim Lernen helfen.

Die fett gedruckten Wörter musst du lernen. Normal gedruckte Wörter solltest du wiedererkennen, wenn du sie hörst oder liest.
Gleich nach jedem neuen englischen Wort steht die Lautschrift in eckigen Klammern. Sie zeigt dir, wie das neue Wort ausgesprochen wird. Wie du diese Lautzeichen liest, siehst du unten.

Englische Laute

Mitlaute

[b]	**b**ed	[p]	**p**icture
[d]	**d**ay	[r]	**r**ed
[ð]	**th**e	[s]	**s**ix
[f]	**f**amily	[ʃ]	**sh**e
[g]	**g**o	[t]	**t**en
[ŋ]	morni**ng**	[tʃ]	lun**ch**
[h]	**h**ouse	[v]	**v**ideo
[j]	**y**ou	[w]	**w**e, **o**ne
[k]	**c**an, mil**k**	[z]	ea**s**y
[l]	**l**etter	[ʒ]	revi**si**on
[m]	**m**an	[dʒ]	pa**ge**
[n]	**n**o	[θ]	**th**ank you

Selbstlaute

[ɑː]	c**a**r
[æ]	**a**pple
[e]	p**e**n
[ə]	**a**gain
[ɜː]	g**ir**l
[ʌ]	b**u**t
[ɪ]	**i**t
[i]	happ**y**
[iː]	t**ea**cher
[ɒ]	d**o**g
[ɔː]	b**a**ll
[ʊ]	b**oo**k
[u]	Jan**u**ary
[uː]	t**oo**, tw**o**

Doppellaute

[aɪ]	**I**, m**y**
[aʊ]	n**ow**, m**ou**se
[eɪ]	n**a**me, th**ey**
[eə]	th**ere**, p**air**
[ɪə]	h**ere**, id**ea**
[əʊ]	hell**o**
[ɔɪ]	b**oy**
[ʊə]	s**ure**

[ː] der vorangehende Laut ist lang, z. B. *you* [juː]

[ˈ] die folgende Silbe wird betont, z. B. *hello* [həˈləʊ]

In jeder *Topic* findest du Übungen zum Vokabellernen sowie einen Kasten mit *Useful phrases*, die dir helfen, dich auf Englisch zu verständigen.

Außerdem gibt es zu jeder *Topic* einen Kasten, in dem du Interessantes zur Landeskunde erfährst.

Auf das *Vocabulary* folgt das *Dictionary*, eine alphabetische Wortliste aller englischen Wörter im Buch. Wenn du ein Wort nicht verstehst, kannst du es hier nachschlagen

Abkürzungen und Zeichen

pl	Plural, Mehrzahl
sg	Singular, Einzahl
infml	umgangssprachlich
10	Auf dieser Seite kommen die Wörter vor.

!	Achtung!	! *Information* hat keine Mehrzahl.
↔	ist das Gegenteil von	permanent ↔ temporary
→	ist verwandt mit	drive → driver
=	entspricht	Dear Jenny = Liebe Jenny

Topic 1 A 'global' language

Englisch als Weltsprache

Auf der Welt gibt es insgesamt circa 6500 bis 7000 Sprachen, wobei jedoch über die Hälfte der Bevölkerung auf der Erde eine der zehn meist gesprochenen Sprachen der Welt spricht.
Seit vielen Jahren gilt Englisch als Weltsprache, weil keine andere Sprache so weit verbreitet ist.
Sie wird häufig auch als so genannte *lingua franca* bezeichnet. Unter einer *lingua franca* versteht man im Allgemeinen eine Verkehrssprache, d. h. eine Sprache, die Menschen mit verschiedenen Muttersprachen, z. B. im Handel, zur Verständigung dient.

Englisch wird heute in über 100 Ländern gesprochen, das entspricht ca. der Hälfte aller Länder auf der Erde. 340 Millionen Menschen sprechen Englisch als Muttersprache. Wenn man Englisch hingegen mit anderen Sprachen vergleicht, so steht es nach Hochchinesisch mit 880 Millionen Muttersprachlern und Spanisch mit 360 Millionen Muttersprachlern nur an dritter Stelle.
In vielen Schulen auf der ganzen Welt wird Englisch zudem als erste Fremdsprache unterrichtet. Man nimmt an, dass etwa 750 Millionen Menschen Englisch als Fremdsprache sprechen.
Schätzungen zufolge kommen demnach rund 2 Milliarden Menschen regelmäßig in Kontakt mit der englischen Sprache.

Überlege dir weitere Situationen, in denen Menschen mit unterschiedlichen Muttersprachen Englisch sprechen. Welche Situationen hast du schon erlebt?
In welchen Ländern wird deine Muttersprache gesprochen? Wie viele Menschen sprechen deine Sprache? Recherchiere im Internet.

Check-in

8	**backpacker** ['bækpækə]	Rucksacktourist/ Rucksacktouristin →	a tourist with a bag that they carry on their back
	Canadian [kə'neɪdiən]	kanadisch; Kanadier/ Kanadierin →	a person who lives in or comes from Canada
	to work out [ˌwɜːk‿'aʊt]	herausfinden, ausarbeiten →	to work → *to work out*
9	**deputy** ['depjəti]	stellvertretend; Stellvertreter/ Stellvertreterin	
	Prime Minister (PM) [ˌpraɪm 'mɪnɪstə]	Premierminister/ Premierministerin	
	minister ['mɪnɪstə]	Minister/Ministerin	
	media *(pl)* ['miːdiə]	Medien →	Books, e-mails and the cinema are all types of *media*.

Aspects

10	**common** ['kɒmən]	gemeinsam, gebräuchlich, verbreitet →	known or used by many people

coaching ['kəʊtʃɪŋ]	Training, Nachhilfe →	special help in a subject or sport
mother tongue ['mʌðə ˌtʌŋ]	Muttersprache	
passion ['pæʃn]	Passion, Leidenschaft	
sponsor ['spɒntsə]	Sponsor/Sponsorin, Förderer/Förderin	
talented ['tæləntɪd]	talentiert, begabt →	If you are *talented*, you are naturally very good at something.
normally ['nɔ:mli]	normalerweise	
fully-qualified [ˌfʊli'kwɒlɪfaɪd]	voll ausgebildet, voll qualifiziert →	A *fully-qualified* teacher has all the necessary qualifications.
coach [kəʊtʃ]	Trainer/Trainerin →	someone who gives special help in a subject or sport
used to *(+ infinitive)* ['ju:s‿tə]	früher; pflegte(n) zu →	We *used to* live in Munich. = Wir wohnten früher in München.
multi-lingual [ˌmʌlti'lɪŋgwəl]	vielsprachig	
session ['seʃn]	Einheit, Sitzung, Stunde	
to **rotate** [rə'teɪt]	rotieren, sich abwechseln	
to **assess** [ə'ses]	bewerten, beurteilen, einschätzen →	The coach *assessed* each player.
promising ['prɒmɪsɪŋ]	viel versprechend	
trial ['traɪəl]	Prüfung, Test	
admission [əd'mɪʃn]	Aufnahme, Zulassung, Eintritt	
idiom ['ɪdiəm]	Redewendung, Idiom, Redensart →	Most *idioms* can't be translated word for word from one language into another.
variation [ˌveərɪ'eɪʃn]	Variation, Verschiedenartigkeit	
lingua franca [ˌlɪŋgwə 'fræŋkə]	Verkehrssprache, Universalsprache →	English is often used as *lingua franca*.
tower ['taʊə]	Kontrollturm, Tower	
to **translate** [trænz'leɪt]	übersetzen	
to **create** [kri'eɪt]	(er)schaffen →	*to create* → creative
e.g. [i:'dʒi:]	zum Beispiel →	for example (Lat. exempli gratia)
Spanglish ['spæŋglɪʃ]	Spanglisch *(Mischung aus Spanisch und Englisch)*	
Hinglish ['hɪŋglɪʃ]	Hinglisch *(Mischung aus Hindi und Englisch)*	
mixture ['mɪkstʃə]	Mischung, Gemisch, Mixtur →	If you put different sweets in a bag you get a *mixture*.
Hindi ['hɪndi:]	Hindi →	a language spoken in India
pukka *(slang)* ['pʌkə]	echt	
Punjabi [pʌn'dʒɑ:bi:]	Punjabi →	a language spoken in parts of India
Urdu ['ʊədu:]	Urdu →	the language spoken in Pakistan
to **spread**, **spread**, **spread** [spred, spred, spred]	(sich) ausbreiten, (sich) verbreiten →	If something *spreads*, it moves to cover a larger and larger area.
rapid ['ræpɪd]	schnell, rasch, rapide	
Asian ['eɪʃn]	asiatisch; Asiate/Asiatin →	Chinese people and people from India are *Asians*.
sub-continent [sʌb'kɒntɪnənt]	Subkontinent	

trend [trend]	Trend, Entwicklung, Richtung	
to list [lɪst]	auflisten	
11 **unilingual** [ˌjuːnɪ'lɪŋgwəl]	einsprachig	
bilingual [baɪ'lɪŋgwəl]	zweisprachig, bilingual →	You need to be *bilingual* to get a good job today.
territory ['terɪtri]	Territorium, Land, Gebiet	
Aboriginal [ˌæbə'rɪdʒnl]	eingeboren, einheimisch	
majority [mə'dʒɒrəti]	Mehrheit(en-) →	the *majority* of us = most of us
Inuktitut [ɪ'nʊktɪtʊt]	Inuktitut *(Sprache der Inuit)* →	The language of the Inuit is *Inuktitut*.
Inuit ['ɪnuɪt]	Inuit	
people, peoples *(pl)* ['piːpl]	Volk	
non-official [ˌnɒnə'fɪʃl]	inoffiziell	
outsourcing ['aʊtsɔːsɪŋ]	Outsourcing *(Ausgliederung von Produktions- oder Dienstleistungen an externe Mitarbeiter)*	
to **reduce** [rɪ'djuːs]	reduzieren, vermindern →	to increase sth ↔ *to reduce sth*
to **transfer** [trænts'fɜː]	transferieren, verlegen; übertragen →	to move (sb or sth) from one place to another
call centre ['kɔːl ˌsentə]	Call-Center	
critic ['krɪtɪk]	Kritiker/Kritikerin	
to **outsource** ['aʊtsɔːs]	ausgliedern, outsourcen	
unemployment [ˌʌnɪm'plɔɪmənt]	Arbeitslosigkeit →	to employ → *unemployment*
to **feel** [fiːl]	*hier:* glauben	
to **provide** (sb with sth) [prə'vaɪd]	bereitstellen, besorgen, liefern →	We'll *provide* you *with* money. = We'll give you the money you need.
worldwide [ˌwɜːld'waɪd]	weltweit →	world → *worldwide*
policy ['pɒləsi]	Grundsatz, Politik, politische Linie	

Canadian English

Canadian English ist ähnlich wie *American English*. Es werden oft die selben Wörter verwendet.

British English	American English/Canadian English	Übersetzung
trousers	*pants* [pænts]	Hose
crisps	*chips*	Chips
chips	*French fries*	Pommes frites
holiday	*vacation*	Ferien
lorry ['lɒri]	*truck*	Lastwagen

Ergänze die Liste in deinem Heft.

Option 1

12	webzine ['webzi:n]	Webmagazin	
	impression [ɪm'preʃn]	Eindruck, Impression	
	these days ['ði:z deɪz]	heutzutage →	In the 1980's nobody had a mobile. *These days* you can't imagine life without one.
	a couple of [ə 'kʌpl‿əv]	einige, ein paar →	*a couple of* = a few
	hardly ['hɑ:dli]	kaum →	! You're working hard. = Du arbeitest hart. I can *hardly* believe it. = Ich kann es kaum glauben.
	to **seem** [si:m]	(er)scheinen, wirken →	The dog *seemed* friendly, but actually it wasn't.
	whatever [wɒt'evə]	was auch immer; egal welche	
	certainly ['sɜ:tnli]	sicher, gewiss	
	future ['fju:tʃə]	zukünftig	
	participant [pɑ:'tɪsɪpənt]	Teilnehmer/Teilnehmerin	
	both ... and ... ['bəʊθ ... ænd]	sowohl ... als auch ... →	The journey over the mountains was *both* long *and* difficult.
	stay [steɪ]	Anwesenheit, Aufenthalt →	Their *stay* at the camp lasted two weeks.
	immersion school [ɪ'mɜ:ʃn ˌsku:l]	Schule, in der in einer Fremdsprache unterrichtet wird	
	sort of ['sɔ:t‿əv]	irgendwie	
	hopeless ['həʊpləs]	hoffnungslos →	helpless – homeless – *hopeless*
	even though [ˌi:vn‿'ðəʊ]	auch wenn; obwohl	
	to **grow up, grew up, grown up** [grəʊ‿'ʌp, gru:‿'ʌp, grəʊn‿'ʌp]	aufwachsen, heranwachsen	
	Zulu ['zu:lu:]	Zulu	
	scholarship ['skɒləʃɪp]	Stipendium →	If you can win a *scholarship* to a school or college, your parents don't have to pay.
	to **manage** ['mænɪdʒ]	bewältigen, handhaben; *hier:* zurechtkommen →	manager → *to manage*
	foul [faʊl]	Foul	
	offside [ˌɒf'saɪd]	im Abseits →	The referee blew his whistle because I was *offside*.
	header ['hedə]	Kopfball	
	Cantonese [ˌkæntə'ni:z]	kantonesisch; Kantonese/Kantonesin	
	as well [əz 'wel]	auch →	another word for 'too' or 'also'
13	**figure** ['fɪgə]	Ziffer, Zahl	
	widespread [waɪdspred]	(weit)verbreitet	
	explorer [ɪk'splɔ:rə]	Forscher/Forscherin; Forschungsreisender/Forschungsreisende →	to explore → *explorer*
	trader ['treɪdə]	Händler/Händlerin →	trade → *trader*
	settler ['setlə]	Siedler/Siedlerin →	somebody who goes to a new country and makes their home there

former ['fɔ:mə]	ehemaliger/ehemalige/ ehemaliges, früherer/ frühere/früheres	
to **remain** [rɪ'meɪn]	(ver)bleiben →	*to remain* = to stay
Commonwealth ['kɒmənwelθ]	Commonwealth →	The 53 former British colonies are called the *Commmonwealth*.
including [ɪn'klu:dɪŋ]	einschließlich, inklusive	
African ['æfrɪkən]	afrikanisch; Afrikaner/ Afrikanerin →	Mali, Ghana and South Africa are all *African* countries.
vocabulary [vəʊ'kæbjəlri]	Wortschatz, Vokabular	
lung [lʌŋ]	Lunge	
disease [dɪ'zi:z]	Krankheit, Erkrankung →	A lot of *diseases* are caused by bad water.
podcast ['pɒdkɑ:st]	Podcast	
to agree on [ə'gri:‿ɒn]	sich einigen auf	
multiple choice [ˌmʌltɪpl 'tʃɔɪs]	Multiple-Choice *(Auswahl aus mehreren Möglichkeiten)*	
footballer ['fʊtbɔ:lə]	Fußballspieler/ Fußballspielerin →	! Das englische Wort *football* kann Fußball oder Football heißen.

s + z

Im Englischen gibt es Wörter, die man sowohl mit ***s*** als auch mit ***z*** schreiben kann: z. B. ***realise/realize, summarise/ summarize*** usw. Früher wurde die Schreibung mit ***s*** eher in Großbritannien verwendet und die Schreibung mit ***z*** eher in den USA. Heutzutage gibt es diese strikte Trennung nicht mehr, weil durch das Fernsehen, das Internet etc. die Grenzen verschwommen sind. Deshalb kommen auch in deinem Schülerbuch beide Schreibweisen vor.
Aber Vorsicht! ***size*** schreibt sich immer mit ***z*** und ***compromise*** immer mit ***s***.

Option 2

14 **secondary school** ['sekəndri ˌsku:l]	weiterführende Schule →	After junior school you go to *secondary school*.
I don't mind. [maɪnd]	Ich habe nichts dagegen., Es ist mir egal.	
to **prefer** [prɪ'fɜ:]	vorziehen, bevorzugen →	to like more/better
junior high school [ˌdʒu:niə 'haɪ ˌsku:l]	Junior High School *(Vorstufe zur High School, meist 7.-9. Klasse)*	
immersion school [ɪ'mɜ:ʃn ˌsku:l]	Schule, in der in einer Fremdsprache unterrichtet wird →	Canadians call bilingual schools *immersion schools*.
manga ['mæŋgə]	Manga *(japanischer Comic)*	
to **copy** ['kɒpi]	abzeichnen, abmalen	
storyboard ['stɔ:ribɔ:d]	Storyboard *(gezeichnete Version eines Drehbuchs)* →	story → *storyboard*
indigenous [ɪn'dɪdʒɪnəs]	einheimisch, eingeboren, Ur- →	Aboriginals are *indigenous* people in Australia.

	animé ['ænɪmeɪ]	animierter Manga	
	to **scan** [skæn]	scannen, abtasten, nach Details durchsuchen →	To look at something (a text etc.) very carefully because you are looking for special details.
	amazed [ə'meɪzd]	erstaunt, verblüfft →	very surprised
	to **exchange** [ɪks'tʃeɪndʒ]	(aus)tauschen, umtauschen	
	that way [ðæt 'weɪ]	auf diese Weise	
	technique [tek'ni:k]	Methode, Technik →	! a *technique* = eine Methode technology = Technik, Technologie
	to **keep up** [ki:p‿'ʌp]	beibehalten, aufrechterhalten, weitermachen mit	
15	**delirious** [dɪ'lɪriəs]	im Delirium; außer sich, irre	
	example [ɪg'zɑ:mpl]	Beispiel	
	drawing ['drɔ:ɪŋ]	Bild, Zeichnung →	to draw → *drawing*
	through to ['θru: tə]	bis hin zu	
	including [ɪn'klu:dɪŋ]	einschließlich, inklusive	
	3D [θri:'di:]	3D-, dreidimensional	
	fascinating ['fæsɪneɪtɪŋ]	faszinierend, spannend	
	Western ['westən]	westlich	
	animation [ænɪ'meɪʃn]	Animation, Zeichentrickfilm	
	must [mʌst]	Muss	
	lover ['lʌvə]	Liebhaber; Geliebter/ Geliebte →	to love → *lover*
	future ['fju:tʃə]	zukünftig →	Tell me about your *future* plans.
	to conduct ['kɒndʌkt]	(durch)führen; dirigieren	
	version ['vɜ:ʃn]	Version, Fassung	

Youth culture

Sammle so viele Wörter wie möglich zum Thema *Youth culture*. Vervollständige die Tabelle in deinem Heft. Du kannst auch weitere Spalten hinzufügen.

comics	*music*	*language*	*communication*	*films/TV*
Manga	*hip hop*	*bling-bling*	*Internet*	*horror*
drawings	*breakdance*	*CU*	*chat*	*animé*
...	...	...	...	...

Option 3

16	**learner** ['lɜ:nə]	Lernender/Lernende →	to learn → *learner*
	dictionary ['dɪkʃnri]	Wörterbuch	
	to **overhear, overheard, overheard** [ˌəʊvə'hɪə, ˌəʊvə'hɜ:d, ˌəʊvə'hɜ:d]	zufällig mitanhören, belauschen →	I *overheard* two men who were planning to rob a bank.

example [ɪɡ'zɑːmpl]	Beispiel	
fusion ['fjuːʒn]	Fusion, Verbindung, Verschmelzung	
exaggerated [ɪɡ'zædʒreɪtɪd]	übertrieben	
unlike [ʌn'laɪk]	anders als, im Gegensatz zu →	like ↔ *unlike*
to **take a look** (at) [ˌteɪk‿ə 'lʊk]	einen Blick werfen (auf) →	Do you want to *take a look at* my new mobile?
immediately [ɪ'miːdiətli]	sofort, gleich →	at once
to **realise** ['rɪəlaɪz]	erkennen, realisieren, begreifen →	Suddenly I *realised* … = Plötzlich wurde mir klar …
television ['telɪvɪʒn]	Fernsehen, Fernseher	
uncool [ʌn'kuːl]	uncool	
doubleclick ['dʌblklɪk]	Doppelklick	
screenager ['skriːneɪdʒə]	Bildschirm-Teenie →	a teenager who sits in front of the computer or television all the time
thug [θʌɡ]	Gangster, Schläger; *hier:* Typ	
along with [ə'lɒŋ wɪð]	zusammen mit, neben	
hood [hʊd]	Kapuze, Kappe →	I pulled on my *hood* because it was raining.
hip hopper ['hɪp ˌhɒpə]	Hip-Hopper/Hip-Hopperin	
expression [ɪk'spreʃn]	Ausdruck, Redewendung →	to express → *expression*
everyday ['evrideɪ]	alltäglich, Alltags-	
among [ə'mʌŋ]	unter (zwischen) →	! Notice the difference: under ≠ *among* He stood *among* the trees = in the middle of the forest, but not necessarily under a tree.
chuddies *(pl) (slang)* ['tʃʌdiz]	*hier:* Hose	
cultural ['kʌltʃrl]	kulturell →	culture → *cultural*
multicultural [ˌmʌlti'kʌltʃrl]	multikulturell	
to **pick out** [pɪk‿'aʊt]	auswählen, aussuchen; *hier:* erkennen →	I could choose a T-shirt, so I *picked out* the red one.
to **catch**, **caught**, **caught** [kætʃ, kɔːt, kɔːt]	hören, aufschnappen	
conversation [ˌkɒnvə'seɪʃn]	Unterhaltung, Gespräch, Konversation →	I couldn't hear much of their *conversation*.
17 versus ['vɜːsəs]	gegen, kontra	
phonetics [fə'netɪks]	Phonetik, Lautschrift	
to challenge ['tʃælɪndʒ]	(heraus)fordern	

Lerntipp: Neues mit altem Vokabular vernetzen

Tipp 1

Wenn du neue Wörter lernst, ist es gut, wenn du dir überlegst, welche ähnlichen Wörter du bereits kennst.

neu	**bekannt**
unlike	*like*
expression	*expressive*
cultural	*culture*
television	*TV, view*

Tipp 2

Wenn dir sonst etwas einfällt, das dir beim Lernen helfen könnte, dann schreib' es auf.

Man kann aus einem Verb ein Nomen machen, indem man z. B. die Endung ***-ion*** anhängt:

*to express → express**ion***

Option 4

18 to **widen** ['waɪdn]	(aus)weiten, erweitern →	They *widened* the bridge when they built the new road.
horizon [hə'raɪzn]	Horizont, Blickfeld	
to **give a talk** [ˌgɪv‿ə 'tɔ:k]	einen Vortrag/eine Rede halten	
asset ['æset]	Vorzug, Vorteil →	His teaching background was a great *asset*.
colleague ['kɒli:g]	Kollege/Kollegin	
presentation [ˌprezn'teɪʃn]	Präsentation, Vortrag	
department [dɪ'pɑ:tmənt]	Abteilung →	The games *department* is the part of a shop that sells games.
present ['preznt]	gegenwärtig, aktuell	
section ['sekʃn]	Sektion, Abschnitt, Abteilung	
personality [ˌpɜ:sn'æləti]	Persönlichkeit, Charakter →	person → *personality*
reliable [rɪ'laɪəbl]	zuverlässig, vertrauenswürdig →	Someone who does what he/she promises is *reliable*.
trustworthy ['trʌstwɜ:ði]	vertrauenswürdig →	If someone is *trustworthy*, you know that you can trust them.
strength [streŋθ]	Stärke, Kraft	
mobile ['məʊbaɪl]	mobil, veränderlich	
weakness ['wi:knəs]	Schwäche →	weak → *weakness*
disabled [dɪ'seɪbld]	behindert →	He wasn't able to run because he was *disabled*.

Wörter mit mehreren Bedeutungen

Im Deutschen wie im Englischen gibt es Wörter, die mehrere Bedeutungen haben. Der Kontext, in dem das Wort steht, zeigt dir die richtige Bedeutung.

mobile (mobil) → *mobile* (Handy)
present (gegenwärtig) → *present* (Geschenk)
…

Finde weitere englische Wörter und überlege dir auch Beispiele auf Deutsch oder in einer anderen Sprache.

assistant [ə'sɪstnt]	Assistent/Assistentin	
conscientious [ˌkɒntʃi'entʃəs]	gewissenhaft	
creative [kri'eɪtɪv]	kreativ →	In *creative* writing exercises you can use your own ideas.
situation [ˌsɪtju'eɪʃn]	Situation →	what is happening at the moment
lift *(BE)* [lɪft]	Lift, Aufzug	
19 **consultant** [kən'sʌltnt]	Berater/Beraterin	
to **communicate** [kə'mju:nɪkeɪt]	kommunizieren, sich verständigen →	The easiest way to *communicate* with people is to speak to them.
to **be afraid (of)** [bi‿ə'freɪd‿əv]	(sich) fürchten (vor), Angst haben (vor) →	I'*m afraid of* dogs.

chaotic [keɪ'ɒtɪk]	chaotisch →	When everything goes wrong at the same time, it can be *chaotic*.
leather ['leðə]	Leder →	the skin of animals that is used to make shoes, bags, etc.
curly ['kɜ:li]	lockig; Lockenkopf	
feedback ['fi:dbæk]	Feedback, Rückmeldung	

Check-out

20 to reconstruct [ˌri:kn'strʌkt]	rekonstruieren, wiederherstellen	

Everyday English: Talking about strengths and weaknesses

Die folgenden *phrases* können dir helfen, wenn du über deine Stärken und Schwächen sprechen möchtest.

I'd say I'm conscientious/reliable/creative/ practical/…	Ich würde sagen, dass ich gewissenhaft/zuverlässig/ kreativ/praktisch veranlagt/ … bin.
I find/don't find it easy to meet people/to learn new skills/…	Es fällt mir leicht/nicht leicht, neue Menschen kennen zu lernen/Ich habe (k)eine schnelle Auffassungsgabe/…
I'm (not so) good with animals/with children/with my hands/…	Ich bin (nicht so) gut im Umgang mit Tieren/im Umgang mit Kindern/Ich bin (nicht) sehr praktisch veranlagt/…
I like working alone/outside/with my hands/…	Ich arbeite gerne allein/draußen/mit meinen Händen/…
I don't like computers/offices/working outside in bad weather/…	Ich mag keine Computer/keine Büros/ Bei schlechtem Wetter arbeite ich nicht gerne draußen/…

Stelle mit einem Partner/einer Partnerin ein Gespräch über deine Stärken/Schwächen nach.

2,18 Sounds: Sentence stress

Wenn du lange Sätze laut liest, ist das manchmal gar nicht so einfach. Hilfreich ist es, die wichtigsten Wörter zu betonen.

a) Hör dir diese Sätze an:

1. Thanks to our **sponsors** we are able to offer **three free places** to **talented** young people who **normally wouldn't** be able to take part.
2. In a recent **interview** one critic **said** that **call**-centre customers had problems with foreign **accents** and that **outsourcing** led to local **unemployment**.

Finde Regeln dafür, welche Wörter nicht betont werden.

b) Finde nun die wichtigen Wörter in diesen Sätzen und lies die Sätze laut. Vergleiche dann mit der Aufnahme.

1. You will learn that most people who learn English as a second or foreign language make mistakes when they speak it or translate into it.
2. In former British colonies like Australia, the US, Canada and India, English has remained the official language.
3. I designed a poster for the club, scanned it for our school website and added a link to my old art forum.
4. Couch potato is a fairly new English (and German!) expression which clearly didn't exist before television was invented.

Topic 2 Living democracy

Das Waffenrecht in den USA

Seit mehr als 200 Jahren ist das Recht, eine Waffe zur Selbstverteidigung zu besitzen und zu tragen, in der amerikanischen Verfassung verankert. Der Umgang mit Waffen wird in über 20000 Waffengesetzen geregelt. Gegner dieses Gesetzes sehen einen Zusammenhang zwischen privatem Waffenbesitz und der hohen Kriminalität in vielen Staaten der USA. Schätzungsweise jeder dritte Schüler an weiterführenden Schulen in den USA besitzt eine Waffe. Jährlich werden 15000 Menschen in den USA mit Schusswaffen ermordet. Immer wieder wird die Diskussion über die Verschärfung des Waffengesetzes angeregt.

Während der Amtszeit von Bill Clinton wurden die Waffengesetze verschärft. 1994 z. B. wurde ein Gesetz in Kraft gesetzt, das die Überprüfung von Waffenkäufern erlaubte oder eine 5-Tage-Frist zwischen Kauf und Aushändigung der Waffe bestimmte. Auch der Verkauf von Waffen mit mehr als 10 Schuss wurde verboten.
Dieses Gesetz wurde 1997 allerdings vom Obersten Gerichtshof in den USA wieder gelockert.
Im Juni 2008 erklärte der *Supreme Court* ein Gesetz im Stadtbezirk Washington für verfassungswidrig. Es hatte Privatbürgern verboten, Waffen zu besitzen. Der Oberste Gerichtshof entschied, dass jeder Bürger ein Recht darauf hat, zu jagen und sich selbst zu verteidigen. Somit müsse es Bürgern in Washington erlaubt sein, eine Waffe zu besitzen. Allerdings gelte dies nicht für Geistigkranke und verurteilte Verbrecher.

Was hältst du von diesem Gesetz? Glaubst du, dass es richtig ist den Besitz von Waffen zu erlauben? Ist es Privatbürgern in Deutschland auch erlaubt, eine Waffe zu besitzen?

Check-in

26	**democracy** [dɪˈmɒkrəsi]	Demokratie →	*Democracy* comes from a Greek word and means that the people have political power.
	Bill of Rights [ˌbɪl‿əv ˈraɪts]	*Teil der am. Verfassung*	
	bill [bɪl]	Gesetz(entwurf)	
	arms *(pl)* [ɑːmz]	Waffen	
	constitution [ˌkɒnstɪˈtjuːʃn]	Verfassung, Grundgesetz; Konstitution	
	election [ɪˈlekʃn]	Wahl →	to elect → *election*
	charter [ˈtʃɑːtə]	Charta, Satzung, Urkunde	
	trial [traɪəl]	Gerichtsverfahren, -verhandlung	
	court [kɔːt]	Hof, Gericht(shof) →	Trials take place in a *court* of law.
	e.g. [iːˈdʒiː]	zum Beispiel →	for example
	to **express** [ɪkˈspres]	ausdrücken, äußern →	Do you feel angry, scared or sad? So how do you *express* those feelings?
	in public [ˈpʌblɪk]	in der Öffentlichkeit	
	basic [ˈbeɪsɪk]	grundlegend, Grund-; einfach →	In the first two years of English you learn a lot of *basic* words and phrases.
27	**journalist** [ˈdʒɜːnlɪst]	Journalist/Journalistin →	A *journalist* writes for a newspaper.

Aspects

28 **husband** ['hʌzbənd]	Ehemann →	wife ↔ *husband*
false teeth [fɔ:ls 'ti:θ]	Zahnprothese, Gebiss	
false [fɔ:ls]	falsch →	true ↔ *false*
blindfolded ['blaɪndfəʊldɪd]	mit verbundenen Augen	
Member of Parliament (MP) [ˌmembə‿əv 'pɑ:ləmənt]	Mitglied des Parlaments; Abgeordneter/ Abgeordnete	
parliament ['pɑ:ləmənt]	Parlament →	! The spelling is different from German.
suit of armour [ˌsu:t‿əv 'ɑ:mə]	Rüstung →	Knights wore *suits of armour* to protect themselves in battle.
Englishman, Englishmen *(pl)* ['ɪŋglɪʃmən, 'ɪŋglɪʃmen]	Engländer	
long bow ['lɒŋ bəʊ]	Langbogen →	English *long bows* played an important role in the Battle of Agincourt.
plague [pleɪg]	Pest, Plage, Seuche	
treason ['tri:zn]	(Landes-)Verrat	
monarch ['mɒnək]	Monarch/Monarchin, Herrscher/Herrscherin	
upside down [ˌʌpsaɪd 'daʊn]	umgedreht, auf den Kopf gestellt →	The kitchen clock is *upside down*.
Middle Ages [ˌmɪdl‿'eɪdʒɪz]	Mittelalter →	the time in history from 1066 to 1485
lady ['leɪdi]	Dame, Frau →	another word for a woman
not either [nɒt 'aɪðə]	keiner/keine/keines →	There were ladies and knights but most people were*n't either* of these.
then [ðen]	damals →	in those times
serf [sɜ:f]	Leibeigener/Leibeigene	
hut [hʌt]	Hütte	
certainly ['sɜ:tnli]	zweifellos, bestimmt, sicher →	It was *certainly* a very dangerous time in England.
soldier ['səʊldʒə]	Soldat/Soldatin →	someone whose job is to fight, usually for his or her country
freeman, freemen *(pl)* ['fri:mən, fri:men]	freier Mann →	free → *freeman*
baron ['bærn]	Baron	
bishop ['bɪʃəp]	Bischof →	The *bishops* had a lot of power and money then.
loyal ['lɔɪəl]	treu, loyal	
to **feed, fed, fed** [fi:d, fed, fed]	ernähren, durchfüttern	
pyramid ['pɪrəmɪd]	Pyramide	
29 to **kidnap** ['kɪdnæp]	kidnappen, entführen →	When a child is *kidnapped*, the criminals usually want money from the child's parents.
militant ['mɪlɪtnt]	militant, aggressiv	
Palestinian [ˌpælə'stɪniən]	palästinensisch; Palästinenser/ Palästinenserin →	A lot of *Palestinians* live in the Gaza Strip.

Democracy

Erstelle ein Cluster zum Thema *Democracy*. Welche Wörter kennst du schon? Welche hast du neu dazu gelernt? Teile die Wörter in verschiedene Gruppen ein (*government, head of state, law* etc.). Finde so viele Wörter wie möglich.

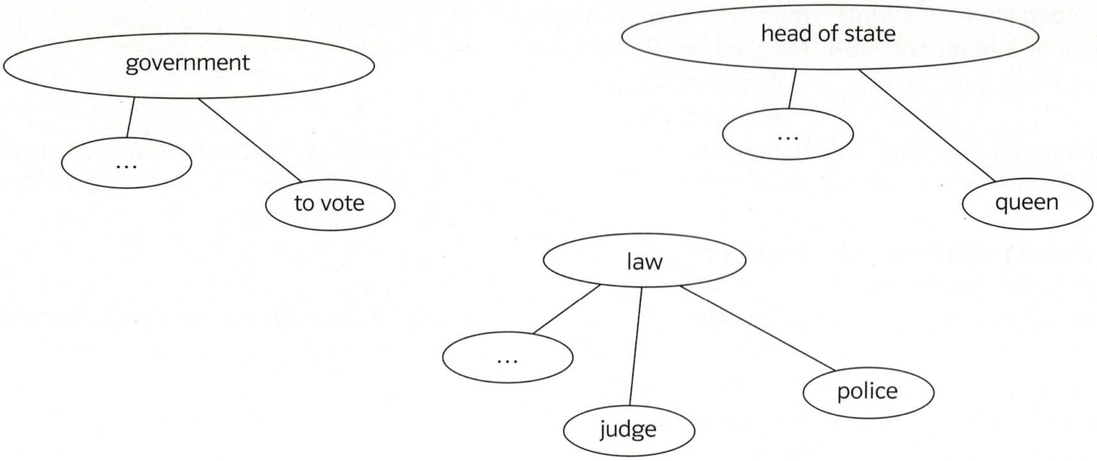

armed [ɑ:md]	bewaffnet →	A soldier can only fight in battle if he is *armed*.
hostage ['hɒstɪdʒ]	Geisel	
situation [ˌsɪtju'eɪʃn]	Situation →	what is happening at the moment
to **stay on** [steɪ‿'ɒn]	dableiben, länger bleiben	
kidnap(ping) ['kɪdnæp(ɪŋ)]	Entführung, Kidnapping	
common ['kɒmən]	gemeinsam, gebräuchlich, verbreitet →	known or used by many people
to **fly out** [flaɪ‿'aʊt]	ausfliegen, evakuieren	
foreigner ['fɒrɪnə]	Ausländer/Ausländerin; Fremder/Fremde →	foreign → *foreigner*
South American [ˌsaʊθ‿ə'merɪkən]	südamerikanisch; Südamerikaner/Südamerikanerin →	Spanish is spoken by many *South Americans*.
to **set free** [set‿'fri:]	freilassen, freisetzen →	to let go
load [ləʊd]	Ladung, Last	
to **be about to** (do sth) [bi‿ə'baʊt tə]	im Begriff sein, etw. zu tun →	I *was about to* leave the house when the phone rang.
to **remain** [rɪ'meɪn]	(ver)bleiben →	*to remain* = to stay
to **adapt to** [ə'dæpt tə]	(sich) anpassen an	
workplace ['wɜ:kpleɪs]	Arbeitsplatz, Arbeitsstätte →	A lot of accidents happen at the *workplace*.

Option 1

30 to **demand** [dɪ'mɑ:nd]	fordern, verlangen	
to **draw up, drew up, drawn up** [drɔ:‿'ʌp, dru:‿'ʌp, drɔ:n‿'ʌp]	aufsetzen, anfertigen, ausarbeiten →	The barons *drew up* a list of rules.

to **force** [fɔ:s]	(er)zwingen →	If you *force* someone to do something, you make them do it.
31 **justice** ['dʒʌstɪs]	Gerechtigkeit, Justiz	
version ['vɜ:ʃn]	Version, Fassung	
common law [ˌkɒmən 'lɔ:]	Gewohnheitsrecht →	*Common law* is law developed by judges through decisions of courts rather than developed through political decisions.
brief [bri:f]	kurz →	another word for 'short'
comic strip ['kɒmɪk strɪp]	Bildgeschichte, Comicstrip	
copy ['kɒpi]	Kopie, Abschrift →	to copy → a *copy*
eye-catching ['aɪkætʃɪŋ]	auffallend, ins Auge stechend	
feature ['fi:tʃə]	Merkmal, Gesichtszug, Charakterzug	

Giving a presentation

Die folgenden Ausdrücke sind nützlich, wenn du eine Präsentation hältst.

Vor der Präsentation	
Today I'd like to talk about …	Heute werde ich über … sprechen.
I'm going to talk about …, … and …	Ich werde über …, … und … sprechen.
First I'll give you some information about …	Zuerst werde ich euch über … informieren.
Then I'll go on with …	Dann spreche ich über …
There'll be time for questions at the end of the presentation.	Am Ende der Präsentation können Fragen gestellt werden.
Während der Präsentation	
My first point is …	Mein erster Punkt ist …
Secondly, …	Zweitens …
Let me add one more point …	Lasst mich einen weiteren Punkt hinzufügen …
It's also important to know …	Es ist auch wichtig zu wissen, dass …
In my opinion …	Meiner Meinung nach …
Many people say/think that …	Viele Menschen sagen/behaupten …
The most important point is …	Der wichtigste Punkt ist …
Have a look at the chart/picture/etc. …	Schaut bitte die Tabelle/das Foto/etc. an …
Nach der Präsentation	
To conclude, you can say …	Zusammenfassend kann man festhalten, dass …
Have you got any questions?	Gibt es Fragen?

Option 2

32 **head of state** [ˌhed‿əv 'steɪt]	Staatsoberhaupt →	A president can be *head of state*.
to **open** ['əʊpn]	eröffnen	
to **read out** [ˌri:d‿'aʊt]	laut vorlesen, verlesen	
throne [θrəʊn]	Thron	
policy ['pɒlɪsi]	Politik, politische Linie, Grundsatz →	The people were not happy with the government's education *policy*.

On the one hand ..., (but) on the other hand ... [ɒn ðəˬ'wʌn ˌhænd ... ɒn ðiˬ'ʌðə ˌhænd ...]	Einerseits ..., andererseits ... →	*On the one hand* he'd like to be a better player, *but on the other hand* he doesn't want to practise hard.
to **elect** [ɪ'lekt]	(aus)wählen →	If you want to be in parliament, you first have to be *elected*.
to **dissolve** [dɪ'zɒlv]	(sich) auflösen	
general ['dʒenrl]	generell, gewöhnlich	
general election [ˌdʒenrlˬɪ'lekʃn]	landesweite Wahl →	MPs are elected in a *general election*.
to **refuse** [rɪ'fju:z]	ablehnen, sich weigern →	to say you will not do or accept something
armed forces [ˌɑ:md 'fɔ:sɪz]	Militär, Streitkräfte	
to **declare** [dɪ'kleə]	erklären, verkünden →	If you *declare* war on someone, you start a war.
treaty ['tri:ti]	(Staats-)Vertrag, Abkommen →	When two countries or nations agree on something, there is an official *treaty*.
nation ['neɪʃn]	Nation, Volk →	national → *nation*
party ['pɑ:ti]	Partei	
to **appoint** [ə'pɔɪnt]	ernennen, berufen, einsetzen	
Prime Minister (PM) [ˌpraɪm 'mɪnɪstə]	Premierminister/ Premierministerin →	The *Prime Minister* has more powers than the Queen.
minister ['mɪnɪstə]	Minister/Ministerin	
well-informed [ˌwelin'fɔ:md]	gut informiert	
unlike [ʌn'laɪk]	anders als, im Gegensatz zu →	like ↔ *unlike*
immunity [ɪ'mju:nəti]	Immunität	

Prepositions

Lerne Verben immer mit der dazugehörigen Präposition. So kannst du dir leichter merken, welche Präposition nach welchem Verb folgt.

to apply for	sich bewerben um/für	*to be worried about*	besorgt sein über
to escape from	fliehen vor	*to point to*	zeigen auf
to be interested in	sich interessieren für	*to be frightened of*	Angst haben vor
to agree to	zustimmen zu	*to believe in*	glauben an
to belong to	gehören zu	*to argue about*	streiten um/über

Finde weitere Verben mit den dazugehörigen Präpositionen und führe die Liste in deinem Heft weiter.

33 to **limit** ['lɪmɪt]	limitieren, begrenzen, beschränken →	limit → *to limit*
federal ['fedrl]	Bundes-; föderal(istisch) →	belonging to the central government of a country, not just of a region or state
representative [ˌreprɪ'zentətɪv]	Vertreter/Vertreterin; Abgeordneter/ Abgeordnete, Repräsentant/ Repräsentantin	

president ['prezɪdnt]	Präsident/Präsidentin	
branch [brɑːntʃ]	Zweig, Ast; Zweigstelle; *hier:* Teil →	A tree has *branches*.
veto ['viːtəʊ]	Veto, Einspruch	
to **approve** [ə'pruːv]	genehmigen, anerkennen, gutheißen	
chief [tʃiːf]	Vorsitzender/Vorsitzende; Häuptling →	the leader of a group (especially of Native Americans)
military ['mɪlɪtri]	Militär, Heer	
troops *(pl)* [truːps]	Truppen →	*'Troops'* is another word for 'soldiers'.
overseas [ˌəʊvə'siːz]	nach/in Übersee, ins/im Ausland	
natural-born [ˌnætʃrl'bɔːn]	gebürtig, von Geburt an →	He was born in Virginia, so he's a *natural-born* American.

Option 3

34 **young** [jʌŋ]	*hier:* minderjährig	
apprentice [ə'prentɪs]	Auszubildender/ Auszubildende, Lehrling	
comment ['kɒment]	Kommentar, Bemerkung →	! Achte auf die Betonung: ['-]
take a joke [ˌteɪk‿ə 'dʒəʊk]	Spaß verstehen	
use [juːs]	Anwendung, Gebrauch, Nutzen	
colleague ['kɒliːg]	Kollege/Kollegin	
safety ['seɪfti]	Sicherheit →	safe → *safety*
to **stress** [stres]	betonen; beanspruchen, belasten →	If you *stress* something, it shows that you think it is very important.
protective [prə'tektɪv]	beschützend; Schutz-	
clothing ['kləʊðɪŋ]	Kleidung →	clothes → *clothing*
task [tɑːsk]	Aufgabe, Auftrag →	a piece of work, especially something that is quite difficult or that you don't enjoy doing
however [haʊ'evə]	jedoch →	The man had lots of money. He wasn't happy, *however*.
supervisor ['suːpəvaɪzə]	Betreuer/Betreuerin, Aufsichtsperson, Vorgesetzter/Vorgesetzte	
opposite ['ɒpəzɪt]	entgegengesetzt, gegenüberliegend	
sex [seks]	Geschlecht, Sexualität →	If someone is of the opposite *sex*, he/she is not the same sex as you.
to **come up behind sb** [ˌkʌm‿ʌp bɪ'haɪnd]	sich jmdm. von hinten nähern	
conversation [ˌkɒnvə'seɪʃn]	Unterhaltung, Gespräch, Konversation	
(work) placement ['pleɪsmənt]	Praktikum →	a position you have for a short time with a company to learn about the work there

department [dɪ'pɑ:tmənt]	Abteilung →	The games *department* is the part of a shop that sells games.
a **while** [ə 'waɪl]	eine Weile →	a little time
ambitious [æm'bɪʃəs]	ehrgeizig →	An *ambitious* person wants to have success or to be rich and famous.
bad language [bæd 'læŋgwɪdʒ]	Schimpfwörter	
to **read out** [ˌri:d‿'aʊt]	laut vorlesen, verlesen →	Can you *read* it *out* to me, please? I haven't got my glasses.
tabloid (newspaper) ['tæblɔɪd]	Boulevardzeitung	
rude [ru:d]	unhöflich, unverschämt →	Wayne isn't just a bully. He's *rude* to the teachers, too.
sexist ['seksɪst]	sexistisch	

Adjektive

Adjektive beziehen sich auf ein Nomen. Sie machen einen Text oder das, was du sagst, interessanter und du kannst mit ihnen z. B. Personen, Dinge oder Situationen genauer beschreiben.

Positive Adjektive	Negative Adjektive	Neutrale Adjektive
special *ambitious* *better* …	*nervous* *bad* *boring* …	*quiet* *tall* *small* …

Finde so viele Adjektive wie möglich und führe die Tabelle in deinem Heft weiter.

35 **sheet** [ʃi:t]	Blatt *(Papier)*; Bettlaken	
well-informed [ˌwelɪn'fɔ:md]	gut informiert →	He reads the paper every day and is always *well-informed*.
firmly ['fɜ:mli]	eindeutig, deutlich, standhaft	
to **treat** [tri:t]	behandeln →	If you don't *treat* your dog right, you'll have trouble with it.
harassment [hə'ræsmənt]	Belästigung, Schikanierung	
bullying ['bʊliɪŋ]	Mobbing	
horseplay ['hɔ:spleɪ]	Unfug	
realistic [ˌrɪə'lɪstɪk]	realistisch →	real → *realistic*
suitable ['su:təbl]	geeignet, passend →	Warm jackets and shoes are *suitable* for cold weather.
role model ['rəʊl ˌmɒdl]	Vorbild	
to **inform** [ɪn'fɔ:m]	informieren, benachrichtigen →	We *informed* the police the next morning.
to **shop sb** [ʃɒp]	jmdn. verpfeifen, jmdn. verraten	
panel (of experts) ['pænl]	Expertenrunde, Gremium	
to distribute [dɪ'strɪbju:t]	verteilen, austeilen	

among [ə'mʌŋ]	unter (zwischen) →	! Notice the difference: under ≠ *among* He stood *among* the trees. = in the middle of the forest, but not necessarily under a tree.

Option 4

36 **ordeal** [ɔ:'di:l]	Feuerprobe, Qual, Tortur →	I don't want to go through that *ordeal* again.
bullet-proof ['bʊlɪtpru:f]	kugelsicher	
bullet ['bʊlɪt]	Geschoss, Kugel	
vest [vest]	Weste	
kidnapper ['kɪdnæpə]	Kidnapper/Kidnapperin, Entführer/Entführerin →	The *kidnappers* sent a text message.
to **force** [fɔ:s]	(er)zwingen →	If you *force* someone to do something, you make them do it.
to **tie** [taɪ]	(an)binden, fesseln →	If you *tie* a dog to a *post*, it can't run away.
hood [hʊd]	Kapuze, Kappe	
sense [sens]	Gefühl	
sunshine ['sʌnʃaɪn]	Sonnenschein →	sun – sunny – *sunshine*
to **point a gun at sb** [ˌpɔɪnt‿ə 'gʌn‿ət]	eine Waffe auf jmdn. richten	
to **be afraid (of)** [bi‿ə'freɪd‿əv]	(sich) fürchten (vor), Angst haben (vor) →	I'*m afraid of* dogs.
My turn had come. [tɜ:n]	Ich war an der Reihe.	
back seat ['bæk si:t]	Rücksitz →	I left my bag on the *back seat* of my car.
to **flicker** ['flɪkə]	flackern, flimmern	
south [saʊθ]	nach Süden	
east [i:st]	nach Osten	
used to *(+ infinitive)* ['ju:s‿tə]	früher; pflegte(n) zu →	We *used to* live in Munich. = Wir wohnten früher in München.
authority [ɔ:'θɒrəti]	Autorität; Behörde	
unimportant [ˌʌnɪm'pɔ:tnt]	unwichtig, unbedeutend	
unharmed [ʌn'hɑ:md]	unverletzt, unbeschädigt →	He came back from the war *unharmed*.
to **convert** ['kɒnvɜ:t]	konvertieren, (um)wandeln	
Islam ['ɪzlɑ:m]	Islam	
to **wage a war** [ˌweɪdʒ‿ə 'wɔ:]	einen Krieg führen	
holy ['həʊli]	heilig	
target ['tɑ:gɪt]	Ziel(scheibe)	
to **reduce** [rɪ'dju:s]	reduzieren, vermindern →	to increase sth ↔ *to reduce sth*
at the heart of [æt ðə 'hɑ:t‿əv]	im Zentrum von	
tension ['tenʃn]	(An-)Spannung →	a nervous feeling that you get when you can't relax
to **be worth** *(+ gerund)* [bi: 'wɜ:θ]	(es) wert sein (zu) →	*It's worth* buying really strong shoes for hiking.
to **appear** [ə'pɪə]	auftauchen, erscheinen	
to **be due** (to do) [bi: 'dju:]	im Begriff sein (zu tun) →	He *is due to* do his first exam next week.
robe [rəʊb]	Robe, Gewand	

scarf, **scarves** *(pl)* [skɑ:f; skɑ:vz]	Schal, Kopftuch	
to **treat** [tri:t]	behandeln	
Islamic [ɪz'læmɪk]	islamisch	
code of behaviour [ˌkəʊd‿əv bɪ'heɪvjə]	Verhaltenskodex →	A *code of behaviour* tells people how they should behave.
behaviour [bɪ'heɪvjə]	Verhalten, Benehmen	
eventually [ɪ'ventʃuəli]	schließlich, endlich →	in the end, at last

Wortbildung I

Mit der Silbe ***un-*** kannst du das Gegenteil von Wörtern bilden.

happy → glücklich	***un**happy* → unglücklich
important → wichtig	***un**important* → unwichtig
to pack → packen	*to **un**pack* → auspacken

Finde in einem Wörterbuch mehr Beispiele und erweitere die Liste in deinem Heft.

37	to **count (for sth)** [kaʊnt]	zählen, etw. gelten	
	to **realise** ['rɪəlaɪz]	erkennen, realisieren, begreifen →	Suddenly I *realised* … = Plötzlich wurde mir klar …
	narrow ['nærəʊ]	eng, schmal →	a *narrow* path
	power cut ['paʊə ˌkʌt]	Stromausfall	
	measured ['meʒəd]	gleichmäßig, gemessen, getragen	
	tone [təʊn]	Ton(fall) →	Don't use that *tone!* = Don't speak to me like that!
	Arabic ['ærəbɪk]	arabisch; Arabisch	
	fighter ['faɪtə]	Kämpfer/Kämpferin →	to fight → *fighter*
	hot spot ['hɒt spɒt]	Krisenherd, Brennpunkt	
	decision [dɪ'sɪʒn]	Entscheidung	
	return [rɪ'tɜ:n]	Rückkehr; Antwort	
	debate [dɪ'beɪt]	Debatte	
	motion ['məʊʃn]	Thema	
	to risk [rɪsk]	riskieren	

Check-out

38	democratic [ˌdemə'krætɪk]	demokratisch

Everyday English: Talking about society

Die folgenden *phrases* können dir helfen, wenn du ein Gespräch zum Thema *society* führst.

I think our government is …	Ich finde unsere Regierung …
I'm glad we don't have … in our country.	Ich bin froh, dass es in unserem Land keine … gibt.
I think it is a good idea for young people to … because …	Ich denke, es ist eine gute Idee, wenn junge Leute …, denn …
If I was in the government, I would fight for change/ …	Wenn ich an der Regierung wäre, würde ich für Veränderungen kämpfen/…
I think the main problems in society today are … and …	Meiner Meinung nach sind die Hauptprobleme in der heutigen Gesellschaft … und …
I think everyone in our society should vote/feel responsible for/…	Ich finde, dass jedes Mitglied unserer Gesellschaft zur Wahl gehen sollte/sich verantwortlich für … fühlen sollte/…

Arbeite mit einem Partner/einer Partnerin und denkt euch ein Gespräch zum Thema *society* aus.

2,19 ## Sounds: Word stress

Schreibe die Wörter in die richtige Spalte.

compact purpose capable princess department ice-cream
repeat themselves colony mistake candidate condition

xX	Xx	xXx	Xxx
express	contract	assistant	flexible
…	…	…	…

Topic 3 Our world in our hands

Alternative Energiegewinnung

Im Allgemeinen versteht man unter dem Begriff „Alternative Energie" Energie, die im Gegensatz zu fossilen Quellen, wie Kohle oder Erdöl, kontinuierlich und unbegrenzt verfügbar ist z. B. Sonnenenergie, Windkraft, Wasserkraft, Biomasse oder die Erdwärme. Alternative Energiegewinnung ist umweltfreundlich, da sie die natürlichen Kreisläufe unserer Erde zur Gewinnung von Energie nutzt. Fossile Energiequellen schaden unserer Umwelt sehr und sind Hauptverursacher des derzeitigen Klimawandels.
Bei der Sonnen- oder auch Solarenergie werden die Sonnenstrahlen durch Sonnenkollektoren oder Solarzellen z. B. auf Dächern aufgenommen und in Strom umgewandelt. Bei der Windkraft geschieht diese Umwandlung durch ein vom Wind angetriebenes Windrad.

An schnell fließenden Flüssen kann man häufig Turbinen oder Wasserräder sehen, die durch das Wasser in Bewegung gesetzt werden und hierbei elektrische Energie erzeugen.
Die Energiegewinnung aus Biomasse erfolgt durch Verbrennen von Sägespänen, Biomüll aus dem Haushalt oder den Ausscheidungen von Tieren, während man bei der Erdwärme durch eine Sonde, die in Hunderte Meter Tiefe reicht, die Wärme der Erdkruste nutzt.
Obwohl die Gewinnung fossiler Energie die Umwelt stark schädigt, ist sie immer noch die meist genutzte Energiequelle auf der Welt.
Für Großbritannien ist vor allem die Windenergie von Interesse – es gibt Behauptungen, dass alle Haushalte in Großbritannien allein durch die Stromgewinnung aus der Windkraft versorgt werden können. Leider ist der Anteil an erneuerbaren Energien immer noch gering und Großbritannien liegt sogar im europaweiten Vergleich auf den hinteren Plätzen.

Welche Art von alternativer Energiegewinnung hast du schon einmal gesehen oder nutzt du/deine Familie? Wie viel Prozent der Energie wird in Deutschland auf alternativen Wegen gewonnen?

Check-in

50	**organic** [ɔ:'gænɪk]	biologisch angebaut, organisch →	This is an *organic* potato field.
	resource [rɪ'zɔ:s]	Ressource, Rohstoff; Quelle →	It's important not to waste the world's natural *resources*.

Aspects

52	to **reduce** [rɪ'dju:s]	reduzieren, vermindern →	to increase sth ↔ *to reduce sth*
	carbon dioxide (CO_2) [ˌkɑ:bn daɪ'ɒksaɪd; si:‿əʊ 'tu:]	Kohlendioxid	
	carbon ['kɑ:bn]	Kohle(nstoff)	
	emission [ɪ'mɪʃn]	Ausstoß, Emission	
	to **provide** (sb with sth) [prə'vaɪd]	bereitstellen, besorgen, liefern →	We'll *provide* you *with* money. = We'll give you the money you need.

biologist [baɪ'ɒlədʒɪst]	Biologe/Biologin	
engineer [ˌendʒɪ'nɪə]	Ingenieur/Ingenieurin, Techniker/Technikerin →	sb whose job is to design, build or repair machines, engines, roads, bridges, etc.
textile ['tekstaɪl]	textil; Textil(-) →	A *textile* factory is a place where cloth is produced.
builder ['bɪldə]	Baufachmann/Baufachfrau, Baumeister/ Baumeisterin	
carbon footprint [ˌkɑ:bn 'fʊtprɪnt]	CO_2 -Bilanz	
footprint ['fʊtprɪnt]	Fußabdruck →	foot → footstep → *footprint*
to **create** [kri'eɪt]	(er)schaffen →	*to create* → creative
to interest ['ɪntrəst]	interessieren →	*to interest* → interested in → interesting
to **leave**, **left**, **left** [li:v, left, left]	hinterlassen	
amount [ə'maʊnt]	Betrag, Menge, Summe →	! Notice the difference: 1. a large *amount* of water (uncountable) 2. a large number of people (countable)
petrol ['petrl]	Benzin, Kraftstoff	

Einen Cartoon beschreiben

Die folgenden *phrases* können dir helfen, wenn du einen Cartoon beschreiben sollst.

The cartoon is about …	Das Thema des Cartoons ist …
The cartoon shows …	Der Cartoon zeigt … auf.
In the cartoon you can see …	Im Cartoon sieht man …
On the left/on the right there is/there are …	Recht/links sieht man …
In the foreground/background you can see …	Vorne/hinten kann man … erkennen.
The meaning of the cartoon is clear/not clear/ …	Die Aussage des Cartoons ist deutlich/undeutlich/…
The message of the cartoon is …	Die Aussage des Cartoons ist …
The cartoon tries to say that …	Der Cartoon versucht … deutlich zu machen.
The caption says …	Die Bildunterschrift lautet …
The character(s) … is/are saying …	Die Person(en) sagt/sagen …

53 **bottled** ['bɒtld]	in Flaschen abgefüllt	
soft drink ['sɒft ˌdrɪŋk]	alkoholfreies Getränk	
wealth [welθ]	Wohlstand, Reichtum →	! Be careful with the pronunciation: The 'ea' in *'wealth'* sounds the same as in 'health'.
tap [tæp]	Wasserhahn	
tap water ['tæp ˌwɔ:tə]	Leitungswasser	
exotic [ɪg'zɒtɪk]	exotisch	
fizzy ['fɪzi]	sprudelnd →	I don't like *fizzy* drinks.
refreshing [rɪ'freʃɪŋ]	erfrischend	
billion ['bɪljən]	Milliarde *(tausend Millionen)*	
plastic ['plæstɪk]	Plastik(-), Kunststoff(-) →	a material that is light and doesn't break easily

	filter ['fɪltə]	Filter	
	lemon ['lemən]	Zitrone(n-)	
	taste [teɪst]	Geschmack →	to taste → *taste*
	to **emit** [ɪ'mɪt]	ausstoßen, absondern	
	to put across [pʊt͜ə'krɒs]	übermitteln →	If you *put across* a message, you tell someone something.
	debate [dɪ'beɪt]	Debatte	
	motion ['məʊʃn]	Thema	

Option 1

54	**excuse** [ɪk'skju:s]	Ausrede, Entschuldigung →	Excuse me! → *excuse*
	special ['speʃl]	Sonderausgabe, -heft →	special → *a special*
	eating ['i:tɪŋ]	Essen	
	to **lose weight** [lu:z 'weɪt]	abnehmen →	He *lost weight* because he was sick.
	to **be aware of** [ˌbi͜ə'weə]	sich … bewusst sein →	If you *are aware of* a fact, you know about it.
	sugar ['ʃʊgə]	Zucker →	You can put it in foods and drinks to make them sweet.
	fat [fæt]	Fett; fett →	Butter is a kind of *fat*.
	disease [dɪ'zi:z]	Krankheit →	A lot of *diseases* can be caused by dirty water and bad food.
	diabetes [ˌdaɪə'bi:ti:z]	Diabetes, Zuckerkrankheit	
	to **treat** [tri:t]	behandeln	
	industrial [ɪn'dʌstriəl]	industriell, Industrie-, gewerblich	
	incinerator [ɪn'sɪnreɪtə]	(Müll-)Verbrennungsanlage →	A lot of rubbish is burnt in *incinerators*.
	request [rɪ'kwest]	Anfrage, Anliegen, Wunsch	

Wortbildung II

Aus Verben kannst du Nomen für Menschen bilden, indem du ***-er*** oder ***-r*** anhängst.

*to play → play**er***	*to dream → dream**er***
*to build → build**er***	*to drive → drive**r***
*to work → work**er***	*to rap → rapp**er***
*to write → write**r***	*to rock → rock**er***
*to sing → sing**er***	*to dance → dance**r***

Aus manchen Verben kannst du zwei Nomen für Menschen bilden: z. B. *employ → employ**er***, employ**ee**.

Finde weitere Beispiele und vervollständige die Liste in deinem Heft.

55	**poisonous** ['pɔɪznəs]	giftig →	*Poisonous* snakes are very dangerous.
	quarry ['kwɒri]	Steinbruch	
	pure [pjʊə]	pur, rein	
	acid rain [ˌæsɪd 'reɪn]	saurer Regen →	*Acid rain* is killing our forests.
	acid ['æsɪd]	sauer; Säure	
	spring fountain [ˌsprɪŋ 'faʊntɪn]	Quelle	

fountain ['faʊntɪn]	(Spring-)Brunnen, Fontäne	
toxic ['tɒksɪk]	giftig, toxisch	
canal [kə'næl]	Kanal →	! Notice the difference: A *canal* looks like a river and is built for boats to carry goods. The English Channel; a TV channel.
butterfly ['bʌtəflaɪ]	Schmetterling →	*Butterflies* can be very colourful.
blackbird ['blækbɜ:d]	Amsel	
stealth bomber [ˌstelθ 'bɒmə]	Tarnkappenbomber →	*Stealth bombers* cost millions.
abundance [ə'bʌndəns]	Überfluss	
to reconsider [ˌri:kn'sɪdə]	überdenken, nochmals überlegen	
repetition [ˌrepɪ'tɪʃn]	Wiederholung	
stanza ['stænzə]	Strophe →	a part of a poem (often four lines or more)

Option 2

56 **cyclone** ['saɪkləʊn]	Zyklon, Wirbelsturm →	strong storm in Asia with wind and rain
survivor [sə'vaɪvə]	Überlebender/Überlebende	
West Asian [ˌwest 'eɪʃn]	westasiatisch; Westasiate/-asiatin	
to **face** [feɪs]	gegenüberliegen, konfrontiert werden mit →	This room *faces* the garden. This is a problem we have to *face*.
shortage ['ʃɔ:tɪdʒ]	Knappheit, Mangel →	short → *shortage*; If there's a *shortage* of something, there isn't enough of it.
dry [draɪ]	trocken →	to dry → *dry*
pond [pɒnd]	Teich →	Fish swim in a *pond*.
well [wel]	Brunnen	
water treatment plant ['wɔ:tə ˌtri:tmənt ˌplɑ:nt]	Wasseraufbereitungs-anlage →	A *water treatment plant* cleans water for drinking.
treatment ['tri:tmənt]	Behandlung, Aufbereitung →	to treat → *treatment*
plant [plɑ:nt]	Anlage, Werk	
resident ['rezɪdnt]	Anwohner/Anwohnerin, Bewohner/Bewohnerin, Ortsansässiger/Ortsansässige →	The *residents* of a town, street, etc. are the people who live in it. Hotel *residents* are the guests staying there.
bucket ['bʌkɪt]	Eimer →	There's a hole in my *bucket*.
pump [pʌmp]	(Luft-)Pumpe	
pipe [paɪp]	Rohr(leitung)	
income ['ɪnkʌm]	Einkommen, Verdienst →	what you earn
to **blame** [bleɪm]	verantwortlich machen, beschuldigen →	Don't *blame* me! It's not my fault. ! False friend: to blame ≠ blamieren
privatisation [ˌpraɪvɪtaɪ'zeɪʃn]	Privatisierung →	private → *privatisation*
to **manage** ['mænɪdʒ]	bewältigen, handhaben →	manager → *to manage*
existing [ɪg'zɪstɪŋ]	existierend, bestehend	
lack (of) [læk]	Mangel (an), Fehlen (von)	
investment [ɪn'vestmənt]	Investition	

Über Sachtexte sprechen I

Die folgenden Sätze können dir helfen, wenn du über Sachtexte (Zeitungsartikel, Reden, Gebrauchsanweisungen, Interviews) sprechen möchtest.

The article/interview/speech … was written in … by …	Der Artikel/das Interview/die Rede/… wurde im Jahr … von … geschrieben.
The text is a typical example of a …	Der Text ist ein typisches Beispiel einer/eines …
It is about …	Er/es handelt von …
It tells … from the point of view of …	Die Fakten werden aus der Sicht des … geschildert.
On the one hand …	Einerseits …
On the other hand …	Andererseits …
At the beginning …	Zu Beginn …
At the end …	Am Ende …
There are … parts.	Es gibt … Abschnitte.

desert ['dezət]	Wüste →	! Be careful with these two words: 1. dessert [dɪ'zɜ:t] = Nachspeise 2. *desert* ['dezət] = Wüste
crop [krɒp]	Feldfrucht; Ernte →	*Crops* are plants like wheat or potatoes that are grown in fields for food.
to **evaporate** [ɪ'væpreɪt]	verdampfen, verdunsten	
pure [pjʊə]	pur, rein	
nuclear-powered [ˌnju:kliə'paʊəd]	atombetrieben →	A lot of people are against plants which are *nuclear-powered*.
to **invest** [ɪn'vest]	investieren →	to put money in something or to buy something because you hope to make a profit investment → *to invest*
57 **non-fiction** [ˌnɒn'fɪkʃn]	Sachliteratur; Sach-	
introduction [ˌɪntrə'dʌkʃn]	Einleitung, Einführung	
fresh water ['freʃ ˌwɔ:tə]	Süßwasser, Trinkwasser →	*fresh water* ↔ salt water
to **shrink, shrank, shrunk** [ʃrɪŋk, ʃræŋk, ʃrʌŋk]	schrumpfen, schwinden; einlaufen →	Oh, no! My pullover has *shrunk*!
increasing [ɪn'kri:sɪŋ]	wachsend, steigend	
aspect ['æspekt]	Aspekt, Gesichtspunkt, Seite	
author ['ɔ:θə]	Autor/Autorin →	We have to get permission from the *author* if we want to publish the story.
reservoir ['rezəvwɑ:]	Stausee, Wasserspeicher	
to affect [ə'fekt]	beeinflussen, beeinträchtigen, betreffen	
generation [ˌdʒenə'reɪʃn]	Generation	

Option 3

58 **direction** [dɪ'rekʃn]	Richtung →	direct → *direction*
leisure ['leʒə]	Freizeit(-); Muße	

Über Sachtexte sprechen II

Die folgenden Sätze können dir helfen, wenn du über Sachtexte (Zeitungsartikel, Reden, Gebrauchsanweisungen, Interviews) sprechen möchtest.

The author uses … to show …	Der Autor/Die Autorin verwendet …, um zu zeigen, dass …
He/she wants to show that …	Er/sie möchte zeigen, dass …
In line … you can see …	In Zeile … kann man sehen, dass …
His/her main argument is …	Sein/ihr Hauptargument ist …
The structure of the text is …	Die Struktur des Texts ist …
The arguments are good/not so good/…	Die Argumente sind gut/nicht so gut/…
This can be seen in lines … where the author …	Man kann dies in den Zeilen … erkennen, da der Autor dort …
The text is special because …	Der Text ist etwas Besonderes, da …
… is a good example to show …	… ist ein gutes Beispiel, um zu zeigen, dass …

58	**according to** [ə'kɔ:dɪŋ tə]	laut, gemäß →	*According to* the weather forecast, it'll be warm and sunny tomorrow. = The weather forecast says that it'll be warm and sunny tomorrow.
	annual ['ænjuəl]	jährlich	
	to **avoid** [ə'vɔɪd]	(ver)meiden	
	to **turn down** [tɜ:n 'daʊn]	herunterdrehen →	*Turn down* the heating, please! It's so hot in here.
	thermostat ['θɜ:məstæt]	Thermostat, Temperaturregler	
	standby ['stændbaɪ]	in Bereitschaft, auf Stand-by	
	to **recycle** [ri:'saɪkl]	recyceln, wiederverwerten →	You can *recycle* bottles, paper and plastic.
	packaging ['pækɪdʒɪŋ]	Verpackung, Packmaterial →	to pack → *packaging*
	to **work out** [ˌwɜ:k‿'aʊt]	herausfinden, ausarbeiten →	If you don't know the answer to a problem (for example in Maths), it's often best to *work* it *out* on paper.
	impact ['ɪmpækt]	Auswirkung, Einfluss	
	ordinary ['ɔ:dnri]	einfach, herkömmlich, normal →	= basic
	use [ju:s]	Verwendung, Nutzung	
	insulation [ˌɪnsjə'leɪʃn]	Isolierung, Dämmung	
	income ['ɪnkʌm]	Einkommen, Verdienst →	what you earn
	average ['ævrɪdʒ]	Durchschnitt(s-)	
	figure ['fɪgə]	Ziffer, Zahl →	Are you sure that *figure* is correct? It seems very high.
59	**total** ['təʊtl]	Gesamtbetrag, Summe	
	clothing ['kləʊðɪŋ]	Kleidung →	clothes → *clothing*
	recreation [ˌri:kri'eɪʃn]	Freizeitaktivitäten, Erholung	
	household ['haʊshəʊld]	Haushalt(s-) →	house → *household*
	to **go green** [ˌgəʊ 'gri:n]	umweltbewusst werden	
	to **get on** [get‿'ɒn]	zurechtkommen, klarkommen →	Was the exam difficult? How did you *get on*?

last [lɑ:st]	zuletzt →	This site was *last* updated two years ago.
to **update** [ʌp'deɪt]	aktualisieren	
to **be supposed to** (do sth) [ˌbi sə'pəʊzd tə]	(etw. tun) sollen	
to **be aware of** [ˌbi‿ə'weə]	sich … bewusst sein →	If you *are aware of* a fact, you know about it.
to **involve** [ɪn'vɒlv]	involvieren, einbeziehen, beteiligen; umfassen	
ethical ['eθɪkl]	ethisch, moralisch →	Our company wouldn't do anything that wasn't *ethical*.
oxygen ['ɒksɪdʒən]	Sauerstoff	
hydrogen ['haɪdrədʒən]	Wasserstoff	
pie diagram ['paɪ ˌdaɪəgræm]	Kuchen-, Tortendiagramm →	The results are shown in a *pie diagram*.
pie [paɪ]	Kuchen; Pastete	
to go into labour [ˌgəʊ‿ɪntə 'leɪbə]	in den Wehen liegen	
panel (of experts) ['pænl]	Expertenrunde, Gremium	

Option 4

60 to **interest** ['ɪntrəst]	interessieren →	*to interest* → interested in → interesting
wanted ['wɒntɪd]	gesucht	
tourism ['tʊərɪzm]	Tourismus, Touristik, Fremdenverkehr →	*Tourism* is very important for our island.
live-in ['lɪvɪn]	mit Unterbringung; im Haus lebend	
flexible ['fleksɪbl]	flexibel, beweglich →	I have *flexible* working hours.
weekly ['wi:kli]	wöchentlich	
update ['ʌpdeɪt]	Update, Aktualisierung	
media *(pl)* ['mi:diə]	Medien →	Books, e-mails and the cinema are all types of *media*.
to **promote sth** [prə'məʊt]	für etw. werben, etw. bewerben	
species, species *(pl)* ['spi:ʃi:z]	Art, Spezies	
excuse [ɪk'skju:s]	Ausrede, Entschuldigung →	Excuse me! → *excuse*
mail [meɪl]	Post →	e-mail → *mail*
postal ['pəʊstl]	postalisch; Post-	
accommodation [əˌkɒmə'deɪʃn]	Unterbringung, Unterkunft →	a place where you can stay (e.g. for a holiday)
excellent ['ekslnt]	exzellent, hervorragend →	very, very good or beautiful
outdoors [ˌaʊt'dɔ:z]	freie Natur; in der freien Natur; draußen →	We are often *outdoors*. We like nature.
to **snorkel** ['snɔ:kl]	schnorcheln	
knowledge ['nɒlɪdʒ]	Wissen, Kenntnisse →	! Watch the pronunciation: to know [əʊ] – *knowledge* [ɒ]
candidate ['kændɪdət]	Kandidat/Kandidatin, Bewerber/Bewerberin →	sb who is trying to get a position, e. g. a job, or is taking part in a test of some kind

60 **wild card** ['waɪld ˌkɑ:d]	Joker; Wildcard	
61 **motto** ['mɒtəʊ]	Motto →	My *motto* is: 'Live and let live!'
to **connect** [kə'nekt]	verbinden, anschließen	
to **browse** [brauz]	durchsuchen, durchstöbern	
site [saɪt]	Ort, Schauplatz; *hier:* Webseite →	I found an interesting *site* about the Great Barrier Reef.
conservation [ˌkɒnsə'veɪʃn]	Bewahrung, Konservierung, Naturschutz	
fund raising ['fʌnd ˌreɪzɪŋ]	Spenden sammeln	
fund [fʌnd]	Fonds; Fundus	
to **raise** [reɪz]	(an)heben; aufbringen, bereitstellen →	to *raise* money = to get money together
to **campaign** [kæm'peɪn]	für etw./jmdn. werben, sich für etw./jmdn. einsetzen	
to **communicate** [kə'mju:nɪkeɪt]	kommunizieren, sich verständigen →	The easiest way to *communicate* with people is to speak to them.
to **inform** [ɪn'fɔ:m]	informieren, benachrichtigen	

Wortbildung III

Mit den Silben ***mis-***, ***de-*** und ***il-*** kannst du Wörter in ihr Gegenteil umkehren.

mis- *use → **mis**use* *understanding → **mis**understanding*	***il-*** *legal → **il**legal*
de- *compression → **de**compression*	***in-*** *dependent → **in**dependent*
im- *possible → **im**possible*	***dis-*** *like → **dis**like*

Finde weitere Beispiele und vervollständige die Liste in deinem Heft.

generator ['dʒenreɪtə]	Generator	
turbine ['tɜ:baɪn]	Turbine	
engineering [ˌendʒɪ'nɪərɪŋ]	Maschinenbau, Technik →	engine → engineer → *engineering*
to **recycle** [ri:'saɪkl]	recyceln, wiederverwerten →	You can *recycle* bottles, paper and plastic.
communications officer [kəmju:nɪ'keɪʃnz ˌɒfɪsə]	Pressesprecher/ Pressesprecherin →	to communicate → *communications officer*
co-operative [kəʊ'ɒprətɪv]	Genossenschaft	
to **prepare** [prɪ'peə]	vorbereiten, zubereiten →	to get something ready
income ['ɪnkʌm]	Einkommen, Verdienst →	what you earn
to brainstorm ['breɪnstɔ:m]	Ideen sammeln	

Check-out

62	to summarize ['sʌmraɪz]	(kurz) zusammenfassen →	Who can *summarize* for the class what the author was trying to say in the article?
	to recognize ['rekəgnaɪz]	erkennen	
63	recycling [riː'saɪklɪŋ]	Recycling, Abfallverwertung	

Everyday English: Talking about the media

Diese *phrases* können dir helfen, wenn du dich über das Thema ‚Medien' unterhalten willst.

My favourite TV programme(s) is/are …	Meine Lieblingsfernsehsendung(en) ist/ sind …
I think newspapers should give us more facts/are too sensationalist/…	Ich denke, Zeitungen sollten mehr Fakten enthalten/sind zu sensationsgierig/…
I get most of my news from …	Ich informiere mich am häufigsten durch/über …
I feel that we don't get enough information about … from TV news programmes.	Ich finde, dass wir nicht genug Informationen über … in den Fernsehnachrichten erhalten.
I'd like to know more about …	Ich möchte gerne mehr über … erfahren.

Arbeite mit einem Partner/einer Partnerin. Denkt euch eine Situation aus und spielt einen Dialog nach.

2,20 Sounds: One sound makes a difference

The Queen Mary isn't a sheep [iː] → it's a ship [ɪ].

a) Hör genau hin und sage, ob du a. oder b. hörst.

1. a. prize	b. price
2. a. bad	b. bat
3. a. dog	b. dock
4. a. man	b. men
5. a. boat	b. bought

b) Teste deine/n Partner/in. Wähle a. oder b. und sage die Wörter. Dein/e Partner/in schreibt auf, was er/sie hört. Hat er/sie dich richtig verstanden?

Topic 4 Choices and decisions

Aufbau einer Firma (ein Beispiel)

Executive board
Verwaltungs- /Aufsichtsrat

Manager
Geschäftsführung

Sales Department	***Purchasing Department***	***Human Resources***	***Manufacturing***	***Finance***
Vertrieb	Einkauf	Personalwesen	Produktion	Rechnungswesen
Verkauf von Waren und Dienstleistungen Kommunikation mit den Kunden	Kontrolle des Lagerbestands Lieferantenauswahl Bestellung der benötigten Dinge …	Stellenausschreibungen Vorstellungsgespräche Personaleinstellung Kündigungen Lohnabrechungen …	Aufbau und Ablauf der Produktion Bedienung der Maschinen …	Planung und Kontrolle der Ausgaben und Einnahmen des Unternehmens …

Kennst du andere Firmen (in Deutschland, England oder einem anderen Land)?
Wie sind diese aufgebaut? Handelt es sich um kleine oder große Firmen?

Check-in

68	**decision** [dɪ'sɪʒn]	Entscheidung →	! Achtung Aussprache: to decide [aɪ] → *decision* [ɪ]
	whether ['weðə]	ob →	*whether* = if (in indirect speech)
	relationship [rɪ'leɪʃnʃɪp]	Beziehung →	The first *relationship* in life is usually between mother and child.

Aspects

70	**legal age** [ˌliːgl‿'eɪdʒ]	gesetzliches Mindestalter	
	table ['teɪbl]	Tabelle	
	to list [lɪst]	auflisten	
	employment [ɪm'plɔɪmənt]	Beschäftigung, Anstellung →	The chance of *employment* = the chance of getting work.
	age of consent [ˌeɪdʒ‿əv kən'sent]	das Alter, in dem man legal Sex haben darf	
	consent [kən'sent]	Zustimmung, Einwilligung	
	marriage ['mærɪdʒ]	Ehe(schließung) →	Jimmy became famous after his *marriage* to a top model.

parental [pə'rentl]	elterlich	
female ['fi:meɪl]	weiblich; Weibchen	
male [meɪl]	männlich; Männchen →	Men and boys are *male*; women and girls are female.
election [ɪ'lekʃn]	Wahl	
criminal responsibility [ˌkrɪmɪnl rɪsˌpɒnsə'bɪləti]	Schuldfähigkeit	
responsibility [rɪsˌpɒnsə'bɪləti]	Verantwortung →	Rights and *responsibilities* go hand in hand.
to **vary** ['veəri]	variieren, schwanken, sich ändern	
spirit ['spɪrɪt]	Spirituose	
tragedy ['trædʒədi]	Tragödie →	a *tragedy* = something very terrible that happens to a person
to **experience** [ɪk'spɪəriənts]	erfahren, erleben	
to **daydream** ['deɪdri:m]	tagträumen	
to **face** [feɪs]	gegenüberliegen, konfrontiert werden mit →	This room *faces* the garden. This is a problem we have to *face*.
bitter ['bɪtə]	verbittert, bitter	
illness ['ɪlnəs]	Krankheit →	Her *illness* is not serious.
restrictive [rɪ'strɪktɪv]	einschränkend, restriktiv	
novel ['nɒvl]	Roman	

Phrasal verbs

Diese Verben solltest du immer zusammen mit ihren Präpositionen lernen.

to grow up → aufwachsen
to look after → sich kümmern um
to look for → suchen nach
to look up → nachschlagen; hinaufschauen
...

to turn on → einschalten
to turn off → ausschalten
to turn over → (sich) umdrehen
to take off → ausziehen; wegbringen, starten
...

71 **future** ['fju:tʃə]	Zukunft →	We can't look into the *future*.
sixth form ['sɪksθ ˌfɔ:m]	Oberstufe	
specialist ['speʃlɪst]	Spezialist/Spezialistin; Fach- →	I think you should talk to a *specialist* before you decide.
horticulture ['hɔ:tɪkʌltʃə]	Gartenbau	
creative [kri'eɪtɪv]	kreativ →	In *creative* writing exercises you can use your own ideas.
agriculture ['ægrɪkʌltʃə]	Agrikultur, Landwirtschaft	
additional [ə'dɪʃnl]	zusätzlich →	There's an *additional* problem: We haven't got any money.
term [tɜ:m]	Trimester *(Einteilung des englischen Schuljahrs)*	
financial [faɪ'næntʃl]	finanziell	
residential [ˌrezɪ'dentʃl]	Wohn-, am Wohnsitz →	They live in a nice, *residential* area.
study ['stʌdi]	Studieren, Studium, Lernen →	I did my *studies* in Berlin.

	to **gain** [geɪn]	erlangen, erwerben; gewinnen →	to get something positive (or an advantage) from doing something
	specific [spə'sɪfɪk]	spezifisch, speziell, bestimmt →	special → *specific*
	time off [ˌtaɪm‿'ɒf]	Freizeit →	She hasn't got a lot of *time off.*
	prospect ['prɒspekt]	Aussicht, Perspektive	
	to **prepare** [prɪ'peə]	vorbereiten, zubereiten →	to get something ready
	self-employment [ˌselfɪm'plɔɪmənt]	Selbstständigkeit →	*Self-employment* is not a good alternative for everybody.
	direction [dɪ'rekʃn]	Richtung	
	flow chart ['fləʊ ˌtʃɑ:t]	Ablauf-, Flussdiagramm	
	site [saɪt]	Ort, Schauplatz; *hier:* Webseite	

Option 1

72	**author** ['ɔ:θə]	Autor/Autorin →	I don't know the *author's* name.
	extremely [ɪk'stri:mli]	extrem, außerordentlich	
	both ... and ... ['bəʊθ ... ænd]	sowohl ... als auch ... →	The journey over the mountains was *both* long *and* difficult.
	to **affect** [ə'fekt]	beeinflussen, beeinträchtigen, betreffen →	! Notice the difference: Technology ***affects*** our lives. Developments in technology have had a huge **effect** on our lives.
	to **surround** [sə'raʊnd]	umgeben, umschließen	
	to **be supposed to** (do sth) [ˌbi sə'pəʊzd tə]	(etw. tun) sollen	
	aspect ['æspekt]	Aspekt, Gesichtspunkt, Seite →	I didn't really think about that *aspect*, but maybe it is important.
	restriction [rɪ'strɪkʃn]	Einschränkung	
	addiction [ə'dɪkʃn]	Abhängigkeit, Sucht	
	to **recognize** ['rekəgnaɪz]	erkennen	
	truthful ['tru:θfl]	wahrhaft, ehrlich →	true → *truthful*

Über fiktionale Texte sprechen I

Die folgenden Sätze können dir helfen, wenn du über fiktionale Texte (Romane, Kurzgeschichten, Gedichte usw.) sprechen möchtest.

The short story/poem/play ... was written ... in ... by	Die Kurzgeschichte/das Gedicht/das Theaterstück ... wurde im Jahr ... von ... geschrieben.
The text is a typical example of	Der Text ist ein typisches Beispiel einer/eines ....
It is about	Er/sie/es handelt von ....
The story is told from the point of view of	Die Geschichte wird aus der Perspektive ... erzählt.
It is set in	Es spielt in/an ....
The atmosphere is	Die Atmosphäre kann als ... beschrieben werden.
The main character(s) is/are	Der/Die Hauptfigur(en) ist/sind ....
There is a conflict between ... and	Es besteht ein Konflikt zwischen ... und ....

	desire [dɪ'zaɪə]	Wunsch, Lust, Verlangen	
	fear [fɪə]	Angst, Furcht →	the feeling you have when you are scared
	romantic [rə'mæntɪk]	romantisch	
	self-worth [ˌself'wɜ:θ]	Selbstwertgefühl, Selbstachtung	
	to **determine** [dɪ'tɜ:mɪn]	bestimmen, entschließen	
	flaw [flɔ:]	Fehler, Defekt	
	to **seem** [si:m]	(er)scheinen, wirken →	The dog *seemed* friendly, but actually it wasn't.
	tempting ['temptɪŋ]	verführerisch, verlockend	
	pregnancy ['pregnəntsi]	Schwangerschaft	
	to **fail a grade** [ˌfeɪl‿ə 'greɪd]	eine Schulnote nicht erreichen →	If you *fail a grade*, you don't get that grade in an exam.
	to **communicate** [kə'mju:nɪkeɪt]	kommunizieren, sich verständigen →	The easiest way to *communicate* with people is to speak to them.
73	to **focus (on)** ['fəʊkəs]	sich konzentrieren (auf) →	When you *focus* your eyes *on* something, you concentrate on it and see it clearly.
	to **slip** [slɪp]	abrutschen, (aus)rutschen	
	to **concentrate** ['kɒntsntreɪt]	(sich) konzentrieren →	If you don't *concentrate* on the traffic while you're driving, you might have an accident.
	to **get along** [ˌget‿ə'lɒŋ]	sich verstehen, zurechtkommen →	My brother and I don't *get along* well.
	in private [ɪn 'praɪvɪt]	insgeheim	
	guidance teacher *(AE)* ['gaɪdənts ˌti:tʃə]	Vertrauenslehrer/ Vertrauenslehrerin →	*BE*: school counselor
	guidance ['gaɪdənts]	Anleitung, Führung, Beratung	
	depressed [dɪ'prest]	deprimiert, bedrückt →	very sad and disappointed with life
	gotten *(AE)* ['gɒtn]	*(Partizip von 'to get')* →	In American English people often say 'gotten' instead of 'got'.
	to **shut sb out** [ʃʌt‿'aʊt]	jmdn. ausschließen	
	to **shut, shut, shut** [ʃʌt, ʃʌt, ʃʌt]	schließen	
	comment ['kɒment]	Kommentar, Bemerkung →	! Achte auf die Betonung: ['-]
	to **go for sth** ['gəʊ fɔ:]	etw. angehen →	Let's *go for* gold this time.
	conclusion [kən'klu:ʒn]	Schluss(folgerung)	
	guide [gaɪd]	Führer/Führerin; Ratgeber	
	feedback ['fi:dbæk]	Feedback, Rückmeldung	

Option 2

74	**automotive** [ˌɔ:tə'məʊtɪv]	Auto-, Fahrzeug- →	*Automotive* firms produce cars, buses, trucks, etc.
	motor ['məʊtəbaɪk]	Motor(-)	
	chief executive officer *(CEO)* [ˌtʃi:f‿ɪgˌzekjətɪv‿'ɒfɪsə; ˌsi: i:'əʊ]	Generaldirektor/ Generaldirektorin; Geschäftsführer/ Geschäftsführerin	
	junior ['dʒu:niə]	Junior, der Jüngere	

internship *(AE)* ['ɪntɜ:nʃɪp]	Praktikum →	*BE:* (work) placement
department [dɪ'pɑ:tmənt]	Abteilung, Branche →	The games *department* is the part of a shop that sells games.
manufacturing [ˌmænjə'fæktʃrɪŋ]	Herstellung, Fertigung	
human resources [ˌhju:mən rɪ'zɔ:sɪz]	Personalabteilung	
resource [rɪ'zɔ:s]	Ressource, Rohstoff; Quelle	
development [dɪ'veləpmənt]	Entwicklung →	to develop → *development*
marketing ['mɑ:kɪtɪŋ]	Marketing, Vermarktung, Vertrieb →	using advertisements etc. to try to sell products
sales *(pl)* [seɪlz]	Vertrieb, Verkauf →	to sell → *sales*
IT [ˌaɪ'ti:]	Informationstechnik, Informatik	
safety ['seɪfti]	Sicherheit →	safe → *safety*
finance ['faɪnænts]	Finanzwesen, Finanzen; Finanz-	
public relations (PR) [ˌpʌblɪk rɪ'leɪʃnz]	Öffentlichkeitsarbeit	
vehicle ['vɪəkl]	Auto, Fahrzeug, Vehikel	
then [ðen]	damals →	in those times
great-grandson [ˌgreɪt'grænsʌn]	Urenkel →	I'm the *great-grandson* of my grandfather's father.
manufacturer [ˌmænjə'fæktʃərə]	Hersteller →	sb who makes sth in a factory
based [beɪst]	ansässig	
sector ['sektə]	Sektor, Abschnitt, (Unternehmens-)Bereich	
to **manufacture** [ˌmænjə'fæktʃə]	fertigen, herstellen, produzieren →	to make in a factory
to **service** ['sɜ:vɪs]	überprüfen, warten →	service → *to service*
worldwide [ˌwɜ:ld'waɪd]	weltweit →	world → *worldwide*
to **market** ['mɑ:kɪt]	vermarkten, vertreiben	
retailer ['ri:teɪlə]	(Einzel-)Händler/Händlerin	
throughout [θru'aʊt]	durchgehend, überall in	
dealer ['di:lə]	Händler/Händlerin →	We bought our car from a *dealer*.
to **supply** [sə'plaɪ]	(be)liefern, ausrüsten	
fleet [fli:t]	Flotte *(Fahrzeug)*	
rental ['rentl]	Miet-, Verleih- →	It's not our car, it's from a *rental* company.
leasing ['li:sɪŋ]	Leasing	
wide [waɪd]	groß, breit, weit →	This table is too *wide*, we can't get it through the door.
range [reɪndʒ]	Auswahl, Angebot	
after-sales service [ˌɑ:ftəseɪlz 'sɜ:vɪs]	Kundendienst	
including [ɪn'klu:dɪŋ]	einschließlich, inklusive →	It's £3,500 *including* tax.
repair [rɪ'peə]	Reparatur	
salesroom ['seɪlzrʊm]	Verkaufsraum →	to sell → sales → *salesroom*

Über fiktionale Texte sprechen II

Die folgenden Sätze können dir helfen, wenn du über fiktionale Texte (Romane, Kurzgeschichten, Gedichte usw.) sprechen möchtest.

The situation between … and … is …	Die Situation zwischen … und … ist …
He/she feels … because …	Er/sie fühlt sich …, da …
Therefore …	Deshalb …
On the one hand …	Einerseits …
On the other hand …	Andererseits …
At the beginning …	Zu Beginn …
Later he/she changes/learns …	Im Verlauf der Geschichte/des Gedichts verändert er/sie sich/lernt er/sie …
At the end …	Am Ende …
This means …	Das bedeutet …
The writer wants to show …	Der Autor/Die Autorin möchte deutlich machen, dass …
The text is special because …	Das Besondere an dem Text ist …

75	**intern** *(AE)* [ˈɪntɜːn]	Praktikant/Praktikantin	
	to **employ sb** [ɪmˈplɔɪ]	jmdn. anstellen, jmdn. beschäftigen →	*to employ* → employer → employee
	to **range** [reɪndʒ]	reichen, rangieren	
	damage assessment [ˌdæmɪdʒ əˈsesmənt]	Schadensfeststellung, Schadensbemessung	
	damage [ˈdæmɪdʒ]	Schaden, Beschädigung →	The storm caused a lot of *damage*.
	assessment [əˈsesmənt]	Bewertung, Einschätzung	
	prototype [ˈprəʊtətaɪp]	Prototyp	
	construction [kənˈstrʌkʃn]	Konstruktion, Aufbau →	He works for a *construction* company.
	body shell [ˈbɒdi ˌʃel]	Karosserie	
	shell [ʃel]	Hülle, Mantel; Muschel	
	frame [freɪm]	Rahmen	
	to **restore** [rɪˈstɔː]	wiederherstellen, restaurieren →	If you *restore* something to its original state, you make it like it used to be.
	Physics [ˈfɪzɪks]	Physik	
	dimension [ˌdaɪˈmenʃn]	Dimension	
	reliable [rɪˈlaɪəbl]	zuverlässig, vertrauenswürdig →	Someone who does what he/she promises is *reliable*.
	flexible [ˈfleksɪbl]	flexibel, beweglich	
	colleague [ˈkɒliːg]	Kollege/Kollegin	
	planning [ˈplænɪŋ]	Planung, Planen	
	to **communicate** [kəˈmjuːnɪkeɪt]	kommunizieren, sich verständigen →	The easiest way to *communicate* with people is to speak to them.
	both … and … [ˈbəʊθ … ænd]	sowohl … als auch … →	The journey over the mountains was *both* long *and* difficult.
	orally [ˈɔːrli]	mündlich	
	in writing [ɪn ˈraɪtɪŋ]	schriftlich	
	organizational [ˌɔːgnaɪˈzeɪʃnl]	organisatorisch →	to organize → *organizational*
	essential [ɪˈsentʃl]	essenziell, entscheidend, unverzichtbar	
	brand [brænd]	Marke(n-)	

auto ['ɔ:təʊ]	Auto(-)	
to scroll down [ˌskrəʊl 'daʊn]	hinunter scrollen	
panel (of experts) ['pænl]	Expertenrunde, Gremium	

Option 3

76	**extract** ['ekstrækt]	Extrakt, Auszug →	An *extract* from a book is just a small part of the story.
	novel ['nɒvl]	Roman	
	introduction [ˌɪntrə'dʌkʃn]	Einleitung, Einführung	
	leukaemia [lju:'ki:miə]	Leukämie, Blutkrebs	
	to **realise** ['rɪəlaɪz]	erkennen, realisieren, begreifen →	Suddenly I *realised* … = Plötzlich wurde mir klar …
	virginity [və'dʒɪnəti]	Jungfräulichkeit	
	to **shamble** ['ʃæmbl]	schlurfen, trotten →	The old man *shambled* along the road.
	to **wipe** [waɪp]	(ab)wischen, abreiben	
	forehead ['fɔ:hed]	Stirn	
	fingernail ['fɪŋgəneɪl]	Fingernagel →	I broke my *fingernail* when I was cleaning the bath.
	shoebox ['ʃu:bɒks]	Schuhkarton	
	to **drape** [dreɪp]	drapieren, behängen	
	to **shrug** (one's shoulders) [ʃrʌg]	mit den Achseln/Schultern zucken →	You can *shrug* your shoulders to show that you don't know or you aren't interested.
	either way [ˌaɪðə 'weɪ]	auf die eine oder andere Art, so oder so →	I don't care *either way*.
	to **separate** ['sepreɪt]	trennen, separieren →	! Careful with the pronunciation: separate (adj.) ['seprət] = getrennt; *to separate* ['sepreɪt] = trennen
	front [frʌnt]	Vor-, Vorder- →	Some houses have a small *front* garden.
	to **hesitate** ['hezɪteɪt]	zögern	
	to **chuck sb** *(coll)* [tʃʌk]	mit jmdm. Schluss machen	
	to **dump sb** [dʌmp]	mit jmdm. Schluss machen, jmdm. den Laufpass geben →	! Two people can agree to *break it off*. But one person *dumps* the other.
	skeleton ['skelɪtn]	Skelett	

Wörter, die in anderen Sprachen ähnlich sind

Manche neuen Wörter kennst du schon aus anderen Sprachen. Das hilft dir, sie dir besser zu merken.

Englisch	Deutsch	Französisch	Türkisch
sport	Sport	sport	spor
university	Universität	université	üniversite
popular	populär	populaire	popüler
automobile	Auto(mobil)	automobile	oto(mobil)

Kennst du noch weitere Wörter oder andere Sprachen? Ergänze die Liste in deinem Heft.

bald [bɔ:ld]	kahl →	My grandad is *bald* but my dad has lots of hair.
disappointing [ˌdɪsə'pɔɪntɪŋ]	enttäuschend	
to **smoulder** ['sməʊldə]	rauchen, qualmen, schwelen	
pile [paɪl]	Stapel, Haufen →	a *pile* of wood
twig [twɪg]	Zweig	
hopeful ['həʊpfl]	hoffnungsvoll →	hope → *hopeful*
to **lick** [lɪk]	(ab)lecken	
damp [dæmp]	feucht →	not quite dry, but not really wet
to **get sth going** [ˌget 'gəʊɪŋ]	etw. in Gang setzen/in Schwung bringen	
to **tip** [tɪp]	(aus)kippen	
upside down [ˌʌpsaɪd 'daʊn]	umgedreht, auf den Kopf gestellt →	Don't turn the bottle *upside down* – there's still some water in it.

Wortbildung IV

Aus manchen Wörtern kannst du durch Anhängen bestimmter Silben viele neue Wörter bilden.

to drink (trinken)	*drink**er** (Trinker)*	*drink**ing** (das Trinken)*	***un**drink**able*** (untrinkbar)
to think	…	…	…
to teach	…	…	…

Finde weitere Wörter und vervollständige die Liste in deinem Heft.

77 **bruise** [bru:z]	Prellung, Quetschung; Bluterguss →	He fell off his bike. Now he has a *bruise* on his leg.
spine [spaɪn]	Wirbelsäule →	He hurt his *spine* when he fell off the ladder.
to **keep a diary** [ˌki:p‿ə 'daɪəri]	ein Tagebuch/einen Terminkalender führen	
pathetic [pə'θetɪk]	Mitleid erregend, erbärmlich	
optimism ['ɒptɪmɪzm]	Optimismus →	Her *optimism* helped her.
to **flare** [fleə]	lodern, flackern	
get-well card [ˌget 'wel ˌkɑ:d]	Gute-Besserung-Karte →	She has lots of *get-well cards* beside her hospital bed.
to **curl** [kɜ:l]	(sich) kräuseln, einrollen	
to **crisp up** [krɪsp‿'ʌp]	aufbacken; *hier:* aufflackern	
to **flake** [fleɪk]	zerfallen, zerbröseln, abbröckeln →	The paint on the doors was *flaking*.
used to *(+ infinitive)* ['ju:s‿tə]	früher; pflegte(n) zu →	We *used to* live in Munich. = Wir wohnten früher in München.
by [baɪ]	neben	
prolific [prə'lɪfɪk]	fruchtbar, produktiv	
to **spit**, **spat**, **spat** [spɪt, spæt, spæt]	spucken, zischen, fauchen →	Please don't *spit* on the floor – it's horrible.
embers *(pl)* ['embəz]	Glut, glimmende Asche	

to **spark** [spɑ:k]	sprühen *(Funken)*; auslösen, entfachen	
to **unburden** [ʌn'bɜ:dn]	entlasten, abladen	
to **drag** [dræg]	ziehen, schleppen →	If you *drag* something, you pull it along.
clump [klʌmp]	Klumpen, Haufen	
bramble ['bræmbl]	Brombeergestrüpp →	There are lots of *brambles* near the river.
to **trawl** [trɔ:l]	mit dem Netz fischen; *hier:* stöbern	
to **scatter** ['skætə]	(sich) zerstreuen, verteilen; auseinanderjagen →	The wind *scattered* the leaves around the garden.
to **get well** [get 'wel]	gesund werden	
image ['ɪmɪdʒ]	(Ab-)Bild, Image, Vorstellung	
self-conscious [ˌself'kɒnʃəs]	befangen, gehemmt →	She is shy and *self-conscious*.
secondary school ['sekəndri ˌsku:l]	weiterführende Schule	
thin [θɪn]	dünn →	If you don't eat enough, you'll get too *thin*.
to **be in remission** [ˌbi_ɪn rɪ'mɪʃn]	auf dem Weg der Besserung sein	
to **whistle** ['wɪsl]	pfeifen	
whistle ['wɪsl]	Pfiff →	I heard a *whistle* behind me and turned round.
desire [dɪ'zaɪə]	Wunsch, Lust, Verlangen	
to **fold** [fəʊld]	falten, knicken, brechen	
to **squash** [skwɑʃ]	zerdrücken, pressen, quetschen	
tight [taɪt]	eng, fest →	These shoes are too *tight*. They hurt my feet.
fist [fɪst]	Faust	
airborne ['eəbɔ:n]	durch die Luft (schwebend), luftübertragen	
still [stɪl]	still, unbewegt	

Fire

Erstelle eine Mind map zum Thema *fire*. Welche Wörter kennst du schon? Welche hast du neu dazu gelernt? Finde so viele Wörter wie möglich und vervollständige die Mind map in deinem Heft.

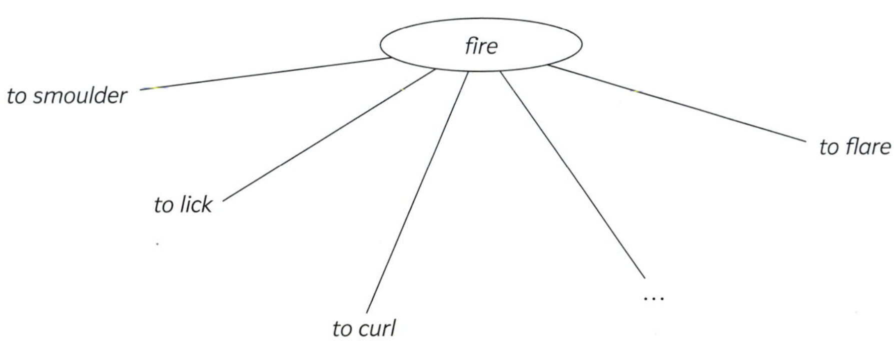

	to **melt** [melt]	schmelzen →	The next morning the snow *had melted*.
	plastic ['plæstɪk]	Plastik(-), Kunststoff(-) →	a material that is light and doesn't break easily
	matter ['mætə]	Materie	
	to **be comprised of** [bi‿kəm'praɪzd‿əv]	bestehen aus, beinhalten →	Our universe is *comprised of* lots of different stars and planets.
	particle ['pɑːtɪkl]	Teilchen, Partikel	
	solid ['sɒlɪd]	fest, solide	
	liquid ['lɪkwɪd]	Flüssigkeit; flüssig →	Water is *liquid* and ice is solid.
	to **alter** ['ɔːltə]	(sich) ändern, (ab)wandeln →	to change
	properly ['prɒpli]	ordentlich, richtig	
	to **seem** [siːm]	(er)scheinen, wirken →	The dog *seemed* friendly, but actually it wasn't.
	grounded ['graʊndɪd]	geerdet, gefestigt	
	to **turn (to)** [tɜːn]	werden (zu) →	His face *turned* green.
	to **drift** [drɪft]	wehen, treiben	
	gravity ['grævəti]	Schwerkraft, Schwere →	In outer space there is no *gravity*.
78	to **surprise** [sə'praɪz]	überraschen	
	pale [peɪl]	blass →	Are you OK? You look very *pale*.
	haloed ['heɪləʊd]	wie von einem Heiligenschein umgeben	
	to **work out** [ˌwɜːk‿'aʊt]	herausfinden, ausarbeiten →	If you don't know the answer to a problem (for example in Maths), it's often best to *work* it *out* on paper.
	diabetic [ˌdaɪə'betɪk]	zuckerkrank; Diabetiker/ Diabetikerin	
	sugar ['ʃʊgə]	Zucker →	You can put it in foods and drinks to make them sweet.
	can [kæn]	Dose	
	to **lean up** [liːn‿'ʌp]	sich aufrichten	
	to **hand** [hænd]	(über)geben, aushändigen →	Could you *hand* me the sugar, please?
	ghostly ['gəʊstli]	geisterhaft	
	charred [tʃɑːd]	verkohlt, verschmort	
	remains *(pl)* [rɪ'meɪnz]	(Über-)Rest →	*remains* = rest
	ash [æʃ]	Asche	
	ashes *(pl)* ['æʃɪz]	Verbrennungsrückstände, Asche	
	moth [mɒθ]	Motte, Falter →	The *moth* flew around the light.
	to **crackle** ['krækl]	knistern, knacken, prasseln	
	to **fizz** [fɪz]	zischen	
	gardening ['gɑːdnɪŋ]	Gärtnern, Gartengestaltung →	garden → *gardening*
	to **dig, dug, dug** [dɪg, dʌg, dʌg]	graben, buddeln	
	startled ['stɑːtld]	verblüfft, alarmiert	
	to **frown** [fraʊn]	die Stirn runzeln →	My dad *frowned* when he read my school report.
	to **be about to** (do sth) [bi‿ə'baʊt tə]	im Begriff sein, etw. zu tun	

	cabbage ['kæbɪdʒ]	Kohl, Kraut	
	runner bean ['rʌnə ˌbi:n]	Stangenbohne	
	to **mention** ['menʃn]	erwähnen →	He forgot to *mention* that he was going on holiday.
	trickle ['trɪkl]	Rinnsal	
	to **get on** [get‿'ɒn]	weiterkommen, vorwärtskommen	
	slightly ['slaɪtli]	geringfügig, leicht	
79	to analyse ['ænlaɪz]	analysieren →	to examine the details of something carefully, in order to understand or explain it
	setting ['setɪŋ]	Schauplatz; Rahmen →	What is the *setting* of the story? = Where and when does it take place?
	to be set (in) [bi 'set]	spielen (in); seinen Schauplatz haben (in) →	The film is about Alaska. It *is set in* Alaska.
	to react [ri'ækt]	reagieren	
	to appear [ə'pɪə]	auftauchen, erscheinen	
	storyline ['stɔ:rileɪn]	Handlung	
	to act out [ækt‿'aʊt]	vorspielen →	to act → *to act out*
	author ['ɔ:θə]	Autor/Autorin	
	to visualize ['vɪʒulaɪz]	visualisieren, sichtbar machen	
	basic ['beɪsɪk]	grundlegend, Grund-; einfach →	base → *basic*
	element ['elɪmənt]	Element →	! Achtung Aussprache
	to arrange [ə'reɪndʒ]	arrangieren, anrichten, einordnen	
	to turn into [ˌtɜ:n‿'ɪntə]	machen zu, verwandeln in	

Check-out

80	to recognize ['rekəgnaɪz]	erkennen	

Everyday English: A job interview

Die folgenden *phrases* helfen dir, wenn du ein Vorstellungsgespräch hast.

I'm still at school./I've left school./did my final exams …	Ich gehe noch zur Schule./Ich habe die Schule verlassen./ Ich habe meinen Abschluss gemacht.
I'm interested in the job/placement/… because …	Ich interessiere mich für die Stelle/das Praktikum /… weil …
I like working outside/with people/with computers/ in a team/…	Ich arbeite gerne im Freien/mit Menschen/mit Computern/in einem Team …
Your website is …	Ihre Website ist …
I'm good at dealing with …	Ich bin gut im Umgang mit …
I'm not so good at dealing with …	Ich bin nicht so gut im Umgang mit …
My hobbies are …	Meine Hobbys sind …
I think … is important.	Ich denke, … ist wichtig.
How much will I be paid?	Wie hoch ist mein Lohn/Gehalt?
When will I have to start work in the morning?	Wann muss ich morgens da sein?
Is there a cafeteria?	Gibt es eine Kantine?
I'd like to train to be a/an …	Ich würde gerne eine Ausbildung zur/zum … machen.
I'd like to work with animals/ …	Ich möchte gerne mit Tieren/… arbeiten.
My 'dream' job would be to be a …	Mein Traumberuf wäre …
I don't want to work as a … all my life.	Ich möchte nicht mein Leben lang als … arbeiten.
I'd like to work abroad/ in …	Ich würde gerne im Ausland /in/auf … arbeiten.

Übe mit deinem Partner/deiner Partnerin ein Vorstellungsgespräch ein.

2,21

Sounds and spelling

a) Manchmal werden zwei Wörter mit unterschiedlicher Schreibweise und Bedeutung genau gleich ausgesprochen. Hör die die Sätze an und sage, welches die korrekte Schreibung ist.

1. [rəʊd]	a. road	b. rode
2. [feə]	a. fair	b. fare
3. ['weðə]	a. whether	b. weather
4. [breɪk]	a. brake	b. break
5. [bɔ:d]	a. bored	b. board
6. [wi:k]	a. weak	b. week

b) Kannst du zwei Schreibweisen für jeden dieser Laute finden?

1. [si:] 2. [ðeə] 3. [nəʊ] 4. [mi:t] 5. [wʊd]

Dictionary

In dieser alphabetischen Liste ist das Vokabular von *Orange Line 1* bis *6* enthalten. Namen werden in einer gesonderten Liste am Ende des Vokabulars aufgelistet.
Das Zeichen ° bei einem Eintrag weist darauf hin, dass das Wort zum rezeptiven Wortschatz zählt.
Die mit * gekennzeichneten Verben sind unregelmäßig.
Wendungen, die aus mehreren Wörtern bestehen, werden meist unter mehreren Stichwörtern aufgeführt.
So ist z. B. *at home* unter *at* und *home* zu finden.
Die Fundstellen verweisen auf das erstmalige Vorkommen der Wörter, z. B.
absent ['æbsnt] abwesend **IV U2,** 27 kommt zum ersten Mal vor in Band IV, Unit 2, Seite 27.
colour ['kʌlə] Farbe **I LUA,** 24 kommt zum ersten Mal vor in Band I, Link-up A, Seite 24.
U = Unit, T = Topic, LU = Link-up, FA = Fakultativer Anhang (nur Namen)

A

a, an [ə; ən] ein/eine **I U1,** 10
a bit [ə 'bɪt] ein bisschen **I U2,** 35
a couple of [ə 'kʌpl‿əv] einige, ein paar **VI T1,** 12
a few [ə 'fju:] einige, ein paar **II U4,** 52
a lot [ə 'lɒt] viel **II U1,** 15
a lot of [ə 'lɒt‿əv] viel/viele, eine Menge **I U2,** 30
a week [ə 'wi:k] pro Woche, in der Woche **II U4,** 52
*to be **able to (do sth)** [bi:‿'eɪbl] fähig sein (zu), können; dürfen **V T2,** 40; **V T3,** 50
to **abolish** [ə'bɒlɪʃ] abschaffen, beseitigen **V T3,** 51
Aboriginal [ˌæbə'rɪdʒnl] eingeboren, einheimisch **VI T1,** 11
Aborigine [ˌæbə'rɪdʒni] Ureinwohner/Ureinwohnerin Australiens, Aborigine **V T1,** 10
about [ə'baʊt] über **I U3,** 40; ungefähr, circa, etwa **III U1,** 11
out and about ['aʊt‿nd‿ə'baʊt] unterwegs °**I U4,** 54
to jump about [ˌdʒʌmp‿ə'baʊt] herumspringen **III U4,** 68
What about ... ? [wɒt‿ə'baʊt] Was ist mit ...?; Wie wäre es mit ...? **I U2,** 30
What's the film about? [wɒts ðə 'fɪlm‿əˌbaʊt] Wovon handelt der Film? °**II U3,** 43
above [ə'bʌv] oben, über, oberhalb **II U5,** 70
abroad [ə'brɔ:d] im/ins Ausland **III U4,** 67
absence ['æbsns] Abwesenheit **IV U2,** 27
absent ['æbsnt] abwesend **IV U2,** 27
absolutely [ˌæbsə'lu:tli] absolut, völlig **III U5,** 88
abundance [ə'bʌndəns] Überfluss **VI T3,** 55
accent ['æksnt] Akzent **II U3,** 36
access ['ækses] Zugang **IV U4,** 69
accha ['ʌtʃʌ] Wirklich? °**VI T1,** 17
accident ['æksɪdnt] Unfall **II U3,** 41
acclaimed [ə'kleɪmd] bejubelt, gefeiert **V T1,** 19
accommodation [əˌkɒmə'deɪʃn] Unterbringung, Unterkunft **VI T3,** 60
according to [ə'kɔ:dɪŋ tə] laut, gemäß **VI T3,** 58
account [ə'kaʊnt] (Bank-)Konto; Bericht **V T4,** 73
acid ['æsɪd] sauer; Säure **VI T3,** 55
acid rain [ˌæsɪd 'reɪn] saurer Regen **VI T3,** 55
across [ə'krɒs] waagerecht *(im Kreuzworträtsel)* °**II U3,** 42; über, hinüber, quer durch/darüber **III U1,** 10; quer durch **IV U3,** 51; im Durchmesser **V T1,** 13
to **act** [ækt] spielen *(Theater)* **I U7,** 90
to act out [ækt‿'aʊt] vorspielen °**VI T4,** 79
action ['ækʃn] Handlung, Aktion **III U1,** 9
active ['æktɪv] aktiv **III U1,** 12
activity [æk'tɪvəti] Aktivität **IV U1,** 14
actor ['æktə] Schauspieler **I U7,** 96
actress ['æktrəs] Schauspielerin **III U2,** 29
actually ['æktʃuəli] eigentlich, tatsächlich **IV U3,** 50
ad [æd] Anzeige, Werbespot, Werbung °**V T1,** 15
to **adapt to** [ə'dæpt tə] (sich) anpassen an **VI T2,** 29
adaptable [ə'dæptəbl] anpassungsfähig **V T3,** 59
adapted [ə'dæptɪd] adaptiert, angepasst °**V T4,** 78
adaptor [ə'dæptə] Adapter **IV U3,** 46
to **add** [æd] hinzufügen, addieren **III U2,** 30
addiction [ə'dɪkʃn] Abhängigkeit, Sucht **VI T4,** 72
additional [ə'dɪʃnl] zusätzlich **VI T4,** 71
address [ə'dres] Adresse **I U5,** 70
adjective ['ædʒəktɪv] Adjektiv, Eigenschaftswort °**I U1,** 22
admission [əd'mɪʃn] Aufnahme, Zulassung, Eintritt **VI T1,** 10
adult ['ædʌlt] Erwachsener/Erwachsene **IV U2,** 27
advanced [əd'vɑ:nst] fortgeschritten **III U4,** 67
advantage [əd'vɑ:ntɪdʒ] Vorteil, Nutzen **V T4,** 75
adventure [əd'ventʃə] Abenteuer **II U6,** 80
adverb ['ædvɜ:b] Adverb °**II U7,** 90
adverb of manner [ˌædvɜ:b‿əv 'mænə] Adverb der Art und Weise °**II U7,** 90
advert ['ædvɜ:t] Anzeige, Werbespot **IV U2,** 26
advertising *(no pl.)* ['ædvətaɪzɪŋ] Werbung, Reklame; Werbe- °**V T1,** 19; °**V T3,** 48
advice [əd'vaɪs] Rat(schlag) **V T1,** 12; **V T3,** 58
careers advice [kə'rɪəz ədˌvaɪs] Berufsberatung **V T3,** 58
to **advise** [əd'vaɪz] raten **III U4,** 69
to **affect** [ə'fekt] beeinflussen, beeinträchtigen, betreffen **VI T4,** 72
I'm **afraid ...** [ˌaɪm‿ə'freɪd] leider, ich fürchte ... **V T4,** 78
to be afraid (of) [bi‿ə'freɪd‿əv] (sich) fürchten (vor), Angst haben (vor) **VI T1,** 19; **VI T2,** 36

English – German

African ['æfrɪkən] afrikanisch; Afrikaner/Afrikanerin **VI T1,** 13
after ['ɑ:ftə] nach **I LUB,** 39; nachdem **III U2,** 30
after dark [ˌɑ:ftə 'dɑ:k] nach Einbruch der Dunkelheit **V T1,** 12
afternoon [ˌɑ:ftə'nu:n] Nachmittag **I U2,** 34
afternoon tea [ˌɑ:ftənu:n 'ti:] Nachmittagstee **I U7,** 94
in the afternoon [ˌɪn ði: ˌɑ:ftə'nu:n] nachmittags, am Nachmittag **I U3,** 47
aftershave ['ɑ:ftəʃeɪv] Aftershave, Rasierwasser **III U3,** 52
again [ə'gen] wieder **I U3,** 48
against [ə'genst] gegen **III U1,** 9
age [eɪdʒ] Alter, Zeitalter **III U3,** 46
age of consent [ˌeɪdʒ‿əv kən'sent] das Alter, in dem man legal Sex haben darf **VI T4,** 70
legal age [ˌli:gl‿'eɪdʒ] gesetzliches Mindestalter **VI T4,** 70
Middle Ages [ˌmɪdl‿'eɪdʒɪz] Mittelalter **VI T2,** 28
of age [əv‿'eɪdʒ] im Alter von **III U4,** 67
agency ['eɪdʒnsi] Agentur, Behörde **IV U3,** 43
agent ['eɪdʒnt] Agent/Agentin, Vertreter/Vertreterin **IV U3,** 50
aggressive [ə'gresɪv] aggressiv **V T2,** 34
ago [ə'gəʊ] vor (*zeitlich*) **II U2,** 26
agony aunt ['ægəni ˌɑ:nt] Kummerkastentante **V T2,** 34
agony uncle ['ægəni ˌʌnkl] Kummerkastenonkel **V T2,** 34
to **agree** [ə'gri:] zustimmen, einer Meinung sein **III U5,** 88
to agree on [ə'gri:‿ɒn] sich einigen auf °**VI T1,** 13
agriculture ['ægrɪkʌltʃə] Agrikultur, Landwirtschaft **VI T4,** 71
air [eə] Luft **II U4,** 55
air traffic controller [ˌeə træfɪk kən'trəʊlə] Fluglotse/Fluglotsin **IV U3,** 51
on the air [ˌɒn ði‿'eə] auf Sendung **II U4,** 55
airborne ['eəbɔ:n] durch die Luft (schwebend), luftübertragen **VI T4,** 77
airport ['eəpɔ:t] Flughafen **II U7,** 89
alarm [ə'lɑ:m] Alarm **II U7,** 90
alarm clock [ə'lɑ:m ˌklɒk] Wecker **I U5,** 75
album ['ælbəm] Album **IV U5,** 77
alcohol ['ælkəhɒl] Alkohol **IV U2,** 27
A-levels *(pl)* ['eɪlevlz] brit. Abitur **III U4,** 67
alien ['eɪliən] Fremder/Fremde, Außerirdischer/Außerirdische **III U5,** 82; fremd, ausländisch **IV U3,** 50
alive [ə'laɪv] lebendig **III U4,** 70
all [ɔ:l] alle/alles; ganz **I U3,** 50
all inclusive [ˌɔ:l‿ɪŋ'klu:sɪv] alles inklusive **IV U4,** 62
all over [ˌɔ:l‿'əʊvə] überall **III U3,** 49
all right [ɔ:l 'raɪt] gut; in Ordnung, alles klar **IV U4,** 68
(not ...) at all [ˌnɒt ... ət‿'ɔ:l] überhaupt (nicht) **IV U2,** 32
in all [ɪn‿'ɔ:l] insgesamt, im Ganzen **III U4,** 63
allegiance [ə'li:dʒns] Treue **IV U2,** 25
to **allow** [ə'laʊ] erlauben, gestatten, zulassen **V T3,** 51
to be allowed to (do sth) [bi:‿ə'laʊd] dürfen **IV U4,** 67
almost ['ɔ:lməʊst] fast, beinahe **III U3,** 45
alone [ə'ləʊn] allein **III U3,** 47
to go it alone [ˌgəʊ‿ɪt‿ə'ləʊn] einen Alleingang starten, es allein schaffen **V T3,** 50
along [ə'lɒŋ] entlang **I U7,** 91
along with [ə'lɒŋ wɪð] zusammen mit, neben **VI T1,** 16
alphabet ['ælfəbet] Alphabet, Abc **I U1,** 15
alphabetical [ˌælfə'betɪkl] alphabetisch **I U6,** 88
already [ɔ:l'redi] schon **I U2,** 34
also ['ɔ:lsəʊ] auch **I U5,** 68
to **alter** ['ɔ:ltə] (sich) ändern, (ab)wandeln **VI T4,** 77
alternative [ɔ:l'tɜ:nətɪv] alternativ; Alternative **V T4,** 70
although [ɔ:l'ðəʊ] obwohl **III U3,** 52
always ['ɔ:lweɪz] immer, ständig **I U1,** 16
a.m. [ˌeɪ'em] vormittags (*Uhrzeit*) **III U3,** 49
amazed [ə'meɪzd] erstaunt, verblüfft **VI T1,** 14
ambassador [æm'bæsədə] Botschafter/ Botschafterin **III U4,** 62
ambitious [æm'bɪʃəs] ehrgeizig **VI T2,** 34
ambulance ['æmbjələnts] Krankenwagen **II U4,** 55
American [ə'merɪkən] amerikanisch; Amerikaner/Amerikanerin **II U4,** 50
American football [əˌmerɪkən 'fʊtbɔ:l] Football **III U1,** 8
Native American [ˌneɪtɪv‿ə'merɪkən] Ureinwohner/Ureinwohnerin Amerikas, Indianer/Indianerin **IV U1,** 9
South American [ˌsaʊθ‿ə'merɪkən] südamerikanisch; Südamerikaner/ Südamerikanerin **VI T2,** 29
among [ə'mʌŋ] unter (zwischen) **VI T1,** 16
amount [ə'maʊnt] Betrag, Menge, Summe **VI T3,** 52
to **analyse** ['ænlaɪz] analysieren °**VI T4,** 79
ancient ['eɪnʃnt] alt **III U1,** 16
and [ænd] und **I U1,** 11
angry ['æŋgri] verärgert, böse **II U1,** 18
to be angry with [bi 'æŋgri wɪð] böse sein auf **II U2,** 26
animal ['ænɪml] Tier **I U6,** 82
animation [ænɪ'meɪʃn] Animation, Zeichentrickfilm **VI T1,** 15
animé ['ænɪmeɪ] animierter Manga **VI T1,** 14
announcement [ə'naʊntsmənt] Ankündigung, Durchsage **III U3,** 52
annual ['ænjuəl] jährlich **VI T3,** 58
anorak ['ænəræk] Anorak **II U6,** 82
another [ə'nʌðə] noch ein/eine, ein anderer/eine andere/ein anderes **II U3,** 44
answer ['ɑ:nsə] Antwort **I U4,** 58
to **answer** ['ɑ:nsə] antworten, beantworten °**I LUA,** 24
answerphone ['ɑ:nsəfəʊn] Anrufbeantworter **III U4,** 69
anti ['æntɪ] gegen-, anti- **V T1,** 12; **V T2,** 38; **V T3,** 49
any ['enɪ] einige; etwas **II U4,** 54
any day ['enɪ deɪ] jeden Tag **IV U2,** 31
anybody ['eniˌbɒdi] jeder (beliebige) **III U5,** 83
anyone ['eniwʌn] jeder (beliebige) **III U5,** 83
anything ['eniθɪŋ] etwas, irgendetwas **I U5,** 66
anyway ['eniweɪ] jedenfalls, sowieso **IV U4,** 68
anywhere ['eniweə] überall, irgendwo **III U3,** 45
apartment *(AE)* [ə'pɑ:tmənt] Wohnung, Apartment **IV U1,** 16
to **appear** [ə'pɪə] auftauchen, erscheinen **VI T2,** 36
apple ['æpl] Apfel **I U1,** 14
applicant ['æplɪkənt] Bewerber/ Bewerberin; Antragsteller/ Antragstellerin **V T1,** 14
application [ˌæplɪ'keɪʃn] Bewerbung, Antrag; Anwendung **V T2,** 32
to **apply (for)** [ə'plaɪ] sich bewerben (um), sich anmelden (zu) **V T1,** 14; **V T2,** 41

to **appoint** [əˈpɔɪnt] ernennen, berufen, einsetzen **VI T2,** 32
apprentice [əˈprentɪs] Auszubildender/Auszubildende, Lehrling **VI T2,** 34
apprenticeship [əˈprentɪʃɪp] Lehre, Ausbildung **V T2,** 41
to **approve** [əˈpruːv] genehmigen, anerkennen, gutheißen **VI T2,** 33
April [ˈeɪprl] April **I U5,** 70
aquarium [əˈkweəriəm] Aquarium **V T4,** 78
Arabic [ˈærəbɪk] arabisch; Arabisch **VI T2,** 37
architect [ˈɑːkɪtekt] Architekt/Architektin **III U2,** 30
area [ˈeəriə] Gebiet; Fläche **II U7,** 94
rest area [ˈrest ˌeəriə] Rastplatz **IV U4,** 65
arena [əˈriːnə] Arena, Stadion **II U2,** 22
to **argue** [ˈɑːgjuː] streiten, argumentieren **III U2,** 34
argument [ˈɑːgjəmənt] Streit; Argument **III U4,** 62
to have an argument [ˌhæv‿ən‿ˈɑːgjəmənt] sich streiten **III U4,** 62
arm [ɑːm] Arm **II U3,** 40; Ärmel **IV U2,** 33
armed [ɑːmd] bewaffnet **VI T2,** 29
armed forces [ˌɑːmd ˈfɔːsɪz] Militär, Streitkräfte **VI T2,** 32
suit of **armour** [ˌsuːt‿əv ˈɑːmə] Rüstung **VI T2,** 28
arms *(pl)* [ɑːmz] Waffen **VI T2,** 26
around [əˈraʊnd] um … herum, umher **II U6,** 78; ungefähr, zirka, etwa **III U3,** 49
See you around! [ˌsiː jə əˈraʊnd] **IV U2,** 28
to hang around *(AE)* [ˌhæŋ‿əˈraʊnd] rumhängen, herumlungern **IV U2,** 32
to **arrange** [əˈreɪndʒ] arrangieren, anrichten, einordnen °**VI T4,** 79
to **arrest** [əˈrest] festnehmen, verhaften **III U5,** 90
to **arrive** [əˈraɪv] ankommen **I U6,** 86
arrow [ˈærəʊ] Pfeil **IV U4,** 62
Art [ɑːt] Kunst **II U1,** 10
article [ˈɑːtɪkl] Artikel **III U2,** 30
artist [ˈɑːtɪst] Künstler/Künstlerin **V T2,** 32
as [æz; əz] als, wie **II U4,** 52
as … as [æz … æz; əz … əz] so … wie … **II U4,** 52
as long as [əz ˈlɒŋ‿əz] solange **I U7,** 94
as soon as [əz ˈsuːn‿əz] sobald **III U4,** 66
as well [əz ˈwel] auch **VI T1,** 12
as well as [əz ˈwel‿əz] sowohl … als auch **III U4,** 67
as [æz; əz] da, weil **V T2,** 33; während **V T4,** 80
ash [æʃ] Asche **VI T4,** 78
ashes *(pl)* [ˈæʃɪz] Verbrennungsrückstände, Asche **VI T4,** 78
Asian [ˈeɪʃn] asiatisch; Asiate/Asiatin **VI T1,** 10
West Asian [ˌwest ˈeɪʃn] westasiatisch; Westasiate/-asiatin **VI T3,** 56
to **ask** [ɑːsk] fragen **I U3,** 44
to ask (for) [ˈɑːsk fə] fragen (nach), bitten (um) **I U4,** 60
*to be **asleep** [ˌbiː‿əˈsliːp] schlafen **II U7,** 94
to fall asleep [ˌfɔːl‿əˈsliːp] einschlafen **V T2,** 38
aspect [ˈæspekt] Aspekt, Gesichtspunkt, Seite **VI T3,** 57; **VI T4,** 72
ass *(AE)* [æs] Hintern, Arsch **IV U5,** 84
assassin [əˈsæsɪn] Mörder **I U1,** 10
assembly [əˈsembli] Versammlung, Morgenappell **II U1,** 10
to **assess** [əˈses] bewerten, beurteilen, einschätzen **VI T1,** 10
assessment [əˈsesmənt] Bewertung, Einschätzung **VI T4,** 75
damage assessment [ˌdæmɪdʒ əˈsesmənt] Schadensfeststellung, Schadensbemessung **VI T4,** 75
asset [ˈæset] Vorzug, Vorteil **VI T1,** 18
assistant [əˈsɪstnt] Assistent/Assistentin **VI T1,** 18
shop assistant [ˈʃɒp‿əˌsɪstnt] Verkäufer/Verkäuferin **II U5,** 67
to **assure** [əˈʃʊə] etw. zusichern, versichern, sicherstellen **V T4,** 80
astronaut [ˈæstrənɔːt] Astronaut/Astronautin **IV U3,** 42
at [æt; ət] in, auf, bei, an **I U1,** 10
at first [ət ˈfɜːst] zuerst, zunächst **II U6,** 80
at home [ət ˈhəʊm] zu Hause **I U2,** 26
at least [ət ˈliːst] wenigstens, mindestens **I U6,** 87
at night [ət ˈnaɪt] nachts **II U3,** 47
at once [ət ˈwʌnts] sofort, plötzlich **II U7,** 94
at the back [ət ðə ˈbæk] hinten, im hinteren Teil **III U1,** 8
at the bottom [ət ðə ˈbɒtəm] im unteren Teil **III U1,** 14
at the front [ət ðə ˈfrʌnt] im vorderen Teil, vorne **III U1,** 8
at the moment [æt ðə ˈməʊmənt] im Augenblick, momentan **I U7,** 90
at the top [ət ðə ˈtɒp] im oberen Teil **III U1,** 14
atmosphere [ˈætməsfɪə] Atmosphäre; Stimmung **V T4,** 74
to **attach** [əˈtætʃ] anbringen, anfügen, anhängen **IV U5,** 78
to **attack** [əˈtæk] angreifen **III U5,** 84
attempt [əˈtempt] Versuch; Anschlag **V T3,** 50
attention [əˈtentʃn] Aufmerksamkeit, Achtung **IV U5,** 77
Attention! [əˈtentʃn] Achtung! °**IV U2,** 31
attitude (to/towards) [ˈætɪtjuːd] Haltung, Einstellung (gegenüber) **V T4,** 73
to **attract** [əˈtrækt] anziehen **IV U4,** 69
attraction [əˈtrækʃn] Attraktion, Sehenswürdigkeit **III U3,** 49
attractive [əˈtræktɪv] attraktiv **IV U2,** 28
audience [ˈɔːdiəns] Publikum **III U4,** 63
audition [ɔːˈdɪʃn] Vorsprechen, Vorsingen, Vortanzen **II U5,** 64
August [ˈɔːgəst] August **I U5,** 70
aunt [ɑːnt] Tante **I U2,** 28
agony aunt [ˈægəni ˌɑːnt] Kummerkastentante **V T2,** 34
Aussie *(Aus)* [ˈɒzi] Australier/Australierin °**V T1,** 13
Australian [ɒsˈtreɪliən] australisch; Australier/Australierin **II U4,** 50
author [ˈɔːθə] Autor/Autorin **VI T3,** 57; **VI T4,** 72
authority [ɔːˈθɒrəti] Autorität; Behörde **VI T2,** 36
auto [ˈɔːtəʊ] Auto(-) °**VI T4,** 75
autograph [ˈɔːtəgrɑːf] Autogramm **I U7,** 96
automatically [ˌɔːtəˈmætɪkli] automatisch **V T3,** 57
automotive [ˌɔːtəˈməʊtɪv] Auto-, Fahrzeug- **VI T4,** 74
autumn [ˈɔːtəm] Herbst **I U6,** 79
average [ˈævrɪdʒ] durchschnittlich **III U5,** 80; Durchschnitt(s-) **VI T3,** 58
to **avoid** [əˈvɔɪd] (ver)meiden **VI T3,** 58
award [əˈwɔːd] Auszeichnung, Preis **IV U5,** 76
*to be **aware** of [ˌbi‿əˈweə] sich … bewusst sein **VI T3,** 54; **VI T3,** 59
away [əˈweɪ] weg **I U3,** 48
to run away [ˌrʌn‿əˈweɪ] wegrennen **I U3,** 48
awesome [ˈɔːsəm] toll **IV U2,** 28
awful [ˈɔːfl] schrecklich, furchtbar **IV U2,** 32

B

baby, babies *(pl)* ['beɪbi; 'beɪbiz] Baby, Säugling **I U6,** 82
back [bæk] Rücken **II U3,** 41
at the back [ət ðə 'bæk] hinten, im hinteren Teil **III U1,** 8
back [bæk] Hinter-, rückwärtig **II U4,** 56
back line [ˌbæk 'laɪn] Grundlinie **III U1,** 10
back seat ['bæk siːt] Rücksitz **VI T2,** 36
back [bæk] zurück **I U3,** 42
to get back (to) [get 'bæk tə] sich melden (bei) **IV U5,** 81
to sit back [ˌsɪt 'bæk] sich zurücklehnen **IV U1,** 16
background ['bækgraʊnd] Hintergrund **IV U1,** 8
backless ['bækləs] rückenfrei **IV U5,** 76
backpacker ['bækpækə] Rucksacktourist/Rucksacktouristin **VI T1,** 8
bacon ['beɪkn] Schinkenspeck **IV U1,** 12
bad [bæd] schlecht **I U5,** 74
bad language [bæd 'læŋgwɪdʒ] Schimpfwörter **VI T2,** 34
bad luck [ˌbæd 'lʌk] Pech **I U4,** 63
badminton ['bædmɪntən] Badminton, Federball **I U3,** 40
bag [bæg] Tasche, Tüte **I U1,** 14
mixed bag ['mɪkst bæg] Vermischtes °**III U1,** 21
school bag ['skuːl bæg] Schultasche, Schulranzen **I U1,** 14
sleeping bag ['sliːpɪŋ ˌbæg] Schlafsack **I U6,** 84
bagel ['beɪgl] Bagel **IV U1,** 12
baguette [bæg'et] Baguette **V T3,** 59
baker ['beɪkə] Bäcker/Bäckerin **III U2,** 32
balance ['bæləns] Gleichgewicht, Balance **V T4,** 74
bald [bɔːld] kahl **VI T4,** 76
ball [bɔːl] Ball **I U1,** 20; Knäuel **IV U1,** 10
balloon [bə'luːn] (Heiß-)Luftballon **V T3,** 50
ballroom ['bɔːlrʊm] Ballsaal **IV U2,** 25
ballroom dancing [ˌbɔːlrʊm 'dɑːntsɪŋ] Gesellschaftstanz **IV U2,** 25
balti ['bɔːlti] *trad. Currygericht in speziellem Gefäß* °**VI T1,** 17
ban [bæn] Verbot, Sperre; Bann **V T3,** 54
to **ban** [bæn] verbieten, ausschließen; (ver)bannen **V T3,** 54
banana [bə'nɑːnə] Banane **II U1,** 15
to go bananas [ˌgəʊ bə'nɑːnəz] verrückt werden, durchdrehen **II U5,** 66
band [bænd] Bande **IV U3,** 50; Band, Kapelle **IV U2,** 33
steel band [ˌstiːl 'bænd] Steelband *(Band, deren Instrumente aus leeren Ölfässern bestehen)* **III U4,** 64
to **bang** [bæŋ] fest klopfen **II U7,** 94
bank [bæŋk] Bank **IV U5,** 84
piggy bank ['pɪgi bæŋk] Sparschwein **II U2,** 23
bannerfish ['bænəfɪʃ] Wimpelfisch **V T4,** 79
bar [bɑː] Bar, Kneipe **IV U2,** 32; Tafel, Riegel, Stück; Stange **V T4,** 76
bistro bar [ˌbiːstrəʊ 'bɑː] Bistro **V T3,** 58
burger bar ['bɜːgə ˌbɑː] Fastfood-Restaurant **I U5,** 68
snack bar ['snæk bɑː] Café, Imbissstube °**IV U1,** 13
barbecue ['bɑːbɪkjuː] Grill(party) **V T1,** 11
to **bark** [bɑːk] bellen **I U3,** 48
barking ['bɑːkɪŋ] Bellen **III U5,** 88
barman, barmen *(pl)* ['bɑːmən, 'bɑːmen] Barmann, Barkeeper **IV U4,** 68
barn [bɑːn] Scheune **II U7,** 88
barn owl ['bɑːn‿aʊl] Schleiereule **II U7,** 94
baron ['bærn] Baron **VI T2,** 28
barrier ['bæriə] Barriere, Sperre, Grenze, Hürde **V T2,** 32; **V T3,** 57
base [beɪs] Base, Grundlinie **III U1,** 14; Station, Basis; Fuß **V T4,** 80
baseball ['beɪsbɔːl] Baseball **III U1,** 9
based [beɪst] ansässig **VI T4,** 74
basement ['beɪsmənt] Kellergeschoss, Untergeschoss **III U3,** 52
basic ['beɪsɪk] grundlegend, Grund-; einfach **VI T2,** 26
basketball ['bɑːskɪtbɔːl] Basketball **I U3,** 40
bass [beɪs] Bass **IV U5,** 80
bat [bæt] Schläger **III U1,** 8
to **bat** [bæt] schlagen **III U1,** 8
bathroom ['bɑːθrʊm] Bad, Badezimmer **I LUA,** 24
batter ['bætə] Schlagmann/Schlagfrau **III U1,** 9
battery ['bætri] Batterie, Akku **II U7,** 95
battle ['bætl] Schlacht, Kampf **IV U5,** 81
to **battle** ['bætl] kämpfen **IV U5,** 81
BC (= before Christ) [biː'siː] vor Christus **III U1,** 15
*to **be** [biː] sein **I U1,** 23
to be able to (do sth) [biː‿'eɪbl] fähig sein (zu), können; dürfen **V T2,** 40; **V T3,** 50
to be about to (do sth) [bi‿ə'baʊt tə] im Begriff sein, etw. zu tun **VI T2,** 29; **VI T4,** 78
to be afraid (of) [bi‿ə'freɪd‿əv] (sich) fürchten (vor), Angst haben (vor) **VI T1,** 19; **VI T2,** 36
to be allowed to (do sth) [biː‿ə'laʊd] dürfen **IV U4,** 67
to be all roses [ˌbiː‿ɔːl 'rəʊzɪz] nur Zuckerschlecken sein °**V T2,** 35
to be angry with [bi 'æŋgri wɪð] böse sein auf **II U2,** 26
to be asleep [ˌbiː‿ə'sliːp] schlafen **II U7,** 94
to be a turn-off ['tɜːnɒf] abtörnend sein, zum Abgewöhnen sein **V T2,** 32
to be aware of [ˌbi‿ə'weə] sich … bewusst sein **VI T3,** 54; **VI T3,** 59
to be cold [biː 'kəʊld] frieren **II U2,** 24
to be comprised of [bi‿kəm'praɪzd‿əv] bestehen aus, beinhalten **VI T4,** 77
to be connected with [kə'nektɪd] verbunden sein mit, in Verbindung stehen mit **V T2,** 33
to be due (to do) [biː 'djuː] im Begriff sein (zu tun) **VI T2,** 36
to be fed up [biː ˌfed‿'ʌp] die Nase voll haben **I U2,** 34
to be frightened (of) [biː 'fraɪtnd] Angst haben (vor) **II U6,** 83
to be fun [biː 'fʌn] Spaß machen **I U3,** 43
to be good with … [biː 'gʊd wɪð] gut mit … umgehen können **I U2,** 34
to be in a hurry [biː‿ɪn‿ə 'hʌri] es eilig haben **I U2,** 30
to be in remission [ˌbi‿ɪn rɪ'mɪʃn] auf dem Weg der Besserung sein **VI T4,** 77
to be into [biː‿'ɪntə] interessiert sein an **IV U1,** 16
to be involved in [biː ɪn'vɒlvd‿ɪn] beteiligt sein an, verwickelt sein in **V T2,** 33
to be lost [biː 'lɒst] sich verirrt haben **III U3,** 46
to be missing [biː 'mɪsɪŋ] fehlen **III U1,** 14
to be nuts about [biː ˌnʌts‿ə'baʊt] verrückt nach … sein **II U1,** 18
to be off [biː‿'ɒf] daneben sein **V T2,** 35
to be off to [biː‿'ɒf tə] auf dem Weg sein zu/nach, gehen zu/nach **V T3,** 50
to be on [biː‿'ɒn] an der Reihe sein; im Gange sein, laufen **II U5,** 70; brennen **II U7,** 94
to be pleased with [biː 'pliːzd wɪð] zufrieden sein mit **I U6,** 87

to be right [bi: 'raɪt] Recht haben **II U4,** 56
to be set (in) [bi 'set] spielen (in); seinen Schauplatz haben (in) °**VI T4,** 79
to be supposed to (do sth) [ˌbi sə'pəʊzd tə] (etw. tun) sollen **VI T3,** 59; **VI T4,** 72
to be trapped [bi: 'træpt] in der Falle sitzen **II U6,** 83
to be unlucky [ˌbi:‿ʌn'lʌki] Pech haben, unglücklich sein **V T3,** 53
to be upset [bi: ʌp'set] aufgeregt sein, bestürzt sein **II U3,** 44
to be worried [bi: 'wʌrid] besorgt sein, beunruhigt sein **I U6,** 87
to be worth *(+ gerund)* [bi: 'wɜ:θ] (es) wert sein (zu) **VI T2,** 36
to be wrong [bi: 'rɒŋ] Unrecht haben **III U3,** 53
beach [bi:tʃ] Strand **III U1,** 10
bean [bi:n] Bohne **II U4,** 54
jelly bean ['dʒeli bi:n] *engl. Süßigkeit* **V T1,** 10
runner bean ['rʌnə ˌbi:n] Stangenbohne **VI T4,** 78
bear [beə] Bär/Bärin **IV U4,** 69
beard [bɪəd] Bart **III U5,** 88
bearings *(pl)* ['beərɪŋz] Position, Kurs, Orientierung **V T4,** 79
*to **beat** [bi:t] besiegen, schlagen **IV U5,** 82
to beat sb up [ˌbi:t‿'ʌp] jmdn. zusammenschlagen, jmdn. verprügeln **V T2,** 34
beautiful ['bju:tɪfl] schön, wunderschön **I U6,** 78
because [bɪ'kɒz] weil **I U2,** 30
because of [bɪ'kɒz‿əv] wegen **V T3,** 55
*to **become** [bɪ'kʌm] werden **III U2,** 29
bed [bed] Bett **I LUA,** 25
bed of roses [bed‿əv 'rəʊzɪz] Zuckerschlecken **V T3,** 58
to get out of bed [ˌget‿aʊt‿əv 'bed] aufstehen **II U7,** 94
bedroom ['bedrʊm] Schlafzimmer **I LUA,** 24
beer [bɪə] Bier **V T2,** 38
before [bɪ'fɔ:] vor, bevor **I LUB,** 39
*to **begin** [bɪ'gɪn] beginnen, anfangen **II U3,** 47
beginning [bɪ'gɪnɪŋ] Anfang, Beginn **III U3,** 49
behaviour [bɪ'heɪvjə] Verhalten, Benehmen **VI T2,** 36
code of behaviour [ˌkəʊd‿əv bɪ'heɪvjə] Verhaltenskodex **VI T2,** 36
behind [bɪ'haɪnd] hinter **I U1,** 18
Belgian ['beldʒən] belgisch; Belgier/Belgierin **IV U1,** 10
to **believe** [bɪ'li:v] glauben **II U1,** 18
bell [bel] Glocke, Klingel **II U2,** 24
The bell rings. [ðə 'bel rɪŋz] Es klingelt. **II U4,** 50
to **belong (to)** [bɪ'lɒŋ] gehören (zu) **IV U2,** 27
below [bɪ'ləʊ] unterhalb, unten **III U3,** 48
bend [bend] Kurve, Biegung, Krümmung **V T3,** 56
beside [bɪ'saɪd] neben, außer **II U1,** 18
best [best] bester/beste/bestes **II U1,** 14; am besten **III U1,** 10
*to **bet** [bet] wetten **II U1,** 14
better ['betə] besser **II U4,** 50
you'd better [jʊd 'betə] du solltest lieber **III U4,** 70
between [bɪ'twi:n] zwischen **I U7,** 90
bhangra [ˌbæŋgrə] *Folkloremusik aus dem Punjab* °**VI T1,** 17
big [bɪg] groß **I U1,** 12
bike [baɪk] Fahrrad **I LUB,** 38
by bike [baɪ 'baɪk] mit dem Fahrrad **I U4,** 57
bilingual [baɪ'lɪŋgwəl] zweisprachig, bilingual **VI T1,** 11
bill [bɪl] Gesetz(entwurf) **VI T2,** 26
Bill of Rights [ˌbɪl‿əv 'raɪts] *Teil der amerikanischen Verfassung* **VI T2,** 26
billion ['bɪljən] Milliarde *(tausend Millionen)* **VI T3,** 53
bin [bɪn] Mülleimer, Mülltonne **III U3,** 46
bio [baɪəʊ] Bio- **V T4,** 75
biocard ['baɪəkɑ:d] Steckbrief °**V T1,** 13
biologist [baɪ'ɒlədʒɪst] Biologe/Biologin **VI T3,** 52
bird [bɜ:d] Vogel **II U4,** 59
birth [bɜ:θ] Geburt **III U1,** 11
birthday ['bɜ:θdeɪ] Geburtstag **I U5,** 68
biscuit ['bɪskɪt] Keks **I U5,** 68
bishop ['bɪʃəp] Bischof **VI T2,** 28
bistro bar [ˌbi:strəʊ 'bɑ:] Bistro **V T3,** 58
bit [bɪt] Stückchen; Auszug, Teil **V T4,** 80
a bit [ə 'bɪt] ein bisschen **I U2,** 35
*to **bite** [baɪt] beißen **V T1,** 12
bitter ['bɪtə] verbittert, bitter **VI T4,** 70
black [blæk] schwarz **I LUA,** 24
Black [blæk] Schwarzer/Schwarze **V T3,** 51
blackbird ['blækbɜ:d] Amsel **VI T3,** 55
blackout *(AE)* ['blækaʊt] Stromausfall **IV U3,** 44
to **blame** [bleɪm] verantwortlich machen, beschuldigen **VI T3,** 56
blanket ['blæŋkɪt] (Woll-)Decke **II U6,** 74
wet blanket [wet 'blæŋkɪt] Miesmacher/Miesmacherin **II U6,** 74
blind [blaɪnd] blind **III U3,** 52
blindfolded ['blaɪndfəʊldɪd] mit verbundenen Augen **VI T2,** 28
bling bling *(slang)* [ˌblɪŋ 'blɪŋ] Klunker **IV U5,** 80
block [blɒk] (Häuser-)Block **V T3,** 50
blog [blɒg] Blog, Internettagebuch **V T1,** 10
bloke [bləʊk] Typ, Kerl **I U7,** 96
blond [blɒnd] blond **II U2,** 28
blond(e)-haired ['blɒndˌheəd] blond **III U2,** 29
blood [blʌd] Blut **III U5,** 86
*to **blow** [bləʊ] blasen **III U1,** 12
to blow up [bləʊ‿'ʌp] aufblasen °**I U5,** 71
blue [blu:] blau **I LUA,** 24
blurred [blɜ:d] verschwommen, undeutlich **V T2,** 38
board [bɔ:d] Tafel, Wandtafel **I U1,** 18
notice board ['nəʊtɪs bɔ:d] schwarzes Brett **III U4,** 66
on board [ɒn 'bɔ:d] an Bord **IV U3,** 51
to **boast** [bəʊst] angeben, prahlen **V T2,** 34
boat [bəʊt] Boot, Schiff **III U2,** 32
body ['bɒdi] Körper **III U5,** 90
body shell ['bɒdi ˌʃel] Karosserie **VI T4,** 75
bomb [bɒm] Bombe **IV U3,** 43
stealth **bomber** ['stelθ ˌbɒmə] Tarnkappenbomber **VI T3,** 55
boogie ['bu:gi] Boogie *(Tanzstil)* °**IV U5,** 84
book [bʊk] Buch **I U1,** 14
exercise book ['eksəsaɪz ˌbʊk] Heft, Übungsheft **I U1,** 14
boot [bu:t] Stiefel **III U5,** 88
rubber boots *(pl)* [ˌrʌbə 'bu:ts] Gummistiefel **II U6,** 74
rugby boot ['rʌgbi bu:t] Rugbyschuh, Stollenschuh **III U1,** 8
border ['bɔ:də] Grenze **IV U4,** 68
bored [bɔ:d] gelangweilt **II U2,** 24
boring ['bɔ:rɪŋ] langweilig **I U1,** 20
natural-**born** [ˌnætʃrl'bɔ:n] gebürtig, von Geburt an **VI T2,** 33
was/were/is/are born [bɔ:n] wurde(n)/wird/werden geboren **III U1,** 11
borough ['bʌrə] Bezirk, Stadtteil **IV U1,** 9
to **borrow** ['bɒrəʊ] borgen, leihen **I U2,** 34
boss [bɒs] Boss, Chef/Chefin **III U1,** 12
both [bəʊθ] beide **III U3,** 52
both … and … ['bəʊθ … ænd] sowohl … als auch … **VI T1,** 12; **VI T4,** 72; **VI T4,** 75

to **bother** ['bɒðə] stören, belästigen **V T4,** 78
bottle ['bɒtl] Flasche **I U5,** 68
bottled ['bɒtld] in Flaschen abgefüllt **VI T3,** 53
bottom ['bɒtəm] Boden, Grund, unterer Teil **III U1,** 14
at the bottom [ət ðə 'bɒtəm] im unteren Teil **III U1,** 14
boulevard ['buːləvɑːd] Boulevard, Prachtstraße **IV U5,** 82
bow [bəʊ] Bogen **IV U4,** 62
long bow ['lɒŋ bəʊ] Langbogen **VI T2,** 28
bowl [bəʊl] Schüssel **II U4,** 50
box, boxes *(pl)* [bɒks; 'bɒksɪz] Kiste, Schachtel, Kasten **I U5,** 68
phone box ['fəʊn ˌbɒks] Telefonzelle **III U3,** 50
boy [bɔɪ] Junge **I U1,** 16
boyfriend ['bɔɪfrend] Freund *(in einer Paarbeziehung)* **III U4,** 63
bracket ['brækɪt] Klammer °**IV U5,** 79
brain(s) [breɪn(z)] Gehirn; Verstand **V T2,** 38
to **brainstorm** ['breɪnstɔːm] Ideen sammeln °**VI T3,** 61
brake [breɪk] Bremse **V T3,** 56
to **brake** [breɪk] (ab)bremsen **V T3,** 56
bramble ['bræmbl] Brombeergestrüpp **VI T4,** 77
branch [brɑːntʃ] Zweig, Ast; Zweigstelle; Teil **VI T2,** 33
brand [brænd] brand- **IV U2,** 25; Marke(n-) °**VI T4,** 75
brave [breɪv] tapfer, mutig **III U5,** 86
bread [bred] Brot **II U4,** 49
break [breɪk] Pause **II U1,** 12
*to **break** [breɪk] (zer)brechen, kaputtmachen **II U5,** 68
to break down [ˌbreɪk 'daʊn] einreißen, abbauen **V T2,** 32
to break out [ˌbreɪk‿'aʊt] ausbrechen **V T3,** 55
to **break-dance** ['breɪkdɑːnts] Breakdance tanzen **I LUB,** 38
breakdown ['breɪkdaʊn] Autopanne; Zusammenbruch **IV U4,** 65
breakfast ['brekfəst] Frühstück **I U3,** 44
breath [breθ] Atem, Atemzug °**III U5,** 86
to take a deep breath [ˌteɪk‿ə 'diːp ˌbreθ] tief Luft holen °**III U5,** 86
to **breathe** [briːð] atmen **V T4,** 74
breathtaking ['breθˌteɪkɪŋ] atemberaubend **V T1,** 19
bridge [brɪdʒ] Brücke **I LUC,** 52
brief [briːf] kurz °**VI T2,** 31

fire **brigade** ['faɪə brɪˌgeɪd] Feuerwehr **III U2,** 32
bright [braɪt] hell, leuchtend, strahlend **V T3,** 57; **V T4,** 72
brilliant ['brɪljənt] toll, prima; leuchtend **II U5,** 70
*to **bring** [brɪŋ] bringen, mitbringen **I U3,** 43
to bring in [brɪŋ‿'ɪn] hereinbringen, mitbringen °**I U7,** 93
to the **brink** [tə ðə 'brɪŋk] an den Rand, bis zur Oberkante **III U4,** 70
British ['brɪtɪʃ] britisch **III U1,** 15
bro [brəʊ] Bruderherz °**IV U2,** 32
broadband ['brɔːdbænd] Breitband(-) **V T1,** 16
broadcast ['brɔːdkɑːst] Sendung; Ausstrahlung **V T1,** 17
to **broadcast** ['brɔːdkɑːst] senden, ausstrahlen **V T1,** 17
brochure ['brəʊʃə] Broschüre, Prospekt °**IV U4,** 61
broke [brəʊk] pleite, abgebrannt **IV U5,** 84
broken ['brəʊkn] kaputt, zerbrochen, gebrochen **I U6,** 84
brother ['brʌðə] Bruder **I LUA,** 25
brown [braʊn] braun **I LUA,** 24
to **browse** [braʊz] durchsuchen, durchstöbern **VI T3,** 61
bruise [bruːz] Prellung, Quetschung; Bluterguss **VI T4,** 77
to **brush** [brʌʃ] putzen, bürsten **IV U3,** 48
brutality [bruː'tæləti] Brutalität **V T3,** 54
speech **bubble** ['spiːtʃ ˌbʌbl] Sprechblase °**III U3,** 47
bucket ['bʌkɪt] Eimer **VI T3,** 56
buddy *(infml)* ['bʌdi] Tauchbegleiter/ Tauchbegleiterin; Kumpel, Kamerad/ Kameradin **V T4,** 79
bug [bʌg] Käfer, Wanze; Bazillus **IV U3,** 50
*to **build** [bɪld] bauen **III U2,** 26
builder ['bɪldə] Baufachmann/ Baufachfrau, Baumeister/ Baumeisterin **VI T3,** 52
building ['bɪldɪŋ] Gebäude **III U2,** 26
light **bulb** ['laɪt bʌlb] Glühbirne **IV U3,** 46
bullet ['bʊlɪt] Geschoss, Kugel **VI T2,** 36
bullet-proof ['bʊlɪtpruːf] kugelsicher **VI T2,** 36
bully ['bʊli] jemand, der andere tyrannisiert **II U3,** 36
to **bully** ['bʊli] tyrannisieren **II U3,** 36
bullying ['bʊliɪŋ] Mobbing **VI T2,** 35
*to go **bump** [gəʊ 'bʌmp] rumsen °**II U7,** 94
burger ['bɜːgə] Hamburger **I U5,** 68

burger bar ['bɜːgə ˌbɑː] Fastfood-Restaurant **I U5,** 68
burglar ['bɜːglə] Einbrecher/ Einbrecherin **II U7,** 90
*to **burn** [bɜːn] (ver)brennen **III U2,** 32
to **bury** ['beri] begraben, beerdigen **III U5,** 86
bus, buses *(pl)* [bʌs; 'bʌsɪz] Bus **I LUC,** 52
bus stop ['bʌs ˌstɒp] Bushaltestelle **I LUC,** 52
on the bus [ˌɒn ðə 'bʌs] im Bus **II U1,** 18
bush [bʊʃ] Busch, Strauch **I U6,** 86
business ['bɪznɪs] Geschäft, Branche **IV U1,** 14
businessman, businessmen *(pl)* ['bɪznɪsmən; 'bɪznɪsmen] Geschäftsmann **III U2,** 28
busy ['bɪzi] beschäftigt, ausgefüllt **I U2,** 34; belebt **III U2,** 28
but [bʌt] aber **I U2,** 26; außer **IV U5,** 84
butter ['bʌtə] Butter **I U7,** 94
butterfly ['bʌtəflaɪ] Schmetterling **VI T3,** 55
button ['bʌtn] Auslöser; Knopf **II U7,** 95
*to **buy** [baɪ] kaufen **I U5,** 66
to **buzz** [bʌz] brummen, summen **V T3,** 57
by [baɪ] bis **II U6,** 78; von **IV U3,** 44; neben **VI T4,** 77
by bike [baɪ 'baɪk] mit dem Fahrrad **I U4,** 57
by far [baɪ 'fɑː] bei weitem **V T2,** 33
by the way [ˌbaɪ ðə 'weɪ] übrigens **IV U4,** 65
bye [baɪ] tschüss **I U1,** 16

C

cabbage ['kæbɪdʒ] Kohl, Kraut **VI T4,** 78
cabin ['kæbɪn] Hütte **IV U4,** 62
cabinet ['kæbɪnət] Kasten, Schrank; Kabinett **IV U5,** 78
cable car ['keɪbl ˌkɑː] Seilbahn **V T1,** 11
café ['kæfeɪ] Café **I U3,** 48
cafeteria [ˌkæfə'tɪəriə] Cafeteria **I U1,** 20
cage [keɪdʒ] Käfig **V T2,** 40
cake [keɪk] Kuchen **I U5,** 68
calendar ['kæləndə] Kalender **I U5,** 71
call [kɔːl] (An-)Ruf **V T2,** 36; **V T3,** 52; **V T4,** 78
call centre ['kɔːl ˌsentə] Call-Center **VI T1,** 11
phone call ['fəʊn ˌkɔːl] (Telefon-)Anruf **V T3,** 52
to **call** [kɔːl] rufen, anrufen, nennen **I U3,** 48

That's what I call .... [ˌðæts wɒt‿ˈaɪ ˌkɔ:l] Das nenne ich .... **II U1,** 14
called [kɔ:ld] genannt **III U5,** 86
caller [ˈkɔ:lə] Anrufer/Anruferin °**III U4,** 69
calm [kɑ:m] ruhig **II U6,** 80
camera [ˈkæmrə] Kamera, Fotoapparat **II U5,** 62
cameraman, cameramen *(pl)* [ˈkæmrəmæn; ˈkæmrəmen] Kameramann **V T2,** 41
camp [kæmp] Camp, Lager **IV U4,** 62
campaign [kæmˈpeɪn] Kampagne; Aktion **V T2,** 39
to **campaign** [kæmˈpeɪn] für etw./jmdn. werben, sich für etw./jmdn. einsetzen **VI T3,** 61
camper [ˈkæmpə] Camper/Camperin **IV U4,** 62
campfire [ˈkæmpfaɪə] Lagerfeuer **IV U4,** 62
camping [ˈkæmpɪŋ] Camping, Zelten **I U6,** 84
can [kæn] Dose **VI T4,** 78
*__can__ [kæn] können, dürfen **I U1,** 19
Canadian [kəˈneɪdiən] kanadisch; Kanadier/Kanadierin **VI T1,** 8
canal [kəˈnæl] Kanal **VI T3,** 55
candidate [ˈkændɪdət] Kandidat/Kandidatin, Bewerber/Bewerberin **VI T3,** 60
candy *(AE)* [ˈkændi] Süßigkeiten **IV U1,** 14
to **canoe** [kəˈnu:] Kanu fahren **III U3,** 46
Cantonese [ˌkɑntəˈni:z] kantonesisch; Kantonese/Kantonesin **VI T1,** 12
canyon [ˈkænjən] Schlucht, Canyon **IV U4,** 60
cap [kæp] Kappe, Mütze **I U5,** 66
capital [ˈkæpɪtl] Hauptstadt **V T1,** 11; Todes-, haupt-, größt-; Kapital- **V T3,** 51
capital crime [ˌkæpɪtl ˈkraɪm] Kapitalverbrechen **V T3,** 51
capital letter [ˌkæpɪtl ˈletə] Großbuchstabe °**II U3,** 37
capsule [ˈkæpsju:l] Kapsel **III U2,** 26
captain [ˈkæptɪn] Kapitän **IV U2,** 25
caption [ˈkæpʃn] Untertitel, Bildunterschrift **IV U2,** 26
car [kɑ:] Auto **I U3,** 49
cable car [ˈkeɪbl ˌkɑ:] Seilbahn **V T1,** 11
carbon [ˈkɑ:bn] Kohle(nstoff) **VI T3,** 52
carbon dioxide (CO_2) [ˌkɑ:bn daɪˈɒksaɪd; si:‿əʊ ˈtu:] Kohlendioxid **VI T3,** 52
carbon footprint [ˌkɑ:bn ˈfʊtprɪnt] CO_2-Bilanz **VI T3,** 52
card [kɑ:d] Karte **I LUB,** 38
get-well card [ˌget ˈwel ˌkɑ:d] Gute-Besserung-Karte **VI T4,** 77
wild card [ˈwaɪld ˌkɑ:d] Joker; Wildcard **VI T3,** 60
*to take **care** [teɪk ˈkeə] aufpassen, sich kümmern **IV U2,** 31
to **care** [keə] sich kümmern, sich interessieren, wichtig nehmen **III U4,** 70
I don't care. [ˌaɪ dəʊnt ˈkeə] Es ist mir egal. **II U4,** 58
career [kəˈrɪə] Beruf, Laufbahn, Karriere **V T3,** 58
careers advice [kəˈrɪəz ədˌvaɪs] Berufsberatung **V T3,** 58
careful [ˈkeəfl] vorsichtig; sorgfältig **II U6,** 80
caretaker [ˈkeəˌteɪkə] Hausmeister/Hausmeisterin **I U1,** 12
carpet [ˈkɑ:pɪt] Teppichboden **IV U5,** 77
carrot [ˈkærət] Karotte, Mohrrübe **II U1,** 15
to **carry** [ˈkæri] tragen **I U6,** 80; befördern **III U2,** 34
cartoon [kɑ:ˈtu:n] Cartoon, Zeichentrickfilm **III U5,** 80
cartoonist [kɑ:ˈtu:nɪst] Karikaturist/Karikaturistin, Cartoonzeichner/Cartoonzeichnerin °**V T4,** 75
pencil **case** [ˈpensl ˌkeɪs] Mäppchen **I U1,** 14
casino [kəˈsi:nəʊ] Casino **IV U4,** 61
castle [ˈkɑ:sl] Schloss, Burg **II U7,** 88
cat [kæt] Katze **I U2,** 26
catalogue [ˈkætlɒg] Katalog °**V T1,** 19
*to **catch** [kætʃ] fangen, erreichen **III U1,** 8; hören, aufschnappen **VI T1,** 16
catcher [ˈkætʃə] Fänger/Fängerin **III U1,** 14
catchy [ˈkætʃi] eingängig **III U5,** 80
category [ˈkætəgri] Kategorie **IV U5,** 77
catering [ˈkeɪtrɪŋ] Gastronomie, Verpflegung, Catering **V T3,** 58
cathedral [kəˈθi:drl] Kathedrale, Dom **III U2,** 28
cattle [ˈkætl] Rind, Rinder **V T1,** 16
cattle station [ˈkætl ˌsteɪʃn] Rinderfarm **V T1,** 16
to **cause** [kɔ:z] verursachen, hervorrufen **V T2,** 34; **V T4,** 74
caviar [ˈkæviɑ:] Kaviar **IV U5,** 84
CD [ˌsi:ˈdi:] CD **I U5,** 69
CD player [ˌsi:ˈdi: ˌpleɪə] CD-Player **II U4,** 56
cell [sell] Zelle **V T3,** 52
cell phone *(AE)* [ˈsel fəʊn] Mobiltelefon, Handy **IV U3,** 44
death watch cell [ˈdeθ ˌwɒtʃ sell] Todeszelle **V T3,** 52
Celsius (C) [ˈselsiəs] Celsius **II U6,** 78
cent [sent] Cent *(Währung)* **IV U1,** 13
centimetre [ˈsentɪˌmi:tə] Zentimeter **III U3,** 48
centre [ˈsentə] Zentrum, Mittelpunkt **I LUC,** 52
call centre [ˈkɔ:l ˌsentə] Call-Center **VI T1,** 11
dive centre [ˈdaɪv ˌsentə] Tauchzentrum **V T1,** 15
information centre [ɪnfəˈmeɪʃn ˌsentə] Informationszentrum **I LUC,** 52
century [ˈsentʃri] Jahrhundert **III U1,** 8
ceremony [ˈserɪməni] Zeremonie **IV U5,** 77
certain [ˈsɜ:tn] bestimmt, sicher **V T3,** 51
certainly [ˈsɜ:tnli] zweifellos, bestimmt, sicher **VI T1,** 12; **VI T2,** 28
certificate [səˈtɪfɪkət] Zertifikat, Bescheinigung, Urkunde, Zeugnis **V T1,** 15
chain [tʃeɪn] Kette **II U3,** 40
chair [tʃeə] Stuhl **I U1,** 18
chairperson [ˈtʃeəˌpɜ:sn] Vorsitzender/Vorsitzende °**V T3,** 53
to **challenge** [ˈtʃælɪndʒ] (heraus)fordern °**VI T1,** 17
chamber [ˈtʃeɪmbə] Kammer, Raum, (Amts-)Zimmer, Saal **V T4,** 81
champagne [ʃæmˈpeɪn] Champagner **IV U5,** 84
chance [tʃɑ:nts] Chance, Aussicht; Möglichkeit, Gelegenheit **V T2,** 32; **V T4,** 72
to take your chance [ˌteɪk jɔ: ˈtʃɑ:ns] etw. wagen, etw. riskieren **III U3,** 53
change [tʃeɪndʒ] Wechselgeld; Änderung **II U4,** 55
change of place [ˌtʃeɪndʒ‿əv ˈpleɪs] Ortswechsel °**III U4,** 65
to **change** [tʃeɪndʒ] (ver)ändern, tauschen, wechseln **II U3,** 42; umsteigen **III U2,** 28
to change your mind [ˌtʃeɪndʒ jə ˈmaɪnd] deine Meinung ändern **III U1,** 17
channel [ˈtʃænl] Kanal; Programm **III U3,** 45
chant [tʃɑ:nt] Sprechgesang **IV U2,** 31
to **chant** [tʃɑ:nt] rhythmisch rufen; singen **IV U2,** 25
chaos [ˈkeɪɒs] Chaos, Durcheinander **IV U4,** 65
chaotic [keɪˈɒtɪk] chaotisch **VI T1,** 19
chaperon [ˈʃæprəʊn] Begleitperson, Anstandswauwau **IV U5,** 84

character ['kærəktə] Charakter; Figur **V T3,** 50
characteristic [ˌkærəktə'rɪstɪk] typisches Merkmal, Charaktereigenschaft **V T3,** 50
charity ['tʃærɪti] Wohltätigkeit, Wohltätigkeitsverein **I U7,** 90
charred [tʃɑ:d] verkohlt, verschmort **VI T4,** 78
chart [tʃɑ:t] Schaubild, Diagramm °**II U4,** 51
flow chart ['fləʊ ˌtʃɑ:t] Ablauf-, Flussdiagramm °**VI T4,** 71
charter ['tʃɑ:tə] Charta, Satzung, Urkunde **VI T2,** 26
charts *(pl)* [tʃɑ:ts] Charts, Hitparade **III U5,** 82
chat [tʃæt] Geplauder, Unterhaltung **I U2,** 33
chat room ['tʃæt rʊm] Chatroom *(Internetforum, wo man sich online unterhalten kann)* **IV U5,** 80
to **chat** [tʃæt] sich unterhalten **I U2,** 33
cheap [tʃi:p] billig **I U5,** 68
to **check** [tʃek] überprüfen **I U6,** 82; untersuchen; kontrollieren **II U3,** 40
to check out [tʃek‿'aʊt] sich etwas ansehen **IV U5,** 80
cheeky ['tʃi:ki] frech, vorlaut **V T2,** 32
to **cheer up** [tʃɪer‿'ʌp] wieder guten Mutes sein **IV U2,** 32
cheerleader ['tʃɪəˌli:də] Cheerleader *(Mädchen, das in einer Gruppe eine Sportmannschaft anfeuert)* **IV U2,** 24
cheerleading ['tʃɪəˌli:dɪŋ] Cheerleading **IV U2,** 32
cheese [tʃi:z] Käse **I U5,** 68
cream cheese [ˌkri:m 'tʃi:z] Frischkäse **IV U1,** 12
chef [ʃef] Koch/Köchin, Küchenchef/-chefin **V T2,** 40; **V T3,** 58
cherry ['tʃeri] Kirsche **IV U1,** 12
chicken ['tʃɪkɪn] Huhn, Hähnchen **II U4,** 49
chief [tʃi:f] Vorsitzender/Vorsitzende; Häuptling **VI T2,** 33
chief executive officer (CEO) [ˌtʃi:f‿ɪgˌzekjətɪv‿'ɒfɪsə; ˌsi: i:'əʊ] Generaldirektor/Generaldirektorin; Geschäftsführer/Geschäftsführerin **VI T4,** 74
child, children *(pl)* [tʃaɪld; 'tʃɪldrɪn] Kind **I U2,** 26
only child ['əʊnli ˌtʃaɪld] Einzelkind **I U2,** 26
to **chill out** [tʃɪl‿'aʊt] sich entspannen, chillen **IV U5,** 80
Chinese [tʃaɪ'ni:z] chinesisch **II U4,** 49
chip *(AE)* [tʃɪp] Chip °**IV U4,** 67
chips *(pl)* [tʃɪps] Pommes frites **II U1,** 14
chocolate ['tʃɒklət] Schokolade **I U1,** 18
choice [tʃɔɪs] (Aus-)Wahl **III U4,** 70
multiple choice [ˌmʌltɪpl 'tʃɔɪs] Multiple-Choice *(Auswahl aus mehreren Möglichkeiten)* °**VI T1,** 13
to **choke** [tʃəʊk] ersticken **III U4,** 70
*to **choose** [tʃu:z] (aus)wählen **I U4,** 54
chorus ['kɔ:rəs] Refrain **IV U5,** 84
Christmas ['krɪsməs] Weihnachten **V T1,** 8
to **chuck sb** *(coll)* [tʃʌk] mit jmdm. Schluss machen **VI T4,** 76
chuddies *(pl) (slang)* ['tʃʌdiz] Hose **VI T1,** 16
church [tʃɜ:tʃ] Kirche **I LUC,** 52
chutney ['tʃʌtni] Chutney, fruchtige Soße °**VI T1,** 17
cigarette [ˌsɪgr'et] Zigarette **V T2,** 38
cinema ['sɪnəmə] Kino **II U1,** 18
circle ['sɜ:kl] Kreis **III U3,** 45
citizen ['sɪtɪzn] (Staats-)Bürger/Bürgerin **V T3,** 55
city ['sɪti] (Groß-)Stadt **II U7,** 89
City Council [ˌsɪti 'kaʊnsl] Stadtrat °**V T2,** 32
City & Guilds [ˌsɪti ənd 'gɪldz] Berufsqualifikation in England °**V T2,** 41
civil ['sɪvl] bürgerlich, zivil, Bürger-, Staats- **V T3,** 51
civil rights *(pl)* [ˌsɪvl 'raɪts] Bürgerrechte **V T3,** 51
Civil Rights Movement (CRM) [ˌsɪvl 'raɪts ˌmu:vmənt] Bürgerrechtsbewegung **V T3,** 54
to **claim** [kleɪm] beanspruchen, (ein)fordern; behaupten **V T1,** 10
to **clap** [klæp] klatschen **I U1,** 15
class [klɑ:s] (Schul-)Klasse **I U1,** 16; Kurs, Unterricht **II U1,** 18
classic ['klæsɪk] klassisch **V T4,** 77
classmate ['klɑ:smeɪt] Klassenkamerad/ Klassenkameradin, Mitschüler/ Mitschülerin **V T1,** 16
classroom ['klɑ:srʊm] Klassenzimmer **I U1,** 16
if-clause ['ɪfklɔ:z] if-Satz °**IV U4,** 62
to **clean** [kli:n] säubern, reinigen **II U3,** 40
cleaning station ['kli:nɪŋ ˌsteɪʃn] Putzerstation **V T4,** 79
clean [kli:n] sauber **III U3,** 46
cleaner ['kli:nə] Raumpfleger/ Raumpflegerin, Putzkraft **IV U4,** 67
clear [klɪə] klar **II U7,** 90
to **click** [klɪk] klicken **II U5,** 64
cliff [klɪf] Klippe **II U7,** 93
climate ['klaɪmət] Klima **V T4,** 70
to **climb** ['klaɪm] klettern, steigen, besteigen **II U2,** 30
clock [klɒk] Uhr **I U4,** 54
alarm clock [ə'lɑ:m ˌklɒk] Wecker **I U5,** 75
o'clock [ə'klɒk] Uhr *(Zeitangabe)* **I U3,** 40
to **close** [kləʊz] schließen, zumachen **I LUC,** 53
close [kləʊs] nahe **III U5,** 90
That was a close one. [ˌðæt wəz‿ə 'kləʊz‿wʌn] Das war knapp. **IV U4,** 68
closed [kləʊzd] zu, geschlossen **IV U3,** 47
closing ['kləʊzɪŋ] (Ab-)Schluss, Schließung **V T1,** 14
clothes *(pl)* [kləʊθs] Kleider, Kleidung **II U2,** 23
clothing ['kləʊðɪŋ] Kleidung **VI T2,** 34; **VI T3,** 59
cloud [klaʊd] Wolke **II U7,** 94
cloudy ['klaʊdi] wolkig **II U6,** 78
club [klʌb] Klub, Verein, Arbeitsgemeinschaft **I LUB,** 39
clue [klu:] Hinweis **II U1,** 13
to have no clue [ˌhæv nəʊ 'klu:] keine Ahnung haben **IV U5,** 84
clump [klʌmp] Klumpen, Haufen **VI T4,** 77
clumsy ['klʌmzi] ungeschickt, tollpatschig **IV U2,** 33
Hey, clumsy! ['klʌmzi] He, du Tollpatsch! **IV U2,** 33
cluster ['klʌstə] Cluster °**IV U2,** 25
coach [kəʊtʃ] Trainer/Trainerin **VI T1,** 10
coaching ['kəʊtʃɪŋ] Training, Nachhilfe **VI T1,** 10
coal [kəʊl] Kohle **V T4,** 74
coast [kəʊst] Küste **II U7,** 88
coastline ['kəʊstlaɪn] Küstenlinie **III U3,** 44
coat [kəʊt] Mantel **II U7,** 90
cockatoo [ˌkɒkə'tu:] Kakadu **V T1,** 19
cocktail ['kɒkteɪl] Cocktail; Gemisch, Mischung **V T2,** 38
cocoa ['kəʊkəʊ] Kakao **V T4,** 71
code [kəʊd] Verschlüsselung, Code **IV U3,** 48
code of behaviour [ˌkəʊd‿əv bɪ'heɪvjə] Verhaltenskodex **VI T2,** 36
coffee ['kɒfi:] Kaffee **IV U1,** 12
coke [kəʊk] Cola **II U4,** 49
cold [kəʊld] kalt **I U4,** 62
to be cold [bi: 'kəʊld] frieren **II U2,** 24
collage [kɒl'ɑ:ʒ] Collage °**IV U5,** 85

colleague ['kɒli:g] Kollege/Kollegin **VI T1,** 18; **VI T2,** 34; **VI T4,** 75
to **collect** [kə'lekt] sammeln **I LUB,** 38; abholen **II U5,** 71
college ['kɒlɪdʒ] College; Institut **III U4,** 67
colony ['kɒləni] Kolonie **V T1,** 10
colored *(AE)* ['kʌləd] bunt, farbig; Farbiger/Farbige **V T3,** 54
colour ['kʌlə] Farbe **I LUA,** 24
coloured ['kʌləd] bunt, farbig **V T4,** 72
colourful ['kʌləfl] bunt, farbig **III U5,** 80
coma ['kəʊmə] Koma **V T2,** 38
to go into a coma ['kəʊmə] ins Koma fallen **V T2,** 38
to **combine** [kəm'baɪn] kombinieren, verbinden **V T2,** 37
*to **come** [kʌm] kommen **I U2,** 33
Come on. [kʌm‿'ɒn] Komm./Kommt. **I U2,** 35
to come down [kʌm 'daʊn] herunterkommen, sich legen **III U1,** 16
to come in [kʌm‿'ɪn] hereinkommen **I U3,** 48
to come over [kʌm‿'əʊvə] herüberkommen **I U2,** 27
to come true [kʌm 'tru:] wahr werden **III U2,** 30
to come up [kʌm‿'ʌp] aufgehen *(Sonne)*, hochkommen; erwähnt werden **V T4,** 78
to come up behind sb [ˌkʌm‿ʌp bɪ'haɪnd] sich jmdm. von hinten nähern **VI T2,** 34
comedy ['kɒmədi] Komödie **III U5,** 80
comfortable ['kʌmpftəbl] komfortabel, bequem **IV U4,** 65
comic ['kɒmɪk] Comic(heft) **I LUB,** 38
comic strip ['kɒmɪk strɪp] Bildgeschichte, Comicstrip °**VI T2,** 31
comment ['kɒment] Kommentar, Bemerkung **VI T2,** 34; **VI T4,** 73
common ['kɒmən] gemeinsam, gebräuchlich, verbreitet **VI T1,** 10; **VI T2,** 29
common law [ˌkɒmən 'lɔ:] Gewohnheitsrecht **VI T2,** 31
Commonwealth ['kɒmənwelθ] Commonwealth **VI T1,** 13
to **communicate** [kə'mju:nɪkeɪt] kommunizieren, sich verständigen **VI T1,** 19; **VI T3,** 61; **VI T4,** 72; **VI T4,** 75
communication [kəˌmju:nɪ'keɪʃn] Kommunikation, Verständigung **V T4,** 70
communications officer [kəmju:nɪ'keɪʃnz ˌɒfɪsə] Pressesprecher/Pressesprecherin **VI T3,** 61
community [kə'mju:nəti] Gemeinde, Gemeinschaft **V T2,** 32; **V T4,** 76
company ['kʌmpəni] Gesellschaft, Firma; Kompanie **III U2,** 34
comparative [kəm'pærətɪv] Komparativ **II U4,** 50
to **compare** [kəm'peə] vergleichen **III U4,** 67
competition [ˌkɒmpə'tɪʃn] Wettbewerb, Turnier **III U1,** 9
to **complete** [kəm'pli:t] vervollständigen **III U2,** 30; ausfüllen, erledigen, fertigstellen **V T2,** 32
completely [kəm'pli:tli] vollständig, völlig, ganz **V T3,** 53
complex ['kɒmpleks] kompliziert, komplex **IV U5,** 78
comprehensive school [kɒmprɪ'hensɪv ˌsku:l] Gesamtschule **III U4,** 66
*to be **comprised of** [bi‿kəm'praɪzd‿əv] bestehen aus, beinhalten **VI T4,** 77
compulsory [kəm'pʌlsri] obligatorisch, zwingend **III U4,** 67
computer [ˌkəm'pju:tə] Computer **I LUA,** 25
to **concentrate** ['kɒntsntreɪt] (sich) konzentrieren **VI T4,** 73
concert ['kɒnsət] Konzert **II U2,** 23
conclusion [kən'klu:ʒn] Schluss(folgerung) °**VI T4,** 73
condition [kən'dɪʃn] Kondition; Bedingung **V T4,** 76
terms and conditions [ˌtɜ:mz‿ənd kən'dɪʃnz] Allgemeine Geschäftsbedingungen (AGB) **V T4,** 76
to **conduct** ['kɒndʌkt] (durch)führen; dirigieren °**VI T1,** 15
conference ['kɒnfrns] Konferenz °**V T4,** 73
confident ['kɒnfɪdnt] selbstsicher, selbstbewusst; überzeugt **V T2,** 33
confused [kən'fju:zd] verwirrt, konfus, verlegen **V T3,** 56
to **connect** [kə'nekt] verbinden, anschließen **VI T3,** 61
to be connected with [kə'nektɪd] verbunden sein mit, in Verbindung stehen mit **V T2,** 33
connection [kə'nekʃn] Verbindung, Beziehung; Anschluss °**V T3,** 51
conqueror ['kɒŋkrə] Eroberer °**III U2,** 31
conscientious [ˌkɒntʃi'entʃəs] gewissenhaft **VI T1,** 18
consent [kən'sent] Zustimmung, Einwilligung **VI T4,** 70
age of consent [ˌeɪdʒ‿əv kən'sent] das Alter, in dem man legal Sex haben darf **VI T4,** 70
conservation [ˌkɒnsə'veɪʃn] Bewahrung, Konservierung, Naturschutz **VI T3,** 61
to **consider** [kən'sɪdə] betrachten, erwägen, bedenken °**V T3,** 53
constitution [ˌkɒnstɪ'tju:ʃn] Verfassung, Grundgesetz; Konstitution **VI T2,** 26
to **construct** [kən'strʌkt] bauen, konstruieren **III U2,** 30
construction [kən'strʌkʃn] Konstruktion, Aufbau **VI T4,** 75
consultant [kən'sʌltnt] Berater/Beraterin **VI T1,** 19
contact ['kɒntækt] Kontakt, Verbindung °**V T1,** 14
to **contact** ['kɒntækt] kontaktieren, sich in Verbindung setzen mit **IV U2,** 27
to **contain** [kən'teɪn] enthalten °**IV U5,** 82
content ['kɒntent] Inhalt **III U4,** 63
context ['kɒntekst] Kontext, Zusammenhang **IV U5,** 82
continent ['kɒntɪnənt] Kontinent, Erdteil **V T1,** 10
sub-continent [sʌb'kɒntɪnənt] Subkontinent **VI T1,** 10
to **continue** [kən'tɪnju:] fortfahren, andauern, weitergehen, weitermachen **V T2,** 38; **V T3,** 50
contract ['kɒntrækt] Vertrag, Abkommen **V T1,** 15
contrast ['kɒntrɑ:st] Kontrast, Gegensatz **III U5,** 80
in contrast to [ɪn 'kɒntrɑ:st tə] im Gegensatz zu **III U5,** 80
to **contrast** [kən'trɑ:st] kontrastieren, gegenüberstellen °**V T3,** 57
control [kən'trəʊl] Kontrolle **IV U3,** 43
remote control [rɪˌməʊt kən'trəʊl] Fernbedienung, Fernsteuerung **IV U3,** 43
to **control** [kən'trəʊl] kontrollieren, beherrschen **IV U3,** 42
air traffic **controller** [ˌeə træfɪk kən'trəʊlə] Fluglotse/Fluglotsin **IV U3,** 51
conversation [ˌkɒnvə'seɪʃn] Unterhaltung, Gespräch, Konversation **VI T1,** 16; **VI T2,** 34
to **convert** ['kɒnvɜ:t] konvertieren, (um)wandeln **VI T2,** 36
convict ['kɒnvɪkt] Sträfling, Gefangener/Gefangene **V T1,** 10
to **convince** [kən'vɪnts] überzeugen °**III U5,** 81
cook [kʊk] Koch/Köchin **III U5,** 82

English – German

to **cook** [kʊk] kochen **IV U3,** 44
cooking ['kʊkɪŋ] Kochen, Koch- **I U3,** 40
cool [ku:l] cool, prima **I U1,** 20; kühl **IV U1,** 16
co-operative [kəʊ'ɒprətɪv] Kooperative **V T4,** 76; Genossenschaft **VI T3,** 61
cop *(AE)* [kɒp] Polizist/Polizistin **IV U1,** 17
to **cope** [kəʊp] zurechtkommen **V T3,** 59
copy ['kɒpi] Kopie, Abschrift **VI T2,** 31
to **copy** ['kɒpi] abschreiben, kopieren **II U5,** 63; abzeichnen, abmalen **VI T1,** 14
coral ['kɒrəl] Koralle; Korallen- **V T4,** 72
cord *(AE)* [kɔ:d] Kabel, Kordel; Schnur **IV U3,** 46
corner ['kɔ:nə] Ecke **V T3,** 56; **V T4,** 81
cornflakes ['kɔ:nfleɪks] Cornflakes **I U5,** 68
Cornish ['kɔ:nɪʃ] kornisch; aus Cornwall **III U3,** 48
to **correct** [kə'rekt] korrigieren, verbessern °**I LUB,** 38
correct [kə'rekt] richtig, korrekt **II U1,** 10
correction [kə'rekʃn] Korrektur °**IV U2,** 30
corridor ['kɒrɪdɔ:] Gang, Flur, Korridor **I U7,** 96
cost [kɒst] Preis, Kosten **IV U4,** 62
cottage ['kɒtɪdʒ] kleines Landhaus, Ferienhaus **III U4,** 64
couch [kaʊtʃ] Couch, Sofa **III U1,** 12
couch potato ['kaʊtʃ pəˌteɪtəʊ] Stubenhocker **III U1,** 12
*__could__ [kʊd] konnte/konnten **II U4,** 52; könnte/könnten **III U1,** 12
City **Council** [ˌsɪti 'kaʊnsl] Stadtrat °**V T2,** 32
counselor ['kaʊnsələ] Berater/Beraterin, Betreuer/Betreuerin **IV U4,** 63
to **count (for sth)** [kaʊnt] zählen, etw. gelten **VI T2,** 37
countdown ['kaʊntdaʊn] Countdown **III U5,** 82
country ['kʌntri] Countrymusik **IV U5,** 77
country, countries *(pl)* ['kʌntri; 'kʌntriz] Land **I U2,** 29
in the country [ˌɪn ðə 'kʌntri] auf dem Land **I U6,** 78
to the country [tʊ ðə 'kʌntri] aufs Land **III U2,** 32
couple ['kʌpl] Paar **IV U3,** 50
a couple of [ə 'kʌpl‿əv] einige, ein paar **VI T1,** 12
courier ['kʊriə] Kurier **III U2,** 34
course [kɔ:s] Gang *(Menü)* **II U4,** 49; Kurs **IV U4,** 62
of course [əv 'kɔ:s] natürlich, selbstverständlich **I U1,** 19
court [kɔ:t] Spielfeld **III U1,** 10; Hof, Gericht(shof) **VI T2,** 26
cousin ['kʌzn] Cousin/Cousine **I U2,** 28
cover ['kʌvə] Einband, Titelseite **II U5,** 64
cow [kaʊ] Kuh **I U6,** 82
cowboy ['kaʊbɔɪ] Rinderhirte, Cowboy **IV U4,** 61
at the **crack of dawn** [ˌkræk‿əv 'dɔ:n] im Morgengrauen **III U2,** 34
to **crackle** ['krækl] knistern, knacken, prasseln **VI T4,** 78
crash [kræʃ] Unfall, Aufprall; Absturz **V T3,** 57; **V T4,** 79
to **crash into** [kræʃ] aufschlagen gegen, gegen etw. krachen **V T3,** 57
to **crawl** [krɔ:l] kriechen, krabbeln, schleichen **III U3,** 53
crazy ['kreɪzi] verrückt **I U7,** 96
to drive crazy [draɪv 'kreɪzi] verrückt machen **II U5,** 71
to **creak** [kri:k] knarren, quietschen **II U7,** 94
cream [kri:m] Creme, Sahne **IV U1,** 12
cream cheese [ˌkri:m 'tʃi:z] Frischkäse **IV U1,** 12
ice-cream [aɪs'kri:m] Eis, Eiscreme **I U7,** 92
to **create** [kri'eɪt] (er)schaffen **VI T1,** 10; **VI T3,** 52
creative [kri'eɪtɪv] kreativ **VI T1,** 18; **VI T4,** 71
creature ['kri:tʃə] Kreatur, Geschöpf, Lebewesen **V T1,** 10; **V T3,** 59; **V T4,** 74; **V T4,** 78
crew [kru:] Crew, Besatzung, Mannschaft **IV U3,** 51
cricket ['krɪkɪt] Kricket **I U7,** 92
crime [kraɪm] Verbrechen; Kriminalität **III U5,** 84
capital crime [ˌkæpɪtl 'kraɪm] Kapitalverbrechen **V T3,** 51
criminal ['krɪmɪnl] Krimineller/Kriminelle, Verbrecher/Verbrecherin; kriminell **V T4,** 73
criminal responsibility [ˌkrɪmɪnl rɪsˌpɒnsə'bɪləti] Schuldfähigkeit **VI T4,** 70
crisp [krɪsp] Kartoffelchip **I U1,** 18
to **crisp up** [krɪsp‿'ʌp] aufbacken; aufflackern **VI T4,** 77
critic ['krɪtɪk] Kritiker/Kritikerin **VI T1,** 11
to **criticise** ['krɪtɪsaɪz] kritisieren **V T1,** 10; **V T3,** 51
crocodile ['krɒkədaɪl] Krokodil **V T1,** 12
crop [krɒp] Feldfrucht; Ernte **VI T3,** 56
to **cross** [krɒs] überqueren, kreuzen **IV U4,** 68
crossword (puzzle) ['krɒswɜ:d 'pʌzl] Kreuzworträtsel °**I U5,** 71
crowd [kraʊd] Menschenmenge **III U1,** 17
crown [kraʊn] Krone **III U2,** 26
cruise [kru:z] Kreuzfahrt **III U3,** 45
cry [kraɪ] Schrei **III U5,** 86
to **cry** [kraɪ] weinen; schreien, rufen **II U3,** 36
crystal ['krɪstl] Kristall; kristall- **V T1,** 19
cultural ['kʌltʃrl] kulturell **VI T1,** 16
culture ['kʌltʃə] Kultur, Bildung **V T2,** 32
cup [kʌp] Tasse, Kelch; Pokal **III U1,** 15
cupboard ['kʌbəd] Küchenschrank, Schrank **I U1,** 18
cupcake ['kʌpkeɪk] rundes Küchlein **IV U1,** 12
to **curl** [kɜ:l] (sich) kräuseln, einrollen **VI T4,** 77
curly ['kɜ:li] lockig; Lockenkopf **VI T1,** 19
current ['kʌrnt] Strömung; Strom **V T4,** 79
up current ['ʌp ˌkʌrnt] gegen die Strömung **V T4,** 79
curriculum [kə'rɪkjələm] Lehrplan, Stundenplan **IV U2,** 24
curriculum vitae (CV) [kə'rɪkjələm 'vi:taɪ] Lebenslauf **V T1,** 15
curry ['kʌri] Curry *(Gewürz oder Gericht)* **II U4,** 49
curtain ['kɜ:tn] Vorhang **IV U3,** 46
curve [kɜ:v] Kurve **III U4,** 70
customer ['kʌstəmə] Kunde/Kundin **III U2,** 34
customs *(pl)* ['kʌstəmz] Zoll **II U7,** 90
power **cut** ['paʊə ˌkʌt] Stromausfall **VI T2,** 37
*to **cut (off)** [kʌt‿'ɒf] (ab)schneiden **IV U3,** 44
cute [kju:t] niedlich, süß **V T1,** 11
to **cycle** ['saɪkl] Rad fahren **III U1,** 12
cyclone ['saɪkləʊn] Zyklon, Wirbelsturm **VI T3,** 56

D

dad [dæd] Papa, Vati **I LUA,** 25
daily ['deɪli] täglich **III U5,** 80
dairy ['deəri] Molkerei **III U2,** 34
damage ['dæmɪdʒ] Schaden, Beschädigung **VI T4,** 75
damage assessment [ˌdæmɪdʒ ə'sesmənt] Schadensfeststellung, Schadensbemessung **VI T4,** 75

to **damage** ['dæmɪdʒ] beschädigen **III U2,** 32
damn [dæm] verdammt **IV U5,** 84
damp [dæmp] feucht **VI T4,** 76
dance [dɑ:nts] Tanz **III U1,** 13
dance floor ['dɑ:nts flɔ:] Tanzfläche **IV U2,** 33
to **dance** [dɑ:nts] tanzen **I U3,** 40
dancehall ['dɑ:ntshɔ:l] Dancehall *(Musikrichtung)* **IV U5,** 77
dancing ['dɑ:ntsɪŋ] Tanzen **IV U2,** 25
ballroom dancing [ˌbɔ:lrʊm 'dɑ:ntsɪŋ] Gesellschaftstanz **IV U2,** 25
danger ['deɪndʒə] Gefahr **V T1,** 12; **V T4,** 78
dangerous ['deɪndʒrəs] gefährlich **II U4,** 56
Danish ['deɪnɪʃ] dänisch; Plundergebäck **IV U1,** 12
to **dare** [deə] wagen, riskieren **IV U2,** 31
dark [dɑ:k] Dunkelheit **III U5,** 88
after dark [ˌɑ:ftə 'dɑ:k] nach Einbruch der Dunkelheit **V T1,** 12
dark [dɑ:k] dunkel **I U2,** 34
date [deɪt] Datum **I U5,** 70; Verabredung **IV U2,** 28
to **date** [deɪt] sich verabreden **IV U2,** 26
daughter ['dɔ:tə] Tochter **IV U5,** 84
dawn [dɔ:n] Morgendämmerung, Tagesanbruch **V T4,** 78
at the crack of dawn [ˌkræk‿əv 'dɔ:n] im Morgengrauen **III U2,** 34
day [deɪ] Tag **I LUB,** 39
any day ['enɪ deɪ] jeden Tag **IV U2,** 31
Have a nice day. [ˌhæv‿ə naɪs 'deɪ] Einen schönen Tag (noch). **II U4,** 55
one day [wʌn 'deɪ] eines Tages **II U3,** 36
sports day ['spɔ:ts deɪ] Sportfest **I U7,** 90
these days ['ði:z deɪz] heutzutage **VI T1,** 12
to have a day off [ˌhæv‿ə 'deɪ‿ɒf] einen Tag frei haben **V T3,** 58
*to **daydream** ['deɪdri:m] tagträumen **VI T4,** 70
dead [ded] tot **III U5,** 86; leer **IV U3,** 47
deadly ['dedli] tödlich, tod- **V T1,** 12
deal [di:l] Handel; Abmachung, Übereinkunft **V T4,** 76
dealer ['di:lə] Händler/Händlerin **VI T4,** 74
dear [dɪə] Schatz *(Anrede)* **III U4,** 70
dear [dɪə] lieb **I U3,** 44
Dear [dɪə] Lieber ..., Liebe ... *(Anrede in Briefen)* **II U3,** 36

death [deθ] Tod, Todesfall **V T1,** 10; **V T3,** 50
death row [ˌdeθ 'rəʊ] Todestrakt **V T3,** 52
death watch cell ['deθ ˌwɒtʃ sell] Todeszelle **V T3,** 52
debate [dɪ'beɪt] Debatte °**VI T2,** 37; °**VI T3,** 53
decade ['dekeɪd] Jahrzehnt **V T1,** 16
December [dɪ'sembə] Dezember **I U5,** 70
to **decide** [dɪ'saɪd] entscheiden **II U5,** 64
decision [dɪ'sɪʒn] Entscheidung **VI T4,** 68
to **declare** [dɪ'kleə] erklären, verkünden **VI T2,** 32
decompression [ˌdi:kəm'preʃn] Dekompression, Druckverminderung **V T4,** 79
decoration [ˌdek'reɪʃn] Dekoration **IV U1,** 14
deep [di:p] tief; dunkel *(Farbe)* **V T4,** 74; **V T4,** 78
to **define** [dɪ'faɪn] definieren °**III U3,** 48
definitely ['defɪnətli] definitiv, bestimmt **IV U2,** 32
definition [ˌdefɪ'nɪʃn] Definition **II U1,** 20
to **defuse** [ˌdi:'fju:z] entschärfen **IV U3,** 43
degree (°) [dɪ'gri:] Grad **II U6,** 78
delayed [dɪ'leɪd] verspätet, verzögert **IV U4,** 65
to **delete** [dɪ'li:t] löschen *(Text)* **II U5,** 63
deli *(AE)* ['deli] Imbissstube, Deli **IV U1,** 12
delirious [dɪ'lɪriəs] im Delirium; außer sich, irre **VI T1,** 15
to **deliver** [dɪ'lɪvə] liefern **III U2,** 34
to **demand** [dɪ'mɑ:nd] fordern, verlangen **VI T2,** 30
democracy [dɪ'mɒkrəsi] Demokratie **VI T2,** 26
democratic [ˌdemə'krætɪk] demokratisch °**VI T2,** 38
demonstration [ˌdemən'streɪʃn] Darstellung, Demonstration °**V T1,** 15; °**V T4,** 75
dentist ['dentɪst] Zahnarzt/Zahnärztin **IV U3,** 50
department [dɪ'pɑ:tmənt] Abteilung, Branche **VI T1,** 18; **VI T2,** 34; **VI T4,** 74
department store [dɪ'pɑ:tmənt stɔ:] Kaufhaus **I LUC,** 52
departure [dɪ'pɑ:tʃə] Abflug, Abreise **II U7,** 90
depressed [dɪ'prest] deprimiert, bedrückt **VI T4,** 73
deputy ['depjəti] stellvertretend; Stellvertreter/Stellvertreterin **VI T1,** 9
to **describe** [dɪ'skraɪb] beschreiben **IV U3,** 51

description [dɪ'skrɪpʃn] Beschreibung °**III U1,** 15
desert ['dezət] Wüste **VI T3,** 56
to **deserve** [dɪ'zɜ:v] verdienen **IV U5,** 84
desi ['desɪ] *richtig asiatisch* °**VI T1,** 17
design [dɪ'zaɪn] Design, Gestaltung **V T2,** 40
to **design** [dɪ'zaɪn] entwerfen; zeichnen **III U2,** 30
designer [dɪ'zaɪnə] Designer/Designerin **IV U5,** 76
interior designer [ɪnˌtɪəriə dɪ'zaɪnə] Innenarchitekt **V T2,** 40
desire [dɪ'zaɪə] Wunsch, Lust, Verlangen **VI T4,** 72; **VI T4,** 77
desk [desk] Schreibtisch **I U1,** 18; Schalter **II U7,** 90
desperate ['desprət] verzweifelt, hoffnungslos **V T2,** 34
dessert [dɪ'zɜ:t] Dessert, Nachtisch **II U4,** 49
to **destroy** [dɪ'strɔɪ] zerstören **III U2,** 32
detail ['di:teɪl] Detail, Einzelheit °**V T1,** 14
detective [dɪ'tektɪv] Detektiv/Detektivin **II U2,** 30
detective story [dɪ'tektɪv ˌstɔ:ri] Krimi **III U5,** 80
store detective ['stɔ: dɪˌtektɪv] Kaufhausdetektiv/Kaufhausdetektivin **II U2,** 30
to **determine** [dɪ'tɜ:mɪn] bestimmen, entschließen **VI T4,** 72
to **develop** [dɪ'veləp] (sich) entwickeln **V T1,** 12
development [dɪ'veləpmənt] Entwicklung **VI T4,** 74
diabetes [ˌdaɪə'bi:ti:z] Diabetes, Zuckerkrankheit **VI T3,** 54
diabetic [ˌdaɪə'betɪk] zuckerkrank; Diabetiker/Diabetikerin **VI T4,** 78
diagram ['daɪəgræm] Diagramm °**III U1,** 14
pie diagram ['paɪ ˌdaɪəgræm] Kuchen-, Tortendiagramm °**VI T3,** 59
dialogue ['daɪəlɒg] Dialog, Gespräch **III U2,** 33
diamond ['daɪəmənd] Diamant **III U5,** 82
diary ['daɪəri] Tagebuch; Terminkalender **III U4,** 64
to keep a diary [ˌki:p‿ə 'daɪəri] ein Tagebuch/einen Terminkalender führen **VI T4,** 77
dictionary ['dɪkʃnri] Wörterbuch **VI T1,** 16
to **die** [daɪ] sterben **III U2,** 31
diet [daɪət] Diät **II U4,** 52
to go on a diet [ˌgəʊ‿ɒn‿ə 'daɪət] eine Diät machen **II U4,** 52

difference ['dɪfrnts] Unterschied **IV U2,** 24
different ['dɪfrnt] anders, verschieden **I U6,** 78
difficult ['dɪfɪklt] schwierig **II U1,** 13
*to **dig** [dɪg] graben, buddeln **VI T4,** 78
to dig up [dɪg‿'ʌp] ausgraben **III U1,** 16
digital ['dɪdʒɪtl] digital **II U5,** 62
dime [daɪm] Zehncentstück *(Währung)* **IV U1,** 13
dimension [ˌdaɪ'menʃn] Dimension **VI T4,** 75
diner *(AE)* ['daɪnə] Imbissstube **IV U4,** 61
dingo ['dɪŋgəʊ] Dingo *(austral. Wildhund)* **V T1,** 10
dining room ['daɪnɪŋ rʊm] Esszimmer, Speisesaal **I LUA,** 24
dinner ['dɪnə] Abendessen, Mittagessen **IV U4,** 65
dinosaur ['daɪnəsɔ:] Dinosaurier **V T4,** 74
carbon **dioxide** (CO_2) [ˌkɑ:bn daɪ'ɒksaɪd; si:‿əʊ 'tu:] Kohlendioxid **VI T3,** 52
diploma [dɪ'pləʊmə] Diplom, Abschlusszeugnis **V T3,** 58
direct [dɪ'rekt] direkt **III U4,** 63
direction [dɪ'rekʃn] Richtung **VI T3,** 58
director [dɪ'rektə] Direktor/Direktorin, Regisseur/Regisseurin **III U5,** 87
dirty ['dɜ:ti] schmutzig **II U1,** 10
disability [ˌdɪsə'bɪləti] Behinderung; Unfähigkeit **V T1,** 14
disabled [dɪ'seɪbld] behindert **VI T1,** 18
disadvantage [ˌdɪsəd'vɑ:ntɪdʒ] Nachteil **V T4,** 75
to **disagree** [ˌdɪsə'gri:] anderer Meinung sein, nicht einverstanden sein °**V T2,** 39
to **disappear** [ˌdɪsə'pɪə] verschwinden **II U6,** 83
disappointed [ˌdɪsə'pɔɪntɪd] enttäuscht **III U4,** 62
disappointing [ˌdɪsə'pɔɪntɪŋ] enttäuschend **VI T4,** 76
disaster [dɪ'zɑ:stə] Desaster, Katastrophe **III U4,** 64
disco ['dɪskəʊ] Disko **I U5,** 74
to **discover** [dɪ'skʌvə] entdecken **IV U3,** 50
discrimination [dɪˌskrɪmɪ'neɪʃn] Diskriminierung; Unterscheidung **V T3,** 49
to **discuss** [dɪ'skʌs] diskutieren, etw. besprechen **V T2,** 40; **V T4,** 75
discussion [dɪ'skʌʃn] Diskussion, Besprechung **V T1,** 16
disease [dɪ'zi:z] Krankheit, Erkrankung **VI T1,** 13; **VI T3,** 54
dislikes *(pl)* [dɪ'slaɪks] Abneigungen °**V T2,** 41
display [dɪ'spleɪ] Ausstellung, Schaukasten, Anzeige °**V T1,** 13; °**V T1,** 19; °**V T2,** 39
to **display** [dɪ'spleɪ] ausstellen, (an)zeigen °**V T1,** 13; °**V T1,** 19; °**V T4,** 77
disrespect [ˌdɪsrɪ'spekt] Respektlosigkeit, Verachtung **IV U5,** 80
to **diss** *(slang)* [dɪs] beleidigen; schneiden **IV U5,** 80
to **dissolve** [dɪ'zɒlv] (sich) auflösen **VI T2,** 32
distance ['dɪstnts] Distanz, Entfernung, Abstand **IV U3,** 51
to **distribute** [dɪ'strɪbju:t] verteilen, austeilen °**VI T2,** 35
dive [daɪv] Tauch-; Tauchgang **V T4,** 80
dive centre ['daɪv ˌsentə] Tauchzentrum **V T1,** 15
to **dive** [daɪv] tauchen **III U3,** 47
diver ['daɪvə] Taucher/Taucherin **V T1,** 9; **V T4,** 79
divine [dɪ'vaɪn] göttlich °**V T4,** 76
diving ['daɪvɪŋ] Tauch-, Tauchen **V T1,** 15; **V T4,** 79
divorced from [dɪ'vɔ:st frəm] geschieden von **I U2,** 28
dizzy ['dɪzi] schwindlig **IV U1,** 16
DJ [ˌdi:'dʒeɪ] DJ **I U2,** 33
*to **do** [du:] machen, tun **I U1,** 15
to do sports [du: 'spɔ:ts] Sport treiben **I U7,** 92
doctor ['dɒktə] Arzt/Ärztin **II U3,** 40
to see a doctor [si:‿ə 'dɒktə] zum Arzt gehen **II U4,** 52
docu soap ['dɒkju ˌsəʊp] Dokusoap **III U5,** 80
documentary [ˌdɒkjə'mentri] Dokumentarfilm **III U5,** 80
dog [dɒg] Hund **I U2,** 27
dog-tired [ˌdɒg'taɪəd] hundemüde **I U3,** 49
to walk the dog [wɔ:k ðə 'dɒg] mit dem Hund spazieren gehen **I U3,** 42
doll [dɒl] Puppe °**IV U3,** 49
dollar ['dɒlə] Dollar *(Währung)* **IV U1,** 12
domino ['dɒmɪnəʊ] Dominospiel °**II U2,** 26
door [dɔ:] Tür **I U1,** 18
next door [ˌnekst 'dɔ:] nebenan **III U1,** 16
doorbell ['dɔ:bel] Türklingel **II U5,** 66
doorstep ['dɔ:step] Türstufe **III U1,** 16
dope *(slang)* [dəʊp] toll °**IV U5,** 84
dot [dɒt] Punkt, Pünktchen **V T4,** 80
double ['dʌbl] Doppelgänger, das Doppelte **I U7,** 97
doubleclick ['dʌblklɪk] Doppelklick **VI T1,** 16
down [daʊn] (nach) unten, herunter, hinunter, nieder **II U2,** 30; senkrecht *(im Kreuzworträtsel)* °**II U3,** 42
Down Under [ˌdaʊn‿'ʌndə] Down Under *(Spitzname für Australien)*; in Australien **V T1,** 10
Go down .... ['gəʊ daʊn] Geh ... entlang. **I LUC,** 53
to come down [kʌm 'daʊn] herunterkommen, sich legen **III U1,** 16
to go down [gəʊ 'daʊn] hinuntergehen, entlanggehen **II U2,** 30
to lie down [laɪ 'daʊn] (sich) hinlegen, niederlegen **III U3,** 52
to sit down [sɪt 'daʊn] sich (hin)setzen **I U1,** 19
to **download** [ˌdaʊn'ləʊd] herunterladen **II U5,** 63
downstairs [ˌdaʊn'steəz] unten, im unteren Stock **I U2,** 27; (die Treppe) hinunter/herunter **III U5,** 85
to **drag** [dræg] ziehen, schleppen **VI T4,** 77
dragon ['drægn] Drache **IV U1,** 14
drama ['drɑ:mə] Theater, Drama **I U3,** 40
dramatic [drə'mætɪk] dramatisch **III U5,** 80
to **drape** [dreɪp] drapieren, behängen **VI T4,** 76
It's a **draw.** [ˌɪts‿ə 'drɔ:] Es steht unentschieden. **III U1,** 12
*to **draw** [drɔ:] zeichnen **I LUB,** 38
to draw up [drɔ:‿'ʌp] aufsetzen, anfertigen, ausarbeiten **VI T2,** 30
drawing ['drɔ:ɪŋ] Bild, Zeichnung **VI T1,** 15
dream [dri:m] Traum **I LUA,** 25
dress [dres] **IV U2,** 25
evening dress ['i:vnɪŋ ˌdres] Abendkleid **IV U5,** 76
to **dress** [dres] sich anziehen **I U3,** 44
to **drift** [drɪft] wehen, treiben **VI T4,** 77
drill [drɪl] Bohrer, Bohrmaschine **IV U1,** 17
drink [drɪŋk] Getränk **I U7,** 95
soft drink ['sɒft ˌdrɪŋk] alkoholfreies Getränk **VI T3,** 53
*to **drink** [drɪŋk] trinken **I U5,** 75
to **drip** [drɪp] tropfen (lassen), tröpfeln **IV U3,** 47
*to **drive** [draɪv] fahren **I U6,** 86
to drive crazy [draɪv 'kreɪzi] verrückt machen **II U5,** 71

driving licence *(BE)* ['draɪvɪŋ ˌlaɪsnts] Führerschein **V T1,** 15
driver ['draɪvə] Fahrer/Fahrerin **I U4,** 54
driver's license *(AE)* ['draɪvəz ˌlaɪsnts] Führerschein **IV U4,** 68
drop [drɒp] Tropfen **V T1,** 13
to **drop** [drɒp] fallen, fallen lassen **II U1,** 18; sinken *(beim Tauchen)* **V T4,** 79
to drop out [ˌdrɒp‿'aʊt] die Schule abbrechen, aussteigen **V T3,** 52
drug [drʌg] Droge; Medikament *(im Amerikanischen)* **IV U2,** 27
drug trafficking [ˌdrʌg 'træfɪkɪŋ] Drogenhandel **V T3,** 51
drummer ['drʌmə] Schlagzeuger/ Schlagzeugerin **IV U5,** 80
drums *(pl)* [drʌmz] Schlagzeug **I U2,** 26
to **dry** [draɪ] trocknen **IV U3,** 44
dry [draɪ] trocken **VI T3,** 56
duck-billed platypus [ˌdʌkbɪld 'plætɪpəs] Schnabeltier **V T1,** 10
*to be **due (to do)** [bi: 'dju:] im Begriff sein (zu tun) **VI T2,** 36
due to ['dju: ˌtʊ/tə] wegen **V T4,** 72
dummy *(AE)* ['dʌmi] Idiot **V T3,** 56
dump [dʌmp] Dreckloch, Müllkippe **II U7,** 88
to **dump** [dʌmp] abladen, auskippen, verklappen **V T4,** 73
to dump sb [dʌmp] mit jmdm. Schluss machen, jmdm. den Laufpass geben **VI T4,** 76
during *(+ noun)* ['djʊərɪŋ] während *(+ Nomen)* **III U1,** 8
dust [dʌst] Staub **V T1,** 10
Dutch [dʌtʃ] niederländisch; Niederländerin/Niederländerinnen **IV U1,** 10
duty ['dju:ti] Pflicht, Aufgabe **V T1,** 11
DVD [di:vi:'di:] DVD **II U5,** 62
DVD player [ˌdi:vi:'di: 'pleɪə] DVD-Player **II U5,** 62
to **dye** [daɪ] färben **II U2,** 28

E

each [i:tʃ] jeder/jede/jedes **III U1,** 8; je, jeweils **III U4,** 63
each other [ˌi:tʃ‿'ʌðə] sich gegenseitig **II U1,** 19
ear [ɪə] Ohr **II U3,** 40
early ['ɜ:li] früh **I U3,** 46
to **earn** [ɜ:n] verdienen **V T1,** 15; **V T3,** 58
earth [ɜ:θ] Erde **IV U3,** 42
east [i:st] Osten **I U4,** 54; nach Osten **VI T2,** 36
easy ['i:zi] einfach, leicht **I U1,** 20
*to **eat** [i:t] essen, fressen **I U3,** 44
eating ['i:tɪŋ] Essen **VI T3,** 54
to **echo** ['ekəʊ] widerhallen **III U5,** 90
eco ['i:kəʊ] Öko-, Umwelt- **V T4,** 72
ecstasy ['ekstəsi] Ecstasy **V T2,** 38
edge [edʒ] Rand, Kante **IV U5,** 82
to **edit** ['edɪt] bearbeiten **IV U2,** 26
editor ['edɪtə] Herausgeber/ Herausgeberin; Redakteur/ Redakteurin; Lektor/Lektorin **V T3,** 53
education [edʒʊ'keɪʃn] Erziehung, Bildung **II U1,** 10
Physical Education (PE) [ˌfɪzɪkl‿edʒʊ'keɪʃn] Sport *(Schulfach)* **II U1,** 10
Religious Education (RE) [rɪˌlɪdʒəs‿edʒʊ'keɪʃn] Religionsunterricht **II U1,** 12
effect [ɪ'fekt] Effekt; (Aus-)Wirkung **V T2,** 38
e.g. [i:'dʒi:] zum Beispiel **VI T1,** 10; **VI T2,** 26
egg [eg] Ei **I U5,** 68
either ... or ... ['aɪðə; 'i:ðə ... ɔ:] entweder ... oder ... **V T2,** 35
either way [ˌaɪðə 'weɪ] auf die eine oder andere Art, so oder so **VI T4,** 76
not ... either [ˌnɒt ... 'aɪðə] auch nicht **III U1,** 17
not either [nɒt 'aɪðə] keiner/keine/ keines **VI T2,** 28
elbow ['elbəʊ] Ellbogen **II U3,** 41
to **elect** [ɪ'lekt] (aus)wählen **VI T2,** 32
election [ɪ'lekʃn] Wahl **VI T2,** 26; **VI T4,** 70
general election [ˌdʒenrl‿ɪ'lekʃn] landesweite Wahl **VI T2,** 32
electric [ɪ'lektrɪk] elektrisch **IV U1,** 17
electrical [ɪ'lektrɪkl] elektrisch **IV U3,** 44
electricity [ˌelɪk'trɪsəti] Elektrizität, Strom **IV U3,** 44
electronics *(pl)* [ˌelek'trɒnɪks] Elektronik **V T2,** 41
element ['elɪmənt] Element °**VI T4,** 79
elementary school *(AE)* [elɪ'mentri ˌsku:l] Grundschule **IV U2,** 30
elephant ['elɪfənt] Elefant **I U7,** 96
else [els] sonst, noch **I U5,** 66
someone else [ˌsʌmwʌn‿'els] jemand anderes °**III U1,** 13
e-mail ['i:meɪl] E-Mail **I U3,** 44
to **e-mail** ['i:meɪl] mailen, per E-Mail schicken **V T2,** 32; E-Mail schreiben **IV U5,** 80
embarrassed [ɪm'bærəst] verlegen **IV U2,** 32
embarrassing [ɪm'bærəsɪŋ] peinlich **II U2,** 26
embers *(pl)* ['embəz] Glut, glimmende Asche **VI T4,** 77
emergency [ɪ'mɜ:dʒnsi] Notfall, Notlage **III U5,** 82
to **emigrate** ['emɪgreɪt] emigrieren, auswandern **IV U1,** 10
emission [ɪ'mɪʃn] Ausstoß, Emission **VI T3,** 52
to **emit** [ɪ'mɪt] austoßen, absondern **VI T3,** 53
to **employ sb** [ɪm'plɔɪ] jmdn. anstellen, jmdn. beschäftigen **VI T4,** 75
employee [ɪm'plɔɪi:] Angestellter/ Angestellte, Mitarbeiter/Mitarbeiterin **V T3,** 58
employer [ɪm'plɔɪə] Arbeitgeber/ Arbeitgeberin **V T3,** 58
employment [ɪm'plɔɪmənt] Beschäftigung, Anstellung **VI T4,** 70
self-employment [ˌselfɪm'plɔɪmənt] Selbstständigkeit **VI T4,** 71
empty ['empti] leer **II U1,** 18
to **encourage** [ɪn'kʌrɪdʒ] ermutigen, unterstützen **V T1,** 14; **V T4,** 73
end [end] Ende, Schluss **II U6,** 84
in the end [ɪn ði:‿'end] schließlich, zum Schluss **II U6,** 80
to **end** [end] enden **I U5,** 76; beenden, abschließen **IV U2,** 28
to end in ['end‿ɪn] enden auf °**II U7,** 90
to end up [ˌend‿'ʌp] enden, landen **IV U4,** 68
ending ['endɪŋ] Ende, Schluss *(einer Geschichte)* °**II U1,** 19
enemy ['enəmi] Feind/Feindin **II U3,** 43
energy ['enədʒi] Energie; Kraft **V T4,** 70
engine ['endʒɪn] Maschine, Motor **III U3,** 56
search engine ['sɜ:tʃ ˌendʒɪn] Suchmaschine °**IV U4,** 61
engineer [ˌendʒɪ'nɪə] Ingenieur/ Ingenieurin, Techniker/Technikerin **VI T3,** 52
mechatronic engineer [mɪkæˌtrɒnɪk endʒɪ'nɪə] Mechatroniker/ Mechatronikerin **V T2,** 41
engineering [ˌendʒɪ'nɪərɪŋ] Maschinenbau, Technik **VI T3,** 61
English ['ɪŋglɪʃ] englisch **I U1,** 11; Engländer/Engländerinnen **IV U1,** 10
Englishman, Englishmen *(pl)* ['ɪŋglɪʃmən, 'ɪŋglɪʃmen] Engländer **VI T2,** 28
to **enjoy** [ɪn'dʒɔɪ] sich erfreuen, genießen **II U6,** 80
enormous [ɪ'nɔ:məs] enorm, riesig **III U5,** 90

English – German

enough [ɪ'nʌf] genug, genügend **III U1,** 12
to **enter** ['entə] sich beteiligen an; eintreten, betreten **III U2,** 30
enterprising ['entəpraɪzɪŋ] geschäftstüchtig, unternehmungslustig **V T3,** 50
to **entertain** [ˌentə'teɪn] unterhalten **IV U5,** 81
entrance ['entrənts] Eingang; Eintritt **IV U4,** 68
entry ['entri] Eintrag °**III U2,** 35
envelope ['envələʊp] Briefumschlag, Umschlag **II U7,** 90
environment [ɪn'vaɪərnmənt] Umwelt, Umgebung **II U6,** 74
environmental [ɪnˌvaɪərn'mentl] Umwelt-, die Umwelt betreffend, umweltbedingt **V T1,** 14; **V T4,** 72
equal ['iːkwəl] gleich(wertig), Gleich- **V T3,** 54
equipment [ɪ'kwɪpmənt] Ausrüstung, Ausstattung **IV U3,** 42
er [ɜː] äh °**I U1,** 12
to **erase** [ɪ'reɪz] löschen, ausradieren **IV U3,** 50
erm [ɜːm] äh °**II U3,** 38
to **escape (from)** [ɪ'skeɪp] flüchten (vor), entkommen **II U6,** 78
especially [ɪ'speʃli] besonders, vor allem **V T3,** 52
essential [ɪ'sentʃl] essenziell, entscheidend, unverzichtbar **VI T4,** 75
etc. [ɪt'setrə] usw., et cetera **II U1,** 10
ethical ['eθɪkl] ethisch, moralisch **VI T3,** 59
eucalyptus [ˌjuːk'lɪptəs] Eukalyptus **V T1,** 10
euro ['jʊərəʊ] Euro *(Währung)* **I U5,** 73
European [ˌjʊərə'piːən] europäisch **III U3,** 55
to **evaporate** [ɪ'væpreɪt] verdampfen, verdunsten **VI T3,** 56
even ['iːvn] selbst, sogar **I U7,** 90
even though [ˌiːvn‿'ðəʊ] auch wenn; obwohl **VI T1,** 12
not even [nɒt‿'iːvn] nicht einmal **III U4,** 64
evening ['iːvnɪŋ] Abend **I U3,** 47
evening dress ['iːvnɪŋ ˌdres] Abendkleid **IV U5,** 76
in the evening [ˌɪn ðiː 'iːvnɪŋ] abends, am Abend **I U3,** 47
that evening [ˌdæt‿'iːvnɪŋ] an diesem Abend **II U1,** 19
this evening [ðɪs 'iːvnɪŋ] heute Abend **III U3,** 52
event [ɪ'vent] Veranstaltung, Ereignis **I U7,** 90
eventually [ɪ'ventʃuəli] schließlich, endlich **VI T2,** 36
ever ['evə] jemals **II U5,** 66
every ['evri] jeder/jede/jedes **I U3,** 40
everybody ['evribɒdi] jeder; alle **IV U2,** 25
everyday ['evrideɪ] alltäglich, Alltags- **VI T1,** 16
everyone ['evriwʌn] jeder **III U3,** 48
everything ['evriθɪŋ] alles **II U4,** 50
everywhere ['evriweə] überall **II U5,** 71
evidence ['evɪdnts] Beweis °**II U6,** 83
exact [ɪg'zækt] genau **III U3,** 49
exaggerated [ɪg'zædʒreɪtɪd] übertrieben **VI T1,** 16
exam [ɪg'zæm] Examen, Prüfung **III U4,** 67
example [ɪg'zɑːmpl] Beispiel **VI T1,** 15; **VI T1,** 16
for example [ˌfər‿ɪg'zɑːmpl] zum Beispiel **III U3,** 48
excellent ['ekslnt] exzellent, hervorragend **VI T3,** 60
except [ɪk'sept] außer **IV U5,** 80
exchange [ɪks'tʃeɪndʒ] (Aus-)Tausch **I U7,** 94
to **exchange** [ɪks'tʃeɪndʒ] (aus)tauschen, umtauschen **VI T1,** 14
excited [ɪk'saɪtɪd] aufgeregt **I U5,** 74
exciting [ɪk'saɪtɪŋ] spannend, aufregend **II U4,** 51
excuse [ɪk'skjuːs] Ausrede, Entschuldigung **VI T3,** 54; **VI T3,** 60
Excuse me! [ɪk'skjuːz miː] Entschuldigung! **I U3,** 42
to **execute** ['eksɪkjuːt] exekutieren, hinrichten; durchführen, ausführen **V T3,** 52
execution [ˌeksɪ'kjuːʃn] Hinrichtung, Exekution; Durchführung **V T3,** 51
exercise ['eksəsaɪz] Übung, Aufgabe **I U1,** 19
exercise book ['eksəsaɪz ˌbʊk] Heft, Übungsheft **I U1,** 14
to **exercise** ['eksəsaɪz] üben, Sport machen **II U4,** 52
exhibition [ˌeksɪ'bɪʃn] Ausstellung, Vorführung **III U2,** 31
to **exist** [ɪg'zɪst] existieren **IV U3,** 43
existing [ɪg'zɪstɪŋ] existierend, bestehend **VI T3,** 56
exit ['eksɪt] Ausgang, Abgang, Ausfahrt **IV U4,** 65
exotic [ɪg'zɒtɪk] exotisch **VI T3,** 53
to **expect** [ɪk'spekt] erwarten **III U2,** 34
expensive [ɪk'spentsɪv] teuer **I U5,** 68
experience [ɪk'spɪəriənts] Erfahrung, Erlebnis **IV U4,** 68
to **experience** [ɪk'spɪəriənts] erfahren, erleben **VI T4,** 70
experiment [ɪk'sperɪmənt] Experiment, Versuch **II U1,** 13
expert ['ekspɜːt] Experte/Expertin **V T1,** 13
to **explain** [ɪk'spleɪn] erklären, erläutern **II U5,** 64
to **explore** [ɪk'splɔː] erkunden, erforschen **IV U3,** 43
explorer [ɪk'splɔːrə] Forscher/Forscherin; Forschungsreisender/Forschungsreisende **VI T1,** 13
export ['ekspɔːt] Export, Ausfuhr **V T4,** 76
to **export** [ɪk'spɔːt] exportieren, ausführen **V T4,** 76
to **express** [ɪk'spres] ausdrücken, äußern **VI T2,** 26
expression [ɪk'spreʃn] Ausdruck, Redewendung **VI T1,** 16
expressive [ɪk'spresɪv] ausdrucksstark °**III U5,** 86
extra ['ekstrə] zusätzlich; Zusatz **III U4,** 68
extract ['ekstrækt] Extrakt, Auszug **VI T4,** 76
extremely [ɪk'striːmli] extrem, außerordentlich **VI T4,** 72
eye [aɪ] Auge **I U2,** 35
eye-catching ['aɪkætʃɪŋ] auffallend, ins Auge stechend °**VI T2,** 31
to keep an eye on sth/sb [ˌkiːp‿ən‿'aɪ‿ɒn] etw./jmdn. im Auge behalten, auf etw./jmdn. aufpassen **V T1,** 11
eyebrow ['aɪbraʊ] Augenbraue **III U4,** 62

F

fabulous ['fæbjələs] fabelhaft, fantastisch **IV U4,** 61
face [feɪs] Gesicht **I U3,** 48
to **face** [feɪs] gegenüberliegen; konfrontiert werden mit **VI T3,** 56; **VI T4,** 70
facility [fə'sɪləti] Anlage, Einrichtung **V T1,** 16
fact [fækt] Fakt, Tatsache **II U2,** 32
fact file (on) ['fækt faɪl] Datei mit Informationen (über) **V T3,** 58
in fact [ɪn 'fækt] in der Tat, genau genommen **II U7,** 94
factory ['fæktri] Fabrik, Werk **IV U3,** 50
factual ['fæktʃʊəl] Sach-, sachlich °**IV U1,** 14

Fahrenheit (F) [ˈfærnhaɪt] Fahrenheit **IV U1,** 16
to **fail** [feɪl] versagen; ausfallen; fehlschlagen **V T3,** 50
to fail a grade [ˌfeɪl‿ə ˈgreɪd] eine Schulnote nicht erreichen **VI T4,** 72
to **faint** [feɪnt] ohnmächtig werden **IV U1,** 17
fair [feə] Messe, Jahrmarkt **I U7,** 90
summer fair [ˈsʌmə ˌfeə] Sommerfest **I U7,** 90
fair [feə] gerecht, fair **III U1,** 16; blond, hell **III U5,** 80
fair trade [ˌfeə ˈtreɪd] fairer Handel **V T4,** 76
fairly [ˈfeəli] ziemlich **I U1,** 10
fall [fɔːl] Fall, Sturz °**V T3,** 48
*to **fall** [fɔːl] fallen, herunterfallen, hinfallen **II U2,** 26
to fall asleep [ˌfɔːl‿əˈsliːp] einschlafen **V T2,** 38
to fall off [fɔːl‿ˈɒf] herunterfallen **II U3,** 40
false [fɔːls] falsch **VI T2,** 28
false teeth [fɔːls ˈtiːθ] Zahnprothese, Gebiss **VI T2,** 28
family [ˈfæmli] Familie **I LUA,** 25
family tree [ˈfæmli triː] Familienstammbaum °**I U2,** 28
famine [ˈfæmɪn] Hungersnot **IV U1,** 10
famous [ˈfeɪməs] berühmt **I U4,** 54
fan [fæn] Fan **II U5,** 66
fantastic [fænˈtæstɪk] fantastisch, großartig **I U7,** 94
far [fɑː] weit **II U6,** 78
by far [baɪ ˈfɑː] bei weitem **V T2,** 33
so far [ˈsəʊ fɑː] bis jetzt °**IV U1,** 17
to go far [gəʊ ˈfɑː] weit kommen, es weit bringen **III U2,** 26
farm [fɑːm] Bauernhof, Farm **I U6,** 78
farmer [ˈfɑːmə] Bauer/Bäuerin, Landwirt/Landwirtin **I U6,** 82
farmhouse [ˈfɑːmhaʊs] Bauernhaus **II U7,** 88
farming [fɑːmɪŋ] Landwirtschaft **V T4,** 75
farther [ˈfɑːðə] weiter **IV U1,** 10
farther and farther [ˈfɑːðə] immer weiter **IV U1,** 10
fascinating [ˈfæsɪneɪtɪŋ] faszinierend, spannend **VI T1,** 15
fashion [ˈfæʃn] Mode **II U6,** 82
fast [fɑːst] schnell **II U4,** 50
fast food [ˌfɑːst ˈfuːd] Schnellimbiss °**II U4,** 50
fast lane [ˈfɑːst ˌleɪn] Überholspur **V T3,** 56
fat [fæt] Fett; fett **VI T3,** 54
father [ˈfɑːðə] Vater **III U3,** 52
faucet *(AE)* [ˈfɔːsɪt] Wasserhahn **IV U3,** 44
fave *(slang)* [feɪv] Liebling(s-); Favorit/Favoritin °**V T2,** 34
favourite [ˈfeɪvrɪt] Lieblings- **I U1,** 12
fear [fɪə] Angst, Furcht **VI T4,** 72
feature [ˈfiːtʃə] Merkmal, Gesichtszug, Charakterzug °**VI T2,** 31
February [ˈfebruəri] Februar **I U5,** 70
federal [ˈfedrl] Bundes-; föderal(istisch) **VI T2,** 33
*to **feed** [fiːd] füttern **I U6,** 80; ernähren, durchfüttern **VI T2,** 28
to be fed up [biː ˌfed‿ˈʌp] die Nase voll haben **I U2,** 34
feedback [ˈfiːdbæk] Feedback, Rückmeldung °**VI T1,** 19; °**VI T4,** 73; °**VI T4,** 79
*to **feel** [fiːl] (sich) fühlen **II U3,** 40; glauben **VI T1,** 11
to feel for [ˈfiːl fə] tasten nach **III U3,** 52
to feel homesick [ˌfiːl ˈhəʊmsɪk] Heimweh haben **IV U4,** 68
to feel sick [fiːl ˈsɪk] Übelkeit verspüren **II U3,** 46
to feel sorry for [fiːl ˈsɒri] Mitleid haben mit, bedauern **III U1,** 16
feeling [ˈfiːlɪŋ] Gefühl **III U4,** 64
female [ˈfiːmeɪl] weiblich; Weibchen **VI T4,** 70
fence [fens] Zaun **V T3,** 49
to **fence sb in** [fens ˈɪn] jmdn. einsperren °**V T3,** 48
ferry [ˈferi] Fähre **III U3,** 45
festival [ˈfestɪvl] Festival, Fest **IV U1,** 14
fetish [ˈfetɪʃ] Fetisch °**IV U5,** 84
few [fjuː] wenige **II U5,** 71
a few [ə ˈfjuː] einige, ein paar **II U4,** 52
fiction [ˈfɪkʃn] Erfindung, Fiktion **III U5,** 80
science fiction [ˌsaɪəns ˈfɪkʃn] Sciencefiction **III U5,** 80
to **fiddle (with)** [ˈfɪdl] herumfummeln (an) **IV U4,** 68
field [fiːld] Feld, Acker **I U6,** 88
sports field [ˈspɔːts fiːld] Sportplatz **I U7,** 92
fierce [fɪəs] bösartig **II U5,** 70
fifth [fɪfθ] Fünftel **III U2,** 32
fight [faɪt] Kampf **III U1,** 16
*to **fight** [faɪt] streiten, kämpfen **III U4,** 69
fighter [ˈfaɪtə] Kämpfer/Kämpferin **VI T2,** 37
fighting [ˈfaɪtɪŋ] Kampf(-) **V T3,** 50
figure [ˈfɪgə] Figur, Gestalt **II U7,** 94; Ziffer, Zahl **VI T1,** 13; **VI T3,** 58
to **fill** [fɪl] füllen **IV U2,** 33
to fill in [fɪl‿ˈɪn] ausfüllen, einsetzen **II U5,** 64
film [fɪlm] Film **II U3,** 43
to **film** [fɪlm] filmen **III U5,** 87
filter [ˈfɪltə] Filter **VI T3,** 53
fin [fɪn] (Schwimm-)Flosse **V T4,** 79
final [ˈfaɪnl] letzter/letzte/letztes **III U5,** 82
finally [ˈfaɪnli] endlich, schließlich **III U2,** 28
finance [ˈfaɪnænts] Finanzwesen, Finanzen; Finanz- **VI T4,** 74
financial [faɪˈnæntʃl] finanziell **VI T4,** 71
*to **find** [faɪnd] finden **I U3,** 48
to find out [faɪnd‿ˈaʊt] herausfinden **I U4,** 62
fine [faɪn] Geldbuße, Geldstrafe **III U2,** 28
fine [faɪn] gut, in Ordnung, fein, schön **I U7,** 94
finger [ˈfɪŋgə] Finger **II U3,** 41
fingernail [ˈfɪŋgəneɪl] Fingernagel **VI T4,** 76
to **finish** [ˈfɪnɪʃ] beenden, erledigen, aufhören **I U2,** 34
fire [faɪə] Feuer, Brand **I U7,** 96; Feuerstelle, Kaminfeuer **III U2,** 32
fire brigade [ˈfaɪə brɪˌgeɪd] Feuerwehr **III U2,** 32
Where's the fire? [ˌweəz ðə ˈfaɪə] Wo brennt's denn? **I U7,** 96
to **fire** [faɪə] (ab)feuern **V T3,** 52
fireplace [ˈfaɪəpleɪs] Kamin **III U5,** 89
firework [ˈfaɪəwɜːk] Feuerwerkskörper; *Plural:* Feuerwerk **IV U1,** 14
firm [fɜːm] Firma **III U1,** 12
firmly [ˈfɜːmli] eindeutig, deutlich, standhaft **VI T2,** 35
first [fɜːst] zuerst; erster/erste/erstes **I U4,** 54
at first [ət ˈfɜːst] zuerst, zunächst **II U6,** 80
first of all [ˌfɜːst‿ɒf‿ˈɔːl] zuerst, zuallererst, zunächst **IV U4,** 66
fish, **fish** *(pl)* [fɪʃ] Fisch **I U6,** 78
to **fish** [fɪʃ] fischen, angeln **I U6,** 82
fisherman, fishermen *(pl)* [ˈfɪʃəmən; ˈfɪʃəmen] Fischer, Angler **V T4,** 78
fishing [ˈfɪʃɪŋ] Fischen, Angeln **I U6,** 78
fist [fɪst] Faust **VI T4,** 77
*to have a **fit** [ˌhæv‿ə ˈfɪt] einen Anfall bekommen, Zustände kriegen **III U4,** 70
to **fit** [fɪt] passen **II U6,** 76
fit [fɪt] fit **II U4,** 52

to **fix (to)** [fɪks] befestigen, anbringen; reparieren **III U2,** 30
to fix [fɪks] manipulieren **IV U2,** 33
to **fizz** [fɪz] zischen **VI T4,** 78
fizzy ['fɪzi] sprudelnd **VI T3,** 53
flag [flæg] Flagge, Fahne **I U2,** 29
to **flake** [fleɪk] zerfallen, zerbröseln, abbröckeln **VI T4,** 77
flame [fleɪm] Flamme **III U2,** 32
flare [fleə] Leuchtfeuer; Lichtschein **IV U3,** 51
to **flare** [fleə] lodern, flackern **VI T4,** 77
flash [flæʃ] Aufblinken, Blitzen **II U7,** 95
flash flood ['flæʃ ˌflʌd] flutartige Überschwemmung, Sintflut **II U6,** 74
to **flash** [flæʃ] blitzen, blinken **IV U1,** 16
flat [flæt] Wohnung **I U2,** 26; flach, platt **IV U1,** 16
flaw [flɔ:] Fehler, Defekt **VI T4,** 72
fleet [fli:t] Flotte *(Fahrzeug)* **VI T4,** 74
First Fleet [ˌfɜ:st 'fli:t] Erste Flotte *(die ersten Schiffe, die Sträflinge nach Australien brachten)* °**V T1,** 11
flexible ['fleksɪbl] flexibel, beweglich **VI T3,** 60; **VI T4,** 75
to **flicker** ['flɪkə] flackern, flimmern **VI T2,** 36
flight [flaɪt] Flug **II U2,** 23
flood [flʌd] Überschwemmung, Hochwasser **II U6,** 74
flash flood ['flæʃ ˌflʌd] flutartige Überschwemmung, Sintflut **II U6,** 74
to **flood** [flʌd] überfluten, überschwemmen **IV U3,** 44
floor [flɔ:] Fußboden **II U5,** 71
dance floor ['dɑ:nts flɔ:] Tanzfläche **IV U2,** 33
flossy *(slang)* ['flɒsi] aufgemotzt °**IV U5,** 84
flow chart ['fləʊ ˌtʃɑ:t] Ablauf-, Flussdiagramm °**VI T4,** 71
flower ['flaʊə] Blume **I U6,** 78
*to **fly** [flaɪ] fliegen **II U7,** 88; wehen **III U3,** 46
to fly out [flaɪ‿'aʊt] ausfliegen, evakuieren **VI T2,** 29
to **focus (on)** ['fəʊkəs] sich konzentrieren (auf) **VI T4,** 73
fog [fɒg] Nebel **II U6,** 78
foggy ['fɒgi] neblig **I U6,** 79
to **fold** [fəʊld] falten, knicken, brechen **VI T4,** 77
folder ['fəʊldə] Ordner, Mappe **I U4,** 60
folk [fəʊk] Volksmusik **IV U5,** 77
folks *(Anrede)* [fəʊks] Leute *(Anrede)* **IV U1,** 16
to **follow** ['fɒləʊ] hinterhergehen, folgen, befolgen **I U7,** 96
following ['fɒləʊɪŋ] folgend/folgender/folgende/folgendes **III U4,** 67
food [fu:d] Essen, Nahrung, Lebensmittel **I U7,** 95
fast food [ˌfɑ:st 'fu:d] Schnellimbiss °**II U4,** 50
foot, feet *(pl)* [fʊt; fi:t] Fuß **I U4,** 54; Fuß *(Längenmaß: 30,48 cm)* **III U1,** 11
on foot [ɒn 'fʊt] zu Fuß **I U4,** 57
football ['fʊtbɔ:l] Fußball **I U1,** 12
American football [əˌmerɪkən 'fʊtbɔ:l] Football **III U1,** 8
footballer ['fʊtbɔ:lə] Fußballspieler/Fußballspielerin °**VI T1,** 13
footprint ['fʊtprɪnt] Fußabdruck **VI T3,** 52
carbon footprint [ˌkɑ:bn 'fʊtprɪnt] CO_2-Bilanz **VI T3,** 52
footstep ['fʊtstep] Schritt **III U3,** 52
for [fɔ:; fə] für **I U1,** 11; seit **II U5,** 69
for ... [fɔ:; fə] ... lang **III U2,** 32
for example [ˌfər‿ɪg'zɑ:mpl] zum Beispiel **III U3,** 48
for hours [fər‿'aʊəz] stundenlang **II U4,** 52
for miles [fə‿'maɪlz] meilenweit **IV U4,** 69
for supper [fə 'sʌpə] zum Abendessen **II U3,** 38
armed **forces** [ˌɑ:md 'fɔ:sɪz] Militär, Streitkräfte **VI T2,** 32
to **force** [fɔ:s] (er)zwingen **VI T2,** 30; **VI T2,** 36
forecast ['fɔ:kɑ:st] Vorhersage *(Wetter)* **II U6,** 78
*to **forecast** ['fɔ:kɑ:st] vorhersagen *(Wetter)* **IV U3,** 43
foreground ['fɔ:graʊnd] Vordergrund **IV U1,** 9
forehead ['fɔ:hed] Stirn **VI T4,** 76
foreign ['fɒrɪn] fremd, ausländisch **II U1,** 10
foreigner ['fɒrɪnə] Ausländer/Ausländerin; Fremder/Fremde **VI T2,** 29
forest ['fɒrɪst] Wald **IV U4,** 62
*to **forget** [fə'get] vergessen **I U4,** 60
*to **forgive** [fə'gɪv] vergeben, verzeihen **V T3,** 52
fork [fɔ:k] Gabel **II U4,** 50
form [fɔ:m] Formular, Form **II U5,** 64
long form ['lɒŋ fɔ:m] Langform °**I U1,** 16
sixth form ['sɪksθ ˌfɔ:m] Oberstufe **VI T4,** 71
to **form** [fɔ:m] formen, bilden **IV U5,** 80; entstehen, sich bilden **V T4,** 74
formal ['fɔ:ml] formal, formell, förmlich **IV U2,** 25
former ['fɔ:mə] ehemaliger/ehemalige/ehemaliges, früherer/frühere/früheres **VI T1,** 13
fortress ['fɔ:trəs] Festung **III U2,** 31
fortune ['fɔ:tʃu:n] Vermögen, Reichtum; Schicksal, Glück **V T3,** 58
forum ['fɔ:rəm] Forum **IV U5,** 80
forward ['fɔ:wəd] nach vorne, vorwärts **IV U1,** 16
to look forward to (+ -ing) [lʊk 'fɔ:wəd] sich freuen auf **V T4,** 81
fossil ['fɒsl] Fossil; fossil, versteinert **V T4,** 72
fossil fuel ['fɒsl ˌfju:əl] fossiler Brennstoff **V T4,** 72
foul [faʊl] Foul **VI T1,** 12
to **found** [faʊnd] gründen **IV U1,** 10
fountain ['faʊntɪn] (Spring-)Brunnen, Fontäne **VI T3,** 55
spring fountain [ˌsprɪŋ 'faʊntɪn] Quelle **VI T3,** 55
frame [freɪm] Rahmen **VI T4,** 75
free [fri:] frei **I U3,** 40; kostenlos, umsonst **IV U1,** 12
freedom ['fri:dəm] Freiheit **IV U1,** 9
freeman, freemen *(pl)* ['fri:mən, fri:men] freier Mann **VI T2,** 28
to **freestyle** *(slang)* ['fri:staɪl] improvisieren **IV U5,** 80
freewheeling [ˌfri:'wi:lɪŋ] locker; freilaufend °**V T3,** 50
French [frentʃ] französisch **II U1,** 18
French fries *(AE)* ['frentʃ ˌfraɪz] Pommes frites **IV U1,** 12
fresh [freʃ] frisch **II U4,** 54
fresh water ['freʃ ˌwɔ:tə] Süßwasser, Trinkwasser **VI T3,** 57
Friday [fraɪdeɪ] Freitag **I LUB,** 39
fridge [frɪdʒ] Kühlschrank **IV U3,** 48
friend [frend] Freund/Freundin **I U1,** 16
to make friends (with) [ˌmeɪk 'frendz] Freundschaft schließen (mit) **IV U4,** 68
friendly ['frendli] freundlich, nett **IV U1,** 14
French **fries** *(AE)* ['frentʃ ˌfraɪz] Pommes frites **IV U1,** 12
to **frighten away** [ˌfraɪtn‿ə'weɪ] abschrecken **II U7,** 88
*to be **frightened** (of) [bi: 'fraɪtnd] Angst haben (vor) **II U6,** 83
frightening ['fraɪtnɪŋ] schrecklich, furchtbar, beängstigend **II U6,** 80
from [frɒm] aus, von **I U1,** 10
divorced from [dɪ'vɔ:st frəm] geschieden von **I U2,** 28
Where are you from? [ˌweər‿ə jə 'frɒm] Woher kommst du? **I U1,** 11

front [frʌnt] Vorderseite **IV U2,** 33; Vor-, Vorder- **VI T4,** 76
at the front [ət ðə 'frʌnt] im vorderen Teil, vorne **III U1,** 8
in front of [ɪn 'frʌnt‿əv] vor **I U3,** 49
to **frown** [fraʊn] die Stirn runzeln **VI T4,** 78
frozen ['frəʊzn] gefroren **IV U4,** 65
fruit [fru:t] Obst, Frucht **II U1,** 15
frustrated [frʌs'treɪtɪd] frustriert **III U4,** 62
fuel ['fju:əl] Treibstoff; Brennmaterial **V T4,** 72
fossil fuel ['fɒsl ˌfju:əl] fossiler Brennstoff **V T4,** 72
to **fulfill** *(AE)* [fʊl'fɪl] erfüllen, genügen **V T3,** 58
full (of) [fʊl] ganz, voll (von/mit) **III U1,** 11
full-time (F/T) [ˌfʊl'taɪm] Vollzeit- **V T1,** 14
fully-qualified [ˌfʊli'kwɒlɪfaɪd] voll ausgebildet, voll qualifiziert **VI T1,** 10
fun [fʌn] Spaß **I U3,** 41
Have fun! [ˌhæv 'fʌn] Viel Spaß! **I U6,** 82
to be fun [bi: 'fʌn] Spaß machen **I U3,** 43
to have fun [ˌhæv 'fʌn] Spaß haben, sich amüsieren **I U6,** 82
fund [fʌnd] Fonds; Fundus **VI T3,** 61
fund raising ['fʌnd ˌreɪzɪŋ] Spenden sammeln **VI T3,** 61
funeral ['fju:nrəl] Beerdigung **II U6,** 76
funk [fʌŋk] Funk *(Musikrichtung)* **IV U5,** 80
funny ['fʌni] komisch, lustig **I LUA,** 25
furious ['fjʊəriəs] wütend **III U3,** 53
furniture ['fɜ:nɪtʃə] Möbel **I LUA,** 25
further ['fɜ:ðə] weiter **V T1,** 11
fuse-box ['fju:zbɒks] Sicherungskasten **III U3,** 53
fusion ['fju:ʒn] Fusion, Verbindung, Verschmelzung **VI T1,** 16
fuss [fʌs] Aufregung, Wirbel **III U4,** 70
future ['fju:tʃə] zukünftig **VI T1,** 12; **VI T1,** 15; Zukunft **VI T4,** 71

G

Gaelic ['geɪlɪk] gälisch **III U3,** 48
to **gain** [geɪn] erlangen, erwerben; gewinnen **VI T4,** 71
gallery ['gælri] Galerie °**V T4,** 77
game [geɪm] Spiel **I U2,** 26
miming game ['maɪmɪŋ geɪm] Pantomime °**I U6,** 81
gang [gæŋ] Gang, Bande **IV U2,** 27
gangster ['gæŋkstə] Gangster/Gangsterin, Verbrecher/Verbrecherin **IV U5,** 80
garden ['gɑ:dn] Garten **I U2,** 26
gardener ['gɑ:dnə] Gärtner/Gärtnerin **III U2,** 34
gardening ['gɑ:dnɪŋ] Gärtnern, Gartengestaltung **VI T4,** 78
gas [gæs] Gas *(BE)*; Benzin *(AE)* **V T3,** 56; **V T4,** 73
greenhouse gas [ˌgri:nhaʊs 'gæs] Treibhausgas **V T4,** 73
natural gas [ˌnætʃrl 'gæs] Erdgas **V T4,** 74
to step on the gas [ˌstep‿ɒn ðə 'gæs] Gas geben **V T3,** 56
gate [geɪt] Tor, Pforte; Gate **II U7,** 90
GCSE [ˌdʒi:si:es'i:] Prüfung zum Abschluss der Sekundarstufe **III U4,** 67
g'day [gə'deɪ] Tag, hallo *(australische Begrüßung)* °**II U1,** 14
general ['dʒenrl] generell, gewöhnlich **VI T2,** 32
general election [ˌdʒenrl‿ɪ'lekʃn] landesweite Wahl **VI T2,** 32
generation [ˌdʒenə'reɪʃn] Generation °**VI T3,** 57
generator ['dʒenreɪtə] Generator **VI T3,** 61
ladies and **gentlemen** [ˌleɪdiz‿n 'dʒentlmən] meine Damen und Herren °**III U2,** 33
Geography [dʒi'ɒgrəfi] Geografie, Erdkunde **II U1,** 10
German ['dʒɜ:mən] deutsch; Deutscher/Deutsche **I U1,** 17
*to **get** [get] kommen, bekommen, besorgen **I U3,** 44; holen **II U2,** 26; werden **II U6,** 83
get-well card [ˌget 'wel ˌkɑ:d] Gute-Besserung-Karte **VI T4,** 77
to get along [ˌget‿ə'lɒŋ] sich verstehen, zurechtkommen **VI T4,** 73
to get away [ˌget‿ə'weɪ] abhauen, wegkommen **V T3,** 56
to get back (to) [get 'bæk tə] sich melden (bei) **IV U5,** 81
to get hungry [get 'hʌŋgri] Hunger bekommen **II U4,** 56
to get interested [get 'ɪntrəstɪd] sich interessieren **III U2,** 35
to get into [get‿'ɪntə] einsteigen in *(Auto)* **I U5,** 75
to get into such a state [getˌɪntə 'sʌtʃ‿ə 'steɪt] durchdrehen, (sich) verrückt machen **III U4,** 70
to get it ['get‿ɪt] bestraft werden **IV U4,** 68
to get lost [get 'lɒst] verloren gehen, sich verirren **I U3,** 48
to get lucky *(AE)* [get 'lʌki] Glück haben **IV U4,** 68
to get off [get‿'ɒf] aussteigen aus **I U4,** 59; wegräumen von, abräumen von **III U4,** 65
to get on [get‿'ɒn] aufsteigen, einsteigen *(in Zug, Bus …)* **III U5,** 86; zurechtkommen, klarkommen **VI T3,** 59; weiterkommen, vorwärtskommen **VI T4,** 78
to get onto [get‿'ɒntə] einsteigen *(Bus)* **II U1,** 19
to get out [get‿'aʊt] aussteigen **I U6,** 86; entkommen **III U3,** 53
to get out of bed [ˌget‿aʊt‿əv 'bed] aufstehen **II U7,** 94
to get ready [get 'redi] sich vorbereiten **II U5,** 68
to get rid of sth/sb [get 'rɪd‿əv] etw./jmdn. loswerden **V T2,** 38
to get … right/wrong [get … 'raɪt/'rɒŋ] richtig/falsch machen **II U3,** 44
to get sth going [ˌget 'gəʊɪŋ] etw. in Gang setzen/in Schwung bringen **VI T4,** 76
to get to know [ˌget tə 'nəʊ] kennen lernen **V T3,** 59
to get up [get‿'ʌp] aufstehen **I U3,** 44
to get well [get 'wel] gesund werden **VI T4,** 77
to get … wrong [get … 'rɒŋ] falsch verstehen °**II U3,** 47
ghost [gəʊst] Geist, Gespenst **I U2,** 34
ghostly ['gəʊstli] geisterhaft **VI T4,** 78
gift [gɪft] Geschenk; Begabung **V T3,** 52
girl [gɜ:l] Mädchen **I U1,** 16
girlfriend ['gɜ:lfrend] Freundin *(in einer Paarbeziehung)* **II U3,** 39
*to **give** [gɪv] geben, schenken **I U4,** 60
to give … a dirty look [ˌgɪv‿ə dɜ:ti 'lʊk] einen vernichtenden Blick zuwerfen **II U1,** 10
to give a talk [ˌgɪv‿ə 'tɔ:k] einen Vortrag/eine Rede halten **VI T1,** 18
to give it a go [ˌgɪv‿ɪt‿ə 'gəʊ] es versuchen **IV U5,** 81
to give up [gɪv‿'ʌp] aufgeben **III U2,** 30
glad [glæd] froh **III U4,** 68
glamorous ['glæmrəs] glamourös **IV U5,** 76
glare [gleə] blendender Glanz, grelles Licht **III U4,** 70
glass [glɑ:s] Glas **II U4,** 50
glasses *(pl)* ['glɑ:sɪz] Brille **IV U3,** 50
glee [gli:] Entzücken **III U4,** 70
global ['gləʊbl] global, Erd- **V T4,** 70

(global) warming [ˌgləʊbl 'wɔ:mɪŋ] (Erd-)Erwärmung **VT4,** 72
globalisation [ˌgləʊblaɪ'zeɪʃn] Globalisierung **VT4,** 73
glove [glʌv] Handschuh **III U1,** 8
to **glow** [gləʊ] leuchten **III U5,** 88
to **go** [gəʊ] gehen **I U1,** 19
gonna (= going to) ['gɒnə] wird/werden °**IV U4,** 68
Go down …. ['gəʊ daʊn] Geh … entlang. **I LUC,** 53
Go left. [gəʊ 'left] Biege nach links ab. **I LUC,** 52
Go right. [gəʊ 'raɪt] Biege nach rechts ab. **I LUC,** 52
to go [tə‿'gəʊ] zum Mitnehmen **IV U1,** 12
to go bananas [ˌgəʊ bə'nɑ:nəz] verrückt werden, durchdrehen **II U5,** 66
to go bump [gəʊ 'bʌmp] rumsen °**II U7,** 94
to go down [gəʊ 'daʊn] hinuntergehen, entlanggehen **II U2,** 30
to go far [gəʊ 'fɑ:] weit kommen, es weit bringen **III U2,** 26
to go for a walk [ˌgəʊ fər‿ə 'wɔ:k] spazieren gehen **III U5,** 88
to go for sth ['gəʊ fɔ:] etw. angehen **VI T4,** 73
to go green [ˌgəʊ 'gri:n] umweltbewusst werden **VI T3,** 59
to go in [gəʊ 'ɪn] hineingehen **II U2,** 26
to go + -ing [gəʊ] … gehen **II U4,** 52
to go into a coma ['kəʊmə] ins Koma fallen **VT2,** 38
to go into labour [ˌgəʊ‿ɪntə 'leɪbə] in den Wehen liegen °**VI T3,** 59
to go it alone [ˌgəʊ‿ɪt‿ə'ləʊn] einen Alleingang starten, es allein schaffen **VT3,** 50
to go off [gəʊ‿'ɒf] losgehen *(Alarm)* **II U7,** 95
to go on [gəʊ‿'ɒn] andauern; weitermachen, weitergehen **IV U1,** 14
to go on a diet [ˌgəʊ‿ɒn‿ə 'daɪət] eine Diät machen **II U4,** 52
to go out [gəʊ‿'aʊt] (hin)ausgehen; erlöschen **II U3,** 38
to go over [gəʊ‿'əʊvə] hinübergehen **II U3,** 38
to go places [ˌgəʊ 'pleɪsɪz] herumreisen **IV U4,** 68
to go red [gəʊ 'red] rot werden **II U1,** 11
to go soft on sb [ˌgəʊ 'sɒft] sich in jmdn. verknallen **VT3,** 50
to go up [gəʊ‿'ʌp] hinaufgehen °**I U4,** 61
to go weak [gəʊ 'wi:k] schwach werden **III U4,** 70
to go (together) with ['gəʊ wɪð] passen zu **III U5,** 81
to go without [ˌgəʊ wɪ'ðaʊt] ohne … auskommen **II U4,** 52
to go wrong [gəʊ 'rɒŋ] schief gehen **II U6,** 85
goal [gəʊl] Tor, Ziel **I U1,** 12
goal post ['gəʊl pəʊst] Torpfosten **III U1,** 15
winning goal ['wɪnɪŋ gəʊl] Siegtreffer **III U4,** 68
goalkeeper ['gəʊlˌki:pə] Torwart **III U1,** 10
goblin ['gɒblɪn] Kobold **II U7,** 90
My **God!** [maɪ 'gɒd] Mein Gott! **II U6,** 82
gold [gəʊld] Gold **II U7,** 90
good [gʊd] gut **I U1,** 16
Good grief! [gʊd 'gri:f] Du liebe Zeit! **II U2,** 28
Good luck! [ˌgʊd 'lʌk] Viel Glück! **I U4,** 63
Good morning! [ˌgʊd 'mɔ:nɪŋ] Guten Morgen! **I U1,** 16
I'm good at … [aɪm 'gʊd‿ət] ich bin gut in … **I U1,** 20
to be good with … [bi: 'gʊd wɪð] gut mit … umgehen können **I U2,** 34
to have a good time [ˌhæv‿ə gʊd 'taɪm] sich amüsieren **I U5,** 75
goodbye [gʊd'baɪ] auf Wiedersehen **I U1,** 19
goods *(pl)* [gʊdz] Güter, Waren **IV U4,** 61
gorge [gɔ:dʒ] Schlucht, Klamm **IV U4,** 60
gossip ['gɒsɪp] Tratsch, Klatsch **IV U2,** 32
to **gossip** ['gɒsɪp] tratschen, klatschen, schwatzen **IV U2,** 32
government ['gʌvnmənt] Regierung **VT1,** 14; **VT3,** 55; **VT4,** 73
to **grab** [græb] greifen, schnappen **III U3,** 53
grade *(AE)* [greɪd] Klasse; Note **IV U2,** 24
to fail a grade [ˌfeɪl‿ə 'greɪd] eine Schulnote nicht erreichen **VI T4,** 72
grader ['greɪdə] -Klässler/Klässlerin **VT2,** 38
to **graduate** ['grædjueɪt] den Schulabschluss machen **IV U2,** 29
grammar ['græmə] Grammatik °**II U1,** 16
grammar school ['græmə ˌsku:l] Gymnasium **III U4,** 67
gramme (g) [græm] Gramm **III U1,** 11
grandad ['grændæd] Opa **I LUA,** 25
grandma ['grændmɑ:] Oma **I LUA,** 25
great-**grandson** [ˌgreɪt'grænsʌn] Urenkel **VI T4,** 74
graph [grɑ:f] Diagramm, Graph, Schaubild °**IV U4,** 69
grass [grɑ:s] Gras **III U1,** 8
grave [greɪv] Grab **III U5,** 81
gravestone ['greɪvstəʊn] Grabstein **III U5,** 86
gravity ['grævəti] Schwerkraft, Schwere **VI T4,** 77
great [greɪt] großartig, toll **I U2,** 26; groß **III U2,** 26
great-grandson [ˌgreɪt'grænsʌn] Urenkel **VI T4,** 74
Greek [gri:k] griechisch; Grieche/Griechin **I U2,** 29
green [gri:n] grün **I LUA,** 24
to go green [ˌgəʊ 'gri:n] umweltbewusst werden **VI T3,** 59
greenhouse ['gri:nhaʊs] Gewächshaus **II U6,** 81
greenhouse gas [ˌgri:nhaʊs 'gæs] Treibhausgas **VT4,** 73
greeting ['gri:tɪŋ] Gruß, Begrüßung °**VT2,** 32
grey [greɪ] grau **III U5,** 89
grid [grɪd] Gitter, Tabelle **III U4,** 67
Good **grief!** [gʊd 'gri:f] Du liebe Zeit! **II U2,** 28
grin [grɪn] Grinsen **VT3,** 56
to **grin** [grɪn] grinsen **VT3,** 56
ground [graʊnd] Boden **II U2,** 26
grounded ['graʊndɪd] geerdet, gefestigt **VI T4,** 77
group [gru:p] Gruppe **I U4,** 54
*to **grow** [grəʊ] wachsen (lassen); anbauen; zunehmen **VT1,** 13; **VT3,** 50; **VT4,** 75; **VT4,** 76
to grow up [grəʊ‿'ʌp] aufwachsen, heranwachsen **VI T1,** 12
grown up [ˌgrəʊn‿'ʌp] erwachsen **VT3,** 52
to **guarantee** [ˌgærn'ti:] garantieren, sicherstellen, bürgen **VT4,** 76
guard [gɑ:d] Wache; Wächter/Wächterin **III U5,** 85
national guard [ˌnæʃnl 'gɑ:d] Nationalgarde °**VT3,** 54
to **guard** [gɑ:d] bewachen **II U7,** 90
guess [ges] Vermutung °**IV U2,** 24
to **guess** [ges] raten, vermuten **III U4,** 66
guest [gest] Gast **III U5,** 85
guidance ['gaɪdənts] Anleitung, Führung, Beratung **VI T4,** 73
guidance teacher *(AE)* ['gaɪdənts ˌti:tʃə] Vertrauenslehrer/Vertrauenslehrerin **VI T4,** 73

guide [gaɪd] Führer/Führerin; Ratgeber °VI T4, 73
guilty ['gɪlti] schuldig VT2, 36; VT3, 52
guitar [gɪ'tɑː] Gitarre IV U5, 80
gun [gʌn] Schusswaffe III U5, 90
to point a gun at sb [ˌpɔɪnt‿ə 'gʌn‿ət] eine Waffe auf jmdn. richten VI T2, 36
gunshot ['gʌnʃɒt] Schuss III U5, 90
guy [gaɪ] Typ, Kerl; *Plural:* Leute IV U2, 32
gym [dʒɪm] Turnhalle I U3, 40

H

Ha! [hɑː] Ha! °III U4, 68
hair [heə] Haar, Haare II U2, 28
hairdresser ['heəˌdresə] Friseur/Friseurin II U2, 28
hairdryer ['heəˌdraɪə] Fön IV U3, 46
half [hɑːf] halb II U6, 83; Hälfte III U2, 32
half an hour [ˌhɑːf‿ən‿'aʊə] eine halbe Stunde II U2, 26
half past (two) ['hɑːf pɑːst] halb (drei) I U3, 40
half-price [ˌhɑːf'praɪs] zum halben Preis III U1, 15
half-sister ['hɑːfˌsɪstə] Halbschwester I U2, 26
half-time [ˌhɑːf'taɪm] Halbzeit III U1, 12
hall [hɔːl] Halle, Saal, Flur I U3, 40
haloed ['heɪləʊd] wie von einem Heiligenschein umgeben VI T4, 78
to screech to a **halt** ['skriːtʃ tʊ‿ə ˌhɒlt] mit quietschenden Reifen zum Stillstand kommen VT3, 50
ham [hæm] Schinken II U4, 49
hand [hænd] Hand II U3, 41
Hands off! [hændz‿'ɒf] Hände weg! II U4, 50
On the one hand ..., (but) on the other hand ... [ɒn ðə‿'wʌn ˌhænd ... ɒn ði‿'ʌðə ˌhænd ...] Einerseits ..., andererseits ... VI T2, 32
to **hand** [hænd] (über)geben, aushändigen VI T4, 78
handbag ['hænbæg] Handtasche III U2, 28
*to **hang around** *(AE)* [ˌhæŋ‿ə'raʊnd] rumhängen, herumlungern IV U2, 32
Hang on! ['hæŋ‿ɒn] Moment mal! Warte mal! I U6, 82
to hang out [hæŋ‿'aʊt] sich herumtreiben III U4, 64
to **happen** ['hæpn] geschehen, passieren I U6, 86
happy ['hæpi] glücklich, froh I U2, 33
harassment [hə'ræsmənt] Belästigung, Schikanierung VI T2, 35
harbor *(AE)* ['hɑːbə] Hafen IV U1, 9
hard [hɑːd] hart, schwierig, stark II U6, 82
to try hard [traɪ‿'hɑːd] sich stark bemühen III U4, 70
hardly ['hɑːdli] kaum VI T1, 12
harm [hɑːm] Schaden, Verletzung III U4, 70
hat [hæt] Hut II U2, 26
hate [heɪt] Hass II U1, 10
to **hate** [heɪt] hassen II U1, 10
*to **have** [hæv] haben I U5, 68
Have a nice day. [ˌhæv‿ə naɪs 'deɪ] Einen schönen Tag (noch). II U4, 55
Have fun! [ˌhæv 'fʌn] Viel Spaß! I U6, 82
to have a day off [ˌhæv‿ə 'deɪ‿ɒf] einen Tag frei haben VT3, 58
to have a fit [ˌhæv‿ə 'fɪt] einen Anfall bekommen, Zustände kriegen III U4, 70
to have a good time [ˌhæv‿ə gʊd 'taɪm] sich amüsieren I U5, 75
to have a look (at) [ˌhæv‿ə 'lʊk] anschauen, einen Blick werfen (auf) IV U2, 26
to have an argument [ˌhæv‿ən‿'ɑːgjəmənt] sich streiten III U4, 62
to have a party [ˌhæv‿ə 'pɑːti] eine Party feiern I U5, 68
to have fun [ˌhæv 'fʌn] Spaß haben, sich amüsieren I U6, 82
to have got [hæv 'gɒt] besitzen, haben I U2, 30
to have no clue [ˌhæv nəʊ 'kluː] keine Ahnung haben IV U5, 84
to have supper [hæv 'sʌpə] zu Abend essen I U3, 44
to have to ['hæv tə] müssen II U5, 64
he [hiː] er I U1, 12
head [hed] Kopf II U3, 36
head of state [ˌhed‿əv 'steɪt] Staatsoberhaupt VI T2, 32
header ['hedə] Kopfball VI T1, 12
heading ['hedɪŋ] Überschrift °III U5, 85
headline ['hedlaɪn] Überschrift, Schlagzeile °VT4, 70
headphones *(pl)* ['hedfəʊnz] Kopfhörer II U4, 56
headquarters *(pl)* [ˌhed'kwɔːtəz] Hauptsitz VT4, 77
headscarf, headscarves *(pl)* ['hedskɑːf; 'hedskɑːvz] Kopftuch VT4, 81
health [helθ] Gesundheit VT2, 38
healthy ['helθi] gesund II U4, 50
*to **hear** [hɪə] hören I U6, 78
heart [hɑːt] Herz IV U5, 82
at the heart of [æt ðə 'hɑːt‿əv] im Zentrum von VI T2, 36
heat [hiːt] Hitze IV U1, 17
to **heat** [hiːt] erhitzen, erwärmen; heizen VT4, 74
heating ['hiːtɪŋ] Heizung II U6, 78
heavy ['hevi] schwer II U4, 51
height [haɪt] Höhe, Größe III U1, 11
helicopter ['helɪˌkɒptə] Helikopter, Hubschrauber II U6, 83
hell [hel] Hölle IV U3, 50
Hello! [he'ləʊ] Hallo! I U1, 10
helmet ['helmət] Helm III U1, 8
help [help] Hilfe I U2, 34
to **help** [help] helfen I U2, 34
helpful ['helpfəl] hilfreich II U5, 71
helpless ['helpləs] hilflos III U3, 52
helpline ['helplaɪn] telefonischer Beratungsdienst, Notruf VT2, 35
her [hɜː] ihr/ihre; sie I U2, 26
Her Majesty [hə 'mædʒəsti] Ihre Majestät °III U5, 90
here [hɪə] hier I U1, 12
Here you are! ['hɪə juː‿ɑː] Bitte schön! I U1, 20
hero, heroes *(pl)* ['hɪərəʊ; 'hɪərəʊz] Held II U3, 43
heroine ['herəʊɪn] Heldin III U5, 80
herself [hɜː'self] sie/sich (selbst) III U4, 67
to **hesitate** ['hezɪteɪt] zögern VI T4, 76
hey [heɪ] he °I U1, 16
Hi! [haɪ] Hi! I U1, 10
Hi, there! ['haɪ ðeə] Hallo! IV U2, 28
*to **hide** [haɪd] (sich) verstecken I U6, 86
high [haɪ] hoch, groß II U2, 30
high-tech [ˌhaɪ'tek] high-tech IV U3, 44
high school ['haɪ ˌskuːl] High School *(weiterführende Schule in den USA, Oberstufe)* IV U2, 24
to **highlight** ['haɪlaɪt] hervorheben, markieren °IV U1, 13
highly ['haɪli] höchst, sehr VT1, 19
highway *(AE)* ['haɪweɪ] Bundesstraße, Highway IV U4, 61
him [hɪm] ihn, ihm I U4, 60
himself [hɪm'self] er/sich (selbst) III U1, 17
Hindi ['hɪndiː] Hindi VI T1, 10
Hinglish ['hɪŋglɪʃ] Hinglisch *(Mischung aus Hindi und Englisch)* VI T1, 10
hint [hɪnt] Hinweis, Spur, Anspielung °III U3, 53
hip [hɪp] Hüfte VT4, 78
hip hop ['hɪp hɒp] Hip-Hop °III U4, 63

hip hopper ['hɪp ˌhɒpə] Hip-Hopper/ Hip-Hopperin **VI T1,** 16
his [hɪz] sein/seine **I LUA,** 25
Hispanic [hɪ'spænɪk] hispanisch, lateinamerikanisch; Hispano-Amerikaner/-Amerikanerin **IV U4,** 68
historical [hɪ'stɒrɪkl] geschichtlich, historisch **V T1,** 14
History ['hɪstəri] Geschichte **II U1,** 10
hit [hɪt] Hit **III U5,** 82
*to **hit** [hɪt] schlagen, treffen **II U3,** 36
hobby, hobbies *(pl)* ['hɒbi; 'hɒbiz] Hobby **I LUB,** 38
hockey ['hɒki] Hockey **II U1,** 16
ice hockey ['aɪs ˌhɒki] Eishockey **II U2,** 23
*to **hold** [həʊld] (fest)halten **IV U5,** 76
holiday ['hɒlədeɪ] Feiertag **IV U4,** 64
holiday(s) ['hɒlədeɪ(z)] Urlaub, Ferien **II U7,** 88
holy ['həʊli] heilig **VI T2,** 36
home [həʊm] Zuhause, Heim; nach Hause **I U1,** 11; Heimat **III U1,** 8
at home [ət 'həʊm] zu Hause **I U2,** 26
home-made [ˌhəʊm'meɪd] selbst gemacht **III U1,** 16
home plate ['həʊm ˌpleɪt] Home Plate **III U1,** 14
to take home [ˌteɪk 'həʊm] nach Hause bringen **I U2,** 35
homecoming ['həʊmkʌmɪŋ] Homecoming *(Schulfest an amerikanischen High Schools)* **IV U2,** 24
homecoming queen [ˌhəʊmkʌmɪŋ 'kwi:n] Ballkönigin **IV U2,** 25
*to feel **homesick** [ˌfi:l 'həʊmsɪk] Heimweh haben **IV U4,** 68
homework ['həʊmwɜ:k] Hausaufgabe(n) **I U1,** 19
homie *(slang)* ['həʊmi] Kumpel **IV U5,** 80
honest ['ɒnɪst] ehrlich **IV U2,** 32
hood [hʊd] Kapuze, Kappe **VI T1,** 16; **VI T2,** 36
to **hoot** [hu:t] schreien, rufen *(Eule)* **II U7,** 94
hope [həʊp] Hoffnung **IV U1,** 10
to **hope** [həʊp] hoffen **I U5,** 72
hopeful ['həʊpfl] hoffnungsvoll **VI T4,** 76
hopeless ['həʊpləs] hoffnungslos **VI T1,** 12
horizon [hə'raɪzn] Horizont, Blickfeld **VI T1,** 18
horoscope ['hɒrəskəʊp] Horoskop **II U6,** 80
horrible ['hɒrəbl] schrecklich, furchtbar **II U2,** 24
horse [hɔ:s] Pferd **I LUB,** 38
horseplay ['hɔ:spleɪ] Unfug **VI T2,** 35
horticulture ['hɔ:tɪkʌltʃə] Gartenbau **VI T4,** 71
hospital ['hɒspɪtl] Krankenhaus **II U3,** 36
host [həʊst] Gastgeber, Talkmaster **III U5,** 82
hostage ['hɒstɪdʒ] Geisel **VI T2,** 29
hot [hɒt] heiß **I U6,** 79; toll; scharf **IV U2,** 28
hot spot ['hɒt spɒt] Krisenherd, Brennpunkt °**VI T2,** 37
hotel [həʊ'tel] Hotel **III U5,** 84
hotline ['hɒtlaɪn] Hotline **IV U4,** 65
hound [haʊnd] Jagdhund **III U5,** 82
hour ['aʊə] Stunde **I U2,** 34
hours *(pl)* ['aʊəz] Öffnungszeiten **I U4,** 62
for hours [fər‿'aʊəz] stundenlang **II U4,** 52
half an hour [ˌhɑ:f‿ən‿'aʊə] eine halbe Stunde **II U2,** 26
house [haʊs] Haus **I LUA,** 25
house-sitter ['haʊsˌsɪtə] Haussitter/ Haussitterin °**IV U1,** 15
household ['haʊshəʊld] Haushalt(s-) **VI T3,** 59
how [haʊ] wie **I U1,** 11
How are you? [ˌhaʊ‿'ɑ: ju:] Wie geht es dir/Ihnen/euch? **I U6,** 83
how many [haʊ 'meni] wie viele **I U5,** 68
How much are … ? [ˌhaʊ 'mʌtʃ‿ɑ:] Wie viel kosten … ? **I U5,** 66
How much is … ? [ˌhaʊ 'mʌtʃ‿ɪz] Wie viel kostet … ? **I U5,** 66
How old are you? [haʊ‿'əʊld‿ɑ: ju:] Wie alt bist du? **I U1,** 11
how to … ['haʊ tə] wie man … °**II U3,** 37
however [haʊ'evə] jedoch **VI T2,** 34
hub [hʌb] Mittelpunkt, Zentrum **IV U1,** 9
huge [hju:dʒ] riesig, gewaltig **III U2,** 30
human ['hju:mən] Mensch; menschlich **IV U3,** 43
human resources [ˌhju:mən rɪ'zɔ:sɪz] Personalabteilung **VI T4,** 74
hundred ['hʌndrəd] hundert **II U2,** 23
hungry ['hʌŋgri] hungrig **II U1,** 14
to get hungry [get 'hʌŋgri] Hunger bekommen **II U4,** 56
hunting ['hʌntɪŋ] Jagen **III U5,** 86
*to be in a **hurry** [bi:‿ɪn‿ə 'hʌri] es eilig haben **I U2,** 30
Hurry up! [ˌhʌri‿'ʌp] Beeil dich! **I U2,** 30
*to **hurt** [hɜ:t] verletzen, weh tun **II U3,** 40
hurt [hɜ:t] verletzt **III U5,** 86
hurtful ['hɜ:tfl] verletzend **IV U2,** 29
husband ['hʌzbənd] Ehemann **VI T2,** 28
hut [hʌt] Hütte **VI T2,** 28
hydrogen ['haɪdrədʒən] Wasserstoff **VI T3,** 59

I

I [aɪ] ich **I U1,** 10
I'd like to [ˌaɪd 'laɪk tə] ich würde gern **II U2,** 22
I don't care. [ˌaɪ dəʊnt 'keə] Es ist mir egal. **II U4,** 58
I don't mind. [maɪnd] Ich habe nichts dagegen., Es ist mir egal. **VI T1,** 14
I'd rather [aɪd 'rɑ:ðə] ich würde lieber **II U2,** 22
I'm afraid … [ˌaɪm‿ə'freɪd] leider, ich fürchte … **V T4,** 78
I'm having … . [aɪm 'hævɪŋ] Ich nehme … . **II U1,** 14
I'm scared. [aɪm 'skeəd] Ich habe Angst. **II U3,** 44
I want my … pierced. [aɪ 'wɒnt maɪ … 'pɪəst] Ich möchte mein … piercen lassen. **III U4,** 62
ice [aɪs] Eis **II U2,** 23
ice-cream [aɪs'kri:m] Eis, Eiscreme **I U7,** 92
ice hockey ['aɪs ˌhɒki] Eishockey **II U2,** 23
ice rink ['aɪs rɪŋk] Eis-/ Schlittschuhbahn **II U2,** 23
icon ['aɪkɒn] Ikone **III U3,** 53
idea [aɪ'dɪə] Idee, Einfall **I LUB,** 38
no idea [ˌnəʊ‿aɪ'dɪə] keine Ahnung **III U3,** 52
ideal [aɪ'dɪəl] ideal, vorbildlich; Ideal **V T2,** 32; **V T4,** 72
to **identify** [aɪ'dentɪfaɪ] erkennen, identifizieren **IV U4,** 62
to identify (with) [aɪ'dentɪfaɪ] sich identifizieren (mit) **V T2,** 35
idiom ['ɪdiəm] Redewendung, Idiom, Redensart **VI T1,** 10
idiot ['ɪdiət] Idiot, Dummkopf **I U1,** 21
if [ɪf] wenn, falls; ob **II U7,** 90
if-clause ['ɪfklɔ:z] if-Satz °**IV U4,** 62
illegal [ɪ'li:gl] illegal, unrechtmäßig, rechtswidrig **IV U3,** 50
illness ['ɪlnəs] Krankheit **VI T4,** 70
to **illustrate** ['ɪləstreɪt] darstellen, zeigen, illustrieren °**V T4,** 70
image ['ɪmɪdʒ] (Ab-)Bild, Image, Vorstellung **VI T4,** 77
to **imagine** [ɪ'mædʒɪn] sich (etwas) vorstellen **III U1,** 12

immediately [ɪ'mi:diətli] sofort, gleich **VI T1,** 16
immersion school [ɪ'mɜ:ʃn ˌsku:l] *Schule, in der in einer Fremdsprache unterrichtet wird* **VI T1,** 12; **VI T1,** 14
immigrant ['ɪmɪgrənt] Immigrant/ Immigrantin, Einwanderer/ Einwanderin **IV U1,** 9
immigration [ˌɪmɪ'greɪʃn] Immigration, Einwanderung **IV U1,** 10
immunity [ɪ'mju:nəti] Immunität **VI T2,** 32
impact ['ɪmpækt] Auswirkung, Einfluss **VI T3,** 58
importance [ɪm'pɔ:tnts] Bedeutung, Wichtigkeit °**V T3,** 59
important [ɪm'pɔ:tnt] wichtig; einflussreich **II U6,** 74
to **impress** [ɪm'pres] beeindrucken **V T2,** 36; **V T2,** 40
impression [ɪm'preʃn] Eindruck, Impression **VI T1,** 12
to **improve** [ɪm'pru:v] (sich) verbessern **V T3,** 51; **V T4,** 73
in [ɪn] in, herein **I U1,** 10; von, aus **V T2,** 33
in all [ɪn‿'ɔ:l] insgesamt, im Ganzen **III U4,** 63
in fact [ɪn 'fækt] in der Tat, genau genommen **II U7,** 94
in front of [ɪn 'frʌnt‿əv] vor **I U3,** 49
in private [ɪn 'praɪvɪt] insgeheim **VI T4,** 73
in public [ɪn 'pʌblɪk] in der Öffentlichkeit **VI T2,** 26
in the end [ɪn ði:‿'end] schließlich, zum Schluss **II U6,** 80
in time [ɪn 'taɪm] rechtzeitig **V T3,** 53
in turn [ɪn 'tɜ:n] abwechselnd, der Reihe nach °**V T3,** 55
in writing [ɪn 'raɪtɪŋ] schriftlich **VI T4,** 75
inch [ɪnʃ] Zoll *(Längenmaß: 2,54 cm)* **III U1,** 11
incident ['ɪntsɪdnt] Vorfall, Ereignis °**V T2,** 42
incinerator [ɪn'sɪnreɪtə] (Müll-)Verbrennungsanlage **VI T3,** 54
to **include** [ɪn'klu:d] einschließen, beinhalten, aufnehmen **IV U5,** 77
including [ɪn'klu:dɪŋ] einschließlich, inklusive **VI T1,** 13; **VI T1,** 15; **VI T4,** 74
all **inclusive** [ˌɔ:l‿ɪŋ'klu:sɪv] alles inklusive **IV U4,** 62
income ['ɪnkʌm] Einkommen, Verdienst **VI T3,** 56; **VI T3,** 58; **VI T3,** 61
to **increase** [ɪn'kri:s] vergrößern; zunehmen, steigen **V T4,** 73
increasing [ɪn'kri:sɪŋ] wachsend, steigend **VI T3,** 57
independent [ˌɪndɪ'pendənt] unabhängig **III U3,** 52
Indian ['ɪndiən] indisch **II U4,** 49
indie ['ɪndi] Indie *(Musikrichtung)* **IV U5,** 80
indigenous [ɪn'dɪdʒɪnəs] einheimisch, eingeboren, Ur- **VI T1,** 14
industrial [ɪn'dʌstriəl] industriell, Industrie-, gewerblich **VI T3,** 54
industry ['ɪndəstri] Industrie **III U5,** 80
influence ['ɪnfluənts] Einfluss **V T4,** 74
to **influence** ['ɪnfluənts] beeinflussen **V T4,** 74
to **inform** [ɪn'fɔ:m] informieren, benachrichtigen **VI T2,** 35; **VI T3,** 61
information [ˌɪnfə'meɪʃn] Information(en) **I LUC,** 52
information centre [ɪnfə'meɪʃn ˌsentə] Informationszentrum **I LUC,** 52
well-**informed** [ˌwelɪn'fɔ:md] gut informiert **VI T2,** 32; **VI T2,** 35
inheritor [ɪn'herɪtə] Erbe/Erbin **III U5,** 88
initiative [ɪ'nɪʃətɪv] Initiative **V T1,** 14
injection [ɪn'dʒekʃn] Injektion, Spritze **V T3,** 52
inner-city ['ɪnəˌsɪti] Innenstadt; innerstädtisch **V T2,** 32
insect ['ɪnsekt] Insekt **V T4,** 76
inside [ɪn'saɪd] innen, drin, nach drinnen **I U5,** 75
inspector [ɪn'spektə] Inspektor **III U5,** 84
to **inspire** [ɪn'spaɪə] inspirieren, anregen **V T3,** 51
instead [ɪn'sted] stattdessen, dafür **V T3,** 56
instead of [ɪn'sted‿əv] statt, anstatt **III U1,** 17
instruction [ɪn'strʌkʃn] Instruktion, Anweisung **IV U1,** 17
instructor [ɪn'strʌktə] Lehrer/Lehrerin, Ausbilder/Ausbilderin **V T1,** 15
insulation [ˌɪnsjə'leɪʃn] Isolierung, Dämmung **VI T3,** 58
insult ['ɪnsʌlt] Beleidigung **V T2,** 34
to **insult** [ɪn'sʌlt] beleidigen **V T2,** 34
insurance [ɪn'ʃʊərns] Versicherung **V T1,** 15
intelligent [ɪn'telɪdʒnt] intelligent, klug, vernünftig **IV U3,** 44
interest ['ɪntrəst] Interesse **V T1,** 15
to **interest** ['ɪntrəst] interessieren **VI T3,** 60
interested ['ɪntrəstɪd] interessiert **II U1,** 18
to get interested [get 'ɪntrəstɪd] sich interessieren **III U2,** 35
interesting ['ɪntrəstɪŋ] interessant **II U4,** 51
interior [ɪn'tɪəriə] das Innere; Innen- **V T2,** 40
interior designer [ɪnˌtɪəriə dɪ'zaɪnə] Innenarchitekt **V T2,** 40
intern *(AE)* ['ɪntɜ:n] Praktikant/ Praktikantin **VI T4,** 75
international [ˌɪntə'næʃnl] international **III U3,** 45
Internet ['ɪntənet] Internet **II U1,** 14
to surf the Internet [ˌsɜ:f ði‿'ɪntənet] im Internet surfen **II U1,** 14
internship *(AE)* ['ɪntɜ:nʃɪp] Praktikum **VI T4,** 74
Interstate *(AE)* [ˌɪntə'steɪt] Autobahn **IV U4,** 61
interview ['ɪntəvju:] Interview **II U1,** 17
to **interview** ['ɪntəvju:] interviewen **II U1,** 17
into ['ɪntə] in; in … hinein **I U3,** 44
to get into [get‿'ɪntə] einsteigen in *(Auto)* **I U5,** 75
to run into [rʌn‿'ɪntə] laufen gegen, stoßen gegen **III U1,** 17
intonation [ˌɪntə'neɪʃn] Satzmelodie °**III U5,** 86
to **introduce** [ˌɪntrə'dju:s] vorstellen, einführen °**V T2,** 35; °**V T4,** 83
introduction [ˌɪntrə'dʌkʃn] Einleitung, Einführung **VI T3,** 57; **VI T4,** 76
Inuit ['ɪnuɪt] Inuit **VI T1,** 11
Inuktitut [ɪ'nʊktɪtʊt] Inuktitut *(Sprache der Inuit)* **VI T1,** 11
to **invent** [ɪn'vent] erfinden **III U4,** 63
invention [ɪn'ventʃn] Erfindung **IV U3,** 43
to **invest** [ɪn'vest] investieren **VI T3,** 56
investigator [ɪn'vestɪgeɪtə] Ermittler/ Ermittlerin **IV U3,** 51
investment [ɪn'vestmənt] Investition **VI T3,** 56
invitation [ˌɪnvɪ'teɪʃn] Einladung **I U5,** 70
to **invite** [ɪn'vaɪt] einladen **I U5,** 68
to **involve** [ɪn'vɒlv] involvieren, einbeziehen, beteiligen; umfassen **VI T3,** 59
to be **involved in** [bi: ɪn'vɒlvd‿ɪn] beteiligt sein an, verwickelt sein in **V T2,** 33
Irish ['aɪrɪʃ] irisch **II U7,** 90; Iren/Irinnen **IV U1,** 10
to **iron** [aɪən] bügeln **II U7,** 90
irregular [ɪ'regjələ] unregelmäßig °**II U2,** 26
Islam ['ɪzlɑ:m] Islam **VI T2,** 36
Islamic [ɪz'læmɪk] islamisch **VI T2,** 36
island ['aɪlənd] Insel **II U6,** 82

islander ['aɪləndə] Inselbewohner/ Inselbewohnerin **V T4,** 81
it [ɪt] es **I U1,** 12
It said .... [ɪt 'sed] Es lautete .... **II U2,** 30
IT [ˌaɪ'tiː] Informationstechnik, Informatik **VI T4,** 74
Italian [ɪ'tæliən] italienisch; Italiener/ Italienerin **I U2,** 29
to **itch** [ɪtʃ] jucken **V T4,** 80
its [ɪts] sein/seine; ihr/ihre **III U1,** 8

J

jacket ['dʒækɪt] Jacke **I U6,** 86
jail [dʒeɪl] Gefängnis **V T1,** 10
jam [dʒæm] Marmelade **I U7,** 94; Jamsession **IV U5,** 81
traffic jam ['træfɪk ˌdʒæm] Stau **III U2,** 26
January ['dʒænjuəri] Januar **I U5,** 70
Japanese [ˌdʒæpn'iːz] japanisch, Japanisch; Japaner/Japanerin **V T2,** 41
jazz [dʒæz] Jazz **II U3,** 45
jealous (of) ['dʒeləs] eifersüchtig, neidisch (auf) **II U3,** 45
jeans *(pl)* [dʒiːnz] Jeans **IV U2,** 25
jelly bean ['dʒeli biːn] *engl. Süßigkeit* **V T1,** 10
jellyfish, **jellyfish** *(pl)* ['dʒelifɪʃ] Qualle **V T1,** 12
jerk *(slang)* [dʒɜːk] Trottel **IV U2,** 28
jersey ['dʒɜːzi] Trikot **III U1,** 12
jewel ['dʒuːəl] Juwel **III U2,** 26
jewellery ['dʒuːəlri] Schmuck **III U5,** 82
job [dʒɒb] Arbeitsstelle, Job **II U6,** 80
on the job [ˌɒn ðə 'dʒɒb] bei der Arbeit **III U5,** 82
to **jog** [dʒɒg] joggen **II U4,** 52
jogger ['dʒɒgə] Jogger/Joggerin **IV U1,** 9
to **join** [dʒɔɪn] beitreten, sich anschließen, verbinden **IV U5,** 81
joke [dʒəʊk] Witz **I U1,** 20
take a joke [ˌteɪk‿ə 'dʒəʊk] Spaß verstehen **VI T2,** 34
to **joke** [dʒəʊk] scherzen, Witze machen **I U6,** 82
journalist ['dʒɜːnlɪst] Journalist/ Journalistin **VI T2,** 27
journey ['dʒɜːni] Reise, Fahrt **II U7,** 90
joy riding ['dʒɔɪ ˌraɪdɪŋ] Joy-Riding *(mit einem gestohlenen Auto durch die Gegend fahren)* °**V T3,** 50
judge [dʒʌdʒ] Richter, Kampfrichter **II U5,** 70
juice [dʒuːs] Saft **IV U2,** 32
July [dʒʊ'laɪ] Juli **I U5,** 70
long **jump** ['lɒŋ ˌdʒʌmp] Weitsprung **I U7,** 90
to **jump** [dʒʌmp] springen **II U2,** 30
to jump about [ˌdʒʌmp‿ə'baʊt] herumspringen **III U4,** 68
to jump up [dʒʌmp‿'ʌp] hochspringen, aufspringen **II U6,** 82
June [dʒuːn] Juni **I U5,** 70
junior ['dʒuːniə] Junior, der Jüngere **VI T4,** 74
junior high school [ˌdʒuːniə 'haɪ ˌskuːl] Junior High School *(Vorstufe zur High School, meist 7.–9. Klasse)* **VI T1,** 14
just [dʒʌst] nur, gerade, einfach **I U2,** 30
justice ['dʒʌstɪs] Gerechtigkeit, Justiz **VI T2,** 31

K

kangaroo [ˌkæŋgr'uː] Känguru **V T1,** 9
*to **keep** [kiːp] (be)halten **II U4,** 55; aufbewahren **IV U3,** 46
Keep out! [kiːp‿'aʊt] Eintritt verboten! **I U2,** 26
to keep a diary [ˌkiːp‿ə 'daɪəri] ein Tagebuch/einen Terminkalender führen **VI T4,** 77
to keep an eye on sth/sb [ˌkiːp‿ən‿'aɪ‿ɒn] etw./jmdn. im Auge behalten, auf etw./jmdn. aufpassen **V T1,** 11
to keep away [ˌkiːp‿ə'weɪ] sich fernhalten, wegbleiben **V T1,** 12
to keep up [kiːp‿'ʌp] beibehalten, aufrechterhalten, weitermachen mit **VI T1,** 14
keeper ['kiːpə] Wärter/Wärterin, Aufseher/Aufseherin; Inhaber/ Inhaberin **V T2,** 40
key [kiː] Schlüssel **II U5,** 67
kick [kɪk] Kick **III U1,** 18
to **kick** [kɪk] treten **I U5,** 74
kickboard ['kɪkbɔːd] Kickboard, Roller **IV U1,** 9
kid [kɪd] Kind **I U3,** 44
You're **kidding.** [ˌjə 'kɪdɪŋ] Du machst Witze. **IV U2,** 32
kidnap(ping) ['kɪdnæp(ɪŋ)] Entführung, Kidnapping **VI T2,** 29
to **kidnap** ['kɪdnæp] kidnappen, entführen **VI T2,** 29
kidnapper ['kɪdnæpə] Kidnapper/ Kidnapperin, Entführer/Entführerin **VI T2,** 36
to **kill** [kɪl] töten; tot machen *(Volleyball)* **III U1,** 10
killer ['kɪlə] Mörder/Mörderin **V T3,** 53
killing ['kɪlɪŋ] Tötung, Töten **V T3,** 53
kilo (kg) ['kɪləʊ] Kilo(gramm) **II U4,** 54
kilometre ['kɪləʊˌmiːtə; kɪ'lɒmɪtə] Kilometer **III U3,** 45
kind [kaɪnd] Art, Sorte **III U2,** 34; freundlich, nett **IV U2,** 32
Kinetoscope [kɪ'netəskəʊp] Kinetoskop °**IV U5,** 78
king [kɪŋ] König **III U2,** 31
kiss [kɪs] Kuss **IV U2,** 28
to **kiss** [kɪs] küssen **III U5,** 80
PE **kit** [ˌpiː‿'iː kɪt] Sportzeug **II U1,** 10
kitchen ['kɪtʃɪn] Küche **I LUA,** 24
knee [niː] Knie **II U3,** 41
knife, knives *(pl)* [naɪf; naɪvz] Messer **II U4,** 50
knight [naɪt] Ritter **II U2,** 22
knock [nɒk] Klopfen, Schlag **I U2,** 34
to **knock** [nɒk] klopfen; stoßen, schlagen **III U5,** 90
to knock out [nɒk‿'aʊt] k.o. schlagen, umhauen **III U1,** 17
*to **know** [nəʊ] wissen, kennen **I U4,** 58
to get to know [ˌget tə 'nəʊ] kennen lernen **V T3,** 59
knowledge ['nɒlɪdʒ] Wissen, Kenntnisse **VI T3,** 60
koala [kəʊ'ɑːlə] Koala **V T1,** 10

L

lab(oratory) [læb; lə'bɒrətri] Labor **II U2,** 23
label ['leɪbl] Etikett; Beschriftung; Siegel **V T4,** 76
organic label [ɔːˌgænɪk 'leɪbl] Biosiegel **V T4,** 76
to **label** ['leɪbl] beschriften, benennen, etikettieren **V T4,** 76
labelling ['leɪblɪŋ] Etikettierung; Beschriftung **V T4,** 76
*to go into **labour** [ˌgəʊ‿ɪntə 'leɪbə] in den Wehen liegen °**VI T3,** 59
lack (of) [læk] Mangel (an), Fehlen (von) **VI T3,** 56
lad [læd] Junge **III U5,** 83
ladder ['lædə] Leiter **III U5,** 85
lady ['leɪdi] Dame, Frau **VI T2,** 28
ladies and gentlemen [ˌleɪdiz‿n 'dʒentlmən] meine Damen und Herren °**III U2,** 33
lake [leɪk] See **III U3,** 57
lamb [læm] Lamm, Lammfleisch **II U4,** 49
lamp [læmp] Lampe, Leuchte **IV U3,** 46
land [lænd] Land **I LUB,** 38
to **land** [lænd] landen **III U3,** 45

landmark ['lændmɑːk] Wahrzeichen, Markstein **III U2,** 30
lane [leɪn] Fahrspur, Gasse **IV U5,** 84
fast lane ['fɑːst ˌleɪn] Überholspur **V T3,** 56
language ['læŋgwɪdʒ] Sprache **I U2,** 29
bad language [bæd 'læŋgwɪdʒ] Schimpfwörter **VI T2,** 34
lantern ['læntən] Laterne **I U7,** 90
laptop ['læptɒp] Laptop **I U2,** 34
large [lɑːdʒ] groß, riesig **I U5,** 66
lassi ['lasɪ] Lassi *(Jogurtgetränk)* **II U4,** 49
to **last** [lɑːst] dauern, anhalten **IV U4,** 68
last [lɑːst] letzter/letzte/letztes **I U7,** 90
last night [lɑːst 'naɪt] gestern Abend/Nacht **II U3,** 37
last [lɑːst] zuletzt **VI T3,** 59
late [leɪt] (zu) spät, verspätet **I U1,** 16
later ['leɪtə] später **I U2,** 30
Latino [lə'tiːnəʊ] Latinomusik; Latino **IV U5,** 77
latte ['lɑːteɪ] Café latte **IV U2,** 32
to **laugh** [lɑːf] lachen **I U5,** 74
to laugh at ['lɑːf‿ət] auslachen, sich lustig machen über **II U3,** 36
launch [lɔːnʃ] Einführung, Start; Abschuss **V T4,** 72
to **launch** [lɔːnʃ] starten, abschießen **IV U3,** 43; einführen, herausbringen **V T4,** 72
law [lɔː] Gesetz(gebung), Recht **V T3,** 51
common law [ˌkɒmən 'lɔː] Gewohnheitsrecht **VI T2,** 31
lawyer ['lɔɪə] Jurist/Juristin; Anwalt/Anwältin **V T3,** 51
layout ['leɪaʊt] Layout, Anordnung °**IV U3,** 48
lead [led] Blei **III U4,** 70
*to **lead** [liːd] (an)führen, leiten **V T3,** 55; **V T4,** 73
leader ['liːdə] Führer/Führerin, Anführer/Anführerin **II U6,** 80
leaf, leaves *(pl)* [liːf; liːvz] Blatt **III U4,** 70
leaflet ['liːflət] Flugblatt, Prospekt **III U4,** 66
to **leak** [liːk] auslaufen, lecken **IV U3,** 44
*to **lean** [liːn] (sich) lehnen **IV U1,** 16
to lean out [liːn‿'aʊt] (sich) hinauslehnen **II U7,** 94
to lean up [liːn‿'ʌp] sich aufrichten **VI T4,** 78
*to **learn** [lɜːn] lernen **I U3,** 40; erfahren **III U1,** 8
learner ['lɜːnə] Lernender/Lernende **VI T1,** 16
leasing ['liːsɪŋ] Leasing **VI T4,** 74
least [liːst] am wenigsten °**IV U5,** 87
at least [ət 'liːst] wenigstens, mindestens **I U6,** 87
leather ['leðə] Leder **VI T1,** 19
*to **leave** [liːv] lassen, verlassen, abfahren **I U3,** 43; (weg)gehen **II U1,** 18; hinterlassen **VI T3,** 52
left [left] linker/linke/linkes; links **I U4,** 55
Go left. [gəʊ 'left] Biege nach links ab. **I LUC,** 52
on the left [ɒn ðə 'left] links **I U2,** 28
to turn left [tɜːn 'left] links abbiegen **II U7,** 97
left [left] übrig **II U4,** 54
leg [leg] Bein **II U3,** 41
legal ['liːgl] legal, rechtlich, Rechts- **IV U3,** 50
legal age [ˌliːgl‿'eɪdʒ] gesetzliches Mindestalter **VI T4,** 70
leisure ['leʒə] Freizeit(-), Muße **VI T3,** 58
lemon ['lemən] Zitrone(n-) **VI T3,** 53
lemonade [ˌlemə'neɪd] Limonade **I U5,** 68
*to **lend** [lend] leihen **II U7,** 90
length [leŋkθ] Länge **IV U3,** 48
leprechaun ['leprəkɔːn] Gnom, Kobold °**II U7,** 90
less [les] weniger **IV U2,** 31
lesson ['lesn] Unterrichtsstunde **I U1,** 15
*to **let** [let] lassen **III U4,** 62
Let's .... [lets] Lasst uns .... **I U1,** 10
to let sb down [let 'daʊn] jmdn. im Stich lassen, jmdn. enttäuschen **V T2,** 37
lethal ['liːθl] tödlich **V T3,** 52
letter ['letə] Buchstabe; Brief **I U1,** 15
capital letter [ˌkæpɪtl 'letə] Großbuchstabe °**II U3,** 37
lettuce ['letɪs] Kopfsalat **II U4,** 54; *(slang)* Geld °**IV U5,** 84
leukaemia [ljuː'kiːmiə] Leukämie, Blutkrebs **VI T4,** 76
level ['levl] Ebene, Niveau **III U4,** 67; Level, Höhe, Pegel **V T2,** 38; **V T4,** 72
driving **licence** *(BE)* ['draɪvɪŋ ˌlaɪsnts] Führerschein **V T1,** 15
driver's **license** *(AE)* ['draɪvəz ˌlaɪsnts] Führerschein **IV U4,** 68
to **lick** [lɪk] (ab)lecken **VI T4,** 76
lie [laɪ] Lüge **V T4,** 78
to **lie** [laɪ] lügen **IV U2,** 33
*to **lie** [laɪ] liegen **III U3,** 52
to lie down [laɪ 'daʊn] (sich) hinlegen, niederlegen **III U3,** 52
life, lives *(pl)* [laɪf; laɪvz] Leben **II U3,** 42
lifeguard ['laɪfgɑːd] Rettungsschwimmer/Rettungsschwimmerin **III U3,** 46
lifestyle ['laɪfstaɪl] Lebensart **IV U5,** 84
lift *(BE)* [lɪft] Lift, Aufzug **VI T1,** 18
to **lift** [lɪft] hochziehen, hochheben **III U2,** 30
light [laɪt] Licht **II U7,** 94
light bulb ['laɪt bʌlb] Glühbirne **IV U3,** 46
light [laɪt] leicht; hell **V T4,** 72
lighting ['laɪtɪŋ] Beleuchtung **V T2,** 41
to **like** [laɪk] mögen, gern haben **I U3,** 44
I'd like to [ˌaɪd 'laɪk tə] ich würde gern **II U2,** 22
would like [wʊd 'laɪk] hätte(n) gern, möchte(n) gern **II U4,** 52
like [laɪk] wie *(Vergleich)* **I U6,** 86
likes *(pl)* [laɪks] Vorlieben °**V T2,** 41
limit ['lɪmɪt] Limit, Grenze, Beschränkung **V T3,** 56
to **limit** ['lɪmɪt] limitieren, begrenzen, beschränken **VI T2,** 33
limousine [ˌlɪmə'ziːn] Limousine **IV U5,** 84
to **limp** [lɪmp] hinken **V T3,** 57
line [laɪn] Zeile, Text, Linie **I U3,** 43; Warteschlange **V T3,** 52
back line [ˌbæk 'lain] Grundlinie **III U1,** 10
ocean **liner** ['əʊʃn ˌlaɪnə] Ozeandampfer **III U3,** 45
lingua franca [ˌlɪŋgwə 'frænkə] Verkehrssprache, Universalsprache **VI T1,** 10
link [lɪŋk] Verbindung, Bindeglied **III U5,** 82; Link, Verknüpfung **V T1,** 14
to **link** [lɪŋk] verbinden °**IV U2,** 26
lion ['laɪən] Löwe **II U5,** 68
sea lion ['siː ˌlaɪən] Seelöwe **V T2,** 40
lip balm ['lɪp bɑːm] Lippenpflegestift **II U6,** 82
liquid ['lɪkwɪd] Flüssigkeit; flüssig **VI T4,** 77
list [lɪst] Liste **I U5,** 68
to **list** [lɪst] auflisten **VI T4,** 70
to **listen** ['lɪsn] zuhören, anhören **I U1,** 11
litre (I) ['liːtə] Liter **V T1,** 13
little ['lɪtl] klein **I U6,** 82; wenig **IV U1,** 10
to **live** [lɪv] wohnen, leben **I U3,** 45
live-in ['lɪvɪn] mit Unterbringung; im Haus lebend **VI T3,** 60
live [laɪv] live **III U4,** 63
living room ['lɪvɪŋ rʊm] Wohnzimmer **I LUA,** 24
load [ləʊd] Ladung, Last **VI T2,** 29
loads of ['ləʊdz‿əv] viele **IV U1,** 16

English – German

loan [ləʊn] Darlehen, Kredit **VT3,** 58
to **loan** [ləʊn] ausleihen, verleihen **VT3,** 58
local ['ləʊkl] lokal, örtlich **III U2,** 28
loch [lɒx] See *(Schottisch)* **III U3,** 57
to **lock** [lɒk] abschließen **III U3,** 53
locker ['lɒkə] Schließfach **II U1,** 10
logbook ['lɒgbʊk] Logbuch **VT4,** 79
logo ['ləʊgəʊ] Logo; Firmenzeichen **VT4,** 76
lonely ['ləʊnli] einsam **III U1,** 16
long [lɒŋ] lang **I U3,** 44
as long as [əz 'lɒŋ‿əz] solange **I U7,** 94
long bow ['lɒŋ bəʊ] Langbogen **VI T2,** 28
long form ['lɒŋ fɔ:m] Langform °**I U1,** 16
long jump ['lɒŋ ˌdʒʌmp] Weitsprung **I U7,** 90
look [lʊk] Blick, Aussehen **II U1,** 10
to give … a dirty look [ˌgɪv‿ə dɜ:ti 'lʊk] einen vernichtenden Blick zuwerfen **II U1,** 10
to have a look (at) [ˌhæv‿ə 'lʊk] anschauen, einen Blick werfen (auf) **IV U2,** 26
to **look** [lʊk] schauen, (aus)sehen **I U1,** 12
to look after [lʊk‿'ɑ:ftə] sich kümmern um, aufpassen auf **II U1,** 14
to look at ['lʊk‿ət] (sich) ansehen **I U6,** 82
to look for ['lʊk fə] suchen (nach) **I U6,** 81
to look forward to (+ -ing) [lʊk 'fɔ:wəd] sich freuen auf **VT4,** 81
to look out (for) [lʊk‿'aʊt] Ausschau halten (nach), suchen (nach) °**III U2,** 32
to look out for [ˌlʊk‿'aʊt fə] sich in Acht nehmen vor **VT1,** 12
to look round [lʊk 'raʊnd] sich umsehen **II U1,** 18
to look up [lʊk‿'ʌp] (hin)aufschauen; nachschlagen **II U2,** 30
*to **lose** [lu:z] verlieren **II U4,** 52
to be lost [bi: 'lɒst] sich verirrt haben **III U3,** 46
to get lost [get 'lɒst] verloren gehen, sich verirren **I U3,** 48
to lose weight [lu:z 'weɪt] abnehmen **VI T3,** 54
a **lot** [ə 'lɒt] viel **II U1,** 15
a lot of [ə 'lɒt‿əv] viel/viele, eine Menge **I U2,** 30
lotta *(slang)* ['lɒtə] viele °**VT2,** 35
parking lot *(AE)* ['pɑ:kɪŋ ˌlɒt] Parkplatz **IV U4,** 68
lots (of) ['lɒts‿əv] viel/viele **II U7,** 88
lots of love [ˌlɒts‿əv 'lʌv] viele Grüße *(am Briefende)* **III U4,** 68
loud [laʊd] laut **II U7,** 91
to say out loud [ˌseɪ‿aʊt 'laʊd] laut sagen °**III U4,** 67
love [lʌv] Liebe; Herzliche Grüße *(am Briefende)* **I U6,** 78
lots of love [ˌlɒts‿əv 'lʌv] viele Grüße *(am Briefende)* **III U4,** 68
to **love** [lʌv] lieben, gern mögen **I U3,** 44
lover ['lʌvə] Liebhaber; Geliebter/Geliebte **VI T1,** 15
low [ləʊ] niedrig, tief **IV U1,** 14
lower ['ləʊə] unterer/untere/unteres **IV U1,** 14
low-cut ['ləʊkʌt] tief ausgeschnitten **IV U5,** 76
loyal ['lɔɪəl] treu, loyal **VI T2,** 28
luck [lʌk] Glück **I U4,** 63
bad luck [ˌbæd 'lʌk] Pech **I U4,** 63
Good luck! [ˌgʊd 'lʌk] Viel Glück! **I U4,** 63
lucky ['lʌki] glücklich **I U1,** 16
luckily ['lʌkɪli] glücklicherweise **IV U2,** 26
to get lucky *(AE)* [get 'lʌki] Glück haben **IV U4,** 68
you're lucky [ˌjʊə 'lʌki] du hast Glück **I U1,** 16
luggage ['lʌgɪdʒ] Gepäck **II U7,** 90
lunch [lʌntʃ] Mittagessen **I U1,** 18
lunchtime ['lʌntʃtaɪm] Mittag, Mittagszeit **I U1,** 19
lung [lʌŋ] Lunge **VI T1,** 13
lyrics ['lɪrɪks] Liedtext °**IV U5,** 82

M

machine [mə'ʃi:n] Maschine, Apparat **III U4,** 66
vending machine ['vendɪŋ məˌʃi:n] Warenautomat **III U4,** 66
washing machine ['wɒʃɪŋ məˌʃi:n] Waschmaschine **IV U3,** 44
mad [mæd] verrückt; wütend **II U1,** 18
magazine [mægə'zi:n] Zeitschrift, Magazin **I U2,** 33
mail [meɪl] Post **VI T3,** 60
to **mail** [meɪl] mailen, per E-Mail schicken **IV U4,** 63
main [meɪn] Haupt- **II U4,** 49
Her **Majesty** [hə 'mædʒəsti] Ihre Majestät °**III U5,** 90
majority [mə'dʒɒrəti] Mehrheit(en-) **VI T1,** 11
*to **make** [meɪk] machen, tun **I U1,** 11
to make friends (with) [ˌmeɪk 'frendz] Freundschaft schließen (mit) **IV U4,** 68
to make it ['meɪk‿ɪt] es schaffen **III U4,** 68
to make sb do sth [meɪk] jmdn. veranlassen, etw. zu tun; jmdn. dafür gewinnen, etw. zu tun **VT3,** 54
to make sure [meɪk 'ʃʊə] sichergehen **II U6,** 82
to make up [meɪk‿'ʌp] erfinden, sich ausdenken **I U4,** 62
make-up ['meɪkʌp] Make-up, Schminke **I U7,** 90
male [meɪl] männlich; Männchen **VI T4,** 70
(shopping) **mall** [mɔ:l] Einkaufszentrum, Einkaufspassage **IV U2,** 32
man, men *(pl)* [mæn; men] Mann **I U4,** 62
to **manage** ['mænɪdʒ] bewältigen, handhaben; zurechtkommen **VI T1,** 12; **VI T3,** 56
management ['mænɪdʒmənt] Management, Geschäftsführung, Verwaltung **VT3,** 58
manager ['mænɪdʒə] Manager/Managerin **I U2,** 26
manga ['mæŋgə] Manga *(japanischer Comic)* **VI T1,** 14
adverb of **manner** [ˌædvɜ:b‿əv 'mænə] Adverb der Art und Weise °**II U7,** 90
mansion ['mænʃn] Villa °**IV U1,** 15
manta ray ['mæntə ˌreɪ] Mantarochen **VT4,** 79
to **manufacture** [ˌmænjə'fæktʃə] fertigen, herstellen, produzieren **VI T4,** 74
manufacturer [ˌmænjə'fæktʃərə] Hersteller **VI T4,** 74
manufacturing [ˌmænjə'fæktʃrɪŋ] Herstellung, Fertigung **VI T4,** 74
many ['meni] viele, etliche **I U5,** 68
how many [haʊ 'meni] wie viele **I U5,** 68
map [mæp] Stadtplan, Landkarte **I LUC,** 52
mind map ['maɪnd mæp] Wörternetz *(eine Art Schaubild)* °**III U1,** 18
maple ['meɪpl] Ahorn **IV U1,** 12
march [mɑ:tʃ] (Fuß-)Marsch **VT3,** 54
to **march** [mɑ:tʃ] marschieren **VT3,** 54
March [mɑ:tʃ] März **I U5,** 70
marijuana [ˌmærɪ'wɑ:nə] Marihuana **VT2,** 38
mark [mɑ:k] Fleck **I U2,** 30; Note *(in der Schule)* **II U3,** 44
to **mark** [mɑ:k] markieren °**II U2,** 29
market ['mɑ:kɪt] Markt **II U2,** 22

to **market** ['mɑ:kɪt] vermarkten, vertreiben **VI T4,** 74
marketing ['mɑ:kɪtɪŋ] Marketing, Vermarktung, Vertrieb **VI T4,** 74
marriage ['mærɪdʒ] Ehe(schließung) **VI T4,** 70
married to ['mærid tə] verheiratet mit **I U2,** 28
to **marry** ['mæri] heiraten **III U2,** 31
masala [me'sɑ:lʌ] Gewürze °**VI T1,** 17
mask [mɑ:sk] Maske; Mundschutz **V T4,** 74
massage ['mæsɑ:ʒ] Massage **V T1,** 13
match [mætʃ] Spiel, Wettkampf **II U2,** 24
to **match** [mætʃ] passen zu; zuordnen, zusammenfügen **III U3,** 50
to match up ['mætʃ‿ʌp] zusammenfügen °**II U4,** 52
mate [meɪt] Kamerad/Kameradin, Kumpel **V T2,** 32; **V T4,** 80
material [mə'tɪəriəl] Material; Stoff **IV U2,** 26
Maths [mæθs] Mathematik **II U1,** 10
matter ['mætə] Angelegenheit, Frage **IV U5,** 80; Materie **VI T4,** 77
no matter [nəʊ 'mætə] egal **IV U5,** 84
What's the matter? [ˌwɒts ðə 'mætə] Was ist los? **III U5,** 88
to **matter** ['mætə] von Bedeutung sein, ausmachen **IV U5,** 80
*__may__ [meɪ] kann/könnte(n) vielleicht **II U4,** 55
May [meɪ] Mai **I U5,** 70
maybe ['meɪbi] vielleicht **I U7,** 96
me [mi:] mich, mir **I LUB,** 38
meal [mi:l] Mahlzeit **II U4,** 52
*to **mean** [mi:n] bedeuten, meinen **I U4,** 55
mean [mi:n] gemein **IV U2,** 33
meaning ['mi:nɪŋ] Bedeutung **III U2,** 33
meanwhile [ˌmi:n'waɪl] mittlerweile, in der Zwischenzeit **V T3,** 50
measured ['meʒəd] gleichmäßig, gemessen, getragen **VI T2,** 37
measurement ['meʒəmənt] Maß, Maßeinheit °**III U3,** 55
meat [mi:t] Fleisch **III U3,** 50
mechanic [mə'kænɪk] Mechaniker/ Mechanikerin **IV U3,** 49
mechatronic engineer [mɪkæˌtrɒnɪk endʒɪ'nɪə] Mechatroniker/ Mechatronikerin **V T2,** 41
media *(pl)* ['mi:diə] Medien **VI T1,** 8; **VI T3,** 60
medium ['mi:diəm] mittel **I U5,** 66
*to **meet** [mi:t] (sich) treffen **I U3,** 45
to meet the needs (of) [ˌmi:t ðə 'ni:dz‿əv] die Bedürfnisse erfüllen (von), den Bedarf decken (von) **V T4,** 75
meeting ['mi:tɪŋ] Treffen, Besprechung **II U1,** 12
mela ['mi:lʌ] *trad. ind. Fest* °**VI T1,** 17
to **melt** [melt] schmelzen **VI T4,** 77
member ['membə] Mitglied **IV U5,** 77
Member of Parliament (MP) [ˌmembə‿əv 'pɑ:ləmənt] Mitglied des Parlaments; Abgeordneter/ Abgeordnete **VI T2,** 28
memory ['memri] Erinnerung; Gedächtnis **IV U3,** 50
menagerie [mə'nædʒri] Menagerie **III U2,** 31
to **mention** ['menʃn] erwähnen **VI T4,** 78
menu ['menju:] Speisekarte, Menü **II U1,** 14
Meow! [mi:'aʊ] Miau! °**I U2,** 35
mess [mes] Durcheinander **III U2,** 35
to **mess around** [ˌmes‿ə'raʊnd] herumalbern **V T2,** 30
to mess sth up [ˌmes‿'ʌp] etw. durcheinanderbringen; etw. vergeigen **V T3,** 52
message ['mesɪdʒ] Nachricht **II U3,** 38
text message ['tekst ˌmesɪdʒ] SMS **I U6,** 80
metal ['metl] Metal *(Musikrichtung)*; Metall **IV U5,** 80
metre (m) ['mi:tə] Meter **III U3,** 48
Mexican ['meksɪkən] mexikanisch; Mexikaner/Mexikanerin **IV U4,** 68
mice *(pl)* [maɪs] Mäuse **I U3,** 45
microphone ['maɪkrəfəʊn] Mikrofon **II U5,** 71
microwave ['maɪkrəʊweɪv] Mikrowelle **IV U3,** 46
middle ['mɪdl] Mitte; Mittel- **III U4,** 64
Middle Ages [ˌmɪdl‿'eɪdʒɪz] Mittelalter **VI T2,** 28
middle school *(AE)* ['mɪdl ˌsku:l] Mittelschule *(weiterführende Schule in den USA, Mittelstufe)* **IV U2,** 30
midnight ['mɪdnaɪt] Mitternacht **II U6,** 78
*__might__ [maɪt] könnte/könnten **IV U4,** 68
mile [maɪl] Meile *(brit. Längenmaß)* **II U6,** 74
for miles [fə‿'maɪlz] meilenweit **IV U4,** 69
militant ['mɪlɪtnt] militant, aggressiv **VI T2,** 29
military ['mɪlɪtri] Militär, Heer **VI T2,** 33
milk [mɪlk] Milch **I U5,** 68
milkman, milkmen *(pl)* ['mɪlkmən; 'mɪlkmen] Milchmann **III U2,** 34
milkshake ['mɪlkʃeɪk] Milchshake **IV U1,** 12
millennium [mɪ'leniəm] Jahrtausend **III U2,** 30
million ['mɪlɪən] Million **II U2,** 23
to **mime** [maɪm] pantomimisch darstellen °**I U6,** 81
miming game ['maɪmɪŋ geɪm] Pantomime °**I U6,** 81
mind [maɪnd] Geist, Verstand **III U5,** 83
He had something on his mind. [maɪnd] Ihn beschäftigte etwas. **III U5,** 83
mind map ['maɪnd mæp] Wörternetz *(eine Art Schaubild)* °**III U1,** 18
to change your mind [ˌtʃeɪndʒ jə 'maɪnd] deine Meinung ändern **III U1,** 17
I don't **mind.** [maɪnd] Ich habe nichts dagegen., Es ist mir egal. **VI T1,** 14
mineral ['mɪnərəl] Mineral- **II U4,** 49
mini ['mɪni] Mini- °**IV U2,** 29
minimum ['mɪnɪməm] Minimum **IV U4,** 62; mindest- **V T3,** 52
minister ['mɪnɪstə] Minister/Ministerin **VI T1,** 9; **VI T2,** 32
Prime Minister (PM) [ˌpraɪm 'mɪnɪstə] Premierminister/Premierministerin **VI T1,** 9; **VI T2,** 32
minute ['mɪnɪt] Minute **I U4,** 64
mirror ['mɪrə] Spiegel **III U4,** 67
to **miss** [mɪs] vermissen, fehlen; verpassen **II U6,** 76; verfehlen **IV U2,** 33
to miss a turn [ˌmɪs‿ə 'tɜ:n] einmal aussetzen °**II U6,** 79
to miss out (on) [mɪss‿'aʊt] vermissen, zu kurz kommen (mit) **IV U4,** 62
Miss [mɪs] Frau *(Anrede)* **I U7,** 94
missing ['mɪsɪŋ] fehlend °**I U4,** 64
to be missing [bi: 'mɪsɪŋ] fehlen **III U1,** 14
mistake [mɪ'steɪk] Fehler **III U5,** 86
mister ['mɪstə] Sie *(Anrede)* **IV U1,** 17
misuse ['mɪsju:s] Missbrauch °**V T2,** 39
mixed bag ['mɪkst bæg] Vermischtes °**III U1,** 21
mixture ['mɪkstʃə] Mischung, Gemisch, Mixtur **VI T1,** 10
to **moan** [məʊn] (sich) (be)klagen **III U1,** 16
mobile ['məʊbaɪl] Handy, Mobiltelefon **I U1,** 11
mobile ['məʊbaɪl] mobil, veränderlich **VI T1,** 18
modal auxiliary verb [ˌməʊdl‿ɔ:g'zɪljəri 'vɜ:b] modales Hilfsverb °**III U3,** 46

model ['mɒdl] Model, Modell **III U2,** 29
role model ['rəʊl ˌmɒdl] Vorbild **VI T2,** 35
modern ['mɒdn] modern **IV U3,** 43
mom *(AE)* [mɒm] Mama, Mutti **IV U4,** 65
moment ['məʊmənt] Moment, Augenblick **I U7,** 90
at the moment [æt ðə 'məʊmənt] im Augenblick, momentan **I U7,** 90
monarch ['mɒnək] Monarch/Monarchin, Herrscher/Herrscherin **VI T2,** 28
monastery ['mɒnəstri] Kloster **III U2,** 31
Monday ['mʌndeɪ] Montag **I LUB,** 39
on Mondays [ɒn 'mʌndeɪz] montags **I LUB,** 39
money ['mʌni] Geld **I U5,** 67
pocket money ['pɒkɪt ˌmʌni] Taschengeld **II U2,** 22
Mongolian [mɒŋ'gəʊliən] mongolisch; Mongole/Mongolin **V T4,** 71
to **monitor** ['mɒnɪtə] überwachen **IV U3,** 43
aerial **monorail** [ˌeəriəl 'mɒnəreɪl] Schwebebahn **V T1,** 18
monster ['mɒnstə] Monster **IV U1,** 12
month [mʌnθ] Monat **I U5,** 70
mood [mu:d] Stimmung, Laune **V T3,** 58
moon [mu:n] Mond **II U7,** 94
moor [mɔ:] Hochmoor **II U6,** 74
more [mɔ:] mehr **I U2,** 29
morning ['mɔ:nɪŋ] Morgen, Vormittag **I U1,** 16
Good morning! [ˌgʊd 'mɔ:nɪŋ] Guten Morgen! **I U1,** 16
in the morning [ˌɪn ðə 'mɔ:nɪŋ] morgens, am Morgen, vormittags **I U3,** 47
the next morning [ðə ˌnekst 'mɔ:nɪŋ] am nächsten Morgen **II U1,** 18
most [məʊst] das meiste, die meisten **I U3,** 44
mostly ['məʊstli] überwiegend, größtenteils, hauptsächlich **IV U1,** 14
motel [məʊ'tel] Motel **°IV U3,** 46
moth [mɒθ] Motte, Falter **VI T4,** 78
mother ['mʌðə] Mutter **III U3,** 52
mother tongue ['mʌðə ˌtʌŋ] Muttersprache **VI T1,** 10
motion ['məʊʃn] Bewegung **IV U5,** 78; Thema **°VI T2,** 37; **°VI T3,** 53
motor ['məʊtəbaɪk] Motor(-) **VI T4,** 74
motorbike ['məʊtəbaɪk] Motorrad **IV U4,** 61
motorway ['məʊtəweɪ] Autobahn **IV U4,** 65
motto ['mɒtəʊ] Motto **VI T3,** 61
mountain ['maʊntɪn] Berg **IV U3,** 50
mouse, mice *(pl)* [maʊs; maɪs] Maus **I U1,** 10
mouth [maʊθ] Mund **II U3,** 41
mouth-to-mouth [ˌmaʊθtə'maʊθ] Mund-zu-Mund-Beatmung **V T1,** 13
move [mu:v] Schritt, Bewegung **IV U2,** 29
to **move** [mu:v] (sich) bewegen; umziehen **II U6,** 78
movement ['mu:vmənt] Bewegung **V T3,** 54
Civil Rights Movement (CRM) [ˌsɪvl 'raɪts ˌmu:vmənt] Bürgerrechtsbewegung **V T3,** 54
movie *(AE)* ['mu:vi] Film **IV U2,** 28
movies *(AE)* ['mu:viz] Kino **IV U2,** 28
MP3 [ˌempi:'θri:] MP3 **II U5,** 62
MP3 player [ˌempi:'θri: ˌpleɪə] MP3-Player **II U5,** 62
Mr ['mɪstə] Herr *(Anrede)* **I U1,** 12
Mrs ['mɪsɪz] Frau *(Anrede)* **I U1,** 12
much [mʌtʃ] viel **I U5,** 66
How much are … ? [ˌhaʊ 'mʌtʃ‿ɑ:] Wie viel kosten … ? **I U5,** 66
How much is … ? [ˌhaʊ 'mʌtʃ‿ɪz] Wie viel kostet … ? **I U5,** 66
multicultural [ˌmʌlti'kʌltʃrl] multikulturell **VI T1,** 16
multi-lingual [ˌmʌlti'lɪŋgwəl] vielsprachig **VI T1,** 10
multinational [ˌmʌlti'næʃnl] multinational **V T4,** 73
multiple choice [ˌmʌltɪpl 'tʃɔɪs] Multiple-Choice *(Auswahl aus mehreren Möglichkeiten)* **°VI T1,** 13
mum [mʌm] Mama, Mutti **I LUA,** 25
mural ['mjʊərl] Graffiti, Wandmalerei **V T2,** 32
murder ['mɜ:də] Mord, Ermordung **V T3,** 51
to **murder** ['mɜ:də] ermorden **III U5,** 88
museum [mju:'zi:əm] Museum **I LUC,** 52
music ['mju:zɪk] Musik **I U2,** 34
musical ['mju:zɪkl] Musical **III U5,** 80
musician [mju:'zɪʃn] Musiker/Musikerin **IV U5,** 80
must [mʌst] Muss **VI T1,** 15
***must** [mʌst] müssen **I U7,** 94
my [maɪ] mein/meine **I U1,** 10
My God! [maɪ 'gɒd] Mein Gott! **II U6,** 82
My name is … . [maɪ 'neɪm‿ɪz] Ich heiße … . **I U1,** 10
My turn had come. [tɜ:n] Ich war an der Reihe. **VI T2,** 36
myself [maɪ'self] ich/mich (selbst) **III U4,** 67
mystery ['mɪstri] Geheimnis, Rätsel **III U3,** 49
myth [mɪθ] Mythos **III U5,** 81

N

naan [nɑ:n] *indisches Fladenbrot* **°VI T1,** 17
name [neɪm] Name **I U1,** 10
My name is … . [maɪ 'neɪm‿ɪz] Ich heiße … . **I U1,** 10
What's your name? [ˌwɒts jə 'neɪm] Wie heißt du? **I U1,** 11
to **name** [neɪm] (be)nennen **IV U1,** 10
narrow ['nærəʊ] eng, schmal **VI T2,** 37
nation ['neɪʃn] Nation, Volk **VI T2,** 32
national ['næʃnl] national **II U6,** 82; landesweit **III U1,** 10
national guard [ˌnæʃnl 'gɑ:d] Nationalgarde **°V T3,** 54
national park [ˌnæʃnl 'pɑ:k] Nationalpark **IV U4,** 60
native ['neɪtɪv] eingeboren, einheimisch, gebürtig **IV U1,** 9
Native American [ˌneɪtɪv‿ə'merɪkən] Ureinwohner/Ureinwohnerin Amerikas, Indianer/Indianerin **IV U1,** 9
natural ['nætʃrl] natürlich, Natur- **V T1,** 18 ; **V T4,** 74
natural-born [ˌnætʃrl'bɔ:n] gebürtig, von Geburt an **VI T2,** 33
natural gas [ˌnætʃrl 'gæs] Erdgas **V T4,** 74
nature ['neɪtʃə] Natur **IV U4,** 62
near [nɪə] in der Nähe von, nahe **I LUC,** 53
nearly ['nɪəli] fast, annähernd **III U1,** 16
neat *(AE)* [ni:t] klasse; hübsch **V T3,** 56
necessary ['nesəsri] notwendig, nötig **°V T2,** 39
need [ni:d] Bedürfnis, Bedarf; Erfordernis **V T4,** 75
to meet the needs (of) [ˌmi:t ðə 'ni:dz‿əv] die Bedürfnisse erfüllen (von), den Bedarf decken (von) **V T4,** 75
to **need** [ni:d] brauchen, benötigen, müssen **II U1,** 21
negative ['negətɪv] negativ, verneint **°III U5,** 82
negative statement [ˌnegətɪv 'steɪtmənt] Verneinung **°III U5,** 82
neighborhood *(AE)* ['neɪbəhʊd] Viertel; Nachbarschaft **IV U1,** 9
neighbour ['neɪbə] Nachbar/Nachbarin **II U7,** 90

neon ['ni:ɒn] neonfarben **IV U1,** 9
nephew ['nefju:] Neffe **III U5,** 88
nervous ['nɜ:vəs] nervös, aufgeregt **II U5,** 71
nervous system ['nɜ:vəs ˌsɪstəm] Nervensystem **V T2,** 38
net [net] Netz **III U1,** 10
neutral ['nju:trl] neutral **V T3,** 53
never ['nevə] nie, niemals **I U3,** 44
new [nju:] neu **I U1,** 10
news *(sg)* [nju:z] Nachricht(en), Neuigkeit(en) **III U3,** 48
breaking news [ˌbreɪkɪŋ 'nju:z] neueste Nachrichten **IV U2,** 24
newsagent ['nju:sˌeɪdʒənt] Zeitschriftenhändler/ Zeitschriftenhändlerin **I LUC,** 52
newspaper ['nju:sˌpeɪpə] Zeitung **III U2,** 28
next [nekst] nächster/nächste/ nächstes **I U5,** 69; als Nächstes °**II U1,** 19
next door [ˌnekst 'dɔ:] nebenan **III U1,** 16
next to ['nekst tə] neben **I U2,** 28
the next morning [ðə ˌnekst 'mɔ:nɪŋ] am nächsten Morgen **II U1,** 18
nice [naɪs] nett **I U1,** 12; schön **II U4,** 54
nickel ['nɪkl] Nickel *(Währung)* **IV U1,** 13
nickname ['nɪkneɪm] Spitzname **IV U5,** 77
night [naɪt] Nacht, Abend **I U3,** 44
at night [ət 'naɪt] nachts **II U3,** 47
last night [lɑ:st 'naɪt] gestern Abend/ Nacht **II U3,** 37
night nurse ['naɪt nɜ:s] Nachtschwester **I U3,** 47
nightmare ['naɪtmeə] Albtraum **V T4,** 72
no [nəʊ] nein, nicht; kein/keine **I U1,** 12
no idea [ˌnəʊ‿aɪ'dɪə] keine Ahnung **III U3,** 52
no one ['nəʊwʌn] niemand **II U2,** 30
No way! [ˌnəʊ‿'weɪ] Auf keinen Fall! **IV U4,** 62
no wonder [nəʊ 'wʌndə] kein Wunder, dass … **V T2,** 39
No. ['nʌmbə] Nummer **V T1,** 10
nobody ['nəʊbədi] niemand **III U5,** 85
noise [nɔɪz] Geräusch, Lärm **I U2,** 35
none [nʌn] keiner/keine **II U7,** 88
non-fiction [ˌnɒn'fɪkʃn] Sachliteratur; Sach- **VI T3,** 57
non-official [ˌnɒnə'fɪʃl] inoffiziell **VI T1,** 11
non-stop [ˌnɒn'stɒp] non-stop, durchgehend, ohne Unterbrechung **V T3,** 50
normal ['nɔ:ml] normal **I U3,** 44
normally ['nɔ:mli] normalerweise **VI T1,** 10
north [nɔ:θ] Norden **I U4,** 55
Norwegian [nɔ:'wi:dʒn] norwegisch; Norweger/Norwegerin **V T4,** 71
nose [nəʊz] Nase **II U3,** 41
not [nɒt] nicht **I U1,** 16
not … yet [jet] noch nicht **II U5,** 66
(not …) at all [ˌnɒt … ət‿'ɔ:l] überhaupt (nicht) **IV U2,** 32
not … either [ˌnɒt … 'aɪðə] auch nicht **III U1,** 17
not either [nɒt 'aɪðə] keiner/keine/ keines **VI T2,** 28
not even [nɒt‿'i:vn] nicht einmal **III U4,** 64
note [nəʊt] Notiz, Anmerkung **II U1,** 11
sick note ['sɪk ˌnəʊt] Krankmeldung **II U2,** 28
to take notes [teɪk 'nəʊts] sich Notizen machen °**II U4,** 55
to **note** [nəʊt] notieren °**IV U1,** 14
nothing ['nʌθɪŋ] nichts **II U4,** 50
notice ['nəʊtɪs] Anschlag, Notiz **III U4,** 66
notice board ['nəʊtɪs bɔ:d] schwarzes Brett **III U4,** 66
to **notice** ['nəʊtɪs] bemerken **III U3,** 48
noun [naʊn] Nomen °**III U1,** 18
novel ['nɒvl] Roman **VI T4,** 76
November [nəʊ'vembə] November **I U5,** 70
now [naʊ] jetzt, nun **I U1,** 20
right now [ˌraɪt 'naʊ] jetzt gleich, in diesem Augenblick **I U7,** 92
nowhere ['nəʊweə] nirgendwo, nirgendwohin **III U4,** 64
nuclear-powered [ˌnju:kliə'paʊəd] atombetrieben **VI T3,** 56
number ['nʌmbə] Nummer, Zahl **I U1,** 11
phone number ['fəʊn ˌnʌmbə] Telefonnummer **I U1,** 11
social security number [ˌsəʊʃl sɪ'kjʊərəti ˌnʌmbə] Sozialversicherungsnummer **IV U3,** 50
nurse [nɜ:s] Krankenschwester, Krankenpfleger **I U3,** 47
night nurse ['naɪt nɜ:s] Nachtschwester **I U3,** 47
nutrition [nju:'trɪʃn] Ernährung(slehre) **V T2,** 40
*to be **nuts about** [bi: ˌnʌts‿ə'baʊt] verrückt nach … sein **II U1,** 18

O

object ['ɒbdʒɪkt] Objekt, Gegenstand **IV U3,** 51
observatory [əb'zɜ:vətri] Observatorium, Sternwarte **I U5,** 73
occasionally [ə'keɪʒnli] gelegentlich **V T2,** 38
ocean ['əʊʃn] Ozean **III U3,** 45
ocean liner ['əʊʃn ˌlaɪnə] Ozeandampfer **III U3,** 45
October [ɒk'təʊbə] Oktober **I U5,** 70
octopus ['ɒktəpəs] Oktopus, Krake **V T1,** 13
Blue Ring Octopus [ˌblu: rɪŋ 'ɒktəpəs] blaugeringelter Krake °**V T1,** 13
odd one out [ɒd wʌn‿'aʊt] das nicht dazu passende (Wort) **II U5,** 72
odour ['əʊdə] Geruch, Duft **V T2,** 32
of [ɒv; əv] von **I U2,** 26
of course [əv 'kɔ:s] natürlich, selbstverständlich **I U1,** 19
off [ɒf] herunter, ab, weg von **II U3,** 36
to be off [bi:‿'ɒf] daneben sein **V T2,** 35
to be off to [bi:‿'ɒf tə] auf dem Weg sein zu/nach, gehen zu/nach **V T3,** 50
to get off [get‿'ɒf] aussteigen aus **I U4,** 59; wegräumen von, abräumen von **III U4,** 65
to have a day off [ˌhæv‿ə 'deɪ‿ɒf] einen Tag frei haben **V T3,** 58
to send off [send‿'ɒf] vom Platz verweisen **III U1,** 15
to take off [ˌteɪk‿'ɒf] ausziehen **III U3,** 52
offer ['ɒfə] Angebot **IV U5,** 81
to **offer** ['ɒfə] anbieten **IV U4,** 62
office ['ɒfɪs] Büro **II U2,** 31
post office ['pəʊst‿ɒfɪs] Postamt **III U2,** 35
officer ['ɒfɪsə] Beamter/Beamtin **III U3,** 45
chief executive officer (CEO) [ˌtʃi:f‿ɪgˌzekjətɪv‿'ɒfɪsə; ˌsi: i:'əʊ] Generaldirektor/Generaldirektorin; Geschäftsführer/Geschäftsführerin **VI T4,** 74
communications officer [kəmju:nɪ'keɪʃnz ˌɒfɪsə] Pressesprecher/Pressesprecherin **VI T3,** 61
official [ə'fɪʃl] offiziell **III U3,** 48; Beamter/Beamtin **IV U1,** 10
offside [ˌɒf'saɪd] im Abseits **VI T1,** 12
often ['ɒfn] oft **I U3,** 44
oh [əʊ] oh °**I U1,** 12
oil [ɔɪl] Öl **V T4,** 71
Oink-oink! [ɔɪŋk‿ɔɪŋk] Grunz! °**I U6,** 82
OK [əʊ'keɪ] o.k. **I U1,** 12
is OK with us [ɪz‿əʊ'keɪ wɪð‿ʌs] ist uns recht **I U6,** 78

We're OK. [ˌwɪər‿əʊ'keɪ] Es geht uns gut. **I U6,** 83
old [əʊld] alt **I U1,** 11
How old are you? [haʊ‿'əʊld‿ɑ: ju:] Wie alt bist du? **I U1,** 11
the **Olympics** *(Olympic Games)* [əʊ'lɪmpɪks; əʊˌlɪmpɪk 'geɪmz] Olympiade, Olympische Spiele **V T1,** 11
on [ɒn] auf, an **I U1,** 14
on board [ɒn 'bɔ:d] an Bord **IV U3,** 51
on foot [ɒn 'fʊt] zu Fuß **I U4,** 57
on Mondays [ɒn 'mʌndeɪz] montags **I LUB,** 39
on record [ɒn 'rekɔ:d] verzeichnet, dokumentiert **III U3,** 46
on the air [ˌɒn ði‿'eə] auf Sendung **II U4,** 55
on the bus [ˌɒn ðə 'bʌs] im Bus **II U1,** 18
on the job [ˌɒn ðə 'dʒɒb] bei der Arbeit **III U5,** 82
on the left [ɒn ðə 'left] links **I U2,** 28
On the one hand ..., (but) on the other hand ... [ɒn ðə‿'wʌn ˌhænd ... ɒn ði‿'ʌðə ˌhænd ...] Einerseits ..., andererseits ... **VI T2,** 32
on the right [ɒn ðə 'raɪt] rechts **I U2,** 28
on time [ɒn 'taɪm] pünktlich **IV U3,** 48
to be on [bi:‿'ɒn] an der Reihe sein; im Gange sein, laufen **II U5,** 70; brennen **II U7,** 94
once [wʌnts] einmal, einst **II U3,** 36
at once [ət 'wʌnts] sofort, plötzlich **II U7,** 94
one day [wʌn 'deɪ] eines Tages **II U3,** 36
one(s) [wʌn(z)] *(Platzhalter für ein Nomen)* **III U2,** 29
online [ˌɒn'laɪn] online, im Internet **V T2,** 34
only ['əʊnli] nur, bloß, erst **I U2,** 26; einziger/einzige/einziges **III U5,** 88
only child ['əʊnli ˌtʃaɪld] Einzelkind **I U2,** 26
onto ['ɒntu:; 'ɒntə] (auf ...) hinauf, auf **II U1,** 19
Oops! [u:ps] Hoppla! Huch! °**I U1,** 20
to **open** ['əʊpn] öffnen, aufmachen **I U1,** 19; sich öffnen, aufgehen **III U5,** 86
open ['əʊpn] offen, geöffnet **II U2,** 23
opera ['ɒprə] Oper **V T1,** 9
to **operate** ['ɒpəreɪt] bedienen; operieren **IV U3,** 43
opinion [ə'pɪnjən] Meinung **IV U1,** 11
opportunity [ˌɒpə'tju:nəti] Gelegenheit, Möglichkeit **V T2,** 32; **V T4,** 70
opposite ['ɒpəzɪt] gegenüber °**II U4,** 49; Gegenteil °**IV U1,** 18; entgegengesetzt, gegenüberliegend **VI T2,** 34
oppression [ə'preʃn] Unterdrückung **IV U1,** 10
optimism ['ɒptɪmɪzm] Optimismus **VI T4,** 77
option ['ɒpʃn] Auswahlmöglichkeit, Option **V T1,** 10; **V T2,** 32; **V T3,** 50; **V T4,** 72
or [ɔ:] oder **I U1,** 11
orally ['ɔ:rli] mündlich **VI T4,** 75
orange ['ɒrɪndʒ] Orange; orange **II U4,** 54
ordeal [ɔ:'di:l] Feuerprobe, Qual, Tortur **VI T2,** 36
order ['ɔ:də] Reihenfolge, Ordnung **IV U3,** 48; Befehl, Anweisung **V T3,** 59
to **order** ['ɔ:də] bestellen **II U4,** 49
ordinary ['ɔ:dnri] einfach, herkömmlich, normal **VI T3,** 58
organic [ɔ:'gænɪk] biologisch angebaut, organisch **V T4,** 76; **VI T3,** 50
organic label [ɔ:ˌgænɪk 'leɪbl] Biosiegel **V T4,** 76
organisation [ˌɔ:gnaɪ'zeɪʃn] Organisation, Unternehmen **V T4,** 76
organizational [ˌɔ:gnaɪ'zeɪʃnl] organisatorisch **VI T4,** 75
to **organize** ['ɔ:gənaɪz] organisieren **I U7,** 90
organizer ['ɔ:gənaɪzə] Organisator/Organisatorin, Veranstalter/Veranstalterin **III U4,** 63
origin ['ɒrɪdʒɪn] Ursprung, Herkunft, Quelle **V T3,** 55
other ['ʌðə] anderer/andere/anderes **I U7,** 91
each other [ˌi:tʃ‿'ʌðə] sich gegenseitig **II U1,** 19
the other way round [ði ˌʌðə‿weɪ 'raʊnd] andersrum, umgekehrt **V T2,** 35
our ['aʊə] unser/unsere **I U2,** 26
ourselves [aʊə'selvz] wir/uns (selbst) **III U4,** 67
out [aʊt] heraus, hinaus, draußen, außerhalb **I U3,** 42
Keep out! [ki:p‿'aʊt] Eintritt verboten! **I U2,** 26
out and about ['aʊt‿nd‿ə'baʊt] unterwegs °**I U4,** 54
out of ['aʊt‿əv] aus ... heraus **I U3,** 49
out of this world [ˌaʊt‿əv ðɪs 'wɜ:ld] nicht von dieser Welt **V T1,** 11
to get out [get‿'aʊt] aussteigen **I U6,** 86; entkommen **III U3,** 53
to hang out [hæŋ‿'aʊt] sich herumtreiben **III U4,** 64
to put out [pʊt‿'aʊt] hinausstellen **III U4,** 65
to sort out [sɔ:t‿'aʊt] klären, regeln *(ein Problem)* **I U2,** 30
to take out [teɪk‿'aʊt] herausnehmen **I U3,** 42
the **Outback** ['aʊtbæk] das Outback *(australisches Hinterland)* **V T1,** 9
outdoors [ˌaʊt'dɔ:z] freie Natur; in der freien Natur; draußen **VI T3,** 60
outer ['aʊtə] äußerer/äußere/äußeres **V T4,** 79
outgoing ['aʊtgəʊɪŋ] aufgeschlossen, kontaktfreudig **V T3,** 59
outrageous [aʊt'reɪdʒəs] gewagt; empörend **IV U5,** 76
outside [aʊt'saɪd] außerhalb, (nach) draußen **I U2,** 30
outsider [ˌaʊt'saɪdə] Außenseiter/Außenseiterin **V T2,** 33
to **outsource** ['aʊtsɔ:s] ausgliedern, outsourcen **VI T1,** 11
outsourcing ['aʊtsɔ:sɪŋ] Outsourcing *(Ausgliederung von Produktions- oder Dienstleistungen an externe Mitarbeiter)* **VI T1,** 11
oven ['ʌvn] Backofen **I U3,** 42
over ['əʊvə] über **I U2,** 26; vorbei, vorüber **II U5,** 70
all over [ˌɔ:l‿'əʊvə] überall **III U3,** 49
over easy [ˌəʊvər‿'i:zi] beidseitig gebraten *(Ei)* **IV U4,** 65
over there [ˌəʊvə 'ðeə] da drüben **I U5,** 66
to come over [kʌm‿'əʊvə] herüberkommen **I U2,** 27
*to **overdo** [ˌəʊvə'du:] übertreiben **IV U2,** 28
*to **overhear** [ˌəʊvə'hɪə] zufällig mitanhören, belauschen **VI T1,** 16
overseas [ˌəʊvə'si:z] nach/in Übersee, ins/im Ausland **VI T2,** 33
*to **overtake** [ˌəʊvə'teɪk] überholen **V T1,** 10; **V T3,** 56
overweight [ˌəʊvə'weɪt] übergewichtig **V T2,** 33
overwhelming [ˌəʊvə'welmɪŋ] überwältigend **IV U4,** 60
to **owe** [əʊ] verdanken, schulden **V T3,** 51
barn **owl** ['bɑ:n‿əʊl] Schleiereule **II U7,** 94
to **own** [əʊn] besitzen **V T3,** 55
own [əʊn] eigener/eigene/eigenes **II U6,** 76
owner ['əʊnə] Besitzer/Besitzerin **II U5,** 71
oxygen ['ɒksɪdʒən] Sauerstoff **VI T3,** 59

P

pacemaker ['peɪsˌmeɪkə] Herzschrittmacher **IV U3,** 43
to **pack** [pæk] packen **I U6,** 80
packaging ['pækɪdʒɪŋ] Verpackung, Packmaterial **VI T3,** 58
packet ['pækɪt] Päckchen, Paket **I U5,** 68
page [peɪdʒ] Seite **I U1,** 19
web page ['web ˌpeɪdʒ] Website, Internetauftritt °**V T1,** 13
pain [peɪn] Schmerz **IV U3,** 50
paint [peɪnt] Farbe **II U3,** 40
to **paint** [peɪnt] (an)malen, (an)streichen **I U7,** 90
painter ['peɪntə] Maler/Malerin °**IV U1,** 15
painting ['peɪntɪŋ] Gemälde **III U5,** 89
pair [peə] Paar °**I U1,** 22
pal [pæl] Kumpel **V T2,** 35
palace ['pælɪs] Palast **III U2,** 26
pale [peɪl] blass **VI T4,** 78
Palestinian [ˌpælə'stɪniən] palästinensisch; Palästinenser/Palästinenserin **VI T2,** 29
palm [pɑːm] Palme; Palm- **V T4,** 74
pancake ['pænkeɪk] Pfannkuchen **IV U1,** 12
panel ['pænl] Tafel, Platte; Element **V T4,** 71
panel (of experts) ['pænl] Expertenrunde, Gremium °**VI T2,** 35; °**VI T3,** 59; °**VI T4,** 75
solar panel [ˌsəʊlə 'pænl] Sonnenkollektor **V T4,** 71
to **panic** ['pænɪk] panisch reagieren, sich aufregen **II U5,** 70
panther ['pæntθə] Panter **II U2,** 25
paper ['peɪpə] Papier; Zeitung; Dokument **IV U1,** 14
parade [pə'reɪd] Parade, Umzug **IV U1,** 14
paradise ['pærəˌdaɪs] Paradies **III U3,** 46
paragraph ['pærəgrɑːf] Paragraf, Absatz °**IV U4,** 66
parent ['peərnt] Elternteil **IV U2,** 27
parental [pə'rentl] elterlich **VI T4,** 70
parents *(pl)* ['peərənts] Eltern **I U2,** 26
park [pɑːk] Park **I U3,** 40
national park [ˌnæʃnl 'pɑːk] Nationalpark **IV U4,** 60
theme park ['θiːm ˌpɑːk] Freizeitpark **IV U2,** 24
to **park** [pɑːk] parken **V T3,** 56
parking lot *(AE)* ['pɑːkɪŋ ˌlɒt] Parkplatz **IV U4,** 68
parliament ['pɑːləmənt] Parlament **VI T2,** 28
Member of Parliament (MP) [ˌmembə‿əv 'pɑːləmənt] Mitglied des Parlaments; Abgeordneter/Abgeordnete **VI T2,** 28
part [pɑːt] Teil **II U3,** 47; Rolle **II U5,** 70
part-time (P/T) [ˌpɑːt'taɪm] Teilzeit- **V T1,** 14
to take part in [teɪk 'pɑːt‿ɪn] teilnehmen an **III U4,** 63
participant [pɑː'tɪsɪpənt] Teilnehmer/Teilnehmerin **VI T1,** 12
particle ['pɑːtɪkl] Teilchen, Partikel **VI T4,** 77
partner ['pɑːtnə] Partner/Partnerin **I U1,** 15
party ['pɑːti] Party, Feier **I U5,** 68; Partei **VI T2,** 32
to have a party [ˌhæv‿ə 'pɑːti] eine Party feiern **I U5,** 68
to **pass** [pɑːs] weitergeben, herüberreichen **II U1,** 18; vorbeigehen (an) **III U5,** 85; bestehen **IV U2,** 30; verabschieden, beschließen **V T3,** 55
passenger ['pæsndʒə] Passagier/Passagierin, Beifahrer/Beifahrerin **III U3,** 45
passion ['pæʃn] Passion, Leidenschaft **VI T1,** 10
passive ['pæsɪv] passiv; Passiv °**IV U3,** 54
passport ['pɑːspɔːt] (Reise-)Pass **III U3,** 50
passports *(pl)* ['pɑːspɔːts] Passkontrolle **III U3,** 50
past [pɑːst] Vergangenheit **II U1,** 13
past perfect [ˌpɑːst 'pɜːfɪkt] Plusquamperfekt °**III U2,** 31
simple past [ˌsɪmpl 'pɑːst] einfache Vergangenheit °**III U2,** 28
past [pɑːst] vorbei, vorüber **I U7,** 97; nach *(Uhrzeit)* **II U1,** 12; vergangen; früherer/frühere/früheres °**IV U1,** 10
half past (two) ['hɑːf pɑːst] halb (drei) **I U3,** 40
pastrami [pəs'trɑːmi] Pastrami **IV U1,** 12
patch [pætʃ] Beet; Fleck, Stelle; Flicken; Augenklappe **V T2,** 39
path [pɑːθ] Pfad, Weg **II U4,** 56
pathetic [pə'θetɪk] Mitleid erregend, erbärmlich **VI T4,** 77
patient ['peɪʃnt] Patient/Patientin **III U5,** 82
pause [pɔːz] Pause °**III U5,** 86
pay [peɪ] Lohn, Gehalt, Bezahlung **V T1,** 14; **V T3,** 55
*to **pay** [peɪ] (be)zahlen **III U5,** 85
to pay (for) [peɪ] bezahlen **IV U2,** 32
payment ['peɪmənt] (Be-/Aus-)Zahlung, Entlohnung **V T4,** 76
PC [ˌpiː'siː] PC **II U5,** 63; Polizeibeamter/Polizeibeamtin °**III U5,** 83
pea [piː] Erbse **II U4,** 54
peace [piːs] Friede **II U7,** 88
peacefully ['piːsfli] friedlich °**V T3,** 55
pear [peə] Birne **II U4,** 54
pedal ['pedl] Pedal **V T3,** 56
peer [pɪə] Gleichaltriger/Gleichaltrige **V T2,** 33
pen [pen] Füller **I U1,** 14
penalty ['penlti] Strafe, Bestrafung; Elfmeter *(Fußball)* **V T3,** 51
pence *(pl)* [pents] Pence *(Währung)* **I U5,** 67
pencil ['pensl] Bleistift **I U1,** 14
pencil case ['pensl ˌkeɪs] Mäppchen **I U1,** 14
penknife, penknives *(pl)* ['pennaɪf; 'pennaɪvz] Taschenmesser **I U6,** 84
people ['piːpl] Leute, Menschen **I U2,** 29
people, peoples *(pl)* ['piːpl] Volk **VI T1,** 11
per [pɜː] pro **III U5,** 80
per cent (%) [pə 'sent] Prozent **IV U4,** 66
percentage [pə'sentɪdʒ] Prozentsatz, prozentualer Anteil **V T2,** 38
perfect ['pɜːfɪkt] perfekt, vollkommen **V T2,** 40
past perfect [ˌpɑːst 'pɜːfɪkt] Plusquamperfekt °**III U2,** 31
to **perform** [pə'fɔːm] aufführen, auftreten **III U4,** 63
performance [pə'fɔːməns] Aufführung, Vorstellung **III U4,** 63
perhaps [pə'hæps] vielleicht **III U5,** 83
period *(AE)* ['pɪəriəd] Unterrichtsstunde; Periode, Zeitabschnitt **IV U2,** 27
permanent ['pɜːmnənt] permanent, dauerhaft **V T1,** 14
permission [pə'mɪʃn] Erlaubnis **IV U2,** 27
person ['pɜːsn] Person **II U3,** 42
personal ['pɜːsnl] persönlich **V T2,** 34
personality [ˌpɜːsn'æləti] Persönlichkeit, Charakter **VI T1,** 18
pesticide ['pestɪsaɪd] Insektenvernichtungsmittel, Pestizid **V T4,** 76
pet [pet] Haustier, Liebling **III U5,** 82
petrol ['petrl] Benzin, Kraftstoff **VI T3,** 52
phone [fəʊn] Telefon **I U1,** 11
cell phone *(AE)* ['sel fəʊn] Mobiltelefon, Handy **IV U3,** 44
phone box ['fəʊn ˌbɒks] Telefonzelle **III U3,** 50
phone call ['fəʊn ˌkɔːl] (Telefon-)Anruf **V T3,** 52

phone number ['fəʊn ˌnʌmbə] Telefonnummer **I U1,** 11
to **phone** [fəʊn] anrufen, telefonieren **I U2,** 33
phonetic [fə'netɪk] phonetisch °**III U5,** 86
phonetics [fə'netɪks] Phonetik, Lautschrift °**VI T1,** 17
photo ['fəʊtəʊ] Foto(grafie) **II U5,** 64
photographer [fə'tɒgrəfə] Fotograf/Fotografin **IV U5,** 77
photography [fə'tɒgrəfi] Fotografie **IV U4,** 62
phrase [freɪz] Redewendung, Ausdruck **IV U5,** 82
physical ['fɪzɪkl] physisch, körperlich **II U1,** 10
Physical Education (PE) [ˌfɪzɪkl͜ edʒʊ'keɪʃn] Sport *(Schulfach)* **II U1,** 10
Physics ['fɪzɪks] Physik **VI T4,** 75
to **pick** [pɪk] pflücken, auswählen **I U6,** 78
to pick on sb ['pɪk͜ ɒn] jmdn. hänseln, jmdn. ärgern, auf jmdm. herumhacken **V T2,** 35
to pick out [pɪk͜ 'aʊt] auswählen, aussuchen; erkennen **VI T1,** 16
to pick up [pɪk͜ 'ʌp] aufheben, abholen **II U1,** 18
picker ['pɪkə] Pflücker/Pflückerin **IV U4,** 68
pickpocket ['pɪkˌpɒkɪt] Taschendieb/Taschendiebin **III U2,** 28
picture ['pɪktʃə] Bild **I U1,** 14; Film **IV U5,** 77
to take pictures [teɪk 'pɪktʃəz] fotografieren, Fotos machen **II U5,** 62
pie [paɪ] Kuchen; Pastete °**VI T3,** 59
pie diagram ['paɪ ˌdaɪəgræm] Kuchen-, Tortendiagramm °**VI T3,** 59
piece [pi:s] Stück **III U2,** 30
pier [pɪə] Pier, Mole **V T4,** 81
I want my … **pierced.** [aɪ 'wɒnt maɪ … 'pɪəst] Ich möchte mein … piercen lassen. **III U4,** 62
pig [pɪg] Schwein **I U6,** 82
piggy bank ['pɪgi bæŋk] Sparschwein **II U2,** 23
pile [paɪl] Stapel, Haufen **VI T4,** 76
pilot ['paɪlət] Pilot/Pilotin **IV U1,** 16
pineapple ['paɪnæpl] Ananas **V T4,** 73
pink [pɪŋk] pink, rosa **I LUA,** 24
pioneer [ˌpaɪə'nɪə] Pionier/Pionierin, Wegbereiter/Wegbereiterin **V T3,** 50
pipe [paɪp] Pfeife **III U5,** 84; Rohr(leitung) **VI T3,** 56
pitch [pɪtʃ] Spielfeld **III U1,** 10
pitcher ['pɪtʃə] Werfer/Werferin **III U1,** 14
to **pivot** ['pɪvət] sich drehen, schwenken **V T4,** 79
pizza ['pi:tsə] Pizza **I U5,** 68
place [pleɪs] Platz, Stelle, Ort **I U2,** 26; Heim, Haus **V T2,** 34
change of place [ˌtʃeɪndʒ͜ əv 'pleɪs] Ortswechsel °**III U4,** 65
to go places [ˌgəʊ 'pleɪsɪz] herumreisen **IV U4,** 68
to take place [teɪk 'pleɪs] stattfinden **III U4,** 63
(work) **placement** ['pleɪsmənt] Praktikum **VI T2,** 34
plague [pleɪg] Pest, Plage, Seuche **VI T2,** 28
plan [plæn] Plan **II U5,** 66
to **plan** [plæn] planen **II U4,** 52
plane [pleɪn] Flugzeug **II U2,** 23
planet ['plænɪt] Planet **IV U3,** 43
planning ['plænɪŋ] Planung, Planen **VI T4,** 75
plant [plɑ:nt] Pflanze **II U6,** 74; Anlage, Werk **VI T3,** 56
water treatment plant ['wɔ:tə ˌtri:tmənt ˌplɑ:nt] Wasseraufbereitungsanlage **VI T3,** 56
to **plant** [plɑ:nt] (an)pflanzen **V T1,** 14
plastic ['plæstɪk] Plastik(-), Kunststoff(-) **VI T3,** 53; **VI T4,** 77
plate [pleɪt] Teller **II U4,** 50
home plate ['həʊm ˌpleɪt] Home Plate **III U1,** 14
platform ['plætfɔ:m] Tribüne **III U2,** 30
play [pleɪ] Theaterstück, Spiel **I U7,** 90
to **play** [pleɪ] spielen **I U1,** 14
player ['pleɪə] Spieler/Spielerin, Mitspieler/Mitspielerin **III U1,** 8
CD player [ˌsi:'di: ˌpleɪə] CD-Player **II U4,** 56
DVD player [ˌdi:vi:'di: 'pleɪə] DVD-Player **II U5,** 62
playground ['pleɪgraʊnd] Schulhof, Spielplatz **I U1,** 18
please [pli:z] bitte **I U1,** 19
*to be **pleased with** [bi: 'pli:zd wɪð] zufrieden sein mit **I U6,** 87
to **pledge** [pledʒ] geloben **IV U2,** 25
to **plough** [plaʊ] pflügen **IV U3,** 43
plug [plʌg] Stecker, Stöpsel **IV U3,** 44
plural ['plʊərəl] Plural, Mehrzahl **I U6,** 88
plus [plʌs] plus, zuzüglich **IV U3,** 48
p.m. [ˌpi:'em] nachmittags *(Uhrzeit)* **III U3,** 47
pocket ['pɒkɪt] Hosen-/Jackentasche **II U2,** 22
pocket money ['pɒkɪt ˌmʌni] Taschengeld **II U2,** 22
podcast ['pɒdkɑ:st] Podcast °**VI T1,** 13
poem ['pəʊɪm] Gedicht **III U4,** 63
poet ['pəʊɪt] Dichter/Dichterin, Poet/Poetin **III U4,** 63
poetry ['pəʊətri] Lyrik **III U4,** 63
poetry slam ['pəʊətri ˌslæm] Poetry Slam *(Gedichtwettbewerb)* **III U4,** 63
point [pɔɪnt] Punkt **II U4,** 53
point of view [ˌpɔɪnt͜ əv 'vju:] Standpunkt; Perspektive °**V T3,** 57
to **point (to)** [pɔɪnt] zeigen (auf), deuten (auf) **IV U1,** 16
to point a gun at sb [ˌpɔɪnt͜ ə 'gʌn͜ ət] eine Waffe auf jmdn. richten **VI T2,** 36
poison ['pɔɪzn] Gift **V T2,** 38
poisonous ['pɔɪznəs] giftig **VI T3,** 55
police [pə'li:s] Polizei **I U6,** 87
policeman, policemen *(pl)* [pə'li:smən; pə'li:smen] Polizist **II U2,** 31
policy ['pɒləsi] Politik, politische Linie; Grundsatz °**VI T1,** 11; **VI T2,** 32
Polish ['pəʊlɪʃ] polnisch **I U2,** 29
polite [pə'laɪt] höflich **II U3,** 39
political [pə'lɪtɪkl] politisch **IV U3,** 50
to **pollute** [pə'lu:t] verschmutzen, verunreinigen **V T4,** 73
pollution [pə'lu:ʃn] (Umwelt-) Verschmutzung **III U2,** 34
pompom ['pɒmpɒm] Pompon *(bunte Quaste der Cheerleader)* **IV U2,** 25
pond [pɒnd] Teich **VI T3,** 56
pony ['pəʊni] Pony **II U6,** 74
pool [pu:l] Schwimmbecken **III U1,** 12
swimming pool ['swɪmɪŋ ˌpu:l] Schwimmbecken; Schwimmbad **III U1,** 12
poor [pɔ:; pʊə] arm **III U5,** 88
pop [pɒp] Popmusik **IV U5,** 77
to **pop** [pɒp] knallen (lassen) **IV U5,** 84
popular ['pɒpjələ] populär, beliebt **II U2,** 23
population [ˌpɒpjə'leɪʃn] Bevölkerung **IV U1,** 14
pork [pɔ:k] Schweinefleisch **II U4,** 49
port [pɔ:t] Hafen **III U3,** 45
to **pose** [pəʊz] (sich) darstellen, posieren **IV U2,** 32
position [pə'zɪʃn] Position **III U3,** 49
positive ['pɒzətɪv] positiv °**V T2,** 37; °**V T2,** 42; °**V T4,** 73
possible ['pɒsəbl] möglich **III U4,** 67
post [pəʊst] Pfosten, Mast **III U1,** 15
goal post ['gəʊl pəʊst] Torpfosten **III U1,** 15
post [pəʊst] Post **V T1,** 17
post office ['pəʊst͜ ɒfɪs] Postamt **III U2,** 35

to **post** [pəʊst] aufgeben *(einen Brief)*, abschicken, posten *(im Internetforum)* **IV U5,** 80
postal ['pəʊstl] postalisch; Post- **VI T3,** 60
postcard ['pəʊstkɑ:d] Postkarte **I U6,** 78
poster ['pəʊstə] Poster, Plakat **I U1,** 11
pot [pɒt] Topf **II U7,** 90
potato, potatoes *(pl)* [pə'teɪtəʊ] Kartoffel **II U4,** 54
couch potato ['kaʊtʃ pə,teɪtəʊ] Stubenhocker **III U1,** 12
pound (£) [paʊnd] Pfund *(Währung)* **I U5,** 66
pound (lb) [paʊnd] Pfund *(Gewicht)* **II U4,** 52
poverty ['pɒvəti] Armut **IV U1,** 10
powder ['paʊdə] Puder, Pulver **III U5,** 89
power ['paʊə] Kraft, Stärke, Macht **II U6,** 74
power cut ['paʊə ˌkʌt] Stromausfall **VI T2,** 37
nuclear-**powered** ['nju:kliəˌpaʊəd] atombetrieben **VI T3,** 56
powerful ['paʊəfl] stark, mächtig, leistungsfähig **V T4,** 73
practical ['præktɪkl] praktisch **V T2,** 40
practice ['præktɪs] Training **III U1,** 16
to **practise** ['præktɪs] üben, proben, praktizieren **II U5,** 66
prayer [preə] Gebet **V T4,** 78
to **prefer** [prɪ'fɜ:] vorziehen, bevorzugen **VI T1,** 14
pregnancy ['pregnəntsi] Schwangerschaft **VI T4,** 72
to **prepare** [prɪ'peə] vorbereiten, zubereiten **VI T3,** 61; **VI T4,** 71
preposition [ˌprepə'zɪʃn] Präposition °**III U1,** 19
present ['preznt] Geschenk **I U5,** 69; Gegenwart, Präsens °**II U2,** 26
present progressive [ˌpreznt prə'gresɪv] Verlaufsform des Präsens/ der Gegenwart °**III U1,** 12
simple present [ˌsɪmpl 'preznt] Gegenwart, Präsens °**IV U4,** 62
to **present** [prɪ'zent] präsentieren; verleihen **IV U5,** 77
present ['preznt] gegenwärtig, aktuell **VI T1,** 18
presentation [ˌprezn'teɪʃn] Präsentation, Vortrag **VI T1,** 18
president ['prezɪdnt] Präsident/ Präsidentin **VI T2,** 33
press [pres] Presse **IV U5,** 77
to **press** [pres] drücken, pressen **II U7,** 95
pressure ['preʃə] Druck, Belastung **V T2,** 33
to **pretend** [prɪ'tend] vorgeben, tun als ob °**III U1,** 13
pretty ['prɪti] ziemlich, ganz schön **IV U4,** 68
price [praɪs] Preis **I U7,** 95
half-price [ˌhɑ:f'praɪs] zum halben Preis **III U1,** 15
pride [praɪd] Stolz; Hochmut **V T3,** 51
primary school ['praɪməri ˌsku:l] Grundschule **III U4,** 67
Prime Minister (PM) [ˌpraɪm 'mɪnɪstə] Premierminister/Premierministerin **VI T1,** 9; **VI T2,** 32
prince [prɪns] Prinz **III U2,** 29
to **print** [prɪnt] drucken **II U5,** 64
prison ['prɪzn] Gefängnis **III U2,** 31
prisoner ['prɪznə] Gefangener/ Gefangene **V T3,** 52
pristine ['prɪsti:n] makellos, rein **IV U5,** 84
private ['praɪvɪt] privat **III U4,** 67
in private [ɪn 'praɪvɪt] insgeheim **VI T4,** 73
privatisation [ˌpraɪvɪtaɪ'zeɪʃn] Privatisierung **VI T3,** 56
prize [praɪz] Preis **IV U2,** 24
pros and cons [ˌprəʊz‿ənd 'kɒnz] Für und Wider, Pro und Kontra, Vor- und Nachteile **IV U4,** 63
probably ['prɒbəbli] wahrscheinlich **II U7,** 88
problem ['prɒbləm] Problem, Schwierigkeit **I U1,** 20
to **produce** [prə'dju:s] herstellen, produzieren, inszenieren *(Theaterstück)* **IV U4,** 62
producer [prə'dju:sə] Produzent/ Produzentin, Erzeuger/Erzeugerin **V T4,** 76
product ['prɒdʌkt] Produkt, Artikel, Ware **V T4,** 73
production [prə'dʌkʃn] Herstellung, Produktion **IV U5,** 77
professional [prə'feʃnl] professionell, beruflich, Berufs- **V T1,** 14
professor [prə'fesə] Professor/ Professorin **V T2,** 38
profile ['prəʊfaɪl] Steckbrief; Profil, Porträt **V T1,** 10; **V T4,** 77
programme ['prəʊgræm] Programm, Sendung **III U5,** 80
progress ['prəʊgres] Fortschritt, Entwicklung **V T1,** 17; **V T4,** 73
project ['prɒdʒekt] Projekt **I U2,** 34
prolific [prə'lɪfɪk] fruchtbar, produktiv **VI T4,** 77
promise ['prɒmɪs] Versprechen °**II U6,** 77
to **promise** ['prɒmɪs] versprechen **II U6,** 77
promising ['prɒmɪsiŋ] viel versprechend **VI T1,** 10
to **promote sth** [prə'məʊt] für etw. werben, etw. bewerben **VI T3,** 60
pronoun ['prəʊnaʊn] Pronomen °**III U4,** 67
reflexive pronoun [rɪ'fleksɪv ˌprəʊnaʊn] Reflexivpronomen °**III U4,** 67
relative pronoun [ˌrelətɪv 'preʊnaʊn] Relativpronomen °**III U3,** 48
properly ['prɒpli] ordentlich, richtig **VI T4,** 77
prospect ['prɒspekt] Aussicht, Perspektive **VI T4,** 71
to **protect** [prə'tekt] (be)schützen **V T1,** 11; **V T4,** 79
protective [prə'tektɪv] beschützend; Schutz- **VI T2,** 34
protest ['prəʊtest] Protest **V T3,** 49
to **protest** [prə'test] protestieren **V T3,** 49
prototype ['prəʊtətaɪp] Prototyp **VI T4,** 75
proud of ['praʊd‿əv] stolz auf **III U4,** 68
to **prove** [pru:v] beweisen, belegen, nachweisen **V T3,** 53
to **provide** (sb with sth) [prə'vaɪd] bereitstellen, besorgen, liefern **VI T1,** 11; **VI T3,** 52
provider [prə'vaɪdə] Anbieter/ Anbieterin, Lieferant/Lieferantin; Provider °**V T1,** 14
to **provoke** [prə'vəʊk] provozieren, reizen; hervorrufen **V T1,** 13
public ['pʌblɪk] öffentlich **IV U1,** 9; in der Öffentlichkeit **VI T2,** 26
public relations (PR) [ˌpʌblɪk rɪ'leɪʃnz] Öffentlichkeitsarbeit **VI T4,** 74
public school [ˌpʌblɪk 'sku:l] staatliche Schule (USA), Privatschule (GB) **IV U2,** 30
to **publish** ['pʌblɪʃ] veröffentlichen, publizieren, verlegen **IV U5,** 78
pudding ['pʊdɪŋ] Pudding; Nachtisch **II U4,** 49
Puerto Rican [ˌpwɜ:tə‿'ri:kən] Puertorikaner/Puertorikanerin °**IV U1,** 14
pukka *(slang)* ['pʌkə] echt **VI T1,** 10
to **pull** [pʊl] ziehen **II U4,** 57
pump [pʌmp] (Luft-)Pumpe **VI T3,** 56
to **punish** ['pʌnɪʃ] (be)strafen **V T3,** 53
punishment ['pʌnɪʃmənt] Strafe **V T3,** 51
Punjabi [pʌn'dʒɑ:bi:] Punjabi **VI T1,** 10
punk [pʌŋk] Punk **III U2,** 35

pupil ['pju:pl] Schüler/Schülerin **I U1,** 10
pure [pjʊə] pur, rein **VI T3,** 55; **VI T3,** 56
purple ['pɜ:pl] lila, violett **I LUA,** 24
to **push** [pʊʃ] stoßen, schieben, drücken **II U3,** 36
*to **put** [pʊt] setzen, stellen, legen **I U3,** 42
to put across [pʊt‿ə'krɒs] übermitteln °**VI T3,** 53
to put down [pʊt 'daʊn] auflegen *(Telefon)*; hinlegen, hinstellen °**II U7,** 89
to put in [pʊt‿'ɪn] einsetzen **II U7,** 95; einschieben **III U4,** 68; hinzufügen **IV U1,** 12
to put on [pʊt‿'ɒn] anziehen, aufsetzen **I U6,** 81; auftragen *(Make-up)* **II U5,** 71
to put out [pʊt‿'aʊt] ausmachen; löschen **III U2,** 32; hinausstellen **III U4,** 65
to put up [pʊt‿'ʌp] aufstellen, aufbauen **I U6,** 84
puzzle ['pʌzl] Rätsel, Puzzle °**I U1,** 15
crossword puzzle ['krɒswɜ:d 'pʌzl] Kreuzworträtsel °**I U5,** 71
pyramid ['pɪrəmɪd] Pyramide °**VI T2,** 28

Q

qualification [ˌkwɒlɪfɪ'keɪʃn] Qualifikation, Befähigung **V T2,** 41
fully-**qualified** [ˌfʊli'kwɒlɪfaɪd] voll ausgebildet, voll qualifiziert **VI T1,** 10
quality ['kwɒləti] Qualität; Eigenschaft °**V T2,** 37
quarry ['kwɒri] Steinbruch **VI T3,** 55
quarter ['kwɔ:tə] Viertel **III U2,** 32; Vierteldollar *(Währung)* **IV U1,** 13
quarters *(pl)* ['kwɔ:təz] Quartier, Unterkunft **V T4,** 79
quarter past ['kwɔ:tə pɑ:st] Viertel nach **I U3,** 42
quarter to ['kwɔ:tə tə] Viertel vor **I U3,** 42
queasy ['kwi:si] empfindlich *(Magen)*, übel **V T2,** 38
queen [kwi:n] Königin **II U5,** 62
homecoming queen [ˌhəʊmkʌmɪŋ 'kwi:n] Ballkönigin **IV U2,** 25
question ['kwestʃn] Frage **I U2,** 31
questionnaire [ˌkwestʃə'neə] Fragebogen °**II U4,** 53
queue [kju:] (Warte-)Schlange **III U2,** 26
quick [kwɪk] schnell **I U6,** 86
quiet [kwaɪət] ruhig, still, leise **I U6,** 78; Ruhe, Stille **II U7,** 88
*to **quit** [kwɪt] aufgeben, mit etw. aufhören; kündigen **V T2,** 39
quite [kwaɪt] ziemlich; ganz, völlig **IV U1,** 17
quiz [kwɪz] Quiz, Rätsel °**I U1,** 13
quota ['kwəʊtə] Quote **IV U1,** 10

R

rabbit ['ræbɪt] Kaninchen **V T1,** 10
race [reɪs] Wettlauf, Rennen **I U7,** 92; Rasse **V T3,** 55
to run a race [ˌrʌn‿ə 'reɪs] einen Wettlauf machen **I U7,** 92
racial ['reɪʃl] Rassen- **V T3,** 49
racing ['reɪsɪŋ] Renn- **III U1,** 12
radio ['reɪdiəʊ] Radio **I U2,** 33; Funk(-) **V T1,** 16
radio show ['reɪdiəʊ ˌʃəʊ] Radiosendung **I U2,** 33
two-way radio [ˌtu:weɪ 'reɪdiəʊ] Funksprechgerät **V T1,** 16
rafting ['rɑ:ftɪŋ] Rafting **IV U4,** 62
raid [reɪd] Razzia; Angriff **IV U4,** 69
rain [reɪn] Regen **II U6,** 78
acid rain [ˌæsɪd 'reɪn] saurer Regen **VI T3,** 55
to **rain** [reɪn] regnen **I U4,** 62
rainy ['reɪni] regnerisch, verregnet **I U6,** 79
to **raise** [reɪz] (an)heben; aufbringen, bereitstellen **VI T3,** 61
fund raising ['fʌnd ˌreɪzɪŋ] Spenden sammeln **VI T3,** 61
rally ['ræli] Jugendtreffen, Versammlung; Rallye **IV U2,** 24
ranch [ræntʃ] Ranch **IV U4,** 61
range [reɪndʒ] Reichweite, Bereich, Auswahl **V T4,** 72; Auswahl, Angebot **VI T4,** 74
to **range** [reɪndʒ] reichen, rangieren **VI T4,** 75
ranger ['reɪndʒə] Wildhüter/Wildhüterin, Ranger/Rangerin **V T1,** 11
rap [ræp] Rap **I U1,** 15
to **rap** [ræp] rappen **I U3,** 40
rape [reɪp] Raps **V T4,** 74
rapid ['ræpɪd] schnell, rasch, rapide **VI T1,** 10
rapper ['ræpə] Rapper/Rapperin **IV U5,** 80
rarely [reəli] selten **V T2,** 33
I'd **rather** [aɪd 'rɑ:ðə] ich würde lieber **II U2,** 22
raw [rɔ:] grob, roh **IV U5,** 84
R&B [ˌɑ:r‿n'bi:] R&B *(Musikrichtung)* **IV U5,** 77
to **reach** [ri:tʃ] erreichen **II U6,** 78
to reach for ['ri:tʃ fə] greifen nach **V T3,** 52
to **react** [ri'ækt] reagieren °**VI T4,** 79
reaction [ri'ækʃn] Reaktion, Resonanz **V T3,** 53
*to **read** [ri:d] lesen **I LUB,** 38
to read out [ˌri:d‿'aʊt] laut vorlesen, verlesen **VI T2,** 32; **VI T2,** 34
reader ['ri:də] Leser/Leserin **V T3,** 53
reading ['ri:dɪŋ] Lesen °**III U5,** 86; Lesung, Lektüre °**V T2,** 37
ready ['redi] fertig, bereit **II U4,** 50
to get ready [get 'redi] sich vorbereiten **II U5,** 68
real [rɪəl] echt, richtig, wirklich **II U3,** 38
to **realise** ['rɪəlaɪz] erkennen, realisieren, begreifen **VI T1,** 16; **VI T2,** 37; **VI T4,** 76
realistic [ˌrɪə'lɪstɪk] realistisch **VI T2,** 35
reality [ri'æləti] Realität, Wirklichkeit **IV U3,** 43
reality show [ri'æləti ˌʃəʊ] Realityshow **III U5,** 80
really ['rɪəli] wirklich **I U2,** 34
reason ['ri:zn] Grund **V T2,** 32; **V T3,** 58
*to **rebuild** [ˌri:'bɪld] wieder aufbauen; wiederherstellen **III U3,** 49
to **receive** [rɪ'si:v] empfangen, erhalten **IV U5,** 79
recent ['ri:snt] kürzlich; neu, neuester/neueste/neuestes; letzter/letzte/letztes **V T3,** 58
recently ['ri:sntli] in letzter Zeit **V T2,** 34
reception [rɪ'sepʃn] Rezeption, Empfang **III U5,** 84
receptionist [rɪ'sepʃnɪst] Empfangschef/Empfangschefin **III U5,** 85
recess *(AE)* ['rɪses] Pause **IV U2,** 27
recipe ['resɪpi:] Rezept **I U7,** 94
to **recognize** ['rekəgnaɪz] erkennen °**VI T3,** 62; **VI T4,** 72; °**VI T4,** 80
to **reconsider** [ˌri:kn'sɪdə] überdenken, nochmals überlegen °**VI T3,** 55
to **reconstruct** [ˌri:kn'strʌkt] rekonstruieren, wiederherstellen °**VI T1,** 20
record ['rekɔ:d] Schallplatte **IV U5,** 77; Aufnahme, Aufzeichnung; Beleg; Akte **V T3,** 59
on record [ɒn 'rekɔ:d] verzeichnet, dokumentiert **III U3,** 46
to **record** [rɪ'kɔ:d] aufnehmen, aufzeichnen **II U5,** 63
recording [rɪ'kɔ:dɪŋ] Aufnahme, Aufzeichnung **IV U3,** 48
recreation [ˌri:kri'eɪʃn] Freizeitaktivitäten, Erholung **VI T3,** 59

to **recycle** [riː'saɪkl] recyceln, wiederverwerten **VI T3,** 58; **VI T3,** 61
recycling [riː'saɪklɪŋ] Recycling, Abfallverwertung °**VI T3,** 63
red [red] rot **I LUA,** 24
red snapper [ˌred 'snæpə] Schnapperfisch, Red Snapper **V T4,** 78
to go red [gəʊ 'red] rot werden **II U1,** 11
to **reduce** [rɪ'djuːs] reduzieren, vermindern **VI T1,** 11; **VI T2,** 36; **VI T3,** 52
reef [riːf] Riff **V T1,** 11; **V T4,** 79
referee [ˌrefr'iː] Schiedsrichter/Schiedsrichterin **III U1,** 12; Referenz *(Person)* **V T1,** 15
reference ['refrns] Referenz; Bezug, Verweis **V T1,** 14
reflexive pronoun [rɪ'fleksɪv ˌprəʊnaʊn] Reflexivpronomen °**III U4,** 67
refrain [rɪ'freɪn] Refrain °**IV U5,** 82
refreshing [rɪ'freʃɪŋ] erfrischend **VI T3,** 53
refrigerator [rɪ'frɪdʒreɪtə] Kühlschrank **IV U3,** 44
to **refuse** [rɪ'fjuːz] ablehnen, sich weigern **VI T2,** 32
reggae ['regeɪ] Reggae **IV U5,** 77
to **register** ['redʒɪstə] sich anmelden **IV U5,** 80; (sich) eintragen **V T4,** 77
registration [ˌredʒɪ'streɪʃn] Registrierung, Erfassung **II U1,** 10
regular ['regjələ] Stammkunde/Stammkundin **III U2,** 35; regelmäßig, regulär **V T1,** 17; **V T3,** 58
to **rehearse** [rɪ'hɜːs] proben *(ein Theaterstück)* **I U7,** 90
public **relations** (PR) [ˌpʌblɪk rɪ'leɪʃnz] Öffentlichkeitsarbeit **VI T4,** 74
relationship [rɪ'leɪʃnʃɪp] Beziehung °**VI T4,** 68
relative pronoun [ˌrelətɪv 'preʊnaʊn] Relativpronomen °**III U3,** 48
to **relax** [rɪ'læks] sich entspannen, sich ausruhen **IV U1,** 16
reliable [rɪ'laɪəbl] zuverlässig, vertrauenswürdig **VI T1,** 18; **VI T4,** 75
religion [rɪ'lɪdʒn] Religion **V T2,** 32; **V T3,** 50
religious [rɪ'lɪdʒəs] religiös **II U1,** 12
Religious Education (RE) [rɪˌlɪdʒəs‿edʒʊ'keɪʃn] Religionsunterricht **II U1,** 12
to **relive** [ˌriː'lɪv] wieder erleben **III U2,** 26
remains *(pl)* [rɪ'meɪnz] (Über-)Rest **VI T4,** 78
to **remain** [rɪ'meɪn] (ver)bleiben **VI T1,** 13; **VI T2,** 29
to **remember** [rɪ'membə] sich erinnern (an), sich merken **I U3,** 49
to **remind** [rɪ'maɪnd] erinnern °**III U3,** 56
to **reminisce** [ˌremɪ'nɪs] zurückdenken, in Erinnerungen schwelgen **IV U5,** 84
*to be in **remission** [ˌbi‿ɪn rɪ'mɪʃn] auf dem Weg der Besserung sein **VI T4,** 77
remote [rɪ'məʊt] fern, abgelegen **V T1,** 16
remote control [rɪˌməʊt kən'trəʊl] Fernbedienung, Fernsteuerung **IV U3,** 43
to **remove** [rɪ'muːv] entfernen **IV U3,** 44
rent [rent] Miete, Pacht **V T3,** 58
to **rent** [rent] mieten, pachten **V T3,** 58
rental ['rentl] Miet-, Verleih- **VI T4,** 74
repair [rɪ'peə] Reparatur **VI T4,** 74
to **repair** [rɪ'peə] reparieren **IV U1,** 17
to **repeat** [rɪ'piːt] wiederholen °**IV U4,** 66
repetition [ˌrepɪ'tɪʃn] Wiederholung °**VI T3,** 55
to **replace** [rɪ'pleɪs] ersetzen **III U3,** 49
reply [rɪ'plaɪ] Antwort, Erwiderung, Entgegnung **V T2,** 34
to **reply** [rɪ'plaɪ] antworten, erwidern, entgegnen **V T2,** 34
report [rɪ'pɔːt] Bericht, Meldung; Zeugnis **IV U2,** 26
to **report** [rɪ'pɔːt] berichten; (sich) melden **IV U3,** 51
reporter [rɪ'pɔːtə] Reporter/Reporterin **I U7,** 92
representative [ˌreprɪ'zentətɪv] Vertreter/Vertreterin, Abgeordneter/Abgeordnete, Repräsentant/Repräsentantin **VI T2,** 33
request [rɪ'kwest] Anfrage, Anliegen, Wunsch **VI T3,** 54
rescue ['reskjuː] Rettung **III U5,** 82
to **rescue** ['reskjuː] retten **II U6,** 83
research [rɪ'sɜːtʃ] Forschung, Recherche, Untersuchung **IV U3,** 43
reservation [ˌrezə'veɪʃn] Reservat; Reservierung **IV U4,** 60
reserve [rɪ'zɜːv] Reserve, Vorrat; Rücklage **V T4,** 74
reservoir ['rezəvwɑː] Stausee, Wasserspeicher °**VI T3,** 57
resident ['rezɪdnt] Anwohner/Anwohnerin, Bewohner/Bewohnerin, Ortsansässiger/Ortsansässige **VI T3,** 56
residential [ˌrezɪ'dentʃl] Wohn-, am Wohnsitz **VI T4,** 71
resource [rɪ'zɔːs] Ressource, Rohstoff; Quelle **VI T3,** 50; **VI T4,** 74
human resources [ˌhjuːmən rɪ'zɔːsɪz] Personalabteilung **VI T4,** 74
respect [rɪ'spekt] Respekt **III U4,** 63
response [rɪ'spɒns] Reaktion, Antwort **III U4,** 63
responsibility [rɪsˌpɒnsə'bɪləti] Verantwortung **VI T4,** 70
criminal responsibility [ˌkrɪmɪnl rɪsˌpɒnsə'bɪləti] Schuldfähigkeit **VI T4,** 70
responsible [rɪs'pɒnsəbl] verantwortlich, verantwortungsvoll °**V T3,** 57
rest [rest] Rest **III U1,** 17
rest area ['rest ˌeəriə] Rastplatz **IV U4,** 65
to **rest** [rest] sich entspannen, sich ausruhen **III U3,** 52
restaurant ['restrənt] Restaurant **II U4,** 55
to **restore** [rɪ'stɔː] wiederherstellen, restaurieren **VI T4,** 75
restriction [rɪ'strɪkʃn] Einschränkung **VI T4,** 72
restrictive [rɪ'strɪktɪv] einschränkend, restriktiv °**VI T4,** 70
restroom *(AE)* ['restrʊm] Toilette **IV U4,** 68
result [rɪ'zʌlt] Ergebnis, Resultat **IV U4,** 66
retailer ['riːteɪlə] (Einzel-)Händler/Händlerin **VI T4,** 74
*to **retell** [riː'tel] nacherzählen, nochmals erzählen °**V T2,** 42; °**V T4,** 81
return [rɪ'tɜːn] Rückkehr; Antwort °**VI T2,** 37
to **return** [rɪ'tɜːn] zurückgehen, zurückkehren **V T2,** 37
to **reverse** [rɪ'vɜːs] umkehren; rückgängig machen; rückwärts fahren **V T3,** 51
review [rɪ'vjuː] Rückblick; Bewertung, Kritik °**V T4,** 74
revision [rɪ'vɪʒn] Wiederholung °**I U2,** 32
*to **rewrite** [ˌriː'raɪt] noch einmal schreiben °**II U4,** 58
rhyme [raɪm] Reim °**I LUA,** 25
rhyming ['raɪmɪŋ] (sich) reimend °**II U4,** 58
rhythm ['rɪðm] Rhythmus **V T3,** 56
rice [raɪs] Reis **II U4,** 49
rich [rɪtʃ] reich **III U2,** 29
*to get **rid of sth/sb** [get 'rɪd‿əv] etw./jmdn. loswerden **V T2,** 38
ride [raɪd] Fahrt, Ritt **III U1,** 18; Mitfahrgelegenheit **IV U4,** 69
*to **ride** [raɪd] fahren, reiten **I LUB,** 38
right [raɪt] Recht **V T3,** 50
Bill of Rights [ˌbɪl‿əv 'raɪts] *Teil der amerikanischen Verfassung* **VI T2,** 26
civil rights *(pl)* [ˌsɪvl 'raɪts] Bürgerrechte **V T3,** 51

Civil Rights Movement (CRM) [ˌsɪvl ˈraɪts ˌmuːvmənt] Bürgerrechtsbewegung **VT3,** 54
right [raɪt] richtig, korrekt **I U1,** 13; rechter/rechte/rechtes; rechts **I U4,** 55; genau, direkt **IV U2,** 32
all right [ɔːl ˈraɪt] gut; in Ordnung, alles klar **IV U4,** 68
Go right. [gəʊ ˈraɪt] Biege nach rechts ab. **I LUC,** 52
on the right [ɒn ðə ˈraɪt] rechts **I U2,** 28
right away [raɪt‿əˈweɪ] sofort, gleich **II U4,** 57
right now [ˌraɪt ˈnaʊ] jetzt gleich, in diesem Augenblick **I U7,** 92
to be right [biː ˈraɪt] Recht haben **II U4,** 56
to get … right [get … ˈraɪt] richtig machen **II U3,** 44
to turn right [tɜːn ˈraɪt] rechts abbiegen **II U7,** 97
rim [rɪm] Radkranz **III U2,** 30
ring [rɪŋ] Ring **III U3,** 47
rubber ring [ˌrʌbə ˈrɪŋ] Schwimmreifen **III U3,** 47
*to **ring** [rɪŋ] klingeln **I U5,** 75; anrufen **III U3,** 51
The bell rings. [ðə ˈbel rɪŋz] Es klingelt. **II U4,** 50
ice **rink** [ˈaɪs rɪŋk] Eis-/Schlittschuhbahn **II U2,** 23
riot [raɪət] Aufruhr, Ausschreitung, Unruhe **VT3,** 55
rise [raɪz] Aufstieg, Anstieg **IV U5,** 78
*to **rise** [raɪz] steigen, wachsen, zunehmen **II U6,** 78
risk [rɪsk] Risiko **IV U3,** 50
to **risk** [rɪsk] riskieren °**VI T2,** 37
rival [ˈraɪvl] Rivale/Rivalin, Konkurrent/Konkurrentin **IV U2,** 32
river [ˈrɪvə] Fluss **I LUC,** 52
road [rəʊd] Straße, Landstraße **I LUC,** 52
road train [ˈrəʊd ˌtreɪn] Fernlaster, Lkw-Zug **VT1,** 10
roadside [ˈrəʊdsaɪd] Straßenrand **IV U4,** 61
to **roar** [rɔː] dröhnen **IV U1,** 16
to **rob** [rɒb] rauben, ausrauben **III U2,** 28
robber [ˈrɒbə] Räuber/Räuberin **IV U3,** 50
robe [rəʊb] Robe, Gewand **VI T2,** 36
robot [ˈrəʊbɒt] Roboter **IV U3,** 43
robotics [rəˈbɒtɪks] Robotertechnik **IV U2,** 31
rock [rɒk] Rockmusik; Stein, Felsen **IV U5,** 77
to **rock** [rɒk] rocken; schaukeln **IV U5,** 84
rocket [ˈrɒkɪt] Rakete **IV U5,** 78
rodeo [rəʊˈdeɪəʊ; ˈrəʊdiəʊ] Rodeo **IV U4,** 61
role [rəʊl] Rolle **II U1,** 10
role model [ˈrəʊl ˌmɒdl] Vorbild **VI T2,** 35
romantic [rəˈmæntɪk] romantisch **VI T4,** 72
roof [ruːf] Dach **I U2,** 26
room [ruːm; rʊm] Zimmer, Raum; Platz **I U1,** 16
chat room [ˈtʃæt rʊm] Chatroom *(Internetforum, wo man sich online unterhalten kann)* **IV U5,** 80
dining room [ˈdaɪnɪŋ rʊm] Esszimmer, Speisesaal **I LUA,** 24
living room [ˈlɪvɪŋ rʊm] Wohnzimmer **I LUA,** 24
bed of **roses** [bed‿əv ˈrəʊzɪz] Zuckerschlecken **VT3,** 58
to be all roses [ˌbiː‿ɔːl ˈrəʊzɪz] nur Zuckerschlecken sein °**VT2,** 35
to **rotate** [rəˈteɪt] rotieren, sich abwechseln **VI T1,** 10
round [raʊnd] Runde **III U2,** 34; (um …) herum **IV U1,** 17
to **round off** [raʊnd‿ˈɒf] abrunden °**IV U4,** 66
route [ruːt; raʊt] Route °**III U2,** 28
row [rəʊ] Reihe **III U1,** 15
death row [ˌdeθ ˈrəʊ] Todestrakt **VT3,** 52
royal [ˈrɔɪəl] königlich **III U2,** 26
RSVP [ˌɑːr‿es viː ˈpiː] um Antwort wird gebeten °**I U5,** 70
rubber [ˈrʌbə] Radiergummi **I U1,** 14; Gummi; Kautschuk **III U3,** 47
rubber boots *(pl)* [ˌrʌbə ˈbuːts] Gummistiefel **II U6,** 74
rubber ring [ˌrʌbə ˈrɪŋ] Schwimmreifen **III U3,** 47
rubbish [ˈrʌbɪʃ] Abfall, Abfälle, Müll **I U6,** 84; Unsinn **II U7,** 94
rucksack [ˈrʌksæk] Rucksack **III U2,** 28
rude [ruːd] unhöflich, unverschämt **VI T2,** 34
rugby [ˈrʌgbi] Rugby **III U1,** 8
rugby boot [ˈrʌgbi buːt] Rugbyschuh, Stollenschuh **III U1,** 8
rule [ruːl] Regel, Vorschrift **I U3,** 43
ruler [ˈruːlə] Lineal **I U1,** 14; Herrscher/Herrscherin **VT3,** 58
run [rʌn] Lauf **II U4,** 57; Run, Runde **III U1,** 9
*to **run** [rʌn] rennen, laufen **I U3,** 48
to run a race [ˌrʌn‿ə ˈreɪs] einen Wettlauf machen **I U7,** 92
to run away [ˌrʌn‿əˈweɪ] wegrennen **I U3,** 48; ablaufen *(Wasser)* **IV U3,** 44
to run into [rʌn‿ˈɪntə] laufen gegen, stoßen gegen **III U1,** 17
to run on [ˈrʌn‿ɒn] laufen mit *(Auto)* **VT4,** 72
to run out [ˌrʌn‿ˈaʊt] ausgehen *(Zeit)*, ablaufen *(Zeit)*; hinausrennen **IV U1,** 10
to run upstairs [ˌrʌn‿ʌpˈsteəz] die Treppe hinaufrennen **III U3,** 53
runaway [ˈrʌnəˌweɪ] Ausreißer/Ausreißerin **III U5,** 83
runner [ˈrʌnə] Läufer/Läuferin **I U7,** 92
runner bean [ˈrʌnə ˌbiːn] Stangenbohne **VI T4,** 78
to **rush** [rʌʃ] eilen, hetzen **VT4,** 81
Russian [ˈrʌʃn] russisch; Russe/Russin **I U2,** 29

S

sacred [ˈseɪkrɪd] heilig **IV U4,** 60
sad [sæd] traurig, bedauerlich **II U1,** 19
safe [seɪf] sicher **III U3,** 46; Safe, Tresor **III U5,** 84
safety [ˈseɪfti] Sicherheit **VI T2,** 34; **VI T4,** 74
to **sail** [seɪl] segeln, fahren *(Schiff)* **III U3,** 45
salad [ˈsæləd] Salat **II U4,** 49
sales *(pl)* [seɪlz] Vertrieb, Verkauf **VI T4,** 74
after-sales service [ˌɑːftəseɪlz ˈsɜːvɪs] Kundendienst **VI T4,** 74
salesroom [ˈseɪlzrʊm] Verkaufsraum **VI T4,** 74
salsa [ˈsælsə] Salsa, würzige Soße °**VI T1,** 17
salt [sɔːlt] Salz **VT1,** 12
saltie *(Aus)* [ˈsɔːlti] Salzwasserkrokodil °**VT1,** 12
the **same** [seɪm] derselbe/dieselbe/dasselbe; gleich **III U1,** 18
sand [sænd] Sand **III U1,** 10
sands *(pl)* [sændz] Strand **VT4,** 78
sandwich [ˈsænwɪdʒ] Sandwich, belegtes Brot **I U1,** 14
sandy [ˈsændɪ] sandig **III U3,** 46
satellite [ˈsætlaɪt] Satellit **IV U3,** 43
Saturday [ˈsætədeɪ] Samstag **I U2,** 34
sauerkraut [ˈsaʊəkraʊt] Sauerkraut **III U2,** 34
sausage [ˈsɒsɪdʒ] Wurst, Würstchen **II U4,** 49
to **save** [seɪv] retten; sparen **II U6,** 80
*to **say** [seɪ] sagen, sprechen **I U1,** 11

It said .... [ɪt 'sed] Es lautete .... **II U2,** 30
to say out loud [ˌseɪ‿aʊt 'laʊd] laut sagen °**III U4,** 67
What does it say? [ˌwɒt dʌz‿ɪt 'seɪ] Was steht da? **II U3,** 44
to **scan** [skæn] scannen, abtasten, nach Details durchsuchen **VI T1,** 14
to **scare** ['skeə] Angst machen **III U4,** 67
scared [skeəd] verängstigt **I U2,** 35
I'm scared. [aɪm 'skeəd] Ich habe Angst. **II U3,** 44
scarf, scarves *(pl)* [skɑːf; skɑːvz] Schal, Kopftuch **VI T2,** 36
scary ['skeəri] unheimlich, gruselig **II U7,** 95
to **scatter** ['skætə] (sich) zerstreuen, verteilen; auseinanderjagen **VI T4,** 77
scene [siːn] Szene, Schauplatz **III U5,** 80
scenery ['siːnri] Landschaft **IV U4,** 60
scholarship ['skɒləʃɪp] Stipendium **VI T1,** 12
school [skuːl] Schule **I U1,** 10; (Fisch-)Schwarm **V T4,** 79
boarding school ['bɔːdɪŋ ˌskuːl] Internat **V T1,** 16
comprehensive school [kɒmprɪ'hensɪv ˌskuːl] Gesamtschule **III U4,** 66
elementary school *(AE)* [elɪ'mentri ˌskuːl] Grundschule **IV U2,** 30
grammar school ['græmə ˌskuːl] Gymnasium **III U4,** 67
high school ['haɪ ˌskuːl] High School *(weiterführende Schule in den USA, Oberstufe)* **IV U2,** 24
immersion school [ɪ'mɜːʃn ˌskuːl] *Schule, in der in einer Fremdsprache unterrichtet wird* **VI T1,** 12; **VI T1,** 14
junior high school [ˌdʒuːniə 'haɪ ˌskuːl] Junior High School *(Vorstufe zur High School, meist 7.–9. Klasse)* **VI T1,** 14
middle school *(AE)* ['mɪdl ˌskuːl] Mittelschule *(weiterführende Schule in den USA, Mittelstufe)* **IV U2,** 30
primary school ['praɪməri ˌskuːl] Grundschule **III U4,** 67
public school [ˌpʌblɪk 'skuːl] staatliche Schule (USA), Privatschule (GB) **IV U2,** 30
school bag ['skuːl bæg] Schultasche, Schulranzen **I U1,** 14
School of the Air [ˌskuːl‿əv ði 'eə] School of the Air *(Fernunterricht per Internet)* °**V T1,** 11
secondary school ['sekəndri ˌskuːl] weiterführende Schule **VI T1,** 14; **VI T4,** 77
Science ['saɪəns] Wissenschaft, Naturwissenschaft **II U1,** 10
science fiction [ˌsaɪəns 'fɪkʃn] Sciencefiction **III U5,** 80
scientific [ˌsaɪən'tɪfɪk] wissenschaftlich **IV U3,** 42
scientist ['saɪəntɪst] Wissenschaftler/Wissenschaftlerin **III U5,** 89
scone [skɒn] Scone *(Gebäck)* **I U7,** 94
score [skɔː] Punktestand, Spielstand **III U1,** 12
(music) score [skɔː] Partitur **IV U5,** 78
to **score** [skɔː] punkten, ein Tor schießen **III U1,** 9
Scottish ['skɒtɪʃ] schottisch **II U3,** 36
to **screech to a halt** ['skriːtʃ tʊ‿ə ˌhɒlt] mit quietschenden Reifen zum Stillstand kommen **V T3,** 50
screen [skriːn] Bildschirm, Leinwand **III U5,** 80
screen shot ['skriːn ˌʃɒt] Screenshot **III U5,** 80
screenager ['skriːneɪdʒə] Bildschirm-Teenie **VI T1,** 16
script [skrɪpt] Drehbuch **III U5,** 81
to **scroll down** [ˌskrəʊl 'daʊn] hinunter scrollen °**VI T4,** 75
sea [siː] Meer **II U7,** 88
sea lion ['siː ˌlaɪən] Seelöwe **V T2,** 40
sea wasp ['siː ˌwɒsp] Seewespe **V T1,** 10
seal [siːl] Seehund, Robbe **V T1,** 13
search [sɜːtʃ] Suche °**IV U4,** 61
search engine ['sɜːtʃ ˌendʒɪn] Suchmaschine °**IV U4,** 61
to **search** [sɜːtʃ] (durch)suchen °**IV U3,** 48
seasick ['siːsɪk] seekrank **IV U1,** 10
seaside ['siːsaɪd] Küste, Meeresküste **III U5,** 82
season ['siːzn] Jahreszeit, Saison **I U6,** 79
seat [siːt] Sitz, Sitzplatz **II U2,** 23
back seat ['bæk siːt] Rücksitz **VI T2,** 36
seaweed ['siːwiːd] Alge, Seetang **V T2,** 38
second ['seknd] Sekunde **I U2,** 30
secondary school ['sekəndri ˌskuːl] weiterführende Schule **VI T1,** 14; **VI T4,** 77
secondly ['sekndli] zweitens **IV U4,** 66
secret ['siːkrət] Geheimnis **III U5,** 87; geheim, heimlich **IV U3,** 50
secretary ['sekrətri] Sekretär/Sekretärin **III U1,** 12
section ['sekʃn] Sektion, Abschnitt, Abteilung **VI T1,** 18
sector ['sektə] Sektor, Abschnitt, (Unternehmens-)Bereich **VI T4,** 74
security [sɪ'kjʊərəti] Sicherheit **IV U3,** 50
social security number [ˌsəʊʃl sɪ'kjʊərəti ˌnʌmbə] Sozialversicherungsnummer **IV U3,** 50
*to **see** [siː] sehen **I U2,** 33; besuchen **II U1,** 19
See you! ['siː jə] Bis dann! Bis .... **I U5,** 70
See you around! [ˌsiː jə ə'raʊnd] Bis dann! Bis .... **IV U2,** 28
to see a doctor [siː‿ə 'dɒktə] zum Arzt gehen **II U4,** 52
you see [jʊ 'siː] weißt du **III U1,** 12
seed [siːd] Saat(korn), Samen **V T4,** 74
seeker ['siːkə] Suchender/Suchende °**V T1,** 14
to **seem** [siːm] (er)scheinen, wirken **VI T1,** 12; **VI T4,** 72; **VI T4,** 77
to **segregate** ['segrɪgeɪt] ausgrenzen, isolieren, trennen **V T3,** 55
segregation [ˌsegrɪ'geɪʃn] (Rassen-)Trennung **V T3,** 54
seldom ['seldəm] selten **III U5,** 80
self-conscious [ˌself'kɒnʃəs] befangen, gehemmt **VI T4,** 77
self-employed [ˌselfɪm'plɔɪd] selbstständig **V T3,** 58
self-employment [ˌselfɪm'plɔɪmənt] Selbstständigkeit **VI T4,** 71
self-worth [ˌself'wɜːθ] Selbstwertgefühl, Selbstachtung **VI T4,** 72
*to **sell** [sel] verkaufen **I U7,** 90
*to **send** [send] schicken **I U6,** 80
to send in [send‿'ɪn] einschicken **II U5,** 64
to send off [send‿'ɒf] vom Platz verweisen **III U1,** 15
sense [sens] Sinn, Bedeutung **III U5,** 88; Gefühl **VI T2,** 36
to **sense** [sens] spüren, fühlen, ahnen **V T1,** 12
sensible ['sensɪbl] vernünftig **III U3,** 46
sentence ['sentənts] Satz °**I U1,** 13; Verurteilung, Urteil, Strafe **V T1,** 10; **V T3,** 52
to **separate** ['sepreɪt] trennen, separieren **VI T4,** 76
September [sep'tembə] September **I U5,** 70
serf [sɜːf] Leibeigener/Leibeigene **VI T2,** 28
series, series *(pl)* ['sɪəriːz] Serie **III U5,** 82
serious ['sɪəriəs] ernst, ernsthaft **IV U5,** 79
servant ['sɜːvnt] Diener/Dienerin **III U5,** 88
to **serve** [sɜːv] servieren; (be)dienen **IV U4,** 65
service ['sɜːvɪs] Service, Dienst **II U6,** 83

English – German

after-sales service [ˌɑ:ftəseɪlz 'sɜ:vɪs] Kundendienst **VI T4,** 74
to **service** ['sɜ:vɪs] überprüfen, warten **VI T4,** 74
session ['seʃn] Veranstaltung **III U4,** 66; Einheit, Sitzung, Stunde **VI T1,** 10
set [set] Satz, Gerät **IV U5,** 81
*to **set** [set] stellen, einstellen **II U7,** 90
to be set (in) [bi 'set] spielen (in); seinen Schauplatz haben (in) °**VI T4,** 79
to set free [set‿'fri:] freilassen, freisetzen **VI T2,** 29
to set off [set‿'ɒf] auslösen *(Alarm)* **II U7,** 95; aufbrechen, sich auf den Weg machen **IV U4,** 68
to set the table [ˌset ðə 'teɪbl] den Tisch decken **II U4,** 50
to set up [set‿'ʌp] einrichten, aufbauen, gründen **IV U5,** 78
setting ['setɪŋ] Schauplatz; Rahmen °**VI T4,** 79
settler ['setlə] Siedler/Siedlerin **VI T1,** 13
several ['sevrl] mehrere, verschiedene **V T1,** 16; **V T3,** 50
sex [seks] Geschlecht, Sexualität, Sex **VI T2,** 34
sexist ['seksɪst] sexistisch **VI T2,** 34
shade [ʃeɪd] Schatten; Schattierung **V T4,** 80
shadow ['ʃædəʊ] Schatten **IV U5,** 82
*to **shake** [ʃeɪk] schütteln, zittern **III U4,** 70
***shall** [ʃæl; ʃəl] sollen **III U4,** 65
to **shamble** ['ʃæmbl] schlurfen, trotten **VI T4,** 76
shape [ʃeɪp] Form, Gestalt **V T4,** 79
share [ʃeə] Anteil, Beteiligung, Portion **V T4,** 76
to **share** [ʃeə] teilen **III U5,** 90
shareholder ['ʃeəˌhəʊldə] Teilhaber/Teilhaberin **V T4,** 77
shark [ʃɑ:k] Hai **V T1,** 13; **V T1,** 18
Great White Shark [ˌɡreɪt waɪt 'ʃɑ:k] Weißer Hai °**V T1,** 13
she [ʃi:] sie **I U1,** 12
shed [ʃed] Schuppen **I U2,** 26
sheep, sheep *(pl)* [ʃi:p] Schaf **I U6,** 78
sheet [ʃi:t] Blatt *(Papier)*; Bettlaken **VI T2,** 35
shelf, shelves *(pl)* [ʃelf; ʃelvz] Regal, Regalbrett **I U2,** 30
shell [ʃel] Hülle, Mantel; Muschel **VI T4,** 75
body shell ['bɒdi ˌʃel] Karosserie **VI T4,** 75
shift [ʃɪft] Schicht, Dienst **V T1,** 14
ship [ʃɪp] Schiff **I U4,** 54
shirt [ʃɜ:t] Hemd **I U3,** 44
shocked [ʃɒkt] geschockt, schockiert **III U5,** 86
shoe [ʃu:] Schuh **I U1,** 12
shoebox ['ʃu:bɒks] Schuhkarton **VI T4,** 76
*to **shoot** [ʃu:t] (ab)schießen, erschießen **V T3,** 55
shop [ʃɒp] Laden, Geschäft **I U2,** 26
shop assistant ['ʃɒp‿əˌsɪstnt] Verkäufer/Verkäuferin **II U5,** 67
sports shop ['spɔ:ts ʃɒp] Sportgeschäft **I U5,** 66
to **shop sb** [ʃɒp] jmdn. verpfeifen, jmdn. verraten **VI T2,** 35
shopping ['ʃɒpɪŋ] Einkaufen, Einkauf **I U5,** 66
shopping mall ['ʃɒpɪŋ mɔ:l] Einkaufszentrum, Einkaufspassage **IV U2,** 32
short [ʃɔ:t] kurz **I U4,** 55
shortage ['ʃɔ:tɪdʒ] Knappheit, Mangel **VI T3,** 56
shorts *(pl)* [ʃɔ:ts] Shorts, kurze Hose **II U1,** 10
shot [ʃɒt] Schuss, Schlag **III U5,** 80; Aufnahme, Foto; Einstellung **V T2,** 41; **V T4,** 79
screen shot ['skri:n ˌʃɒt] Screenshot **III U5,** 80
***should** [ʃʊd] sollte/sollten **II U4,** 52
shoulder ['ʃəʊldə] Schulter **IV U2,** 33
to **shout** [ʃaʊt] schreien, rufen **I U1,** 15
show [ʃəʊ] Show, Sendung, Schau **I U2,** 33
radio show ['reɪdiəʊ ˌʃəʊ] Radiosendung **I U2,** 33
reality show [ri'æləti ˌʃəʊ] Realityshow **III U5,** 80
talk show ['tɔ:k ˌʃəʊ] Talkshow **III U5,** 80
*to **show** [ʃəʊ] zeigen **I U4,** 65
shower ['ʃaʊə] Regenguss; Dusche **II U6,** 74
show-off ['ʃəʊ‿ɒf] Angeber/Angeberin °**V T3,** 57
*to **shrink** [ʃrɪŋk] schrumpfen, schwinden; einlaufen **VI T3,** 57
to **shrug (one's shoulders)** [ʃrʌɡ] mit den Achseln/Schultern zucken **VI T4,** 76
to **shuffle** ['ʃʌfl] mischen °**II U6,** 79
*to **shut** [ʃʌt] schließen **VI T4,** 73
to shut sb out [ʃʌt‿'aʊt] jmdn. ausschließen **VI T4,** 73
shutter ['ʃʌtə] Verschluss, Klappe, Blende **IV U5,** 78
shuttle ['ʃʌtl] Raumfähre **IV U3,** 43
shy [ʃaɪ] schüchtern **III U4,** 66
sick [sɪk] krank **II U3,** 46
sick note ['sɪk ˌnəʊt] Krankmeldung **II U2,** 28
to feel sick [fi:l 'sɪk] Übelkeit verspüren **II U3,** 46
side [saɪd] Seite **III U3,** 52
sunny side up [ˌsʌni saɪd‿'ʌp] Spiegelei **IV U4,** 65
sidewalk *(AE)* ['saɪdwɔ:k] Gehweg °**IV U1,** 15
sight [saɪt] Sehenswürdigkeit; Sicht, Anblick **IV U4,** 61
sign [saɪn] Zeichen, Schild **I U2,** 26
vital signs *(pl)* [ˌvaɪtl 'saɪnz] Lebenszeichen **IV U5,** 82
to **sign** [saɪn] unterschreiben **II U5,** 66
signal ['sɪɡnl] Signal **II U2,** 26; Zeichen **III U1,** 10
to **signal** ['sɪɡnl] signalisieren, ein Zeichen geben **III U3,** 48
silence ['saɪlənts] Stille, Ruhe, Schweigen **V T3,** 57
silly ['sɪli] dumm; Dummkopf **II U1,** 11
similar ['sɪmɪlə] ähnlich °**III U4,** 62
simple ['sɪmpl] einfach, simpel **IV U3,** 51
simple past [ˌsɪmpl 'pɑ:st] einfache Vergangenheit °**III U2,** 28
since [sɪnts] seit, seitdem **III U2,** 34
*to **sing** [sɪŋ] singen **I U2,** 33
singer ['sɪŋə] Sänger/Sängerin **II U1,** 14
single ['sɪŋɡl] einzeln; individuell **V T2,** 34
sink [sɪŋk] Waschbecken *(im Amerikanischen)*, Spülbecken **IV U3,** 44
to **sip** [sɪp] schluckweise trinken **IV U5,** 84
Sir [sɜ:] Sir *(Anrede für einen Ritter)* °**III U5,** 87
sis [sɪs] Schwesterchen °**III U4,** 65
sissy ['sɪsi] Jammerlappen **V T2,** 34
sister ['sɪstə] Schwester **I LUA,** 25
half-sister ['hɑ:fˌsɪstə] Halbschwester **I U2,** 26
*to **sit** [sɪt] sitzen **I U3,** 48
to sit back [ˌsɪt 'bæk] sich zurücklehnen **IV U1,** 16
to sit down [sɪt 'daʊn] sich (hin)setzen **I U1,** 19
to sit with ['sɪt wɪθ] sich setzen zu **I U5,** 74
sitcom ['sɪtkɒm] Situationskomödie **III U5,** 82
site [saɪt] Ort, Schauplatz; Webseite **VI T3,** 61
situation [ˌsɪtju'eɪʃn] Situation **VI T1,** 18; **VI T2,** 29
six-pack ['sɪkspæk] Waschbrettbauch **V T2,** 32

sixth form [ˈsɪksθ ˌfɔːm] Oberstufe **VI T4,** 71
size [saɪz] (Kleider-)Größe **III U5,** 90
to **skate** [skeɪt] Inlineskates fahren, skaten **I LUB,** 38
skateboard [ˈskeɪtbɔːd] Skateboard **I U4,** 54
skater [ˈskeɪtə] Skater/Skaterin **VT2,** 35
skates *(pl)* [skeɪts] Inlineskates **I U4,** 54
skeleton [ˈskelɪtn] Skelett **VI T4,** 76
skiing [ˈskiːɪŋ] Skifahren **IV U4,** 66
skill [skɪl] Fertigkeit, Geschick **VT1,** 15; **VT2,** 32
to **skim** [skɪm] überfliegen °**III U2,** 32
skimming [ˈskɪmɪŋ] Überfliegen °**III U2,** 32
skin [skɪn] Haut; Fell **VT1,** 13
skirt [skɜːt] Rock **II U1,** 10
sky [skaɪ] Himmel **II U7,** 94
skyscraper [ˈskaɪˌskreɪpə] Wolkenkratzer **IV U1,** 9
poetry **slam** [ˈpəʊətri ˌslæm] Poetry Slam *(Gedichtwettbewerb)* **III U4,** 63
slamster [ˈslæmstə] Teilnehmer/Teilnehmerin an einem Poetry Slam **III U4,** 63
slang [slæŋ] Slang **IV U5,** 80
slavery [ˈsleɪvri] Sklaverei **VT3,** 54
sleep [sliːp] Schlaf **IV U3,** 48
*to **sleep** [sliːp] schlafen **I U3,** 46
sleeping bag [ˈsliːpɪŋ ˌbæg] Schlafsack **I U6,** 84
sleepy [ˈsliːpi] schläfrig, verschlafen **II U7,** 94
slice [slaɪs] Scheibe **IV U1,** 12
slightly [ˈslaɪtli] geringfügig, leicht °**VI T4,** 78
slip [slɪp] Beleg, Schein **IV U2,** 27
to **slip** [slɪp] abrutschen, (aus)rutschen **VI T4,** 73
slogan [ˈsləʊgən] Slogan, Werbespruch °**VT2,** 39
to **slow down** [ˌsləʊ ˈdaʊn] bremsen, verlangsamen; langsamer werden **VT2,** 38
slow [sləʊ] langsam **I U2,** 34
slug [slʌg] Nacktschnecke **VT3,** 59
small [smɔːl] klein **I U2,** 26
smart [smɑːt] schlau, klug **IV U3,** 42
smell [smel] Geruch, Gestank **III U5,** 88
*to **smell** [smel] riechen **III U2,** 32
smile [smaɪl] Lächeln **VT2,** 32; **VT3,** 56
to **smile** [smaɪl] lächeln **I U3,** 43
smoke [sməʊk] Rauch **III U2,** 32
to **smoke** [sməʊk] rauchen **III U5,** 84
smoking [ˈsməʊkɪŋ] Rauchen **VT2,** 38
to **smoulder** [ˈsməʊldə] rauchen, qualmen, schwelen **VI T4,** 76

smuggler [ˈsmʌglə] Schmuggler/Schmugglerin **III U3,** 45
snack [snæk] Imbiss, Snack **II U4,** 55
snack bar [ˈsnæk bɑː] Café, Imbissstube °**IV U1,** 13
snake [sneɪk] Schlange **VT1,** 12
Brown Snake [ˌbraʊn ˈsneɪk] Braunschlange, Braunotter °**VT1,** 12
red **snapper** [ˌred ˈsnæpə] Schnapperfisch, Red Snapper **VT4,** 78
snapshot [ˈsnæpʃɒt] Schnappschuss **IV U1,** 16
sneak [sniːk] Petzer/Petze **VT2,** 35
to **sneak on sb** [sniːk] jmdn. verpetzen **VT2,** 34
to **sniff** [snɪf] schnüffeln, schnuppern **III U5,** 90
to **snorkel** [ˈsnɔːkl] schnorcheln **VI T3,** 60
snow [snəʊ] Schnee **II U6,** 79
to **snow** [snəʊ] schneien **II U6,** 79
snowboarding [ˈsnəʊbɔːdɪŋ] Snowboarden **VT3,** 48
snowy [ˈsnəʊi] verschneit **I U6,** 79
so [səʊ] so, also, deshalb **I U2,** 26
so-called [ˌsəʊˈkɔːld] so genannt **VT4,** 72
so far [ˈsəʊ fɑː] bis jetzt °**IV U1,** 17
soap [səʊp] Seifenoper, Seife **I U7,** 97
docu soap [ˈdɒkju ˌsəʊp] Dokusoap **III U5,** 80
soccer *(AE)* [ˈsɒkə] Fußball **IV U2,** 31
social [ˈsəʊʃl] sozial, gesellschaftlich **IV U3,** 50
social security number [ˌsəʊʃl sɪˈkjʊərəti ˌnʌmbə] Sozialversicherungsnummer **IV U3,** 50
to **socialize** [ˈsəʊʃlaɪz] ausgehen, unter die Leute kommen **VT2,** 31
society [səˈsaɪəti] Gesellschaft; Verein **VT3,** 55
socket [ˈsɒkɪt] Steckdose **IV U3,** 46
sofa [ˈsəʊfə] Sofa, Couch **I LUA,** 25
soft [sɒft] leise; weich, sanft **II U7,** 94
soft drink [ˈsɒft ˌdrɪŋk] alkoholfreies Getränk **VI T3,** 53
to go soft on sb [ˌgəʊ ˈsɒft] sich in jmdn. verknallen **VT3,** 50
softy [ˈsɒfti] Weichei **VT2,** 35
solar [ˈsəʊlə] Sonnen-, solar **VT4,** 71
solar panel [ˌsəʊlə ˈpænl] Sonnenkollektor **VT4,** 71
soldier [ˈsəʊldʒə] Soldat/Soldatin **VI T2,** 28
solid [ˈsɒlɪd] fest, solide **VI T4,** 77
solo [ˈsəʊləʊ] allein, Allein-, solo, Solo- **VT3,** 50
solution [səˈluːʃn] Lösung °**VT2,** 35
to **solve** [sɒlv] lösen **III U5,** 88

some [sʌm] etwas **II U1,** 13
somebody [ˈsʌmbədi] jemand **III U5,** 83
somehow [ˈsʌmhaʊ] irgendwie **IV U4,** 69
someone [ˈsʌmwʌn] jemand **II U5,** 70
someone else [ˌsʌmwʌn‿ˈels] jemand anderes °**III U1,** 13
something [ˈsʌmθɪŋ] etwas **II U4,** 56
sometimes [ˈsʌmtaɪmz] manchmal **I U3,** 44
somewhere [ˈsʌmweə] irgendwo **II U4,** 57
son [sʌn] Sohn **III U5,** 86
song [sɒŋ] Lied **I U2,** 33
soon [suːn] bald **I U6,** 78
as soon as [əz ˈsuːn‿əz] sobald **III U4,** 66
sorry [ˈsɒri] Tut mir leid. Entschuldigung. **I U1,** 12
I'm sorry about .... [aɪm ˈsɒri‿əˌbaʊt] Es tut mir leid wegen .... °**II U3,** 39
to feel sorry for [fiːl ˈsɒri] Mitleid haben mit, bedauern **III U1,** 16
sort [sɔːt] Art, Sorte **IV U1,** 16
sort of [ˈsɔːt‿əv] irgendwie **VI T1,** 12
to **sort** [sɔːt] sortieren °**I U1,** 21
to sort out [sɔːt‿ˈaʊt] klären, regeln *(ein Problem)* **I U2,** 30
soul [səʊl] Soulmusik; Seele **IV U5,** 77
sound [saʊnd] Ton, Geräusch, Klang **I U6,** 85
to **sound** [saʊnd] klingen, sich anhören **III U5,** 88
soup [suːp] Suppe **II U1,** 15
sour [ˈsaʊə] sauer **II U4,** 49
source [sɔːs] Quelle; Grund **VT4,** 77
south [saʊθ] Süden **I U4,** 55; nach Süden **VI T2,** 36
South American [ˌsaʊθ‿əˈmerɪkən] südamerikanisch; Südamerikaner/Südamerikanerin **VI T2,** 29
southwest [ˌsaʊθˈwest] Südwesten **II U6,** 78
souvenir [ˌsuːvəˈnɪə] Souvenir, Andenken **III U2,** 29
soy [sɔɪ] Soja(-) **VT4,** 74
spa [spɑː] Wellness-Center, Spa **VT4,** 80
space [speɪs] Raum, Platz; Weltraum **IV U3,** 42
outer space [ˌaʊtə ˈspeɪs] Weltraum, Weltall **IV U3,** 42
space station [ˈspeɪs ˌsteɪʃn] Weltraumstation **IV U3,** 42
spaceship [ˈspeɪsʃɪp] Raumschiff **IV U3,** 43
spaghetti [spəˈgeti] Spaghetti **II U1,** 13
spam [spæm] Spam *(unerwünschte Werbe-E-Mails)* **VT4,** 73

Spanglish ['spæŋglɪʃ] Spanglisch *(Mischung aus Spanisch und Englisch)* **VI T1,** 10
Spanish ['spænɪʃ] spanisch, Spanisch **IV U4,** 68
spark [spɑ:k] Funke(n) **III U2,** 32
to **spark** [spɑ:k] sprühen *(Funken)*; auslösen, entfachen **VI T4,** 77
*to **speak** [spi:k] sprechen **I U4,** 62
It's ... speaking. [ɪts ... 'spi:kɪŋ] Hier spricht .... **III U4,** 69
speaker ['spi:kə] Sprecher/Sprecherin **III U3,** 45
special ['speʃl] besonders, speziell **III U4,** 63; Spezialität **IV U1,** 12; Sonderausgabe, -heft **VI T3,** 54
specialist ['speʃlɪst] Spezialist/Spezialistin; Fach- **VI T4,** 71
species, **species** *(pl)* ['spi:ʃi:z] Art, Spezies **VI T3,** 60
specific [spə'sɪfɪk] spezifisch, speziell, bestimmt **VI T4,** 71
spectacular [spek'tækjələ] spektakulär **III U2,** 26
speech [spi:tʃ] (An-)Sprache, Rede; Sprechen **V T3,** 54
speech bubble ['spi:tʃ ˌbʌbl] Sprechblase °**III U3,** 47
speed [spi:d] Geschwindigkeit, Tempo; Eile **V T3,** 56; **V T4,** 72
*to **spell** [spel] buchstabieren **I U4,** 60
spelling ['spelɪŋ] Orthographie, Rechtschreibung °**II U3,** 43
*to **spend** [spend] verbringen; ausgeben **I U6,** 83
spice [spaɪs] Gewürz °**VI T1,** 17
spicy ['spaɪsi] würzig, pikant **II U4,** 49
spider ['spaɪdə] Spinne **V T1,** 12
Sydney Funnel Web Spider ['sɪdni ˌfʌnl web 'spaɪdə] australische Trichternetzspinne °**V T1,** 12
spin-off ['spɪn‿ɒf] Nebenprodukt **IV U3,** 43
spine [spaɪn] Wirbelsäule **VI T4,** 77
spirit ['spɪrɪt] Geist; Stimmung **V T3,** 50; Spirituose **VI T4,** 70
*to **spit** [spɪt] spucken, zischen, fauchen **VI T4,** 77
*to **split** [splɪt] (sich) (auf)teilen, spalten °**V T3,** 53
to **spoil** [spɔɪl] zerstören, verderben; verwöhnen **V T3,** 56
sponge [spʌndʒ] Schwamm **I U7,** 90
sponsor ['spɒntsə] Sponsor/Sponsorin, Förderer/Förderin **VI T1,** 10
spooky ['spu:ki] unheimlich **I U2,** 35
spoon [spu:n] Löffel **II U4,** 50
sport [spɔ:t] Sport **I U1,** 12
sports day ['spɔ:ts deɪ] Sportfest **I U7,** 90
sports field ['spɔ:ts fi:ld] Sportplatz **I U7,** 92
sports shop ['spɔ:ts ʃɒp] Sportgeschäft **I U5,** 66
to do sports [du: 'spɔ:ts] Sport treiben **I U7,** 92
sporty ['spɔ:ti] sportlich **III U2,** 29
hot **spot** ['hɒt spɒt] Krisenherd, Brennpunkt °**VI T2,** 37
to **spot** [spɒt] entdecken, erkennen °**IV U4,** 67
to **spray** [spreɪ] (be)sprühen, lackieren **IV U4,** 68
*to **spread** [spred] (sich) ausbreiten, (sich) verbreiten **VI T1,** 10
spring [sprɪŋ] Frühling **I U6,** 78
spring fountain [ˌsprɪŋ 'faʊntɪn] Quelle **VI T3,** 55
square [skweə] Quadrat(-) **V T1,** 16
to **squash** [skwɑʃ] zerdrücken, pressen, quetschen **VI T4,** 77
stadium ['steɪdiəm] Stadion **III U1,** 8
staff [stɑ:f] Personal; Kollegium **IV U4,** 67
stage [steɪdʒ] Stadium, Station, Abschnitt **V T2,** 38
stairs *(pl)* [steəz] Treppe **III U3,** 52
stall [stɔ:l] Stand, Bude **I U7,** 90
stall holder ['stɔ:l ˌhəʊldə] Standbesitzer/Standbesitzerin **II U4,** 54
white elephant stall [ˌwaɪt 'elɪfənt stɔ:l] Trödelstand **I U7,** 96
stamp [stæmp] Briefmarke **III U3,** 47
stand [stænd] Tribüne **III U1,** 9
*to **stand** [stænd] stehen **III U3,** 49
standby ['stændbaɪ] in Bereitschaft, auf Stand-by **VI T3,** 58
stanza ['stænzə] Strophe °**VI T3,** 55
star [stɑ:] Star; Stern **III U1,** 12
word star ['wɜ:d stɑ:] Wortstern °**I U1,** 22
start [stɑ:t] Anfang, Beginn, Start **II U1,** 10
to **start** [stɑ:t] anfangen, starten **I U3,** 44
to start up [stɑ:t‿'ʌp] eröffnen **IV U2,** 32
starter ['stɑ:tə] Vorspeise **II U4,** 49
startled ['stɑ:tld] verblüfft, alarmiert **VI T4,** 78
state [steɪt] Staat, Land; staatlich; Zustand **III U4,** 67
head of state [ˌhed‿əv 'steɪt] Staatsoberhaupt **VI T2,** 32
state-of-the-art [ˌsteɪtəvði'ɑ:t] auf dem neuesten Stand **V T1,** 16
to get into such a state [get‿ɪntə 'sʌtʃ‿ə 'steɪt] durchdrehen, (sich) verrückt machen **III U4,** 70
statement ['steɪtmənt] Aussage, Behauptung °**III U5,** 82
negative statement [ˌnegətɪv 'steɪtmənt] Verneinung °**III U5,** 82
station ['steɪʃn] Wache, Station, Bahnhof **I U6,** 87; (Radio-/Fernseh-)Sender **V T3,** 52
cattle station ['kætl ˌsteɪʃn] Rinderfarm **V T1,** 16
cleaning station ['kli:nɪŋ ˌsteɪʃn] Putzerstation **V T4,** 79
space station ['speɪs ˌsteɪʃn] Weltraumstation **IV U3,** 42
stationery ['steɪʃnri] Schreibwaren **V T1,** 17
statistical [stə'tɪstɪkl] statistisch °**V T4,** 74
statistics *(pl)* [stə'tɪstɪks] Statistik °**IV U4,** 66
statue ['stætʃu:] Statue, Standbild **IV U5,** 77
stay [steɪ] Anwesenheit, Aufenthalt **VI T1,** 12
to **stay** [steɪ] bleiben **I U4,** 60
to stay on [steɪ‿'ɒn] dableiben, länger bleiben **VI T2,** 29
to stay out [steɪ‿'aʊt] wegbleiben **III U4,** 69
to stay with ['steɪ wɪð] wohnen bei **I U6,** 78
*to **steal** [sti:l] stehlen **II U4,** 57
stealth bomber [ˌstelθ 'bɒmə] Tarnkappenbomber **VI T3,** 55
steel band [ˌsti:l 'bænd] Steelband *(Band, deren Instrumente aus leeren Ölfässern bestehen)* **III U4,** 64
steelworker ['sti:lˌwɜ:kə] Stahlarbeiter/Stahlarbeiterin °**IV U1,** 15
step [step] Stufe, Schritt **IV U1,** 9
to **step** [step] treten, steigen, gehen **IV U2,** 33
to step on the gas [ˌstep‿ɒn ðə 'gæs] Gas geben **V T3,** 56
stepdad ['stepdæd] Stiefvater **I U2,** 26
stick [stɪk] Stock **II U2,** 26
*to **stick** [stɪk] kleben; stecken **IV U4,** 68
sticker ['stɪkə] Aufkleber, Sticker °**V T2,** 39
still (picture) ['stɪl ˌpɪktʃə] Standfoto **IV U5,** 78
still [stɪl] noch, immer noch **II U1,** 21; dennoch **IV U2,** 28; still, unbewegt **VI T4,** 77
*to **sting** [stɪŋ] stechen, beißen **V T1,** 10
*to **stink** [stɪŋk] stinken **V T2,** 40

stinking ['stɪŋkɪŋ] stinkend; stinkig **V T4,** 81
stomach ['stʌmək] Magen, Bauch **II U3,** 41
stone [stəʊn] Stein **II U6,** 82; *brit. Gewichtseinheit* (= 6,35 kg) **III U1,** 11
stop [stɒp] Halt, Haltestelle **I LUC,** 52
bus stop ['bʌs ˌstɒp] Bushaltestelle **I LUC,** 52
to **stop** [stɒp] aufhören (mit), anhalten **I U3,** 42
to stop + -ing [stɒp] aufhören etw. zu tun **II U4,** 52
to stop sb from [stɒp] jmdn. abhalten von **V T3,** 53
store [stɔ:] Kaufhaus, Geschäft, Laden **II U2,** 30
department store [dɪ'pɑ:tmənt stɔ:] Kaufhaus **I LUC,** 52
store detective ['stɔ: dɪˌtektɪv] Kaufhausdetektiv/Kaufhausdetektivin **II U2,** 30
to **store** [stɔ:] speichern, lagern **V T4,** 75
storm [stɔ:m] Sturm **II U6,** 81
stormy ['stɔ:mi] stürmisch **II U6,** 78
story ['stɔ:ri] Geschichte, Erzählung **I U1,** 21
detective story [dɪ'tektɪv ˌstɔ:ri] Krimi **III U5,** 80
storyboard ['stɔ:ribɔ:d] Storyboard *(gezeichnete Version eines Drehbuchs)* **VI T1,** 14
storyline ['stɔ:rileɪn] Handlung °**VI T4,** 79
straight [streɪt] gerade, direkt **IV U2,** 27
stranded ['strændɪd] gestrandet **IV U4,** 65
strange [streɪndʒ] merkwürdig, seltsam **I U2,** 35
stranger ['streɪndʒə] Fremder/Fremde **III U3,** 47
straw [strɔ:] Stroh **III U2,** 32
strawberry ['strɔ:bri] Erdbeere **IV U1,** 12
stream [stri:m] Bach **II U6,** 82
street [stri:t] Straße **I LUC,** 52
streetwise ['stri:twaɪz] clever, gewieft, raffiniert **V T2,** 34
strength [streŋθ] Stärke, Kraft **VI T1,** 18
stress [stres] Stress; Betonung **IV U3,** 48
to **stress** [stres] betonen; beanspruchen, belasten **VI T2,** 34
strict [strɪkt] streng, strikt **III U4,** 62
*to **strike** [straɪk] auffallen; schlagen; streiken °**V T4,** 70
string [strɪŋ] Schnur, Kordel, Bindfaden **IV U5,** 78

comic **strip** ['kɒmɪk strɪp] Bildgeschichte, Comicstrip °**VI T2,** 31
stroke [strəʊk] Schlag(anfall) **III U4,** 70
strong [strɒŋ] stark **III U5,** 86
struggle (for sth) ['strʌgl] Kampf (um); Anstrengung **V T3,** 55
to **struggle** ['strʌgl] kämpfen, ringen, sich anstrengen **V T3,** 55
student ['stju:dnt] Student/Studentin, Schüler/Schülerin **IV U2,** 24
studio ['stju:diəʊ] Studio **I U2,** 33
study ['stʌdi] Studieren, Studium, Lernen **VI T4,** 71
studies *(pl)* ['stʌdiz] Studium; Lernen **V T2,** 41
to **study** ['stʌdi] studieren; lernen **II U6,** 74
stuff [stʌf] Zeug, Sachen **IV U4,** 68
to **stun** [stʌn] betäuben, lähmen; verblüffen **V T4,** 78
stupid ['stju:pɪd] dumm, blöd **I U2,** 35
style [staɪl] Stil; Frisur **III U2,** 35
sub-continent [sʌb'kɒntɪnənt] Subkontinent **VI T1,** 10
subject ['sʌbdʒɪkt] Schulfach; Thema **II U1,** 13
to **substitute** ['sʌbstɪtju:t] auswechseln, ersetzen **III U1,** 17
suburb ['sʌbɜ:b] Vorort **IV U5,** 80
success [sək'ses] Erfolg **III U5,** 80
successful [sək'sesfl] erfolgreich **V T1,** 14; **V T3,** 51
such [sʌtʃ] solch **III U4,** 70
such as ['sʌtʃ‿æz] wie **IV U1,** 14
It **sucks that ...** [ɪt 'sʌks] Es ist ätzend, dass ... **V T2,** 35
That sucks! [ðæt 'sʌks] Das ist ätzend! **V T2,** 36
sudden ['sʌdn] plötzlich **III U4,** 70
suddenly ['sʌdnli] plötzlich, auf einmal **I U2,** 35
to **suffer** ['sʌfə] leiden, aushalten, erdulden **V T3,** 54
sugar ['ʃʊgə] Zucker **VI T3,** 54; **VI T4,** 78
to **suggest** [sə'dʒest] vorschlagen **III U4,** 69
suggestion [sə'dʒestʃn] Vorschlag, Anregung °**II U4,** 53
suit [su:t] Anzug **IV U2,** 33
suit of armour [ˌsu:t‿əv 'ɑ:mə] Rüstung **VI T2,** 28
to **suit** [su:t] passen (zu) **V T3,** 59
suitable ['su:təbl] geeignet, passend **VI T2,** 35
to **sum up** [ˌsʌm‿'ʌp] zusammenfassen °**V T2,** 30
to **summarize** ['sʌməraɪz] (kurz) zusammenfassen °**VI T3,** 62

summary ['sʌmri] Zusammenfassung °**III U3,** 49
summer ['sʌmə] Sommer **I U6,** 79
summer fair ['sʌmə ˌfeə] Sommerfest **I U7,** 90
sun [sʌn] Sonne **III U3,** 46
Sunday ['sʌndeɪ] Sonntag **I LUB,** 39
sunny ['sʌni] sonnig **I U6,** 79
sunny side up [ˌsʌni saɪd‿'ʌp] Spiegelei **IV U4,** 65
sunset ['sʌnset] Sonnenuntergang **V T1,** 12
sunshine ['sʌnʃaɪn] Sonnenschein **VI T2,** 36
suntan ['sʌntæn] Sonnenbräune **II U1,** 14
superb [su:'pɜ:b] großartig, herrlich **V T1,** 19
superlative [su:'pɜ:lətɪv] Superlativ **II U4,** 50
supermarket ['su:pəˌmɑ:kɪt] Supermarkt **I LUC,** 52
supervisor ['su:pəvaɪzə] Betreuer/Betreuerin, Aufsichtsperson, Vorgesetzter/Vorgesetzte **VI T2,** 34
supper ['sʌpə] Abendessen **I U3,** 44
for supper [fə 'sʌpə] zum Abendessen **II U3,** 38
to have supper [hæv 'sʌpə] zu Abend essen **I U3,** 44
supply [sə'plaɪ] Vorrat, Bestand, Versorgung **V T4,** 74
to **supply** [sə'plaɪ] beschaffen, besorgen, bereitstellen **V T1,** 17; **V T4,** 74; (be)liefern, ausrüsten **VI T4,** 74
support [sə'pɔ:t] Unterstützung, Hilfe **V T1,** 14; **V T1,** 17; **V T3,** 52; **V T4,** 76
to **support** [sə'pɔ:t] unterstützen, stützen **IV U5,** 84
supporter [sə'pɔ:tə] Anhänger/Anhängerin **IV U2,** 25
*to **be supposed to (do sth)** [ˌbi sə'pəʊzd tə] (etw. tun) sollen **VI T3,** 59; **VI T4,** 72
supreme [su:'pri:m] höchster/höchste/höchstes, oberster/oberste/oberstes **V T3,** 58
sure [ʃʊə] sicher **I U1,** 16
to make sure [meɪk 'ʃʊə] sichergehen **II U6,** 82
to **surf** [sɜ:f] (wind)surfen **II U1,** 14
to surf the Internet [ˌsɜ:f ði‿'ɪntənet] im Internet surfen **II U1,** 14
surface ['sɜ:fɪs] (Ober-)Fläche **V T4,** 74
surfing ['sɜ:fɪŋ] Wellenreiten, Surfen **II U1,** 14
to **surprise** [sə'praɪz] überraschen **VI T4,** 78
surprised [sə'praɪzd] überrascht, erstaunt **II U1,** 18

English – German

surprising [sə'praɪzɪŋ] überraschend **II U7,** 96
to **surround** [sə'raʊnd] umgeben, umschließen **VI T4,** 72
survey ['sɜːveɪ] Umfrage **I U4,** 56
survival [sə'vaɪvl] Überleben **III U4,** 66
to **survive** [sə'vaɪv] überleben, bestehen, durchstehen **V T4,** 75
survivor [sə'vaɪvə] Überlebender/Überlebende **VI T3,** 56
suspect ['sʌspekt] Verdächtigter/Verdächtigte **III U5,** 84
suspense [sə'spens] Spannung **IV U3,** 50
swap [swɒp] Tausch **II U7,** 88
to **swap** [swɒp] tauschen **I LUB,** 38
sweatshirt ['swetʃɜːt] Sweatshirt **II U1,** 10
sweet [swiːt] süß **I LUA,** 24; Bonbon, Süßigkeit **II U4,** 53
to **swerve** [swɜːv] ausweichen, ausscheren **III U4,** 70; ausbrechen *(Fahrzeug)* **V T3,** 56
*to **swim** [swɪm] schwimmen **I LUB,** 38
swimmer ['swɪmə] Schwimmer/Schwimmerin **III U3,** 45
swimming pool ['swɪmɪŋ ˌpuːl] Schwimmbecken; Schwimmbad **III U1,** 12
swimsuit ['swɪmsuːt] Badeanzug **III U1,** 12
switch [swɪtʃ] Schalter **IV U3,** 46
to **switch off** [ˌswɪtʃ‿'ɒf] ausschalten **IV U1,** 17
to switch on [ˌswɪtʃ‿'ɒn] einschalten, anmachen **IV U3,** 44
symbol ['sɪmbl] Symbol, Sinnbild, Zeichen **IV U1,** 9
synonym ['sɪnənɪm] Synonym **IV U5,** 87
syrup ['sɪrəp] Sirup **IV U1,** 12
system ['sɪstəm] System **III U4,** 67
nervous system ['nɜːvəs ˌsɪstəm] Nervensystem **V T2,** 38

T

table ['teɪbl] Tisch **I U1,** 18; Tabelle **VI T4,** 70
table-tennis ['teɪblˌtenɪs] Tischtennis **II U7,** 88
to set the table [ˌset ðə 'teɪbl] den Tisch decken **II U4,** 50
tabloid (newspaper) ['tæblɔɪd] Boulevardzeitung **VI T2,** 34
tail [teɪl] Schwanz, Schweif; Heck **V T1,** 13
*to **take** [teɪk] nehmen, mitnehmen, wegnehmen, bringen **I U3,** 42; dauern, *(Zeit)* brauchen **III U3,** 45
to take a deep breath [ˌteɪk‿ə 'diːp ˌbreθ] tief Luft holen °**III U5,** 86
to take a joke [ˌteɪk‿ə 'dʒəʊk] Spaß verstehen **VI T2,** 34
to take a look (at) [ˌteɪk‿ə 'lʊk] einen Blick werfen (auf) **VI T1,** 16
to take care [teɪk 'keə] aufpassen, sich kümmern **IV U2,** 31
to take home [ˌteɪk 'həʊm] nach Hause bringen **I U2,** 35
to take notes [teɪk 'nəʊts] sich Notizen machen °**II U4,** 55
to take off [ˌteɪk‿'ɒf] wegbringen, fortschaffen **III U1,** 17; ausziehen **III U3,** 52; abheben, starten, abfliegen **IV U1,** 16
to take on sth/sb [teɪk‿'ɒn] es mit etw./jmdm. aufnehmen, antreten gegen etw./jmdn. **V T2,** 35
to take out [teɪk‿'aʊt] herausnehmen **I U3,** 42
to take part in [teɪk 'pɑːt‿ɪn] teilnehmen an **III U4,** 63
to take pictures [teɪk 'pɪktʃəz] fotografieren, Fotos machen **II U5,** 62
to take place [teɪk 'pleɪs] stattfinden **III U4,** 63
to take your chance [ˌteɪk jɔː 'tʃɑːns] etw. wagen, etw. riskieren **III U3,** 53
takeaway ['teɪkəweɪ] Restaurant mit Straßenverkauf; Essen zum Mitnehmen **II U4,** 48
talent ['tælənt] Talent **V T2,** 40
talented ['tæləntɪd] talentiert, begabt **VI T1,** 10
talk [tɔːk] Vortrag, Rede **III U1,** 14
sales talk ['seɪlz tɔːk] Verkaufsgespräch °**V T1,** 19
talk show ['tɔːk ˌʃəʊ] Talkshow **III U5,** 80
to give a talk [ˌɡɪv‿ə 'tɔːk] einen Vortrag/eine Rede halten **VI T1,** 18
to **talk** [tɔːk] sprechen, reden **I U1,** 10
to talk to ['tɔːk tə] sprechen mit, reden mit **II U2,** 28
talkie ['tɔːki] Tonfilm **IV U5,** 78
tall [tɔːl] groß, hoch **II U3,** 36
tank [tæŋk] Tank, Kessel; Panzer **V T4,** 72
tanker ['tæŋkə] Tanker **V T4,** 71
tap [tæp] Wasserhahn **VI T3,** 53
tap water ['tæp ˌwɔːtə] Leitungswasser **VI T3,** 53
target ['tɑːɡɪt] Ziel(scheibe) **VI T2,** 36
task [tɑːsk] Aufgabe, Auftrag **VI T2,** 34
taste [teɪst] Geschmack **VI T3,** 53
to **taste** [teɪst] schmecken **I U7,** 94
tasty ['teɪsti] schmackhaft **II U4,** 50
Pizza is tastier. ['piːtsə ɪz ˌteɪstɪə] Pizza schmeckt besser. **II U4,** 50
tattoo [tæt'uː] Tätowierung **III U4,** 62
tax [tæks] Steuer, Abgabe, Gebühr **V T3,** 53
taxi ['tæksi] Taxi **III U2,** 34
taxman *(infml)* ['tæksmæn] Finanzamt **V T3,** 59
tea [tiː] Tee, Abendessen **I U7,** 94
afternoon tea [ˌɑːftənuːn 'tiː] Nachmittagstee **I U7,** 94
*to **teach** [tiːtʃ] unterrichten, lehren **I LUB,** 38
teacher ['tiːtʃə] Lehrer/Lehrerin **I U1,** 12
guidance teacher *(AE)* ['ɡaɪdənts ˌtiːtʃə] Vertrauenslehrer/Vertrauenslehrerin **VI T4,** 73
team [tiːm] Mannschaft, Team **II U2,** 23
tear [tɪə] Träne **V T4,** 80
technical ['teknɪkl] technisch; handwerklich, fachlich **V T2,** 41
technique [tek'niːk] Methode, Technik **VI T1,** 14
Technology [tek'nɒlədʒi] Technik **II U1,** 10
teen [tiːn] Jugendlicher/Jugendliche **II U6,** 80
teenage ['tiːneɪdʒ] jugendlich **III U4,** 63
teenager ['tiːnˌeɪdʒə] Teenager, Jugendlicher/Jugendliche **III U2,** 28
television ['telɪvɪʒn] Fernsehen, Fernseher **VI T1,** 16
*to **tell** [tel] erzählen, sagen **I U3,** 49
temperature ['temprətʃə] Temperatur **II U6,** 78
temporary ['temprəri] vorübergehend, temporär, befristet **V T1,** 15; **V T3,** 59
tempting ['temptɪŋ] verführerisch, verlockend **VI T4,** 72
tenant ['tenənt] Mieter/Mieterin °**V T3,** 49
tennis ['tenɪs] Tennis **III U1,** 12
table-tennis ['teɪblˌtenɪs] Tischtennis **II U7,** 88
tense [tens] Zeit, Zeitform *(grammatisch)* °**III U2,** 39
tension ['tenʃn] (An-)Spannung **VI T2,** 36
tent [tent] Zelt **I U6,** 84
term [tɜːm] Bedingung; Begriff, Bezeichnung **V T4,** 76; Trimester *(Einteilung des englischen Schuljahrs)* **VI T4,** 71
terms and conditions [ˌtɜːmz‿ənd kən'dɪʃnz] Allgemeine Geschäftsbedingungen (AGB) **V T4,** 76
terrible ['terəbl] schrecklich, furchtbar **I U2,** 35
territory ['terɪtri] Territorium, Land, Gebiet **VI T1,** 11

terrorism ['terərɪsm] Terrorismus **V T3,** 51
test [test] Test, Klassenarbeit **II U3,** 44
to **test** [test] testen, prüfen **V T4,** 72
text [tekst] Text °**I U2,** 27
text message ['tekst ˌmesɪdʒ] SMS **I U6,** 80
to **text** [tekst] Textnachricht (SMS) schicken, simsen **III U4,** 64
textbook ['teksbʊk] Schulbuch **IV U3,** 48
textile ['tekstaɪl] textil; Textil(-) **VI T3,** 52
thali ['θɑːli] *indisches Gericht* °**VI T1,** 17
than [ðæn] als **I U4,** 55
to **thank** [θæŋk] danken **I U4,** 60
thank you ['θæŋk juː] danke **I U1,** 12
thanks [θæŋks] danke **II U2,** 26
thanks to ['θæŋks tə] dank (dir/ ihnen), wegen **III U2,** 28
that [ðæt] das, jenes **I U1,** 12
that (bad) ['ðæt bæd] so (schlimm) **II U2,** 24
that evening [ˌdæt‿'iːvnɪŋ] an diesem Abend **II U1,** 19
That's what I call .... [ˌðæts wɒt‿'aɪ ˌkɔːl] Das nenne ich .... **II U1,** 14
that's why ['ðæts ˌwaɪ] deshalb **II U1,** 18
that way [ðæt 'weɪ] auf diese Weise **VI T1,** 14
to **thaw** [θɔː] auftauen **IV U4,** 65
the [ðə; ði] der/die/das **I U1,** 11
theater *(AE)* ['θɪətə] Theater; Kino **IV U1,** 9
their [ðeə] ihr/ihre **I U2,** 30
them [ðem] sie, ihnen **I U4,** 60
theme park ['θiːm ˌpɑːk] Freizeitpark **IV U2,** 24
themselves [ðəm'selvz] sie/sich (selbst) **III U4,** 67
then [ðen] dann **I LUB,** 38; damals **VI T2,** 28; **VI T4,** 74
there [ðeə] dort, da **I U2,** 26
over there [ˌəʊvə 'ðeə] da drüben **I U5,** 66
there are [ðeər‿'ɑː] da sind, es gibt **I U2,** 32
there is [ðeər‿'ɪz] da ist, es gibt **I U2,** 32
thermostat ['θɜːməstæt] Thermostat, Temperaturregler **VI T3,** 58
these [ðiːz] diese, diese hier **I U6,** 84
these days ['ðiːz deɪz] heutzutage **VI T1,** 12
they [ðeɪ] sie (*Mehrzahl)* **I U1,** 16; man **III U1,** 8
thick [θɪk] dick *(nicht für Personen)*; dumm **III U1,** 16
thin [θɪn] dünn **VI T4,** 77
thing [θɪŋ] Sache, Ding **I U3,** 40
*to **think** [θɪŋk] denken **I U3,** 49; glauben **II U4,** 50
to think about ['θɪŋk‿əˌbaʊt] nachdenken über, denken an °**II U7,** 95
to think of ['θɪŋk‿əv] denken an °**II U3,** 39
to think up [θɪŋk‿'ʌp] (sich) ausdenken **IV U2,** 26
third [θɜːd] dritter/dritte/drittes **I U5,** 70; Drittel **V T2,** 33; **V T3,** 52; **V T3,** 58
this [ðɪs] dieser/diese/dieses **I U1,** 12
this evening [ðɪs 'iːvnɪŋ] heute Abend **III U3,** 52
thorn [θɔːn] Dorn **V T2,** 35
those [ðəʊz] diese dort, jene **I U6,** 84
though [ðəʊ] trotzdem, dennoch **IV U5,** 84
even though [ˌiːvn‿'ðəʊ] auch wenn; obwohl **VI T1,** 12
thought [θɔːt] Gedanke **IV U3,** 50
thoughtful ['θɔːtfl] aufmerksam, fürsorglich **IV U2,** 28
thousand ['θaʊznd] tausend **II U2,** 23
thread [θred] Zwirn, Garn, Faden **IV U1,** 10
threat [θret] (Be-)Drohung, Gefahr **V T2,** 35; **V T3,** 54; **V T4,** 74
thriller ['θrɪlə] Thriller **III U5,** 80
throne [θrəʊn] Thron **VI T2,** 32
through [θruː] durch **II U4,** 57
through to ['θruː tə] bis hin zu **VI T1,** 15
throughout [θru'aʊt] durchgehend, überall in **VI T4,** 74
throw [θrəʊ] Wurf **III U1,** 18
*to **throw** [θrəʊ] werfen **I U3,** 49
thug [θʌg] Gangster, Schläger; Typ **VI T1,** 16
Thursday ['θɜːzdeɪ] Donnerstag **I LUB,** 39
to **tick** [tɪk] abhaken °**II U5,** 65
ticket ['tɪkɪt] Ticket, Fahrschein, Eintrittskarte **I U7,** 90
to **tie** [taɪ] (an)binden, fesseln **VI T2,** 36
tied [taɪd] gebunden **V T2,** 38
tiger ['taɪgə] Tiger **I U2,** 26
tight [taɪt] eng, fest **VI T4,** 77
tikka ['tikʌ] *Fleisch in würz. Soße* °**VI T1,** 17
till [tɪl] bis **IV U4,** 68
time [taɪm] Zeit **I U2,** 30; Mal **II U1,** 18
in time [ɪn 'taɪm] rechtzeitig **V T3,** 53
on time [ɒn 'taɪm] pünktlich **IV U3,** 48
time is up [ˌtaɪm‿əz‿'ʌp] die Zeit ist abgelaufen **V T3,** 52
time off [taɪm‿'ɒf] Freizeit **VI T4,** 71
to have a good time [ˌhæv‿ə gʊd 'taɪm] sich amüsieren **I U5,** 75
What's the time, please? [ˌwɒts ðə 'taɪm ˌpliːz] Wie viel Uhr ist es, bitte?; Wie spät ist es, bitte? **I U3,** 42
to **time** [taɪm] stoppen, die Zeit nehmen **I U7,** 92
timeline ['taɪmlaɪn] Zeitleiste °**I U4,** 63
timetable ['taɪmteɪbl] Stundenplan, Fahrplan **II U1,** 12
tin [tɪn] Dose, Büchse **III U2,** 34
tiny ['taɪni] winzig **I LUA,** 25
tip [tɪp] Tipp **II U4,** 52; Trinkgeld **IV U1,** 12
to **tip** [tɪp] (aus)kippen **VI T4,** 76
tired ['taɪəd] müde **II U3,** 38
dog-tired [ˌdɒg'taɪəd] hundemüde **I U3,** 49
title ['taɪtl] Titel, Überschrift **II U3,** 42; Bezeichnung **V T1,** 15
to [tʊ; tə] zu, nach, bis **I U1,** 19
toast [təʊst] Toast **IV U1,** 12
tobacco [tə'bækəʊ] Tabak **IV U2,** 27
today [tə'deɪ] heute **I U2,** 29
toe [təʊ] Zeh **II U3,** 41
together [tə'geðə] zusammen, miteinander **I LUB,** 38
toilet ['tɔɪlɪt] Toilette **I U1,** 19
tomato, tomatoes *(pl)* [tə'mɑːtəʊ; tə'mɑːtəʊz] Tomate **I U5,** 68
tomorrow [tə'mɒrəʊ] morgen **II U1,** 18
ton [tʌn] Tonne (*Gewicht)* **III U3,** 49
tone [təʊn] Ton(fall) **VI T2,** 37
tongue [tʌŋ] Zunge **III U4,** 62
mother tongue ['mʌðə ˌtʌŋ] Muttersprache **VI T1,** 10
tongue twister ['tʌŋ ˌtwɪstə] Zungenbrecher °**II U4,** 55
tonight [tə'naɪt] heute Abend, heute Nacht **I U6,** 84
too [tuː] auch **I U1,** 10; zu **I U5,** 66
tooth, teeth *(pl)* [tuːθ; tiːθ] Zahn **III U5,** 86
false teeth [fɔːls 'tiːθ] Zahnprothese, Gebiss **VI T2,** 28
toothache ['tuːθeɪk] Zahnschmerzen **IV U3,** 50
top [tɒp] oberer Teil **III U1,** 14
at the top [ət ðə 'tɒp] im oberen Teil **III U1,** 14
topic ['tɒpɪk] Thema **I U2,** 33
torch, torches *(pl)* [tɔːtʃ; 'tɔːtʃɪz] Taschenlampe, Fackel **I U6,** 84
torn [tɔːn] hin- und hergerissen, zerrissen **V T2,** 36
total ['təʊtl] total, gesamt, vollständig **V T2,** 38; Gesamtbetrag, Summe **VI T3,** 59
to **touch** [tʌtʃ] berühren; antippen **III U3,** 53
tough [tʌf] hart, rau, zäh **III U5,** 80

tour [tʊə] Tour, Fahrt, Reise **IV U1,** 16
tourism ['tʊərɪzm] Tourismus, Touristik, Fremdenverkehr **VI T3,** 60
tourist ['tʊərɪst] Tourist/Touristin **III U2,** 28
towards [tə'wɔ:dz] in Richtung, auf … zu, darauf zu **III U5,** 90
tower ['taʊə] Turm **III U2,** 26; Kontrollturm, Tower **VI T1,** 10
town [taʊn] Stadt **I U3,** 41
toxic ['tɒksɪk] giftig, toxisch **VI T3,** 55
toy [tɔɪ] Spielzeug **III U2,** 28
track [træk] Spur; Gleis **IV U4,** 62
tractor ['træktə] Traktor **IV U3,** 43
trade [treɪd] Handel **V T4,** 70
fair trade [ˌfeə 'treɪd] fairer Handel **V T4,** 76
trader ['treɪdə] Händler/Händlerin **VI T1,** 13
tradition [trə'dɪʃn] Tradition **III U2,** 34
traditional [trə'dɪʃnl] traditionell **V T4,** 71
traffic ['træfɪk] Verkehr **III U2,** 26
air traffic controller [ˌeə træfɪk kən'trəʊlə] Fluglotse/Fluglotsin **IV U3,** 51
traffic jam ['træfɪk ˌdʒæm] Stau **III U2,** 26
tragedy ['trædʒədi] Tragödie **VI T4,** 70
train [treɪn] Zug **I U4,** 54
road train ['rəʊd ˌtreɪn] Fernlaster, Lkw-Zug **V T1,** 10
to **train** [treɪn] eine Ausbildung machen **III U2,** 34; trainieren **IV U2,** 32; ausbilden; lernen **V T3,** 59
trainer ['treɪnə] Trainer/Trainerin **V T1,** 14
training ['treɪnɪŋ] Training, Ausbildung **III U4,** 68
to **transfer** [trænts'fɜ:] transferieren, verlegen; übertragen **VI T1,** 11
to **translate** [trænz'leɪt] übersetzen **VI T1,** 10
transport ['træntspɔ:t] Transport **I U4,** 57; Verkehr(smittel) **III U2,** 36
to **transport** [træn'spɔ:t] transportieren **IV U4,** 61
*to be **trapped** [bi: 'træpt] in der Falle sitzen **II U6,** 83
travel ['trævl] Reise **III U5,** 82
to **travel** ['trævl] reisen **III U3,** 44
to **trawl** [trɔ:l] mit dem Netz fischen; stöbern **VI T4,** 77
tray [treɪ] Tablett °**VI T1,** 17
treason ['tri:zn] (Landes-)Verrat **VI T2,** 28
to **treat** [tri:t] behandeln **VI T2,** 35; **VI T2,** 36; **VI T3,** 54
treatment ['tri:tmənt] Behandlung, Aufbereitung **VI T3,** 56
water treatment plant ['wɔ:tə ˌtri:tmənt ˌplɑ:nt] Wasseraufbereitungsanlage **VI T3,** 56
treaty ['tri:ti] (Staats-)Vertrag, Abkommen **VI T2,** 32
tree [tri:] Baum **I U1,** 20
family tree ['fæmli tri:] Familienstammbaum °**I U2,** 28
trend [trend] Trend, Entwicklung, Richtung °**VI T1,** 10
trendy ['trendi] modisch **III U2,** 26
trial ['traɪəl] Prüfung, Test **VI T1,** 10; Gerichtsverfahren, -verhandlung **VI T2,** 26
tribe [traɪb] (Volks-)Stamm **IV U4,** 60
trick [trɪk] Trick, Streich **I U3,** 40
trickle ['trɪkl] Rinnsal **VI T4,** 78
trip [trɪp] Ausflug, Reise **I U6,** 80
trolley ['trɒli] Gepäck-/Einkaufswagen, Handkarren **III U3,** 50
troops *(pl)* [tru:ps] Truppen **VI T2,** 33
trophy ['trəʊfi] Trophäe, Preis **IV U5,** 77
trouble ['trʌbl] Schwierigkeiten, Ärger **I U2,** 30
trousers *(pl)* ['traʊzəz] Hose **II U1,** 10
truck *(AE)* [trʌk] Lastwagen, Truck **IV U4,** 61
trucker *(AE)* ['trʌkə] Lastwagenfahrer/Lastwagenfahrerin, Trucker **IV U4,** 61
truckie *(Aus)* ['trʌki] Trucker/Truckerin, Lastwagenfahrer/Lastwagenfahrerin **V T1,** 10
true [tru:] wahr **II U1,** 18
to come true [kʌm 'tru:] wahr werden **III U2,** 30
trunk *(AE)* [trʌŋk] Kofferraum **IV U4,** 65
trust [trʌst] Vertrauen **III U5,** 88
to **trust** [trʌst] vertrauen **III U3,** 52
trustworthy ['trʌstwɜ:ði] vertrauenswürdig **VI T1,** 18
truth [tru:θ] Wahrheit **V T1,** 10
truthful ['tru:θfl] wahrhaft, ehrlich **VI T4,** 72
to **try** [traɪ] versuchen, probieren **II U1,** 10
to try hard [traɪ‿'hɑ:d] sich stark bemühen **III U4,** 70
tryout ['traɪaʊt] Auswahlverfahren **IV U2,** 24
T-shirt ['ti:ʃɜ:t] T-Shirt **I U2,** 30
tucker ['tʌkə] Essen *(australischer Ausdruck)* °**II U1,** 14
Tuesday ['tju:zdeɪ] Dienstag **I LUB,** 39
tug [tʌg] Ziehen, Zupfen **III U3,** 52
tumble drier ['tʌmbl ˌdraɪə] Wäschetrockner **IV U3,** 44
tunnel ['tʌnl] Tunnel, Unterführung **I U4,** 54
turbine ['tɜ:baɪn] Turbine **VI T3,** 61
turkey ['tɜ:ki] Truthahn, Pute **IV U1,** 12
Turkish ['tɜ:kɪʃ] türkisch **I U2,** 29
in **turn** [ɪn 'tɜ:n] abwechselnd, der Reihe nach °**V T3,** 55
It's your turn. [ɪts jɔ: 'tɜ:n] Du bist dran. **II U1,** 13
My turn had come. [tɜ:n] Ich war an der Reihe. **VI T2,** 36
to **turn** [tɜ:n] sich umdrehen **III U5,** 86
to turn (to) [tɜ:n] werden (zu) **VI T4,** 77
to turn back [tɜ:n 'bæk] umkehren, zurückgehen **II U1,** 19
to turn down [tɜ:n 'daʊn] herunterdrehen **VI T3,** 58
to turn into [ˌtɜ:n‿'ɪntə] machen zu, verwandeln in °**VI T4,** 79
to turn left/right [tɜ:n 'left/'raɪt] links/rechts abbiegen **II U7,** 97
to turn off [tɜ:n‿'ɒf] abschalten, ausschalten **I U5,** 75
to turn on [ˌtɜ:n‿'ɒn] einschalten, anmachen **IV U3,** 46
to turn over [ˌtɜ:n‿'əʊvə] (sich) umdrehen **II U7,** 94
to turn round [tɜ:n 'raʊnd] (sich) umdrehen **II U1,** 18
to turn sb off [tɜ:n‿'ɒf] jmdn. abtörnen **V T2,** 32
to be a **turn-off** ['tɜ:nɒf] abtörnend sein, zum Abgewöhnen sein **V T2,** 32
turnover ['tɜ:nˌəʊvə] Umsatz, Absatz **V T4,** 77
TV [ˌti:'vi:] Fernsehen, Fernseher **I LUA,** 25
twice [twaɪs] zweimal **III U5,** 80
twig [twɪg] Zweig **VI T4,** 76
twin [twɪn] Zwilling(s-) **V T2,** 34
type [taɪp] Typ, Art, Sorte **IV U4,** 66
typically ['tɪpɪkli] typisch °**V T1,** 11

U

ultra ['ʌltrə] ultra- **V T1,** 19
umbrella [ʌm'brelə] Regenschirm **II U6,** 81
umpire ['ʌmpaɪə] Schiedsrichter/Schiedsrichterin **III U1,** 12
to **unburden** [ʌn'bɜ:dn] entlasten, abladen **VI T4,** 77
uncle ['ʌŋkl] Onkel **I U2,** 28
agony uncle ['ægəni ˌʌnkl] Kummerkastenonkel **V T2,** 34
uncool [ʌn'ku:l] uncool **VI T1,** 16

under ['ʌndə] unter **I U1,** 18
undercover [ˌʌndə'kʌvə] geheim, verdeckt **IV U3,** 50
underground ['ʌndəgraʊnd] U-Bahn **III U2,** 27
to **underline** [ˌʌndə'laɪn] unterstreichen **II U1,** 18
*to **understand** [ˌʌndə'stænd] verstehen **III U3,** 53
understanding [ˌʌndə'stændɪŋ] Verständigung; Verständnis **V T4,** 70
underwater [ˌʌndə'wɔ:tə] Unterwasser- **IV U4,** 62
unemployment [ˌʌnɪm'plɔɪmənt] Arbeitslosigkeit **VI T1,** 11
unfair [ʌn'feə] ungerecht, unfair °**III U4,** 62
unforgettable [ˌʌnfə'getəbl] unvergesslich **V T1,** 19
unfriendly [ʌn'frendli] unfreundlich **IV U5,** 83
unhappy [ʌn'hæpi] unglücklich **I U2,** 33
unharmed [ʌn'hɑ:md] unverletzt, unbeschädigt **VI T2,** 36
unhealthy [ʌn'helθi] ungesund **II U4,** 53
uniform ['ju:nɪfɔ:m] Uniform **I U3,** 44
unilingual [ˌju:nɪ'lɪŋgwəl] einsprachig **VI T1,** 11
unimportant [ˌʌnɪm'pɔ:tnt] unwichtig, unbedeutend **VI T2,** 36
union ['ju:njən] Liga; Vereinigung, Union **III U1,** 11
unique [ju:'ni:k] einzig(artig), einmalig **V T1,** 19
unit ['ju:nɪt] Kapitel, Einheit °**III U5,** 93
universe ['ju:nɪvɜ:s] Universum, Weltraum **V T3,** 58
university [ˌju:nɪ'vɜ:səti] Universität **III U2,** 31
unknown [ʌn'nəʊn] unbekannt °**IV U1,** 14
unless [ən'les] es sei denn, (dass) … **V T1,** 12; **V T2,** 35
unlike [ʌn'laɪk] anders als, im Gegensatz zu **VI T1,** 16; **VI T2,** 32
*to be **unlucky** [ˌbi:‿ʌn'lʌki] Pech haben, unglücklich sein **V T3,** 53
until [ʌn'tɪl; n'tɪl] bis **II U4,** 56
*to **unwind** [ʌn'waɪnd] sich abwickeln **IV U1,** 10
up [ʌp] auf, hinauf, oben **II U2,** 30
  Hurry up! [ˌhʌri‿'ʌp] Beeil dich! **I U2,** 30
  to get up [get‿'ʌp] aufstehen **I U3,** 44
  to give up [gɪv‿'ʌp] aufgeben **III U2,** 30
  to go up [gəʊ‿'ʌp] hinaufgehen °**I U4,** 61
  to wake up [weɪk‿'ʌp] aufwecken; aufwachen **I U3,** 48
  to walk up to [wɔ:k‿'ʌp tə] hingehen, zugehen auf **III U5,** 87
  up current ['ʌp ˌkʌrnt] gegen die Strömung **V T4,** 79
  up to ['ʌp tə] bis zu **III U3,** 49
  What's up? [ˌwɒts‿'ʌp] Was ist los? **I U1,** 16
update ['ʌpdeɪt] Update, Aktualisierung **VI T3,** 60
to **update** [ʌp'deɪt] aktualisieren **VI T3,** 59
upper ['ʌpə] oberer/obere/oberes **IV U2,** 30
*to **upset** [ʌp'set] erschrecken, durcheinanderbringen, umstoßen **III U4,** 64
*to be **upset** [bi: ʌp'set] aufgeregt sein, bestürzt sein **II U3,** 44
upside down [ˌʌpsaɪd 'daʊn] umgedreht, auf den Kopf gestellt **VI T2,** 28; **VI T4,** 76
upstairs [ʌp'steəz] oben, im oberen Stock **I U2,** 27; (die Treppe) hinauf/herauf **III U5,** 85
  to run upstairs [ˌrʌn‿ʌp'steəz] die Treppe hinaufrennen **III U3,** 53
Urdu ['ʊədu:] Urdu **VI T1,** 10
urgent ['ɜ:dʒnt] dringend **V T2,** 34
us [ʌs] uns **I U4,** 60
use [ju:s] Anwendung, Gebrauch, Nutzen **VI T2,** 34; Verwendung, Nutzung **VI T3,** 58
to **use** [ju:z] benutzen, verwenden **I U4,** 54
  used to (+ infinitive) ['ju:s‿tə] früher; pflegte(n) zu **VI T1,** 10; **VI T2,** 36; **VI T4,** 77
useful ['ju:sfl] nützlich **IV U3,** 47
useless ['ju:sləs] nutzlos **III U4,** 64
usual ['ju:ʒl] üblich, gewöhnlich **V T2,** 34
  usually ['ju:ʒli] normalerweise, gewöhnlich **II U4,** 53

V

vacancy ['veɪknsi] Stellenangebot, offene Stelle; freies Zimmer **V T1,** 14
vacation *(AE)* [və'keɪʃn] Ferien, Urlaub **IV U1,** 12
valid ['vælɪd] gültig, zulässig **V T1,** 15
valuable ['væljuəbl] wertvoll **III U2,** 26
van [væn] Lieferwagen **I U6,** 86
variation [ˌveərɪ'eɪʃn] Variation, Verschiedenartigkeit **VI T1,** 10
to **vary** ['veəri] variieren, schwanken, sich ändern **VI T4,** 70
vast [vɑ:st] riesig, ausgedehnt **IV U4,** 61
vegetable ['vedʒtəbl] Gemüse **II U1,** 15
vehicle ['vɪəkl] Auto, Fahrzeug, Vehikel **VI T4,** 74
vending machine ['vendɪŋ məˌʃi:n] Warenautomat **III U4,** 66
venom ['venəm] Gift *(z. B. von Schlangen und Insekten)*; Bosheit **V T1,** 12
verb [vɜ:b] Verb °**II U1,** 20
  modal auxiliary verb [ˌməʊdl‿ɔ:g'zɪljəri 'vɜ:b] modales Hilfsverb °**III U3,** 46
verse [vɜ:s] Strophe, Vers **V T3,** 51
version ['vɜ:ʃn] Version, Fassung **VI T2,** 31
versus ['vɜ:səs] gegen, kontra °**VI T1,** 17
very ['veri] sehr **I U1,** 20; aller- **IV U1,** 16
vest [vest] Weste **VI T2,** 36
veto ['vi:təʊ] Veto, Einspruch **VI T2,** 33
via [vaɪə] via, über, per **V T1,** 15
victim ['vɪktɪm] Opfer **V T3,** 51
video ['vɪdiəʊ] Video **I LUB,** 38
view [vju:] Aussicht, Sicht **III U2,** 26
  point of view [ˌpɔɪnt‿əv 'vju:] Standpunkt; Perspektive °**V T3,** 57
to **view** [vju:] anschauen, betrachten **IV U5,** 80
viewer ['vju:ə] Zuschauer/Zuschauerin **III U5,** 80
villa ['vɪlə] Villa; Landhaus **V T4,** 79
village ['vɪlɪdʒ] Dorf **III U4,** 64
vinegar ['vɪnɪgə] Essig **V T1,** 12
violence ['vaɪəlnts] Gewalt(tätigkeit) **V T2,** 32; **V T3,** 51
violent ['vaɪəlnt] gewaltsam, gewalttätig, brutal **V T3,** 51
virginity [və'dʒɪnəti] Jungfräulichkeit **VI T4,** 76
virtual ['vɜ:tʃuəl] virtuell **IV U3,** 43
visa, visas *(pl)* ['vi:zə] Visum *(Plural: Visa)*, Einreisebewilligung **IV U3,** 50
  working visa ['wɜ:kɪŋ ˌvi:zə] Arbeitserlaubnis **V T1,** 15
visit ['vɪzɪt] Besuch **I U7,** 94
to **visit** ['vɪzɪt] besuchen, besichtigen **I U4,** 54
visitor ['vɪzɪtə] Besucher/Besucherin **I U4,** 55
to **visualize** ['vɪʒulaɪz] visualisieren, sichtbar machen °**VI T4,** 79
visuals *(pl)* ['vɪʒuəlz] Bildmaterial °**V T2,** 39
vital ['vaɪtl] lebenswichtig, unerlässlich; Lebens- **IV U5,** 82
  vital signs *(pl)* [ˌvaɪtl 'saɪnz] Lebenszeichen **IV U5,** 82
vocabulary [vəʊ'kæbjəlri] Wortschatz, Vokabular **VI T1,** 13
voice [vɔɪs] Stimme **II U2,** 31

volleyball ['vɒlibɔ:l] Volleyball **I U3,** 40
volunteer [ˌvɒlən'tɪə] Freiwilliger/ Freiwillige; freiwillig **IV U5,** 81
to **volunteer** [ˌvɒlən'tɪə] sich freiwillig melden **V T2,** 40
vote [vəʊt] Abstimmung; Stimme **IV U2,** 33
to **vote (for)** [vəʊt] abstimmen, wählen, stimmen (für) **IV U2,** 32
V-shaped ['vi:ˌʃeɪpt] V-förmig **IV U3,** 51

W

to **wage a war** [ˌweɪdʒ‿ə 'wɔ:] einen Krieg führen **VI T2,** 36
to **wait** [weɪt] warten **I U5,** 69
to wait for ['weɪt fɔ:] warten auf **I U6,** 86
waiter ['weɪtə] Kellner, Bedienung **II U4,** 55
*to **wake** [weɪk] (auf)wecken **II U7,** 94
to wake up [weɪk‿'ʌp] aufwecken; aufwachen **I U3,** 48
walk [wɔ:k] Spaziergang **III U1,** 12
to go for a walk [ˌgəʊ fər‿ə 'wɔ:k] spazieren gehen **III U5,** 88
to **walk** [wɔ:k] gehen, laufen **I U4,** 54
to walk the dog [wɔ:k ðə 'dɒg] mit dem Hund spazieren gehen **I U3,** 42
to walk up to [wɔ:k‿'ʌp tə] hingehen, zugehen auf **III U5,** 87
walkway ['wɔ:kweɪ] Steg, Weg **V T4,** 79
wall [wɔ:l] Wand, Mauer **I U1,** 18
wallet ['wɒlɪt] Brieftasche, Geldbeutel **II U4,** 56
wannabe *(slang)* ['wɒnəbi:] Möchtegern(-) °**V T2,** 35
to **want (to)** ['wɒnt tə] wollen, mögen **I U4,** 54
wanna *(slang)* ['wɒnə] wollen, mögen °**V T3,** 56
to want sb to do sth [wɒnt] wollen, dass jemand etwas tut **III U4,** 62
wanted ['wɒntɪd] gesucht **VI T3,** 60
war [wɔ:] Krieg **IV U1,** 10
to wage a war [ˌweɪdʒ‿ə 'wɔ:] einen Krieg führen **VI T2,** 36
World War II [ˌwɜ:ld ˌwɔ: 'tu:] der Zweite Weltkrieg **V T3,** 51
wardrobe ['wɔ:drəʊb] Kleiderschrank, Garderobe **I U2,** 30
to **warm up** [wɔ:m‿'ʌp] **IV U2,** 32
warm [wɔ:m] warm **II U2,** 25
(global) **warming** [ˌgləʊbl 'wɔ:mɪŋ] (Erd-)Erwärmung **V T4,** 72
to **warn** [wɔ:n] warnen, ermahnen °**IV U4,** 72
warning ['wɔ:nɪŋ] Warn-; Warnung **IV U3,** 48
to **wash** [wɒʃ] (sich) waschen **I U3,** 44
washing machine ['wɒʃɪŋ məˌʃi:n] Waschmaschine **IV U3,** 44
waste [weɪst] Abfall; Verschwendung **V T4,** 75
to **waste** [weɪst] verschwenden **IV U2,** 32
watch [wɒtʃ] Armbanduhr **V T1,** 11
to **watch** [wɒtʃ] ansehen, beobachten **I LUB,** 38; achten auf **II U2,** 31
water ['wɔ:tə] Wasser **I U5,** 68
fresh water ['freʃ ˌwɔ:tə] Süßwasser, Trinkwasser **VI T3,** 57
tap water ['tæp ˌwɔ:tə] Leitungswasser **VI T3,** 53
water treatment plant ['wɔ:tə ˌtri:tmənt ˌplɑ:nt] Wasseraufbereitungsanlage **VI T3,** 56
wave [weɪv] Welle **III U4,** 70
to **wave** [weɪv] winken, schwenken **II U6,** 83
way [weɪ] Weg **I U3,** 42; Art, Weise **III U3,** 49
by the way [ˌbaɪ ðə 'weɪ] übrigens **IV U4,** 65
either way [ˌaɪðə 'weɪ] auf die eine oder andere Art, so oder so **VI T4,** 76
He is on his way to .... [ˌhi:‿ɪz‿ɒn hɪz 'weɪ tə] Er ist auf dem Weg zu .... **I U3,** 42
No way! [ˌnəʊ‿'weɪ] Auf keinen Fall! **IV U4,** 62
the other way round [ði ˌʌðə‿weɪ 'raʊnd] andersrum, umgekehrt **V T2,** 35
we [wi:] wir **I U1,** 16
weak [wi:k] schwach **III U4,** 70
to go weak [gəʊ 'wi:k] schwach werden **III U4,** 70
weakness ['wi:knəs] Schwäche **VI T1,** 18
wealth [welθ] Wohlstand, Reichtum **VI T3,** 53
*to **wear** [weə] anhaben, tragen **I U3,** 45
weather ['weðə] Wetter **II U1,** 14
weatherman, weathermen *(pl)* ['weðəmən; 'weðəmen] Meteorologe °**II U6,** 78
web page ['web ˌpeɪdʒ] Website, Internetauftritt °**V T1,** 13
webcam ['webkæm] Webcam **V T1,** 16
website ['websaɪt] Website, Internetauftritt **II U5,** 64
webzine ['webzi:n] Webmagazin °**VI T1,** 12
Wednesday ['wenzdeɪ] Mittwoch **I LUB,** 39
week [wi:k] Woche **I LUB,** 39
a week [ə 'wi:k] pro Woche, in der Woche **II U4,** 52
weekday ['wi:kdeɪ] Wochentag, Werktag **V T1,** 14
weekend [ˌwi:k'end] Wochenende **I U3,** 45
weekly ['wi:kli] wöchentlich **VI T3,** 60
to **weigh** [weɪ] wiegen **V T2,** 40
weight [weɪt] Gewicht **III U1,** 11
to lose weight [lu:z 'weɪt] abnehmen **VI T3,** 54
to **welcome** ['welkəm] willkommen heißen **I U7,** 90
Welcome (to) ... ['welkəm tə] Willkommen (in) ... **III U4,** 67
You're welcome. [jʊə 'welkəm] Bitte sehr!, Gern geschehen! **I U1,** 19
well [wel] gut **III U1,** 16; Brunnen **VI T3,** 56
as well [əz 'wel] auch **VI T1,** 12
as well as [əz 'wel‿əz] sowohl ... als auch **III U4,** 67
to get well [get 'wel] gesund werden **VI T4,** 77
Well done! [ˌwel 'dʌn] Gut gemacht! **III U3,** 47
well-informed [ˌwelin'fɔ:md] gut informiert **VI T2,** 32; **VI T2,** 35
well [wel] also, na ja, nun gut **I U2,** 29
Welsh [welʃ] walisisch; Waliser/ Waliserin **III U3,** 48
west [west] Westen **I U4,** 54
West Asian [ˌwest 'eɪʃn] westasiatisch; Westasiate/-asiatin **VI T3,** 56
western ['westən] Western **IV U5,** 78; westlich **VI T1,** 15
wet [wet] nass **II U6,** 74
wet blanket [wet 'blæŋkɪt] Miesmacher/Miesmacherin **II U6,** 74
wetsuit ['wetsu:t] Taucheranzug, Neoprenanzug **V T4,** 79
what [wɒt] welcher/welche/welches **I LUA,** 25; was **I U1,** 11
What about ... ? [wɒt‿ə'baʊt] Was ist mit ...?; Wie wäre es mit ...? **I U2,** 30
What a laugh! [ˌwɒt‿ə 'lɑ:f] Wie lustig! **III U1,** 17
What a week! [ˌwɒt‿ə 'wi:k] Was für eine Woche! **II U2,** 22
What does it say? [ˌwɒt dʌz‿ɪt 'seɪ] Was steht da? **II U3,** 44
What's the film about? [wɒts ðə 'fɪlm‿əˌbaʊt] Wovon handelt der Film? °**II U3,** 43
What's the matter? [ˌwɒts ðə 'mætə] Was ist los? **III U5,** 88
What's the time, please? [ˌwɒts ðə 'taɪm ˌpli:z] Wie viel Uhr ist es, bitte?; Wie spät ist es, bitte? **I U3,** 42

What's up? [ˌwɒtsˈʌp] Was ist los? **I U1,** 16
What's your name? [ˌwɒts jə ˈneɪm] Wie heißt du? **I U1,** 11
What the heck … ? [ˌwɒt ðə ˈhek] Was zum Teufel … ? **III U4,** 70
whatever [wɒtˈevə] was auch immer; egal welche **VI T1,** 12
whatsoever [ˌwɒtsəʊˈevə] überhaupt, was auch immer; welche **V T2,** 39
wheel [wiːl] Rad **III U2,** 30; Steuer(rad) **V T3,** 56
wheelbarrow [ˈwiːlˌbærəʊ] Schubkarre **V T4,** 78
when [wen] wenn, als; wann **I U2,** 33
where [weə] wo, wohin **I U1,** 11
Where are you from? [ˌweər‿ə jə ˈfrɒm] Woher kommst du? **I U1,** 11
Where's the fire? [ˌweəz ðə ˈfaɪə] Wo brennt's denn? **I U7,** 96
whether [ˈweðə] ob °**VI T4,** 68
which [wɪtʃ] welcher/welche/welches **II U1,** 14; der/dem/den/die/das *(Relativpronomen)* **II U3,** 42
a **while** [ə ˈwaɪl] eine Weile **VI T2,** 34
while [waɪl] während **III U5,** 85
to **whisper** [ˈwɪspə] (zu)flüstern **II U1,** 18
whistle [ˈwɪsl] Trillerpfeife **III U1,** 12; Pfiff **VI T4,** 77
to **whistle** [ˈwɪsl] pfeifen **VI T4,** 77
white [waɪt] weiß **I LUA,** 24
white elephant stall [ˌwaɪt ˈelɪfənt stɔːl] Trödelstand **I U7,** 96
whiteboard [ˈwaɪtbɔːd] Whiteboard, Weißwandtafel **V T1,** 16
whitewater [ˈwaɪtwɔːtə] Wildwasser **IV U4,** 62
who [huː] wer, wem, wen **I U5,** 70; der/dem/den/die *(Relativpronomen)* **II U3,** 42
whole [həʊl] ganz **IV U3,** 51
whom [huːm] wem, wen **III U3,** 52
whose [huːz] wessen **II U5,** 68; dessen, deren *(Relativpronomen)* **III U3,** 48
why [waɪ] warum **I U5,** 70
wicked [ˈwɪkɪd] großartig **II U5,** 70
wide [waɪd] groß, breit, weit **VI T4,** 74
to **widen** [ˈwaɪdn] (aus)weiten, erweitern **VI T1,** 18
widespread [waɪdspred] (weit)verbreitet **VI T1,** 13
wife, wives *(pl)* [waɪf; waɪvz] Ehefrau **III U5,** 86
wig [wɪɡ] Perücke **II U2,** 28
wild [waɪld] wild **III U2,** 31
wild card [ˈwaɪld ˌkɑːd] Joker; Wildcard **VI T3,** 60
wildlife [ˈwaɪldlaɪf] wild lebende Tiere **V T1,** 19
*__will ('ll), won't__ [wɪl; wəʊnt] werden/werden nicht *(futurisch)* **II U6,** 76
*to **win** [wɪn] gewinnen, siegen **II U7,** 91
wind [wɪnd] Wind **I U2,** 35
windmill [ˈwɪnmɪl] Windmühle; Windrad, Windkraftanlage **V T4,** 71
window [ˈwɪndəʊ] Fenster **I U1,** 18
to **windsurf** [ˈwɪndsɜːf] windsurfen **III U3,** 46
windy [ˈwɪndi] windig **I U6,** 79
wing [wɪŋ] Flügel **V T4,** 79
winner [ˈwɪnə] Gewinner/Gewinnerin, Sieger/Siegerin **III U4,** 63
winter [ˈwɪntə] Winter **I U6,** 79
to **wipe** [waɪp] (ab)wischen, abreiben **VI T4,** 76
wish [wɪʃ] Wunsch **III U4,** 63
to **wish** [wɪʃ] wünschen **III U4,** 68
with [wɪð] mit **I U1,** 14; bei **II U1,** 11
to go (together) with [ˈɡəʊ wɪð] passen zu **III U5,** 81
within [wɪˈðɪn] innerhalb **III U2,** 28
without [wɪˈðaʊt] ohne **I U4,** 54
to go without [ˌɡəʊ wɪˈðaʊt] ohne … auskommen **II U4,** 52
wizard [ˈwɪzəd] Zauberer **II U5,** 69
wolf, wolves *(pl)* [wʊlf; wʊlvz] Wolf **III U5,** 86
woman, women *(pl)* [ˈwʊmən; ˈwɪmɪn] Frau **I U4,** 62
no **wonder** [nəʊ ˈwʌndə] kein Wunder, dass … **V T2,** 39
to **wonder** [ˈwʌndə] sich Gedanken machen, sich fragen **V T3,** 52; **V T4,** 72
wood [wʊd] Holz **III U2,** 32; Wald **IV U4,** 62
wooden [ˈwʊdn] hölzern **III U3,** 49
Woof! [wʊf] Wau! °**I U2,** 27
word [wɜːd] Wort **I U1,** 15
word star [ˈwɜːd stɑː] Wortstern °**I U1,** 22
work [wɜːk] Arbeit **I U3,** 47
(work) placement [ˈpleɪsmənt] Praktikum **VI T2,** 34
to **work** [wɜːk] arbeiten, funktionieren **I U3,** 48
to work out [ˌwɜːk‿ˈaʊt] herausfinden, ausarbeiten **VI T3,** 58; **VI T4,** 78
worker [ˈwɜːkə] Arbeiter/Arbeiterin, Angestellter/Angestellte **IV U3,** 50
workman, workmen *(pl)* [ˈwɜːkmən; ˈwɜːkmen] Handwerker **IV U1,** 17
workplace [ˈwɜːkpleɪs] Arbeitsplatz, Arbeitsstätte **VI T2,** 29
worksheet [ˈwɜːkʃiːt] Arbeitsblatt **I U4,** 58
workshop [ˈwɜːkʃɒp] Workshop, Werkstatt **III U4,** 63
world [wɜːld] Erde, Welt **III U2,** 26
out of this world [ˌaʊt‿əv ðɪs ˈwɜːld] nicht von dieser Welt **V T1,** 11
World War II [ˌwɜːld ˌwɔː ˈtuː] der Zweite Weltkrieg **V T3,** 51
worldwide [ˌwɜːldˈwaɪd] weltweit **VI T1,** 11; **VI T4,** 74
*to be **worried** [biː ˈwʌrid] besorgt sein, beunruhigt sein **I U6,** 87
worry [ˈwʌri] Sorge °**III U4,** 64
to **worry** [ˈwʌri] sich Sorgen machen **I U6,** 82; ängstigen, beunruhigen **II U3,** 45
worse [wɜːs] schlimmer, schlechter **II U4,** 50
worst [wɜːst] schlimmster/schlimmste/schlimmstes, schlechtester/schlechteste/schlechtestes **II U4,** 50
self-**worth** [ˌselfˈwɜːθ] Selbstwertgefühl, Selbstachtung **VI T4,** 72
*to be **worth** *(+ gerund)* [biː ˈwɜːθ] (es) wert sein (zu) **VI T2,** 36
***would** [wʊd] würde/würden **III U3,** 53
would like [wʊd ˈlaɪk] hätte(n) gern, möchte(n) gern **II U4,** 52
wreck [rek] Wrack **III U4,** 70
*to **write** [raɪt] schreiben **I U3,** 43
in writing [ɪn ˈraɪtɪŋ] schriftlich **VI T4,** 75
to write down [ˈraɪt ˌdaʊn] aufschreiben °**I LUB,** 38
writer [ˈraɪtə] Schriftsteller/Schriftstellerin, Verfasser/Verfasserin °**V T3,** 53
writing [ˈraɪtɪŋ] Schreiben °**III U4,** 68
wrong [rɒŋ] falsch **I U1,** 16
to be wrong [biː ˈrɒŋ] Unrecht haben **III U3,** 53
to get … wrong [ɡet … ˈrɒŋ] falsch machen **II U3,** 44; falsch verstehen °**II U3,** 47
to go wrong [ɡəʊ ˈrɒŋ] schief gehen **II U6,** 85

Y

ya *(slang)* [jə] du °**V T2,** 35
yard [jɑːd] Elle *(Längenmaß: 0,914 m)* **III U3,** 48
yarn [jɑːn] Garn, Faden **IV U1,** 10
to **yawn** [jɔːn] gähnen **V T3,** 50
yeah *(slang)* [jeə] ja **IV U1,** 16
year [jɪə] Jahr, Jahrgangsstufe **I U1,** 10
year-old [ˌjɪər‿ˈəʊld] -jährig; -Jähriger/-Jährige **III U4,** 63

yearbook ['jɪəbʊk] Jahrbuch **IV U2,** 24
yellow ['jeləʊ] gelb **I LUA,** 24
yes [jes] ja **I U1,** 12
yesterday ['jestədeɪ] gestern **II U2,** 26
not … **yet** [jet] noch nicht **II U5,** 66
yoghurt ['jɒgət] Joghurt °**VI T1,** 17
you [ju:; jə] du, ihr **I U1,** 11; dich, dir, Sie, Ihnen, euch **I LUB,** 38; man **III U1,** 8
Here you are! ['hɪə ju:‿ɑ:] Bitte schön! **I U1,** 20
thank you ['θæŋk ju:] danke **I U1,** 12
you'd better [jʊd 'betə] du solltest lieber **III U4,** 70
You're kidding. [jə 'kɪdɪŋ] Du machst Witze. **IV U2,** 32
you're lucky [jʊə 'lʌki] du hast Glück **I U1,** 16
You're welcome. [jʊə 'welkəm] Bitte sehr!, Gern geschehen! **I U1,** 19
you see [jʊ 'si:] weißt du **III U1,** 12
young [jʌŋ] jung **I U3,** 45; minderjährig **VI T2,** 34
your [jɔ:] dein/deine, euer/eure, Ihr/Ihre **I U1,** 11
Yours [jɔ:z] Dein …/Deine …/Euer …/Eure … *(in Briefen)* **II U3,** 36
Yours faithfully [ˌjɔ:z 'feɪθfʊli] Mit freundlichen Grüßen **VT3,** 53
yourself [jɔ:'self] du/dich (selbst) **III U4,** 67
yourselves [jɔ:'selvz] ihr/euch/Sie/sich (selbst) **III U4,** 67
youth [ju:θ] Jugend **II U3,** 38
Yuk! [jʌk] Igitt! **IV U2,** 32
yukky ['jʌki] ekelhaft **III U4,** 66

Z

zone [zəʊn] Zone **IV U2,** 27
zoo [zu:] Zoo, Tierpark **II U2,** 22
zookeeper ['zu:ˌki:pə] Tierpfleger/Tierpflegerin, Wärter/Wärterin **II U2,** 26
Zulu ['zu:lu:] Zulu **VI T1,** 12

Boys' names

Abdur ['æbdʊə] **VI T4,** 75
Abu ['ɑ:bu:] **VT4,** 79
Adam ['ædəm] **VI T4,** 76
Alan ['ælən] **VI T2,** 29
Ali ['ɑ:li] **VI T1,** 18
Andrew ['ændru:] **VI T3,** 56
Andy ['ændi] **III U4,** 69
Angus ['æŋgəs] **II FA,** 103
Arthur ['ɑ:θə] **III FA,** 100
Ben [ben] **I U2,** 27
Bob [bɒb] **I U6,** 78
Brad [bræd] **IV U2,** 26
Brandon ['brændən] **IV U1,** 16
Burt [bɜ:t] **II U4,** 55
Cal [kæl] **IV U2,** 32
Carl [kɑ:l] **VI T4,** 75
Carly ['kɑ:li] **IV U5,** 80
Cavendish ['kævndɪʃ] **VI T4,** 74
Chandler ['tʃændlə] **II U3,** 37
Charles [tʃɑ:lz] **III U5,** 88
Charlie ['tʃɑ:li] **I U2,** 33
Damian ['deɪmiən] **VT3,** 53
Daniel ['dænjəl] **II U4,** 51
Dave [deɪv] **III U1,** 9
David ['deɪvɪd] **I U2,** 28
Davy ['deɪvi] **VT1,** 15
Derek ['derɪk] **II U4,** 51
Dicken ['dɪkn] **II FA,** 110
Diego [di'eɪgəʊ] **IV U1,** 12
Don [dɒn] **VT1,** 17
Donny ['dɒni] **IV U4,** 68
Douglas ['dʌgləs] **II FA,** 102
Drew [dru:] **VI T1,** 17
Ector ['ektə] **III FA,** 100
Emilio [ɪ'mɪliəʊ] **VT3,** 58
Eric ['erɪk] **I FA,** 102
Faruq [fə'ru:k] **VT4,** 78
Fayed [feɪ'ed] **VI T2,** 37
Frank [fræŋk] **IV U1,** 16
Fred [fred] **III U3,** 47
Henry ['henri] **II FA,** 114
Homer ['həʊmə] **VI T4,** 74
Ian ['i:ən] **III U5,** 87
Jack [dʒæk] **I FA,** 102
Jaden ['dʒeɪdn] **VT2,** 36
Jake [dʒeɪk] **II U1,** 14
Jamal [dʒə'mɑ:l] **III U4,** 65
James [dʒeɪmz] **I U2,** 28
Jamie ['dʒeɪmi] **III U1,** 12
Jay [dʒeɪ] **IV U2,** 32
Jeff [dʒef] **VT2,** 34
Jim [dʒɪm] **I U5,** 73
Jo [dʒəʊ] **I FA,** 105
Joel ['dʒəʊəl] **VT4,** 79
Joey ['dʒəʊi] **II U3,** 37
John [dʒɒn] **I U4,** 57
Jojo ['dʒəʊdʒəʊ] **IV U5,** 81
Jordan ['dʒɔ:dn] **VT2,** 41
José [həʊ'zeɪ] **IV U1,** 12
Judd [dʒʌd] **VT2,** 32
Jude [dʒu:d] **VI T3,** 54
Justin ['dzʌstɪn] **VI T3,** 58
Karim [kə'ri:m] **VT2,** 40
Kay [keɪ] **III FA,** 100
Kit [kɪt] **IV U4,** 65
Kofi ['kəʊfi] **VT4,** 73
Larry ['læri] **IV U2,** 26
Leo ['lɪ:əʊ] **III U1,** 16
Leon ['li:ɒn] **III U1,** 11
Leroy ['li:rɔɪ] **III U4,** 70
Llywelyn [lə'welɪn] **III U5,** 86
Marc [mɑ:k] **III U4,** 63
Mark [mɑ:k] **I U4,** 61
Mat [mæt] **VT1,** 20
Matt [mæt] **II U2,** 31
Max [mæks] **VT3,** 50
Miggie ['mɪgi] **VT2,** 36
Mike [maɪk] **III U4,** 72
Miles [maɪlz] **IV U2,** 32
Nelson ['nelsn] **I U1,** 13
Pablo ['pɑ:bləʊ] **IV U4,** 67
Patrick ['pætrɪk] **II U7,** 88
Paul [pɔ:l] **I U6,** 85
Pete [pi:t] **II U1,** 11
Peter ['pi:tə] **I U4,** 61
Phil [fɪl] **I U2,** 28
Raj [rɑ:dʒ] **VI T1,** 17
Ray [reɪ] **III U4,** 68
Reece [ri:s] **III U4,** 69
Reg [redʒ] **III U2,** 34
Richard ['rɪtʃəd] **I U2,** 27
Rick [rɪk] **IV U4,** 68
Rico ['ri:kəʊ] **IV U3,** 55
Rob [rɒb] **I U2,** 26
Robert ['rɒbət] **II U4,** 51
Rod [rɒd] **VT3,** 61
Rodger ['rɒdʒə] **III U5,** 89
Roger ['rɒdʒə] **II U3,** 36
Ron [rɒn] **IV U2,** 29
Ross [rɒs] **II U3,** 37
Sam [sæm] **I U1,** 16
Sean [ʃɔ:n] **VI T1,** 14; **VI T4,** 72
Sebastian [sɪ'bæstiən] **VT2,** 33
Stan [stæn] **VT4,** 72
Steve [sti:v] **I U1,** 23
Stu [stu:] **IV U2,** 29
Ted [ted] **I U2,** 26
Terry ['teri] **I U1,** 10
Thomas ['tɒməs] **I LUA,** 25
Tim [tɪm] **I LUA,** 25
Todd [tɒd] **II U3,** 36
Tom [tɒm] **I U1,** 10
Tony ['təʊni] **I LUA,** 25
Tyler ['taɪlə] **IV U2,** 29
Uther ['ju:θə] **III FA,** 100
Wai [hwaɪ] **VI T1,** 14
William ['wɪljəm] **VT1,** 11
Zach [zæk] **VT2,** 36; **VT4,** 79
Zachariya [ˌzækr'aɪə] **VT4,** 81

Girls' names

Abby ['æbi] **IV U4,** 62
Alison ['ælɪsən] **II U5,** 67
Alysha [ə'lɪʃə] **IV U2,** 32
Amanda [ə'mændə] **III U5,** 87
Amber ['æmbə] **V T4,** 79
Andrea ['ændriə] **VI T1,** 12
Anna ['ænə] **I U3,** 47
Barbara ['bɑ:brə] **III U1,** 12
Bee [bi:] **VI T3,** 59
Brenda ['brendə] **IV U2,** 35
Carmen ['kɑ:mən] **V T4,** 73
Carrie ['kæri] **III U4,** 64
Chloé ['kləʊi] **V T2,** 36
Cindy ['sɪndi] **IV U4,** 65
Connie ['kɒni] **V T1,** 15
Cora ['kɔ:rə] **V T1,** 20
Daisy ['deɪzi] **III U4,** 64
Debbie ['debi] **II U3,** 36
Denise [də'ni:z] **IV U4,** 68
Donna ['dɒnə] **IV U2,** 32
Dorothy ['dɒrəθi] **II U5,** 68
Elena ['elɪnə] **I U2,** 28
Elizabeth [ɪ'lɪzəbəθ] **III U2,** 29
Ellie ['eli] **V T2,** 40
Elsa ['elsə] **VI T3,** 59
Em [em] **II FA,** 114
Emma ['emə] **I U1,** 12
Eva ['i:və] **VI T3,** 59
Farah ['fɑ:rə] **I U2,** 26
Faye [feɪ] **VI T1,** 12
Fiona [fi'əʊnə] **I U1,** 23
Glinda ['glɪndə] **II FA,** 114
Grace [greɪs] **I U2,** 26
Helen ['helən] **II U7,** 88
Igraine [ɪ'greɪn] **III FA,** 100
Jade [dʒeɪd] **I U2,** 27
Jamilla [dʒə'mɪlə] **VI T3,** 57
Jane [dʒeɪn] **III U2,** 33
Jenna ['dʒenə] **III U4,** 69
Jenny ['dʒeni] **I U4,** 57
Jo [dʒəʊ] **V T3,** 58
Julia ['dʒu:liə] **III U2,** 30
Julie ['dʒu:li] **III U4,** 72
Kate [keɪt] **I U4,** 57
Kath [kæθ] **I U6,** 78
Kayla ['keɪlə] **V T3,** 50
Kim [kɪm] **IV U1,** 16
Kylie ['kaɪli] **V T1,** 17
Laura ['lɔ:rə] **II U1,** 11
Lauren ['lɔ:rən] **III U4,** 64
Lisa ['li:sə] **I U1,** 10
Louise [lu'i:z] **VI T4,** 77
Lucille [lu:'si:l] **V T3,** 53
Lucy ['lu:si] **V T3,** 50
Lynn [lɪn] **IV U4,** 63
Marcia ['mɑ:siə] **III U1,** 12
Marg [mɑ:dʒ] **III U5,** 85
Margaret ['mɑ:grət] **V T1,** 11
Maria [mə'ri:ə] **I U2,** 28
Marita [mə'ri:tə] **IV U4,** 68
Mariya [mə'ri:ə] **IV U2,** 35
Mary ['meəri] **I U4,** 57
Maude [mɔ:d] **VI T3,** 57
Maxi ['mæksi] **IV U4,** 65
Mei [meɪ] **VI T1,** 14
Mel [mel] **VI T4,** 75
Mia ['mi:ə] **VI T1,** 18
Monika ['mɒnɪkə] **II U3,** 37
Nadine [neɪ'di:n] **I U1,** 13
Nancy ['nænsi] **III U1,** 9
Nasreen [nʌs'ri:n] **I U2,** 26
Nicola ['nɪklə] **I FA,** 100
Nicole [nɪ'kəʊl] **II U3,** 36
Nina ['ni:nə] **IV U2,** 29
Nyla ['naɪlə] **III U4,** 64
Olivia [ɒ'lɪviə] **V T2,** 40
Pat [pæt] **II U1,** 16
Paula ['pɔ:lə] **III U1,** 11
Paula-Jo [ˌpɔ:lə'dʒəʊ] **IV U2,** 29
Phoebe ['fi:bi] **II U3,** 37
Polly ['pɒli] **III U5,** 85
Pru [pru:] **III U2,** 35
Rachel ['reɪtʃl] **II U3,** 37
Rebecca [rɪ'bekə] **IV U2,** 29
Ruby ['ru:bi] **III U4,** 65
Sally ['sæli] **I U6,** 85
Sandra ['sændrə] **IV U2,** 25
Sandy ['sændi] **IV U4,** 68
Sarah ['seərə] **I U2,** 28
Sharleen [ʃə'li:n] **IV U2,** 32
Sharon ['ʃærən] **V T1,** 17
Sheila ['ʃi:lə] **III U1,** 15
Stella ['stelə] **II FA,** 104
Sue [su:] **I U2,** 27
Susan ['su:zn] **I U2,** 28
Suzanne [su:'zæn] **I U1,** 11
Tamara [tə'mɑ:rə] **I LUA,** 25
Tammy ['tæmi] **IV U2,** 29
Terri ['teri] **IV U2,** 29
Tess [tes] **I U6,** 85
Tessa ['tesə] **VI T4,** 70
Tilly ['tɪli] **I LUA,** 25
Tina ['ti:nə] **I LUA,** 25
Tracy ['treɪsi] **I U2,** 28
Trina ['tri:nə] **III U1,** 15
Virginia [və'dʒɪnjə] **III FA,** 112
Zahra ['zeərə] **V T4,** 78
Zameera [zə'mi:rə] **V T4,** 73
Zoey ['zəʊi] **VI T4,** 70
Zola ['zəʊlə] **VI T3,** 59

Surnames

Akodu [ə'kəʊdʊ] **III U4,** 68
Badawi [bə'dɑ:wi] **VI T4,** 75
Balmain ['bælmeɪn] **V T1,** 11
Barber ['bɑ:bə] **VI T3,** 56
Barlow ['bɑ:ləʊ] **VI T3,** 57
Barnes ['bɑ:nz] **III U1,** 16
Barnfield ['bɑ:nfi:ld] **III U2,** 30
Barrymore ['bærimɔ:] **III U5,** 88
Baskerville ['bæskəvɪl] **III U5,** 82
Beem [bi:m] **V T2,** 38
Bell [bel] **II U4,** 52
Berry [beri] **III U1,** 9
Black [blæk] **II U1,** 11
Bland [blænd] **II FA,** 108
Bradshaw ['brædʃɔ:] **V T1,** 17
Brook [brʊk] **I U1,** 12
Brown [braʊn] **II U1,** 11
Buah ['bʊə] **V T4,** 77
Burns [bɜ:nz] **III U5,** 83
Cage [keɪdʒ] **III U1,** 9
Canterville ['kæntəvɪl] **III FA,** 110
Carter ['kɑ:tə] **I U1,** 12
Cartwright ['kɑ:traɪt] **III U2,** 34
Clarke [klɑ:k] **III U3,** 52
Covey ['kʌvi] **VI T4,** 72
Dawson ['dɔ:sn] **V T1,** 11
Dhlomo ['dləʊmə] **VI T1,** 12
Downey ['daʊni] **V T1,** 17
Downham ['daʊnəm] **VI T4,** 76
Fisher ['fɪʃə] **V T4,** 73
Fox [fɒks] **IV U3,** 52
George [dʒɔ:dʒ] **III U1,** 11
Glenn [glen] **III U4,** 70
Grant [grɑ:nt] **V T3,** 53
Gruntle ['grʌntl] **II FA,** 108
Gulch [gʌltʃ] **II FA,** 114
Gusman ['gʌzmən] **IV U4,** 67
Hall [hɔ:l] **III U5,** 87
Hassan [hə'sɑ:n] **VI T1,** 18
Hooker ['hʊkə] **VI T3,** 56
Howard ['haʊəd] **II U1,** 14
Hunter ['hʌntə] **I U6,** 82
Jackson ['dʒæksn] **I U1,** 10
Jiayi [ˌdʒɪ'aɪ] **VI T1,** 12
Johnson ['dʒɒntsn] **V T3,** 53
Johnston ['dʒɒnstn] **VI T2,** 29
Jones [dʒəʊnz] **III U4,** 70
Keenan ['ki:nən] **VI T3,** 54
Khan [kɑ:n] **VI T3,** 57
King [kɪŋ] **VI T1,** 14
Lean [li:n] **I FA,** 104
Longbow ['lɒŋbəʊ] **VI T4,** 74
MacDonald [mək'dɒnld] **IV U2,** 24
Mahal [mə'hæl] **VI T1,** 10
Mangold ['mæŋgəʊld] **III U5,** 85
Marco ['mɑ:kəʊ] **II U1,** 11

Marks [mɑ:ks] **III U2,** 30
Martin ['mɑ:tɪn] **I FA,** 106
McArthur [mək'ɑ:θə] **II FA,** 102
McGough [mə'gɒf] **VI T3,** 55
Monte ['mɒnteɪ] **I U2,** 28
Morley ['mɔ:li] **III U4,** 64
Muir [mjʊə] **II FA,** 103
Newitt ['nju:ɪt] **III U5,** 84
Newman ['nju:mən] **I U1,** 12
O'Brien [əʊ'braɪən] **II U7,** 88
Otis ['əʊtɪs] **III FA,** 110
Pilch [pɪltʃ] **I U2,** 28
Pinovski [paɪ'nɒvski] **VI T4,** 75
Reeves [ri:vz] **V T4,** 72
Richards ['rɪtʃədz] **II U3,** 45
Robbins ['rɒbɪnz] **III U3,** 51
Rose [rəʊz] **I U4,** 60
Rowlatt ['rəʊlæt] **VI T3,** 58
Simpson ['sɪmpsən] **III U5,** 82
Smith [smɪθ] **III U4,** 63
Spencer ['spentsə] **I U2,** 28
Stapleton ['steɪpltən] **III U5,** 89
Stavros ['stʌvrəs] **I U2,** 28
Taylor ['teɪlə] **I U1,** 10
Tiny ['taɪni] **I LUA,** 25
Walters ['wɒltəz] **V T1,** 10
Wang [wæŋ] **VI T1,** 18
Watson ['wɒtsn] **III U5,** 81
White [waɪt] **III U2,** 33
Wilkins ['wɪlkɪnz] **III U4,** 70
Willis ['wɪlɪs] **III U5,** 87
Yu [ju:] **VI T1,** 14
Ziebarth ['tsi:bət] **VI T1,** 12

Place names

Abergavenny [ˌæbəgə'veni] **III U1,** 11
Acton ['æktən] **III U2,** 34
Adelaide ['ædleɪd] **V T1,** 17
Alice Springs [ˌælɪs 'sprɪŋz] **V T1,** 16
Anchorage ['æŋkrɪdʒ] **IV U4,** 64
Ash Street ['æʃ ˌstri:t] **V T3,** 56
Atlanta [ət'læntə] **IV U5,** 80
Austin ['ɒstɪn] **IV U5,** 80
Avondale ['eɪvndeɪl] **III U5,** 81
Ayers Rock [ˌeəz 'rɒk] **V T1,** 9
Baker Street ['beɪkə ˌstri:t] **III U5,** 88
Barcelona [ˌbɑ:sl'əʊnə] **III U1,** 15
Bath [bɑ:θ] **I U6,** 79
Bollywood ['bɒliwʊd] **III U5,** 80
Bondi Beach [ˌbɒndaɪ 'bi:tʃ] **V T1,** 8
Boston ['bɒstn] **III U1,** 15
Boulder Way ['bəʊldə ˌweɪ] **VI T4,** 74
Brighton ['braɪtn] **III U3,** 44
Brisbane ['brɪzbən] **V T1,** 14
Bristol ['brɪstl] **I U1,** 12
Bronx [brɒŋks] **IV U1,** 9
Brooklyn ['brʊklɪn] **IV U1,** 9
Cairns [keənz] **V T1,** 15
Camden ['kæmdən] **II U2,** 22
Canberra ['kænbrə] **V T1,** 11
Castle Garden [ˌkɑ:sl 'gɑ:dn] **IV U1,** 10
Central Park [ˌsentrl 'pɑ:k] **IV U1,** 8
Chicago [ʃɪ'kɑ:gəʊ] **III U1,** 9
Chinatown ['tʃaɪnətaʊn] **IV U1,** 9
Cornwall ['kɔ:nwɔ:l] **II U6,** 78
Covent Garden [ˌkɒvnt 'gɑ:dn] **III U2,** 28
Dallas ['dæləs] **V T3,** 51
Dartmoor ['dɑ:tmɔ:] **III U5,** 88
Denver ['denvə] **IV U4,** 64
Devon ['devn] **II U6,** 78
Dover ['dəʊvə] **III U3,** 44
Dublin ['dʌblɪn] **II U7,** 88
Eastbourne ['i:stbɔ:n] **III U3,** 44
Ellis Island [ˌelɪs 'aɪlənd] **IV U1,** 9
Exmoor ['eksmɔ:] **II ZI,** 8
Folkestone ['fəʊkstən] **III U3,** 44
Forest Springs [ˌfɒrɪst 'sprɪŋz] **IV U4,** 62
Franklin ['fræŋklɪn] **V T1,** 14
Gaza City [ˌgɑ:zə 'sɪti] **VI T2,** 29
Glasgow ['glɑ:zgəʊ] **II FA,** 102
Goldcoast ['gəʊldˌkəʊst] **V T1,** 14
Grand Canyon [ˌgrænd 'kænjən] **IV U4,** 60
Great Barrier Reef [ˌgreɪt ˌbæriə 'ri:f] **V T1,** 9
Greenwich ['grenɪdʒ] **I U1,** 10
Greenwich Village [ˌgrenɪdʒ 'vɪlɪdʒ] **IV U1,** 16
Hamburg ['hæmbɜ:g] **VI T1,** 12
Hastings ['heɪstɪŋz] **III U3,** 44
Heathrow [ˌhi:θ'rəʊ] **III U3,** 45
Hollyoaks ['hɒliəʊks] **III U5,** 82
Hollywood ['hɒliwʊd] **III U5,** 80
Hong Kong [ˌhɒŋ 'kɒŋ] **VI T1,** 12
Honolulu [ˌhɒn'lu:lu:] **IV U4,** 64
Houston ['hju:stn] **V T3,** 52
Istanbul [ˌɪstæn'bʊl] **I U1,** 13
Kent [kent] **III U3,** 57
Kilkenny [kɪl'keni] **II U7,** 93
King's Road ['kɪŋz ˌrəʊd] **III U2,** 26
Kumasi [kʊ'mæsi] **V T4,** 77
Las Vegas [ˌlæs 'veɪgəs] **IV U4,** 61
Limerick ['lɪmrɪk] **II ZI,** 8
Lincoln ['lɪŋkən] **VI T2,** 31
Little Oyster Island [ˌlɪtl ˌɔɪstər ˌaɪlənd] **IV U1,** 10
Liverpool ['lɪvəpu:l] **V T1,** 11
Loch Ness [ˌlɒx 'nes] **II ZI,** 8
London ['lʌndən] **I U1,** 10
Los Angeles (LA) [lɒs ˌændʒɪli:z] **IV U4,** 61
Madrid [mə'drɪd] **I U1,** 13
Manchester ['mæntʃɪstə] **III U2,** 39
Manhattan [mæn'hætn] **IV U1,** 8
Marble Arch ['mɑ:bl ˌɑ:tʃ] **III U2,** 28
Medicine Hat ['medsn ˌhæt] **VI T1,** 14
Memphis ['memfɪs] **V T3,** 51
Mexico City [ˌmeksɪkəʊ 'sɪti] **IV U4,** 69
Miami [maɪ'æmi] **IV U4,** 64
Moher ['məʊhə] **II U7,** 93
Mongolia [mɒŋ'gəʊliə] **V T4,** 71
Montgomery [mən'gʌmri] **V T3,** 54
Montreal [ˌmɒntri'ɔ:l] **VI T1,** 14
Moscow ['mɒskəʊ] **III U3,** 52
Nairobi [naɪ'rəʊbi] **I U1,** 13
Neston ['nestn] **I U6,** 78
Nevada [nə'vɑ:də] Nevada **IV U3,** 51
New Amsterdam [ˌnju: æmstə'dæm] **IV U1,** 10
New York [ˌnju: 'jɔ:k] **I U4,** 55
New York City (NYC) [ˌnju: jɔ:k 'sɪti] **IV U1,** 8
New York Harbor [ˌnju: jɔ:k 'hɑ:bə] **IV U1,** 9
Nottingham ['nɒtɪŋəm] **II U2,** 25
Paris ['pærɪs] **I U1,** 13
Perth [pɜ:θ] **II ZI,** 8
Philadelphia [ˌfɪlə'delfiə] **V T2,** 32
Phoenix ['fi:nɪks] **IV U3,** 51
Piccadilly Circus [ˌpɪkədɪli 'sɜ:kəs] **III U2,** 28
Prescott ['preskət] **IV U3,** 51
Queens [kwi:nz] **IV U1,** 9
Rome [rəʊm] **IV U1,** 18
Round Rock [ˌraʊnd 'rɒk] **IV U5,** 80
Sacramento [ˌsækrə'mentəʊ] **III U1,** 11
Salisbury ['sɔ:lzbri] **III U3,** 44
San Francisco [ˌsæn frən'sɪskəʊ] **IV U4,** 64
Santa Rosa [ˌsæntə 'rəʊzə] **V T4,** 72
Seattle [si'ætl] **IV U4,** 64
Shanghai [ˌʃæŋ'haɪ] **V T3,** 51
Shannon ['ʃænən] **II U7,** 93
Sherwood Forest [ˌʃɜ:wʊd 'fɒrɪst] **II FA,** 110
Shoreditch [ʃɔ:'dɪtʃ] **III U2,** 35
Southampton [saʊ'θæmtən] **III U3,** 44
Staten Island [ˌstætn ˌaɪlənd] **IV U1,** 9
Stonehenge [stəʊn'hendʒ] **III U3,** 45
Sydney ['sɪdni] **V T1,** 8
Sydney Cove [ˌsɪdni 'kəʊv] **V T1,** 10
Tarr Steps [tɑ: 'steps] **II U6,** 82
the **Thames** [temz] **I U4,** 54
Tokyo ['təʊkiəʊ] **I U1,** 13
Townsville ['taʊnzvɪl] **V T1,** 11
Tucson ['tu:sɒn] **IV U3,** 51
Twickenham ['twɪknəm] **III U1,** 8
Uluru [u:'lu:ru:] Uluru = Ayers Rock *(heiliger Berg der Aborigines)* **V T1,** 9
Valley of the Sun [ˌvæli ˌəv ˌðə ˌsʌn] **IV U3,** 51
Vancouver [væn'ku:və] **VI T1,** 11

Washington ['wɒʃɪŋtən] **V T3,** 54
Westminster ['wesmɪnstə] **VI T2,** 32
White Hart Lane [ˌwaɪt hɑ:t 'leɪn] **III U1,** 16
Wildcroft ['waɪldkrɒft] **I FA,** 100
Wiltshire ['wɪltʃə] **I U6,** 78
Wimbledon ['wɪmbldn] **III U1,** 15
Winnipeg ['wɪnɪpeg] **VI T1,** 11
Wordsworth Way [ˌwɜ:dzwəθ 'weɪ] **V T1,** 11
York [jɔ:k] **VI T2,** 28

Geographical names

Africa ['æfrɪkə] **V T4,** 71
Alberta [æl'bɜ:tə] **VI T1,** 14
Alabama [ˌælə'bæmə] **V T3,** 54
America [ə'merɪkə] **II U3,** 36
Arizona [ˌærɪ'zəʊnə] **IV U3,** 51
Asia ['eɪʃə] Asien **VI T1,** 10
Australia [ɒs'treɪliə] Australien **II ZI,** 8
Belgium ['beldʒəm] Belgien **IV U1,** 10
Blue Mountains [blu: 'maʊntɪnz] **V T1,** 19
Brazil [brə'zɪl] **VI T3,** 53
Britain ['brɪtn] **II FA,** 102
British Columbia (B.C.) [ˌbrɪtɪʃ kə'lʌmbiə] **VI T1,** 14
British Isles [ˌbrɪtɪʃ 'aɪlz] Britische Inseln **II ZI,** 8
California [ˌkælɪ'fɔ:niə] **III U1,** 11
Canada ['kænədə] Kanada **III U5,** 88
China ['tʃaɪnə] China **III U1,** 15
Colorado [ˌkɒlr'ɑ:dəʊ] **IV U4,** 65
East Africa [i:st‿'æfrɪkə] **VI T3,** 51
Eastern Europe [ˌi:stn 'jʊərəp] Osteuropa **IV U1,** 10
England ['ɪŋglənd] England **I U2,** 29
Ethiopia [i:θi'əʊpiə] **VI T3,** 51
Europe ['jʊərəp] Europa **IV U1,** 10
Fiji ['fi:dʒi:] **VI T3,** 53
Florida ['flɒrɪdə] **IV U3,** 55
France [frɑ:nts] Frankreich **IV U5,** 78
Gaza ['gɑ:zə] **VI T2,** 29
Gaza Strip [ˌgɑ:zə 'strɪp] **VI T2,** 29
Germany ['dʒɜ:məni] Deutschland **I U2,** 29
Ghana ['gɑ:nə] **V T4,** 71
Greece [gri:s] Griechenland **I U2,** 29
Gulf States [ˌgʌlf 'steɪts] **VI T1,** 10
Gway Chaung [ˌgweɪ 'tʃɔ:ŋ] **VI T3,** 56
Hamilton Island [ˌhæmltən 'aɪlənd] **VI T3,** 60
Hawaii [hə'waɪ] **IV U4,** 66
India ['ɪndiə] Indien **III U1,** 13
Iran [ɪ'rɑ:n] **V T3,** 51
Ireland ['aɪələnd] Irland **II U6,** 85
Irish Sea [ˌaɪrɪʃ 'si:] **III U3,** 44
Isle of Dogs [ˌaɪl‿əv 'dɒgz] **I U4,** 54
Isle of Wight [ˌaɪl‿əv 'waɪt] **III U3,** 44
Israel ['ɪzreɪl] **VI T2,** 27
Italy ['ɪtəli] Italien **I U2,** 29
Jamaica [dʒə'meɪkə] Jamaica **IV U5,** 81
Japan [dʒə'pæn] **V T2,** 41
Kansas ['kænzəs] **II FA,** 114
Lebanon ['lebənən] **VI T2,** 27
Maldives ['mɔ:ldi:vz] die Malediven **V T4,** 72
Manitoba [mænɪ'təʊbə] **VI T1,** 11
Mars [mɑ:s] **VI T1,** 18
Mexico ['meksɪkəʊ] Mexiko **IV U1,** 10
Michigan ['mɪʃɪgən] **VI T4,** 74
Middle East [ˌmɪdl‿'i:st] Mittlerer Osten **VI T3,** 54
Murray-Darling [ˌmʌri'dɑ:lɪŋ] **VI T3,** 57
Myanmar ['mjænmɑ:] Myanmar (Burma) **VI T3,** 56
Netherlands ['neðələndz] Niederlande **V T4,** 76
New Jersey [ˌnju: 'dʒɜ:zi] **IV U5,** 78
New Mexico [ˌnju: 'meksɪkəʊ] **IV U4,** 65
New Brunswick [ˌnju: 'brʌnzwɪk] Neubraunschweig **VI T1,** 11
New South Wales [ˌnju: ˌsaʊθ 'weɪlz] **V T1,** 18
New Zealand [ˌnju: 'zi:lənd] **VI T3,** 54
North Sea [ˌnɔ:θ 'si:] Nordsee **III U3,** 44
Northern Ireland [ˌnɔ:ðn‿'aɪələnd] **II U7,** 89
Northwest Territories [ˌnɔ:θwest 'teritriz] Nordwestterritorien **VI T1,** 11
Nunavut ['nu:nəvət] Nunavit *(Region in Kanada)* **VI T1,** 11
Oman [ə'mɑ:n] Oman **VI T3,** 56
Oz [ɒz] Oz *(Spitzname für Australien)* **V T1,** 8
Philippines ['fɪlɪpi:nz] Philippinen **IV U1,** 10
Poland ['pəʊlənd] Polen **I U2,** 29
Quebec [kwɪ'bek] **VI T1,** 11
Queensland ['kwi:nzlənd] **VI T3,** 60
Republic of Ireland [rɪˌpʌblɪk‿əv‿'aɪələnd] Republik Irland **II U7,** 88
Rockies (Rocky Mountains) ['rɒkiz] **V T3,** 48
Rocky Mountains [ˌrɒki 'maʊntɪnz] **I U7,** 100
Russia ['rʌʃə] Russland **I U2,** 29
Sahara [sə'hɑ:rə] **VI T3,** 56
Scilly Isles ['sɪli ˌaɪlz] **II U6,** 78
Scotland ['skɒtlənd] Schottland **II ZI,** 8
South Africa [ˌsaʊθ‿'æfrɪkə] Südafrika **VI T1,** 8; **VI T2,** 26; **VI T3,** 54
South England [ˌsaʊθ 'ɪŋglənd] Südengland **III U3,** 44
Spain [speɪn] Spanien **III U1,** 15
Tasmania [tæz'meɪniə] **V T1,** 14
Tenerife ['tenəri:f] Teneriffa **VI T3,** 56
Tennessee [ˌtenə'si:] **V T3,** 51
Texas ['teksəs] **IV U1,** 16
Turkey ['tɜ:ki] Türkei **I U2,** 29
UAE (United Arab Emirates) [ˌju:eɪ'i:] Vereinigte Arabische Emirate **VI T3,** 56
UK [ju:'keɪ] **III U1,** 11
United Kingdom (UK) [ju:ˌnaɪtɪd 'kɪŋdəm] Vereinigtes Königreich von Großbritannien und Nordirland **III U3,** 44
US [ju:'es] **IV U1,** 9
USA [ˌju:es'eɪ] **III U1,** 11
Utah ['ju:tɑ:] **IV U4,** 73
Vermont [və'mɒnt] **VI T2,** 28
Wales [weɪlz] Wales **II ZI,** 8
Western Australia [ˌwestən ɒs'treɪliə] **II U1,** 14

Other names

Academy Award [əˌkædəmi ə'wɔ:d] **IV U5,** 77
American Fox News Network [əˌmerɪkn ˌfɒks nju:z 'netwɜ:k] **VI T2,** 36
Apache Lake [əˌpætʃi 'leɪk] **IV U4,** 68
Aquarius [ə'kweəriəs] Wassermann **II U6,** 80
Aqua Vitens Rand Ltd (AVRL) [ˌækwə ˌvaɪtnz ˌrænd 'lɪmɪtɪd (ˌeɪvi:ɑ:r'el)] **VI T3,** 56
Arsenal ['ɑ:snl] **III U1,** 16
Bakerloo Line [ˌbeɪkəl'u: ˌlaɪn] **III U2,** 28
BBC [ˌbi:bi:'si:] **III U5,** 82
Beatles ['bi:tlz] **IV U5,** 79
Big Ben [ˌbɪg 'ben] **III U2,** 26
Billabong ['bɪləbɒŋ] **IV U4,** 62
Birdy ['bɜ:di] **III U5,** 95
Boxing Day ['bɒksɪŋ ˌdeɪ] **I FA,** 114
British Airways (BA) [ˌbrɪtɪʃ 'eəweɪz] **III U2,** 30
Brooklyn Bridge [ˌbrʊklɪn 'brɪdʒ] **IV U1,** 9
Buckingham Bridge [ˌbʌkɪŋəm 'brɪdʒ] **III U2,** 33
Buckingham Palace [ˌbʌkɪŋəm 'pælɪs] **II U3,** 47
Cadillac ['kædɪlæk] **IV U4,** 68
Carbon Trust [ˌkɑ:bn 'trʌst] **VI T3,** 58
Chevy ['tʃevi] **V T3,** 56
Chunnel ['tʃʌnl] Tunnel durch den Ärmelkanal **III U3,** 45
Circle Line ['sɜ:kl ˌlaɪn] **III U2,** 28
Concorde ['kɒŋkɔ:d] **III U2,** 38
Congress ['kɒŋgres] *(Parlament in den USA)* **VI T2,** 33

Countdown ['kaʊntdaʊn] **III U5,** 82
Cutty Sark [ˌkʌti 'sɑːk] **I U4,** 54
Cutty Sark Gardens [kʌti ˌsɑːk 'gɑːdnz] **I U4,** 54
Discman ['dɪskmən] Discman **I U2,** 30
DLR [ˌdiː‿el‿'ɑː] **I U4,** 55
Docklands Light Railway ['dɒkləndz ˌlaɪt 'reɪlweɪ] **I U4,** 55
Eagle ['iːgl] **VI T4,** 74
East India Company [ˌiːst ˌɪndiə 'kʌmpəni] **VI T1,** 13
Embankment [ɪm'bæŋkmənt] **III U2,** 28
Empire State Building [ˌempaɪə 'steɪt ˌbɪldɪŋ] **IV U1,** 8
Eurofoot ['jʊərəʊˌfʊt] **VI T1,** 10
European Union [ˌjʊərə'piːən 'juːnjən] **III U3,** 55
FA Cup [ˌef‿eɪ 'kʌp] Pokal des englischen Fußballverbands, vgl. DFB-Pokal **III U1,** 15
Fairtrade [ˌfeə'treɪd] **V T4,** 76
Flying Doctor Service [ˌflaɪɪŋ 'dɒktə ˌsɜːvɪs] **V T1,** 16
Friar Tuck [ˌfraɪə 'tʌk] **II FA,** 110
GMT ['dʒiːem'tiː] **I U4,** 55
GPS [ˌdʒiːpiː'es] **IV U3,** 43
Grammy Award [ˌgræmi ə'wɔːd] **IV U5,** 77
Great Barrier Reef Marine Park [ˌgreɪt ˌbæriə 'riːf mə'riːn ˌpɑːk] **V T1,** 11
Green Corps ['griːn ˌkɔː] **V T1,** 14
Greenroad ['griːnrəʊd] **VI T4,** 74
Greenwich Mean Time [ˌgrenɪdʒ 'miːn taɪm] **I U4,** 55
Hamas [hæm'æs] **VI T2,** 37
Harbour Bridge ['hɑːbə ˌbrɪdʒ] **V T1,** 19
Harrods ['hærədz] **II U2,** 23
Harry Potter [ˌhæri 'pɒtə] **II U1,** 11
House of Commons [ˌhaʊs‿əv 'kɒmənz] *(britisches Unterhaus)* **VI T2,** 28
House of Lords [ˌhaʊs‿əv 'lɔːdz] *(britisches Oberhaus)* **VI T2,** 32
House of Representatives [ˌhaʊs‿əv reprɪ'zentətɪvz] *US-amerikanisches Unterhaus* **VI T2,** 33
Houses of Parliament [ˌhaʊzɪz‿əv 'pɑːləmənt] **I FA,** 114
IBM [ˌaɪbiː'em] **V T3,** 50
IRIN *(Integrated Regional Information Networks)* [ˌaɪɑːriː'en] **VI T3,** 56
KRAZY ['kreɪzi] **VI T1,** 15
Little John [ˌlɪtl 'dʒɒn] **II FA,** 110
London Dungeon [ˌlʌndən 'dʌndʒn] **III U2,** 26
London Bridge [ˌlʌndən 'brɪdʒ] **III U2,** 32
London Eye [ˌlʌndən‿'aɪ] **III U2,** 26
London Knights [ˌlʌndən 'naɪts] **II U2,** 22
Lord of the Rings [ˌlɔːd‿əv ðə‿'rɪŋz] **IV U5,** 79
Magna Carta [ˌmægnə 'kɑːtə] **VI T2,** 26
Maid Marian [ˌmeɪd 'mæriən] **II FA,** 110
Man U ['mæn juː] **III U5,** 82
Meridian Line [mə'rɪdiən 'laɪn] **I U4,** 54
Merlin ['mɜːlɪn] **III FA,** 100
Mohawk ['məʊhɔːk] **IV U1,** 9
Monument ['mɒnjəmənt] **III U2,** 28
MTV [ˌemtiː'viː] **I U6,** 82
Nargis ['nɑːdʒɪs] **VI T3,** 56
NASA ['næsə] NASA *(US-Weltraumbehörde)* **IV U3,** 43
Newsnight ['njuːznaɪt] **VI T3,** 58
New Stone Age ['njuː ˌstəʊn ˌeɪdʒ] Jungsteinzeit **III U3,** 49
Nobel Peace Prize [ˌnəʊbel 'piːs ˌpraɪz] **V T3,** 55
NVQ (National Vocational Qualification) [ˌenviː'kjuː] Berufsqualifikation in England **°V T2,** 40
Oscar ['ɒskə] **IV U5,** 77
Oxford English Dictionary [ˌɒksfəd ˌɪŋglɪʃ 'dɪkʃnri] **VI T1,** 13
PADI *(Professional Association of Diving Instructors)* ['pædi] PADI *(internationaler Tauchverband)* **V T1,** 15
Palace of Westminster [ˌpælɪs‿əv 'wesmɪnstə] **III U2,** 26
PowerPoint ['paʊəpɔɪnt] **V T2,** 41
Robin Hood [ˌrɒbɪn 'hʊd] **II FA,** 110
Route 66 [ruːt] **IV U4,** 61
Royal Family ['rɔɪəl 'fæmli] **III U2,** 26
Royal National Park [ˌrɔɪəl ˌnæʃnl 'pɑːk] **V T1,** 10
Royal Observatory [ˌrɔɪəl əb'zɜːvətri] **I U4,** 55
Seaview Secondary [ˌsiːvjuː 'sekəndri] **VI T1,** 14
Senate ['senɪt] *(US-amerikanisches Oberhaus)* **VI T2,** 33
Skywalk ['skaɪwɔːk] **IV U4,** 60
Solitaire [ˌsɒlɪ'teə] **VI T2,** 34
Speaker's Corner [ˌspiːkəz 'kɔːnə] **VI T2,** 27
Statue of Liberty [ˌstætʃuː‿əv 'lɪbəti] **IV U1,** 8
St James's Park [snt ˌdʒeɪmzɪz 'pɑːk] **III U2,** 28
St Paul's Cathedral [snt ˌpɔːlz 'kəθiːdrl] **III U2,** 28
Surpreme Court [suːˌpriːm 'kɔːt] *oberster Gerichtshof der USA* **VI T2,** 33
Swallow ['swɒləʊ] **VI T4,** 74
Sydneysider ['sɪdniˌsaɪdə] **V T1,** 18
Sydney Tower [ˌsɪdni 'taʊə] **V T1,** 18
Thanksgiving [ˌθæŋks'gɪvɪŋ] **IV U4,** 64
The Guardian [ðə 'gɑːdiən] **VI T3,** 56; **VI T3,** 61
Times Square [ˌtaɪmz 'skweə] **IV U1,** 9
Titanic [taɪ'tænɪk] **III U3,** 45
Tower Bridge [ˌtaʊə 'brɪdʒ] **V T4,** 77
Tower of London [ˌtaʊər‿əv 'lʌndən] **III U2,** 26
Transfair ['trænsfeə] **V T4,** 76
Tube [tjuːb] **III U2,** 26
UFO *(Unidentified Flying Object)* ['juːef'əʊ] **IV U3,** 51
UN (United Nations) [juː'en] **VI T2,** 26
UNICEF ['juːnɪsef] **VI T3,** 56
University of Michigan [juːnɪˌvɜːsəti‿əv 'mɪʃɪgən] **V T2,** 38
University of Surrey [ˌjuːnɪvɜːsəti‿əv 'sʌri] **VI T3,** 58
Wembley Stadium ['wembli 'steɪdiəm] **III U1,** 12
White House ['waɪt ˌhaʊs] **II U3,** 43
William the Conqueror [ˌwɪljəm ðə 'kɒŋkrə] **III U2,** 31
Will Scarlet [ˌwɪl 'skɑːlət] **II FA,** 110
Wizard of Oz [ˌwɪzəd əv‿'ɒz] **°II U5,** 64
YouTube ['juːtjuːb] **V T2,** 41

Famous names

Abraham Lincoln [ˌeɪbrəhæm 'lɪŋkən] **VI T2,** 33
Angelina Jolie [ˌændʒ'liːnə 'dʒəʊli] **III U2,** 29
Annie Moore [ˌæni 'mɔː] **IV U1,** 10
Arthur Conan Doyle [ˌɑːθə ˌkəʊnən 'dɔɪl] **III U5,** 87
Barack Obama [ˌbærək əʊ'bɑːmə] **VI T2,** 33
Bono ['bəʊnəʊ] **V T3,** 51
B Section ['biː ˌsekʃn] **IV U5,** 84
Captain Cook [ˌkæptɪn kʊk] **VI T1,** 13
50 Cent [ˌfɪfti 'sent] **VI T1,** 8
Charlie Chaplin [ˌtʃɑːli 'tʃæplɪn] **III U4,** 72
Derrek Lee [ˌderɪk 'liː] **III U1,** 9
Eadweard Muybridge [ˌedwəd 'maɪbrɪdʒ] **IV U5,** 78
Edwin Porter [ˌedwɪn 'pɔːtə] **IV U5,** 78
Fergie ['fɜːgi] **IV U5,** 84
Georges Méliès [ˌʒɔːʒ mel'jeɪ] **IV U5,** 78
Green Day ['griːn ˌdeɪ] **IV U5,** 77
James Cook [ˌdʒeɪmz 'kʊk] **V T1,** 10
Jamie Oliver [ˌdʒeɪmi 'ɒlɪvə] **V T2,** 40
Jennifer Hudson [ˌdʒenɪfə 'hʌdsn] **IV U5,** 76
John F. Kennedy [ˌdʒɒn‿ef 'kenədi] **VI T2,** 33
Lil Jon [ˌlɪl 'dʒɒn] **IV U5,** 80
Ludacris ['luːdəkrɪs] **IV U5,** 84

Madonna [mə'dɒnə] **III U2,** 29
Malcolm X [ˌmælkəm‿'eks] **V T3,** 55
Martin Luther King [ˌmɑ:tɪn ˌlu:θə 'kɪŋ] **V T3,** 51
Napoleon [nə'pəʊliən] **II U5,** 62
Naomi Campbell [ˌneɪəmi: 'kæmbl] **III U2,** 29
Nelly Furtado [ˌneli fə'tɑ:dəʊ] **IV U5,** 77
Nelson Mandela [ˌnəlsn mæn'delə] **VI T2,** 26
Nicole Kidman [nɪˌkəʊl 'kɪdmən] **IV U5,** 76
Queen Elizabeth [ˌkwi:n‿ɪ'lɪzəbəθ] **I U5,** 73
Robbie Williams [ˌrɒbi 'wɪljəmz] **II U1,** 14
Robin Leach [ˌrɒbɪn 'li:tʃ] **IV U5,** 84
Rosa Parks [ˌrəʊzə 'pɑ:ks] **V T3,** 54
Samuel Ellis [ˌsæmjʊəl‿'elɪs] **IV U1,** 10
Sean Paul [ˌʃɔ:n 'pɔ:l] **IV U5,** 77
Shakespeare ['ʃeɪkspɪə] **II U5,** 62
Sherlock Holmes [ˌʃɜ:lɒk 'həʊmz] **III U5,** 82
Steve Fossett [sti:v 'fɒsət] **V T3,** 50
Thomas Edison [ˌtɒməs‿'edɪsn] **IV U5,** 78
U2 [ju'tu:] **V T3,** 51
Zandra Rhodes [ˌzændrə 'rəʊdz] **IV U5,** 76
Zeng Peiyan [ˌtseŋg 'peɪən] **VI T1,** 9

A

ab off [ɒf]
abbauen to break down [ˌbreɪk ˈdaʊn]
Abbild image [ˈɪmɪdʒ]
die Schule abbrechen to drop out [ˌdrɒp‿ˈaʊt]
abbremsen to brake [breɪk]
abbröckeln to flake [fleɪk]
Abc alphabet [ˈælfəbet]
Abend evening [ˈiːvnɪŋ]; night [naɪt]
am Abend in the evening [ˌɪn ðiː ˈiːvnɪŋ]
an diesem Abend that evening [ˌðæt‿ˈiːvnɪŋ]
heute Abend this evening [ðɪs ˈiːvnɪŋ]; tonight [təˈnaɪt]
zu Abend essen to have supper [hæv ˈsʌpə]
Abendessen dinner [ˈdɪnə]; supper [ˈsʌpə]; tea [tiː]
zum Abendessen for supper [fə ˈsʌpə]
Abendkleid evening dress [ˈiːvnɪŋ ˌdres]
abends in the evening [ˌɪn ðiː ˈiːvnɪŋ]
Abenteuer adventure [ədˈventʃə]
aber but [bʌt]
abfahren to leave [liːv]
Abfall rubbish [ˈrʌbɪʃ]; waste [weɪst]
Abfälle rubbish [ˈrʌbɪʃ]
abfeuern to fire [faɪə]
abfliegen to take off [ˌteɪk‿ˈɒf]
Abflug departure [dɪˈpɑːtʃə]
Abgabe tax [tæks]
Abgang exit [ˈeksɪt]
abgebrannt broke [brəʊk]
in Flaschen **abgefüllt** bottled [ˈbɒtld]
abgelegen remote [rɪˈməʊt]
Abgeordneter/Abgeordnete representative [ˌreprɪˈzentətɪv]; Member of Parliament (MP) [ˌmembə‿əv ˈpɑːləmənt]
zum **Abgewöhnen sein** to be a turn-off [ˈtɜːnɒf]
jmdn. **abhalten von** to stop sb from [stɒp]
Abhängigkeit addiction [əˈdɪkʃn]
abhauen to get away [ˌget‿əˈweɪ]
abheben to take off [ˌteɪk‿ˈɒf]
abholen to collect [kəˈlekt]; to pick up [pɪk‿ˈʌp]
Abitur A-levels *(pl)* [ˈeɪlevlz]
Abkommen contract [ˈkɒntrækt]; treaty [ˈtriːti]
abladen to dump [dʌmp]; to unburden [ʌnˈbɜːdn]
ablaufen *(Wasser)* to run away [ˌrʌn‿əˈweɪ]
ablaufen *(Zeit)* to run out [ˌrʌn‿ˈaʊt]
ablecken to lick [lɪk]
ablehnen to refuse [rɪˈfjuːz]
Abmachung deal [diːl]
abmalen to copy [ˈkɒpi]
abnehmen to lose weight [luːz ˈweɪt]
Aborigine Aborigine [ˌæbəˈrɪdʒni]
abräumen von to get off [get‿ˈɒf]
abreiben to wipe [waɪp]
Abreise departure [dɪˈpɑːtʃə]
abrutschen to slip [slɪp]
Absatz turnover [ˈtɜːnˌəʊvə]
abschaffen to abolish [əˈbɒlɪʃ]
abschalten to turn off [tɜːn‿ˈɒf]
abschicken to post [pəʊst]
abschießen to shoot [ʃuːt]
abschließen to lock [lɒk]
Abschluss closing [ˈkləʊzɪŋ]
Abschlusszeugnis diploma [dɪˈpləʊmə]
schneiden to cut (off) [kʌt‿ˈɒf]
Abschnitt section [ˈsekʃn]; sector [ˈsektə]; stage [steɪdʒ]
abschrecken to frighten away [ˌfraɪtn‿əˈweɪ]
abschreiben to copy [ˈkɒpi]
Abschrift copy [ˈkɒpi]
Abschuss launch [lɔːnʃ]
im **Abseits** offside [ˌɒfˈsaɪd]
absolut absolutely [ˌæbsəˈluːtli]
absondern to emit [ɪˈmɪt]
Abstand distance [ˈdɪstnts]
abstimmen to vote (for) [vəʊt]
Abstimmung vote [vəʊt]
Absturz crash [kræʃ]
abtasten to scan [skæn]
Abteilung department [dɪˈpɑːtmənt]; section [ˈsekʃn]
jmdn. **abtörnen** to turn sb off [tɜːn‿ˈɒf]
abtörnend sein to be a turn-off [ˈtɜːnɒf]
abwandeln to alter [ˈɔːltə]
sich **abwechseln** to rotate [rəˈteɪt]
abwesend absent [ˈæbsnt]
Abwesenheit absence [ˈæbsns]
sich **abwickeln** to unwind [ʌnˈwaɪnd]
abwischen to wipe [waɪp]
abzeichnen to copy [ˈkɒpi]
achten auf to watch [wɒtʃ]
Achtung attention [əˈtentʃn]
Acker field [fiːld]
Adapter adaptor [əˈdæptə]
addieren to add [æd]
Adresse address [əˈdres]
Afrikaner/Afrikanerin African [ˈæfrɪkən]
afrikanisch African [ˈæfrɪkən]
Aftershave aftershave [ˈɑːftəʃeɪv]
Agent/Agentin agent [ˈeɪdʒnt]
Agentur agency [ˈeɪdʒnsi]
aggressiv aggressive [əˈgresɪv]; militant [ˈmɪlɪtnt]
Agrikultur agriculture [ˈægrɪkʌltʃə]
ahnen to sense [sens]
Ahorn maple [ˈmeɪpl]
Akku battery [ˈbætri]
Akte record [ˈrekɔːd]
Aktion action [ˈækʃn]; campaign [kæmˈpeɪn]
aktiv active [ˈæktɪv]
Aktivität activity [ækˈtɪvəti]
aktualisieren to update [ʌpˈdeɪt]
Aktualisierung update [ˈʌpdeɪt]
aktuell present [ˈpreznt]
Akzent accent [ˈæksnt]
Alarm alarm [əˈlɑːm]
alarmiert startled [ˈstɑːtld]
Albtraum nightmare [ˈnaɪtmeə]
Album album [ˈælbəm]
Alge seaweed [ˈsiːwiːd]
Alkohol alcohol [ˈælkəhɒl]
alkoholfreies Getränk soft drink [ˈsɒft ˌdrɪŋk]
alle all [ɔːl]; everybody [ˈevribɒdi]
aller- very [ˈveri]
allein alone [əˈləʊn]; solo [ˈsəʊləʊ]
es allein schaffen to go it alone [ˌgəʊ‿ɪt‿əˈləʊn]
Allein- solo [ˈsəʊləʊ]
einen **Alleingang starten** to go it alone [ˌgəʊ‿ɪt‿əˈləʊn]
alles all [ɔːl]; everything [ˈevriθɪŋ]
alles klar all right [ɔːl ˈraɪt]
alltäglich everyday [ˈevrideɪ]
Alltags- everyday [ˈevrideɪ]
Alphabet alphabet [ˈælfəbet]
alphabetisch alphabetical [ˌælfəˈbetɪkl]
als as [æz; əz]
als *(Vergleich)* than [ðæn]
als *(zeitlich)* when [wen]
also so [səʊ]; well [wel]
alt ancient [ˈeɪnʃnt]; old [əʊld]
Alter age [eɪdʒ]
das Alter, in dem man legal Sex haben darf age of consent [ˌeɪdʒ‿əv kənˈsent]
im Alter von of age [əv‿ˈeɪdʒ]
alternativ alternative [ɔːlˈtɜːnətɪv]
Alternative alternative [ɔːlˈtɜːnətɪv]
Amerikaner American [əˈmerɪkən]
Hispano-Amerikaner/-Amerikanerin Hispanic [hɪˈspænɪk]
amerikanisch American [əˈmerɪkən]
Amsel blackbird [ˈblækbɜːd]
Amtszimmer chamber [ˈtʃeɪmbə]
sich **amüsieren** to have a good time [ˌhæv‿ə gʊd ˈtaɪm]; to have fun [ˌhæv ˈfʌn]
an at [æt; ət]; on [ɒn]
an sein to be on [biː‿ˈɒn]

Ananas pineapple ['paɪnæpl]

anbauen to grow [grəʊ]

anbieten to offer ['ɒfə]

anbinden to tie [taɪ]

Anblick sight [saɪt]

anbringen to attach [ə'tætʃ]; to fix (to) [fɪks]

andauern to continue [kən'tɪnju:]; to go on [gəʊ‿'ɒn]

Andenken souvenir [ˌsu:və'nɪə]

anderer/andere/anderes other ['ʌðə]
ein anderer/eine andere/ein anderes another [ə'nʌðə]

Einerseits ..., andererseits ... On the one hand ..., (but) on the other hand ... [ɒn ðə‿'wʌn ˌhænd ... ɒn ði‿'ʌðə ˌhænd ...]

ändern to alter ['ɔ:ltə]; to change [tʃeɪndʒ]
sich ändern to alter ['ɔ:ltə]; to vary ['veəri]

anders different ['dɪfrnt]
anders als unlike [ʌn'laɪk]

andersrum the other way round [ði ˌʌðə‿weɪ 'raʊnd]

Änderung change [tʃeɪndʒ]

anerkennen to approve [ə'pru:v]

Anfang beginning [bɪ'gɪnɪŋ]; start [stɑ:t]

anfangen to begin [bɪ'gɪn]; to start [stɑ:t]

anfertigen to draw up [drɔ:‿'ʌp]

Anfrage request [rɪ'kwest]

anfügen to attach [ə'tætʃ]

anführen to lead [li:d]

Anführer/Anführerin leader ['li:də]

angeben to boast [bəʊst]

Angebot offer ['ɒfə]; range [reɪndʒ]

etw. **angehen** to go for sth ['gəʊ fɔ:]

Angelegenheit matter ['mætə]

angeln to fish [fɪʃ]

Angeln fishing ['fɪʃɪŋ]

Angestellter/Angestellte employee [ɪm'plɔɪi:]; worker ['wɜ:kə]

Angler fisherman, fishermen *(pl)* ['fɪʃəmən; 'fɪʃəmen]

angreifen to attack [ə'tæk]

Angriff raid [reɪd]

Angst fear [fɪə]
Angst haben (vor) to be afraid (of) [bi‿ə'freɪd‿əv]; to be frightened (of) [bi: 'fraɪtnd]
Angst machen to scare ['skeə]
Ich habe Angst. I'm scared. [aɪm 'skeəd]

ängstigen to worry ['wʌri]

anhaben to wear [weə]

anhalten to stop [stɒp]

anhängen to attach [ə'tætʃ]

Anhänger/Anhängerin supporter [sə'pɔ:tə]

anheben to raise [reɪz]

anhören to listen ['lɪsn]
sich anhören to sound [saʊnd]

Animation animation [ænɪ'meɪʃn]

animierter Manga animé ['ænɪmeɪ]

fest **anklopfen** to bang [bæŋ]

ankommen to arrive [ə'raɪv]

Ankündigung announcement [ə'naʊntsmənt]

Anlage facility [fə'sɪləti]; plant [plɑ:nt]

Anleitung guidance ['gaɪdənts]

Anliegen request [rɪ'kwest]

anmachen to switch on [ˌswɪtʃ‿'ɒn]; to turn on [ˌtɜ:n‿'ɒn]

anmalen to paint [peɪnt]

anmelden to register ['redʒɪstə]
sich anmelden to register ['redʒɪstə]
sich anmelden (zu) to apply (for) [ə'plaɪ]

Anmerkung note [nəʊt]

annähernd nearly ['nɪəli]

Anorak anorak ['ænəræk]

anpassen an to adapt to [ə'dæpt tə]
sich anpassen an to adapt to [ə'dæpt tə]

anpassungsfähig adaptable [ə'dæptəbl]

anpflanzen to plant [plɑ:nt]

anregen to inspire [ɪn'spaɪə]

Anregung suggestion [sə'dʒestʃn]

Anruf call [kɔ:l]

Anrufbeantworter answerphone ['ɑ:nsəfəʊn]

anrufen to call [kɔ:l]; to phone [fəʊn]; to ring [rɪŋ]

ansässig based [beɪst]

anschauen to have a look (at) [ˌhæv‿ə 'lʊk]; to view [vju:]

Anschlag attempt [ə'tempt]

anschließen to connect [kə'nekt]
sich anschließen to join [dʒɔɪn]

ansehen to look at ['lʊk‿ət]; to watch [wɒtʃ]
sich ansehen to look at ['lʊk‿ət]; to check out [tʃek‿'aʊt]

Anspannung tension ['tenʃn]

Ansprache speech [spi:tʃ]

Anstandswauwau chaperon ['ʃæprəʊn]

anstatt instead of [ɪn'sted‿əv]

jmdn. **anstellen** to employ sb [ɪm'plɔɪ]

Anstellung employment [ɪm'plɔɪmənt]

Anstieg rise [raɪz]

anstreichen to paint [peɪnt]

sich **anstrengen** to struggle ['strʌgl]

Anstrengung struggle (for sth) ['strʌgl]

Anteil share [ʃeə]

anti- anti ['æntɪ]

antippen to touch [tʌtʃ]

Antrag application [ˌæplɪ'keɪʃn]

Antragsteller/Antragstellerin applicant ['æplɪkənt]

antreten gegen etw./jmdn. to take on sth/sb [teɪk‿'ɒn]

Antwort answer ['ɑ:nsə]; reply [rɪ'plaɪ]; response [rɪ'spɒns]

antworten to reply [rɪ'plaɪ]

Anwalt/Anwältin lawyer ['lɔɪə]

Anweisung instruction [ɪn'strʌkʃn]; order ['ɔ:də]

Anwendung application [ˌæplɪ'keɪʃn]; use [ju:s]

Anwesenheit stay [steɪ]

Anwohner/Anwohnerin resident ['rezɪdnt]

Anzeige advert ['ædvɜ:t]

anziehen to attract [ə'trækt]; to put on [pʊt‿'ɒn]
sich anziehen to dress [dres]

Anzug suit [su:t]

Apartment apartment *(AE)* [ə'pɑ:tmənt]

Apfel apple ['æpl]

Apparat machine [mə'ʃi:n]

April April ['eɪprl]

Aquarium aquarium [ə'kweəriəm]

arabisch Arabic ['ærəbɪk]

Arabisch Arabic ['ærəbɪk]

Arbeit work [wɜ:k]

arbeiten to work [wɜ:k]

Arbeiter/Arbeiterin worker ['wɜ:kə]

Arbeitgeber/Arbeitgeberin employer [ɪm'plɔɪə]

Arbeitsblatt worksheet ['wɜ:kʃi:t]

Arbeitserlaubnis working visa ['wɜ:kɪŋ ˌvi:zə]

Arbeitsgemeinschaft club [klʌb]

Arbeitslosigkeit unemployment [ˌʌnɪm'plɔɪmənt]

Arbeitsplatz workplace ['wɜ:kpleɪs]

Arbeitsstätte workplace ['wɜ:kpleɪs]

Arbeitsstelle job [dʒɒb]

Architekt/Architektin architect ['ɑ:kɪtekt]

Arena arena [ə'ri:nə]

Ärger trouble ['trʌbl]

jmdn. **ärgern** to pick on sb ['pɪk‿ɒn]

Argument argument ['ɑ:gjəmənt]

argumentieren to argue ['ɑ:gju:]

arm poor [pɔ:; pʊə]

Arm arm [ɑ:m]

Armbanduhr watch [wɒtʃ]

Ärmel arm [ɑ:m]

Armut poverty ['pɒvəti]

Arsch ass *(AE)* [æs]

Art kind [kaɪnd]; sort [sɔ:t]; species,

species *(pl)* ['spi:ʃi:z]; type [taɪp]; way [weɪ]
auf die eine oder andere Art either way [ˌaɪðə 'weɪ]
Artikel article ['ɑ:tɪkl]
Arzt/Ärztin doctor ['dɒktə]
zum Arzt gehen to see a doctor [si:‿ə 'dɒktə]
Asche ash [æʃ]; ashes *(pl)* ['æʃɪz]
glimmende Asche embers *(pl)* ['embəz]
Asiate/Asiatin Asian ['eɪʃn]
asiatisch Asian ['eɪʃn]
Aspekt aspect ['æspekt]
Assistent/Assistentin assistant [ə'sɪstnt]
Ast branch [brɑ:ntʃ]
Astronaut/Astronautin astronaut ['æstrənɔ:t]
atemberaubend breathtaking ['breθˌteɪkɪŋ]
atmen to breathe [bri:ð]
Atmosphäre atmosphere ['ætməsfɪə]
atombetrieben nuclear-powered ['nju:kliəˌpaʊəd]
Attraktion attraction [ə'trækʃn]
attraktiv attractive [ə'træktɪv]
auch also ['ɔ:lsəʊ]; as well [əz 'wel]; too [tu:]
auch wenn even though [ˌi:vn‿'ðəʊ]
sowohl … als auch as well as [əz 'wel‿əz]
auf at [æt; ət]; on [ɒn]; onto ['ɒntu:; 'ɒntə]; up [ʌp]
auf dem Land in the country [ˌɪn ðə 'kʌntri]
auf einmal suddenly ['sʌdnli]
auf Sendung on the air [ˌɒn ði‿'eə]
auf Wiedersehen goodbye [gʊd'baɪ]
auf … zu towards [tə'wɔ:dz]
auf … hinauf onto ['ɒntu:; 'ɒntə]
aufbacken to crisp up [krɪsp‿'ʌp]
Aufbau construction [kən'strʌkʃn]
aufbauen to put up [pʊt‿'ʌp]; to set up [set‿'ʌp]
wieder aufbauen to rebuild [ˌri:'bɪld]
Aufbereitung treatment ['tri:tmənt]
aufbewahren to keep [ki:p]
Aufblinken flash [flæʃ]
aufbrechen to set off [set‿'ɒf]
aufbringen to raise [reɪz]
Aufenthalt stay [steɪ]
aufflackern to crisp up [krɪsp‿'ʌp]
aufführen to perform [pə'fɔ:m]
Aufführung performance [pə'fɔ:məns]
Aufgabe exercise ['eksəsaɪz]; task [tɑ:sk]
aufgeben to give up [gɪv‿'ʌp]; to quit [kwɪt]; *(einen Brief)* to post [pəʊst]
aufgehen to open ['əʊpn]; *(Sonne)* to come up [kʌm‿'ʌp]
aufgeregt excited [ɪk'saɪtɪd]; nervous ['nɜ:vəs]
aufgeregt sein to be upset [bi: ʌp'set]
aufgeschlossen outgoing ['aʊtgəʊɪŋ]
aufheben to pick up [pɪk‿'ʌp]
aufhören to finish ['fɪnɪʃ]; to stop [stɒp]
aufhören etw. zu tun to stop + -ing [stɒp]
aufhören mit to stop [stɒp]; to quit [kwɪt]
auflisten to list [lɪst]
auflösen to dissolve [dɪ'zɒlv]
sich auflösen to dissolve [dɪ'zɒlv]
aufmachen to open ['əʊpn]
aufmerksam thoughtful ['θɔ:tfl]
Aufmerksamkeit attention [ə'tentʃn]
Aufnahme admission [əd'mɪʃn]; record ['rekɔ:d]; recording [rɪ'kɔ:dɪŋ]; shot [ʃɒt]
aufnehmen to include [ɪn'klu:d]; to record [rɪ'kɔ:d]
es mit etw./jmdm. aufnehmen to take on sth/sb [teɪk‿'ɒn]
aufpassen to take care [teɪk 'keə]
aufpassen auf to look after [lʊk‿'ɑ:ftə]
Aufprall crash [kræʃ]
aufrechterhalten to keep up [ki:p‿'ʌp]
sich **aufregen** to panic ['pænɪk]
aufregend exciting [ɪk'saɪtɪŋ]
Aufregung fuss [fʌs]
sich **aufrichten** to lean up [li:n‿'ʌp]
Aufruhr riot [raɪət]
aufschauen to look up [lʊk‿'ʌp]
aufschlagen gegen to crash into [kræʃ]
aufschnappen to catch [kætʃ]
Aufseher/Aufseherin keeper ['ki:pə]
aufsetzen to draw up [drɔ:‿'ʌp]; to put on [pʊt‿'ɒn]
Aufsichtsperson supervisor ['su:pəvaɪzə]
aufspringen to jump up [dʒʌmp‿'ʌp]
aufstehen to get out of bed [ˌget‿aʊt‿əv 'bed]; to get up [get‿'ʌp]
aufsteigen to get on [get‿'ɒn]
aufstellen to put up [pʊt‿'ʌp]
Aufstieg rise [raɪz]
auftauchen to appear [ə'pɪə]
auftauen to thaw [θɔ:]
Auftrag task [tɑ:sk]
auftragen *(Make-up)* to put on [pʊt‿'ɒn]
auftreten to perform [pə'fɔ:m]
aufwachen to wake up [weɪk‿'ʌp]
aufwachsen to grow up [grəʊ‿'ʌp]
aufwärmen to warm up [wɔ:m‿'ʌp]
sich aufwärmen to warm up [wɔ:m‿'ʌp]
aufwecken to wake [weɪk]; to wake up [weɪk‿'ʌp]
aufzeichnen to record [rɪ'kɔ:d]
Aufzeichnung record ['rekɔ:d]; recording [rɪ'kɔ:dɪŋ]
Aufzug lift *(BE)* [lɪft]
Auge eye [aɪ]
etw./jmdn. im Auge behalten to keep an eye on sth/sb [ˌki:p‿ən‿'aɪ‿ɒn]
Augenblick moment ['məʊmənt]
im Augenblick at the moment [æt ðə 'məʊmənt]
in diesem Augenblick right now [ˌraɪt 'naʊ]
Augenbraue eyebrow ['aɪbraʊ]
Augenklappe patch [pætʃ]
August August ['ɔ:gəst]
aus from [frɒm]; in [ɪn]
aus … heraus out of ['aʊt‿əv]
ausarbeiten to draw up [drɔ:‿'ʌp]; to work out [ˌwɜ:k‿'aʊt]
ausbilden to train [treɪn]
Ausbilder/Ausbilderin instructor [ɪn'strʌktə]
Ausbildung apprenticeship [ə'prentɪʃɪp]; training ['treɪnɪŋ]
eine Ausbildung machen to train [treɪn]
ausbrechen to break out [ˌbreɪk‿'aʊt]; *(Fahrzeug)* to swerve [swɜ:v]
ausbreiten to spread [spred]
sich ausbreiten to spread [spred]
auschecken to check out [tʃek‿'aʊt]
ausdenken to think up [θɪŋk‿'ʌp]
sich ausdenken to think up [θɪŋk‿'ʌp]; to make up [meɪk‿'ʌp]
Ausdruck expression [ɪk'spreʃn]; phrase [freɪz]
ausdrücken to express [ɪk'spres]
auseinanderjagen to scatter ['skætə]
Ausfahrt exit ['eksɪt]
ausfallen to fail [feɪl]
ausfliegen to fly out [flaɪ‿'aʊt]
Ausflug trip [trɪp]
Ausfuhr export ['ekspɔ:t]
ausführen to execute ['eksɪkju:t]; to export [ɪk'spɔ:t]
ausfüllen to complete [kəm'pli:t]; to fill in [fɪl‿'ɪn]
Ausgang exit ['eksɪt]
ausgeben to spend [spend]
voll **ausgebildet** fully-qualified [ˌfʊli'kwɒlɪfaɪd]
ausgedehnt vast [vɑ:st]
ausgehen to go out [gəʊ‿'aʊt]; to socialize ['səʊʃlaɪz]; *(Zeit)* to run out [ˌrʌn‿'aʊt]
ausgliedern to outsource ['aʊtsɔ:s]

ausgraben to dig up [dɪɡ‿'ʌp]
ausgrenzen to segregate ['segrɪɡeɪt]
aushalten to suffer ['sʌfə]
aushändigen to hand [hænd]
auskippen to dump [dʌmp]; to tip [tɪp]
ohne ... **auskommen** to go without [ˌɡəʊ wɪ'ðaʊt]
auslachen to laugh at ['lɑ:f‿ət]
im **Ausland** abroad [ə'brɔ:d]; overseas [ˌəʊvə'si:z]
ins Ausland abroad [ə'brɔ:d]; overseas [ˌəʊvə'si:z]
Ausländer/Ausländerin foreigner ['fɒrɪnə]
ausländisch alien ['eɪliən]; foreign ['fɒrɪn]
auslaufen to leak [li:k]
ausleihen to loan [ləʊn]
auslösen to spark [spɑ:k]; *(Alarm)* to set off [set‿'ɒf]
Auslöser button ['bʌtn]
ausmachen to matter ['mætə]; to put out [pʊt‿'aʊt]
ausradieren to erase [ɪ'reɪz]
ausrauben to rob [rɒb]
Ausrede excuse [ɪk'skju:s]
Ausreißer/Ausreißerin runaway ['rʌnəˌweɪ]
sich **ausruhen** to relax [rɪ'læks]; to rest [rest]
ausrüsten to supply [sə'plaɪ]
Ausrüstung equipment [ɪ'kwɪpmənt]
ausrutschen to slip [slɪp]
ausschalten to switch off [ˌswɪtʃ‿'ɒf]; to turn off [tɜ:n‿'ɒf]
Ausschau halten nach to look out for [ˌlʊk‿'aʊt fə]
ausscheren to swerve [swɜ:v]
ausschließen to ban [bæn]
jmdn. ausschließen to shut sb out [ʃʌt‿'aʊt]
Ausschreitung riot [raɪət]
aussehen to look [lʊk]
Aussehen look [lʊk]
Außenseiter/Außenseiterin outsider [ˌaʊt'saɪdə]
außer beside [bɪ'saɪd]; but [bʌt]; except [ɪk'sept]
außer sich delirious [dɪ'lɪriəs]
äußerer/äußere/äußeres outer ['aʊtə]
außerhalb outside [aʊt'saɪd]
Außerirdischer/Außerirdische alien ['eɪliən]
äußern to express [ɪk'spres]
außerordentlich extremely [ɪk'stri:mli]
Aussicht chance [tʃɑ:nts]; prospect ['prɒspekt]; view [vju:]
Ausstattung equipment [ɪ'kwɪpmənt]
aussteigen to drop out [ˌdrɒp‿'aʊt]; to get out [get‿'aʊt]
aussteigen aus to get off [get‿'ɒf]
Ausstellung exhibition [ˌeksɪ'bɪʃn]
Ausstoß emission [ɪ'mɪʃn]
ausstrahlen to broadcast ['brɔ:dkɑ:st]
Ausstrahlung broadcast ['brɔ:dkɑ:st]
aussuchen to pick out [pɪk‿'aʊt]
Austausch exchange [ɪks'tʃeɪndʒ]
austauschen to exchange [ɪks'tʃeɪndʒ]
austoßen to emit [ɪ'mɪt]
Australier Australian [ɒs'treɪliən]
australisch Australian [ɒs'treɪliən]
Auswahl choice [tʃɔɪs]; range [reɪndʒ]
auswählen to choose [tʃu:z]; to elect [ɪ'lekt]; to pick out [pɪk‿'aʊt]
Auswahlmöglichkeit option ['ɒpʃn]
Auswahlverfahren tryout ['traɪaʊt]
auswandern to emigrate ['emɪɡreɪt]
auswechseln to substitute ['sʌbstɪtju:t]
ausweichen to swerve [swɜ:v]
ausweiten to widen ['waɪdn]
Auswirkung effect [ɪ'fekt]; impact ['ɪmpækt]
Auszahlung payment ['peɪmənt]
Auszeichnung award [ə'wɔ:d]
ausziehen to take off [ˌteɪk‿'ɒf]
Auszubildender/Auszubildende apprentice [ə'prentɪs]
Auszug bit [bɪt]; extract ['ekstrækt]
Auto car [kɑ:]; vehicle ['vɪəkl]
Auto- automotive [ˌɔ:tə'məʊtɪv]
Autobahn Interstate *(AE)* [ˌɪntə'steɪt]; motorway ['məʊtəweɪ]
Autogramm autograph ['ɔ:təɡrɑ:f]
automatisch automatically [ˌɔ:tə'mætɪkli]
Autopanne breakdown ['breɪkdaʊn]
Autor/Autorin author ['ɔ:θə]
Autorität authority [ɔ:'θɒrəti]

B

Baby baby, babies *(pl)* ['beɪbi; 'beɪbiz]
Bach stream [stri:m]
Bäcker/Bäckerin baker ['beɪkə]
Backofen oven ['ʌvn]
Badeanzug swimsuit ['swɪmsu:t]
Badezimmer bathroom ['bɑ:θrʊm]
Badminton badminton ['bædmɪntən]
Bagel bagel ['beɪɡl]
Baguette baguette [bæɡ'et]
Bahnhof station ['steɪʃn]
Bahnsteig platform ['plætfɔ:m]
Balance balance ['bæləns]
bald soon [su:n]
Ball ball [bɔ:l]
Ballkönigin homecoming queen [ˌhəʊmkʌmɪŋ 'kwi:n]
Ballsaal ballroom ['bɔ:lrʊm]
Banane banana [bə'nɑ:nə]
Band band [bænd]
Bande band [bænd]; gang [ɡæŋ]
Bank bank [bæŋk]
Bankkonto account [ə'kaʊnt]
Bann ban [bæn]
bannen to ban [bæn]
Bar bar [bɑ:]
Bär/Bärin bear [beə]
Barkeeper barman, barmen *(pl)* ['bɑ:mən, 'bɑ:men]
Barmann barman, barmen *(pl)* ['bɑ:mən, 'bɑ:men]
Baron baron ['bærn]
Barriere barrier ['bæriə]
Bart beard [bɪəd]
Base base [beɪs]
Baseball baseball ['beɪsbɔ:l]
Basis base [beɪs]
Basketball basketball ['bɑ:skɪtbɔ:l]
Bass bass [beɪs]
Batterie battery ['bætri]
Bauch stomach ['stʌmək]
bauen to build [bɪld]; to construct [kən'strʌkt]
Bauer/Bäuerin farmer ['fɑ:mə]
Bauernhaus farmhouse ['fɑ:mhaʊs]
Bauernhof farm [fɑ:m]
Baufachmann/Baufachfrau builder ['bɪldə]
Baum tree [tri:]
Baumeister/Baumeisterin builder ['bɪldə]
Bazillus bug [bʌɡ]
beabsichtigen to aim ['eɪm]
Beamter/Beamtin officer ['ɒfɪsə]; official [ə'fɪʃl]
beängstigend frightening ['fraɪtnɪŋ]
beanspruchen to claim [kleɪm]; to stress [stres]
bearbeiten to edit ['edɪt]
Mund-zu-Mund-**Beatmung** mouth-to-mouth [ˌmaʊθtə'maʊθ]
Bedarf need [ni:d]
bedauerlich sad [sæd]
bedauern to feel sorry for [fi:l 'sɒri]
bedeuten to mean [mi:n]
Bedeutung meaning ['mi:nɪŋ]; sense [sens]
von Bedeutung sein to matter ['mætə]
bedienen to operate ['ɒpəreɪt]; to serve [sɜ:v]
Bedienung waiter ['weɪtə]

Bedingung condition [kən'dɪʃn]; term [tɜ:m]
Bedrohung threat [θret]
bedrückt depressed [dɪ'prest]
Bedürfnis need [ni:d]
Beeil dich! Hurry up! [ˌhʌri‿'ʌp]
beeindrucken to impress [ɪm'pres]
beeinflussen to affect [ə'fekt]; to influence ['ɪnfluənts]
beeinträchtigen to affect [ə'fekt]
beenden to end [end]; to finish ['fɪnɪʃ]
beerdigen to bury ['beri]
Beerdigung funeral ['fju:nrəl]
Beet patch [pætʃ]
Befähigung qualification [ˌkwɒlɪfɪ'keɪʃn]
befangen self-conscious [ˌself'kɒnʃəs]
Befehl order ['ɔ:də]
befestigen to fix (to) [fɪks]
befolgen to follow ['fɒləʊ]
befördern to carry ['kæri]
befristet temporary ['temprəri]
begabt talented ['tæləntɪd]
Begabung gift [gɪft]
Beginn beginning [bɪ'gɪnɪŋ]; start [stɑ:t]
beginnen to begin [bɪ'gɪn]; to start [stɑ:t]
Begleitperson chaperon ['ʃæprəʊn]
begraben to bury ['beri]
begreifen to realise ['rɪəlaɪz]
begrenzen to limit ['lɪmɪt]
Begriff term [tɜ:m]
behalten to keep [ki:p]
behandeln to treat [tri:t]
Behandlung treatment ['tri:tmənt]
behängen to drape [dreɪp]
behaupten to claim [kleɪm]
beherrschen to control [kən'trəʊl]
behindert disabled [dɪ'seɪbld]
Behinderung disability [ˌdɪsə'bɪləti]
Behörde agency ['eɪdʒnsi]; authority [ɔ:'θɒrəti]
bei at [æt; ət]; with [wɪð]
  bei weitem by far [baɪ 'fɑ:]
beibehalten to keep up [ki:p‿'ʌp]
beide both [bəʊθ]
Beifahrer/Beifahrerin passenger ['pæsndʒə]
Bein leg [leg]
beinahe almost ['ɔ:lməʊst]
beinhalten to be comprised of [bi‿kəm'praɪzd‿əv]; to include [ɪn'klu:d]
Beispiel example [ɪg'zɑ:mpl]
  zum Beispiel e.g. [i:'dʒi:]; for example [ˌfər‿ɪg'zɑ:mpl]
beißen to bite [baɪt]; to sting [stɪŋ]
beitreten to join [dʒɔɪn]
bejubelt acclaimed [ə'kleɪmd]
wohl **bekannt** well-known [ˌwel'nəʊn]
sich **beklagen** to moan [məʊn]
bekommen to get [get]
belasten to stress [stres]
belästigen to bother ['bɒðə]
Belästigung harassment [hə'ræsmənt]
Belastung pressure ['preʃə]
belauschen to overhear [ˌəʊvə'hɪə]
belebt busy ['bɪzi]
Beleg record ['rekɔ:d]; slip [slɪp]
belegen to prove [pru:v]
beleidigen to diss *(slang)* [dɪs]; to insult [ɪn'sʌlt]
Beleidigung insult ['ɪnsʌlt]
Beleuchtung lighting ['laɪtɪŋ]
Belgier/Belgierin Belgian ['beldʒən]
belgisch Belgian ['beldʒən]
beliebt popular ['pɒpjələ]
beliefern to supply [sə'plaɪ]
bellen to bark [bɑ:k]
Bellen barking ['bɑ:kɪŋ]
bemerken to notice ['nəʊtɪs]
Bemerkung comment ['kɒment]
sich stark **bemühen** to try hard [traɪ‿'hɑ:d]
benachrichtigen to inform [ɪn'fɔ:m]
Benehmen behaviour [bɪ'heɪvjə]
benennen to label ['leɪbl]; to name [neɪm]
benötigen to need [ni:d]
benutzen to use [ju:z]
Benzin petrol ['petrl]; *(AE)* gas [gæs]
beobachten to watch [wɒtʃ]
bequem comfortable ['kʌmpftəbl]
Berater/Beraterin consultant [kən'sʌltnt]; counselor ['kaʊnsələ]
Beratung guidance ['gaɪdənts]
telefonischer **Beratungsdienst** helpline ['helplaɪn]
Bereich range [reɪndʒ]; sector ['sektə]
bereit ready ['redi]
in **Bereitschaft** standby ['stændbaɪ]
bereitstellen to provide (sb with sth) [prə'vaɪd]; to raise [reɪz]; to supply [sə'plaɪ]
Berg mountain ['maʊntɪn]
Bericht account [ə'kaʊnt]; report [rɪ'pɔ:t]
berichten to report [rɪ'pɔ:t]
Beruf career [kə'rɪə]
berufen to appoint [ə'pɔɪnt]
beruflich professional [prə'feʃnl]
Berufs- professional [prə'feʃnl]
Berufsberatung careers advice [kə'rɪəz ədˌvaɪs]
berühmt famous ['feɪməs]; well-known [ˌwel'nəʊn]
berühren to touch [tʌtʃ]
Besatzung crew [kru:]
beschädigen to damage ['dæmɪdʒ]
Beschädigung damage ['dæmɪdʒ]
beschaffen to supply [sə'plaɪ]
jmdn. **beschäftigen** to employ sb [ɪm'plɔɪ]
beschäftigt busy ['bɪzi]
Beschäftigung employment [ɪm'plɔɪmənt]
Bescheinigung certificate [sə'tɪfɪkət]
beschließen to pass [pɑ:s]
beschränken to limit ['lɪmɪt]
Beschränkung limit ['lɪmɪt]
beschreiben to describe [dɪ'skraɪb]
beschriften to label ['leɪbl]
Beschriftung label ['leɪbl]; labelling ['leɪblɪŋ]
beschuldigen to blame [bleɪm]
beschützen to protect [prə'tekt]
beschützend protective [prə'tektɪv]
beseitigen to abolish [ə'bɒlɪʃ]
besichtigen to visit ['vɪzɪt]
besiegen to beat [bi:t]
besitzen to have got [hæv 'gɒt]; to own [əʊn]
Besitzer/Besitzerin owner ['əʊnə]
besonders special ['speʃl]; especially [ɪ'speʃli]
besorgen to get [get]; to provide (sb with sth) [prə'vaɪd]; to supply [sə'plaɪ]
besorgt sein to be worried [bi: 'wʌrid]
etw. **besprechen** to discuss [dɪ'skʌs]
Besprechung discussion [dɪ'skʌʃn]; meeting ['mi:tɪŋ]
besprühen to spray [spreɪ]
besser better ['betə]
auf dem Weg der **Besserung sein** to be in remission [ˌbi‿ɪn rɪ'mɪʃn]
Bestand supply [sə'plaɪ]
bestehen to pass [pɑ:s]; to survive [sə'vaɪv]
  bestehen aus to be comprised of [bi‿kəm'praɪzd‿əv]
bestehend existing [ɪg'zɪstɪŋ]
besteigen to climb ['klaɪm]
bestellen to order ['ɔ:də]
bester/beste/bestes best [best]
  am besten best [best]
bestimmen to determine [dɪ'tɜ:mɪn]
bestimmt certain ['sɜ:tn]; certainly ['sɜ:tnli]; definitely ['defɪnətli]; specific [spə'sɪfɪk]
bestrafen to punish ['pʌnɪʃ]
  bestraft werden to get it ['get‿ɪt]
Bestrafung penalty ['penlti]; punishment ['pʌnɪʃmənt]
bestürzt sein to be upset [bi: ʌp'set]

Besuch visit ['vɪzɪt]
besuchen to see [si:]; to visit ['vɪzɪt]
Besucher/Besucherin visitor ['vɪzɪtə]
betäuben to stun [stʌn]
beteiligen to involve [ɪn'vɒlv]
sich beteiligen an to enter ['entə]
beteiligt sein an to be involved in [bi: ɪn'vɒlvd‿ɪn]
Beteiligung share [ʃeə]
betonen to stress [stres]
Betonung stress [stres]
betrachten to view [vju:]
Betrag amount [ə'maʊnt]
betreffen to affect [ə'fekt]
betreten to enter ['entə]
Betreuer/Betreuerin counselor ['kaʊnsələ]; supervisor ['su:pəvaɪzə]
Bett bed [bed]
Bettlaken sheet [ʃi:t]
beunruhigen to worry ['wʌri]
beunruhigt sein to be worried [bi: 'wʌrid]
beurteilen to assess [ə'ses]
Bevölkerung population [ˌpɒpjə'leɪʃn]
bevor before [bɪ'fɔ:]
bevorzugen to prefer [prɪ'fɜ:]
bewachen to guard [gɑ:d]
bewaffnet armed [ɑ:md]
Bewahrung conservation [ˌkɒnsə'veɪʃn]
bewältigen to manage ['mænɪdʒ]
bewegen to move [mu:v]
sich bewegen to move [mu:v]
beweglich flexible ['fleksɪbl]
Bewegung motion ['məʊʃn]; move [mu:v]; movement ['mu:vmənt]
beweisen to prove [pru:v]
etw. **bewerben** to promote sth [prə'məʊt]
sich bewerben (um) to apply (for) [ə'plaɪ]
Bewerber/Bewerberin applicant ['æplɪkənt]; candidate ['kændɪdət]
Bewerbung application [ˌæplɪ'keɪʃn]
bewerten to assess [ə'ses]
Bewertung assessment [ə'sesmənt]
Bewohner/ Bewohnerin resident ['rezɪdnt]
sich ... **bewusst sein** to be aware of [ˌbi‿ə'weə]
bezahlen to pay (for) [peɪ]
Bezahlung pay [peɪ]; payment ['peɪmənt]
Bezeichnung term [tɜ:m]; title ['taɪtl]
Bezirk borough ['bʌrə]
Bezug reference ['refrns]
Biegung bend [bend]
Bier beer [bɪə]
Bild drawing ['drɔ:ɪŋ]; image ['ɪmɪdʒ]; picture ['pɪktʃə]
bilden to form [fɔ:m]
sich bilden to form [fɔ:m]
Bildschirm screen [skri:n]
Bildschirm-Teenie screenager ['skri:neɪdʒə]
Bildung culture ['kʌltʃə]; education [edʒʊ'keɪʃn]
Bildunterschrift caption ['kæpʃn]
bilingual bilingual [baɪ'lɪŋgwəl]
billig cheap [tʃi:p]
Bindeglied link [lɪŋk]
binden to tie [taɪ]
Bindfaden string [strɪŋ]
Bio- bio [baɪəʊ]
Biologe/Biologin biologist [baɪ'ɒlədʒɪst]
biologisch angebaut organic [ɔ:'gænɪk]
Biosiegel organic label [ɔ:ˌgænɪk 'leɪbl]
Birne pear [peə]
bis till [tɪl]; to [tʊ; tə]; until [ʌn'tɪl; n'tɪl]
Bis dann! See you! ['si: jə]; See you around! [ˌsi: jə ə'raʊnd]
bis hin zu through to ['θru: tə]
bis zu up to ['ʌp tə]
Bischof bishop ['bɪʃəp]
ein **bisschen** a bit [ə 'bɪt]
Bistro bistro bar [ˌbi:strəʊ 'bɑ:]
bitte please [pli:z]
Bitte schön! Here you are! ['hɪə ju:‿ɑ:]
Bitte sehr! You're welcome. [jʊə 'welkəm]
bitten um to ask (for) ['ɑ:sk fə]
bitter bitter ['bɪtə]
blasen to blow [bləʊ]
blass pale [peɪl]
Blatt leaf, leaves *(pl)* [li:f; li:vz]; *(Papier)* sheet [ʃi:t]
blau blue [blu:]
Blei lead [led]
bleiben to remain [rɪ'meɪn]; to stay [steɪ]
länger bleiben to stay on [steɪ‿'ɒn]
Bleistift pencil ['pensl]
Blende shutter ['ʃʌtə]
Blick look [lʊk]
einen Blick werfen (auf) to have a look (at) [ˌhæv‿ə 'lʊk]; to take a look (at) [ˌteɪk‿ə 'lʊk]
einen vernichtenden Blick zuwerfen to give ... a dirty look [ˌgɪv‿ə dɜ:ti 'lʊk]
Blickfeld horizon [hə'raɪzn]
blind blind [blaɪnd]
blinken to flash [flæʃ]
blitzen to flash [flæʃ]
Blitzen flash [flæʃ]
Block block [blɒk]
blöd stupid ['stju:pɪd]
Blog blog [blɒg]
blond blond [blɒnd]; blond(e)-haired ['blɒndˌheəd]; fair [feə]
bloß only ['əʊnli]
Blume flower ['flaʊə]
Blut blood [blʌd]
Bluterguss bruise [bru:z]
Blutkrebs leukaemia [lju:'ki:miə]
Boden bottom ['bɒtəm]; ground [graʊnd]
Bogen bow [bəʊ]
Bohne bean [bi:n]
Bohrer drill [drɪl]
Bohrmaschine drill [drɪl]
Bombe bomb [bɒm]
Bonbon sweet [swi:t]
Boot boat [bəʊt]
an **Bord** on board [ɒn 'bɔ:d]
borgen to borrow ['bɒrəʊ]
bösartig fierce [fɪəs]
böse angry ['æŋgri]
böse sein auf to be angry with [bi 'æŋgri wɪð]
Bosheit venom ['venəm]
Boss boss [bɒs]
Botschafter, Botschafterin ambassador [æm'bæsədə]
Boulevard boulevard ['bu:ləvɑ:d]
Boulevardzeitung tabloid (newspaper) ['tæblɔɪd]
Branche business ['bɪznɪs]; department [dɪ'pɑ:tmənt]
brand- brand [brænd]
Brand fire [faɪə]
brauchen to need [ni:d]; *(Zeit)* to take [teɪk]
braun brown [braʊn]
Breakdance tanzen to break-dance ['breɪkdɑ:nts]
brechen to break [breɪk]; to fold [fəʊld]
breit wide [waɪd]
Breitband(-) broadband ['brɔ:dbænd]
Bremse brake [breɪk]
bremsen to brake [breɪk]; to slow down [ˌsləʊ 'daʊn]
brennen to burn [bɜ:n]; *(Licht)* to be on [bi:‿'ɒn]
Brennmaterial fuel ['fju:əl]
fossiler **Brennstoff** fossil fuel ['fɒsl ˌfju:əl]
schwarzes **Brett** notice board ['nəʊtɪs bɔ:d]
Brief letter ['letə]
Briefmarke stamp [stæmp]
Brieftasche wallet ['wɒlɪt]
Briefumschlag envelope ['envələʊp]
Brille glasses *(pl)* ['glɑ:sɪz]
bringen to bring [brɪŋ]; to take [teɪk]
nach Hause bringen to take home [ˌteɪk 'həʊm]

britisch British ['brɪtɪʃ]
Brombeergestrüpp bramble ['bræmbl]
Brot bread [bred]
belegtes Brot sandwich ['sænwɪdʒ]
Brücke bridge [brɪdʒ]
Bruder brother ['brʌðə]
brummen to buzz [bʌz]
Brunnen fountain ['faʊntɪn]; well [wel]
brutal violent ['vaɪələnt]
Brutalität brutality [bru:'tæləti]
Buch book [bʊk]
Büchse tin [tɪn]
Buchstabe letter ['letə]
buchstabieren to spell [spel]
buddeln to dig [dɪg]
Bude stall [stɔ:l]
bügeln to iron [aɪən]
Bundes- federal ['fedrl]
Bundesstraße highway *(AE)* ['haɪweɪ]
bunt colored *(AE)* ['kʌləd]; coloured ['kʌləd]; colourful ['kʌləfl]
Burg castle ['kɑ:sl]
bürgen to guarantee [ˌgærn'ti:]
Bürger/Bürgerin citizen ['sɪtɪzn]
Bürger- civil ['sɪvl]
bürgerlich civil ['sɪvl]
Bürgerrechte civil rights *(pl)* [ˌsɪvl 'raɪts]
Bürgerrechtsbewegung Civil Rights Movement (CRM) [ˌsɪvl 'raɪts ˌmu:vmənt]
Büro office ['ɒfɪs]
bürsten to brush [brʌʃ]
Bus bus, buses *(pl)* [bʌs; 'bʌsɪz]
im Bus on the bus [ˌɒn ðə 'bʌs]
Busch bush [bʊʃ]
Bushaltestelle bus stop ['bʌs ˌstɒp]
Butter butter ['bʌtə]

C

Café café ['kæfeɪ]
Café latte latte ['lɑ:teɪ]
Cafeteria cafeteria [ˌkæfə'tɪəriə]
Call-Center call centre ['kɔ:l ˌsentə]
Camp camp [kæmp]
Camper/Camperin camper ['kæmpə]
Camping camping ['kæmpɪŋ]
Canyon canyon ['kænjən]
Cartoon cartoon [kɑ:'tu:n]
Casino casino [kə'si:nəʊ]
Catering catering ['keɪtrɪŋ]
CD CD [ˌsi:'di:]
CD-Player CD player [ˌsi:'di: ˌpleɪə]
Celsius Celsius (C) ['selsiəs]
Cent *(Währung)* cent [sent]
Champagner champagne [ʃæm'peɪn]
Chance chance [tʃɑ:nts]
Chaos chaos ['keɪɒs]
chaotisch chaotic [keɪ'ɒtɪk]
Charakter character ['kærəktə]; personality [ˌpɜ:sn'æləti]
Charaktereigenschaft characteristic [ˌkærəktə'rɪstɪk]
Charta charter ['tʃɑ:tə]
Charts charts *(pl)* [tʃɑ:ts]
Chatroom *(Internetforum, wo man sich online unterhalten kann)* chat room ['tʃæt rʊm]
Cheerleader *(Mädchen, das in einer Gruppe eine Sportmannschaft anfeuert)* cheerleader ['tʃɪəˌli:də]
Cheerleading cheerleading ['tʃɪəˌli:dɪŋ]
Chef/Chefin boss [bɒs]
chillen to chill out [tʃɪl‿'aʊt]
chinesisch Chinese [tʃaɪ'ni:z]
circa about [ə'baʊt]
clever streetwise ['stri:twaɪz]
CO_2-Bilanz carbon footprint [ˌkɑ:bn 'fʊtprɪnt]
Cocktail cocktail ['kɒkteɪl]
Code code [kəʊd]
Cola coke [kəʊk]
College college ['kɒlɪdʒ]
Comic comic ['kɒmɪk]
Comicheft comic ['kɒmɪk]
Commonwealth Commonwealth ['kɒmənwelθ]
Computer computer [ˌkəm'pju:tə]
cool cool [ku:l]
Cornflakes cornflakes ['kɔ:nfleɪks]
aus **Cornwall** Cornish ['kɔ:nɪʃ]
Couch couch [kaʊtʃ]; sofa ['səʊfə]
Countdown countdown ['kaʊntdaʊn]
Countrymusik country ['kʌntri]
Cousin/Cousine cousin ['kʌzn]
Cowboy cowboy ['kaʊbɔɪ]
Creme cream [kri:m]
Crew crew [kru:]
Curry *(Gewürz oder Gericht)* curry ['kʌri]

D

da there [ðeə]
da drüben over there [ˌəʊvə 'ðeə]
da ist there is [ðeər‿'ɪz]
da sind there are [ðeər‿'ɑ:]
da as [æz; əz]
dableiben to stay on [steɪ‿'ɒn]
Dach roof [ru:f]
dafür instead [ɪn'sted]
damals then [ðen]
Dame lady ['leɪdi]
Dämmung insulation [ˌɪnsjə'leɪʃn]
Dancehall *(Musikrichtung)* dancehall ['dɑ:ntshɔ:l]
daneben sein to be off [bi:‿'ɒf]
dänisch Danish ['deɪnɪʃ]
dank thanks to ['θæŋks tə]
danke thanks [θæŋks]; thank you ['θæŋk ju:]
danken to thank [θæŋk]
dann then [ðen]
darauf zu towards [tə'wɔ:dz]
Darlehen loan [ləʊn]
darstellen to pose [pəʊz]
sich darstellen to pose [pəʊz]
quer **darüber** across [ə'krɒs]
das the [ðə; ði]; that [ðæt]
Das nenne ich .... That's what I call .... [ˌðæts wɒt‿'aɪ ˌkɔ:l]
Datei mit Informationen (über) fact file (on) ['fækt faɪl]
Datum date [deɪt]
dauerhaft permanent ['pɜ:mnənt]
dauern to last [lɑ:st]; to take [teɪk]
Decke blanket ['blæŋkɪt]
Defekt flaw [flɔ:]
definitiv definitely ['defɪnətli]
dein/deine your [jɔ:]
Dein ... *(in Briefen)* Yours [jɔ:z]
Deine ... *(in Briefen)* Yours [jɔ:z]
Dekompression decompression [ˌdi:kəm'preʃn]
Dekoration decoration [ˌdek'reɪʃn]
Deli deli *(AE)* ['deli]
im **Delirium** delirious [dɪ'lɪriəs]
Demokratie democracy [dɪ'mɒkrəsi]
denken to think [θɪŋk]
dennoch though [ðəʊ]; still [stɪl]
deprimiert depressed [dɪ'prest]
der the [ðə; ði]
der/dem/den/die *(Relativpronomen)* who [hu:]
der/dem/den/die/das *(Relativpronomen)* which [wɪtʃ]
deren whose [hu:z]
derselbe/dieselbe/dasselbe the same [seɪm]
Desaster disaster [dɪ'zɑ:stə]
deshalb that's why ['ðæts ˌwaɪ]
Design design [dɪ'zaɪn]
Designer/Designerin designer [dɪ'zaɪnə]
dessen whose [hu:z]
Dessert dessert [dɪ'zɜ:t]
Detektiv/Detektivin detective [dɪ'tektɪv]
deuten (auf) to point (to) [pɔɪnt]
deutlich firmly ['fɜ:mli]
deutsch German ['dʒɜ:mən]
Deutscher/Deutsche German ['dʒɜ:mən]
Dezember December [dɪ'sembə]
Diabetes diabetes [ˌdaɪə'bi:ti:z]

Diabetiker/Diabetikerin diabetic [ˌdaɪə'betɪk]
Dialog dialogue ['daɪəlɒg]
Diamant diamond ['daɪəmənd]
Diät diet [daɪət]
eine Diät machen to go on a diet [ˌgəʊ‿ɒn‿ə 'daɪət]
dich you [ju:; jə]
dich (selbst) yourself [jɔ:'self]
Dichter/Dichterin poet ['pəʊɪt]
dick thick [θɪk]
die the [ðə; ði]
dienen to serve [sɜ:v]
Diener/Dienerin servant ['sɜ:vnt]
Dienst service ['sɜ:vɪs]
Dienstag Tuesday ['tju:zdeɪ]
dies this [ðɪs]
diese these [ði:z]
diese dort those [ðəʊz]
diese hier these [ði:z]
dieser/diese/dieses this [ðɪs]
an diesem Abend that evening [ˌdæt‿'i:vnɪŋ]
digital digital ['dɪdʒɪtl]
Dimension dimension [ˌdaɪ'menʃn]
Ding thing [θɪŋ]
Dingo *(austral. Wildhund)* dingo ['dɪŋgəʊ]
Dinosaurier dinosaur ['daɪnəsɔ:]
Diplom diploma [dɪ'pləʊmə]
dir you [ju:; jə]
direkt direct [dɪ'rekt]; right [raɪt]; straight [streɪt]
Direktor/Direktorin director [dɪ'rektə]
Disko disco ['dɪskəʊ]
Diskriminierung discrimination [dɪˌskrɪmɪ'neɪʃn]
Diskussion discussion [dɪ'skʌʃn]
diskutieren to discuss [dɪ'skʌs]
Distanz distance ['dɪstnts]
DJ DJ [ˌdi:'dʒeɪ]
Dokument paper ['peɪpə]
Dokumentarfilm documentary [ˌdɒkjə'mentri]
dokumentiert on record [ɒn 'rekɔ:d]
Dokusoap docu soap ['dɒkju ˌsəʊp]
Dollar *(Währung)* dollar ['dɒlə]
Dom cathedral [kə'θi:drl]
Donnerstag Thursday ['θɜ:zdeɪ]
Doppelgänger double ['dʌbl]
Doppelklick doubleclick ['dʌblklɪk]
das **Doppelte** double ['dʌbl]
Dorf village ['vɪlɪdʒ]
Dorn thorn [θɔ:n]
dort there [ðeə]
Dose can [kæn]; tin [tɪn]
Down Under *(Spitzname für Australien)* Down Under [ˌdaʊn‿'ʌndə]

Drache dragon ['drægn]
Drama drama ['drɑ:mə]
dramatisch dramatic [drə'mætɪk]
drapieren to drape [dreɪp]
draußen outdoors [ˌaʊt'dɔ:z]; outside [aʊt'saɪd]
Drehbuch script [skrɪpt]
drehen to turn [tɜ:n]
sich drehen to pivot ['pɪvət]
dreidimensional 3D [θri:'di:]
drin inside [ɪn'saɪd]
dringend urgent ['ɜ:dʒnt]
Drittel third [θɜ:d]
dritter/dritte/drittes third [θɜ:d]
Droge drug [drʌg]
Drogenhandel drug trafficking [ˌdrʌg 'træfɪkɪŋ]
dröhnen to roar [rɔ:]
Drohung threat [θret]
Druck pressure ['preʃə]
drücken to press [pres]; to push [pʊʃ]
drucken to print [prɪnt]
Druckverminderung decompression [ˌdi:kəm'preʃn]
du you [ju:; jə]
du (selbst) yourself [jɔ:'self]
Du bist dran. It's your turn. [ɪts jɔ: 'tɜ:n]
Duft odour ['əʊdə]
dumm silly ['sɪli]; stupid ['stju:pɪd]; thick [θɪk]
Dummkopf idiot ['ɪdɪət]; silly ['sɪli]
dunkel dark [dɑ:k]; *(Farbe)* deep [di:p]
Dunkelheit dark [dɑ:k]
dünn thin [θɪn]
durch through [θru:]
quer durch across [ə'krɒs]
durchdrehen to get into such a state [get‿ɪntə 'sʌtʃ‿ə 'steɪt]; to go bananas [ˌgəʊ bə'nɑ:nəz]
Durcheinander chaos ['keɪɒs]; mess [mes]
durcheinanderbringen to upset [ʌp'set]
etw. durcheinanderbringen to mess sth up [ˌmes‿'ʌp]
durchführen to execute ['eksɪkju:t]
Durchführung execution [ˌeksɪ'kju:ʃn]
durchfüttern to feed [fi:d]
durchgehend non-stop [ˌnɒn'stɒp]; throughout [θru'aʊt]
im **Durchmesser** across [ə'krɒs]
Durchsage announcement [ə'naʊntsmənt]
Durchschnitt average ['ævrɪdʒ]
durchschnittlich average ['ævrɪdʒ]
Durchschnitts- average ['ævrɪdʒ]
durchstehen to survive [sə'vaɪv]

durchstöbern to browse [braʊz]
durchsuchen to browse [braʊz]
nach Details durchsuchen to scan [skæn]
dürfen can [kæn]; to be able to (do sth) [bi:‿'eɪbl]; to be allowed to (do sth) [bi:‿ə'laʊd]
nicht dürfen mustn't ['mʌsnt]
Dusche shower ['ʃaʊə]
DVD DVD [di:vi:'di:]
DVD-Player DVD player [ˌdi:vi:'di: 'pleɪə]

E

Ebene level ['levl]
echt pukka *(slang)* ['pʌkə]; real [rɪəl]
Ecke corner ['kɔ:nə]
Ecstasy ecstasy ['ekstəsi]
Effekt effect [ɪ'fekt]
egal welche whatever [wɒt'evə]
Es ist mir egal. I don't care. [ˌaɪ dəʊnt 'keə]; I don't mind. [maɪnd]
Ehe marriage ['mærɪdʒ]
Ehefrau wife, wives *(pl)* [waɪf; waɪvz]
ehemaliger/ehemalige/ehemaliges former ['fɔ:mə]
Ehemann husband ['hʌzbənd]
Eheschließung marriage ['mærɪdʒ]
ehrgeizig ambitious [æm'bɪʃəs]
ehrlich honest ['ɒnɪst]; truthful ['tru:θfl]
Ei egg [eg]
eifersüchtig (auf) jealous (of) ['dʒeləs]
eigener/eigene/eigenes own [əʊn]
eigentlich actually ['æktʃuəli]
Eile speed [spi:d]
eilen to rush [rʌʃ]
es **eilig haben** to be in a hurry [bi:‿ɪn‿ə 'hʌri]
Eimer bucket ['bʌkɪt]
ein/eine a, an [ə; ən]
ein paar a couple of [ə 'kʌpl‿əv]; a few [ə 'fju:]
einander each other [ˌi:tʃ‿'ʌðə]
Einband cover ['kʌvə]
einbeziehen to involve [ɪn'vɒlv]
Einbrecher/Einbrecherin burglar ['bɜ:glə]
eindeutig firmly ['fɜ:mli]
Eindruck impression [ɪm'preʃn]
Einerseits . . . , andererseits . . . On the one hand . . . , (but) on the other hand . . . [ɒn ðə‿'wʌn ˌhænd . . . ɒn ði‿'ʌðə ˌhænd . . .]
einfach basic ['beɪsɪk]; easy ['i:zi]; ordinary ['ɔ:dnri]; simple ['sɪmpl]
Einfall idea [aɪ'dɪə]

German – English

Einfluss impact ['ɪmpækt]; influence ['ɪnfluənts]
einflussreich important [ɪm'pɔ:tnt]
einfordern to claim [kleɪm]
einführen to launch [lɔ:nʃ]
Einführung introduction [ˌɪntrə'dʌkʃn]; launch [lɔ:nʃ]
Eingang entrance ['entrənts]
eingängig catchy ['kætʃi]
eingeboren Aboriginal [ˌæbə'rɪdʒnl]; indigenous [ɪn'dɪdʒɪnəs]; native ['neɪtɪv]
einheimisch Aboriginal [ˌæbə'rɪdʒnl]; indigenous [ɪn'dɪdʒɪnəs]; native ['neɪtɪv]
Einheit session ['seʃn]
einige a couple of [ə 'kʌpl‿əv]; a few [ə 'fju:]; any ['enɪ]; some [sʌm]
Einkauf shopping ['ʃɒpɪŋ]
Einkaufen shopping ['ʃɒpɪŋ]
Einkaufspassage (shopping) mall [mɔ:l]
Einkaufswagen trolley ['trɒli]
Einkaufszentrum (shopping) mall [mɔ:l]
Einkommen income ['ɪnkʌm]
einladen to invite [ɪn'vaɪt]
Einladung invitation [ˌɪnvɪ'teɪʃn]
einlaufen to shrink [ʃrɪŋk]
Einleitung introduction [ˌɪntrə'dʌkʃn]
einmal once [wʌnts]
einmalig unique [ju:'ni:k]
Einreisebewilligung visa, visas *(pl)* ['vi:zə]
einreißen to break down [ˌbreɪk 'daʊn]
einrichten to set up [set‿'ʌp]
Einrichtung facility [fə'sɪləti]
einrollen to curl [kɜ:l]
einsam lonely ['ləʊnli]
einschalten to switch on [ˌswɪtʃ‿'ɒn]; to turn on [ˌtɜ:n‿'ɒn]
einschätzen to assess [ə'ses]
Einschätzung assessment [ə'sesmənt]
einschicken to send in [send‿'ɪn]
einschieben to put in [pʊt‿'ɪn]
einschlafen to fall asleep [ˌfɔ:l‿ə'sli:p]
einschließlich including [ɪn'klu:dɪŋ]
Einschränkung restriction [rɪ'strɪkʃn]
einsetzen to appoint [ə'pɔɪnt]; to fill in [fɪl‿'ɪn]; to put in [pʊt‿'ɪn]
sich für etw./jmdn. einsetzen to campaign [kæm'peɪn]
einsprachig unilingual [ˌju:nɪ'lɪŋgwəl]
Einspruch veto ['vi:təʊ]
einst once [wʌnts]
einsteigen *(in Zug, Bus ...)* to get on [get‿'ɒn]; *(Bus)* to get onto [get‿'ɒntə]; *(Auto)* to get into [get‿'ɪntə]
einstellen to set [set]
Einstellung shot [ʃɒt]
Einstellung (gegenüber) attitude (to/towards) ['ætɪtju:d]
eintragen to register ['redʒɪstə]
sich eintragen to register ['redʒɪstə]
eintreten to enter ['entə]
Eintritt admission [əd'mɪʃn]; entrance ['entrənts]
Eintritt verboten! Keep out! [ki:p‿'aʊt]
Eintrittskarte ticket ['tɪkɪt]
Einwanderer/Einwanderin immigrant ['ɪmɪgrənt]
Einwanderung immigration [ˌɪmɪ'greɪʃn]
Einwilligung consent [kən'sent]
Einzelhändler/Einzelhändlerin retailer ['ri:teɪlə]
Einzelkind only child ['əʊnli ˌtʃaɪld]
einzeln single ['sɪŋgl]
einzig unique [ju:'ni:k]
einzigartig unique [ju:'ni:k]
einziger/einzige/einziges only ['əʊnli]
Eis ice [aɪs]; ice-cream [aɪs'kri:m]
Eisbahn ice rink ['aɪs rɪŋk]
Eiscreme ice-cream [aɪs'kri:m]
Eishockey ice hockey ['aɪs ˌhɒki]
ekelhaft yukky ['jʌki]
Elefant elephant ['elɪfənt]
elektrisch electric [ɪ'lektrɪk]; electrical [ɪ'lektrɪkl]
Elektrizität electricity [ˌelɪk'trɪsəti]
Elektronik electronics *(pl)* [ˌelek'trɒnɪks]
Element panel ['pænl]
Elfmeter *(Fußball)* penalty ['penlti]
Ellbogen elbow ['elbəʊ]
Elle *(Längenmaß: 0,914 m)* yard [jɑ:d]
elterlich parental [pə'rentl]
Eltern parents *(pl)* ['peərənts]
Elternteil parent ['peərnt]
E-Mail e-mail ['i:meɪl]
E-Mail schreiben to e-mail ['i:meɪl]
per E-Mail schicken to e-mail ['i:meɪl]; to mail [meɪl]
emigrieren to emigrate ['emɪgreɪt]
Emission emission [ɪ'mɪʃn]
Empfang reception [rɪ'sepʃn]
empfangen to receive [rɪ'si:v]
Empfangschef/Empfangschefin receptionist [rɪ'sepʃnɪst]
empfindlich *(Magen)* queasy ['kwi:si]
empörend outrageous [aʊt'reɪdʒəs]
Ende end [end]
enden to end [end]; to end up [ˌend‿'ʌp]
endlich eventually [ɪ'ventʃuəli]; finally ['faɪnli]
Energie energy ['enədʒi]
eng narrow ['nærəʊ]; tight [taɪt]
Engländer Englishman, Englishmen *(pl)* ['ɪŋglɪʃmən, 'ɪŋglɪʃmen]
Engländer/Engländerinnen English ['ɪŋglɪʃ]
englisch English ['ɪŋglɪʃ]
enorm enormous [ɪ'nɔ:məs]
entdecken to discover [dɪ'skʌvə]
entfachen to spark [spɑ:k]
entfernen to remove [rɪ'mu:v]
Entfernung distance ['dɪstnts]
entführen to kidnap ['kɪdnæp]
Entführer/Entführerin kidnapper ['kɪdnæpə]
Entführung kidnap(ping) ['kɪdnæp(ɪŋ)]
entgegengesetzt opposite ['ɒpəzɪt]
entgegnen to reply [rɪ'plaɪ]
Entgegnung reply [rɪ'plaɪ]
entkommen to escape (from) [ɪ'skeɪp]; to get out [get‿'aʊt]
entlang along [ə'lɒŋ]
entlanggehen to go down [gəʊ 'daʊn]
entlasten to unburden [ʌn'bɜ:dn]
Entlohnung payment ['peɪmənt]
entschärfen to defuse [ˌdi:'fju:z]
entscheiden to decide [dɪ'saɪd]
entscheidend essential [ɪ'sentʃl]
Entscheidung decision [dɪ'sɪʒn]
entschließen to determine [dɪ'tɜ:mɪn]
Entschuldigung excuse [ɪk'skju:s]
Entschuldigung! Excuse me! [ɪk'skju:z mi:]
sich **entspannen** to chill out [tʃɪl‿'aʊt]; to relax [rɪ'læks]; to rest [rest]
entstehen to form [fɔ:m]
jmdn. **enttäuschen** to let sb down [let 'daʊn]
enttäuschend disappointing [ˌdɪsə'pɔɪntɪŋ]
enttäuscht disappointed [ˌdɪsə'pɔɪntɪd]
entweder ... oder ... either ... or ... ['aɪðə; 'i:ðə ... ɔ:]
entwerfen to design [dɪ'zaɪn]
entwickeln to develop [dɪ'veləp]
sich entwickeln to develop [dɪ'veləp]
Entwicklung development [dɪ'veləpmənt]; progress ['prəʊgres]
Entzücken glee [gli:]
er he [hi:]
er (selbst) himself [hɪm'self]
erbärmlich pathetic [pə'θetɪk]
Erbe/Erbin inheritor [ɪn'herɪtə]
Erbse pea [pi:]
Erd- global ['gləʊbl]
Erdbeere strawberry ['strɔ:bri]
Erde earth [ɜ:θ]; world [wɜ:ld]
Erderwärmung (global) warming [ˌgləʊbl 'wɔ:mɪŋ]
Erdgas natural gas [ˌnætʃrl 'gæs]
Erdkunde Geography [dʒi'ɒgrəfi]

Erdteil continent ['kɒntɪnənt]
erdulden to suffer ['sʌfə]
Ereignis event [ɪ'vent]
erfahren to experience [ɪk'spɪəriənts]; to learn [lɜ:n]
Erfahrung experience [ɪk'spɪəriənts]
Erfassung registration [ˌredʒɪ'streɪʃn]
erfinden to invent [ɪn'vent]; to make up [meɪk‿'ʌp]
Erfindung fiction ['fɪkʃn]; invention [ɪn'ventʃn]
Erfolg success [sək'ses]
erfolgreich successful [sək'sesfl]
Erfordernis need [ni:d]
erforschen to explore [ɪk'splɔ:]
sich **erfreuen** to enjoy [ɪn'dʒɔɪ]
erfrischend refreshing [rɪ'freʃɪŋ]
erfüllen to fulfill *(AE)* [fʊl'fɪl]
Ergebnis result [rɪ'zʌlt]
erhalten to receive [rɪ'si:v]
erhitzen to heat [hi:t]
Erholung recreation [ˌri:kri'eɪʃn]
sich **erinnern (an)** to remember [rɪ'membə]
Erinnerung memory ['memri]
in Erinnerungen schwelgen to reminisce [ˌremɪ'nɪs]
erkennen to identify [aɪ'dentɪfaɪ]; to realise ['rɪəlaɪz]; to recognize ['rekəgnaɪz]
erklären to declare [dɪ'kleə]; to explain [ɪk'spleɪn]
Erkrankung disease [dɪ'zi:z]
erkunden to explore [ɪk'splɔ:]
erlangen to gain [geɪn]
erlauben to allow [ə'laʊ]
Erlaubnis permission [pə'mɪʃn]
erläutern to explain [ɪk'spleɪn]
erleben to experience [ɪk'spɪəriənts]
wieder erleben to relive [ˌri:'lɪv]
Erlebnis experience [ɪk'spɪəriənts]
erledigen to complete [kəm'pli:t]; to finish ['fɪnɪʃ]
erlöschen to go out [gəʊ‿'aʊt]
Ermittler/Ermittlerin investigator [ɪn'vestɪgeɪtə]
ermorden to murder ['mɜ:də]
Ermordung murder ['mɜ:də]
ermutigen to encourage [ɪn'kʌrɪdʒ]
ernähren to feed [fi:d]
Ernährung nutrition [nju:'trɪʃn]
Ernährungslehre nutrition [nju:'trɪʃn]
ernennen to appoint [ə'pɔɪnt]
ernst serious ['sɪəriəs]
ernsthaft serious ['sɪəriəs]
Ernte crop [krɒp]
eröffnen to start up [stɑ:t‿'ʌp]
erreichen to catch [kætʃ]; to reach [ri:tʃ]
erschaffen to create [kri'eɪt]
erscheinen to appear [ə'pɪə]; to seem [si:m]
erschießen to shoot [ʃu:t]
erschrecken to scare ['skeə]; to upset [ʌp'set]
ersetzen to replace [rɪ'pleɪs]; to substitute ['sʌbstɪtju:t]
erst only ['əʊnli]
erstaunt amazed [ə'meɪzd]; surprised [sə'praɪzd]
erster/erste/erstes first [fɜ:st]
ersticken to choke [tʃəʊk]
erwachsen grown up [ˌgrəʊn‿'ʌp]
Erwachsener/Erwachsene adult ['ædʌlt]
erwähnen to mention ['menʃn]
erwähnt werden to come up [kʌm‿'ʌp]
erwärmen to heat [hi:t]
Erwärmung (global) warming [ˌgləʊbl 'wɔ:mɪŋ]
erwarten to expect [ɪk'spekt]
erweitern to widen ['waɪdn]
erwerben to gain [geɪn]
erwidern to reply [rɪ'plaɪ]
Erwiderung reply [rɪ'plaɪ]
erzählen to tell [tel]
Erzählung story ['stɔ:ri]
Erzeuger/Erzeugerin producer [prə'dju:sə]
Erziehung education [edʒʊ'keɪʃn]
erzwingen to force [fɔ:s]
es it [ɪt]
es gibt there are [ðeər‿'ɑ:]; there is [ðeər‿'ɪz]
Es lautete .... It said .... [ɪt 'sed]
es sei denn, (dass) ... unless [ən'les]
essen to eat [i:t]
Essen eating ['i:tɪŋ]; food [fu:d]
Essen zum Mitnehmen takeaway ['teɪkəweɪ]
essenziell essential [ɪ'sentʃl]
Essig vinegar ['vɪnɪgə]
Esszimmer dining room ['daɪnɪŋ rʊm]
et cetera etc. [ɪt'setrə]
ethisch ethical ['eθɪkl]
Etikett label ['leɪbl]
etikettieren to label ['leɪbl]
Etikettierung labelling ['leɪblɪŋ]
etliche many ['meni]
etwa about [ə'baʊt]; around [ə'raʊnd]
etwas any ['enɪ]; anything ['eniθɪŋ]; some [sʌm]; something ['sʌmθɪŋ]
euch you [ju:; jə]
euch (selbst) yourselves [jɔ:'selvz]
euer/eure your [jɔ:]
Euer ... *(in Briefen)* Yours [jɔ:z]
Eure ... *(in Briefen)* Yours [jɔ:z]
Eukalyptus eucalyptus [ˌju:k'lɪptəs]
Euro *(Währung)* euro ['jʊərəʊ]
europäisch European [ˌjʊərə'pi:ən]
evakuieren to fly out [flaɪ‿'aʊt]
Examen exam [ɪg'zæm]
exekutieren to execute ['eksɪkju:t]
Exekution execution [ˌeksɪ'kju:ʃn]
existieren to exist [ɪg'zɪst]
existierend existing [ɪg'zɪstɪŋ]
exotisch exotic [ɪg'zɒtɪk]
Experiment experiment [ɪk'sperɪmənt]
Experte/Expertin expert ['ekspɜ:t]
Export export ['ekspɔ:t]
exportieren to export [ɪk'spɔ:t]
Extrakt extract ['ekstrækt]
extrem extremely [ɪk'stri:mli]
exzellent excellent ['ekslnt]

F

fabelhaft fabulous ['fæbjələs]
Fabrik factory ['fæktri]
Fach- specialist ['speʃlɪst]
fachlich technical ['teknɪkl]
Fackel torch, torches *(pl)* [tɔ:tʃ; 'tɔ:tʃɪz]
Faden thread [θred]; yarn [jɑ:n]
fähig sein (zu) to be able to (do sth) [bi:‿'eɪbl]
Fahne flag [flæg]
Fähre ferry ['feri]
fahren to drive [draɪv]; to ride [raɪd]; *(Schiff)* to sail [seɪl]
rückwärts fahren to reverse [rɪ'vɜ:s]
Fahrenheit Fahrenheit (F) ['færnhaɪt]
Fahrer/Fahrerin driver ['draɪvə]
Fahrplan timetable ['taɪmteɪbl]
Fahrrad bike [baɪk]
mit dem Fahrrad by bike [baɪ 'baɪk]
Fahrschein ticket ['tɪkɪt]
Fahrspur lane [leɪn]
Fahrt journey ['dʒɜ:ni]; ride [raɪd]; tour [tʊə]
Fahrzeug vehicle ['vɪəkl]
Fahrzeug- automotive [ˌɔ:tə'məʊtɪv]
fair fair [feə]
fairer Handel fair trade [ˌfeə 'treɪd]
Fakt fact [fækt]
in der **Falle sitzen** to be trapped [bi: 'træpt]
fallen to drop [drɒp]; to fall [fɔ:l]
fallen lassen to drop [drɒp]
falls if [ɪf]
falsch false [fɔ:ls]; wrong [rɒŋ]
falsch machen to get ... wrong [get ... 'rɒŋ]
falten to fold [fəʊld]
Falter moth [mɒθ]
Familie family ['fæmli]

Fan fan [fæn]
fangen to catch [kætʃ]
Fänger/Fängerin catcher ['kætʃə]
fantastisch fabulous ['fæbjələs]; fantastic [fæn'tæstɪk]
Farbe colour ['kʌlə]; paint [peɪnt]
färben to dye [daɪ]
farbig colored *(AE)* ['kʌləd]; coloured ['kʌləd]; colourful ['kʌləfl]
Farbiger/Farbige colored *(AE)* ['kʌləd]
Farm farm [fɑ:m]
Fassung version ['vɜ:ʃn]
fast almost ['ɔ:lməʊst]; nearly ['nɪəli]
Fastfood-Restaurant burger bar ['bɜ:gə ˌbɑ:]
faszinierend fascinating ['fæsɪneɪtɪŋ]
fauchen to spit [spɪt]
Faust fist [fɪst]
Februar February ['februəri]
Federball badminton ['bædmɪntən]
fehlen to be missing [bi: 'mɪsɪŋ]; to miss [mɪs]
Fehlen (von) lack (of) [læk]
Fehler flaw [flɔ:]; mistake [mɪ'steɪk]
fehlschlagen to fail [feɪl]
Feier party ['pɑ:ti]
eine **Party feiern** to have a party [ˌhæv‿ə 'pɑ:ti]
Feiertag holiday ['hɒlədeɪ]
fein fine [faɪn]
Feind/Feindin enemy ['enəmi]
Feld field [fi:ld]
Feldfrucht crop [krɒp]
Fell skin [skɪn]
Felsen rock [rɒk]
Fenster window ['wɪndəʊ]
Ferien holiday(s) ['hɒlədeɪ(z)]; vacation *(AE)* [və'keɪʃn]
Ferienhaus cottage ['kɒtɪdʒ]
fern remote [rɪ'məʊt]
Fernbedienung remote control [rɪˌməʊt kən'trəʊl]
sich **fernhalten** to keep away [ˌki:p‿ə'weɪ]
Fernlaster road train ['rəʊd ˌtreɪn]
Fernsehen television ['telɪvɪʒn]; TV [ˌti:'vi:]
Fernseher television ['telɪvɪʒn]; TV [ˌti:'vi:]
Fernsehsender station ['steɪʃn]
Fernsteuerung remote control [rɪˌməʊt kən'trəʊl]
fertig ready ['redi]
fertigen to manufacture [ˌmænjə'fæktʃə]
Fertigkeit skill [skɪl]
fertigstellen to complete [kəm'pli:t]
Fertigung manufacturing [ˌmænjə'fæktʃrɪŋ]
fesseln to tie [taɪ]
fest solid ['sɒlɪd]; tight [taɪt]
Fest festival ['festɪvl]
festhalten to hold [həʊld]
Festival festival ['festɪvl]
festnehmen to arrest [ə'rest]
Festung fortress ['fɔ:trəs]
fett fat [fæt]
Fett fat [fæt]
feucht damp [dæmp]
Feuer fire [faɪə]
feuern to fire [faɪə]
Feuerprobe ordeal [ɔ:'di:l]
Feuerstelle fire [faɪə]
Feuerwehr fire brigade ['faɪə brɪˌgeɪd]
Feuerwerk fireworks *(pl)* ['faɪəwɜ:ks]
Feuerwerkskörper firework ['faɪəwɜ:k]
Figur character ['kærəktə]; figure ['fɪgə]
Fiktion fiction ['fɪkʃn]
Film film [fɪlm]; movie *(AE)* ['mu:vi]; picture ['pɪktʃə]
filmen to film [fɪlm]
Filter filter ['fɪltə]
Finanz- finance ['faɪnænts]
Finanzamt taxman *(infml)* ['tæksmæn]
Finanzen finance ['faɪnænts]
finanziell financial [faɪ'næntʃl]
Finanzwesen finance ['faɪnænts]
finden to find [faɪnd]
Finger finger ['fɪŋgə]
Fingernagel fingernail ['fɪŋgəneɪl]
Firma company ['kʌmpəni]; firm [fɜ:m]
Firmenzeichen logo ['ləʊgəʊ]
Fisch fish, fish *(pl)* [fɪʃ]
fischen to fish [fɪʃ]
mit dem Netz fischen to trawl [trɔ:l]
Fischen fishing ['fɪʃɪŋ]
Fischer fisherman, fishermen *(pl)* ['fɪʃəmən; 'fɪʃəmen]
Fischschwarm school [sku:l]
fit fit [fɪt]
flach flat [flæt]
Fläche area ['eəriə]; surface ['sɜ:fɪs]
flackern to flare [fleə]; to flicker ['flɪkə]
Flagge flag [flæg]
Flamme flame [fleɪm]
Flasche bottle ['bɒtl]
in Flaschen abgefüllt bottled ['bɒtld]
Fleck mark [mɑ:k]; patch [pætʃ]
Fleisch meat [mi:t]
flexibel flexible ['fleksɪbl]
Flicken patch [pætʃ]
fliegen to fly [flaɪ]
flimmern to flicker ['flɪkə]
Flosse fin [fɪn]
Flotte *(Fahrzeug)* fleet [fli:t]
flüchten (vor) to escape (from) [ɪ'skeɪp]
Flug flight [flaɪt]
Flugblatt leaflet ['li:flət]
Flügel wing [wɪŋ]
Flughafen airport ['eəpɔ:t]
Fluglotse/Fluglotsin air traffic controller [ˌeə træfɪk kən'trəʊlə]
Flugzeug plane [pleɪn]
Flur corridor ['kɒrɪdɔ:]; hall [hɔ:l]
Fluss river ['rɪvə]
flüssig liquid ['lɪkwɪd]
Flüssigkeit liquid ['lɪkwɪd]
flüstern to whisper ['wɪspə]
flutartige Überschwemmung flash flood ['flæʃ ˌflʌd]
föderal federal ['fedrl]
föderalistisch federal ['fedrl]
folgen to follow ['fɒləʊ]
folgend/folgender/folgende/folgendes following ['fɒləʊɪŋ]
Fön hairdryer ['heəˌdraɪə]
Fonds fund [fʌnd]
Fontäne fountain ['faʊntɪn]
Football American football [əˌmerɪkən 'fʊtbɔ:l]
Förderer/Förderin sponsor ['spɒntsə]
fordern to claim [kleɪm]; to demand [dɪ'mɑ:nd]
Form form [fɔ:m]; shape [ʃeɪp]
formal formal ['fɔ:ml]
formell formal ['fɔ:ml]
formen to form [fɔ:m]
förmlich formal ['fɔ:ml]
Formular form [fɔ:m]
Forscher/Forscherin explorer [ɪk'splɔ:rə]
Forschung research [rɪ'sɜ:tʃ]
Forschungsreisender/Forschungsreisende explorer [ɪk'splɔ:rə]
fortfahren to continue [kən'tɪnju:]
fortgeschritten advanced [əd'vɑ:nst]
fortschaffen to take off [ˌteɪk‿'ɒf]
Fortschritt progress ['prəʊgres]
Forum forum ['fɔ:rəm]
fossil fossil ['fɒsl]
fossiler Brennstoff fossil fuel ['fɒsl ˌfju:əl]
Fossil fossil ['fɒsl]
Foto photo ['fəʊtəʊ]; shot [ʃɒt]
Fotos machen to take pictures [teɪk 'pɪktʃəz]
Fotoapparat camera ['kæmrə]
Fotograf/Fotografin photographer [fə'tɒgrəfə]
Fotografie photo ['fəʊtəʊ]; photography [fə'tɒgrəfi]
fotografieren to take pictures [teɪk 'pɪktʃəz]
Foul foul [faʊl]

Frage matter ['mætə]; question ['kwestʃn]
fragen to ask [ɑ:sk]
fragen nach to ask (for) ['ɑ:sk fə]
sich fragen to wonder ['wʌndə]
französisch French [frentʃ]
Frau lady ['leɪdi]; woman, women *(pl)* ['wʊmən; 'wɪmɪn]
Frau *(Anrede)* Miss [mɪs]; Mrs ['mɪsɪz]
frech cheeky ['tʃi:ki]
frei free [fri:]
freier Mann freeman, freemen *(pl)* ['fri:mən, fri:men]
Freiheit freedom ['fri:dəm]
freilassen to set free [set‿'fri:]
freisetzen to set free [set‿'fri:]
Freitag Friday [fraɪdeɪ]
freiwillig volunteer [ˌvɒlən'tɪə]
sich freiwillig melden to volunteer [ˌvɒlən'tɪə]
Freiwilliger/Freiwillige volunteer [ˌvɒlən'tɪə]
Freizeit leisure ['leʒə]; time off [taɪm‿'ɒf]
Freizeit- leisure ['leʒə]
Freizeitaktivitäten recreation [ˌri:kri'eɪʃn]
Freizeitpark theme park ['θi:m ˌpɑ:k]
fremd alien ['eɪliən]; foreign ['fɒrɪn]
Fremdenverkehr tourism ['tʊərɪzm]
Fremder/Fremde alien ['eɪliən]; foreigner ['fɒrɪnə]; stranger ['streɪndʒə]
fressen to eat [i:t]
sich **freuen auf** to look forward to (+ -ing) [lʊk 'fɔ:wəd]
Freund/Freundin friend [frend]
Freund *(in einer Paarbeziehung)* boyfriend ['bɔɪfrend]
Freundin *(in einer Paarbeziehung)* girlfriend ['gɜ:lfrend]
freundlich friendly ['frendli]; kind [kaɪnd]
Freundschaft schließen (mit) to make friends (with) [ˌmeɪk 'frendz]
Friede peace [pi:s]
frieren to be cold [bi: 'kəʊld]
frisch fresh [freʃ]
Frischkäse cream cheese [ˌkri:m 'tʃi:z]
Friseur/Friseurin hairdresser ['heəˌdresə]
Frisur style [staɪl]
froh glad [glæd]; happy ['hæpi]
Frucht fruit [fru:t]
fruchtbar prolific [prə'lɪfɪk]
früh early ['ɜ:li]
früherer/frühere/früheres former ['fɔ:mə]
Frühling spring [sprɪŋ]
Frühstück breakfast ['brekfəst]
frustriert frustrated [frʌs'treɪtɪd]
fühlen to feel [fi:l]; to sense [sens]
sich fühlen to feel [fi:l]
führen to lead [li:d]
Führer/Führerin leader ['li:də]
Führerschein driver's license *(AE)* ['draɪvəz ˌlaɪsnts]; driving licence *(BE)* ['draɪvɪŋ ˌlaɪsnts]
Führung guidance ['gaɪdənts]
füllen to fill [fɪl]
Füller pen [pen]
Fundus fund [fʌnd]
Fünftel fifth [fɪfθ]
Funk(-) radio ['reɪdiəʊ]
Funk *(Musikrichtung)* funk [fʌŋk]
Funke spark [spɑ:k]
Funken spark [spɑ:k]
Funksprechgerät two-way radio [ˌtu:weɪ 'reɪdiəʊ]
funktionieren to work [wɜ:k]
für for [fɔ:; fə]
Für und Wider pros and cons [ˌprəʊz‿ənd 'kɒnz]
Furcht fear [fɪə]
furchtbar awful ['ɔ:fl]; frightening ['fraɪtnɪŋ]; horrible ['hɒrəbl]; terrible ['terəbl]
(sich) **fürchten (vor)** to be afraid (of) [bi‿ə'freɪd‿əv]
fürsorglich thoughtful ['θɔ:tfl]
Fusion fusion ['fju:ʒn]
Fuß foot, feet *(pl)* [fʊt; fi:t]; *(Längenmaß: 30,48 cm)* foot, feet *(pl)* [fʊt; fi:t]
zu Fuß on foot [ɒn 'fʊt]
Fußabdruck footprint ['fʊtprɪnt]
Fußball football ['fʊtbɔ:l]; soccer *(AE)* ['sɒkə]
Fußboden floor [flɔ:]
Fußmarsch march [mɑ:tʃ]
füttern to feed [fi:d]

G

Gabel fork [fɔ:k]
gähnen to yawn [jɔ:n]
gälisch Gaelic ['geɪlɪk]
Gang corridor ['kɒrɪdɔ:]; *(Menü)* course [kɔ:s]; gang [gæŋ]
etw. in Gang setzen to get sth going [ˌget 'gəʊɪŋ]
Gangster/Gangsterin gangster ['gæŋkstə]; thug [θʌg]
ganz all [ɔ:l]; full (of) [fʊl]; whole [həʊl]; completely [kəm'pli:tli]
ganz schön pretty ['prɪti]
im Ganzen in all [ɪn‿'ɔ:l]
garantieren to guarantee [ˌgærn'ti:]
Garderobe wardrobe ['wɔ:drəʊb]
Garn thread [θred]; yarn [jɑ:n]
Garten garden ['gɑ:dn]
Gartenbau horticulture ['hɔ:tɪkʌltʃə]
Gartengestaltung gardening ['gɑ:dnɪŋ]
Gärtner/Gärtnerin gardener ['gɑ:dnə]
Gärtnern gardening ['gɑ:dnɪŋ]
Gas gas [gæs]
Gas geben to step on the gas [ˌstep‿ɒn ðə 'gæs]
Gasse lane [leɪn]
Gast guest [gest]
Gastgeber host [həʊst]
Gastronomie catering ['keɪtrɪŋ]
Gate gate [geɪt]
Gebäude building ['bɪldɪŋ]
geben to hand [hænd]; to give [gɪv]
Gebet prayer [preə]
Gebiet area ['eəriə]; territory ['terɪtri]
Gebiss false teeth [fɔ:ls 'ti:θ]
Gebrauch use [ju:s]
gebräuchlich common ['kɒmən]
gebrochen broken ['brəʊkn]
Gebühr tax [tæks]
gebunden tied [taɪd]
Geburt birth [bɜ:θ]
von Geburt an natural-born [ˌnætʃrl'bɔ:n]
gebürtig native ['neɪtɪv]; natural-born [ˌnætʃrl'bɔ:n]
Geburtstag birthday ['bɜ:θdeɪ]
Gedächtnis memory ['memri]
Gedanke thought [θɔ:t]
sich Gedanken machen to wonder ['wʌndə]
Gedicht poem ['pəʊɪm]
geeignet suitable ['su:təbl]
geerdet grounded ['graʊndɪd]
Gefahr danger ['deɪndʒə]
gefährlich dangerous ['deɪndʒrəs]
Gefangener/Gefangene convict ['kɒnvɪkt]; prisoner ['prɪznə]
Gefängnis jail [dʒeɪl]; prison ['prɪzn]
gefeiert acclaimed [ə'kleɪmd]
gefestigt grounded ['graʊndɪd]
gefroren frozen ['frəʊzn]
Gefühl feeling ['fi:lɪŋ]; sense [sens]
gegen- anti ['æntɪ]
gegen against [ə'genst]
Gegensatz contrast ['kɒntrɑ:st]
im Gegensatz zu in contrast to [ɪn 'kɒntrɑ:st tə]; unlike [ʌn'laɪk]
sich **gegenseitig** each other [ˌi:tʃ‿'ʌðə]
Gegenstand object ['ɒbdʒɪkt]

German – English

gegenüberliegen to face [feɪs]
gegenüberliegend opposite ['ɒpəzɪt]
gegenwärtig present ['preznt]
Gehalt pay [peɪ]
geheim secret ['si:krət]
Geheimnis mystery ['mɪstri]; secret ['si:krət]
gehemmt self-conscious [ˌself'kɒnʃəs]
gehen to go [gəʊ]; to leave [li:v]; to step [step]; to walk [wɔ:k]
gehen zu/nach to be off to [bi:‿'ɒf tə]
Gehirn brain(s) [breɪn(z)]
gehören (zu) to belong (to) [bɪ'lɒŋ]
Geisel hostage ['hɒstɪdʒ]
Geist ghost [gəʊst]; mind [maɪnd]; spirit ['spɪrɪt]
geisterhaft ghostly ['gəʊstli]
gelangweilt bored [bɔ:d]
gelb yellow ['jeləʊ]
Geld money ['mʌni]
Geldbeutel wallet ['wɒlɪt]
Geldbuße fine [faɪn]
Geldstrafe fine [faɪn]
Gelegenheit chance [tʃɑ:nts]; opportunity [ˌɒpə'tju:nəti]
gelegentlich occasionally [ə'keɪʒnli]
Geliebter/Geliebte lover ['lʌvə]
geloben to pledge [pledʒ]
etw. **gelten** to count (for sth) [kaʊnt]
Gemälde painting ['peɪntɪŋ]
gemäß according to [ə'kɔ:dɪŋ tə]
gemein mean [mi:n]
Gemeinde community [kə'mju:nəti]
gemeinsam common ['kɒmən]
Gemeinschaft community [kə'mju:nəti]
gemessen measured ['meʒəd]
Gemisch cocktail ['kɒkteɪl]; mixture ['mɪkstʃə]
Gemüse vegetable ['vedʒtəbl]
genannt called [kɔ:ld]
genau exact [ɪg'zækt]; exactly [ɪg'zæktli]; right [raɪt]
genau genommen in fact [ɪn 'fækt]
genehmigen to approve [ə'pru:v]
Generaldirektor/Generaldirektorin chief executive officer (CEO) [ˌtʃi:f‿ɪgˌzekjətɪv‿'ɒfɪsə; ˌsi: i:'əʊ]
Generator generator ['dʒenreɪtə]
generell general ['dʒenrl]
genießen to enjoy [ɪn'dʒɔɪ]
Genossenschaft co-operative [kəʊ'ɒprətɪv]
genug enough [ɪ'nʌf]
genügend enough [ɪ'nʌf]
geöffnet open ['əʊpn]
Geografie Geography [dʒi'ɒgrəfi]
Gepäck luggage ['lʌgɪdʒ]
Gepäckwagen trolley ['trɒli]

Geplauder chat [tʃæt]
gerade straight [streɪt]
Geräusch noise [nɔɪz]; sound [saʊnd]
gerecht fair [feə]
Gerechtigkeit justice ['dʒʌstɪs]
Gericht court [kɔ:t]
Gerichtshof court [kɔ:t]
Gerichtsverfahren trial [traɪəl]
Gerichtsverhandlung trial [traɪəl]
gern haben to like [laɪk]
gern mögen to love [lʌv]
Gern geschehen! You're welcome. [jʊə 'welkəm]
Geruch odour ['əʊdə]; smell [smel]
gesamt total ['təʊtl]
Gesamtbetrag total ['təʊtl]
Gesamtschule comprehensive school [kɒmprɪ'hensɪv ˌsku:l]
Geschäft business ['bɪznɪs]; shop [ʃɒp]; store [stɔ:]
Geschäftsführer/Geschäftsführerin chief executive officer (CEO) [ˌtʃi:f‿ɪgˌzekjətɪv‿'ɒfɪsə; ˌsi: i:'əʊ]
Geschäftsführung management ['mænɪdʒmənt]
Geschäftsmann businessman, businessmen *(pl)* ['bɪznɪsmən; 'bɪznɪsmen]
geschäftstüchtig enterprising ['entəpraɪzɪŋ]
geschehen to happen ['hæpn]
Geschenk gift [gɪft]; present ['preznt]
Geschichte History ['hɪstəri]; story ['stɔ:ri]
geschichtlich historical [hɪ'stɒrɪkl]
Geschick skill [skɪl]
geschieden von divorced from [dɪ'vɔ:st frəm]
Geschlecht sex [seks]
geschlossen closed [kləʊzd]
Geschmack taste [teɪst]
geschockt shocked [ʃɒkt]
Geschöpf creature ['kri:tʃə]
Geschoss bullet ['bʊlɪt]
Geschwindigkeit speed [spi:d]
Gesellschaft company ['kʌmpəni]; society [sə'saɪəti]
gesellschaftlich social ['səʊʃl]
Gesellschaftstanz ballroom dancing [ˌbɔ:lrʊm 'dɑ:ntsɪŋ]
Gesetz bill [bɪl]; law [lɔ:]
Gesetzentwurf bill [bɪl]
Gesetzgebung law [lɔ:]
gesetzliches Mindestalter legal age [ˌli:gl‿'eɪdʒ]
Gesicht face [feɪs]
Gesichtspunkt aspect ['æspekt]
Gespenst ghost [gəʊst]

Gespräch conversation [ˌkɒnvə'seɪʃn]; dialogue ['daɪəlɒg]
Gestalt figure ['fɪgə]; shape [ʃeɪp]
Gestaltung design [dɪ'zaɪn]
Gestank smell [smel]
gestatten to allow [ə'laʊ]
gestern yesterday ['jestədeɪ]
gestern Abend last night [lɑ:st 'naɪt]
gestern Nacht last night [lɑ:st 'naɪt]
gestrandet stranded ['strændɪd]
gesucht wanted ['wɒntɪd]
gesund healthy ['helθi]
gesund werden to get well [get 'wel]
Gesundheit health [helθ]
getragen measured ['meʒəd]
Getränk drink [drɪŋk]
alkoholfreies Getränk soft drink ['sɒft ˌdrɪŋk]
Gewächshaus greenhouse ['gri:nhaʊs]
gewagt outrageous [aʊt'reɪdʒəs]
Gewalt violence ['vaɪəlnts]
gewaltig huge [hju:dʒ]
gewaltsam violent ['vaɪəlnt]
gewalttätig violent ['vaɪəlnt]
Gewalttätigkeit violence ['vaɪəlnts]
Gewand robe [rəʊb]
gewerblich industrial [ɪn'dʌstriəl]
Gewicht weight [weɪt]
gewieft streetwise ['stri:twaɪz]
gewinnen to gain [geɪn]; to win [wɪn]
jmdn. dafür gewinnen, etw. zu tun to make sb do sth [meɪk]
Gewinner/Gewinnerin winner ['wɪnə]
gewiss certainly ['sɜ:tnli]
gewissenhaft conscientious [ˌkɒntʃi'entʃəs]
Gewohnheitsrecht common law [ˌkɒmən 'lɔ:]
gewöhnlich general ['dʒenrl]; usual ['ju:ʒl]; usually ['ju:ʒli]
Gift poison ['pɔɪzn]; *(von Schlangen und Insekten)* venom ['venəm]
giftig poisonous ['pɔɪznəs]; toxic ['tɒksɪk]
Gitarre guitar [gɪ'tɑ:]
Gitter grid [grɪd]
glamourös glamorous ['glæmrəs]
Glas glass [glɑ:s]
glauben to believe [bɪ'li:v]; to feel [fi:l]; to think [θɪŋk]
gleich equal ['i:kwəl]; the same [seɪm]
gleich immediately [ɪ'mi:diətli]; right away [raɪt‿ə'weɪ]
Gleich- equal ['i:kwəl]
Gleichaltriger/Gleichaltrige peer [pɪə]
Gleichgewicht balance ['bæləns]
gleichmäßig measured ['meʒəd]
gleichwertig equal ['i:kwəl]

Gleis track [træk]
global global ['gləʊbl]
Globalisierung globalisation [ˌgləʊblaɪ'zeɪʃn]
Glocke bell [bel]
Glück fortune ['fɔ:tʃu:n]; luck [lʌk]
Glück haben to get lucky *(AE)* [get 'lʌki]
du hast Glück you're lucky [ˌjʊə 'lʌki]
Viel Glück! Good luck! [ˌgʊd 'lʌk]
glücklich happy ['hæpi]; lucky ['lʌki]
glücklicherweise luckily ['lʌkɪli]
Glühbirne light bulb ['laɪt bʌlb]
Glut embers *(pl)* ['embəz]
Gold gold [gəʊld]
Mein **Gott!** My God! [maɪ 'gɒd]
Grab grave [greɪv]
graben to dig [dɪg]
Grabstein gravestone ['greɪvstəʊn]
Grad degree (°) [dɪ'gri:]
Graffiti mural ['mjʊərl]
Gramm gramme (g) [græm]
Gras grass [grɑ:s]
grau grey [greɪ]
greifen to grab [græb]
greifen nach to reach for ['ri:tʃ fə]
Grenze barrier ['bæriə]; border ['bɔ:də]; limit ['lɪmɪt]
Grieche/Griechin Greek [gri:k]
griechisch Greek [gri:k]
Grill barbecue ['bɑ:bɪkju:]
Grillparty barbecue ['bɑ:bɪkju:]
grinsen to grin [grɪn]
Grinsen grin [grɪn]
grob raw [rɔ:]
groß big [bɪg]; great [greɪt]; large [lɑ:dʒ]; tall [tɔ:l]; wide [waɪd]
großartig fantastic [fæn'tæstɪk]; great [greɪt]; superb [su:'pɜ:b]; wicked ['wɪkɪd]
Größe height [haɪt]; size [saɪz]
Großstadt city ['sɪti]
größt- capital ['kæpɪtl]
größtenteils mostly ['məʊstli]
grün green [gri:n]
Grund bottom ['bɒtəm]; reason ['ri:zn]
Grund- basic ['beɪsɪk]
gründen to found [faʊnd]; to set up [set‿'ʌp]
Grundgesetz constitution [ˌkɒnstɪ'tju:ʃn]
grundlegend basic ['beɪsɪk]
Grundlinie back line [ˌbæk 'lain]; base [beɪs]
Grundsatz policy ['pɒlɪsi]
Grundschule elementary school *(AE)* [elɪ'mentri ˌsku:l]; primary school ['praɪməri ˌsku:l]
Gruppe group [gru:p]
gruselig scary ['skeəri]
Mit freundlichen **Grüßen** Yours faithfully [ˌjɔ:z 'feɪθfʊli]
grüßen to greet [gri:t]
gültig valid ['vælɪd]
Gummi rubber ['rʌbə]
Gummistiefel rubber boots *(pl)* [ˌrʌbə 'bu:ts]
gut all right [ɔ:l 'raɪt]; fine [faɪn]; good [gʊd]
Gute-Besserung-Karte get-well card [ˌget 'wel ˌkɑ:d]
Es geht uns gut. We're OK. [ˌwɪər‿əʊ'keɪ]
Guten Morgen! Good morning! [ˌgʊd 'mɔ:nɪŋ]
gut informiert well-informed [ˌwelin'fɔ:md]
gut mit … umgehen können to be good with … [bi: 'gʊd wɪð]
ich bin gut in … I'm good at … [aɪm 'gʊd‿ət]
Güter goods *(pl)* [gʊdz]
gutheißen to approve [ə'pru:v]
Gymnasium grammar school ['græmə ˌsku:l]

H

Haar, Haare hair [heə]
haben to have [hæv]; to have got [hæv 'gɒt]
keine Ahnung haben to have no clue [ˌhæv nəʊ 'klu:]
Hafen harbor *(AE)* ['hɑ:bə]; port [pɔ:t]
Hähnchen chicken ['tʃɪkɪn]
Hai shark [ʃɑ:k]
halb half [hɑ:f]
halb (drei) half past (two) ['hɑ:f pɑ:st]
eine halbe Stunde half an hour [ˌhɑ:f‿ən‿'aʊə]
zum halben Preis half-price [ˌhɑ:f'praɪs]
Halbschwester half-sister ['hɑ:fˌsɪstə]
Halbzeit half-time [ˌhɑ:f'taɪm]
Hälfte half [hɑ:f]
Halle hall [hɔ:l]
Hallo! Hello! [he'ləʊ]; Hi, there! ['haɪ ðeə]
halten to hold [həʊld]; to keep [ki:p]
Haltestelle stop [stɒp]
Haltung (gegenüber) attitude (to/towards) ['ætɪtju:d]
Hand hand [hænd]
Hände weg! Hands off! [hændz‿'ɒf]
Handel deal [di:l]; trade [treɪd]
fairer Handel fair trade [ˌfeə 'treɪd]
handhaben to manage ['mænɪdʒ]
Handkarren trolley ['trɒli]
Händler/Händlerin dealer ['di:lə]; retailer ['ri:teɪlə]; trader ['treɪdə]
Handlung action ['ækʃn]
Handschuh glove [glʌv]
Handtasche handbag ['hænbæg]
Handwerker workman, workmen *(pl)* ['wɜ:kmən; 'wɜ:kmen]
handwerklich technical ['teknɪkl]
Handy cell phone *(AE)* ['sel fəʊn]; mobile ['məʊbaɪl]
jmdn. **hänseln** to pick on sb ['pɪk‿ɒn]
hart hard [hɑ:d]; tough [tʌf]
Hass hate [heɪt]
hassen to hate [heɪt]
hätte(n) gern would like [wʊd 'laɪk]
Haufen clump [klʌmp]; pile [paɪl]
Haupt- capital ['kæpɪtl]; main [meɪn]
Häuptling chief [tʃi:f]
hauptsächlich mostly ['məʊstli]
Hauptsitz headquarters *(pl)* [ˌhed'kwɔ:təz]
Hauptstadt capital ['kæpɪtl]
Haus house [haʊs]; place [pleɪs]
im Haus lebend live-in ['lɪvɪn]
zu Hause at home [ət 'həʊm]
Hausaufgabe/Hausaufgaben homework ['həʊmwɜ:k]
Häuserblock block [blɒk]
Haushalt household ['haʊshəʊld]
Haushalts- household ['haʊshəʊld]
Hausmeister/Hausmeisterin caretaker ['keəˌteɪkə]
Haustier pet [pet]
Haut skin [skɪn]
heben to raise [reɪz]
Heck tail [teɪl]
Heer military ['mɪlɪtri]
Heft exercise book ['eksəsaɪz ˌbʊk]
heilig holy ['həʊli]; sacred ['seɪkrɪd]
wie von einem **Heiligenschein umgeben** haloed ['heɪləʊd]
Heim home [həʊm]; place [pleɪs]
Heimat home [həʊm]
heimlich secret ['si:krət]
Heimweh haben to feel homesick [ˌfi:l 'həʊmsɪk]
heiraten to marry ['mæri]
heiß hot [hɒt]
Ich **heiße** …. My name is …. [maɪ 'neɪm‿ɪz]
Heißluftballon balloon [bə'lu:n]
heizen to heat [hi:t]
Heizung heating ['hi:tɪŋ]
Held hero, heroes *(pl)* ['hɪərəʊ; 'hɪərəʊz]
Heldin heroine ['herəʊɪn]

helfen to help [help]
Helikopter helicopter ['helɪˌkɒptə]
hell bright [braɪt]; fair [feə]; light [laɪt]
Helm helmet ['helmət]
Hemd shirt [ʃɜ:t]
heranwachsen to grow up [grəʊ‿'ʌp]
(die Treppe) **herauf** upstairs [ʌp'steəz]
heraus out [aʊt]
herausbringen to launch [lɔ:nʃ]
herausfinden to find out [faɪnd‿'aʊt]; to work out [ˌwɜ:k‿'aʊt]
Herausgeber/Herausgeberin editor ['edɪtə]
herausnehmen to take out [teɪk‿'aʊt]
Herbst autumn ['ɔ:təm]
herein in [ɪn]
hereinkommen to come in [kʌm‿'ɪn]
herkömmlich ordinary ['ɔ:dnri]
Herkunft origin ['ɒrɪdʒɪn]
Herr *(Anrede)* Mr ['mɪstə]
herrlich superb [su:'pɜ:b]
Herrscher/Herrscherin monarch ['mɒnək]; ruler ['ru:lə]
herstellen to manufacture [ˌmænjə'fæktʃə]; to produce [prə'dju:s]
Hersteller manufacturer [ˌmænjə'fæktʃərə]
Herstellung manufacturing [ˌmænjə'fæktʃrɪŋ]; production [prə'dʌkʃn]
herüberkommen to come over [kʌm‿'əʊvə]
herüberreichen to pass [pɑ:s]
(um ...) **herum** round [raʊnd]; around [ə'raʊnd]
herumalbern to mess around [ˌmes‿ə'raʊnd]
herumfummeln (an) to fiddle (with) ['fɪdl]
auf jmdm. **herumhacken** to pick on sb ['pɪk‿ɒn]
herumlungern to hang around *(AE)* [ˌhæŋ‿ə'raʊnd]
herumreisen to go places [ˌgəʊ 'pleɪsɪz]
herumspringen to jump about [ˌdʒʌmp‿ə'baʊt]
sich **herumtreiben** to hang out [hæŋ‿'aʊt]
herunter down [daʊn]; off [ɒf]
(die Treppe) herunter downstairs [ˌdaʊn'steəz]
herunterdrehen to turn down [tɜ:n 'daʊn]
herunterfallen to fall off [fɔ:l‿'ɒf]; to fall [fɔ:l]
herunterkommen to come down [kʌm 'daʊn]
herunterladen to download [ˌdaʊn'ləʊd]
hervorragend excellent ['ekslnt]
hervorrufen to cause [kɔ:z]
Herz heart [hɑ:t]
Herzliche Grüße love [lʌv]
Herzschrittmacher pacemaker ['peɪsˌmeɪkə]
hetzen to rush [rʌʃ]
heute today [tə'deɪ]
heute Abend tonight [tə'naɪt]
heute Nacht tonight [tə'naɪt]
heutzutage these days ['ði:z deɪz]
Hi! Hi! [haɪ]
hier here [hɪə]
High School *(weiterführende Schule in den USA, Oberstufe)* high school ['haɪ ˌsku:l]
high-tech high-tech [ˌhaɪ'tek]
Highway highway *(AE)* ['haɪweɪ]
Hilfe help [help]; support [sə'pɔ:t]
hilflos helpless ['helpləs]
hilfreich helpful ['helpfəl]
Himmel sky [skaɪ]
hinauf up [ʌp]
(die Treppe) hinauf upstairs [ʌp'steəz]
die Treppe **hinaufrennen** to run upstairs [ˌrʌn‿ʌp'steəz]
hinaufschauen to look up [lʊk‿'ʌp]
hinaus out [aʊt]
hinausgehen to go out [gəʊ‿'aʊt]
hinauslehnen to lean out [li:n‿'aʊt]
sich hinauslehnen to lean out [li:n‿'aʊt]
hinausrennen to run out [ˌrʌn‿'aʊt]
hinausstellen to put out [pʊt‿'aʊt]
Hindi Hindi ['hɪndi:]
hineingehen to go in [gəʊ 'ɪn]
hinfallen to fall [fɔ:l]
hingehen to walk up to [wɔ:k‿'ʌp tə]
Hinglisch *(Mischung aus Hindi und Englisch)* Hinglish ['hɪŋglɪʃ]
hinken to limp [lɪmp]
hinlegen to lie down [laɪ 'daʊn]
sich hinlegen to lie down [laɪ 'daʊn]
hinrichten to execute ['eksɪkju:t]
Hinrichtung execution [ˌeksɪ'kju:ʃn]
sich **hinsetzen** to sit down [sɪt 'daʊn]
hinten at the back [ət ðə 'bæk]
hinter behind [bɪ'haɪnd]
Hinter- back [bæk]
Hintergrund background ['bækgraʊnd]
hinterhergehen to follow ['fɒləʊ]
hinterlassen to leave [li:v]
Hintern ass *(AE)* [æs]
hinüber across [ə'krɒs]
hinübergehen to go over [gəʊ‿'əʊvə]
hin- und hergerissen torn [tɔ:n]
hinunter down [daʊn]
(die Treppe) hinunter downstairs [ˌdaʊn'steəz]
hinuntergehen to go down [gəʊ 'daʊn]
Hinweis clue [klu:]
hinzufügen to add [æd]; to put in [pʊt‿'ɪn]
Hip-Hopper/Hip-Hopperin hip hopper ['hɪp ˌhɒpə]
hispanisch Hispanic [hɪ'spænɪk]
historisch historical [hɪ'stɒrɪkl]
Hit hit [hɪt]
Hitparade charts *(pl)* [tʃɑ:ts]
Hitze heat [hi:t]
Hobby hobby, hobbies *(pl)* ['hɒbi; 'hɒbiz]
hoch high [haɪ]; tall [tɔ:l]
hochheben to lift [lɪft]
hochkommen to come up [kʌm‿'ʌp]
Hochmoor moor [mɔ:]
Hochmut pride [praɪd]
hochspringen to jump up [dʒʌmp‿'ʌp]
höchst highly ['haɪli]
höchster/höchste/höchstes supreme [su:'pri:m]
Hochwasser flood [flʌd]
hochziehen to lift [lɪft]
Hockey hockey ['hɒki]
Hof court [kɔ:t]
hoffen to hope [həʊp]
Hoffnung hope [həʊp]
hoffnungslos desperate ['desprət]; hopeless ['həʊpləs]
hoffnungsvoll hopeful ['həʊpfl]
höflich polite [pə'laɪt]
Höhe height [haɪt]; level ['levl]
holen to get [get]
Hölle hell [hel]
Holz wood [wʊd]
hölzern wooden ['wʊdn]
Homecoming *(Schulfest an amerikanischen High Schools)* homecoming ['həʊmkʌmɪŋ]
hören to hear [hɪə]
Horizont horizon [hə'raɪzn]
Horoskop horoscope ['hɒrəskəʊp]
Hose trousers *(pl)* ['traʊzəz]
kurze Hose shorts *(pl)* [ʃɔ:ts]
Hosentasche pocket ['pɒkɪt]
Hotel hotel [həʊ'tel]
Hotline hotline ['hɒtlaɪn]
hübsch neat *(AE)* [ni:t]
Hubschrauber helicopter ['helɪˌkɒptə]
Hüfte hip [hɪp]
Huhn chicken ['tʃɪkɪn]
Hülle shell [ʃel]
Hund dog [dɒg]
mit dem Hund spazieren gehen to walk the dog [wɔ:k ðə 'dɒg]

hundemüde dog-tired [ˌdɒg'taɪəd]
hundert hundred ['hʌndrəd]
Hunger bekommen to get hungry [get 'hʌŋgri]
Hungersnot famine ['fæmɪn]
hungrig hungry ['hʌŋgri]
Hürde barrier ['bæriə]
Hut hat [hæt]
Hütte cabin ['kæbɪn]; hut [hʌt]

I

ich I [aɪ]
ich fürchte I'm afraid ... [ˌaɪm‿ə'freɪd]
Ich habe nichts dagegen. I don't mind. [maɪnd]
Ich heiße .... My name is .... [maɪ 'neɪm‿ɪz]
Ich nehme .... I'm having .... [aɪm 'hævɪŋ]
ich würde gern I'd like to [ˌaɪd 'laɪk tə]
ich würde lieber I'd rather [aɪd 'rɑːðə]
ideal ideal [aɪ'dɪəl]
Ideal ideal [aɪ'dɪəl]
Idee idea [aɪ'dɪə]
identifizieren to identify [aɪ'dentɪfaɪ]
sich identifizieren (mit) to identify (with) [aɪ'dentɪfaɪ]
Idiom idiom ['ɪdiəm]
Idiot dummy *(AE)* ['dʌmi]; idiot ['ɪdɪət]
Igitt! Yuk! [jʌk]
ihm him [hɪm]
ihn him [hɪm]
ihnen them [ðem]
Ihnen you [juː; jə]
ihr you [juː; jə]
ihr/euch/Sie/sich (selbst) yourselves [jɔː'selvz]
ihr/ihre her [hɜː]; its [ɪts]; their [ðeə]
Ihr/Ihre your [jɔː]
Ikone icon ['aɪkɒn]
illegal illegal [ɪ'liːgl]
im Abseits offside [ˌɒf'saɪd]
im Begriff sein (zu tun) to be due (to do) [biː 'djuː]; to be about to (do sth) [bi‿ə'baʊt tə]
im Gange sein to be on [biː‿'ɒn]
im Überfluss abundant [ə'bʌndənt]
im unteren Teil at the bottom [ət ðə 'bɒtəm]
im vorderen Teil at the front [ət ðə 'frʌnt]
Image image ['ɪmɪdʒ]
Imbiss snack [snæk]
Imbissstube deli *(AE)* ['deli]; diner *(AE)* ['daɪnə]
immer always ['ɔːlweɪz]
immer noch still [stɪl]
Immigrant/Immigrantin immigrant ['ɪmɪgrənt]
Immigration immigration [ˌɪmɪ'greɪʃn]
Immunität immunity [ɪ'mjuːnəti]
Impression impression [ɪm'preʃn]
improvisieren to freestyle *(slang)* ['friːstaɪl]
in at [æt; ət]; in [ɪn]; into ['ɪntə]
in Australien Down Under [ˌdaʊn‿'ʌndə]
in ... hinein into ['ɪntə]
Indianer/Indianerin Native American [ˌneɪtɪv‿ə'merɪkən]
Indie *(Musikrichtung)* indie ['ɪndi]
indisch Indian ['ɪndiən]
individuell single ['sɪŋgl]
Industrie industry ['ɪndəstri]
Industrie- industrial [ɪn'dʌstriəl]
industriell industrial [ɪn'dʌstriəl]
Informatik IT [ˌaɪ'tiː]
Information/Informationen information [ˌɪnfə'meɪʃn]
Informationstechnik IT [ˌaɪ'tiː]
Informationszentrum information centre [ɪnfə'meɪʃn ˌsentə]
informieren to inform [ɪn'fɔːm]
Ingenieur/Ingenieurin engineer [ˌendʒɪ'nɪə]
Inhaber/Inhaberin keeper ['kiːpə]
Inhalt content ['kɒntent]
Initiative initiative [ɪ'nɪʃətɪv]
Injektion injection [ɪn'dʒekʃn]
inklusive including [ɪn'kluːdɪŋ]
alles inklusive all inclusive [ˌɔːl‿ɪŋ'kluːsɪv]
Inlineskates skates *(pl)* [skeɪts]
Inlineskates fahren to skate [skeɪt]
innen inside [ɪn'saɪd]
Innen- interior [ɪn'tɪəriə]
Innenarchitekt interior designer [ɪnˌtɪəriə dɪ'zaɪnə]
Innenstadt inner-city ['ɪnəˌsɪti]
das **Innere** interior [ɪn'tɪəriə]
innerhalb within [wɪ'ðɪn]
innerstädtisch inner-city ['ɪnəˌsɪti]
inoffiziell non-official [ˌnɒnə'fɪʃl]
Insekt insect ['ɪnsekt]
Insektenvernichtungsmittel pesticide ['pestɪsaɪd]
Insel island ['aɪlənd]
Inselbewohner/Inselbewohnerin islander ['aɪləndə]
insgeheim in private [ɪn 'praɪvɪt]
insgesamt in all [ɪn‿'ɔːl]
Inspektor inspector [ɪn'spektə]
inspirieren to inspire [ɪn'spaɪə]
Institut college ['kɒlɪdʒ]
Instruktion instruction [ɪn'strʌkʃn]
inszenieren to produce [prə'djuːs]
intelligent intelligent [ɪn'telɪdʒnt]
interessant interesting ['ɪntrəstɪŋ]
Interesse interest ['ɪntrəst]
interessieren to interest ['ɪntrəst]
sich interessieren to get interested [get 'ɪntrəstɪd]
interessiert interested ['ɪntrəstɪd]
interessiert sein an to be into [biː‿'ɪntə]
Internat boarding school ['bɔːdɪŋ ˌskuːl]
international international [ˌɪntə'næʃnl]
Internet Internet ['ɪntənet]
im Internet online [ˌɒn'laɪn]
im Internet surfen to surf the Internet [ˌsɜːf ði‿'ɪntənet]
Internetauftritt website ['websaɪt]
Internettagebuch blog [blɒg]
Interview interview ['ɪntəvjuː]
interviewen to interview ['ɪntəvjuː]
Inuit Inuit ['ɪnuɪt]
Inuktitut *(Sprache der Inuit)* Inuktitut [ɪ'nʊktɪtʊt]
investieren to invest [ɪn'vest]
Investition investment [ɪn'vestmənt]
involvieren to involve [ɪn'vɒlv]
Iren/Irinnen Irish ['aɪrɪʃ]
irgendetwas anything ['eniθɪŋ]; something ['sʌmθɪŋ]
irgendjemand anybody ['eniˌbɒdi]; anyone ['eniwʌn]
irgendwie somehow ['sʌmhaʊ]; sort of ['sɔːt‿əv]
irgendwo anywhere ['eniweə]; somewhere ['sʌmweə]
irisch Irish ['aɪrɪʃ]
irre delirious [dɪ'lɪriəs]
Islam Islam ['ɪzlɑːm]
islamisch Islamic [ɪz'læmɪk]
isolieren to segregate ['segrɪgeɪt]
Isolierung insulation [ˌɪnsjə'leɪʃn]
Italiener/Italienerin Italian [ɪ'tæliən]
italienisch Italian [ɪ'tæliən]

J

ja yes [jes]; yeah *(slang)* [jeə]
Jacke jacket ['dʒækɪt]
Jackentasche pocket ['pɒkɪt]
Jagdhund hound [haʊnd]
Jagen hunting ['hʌntɪŋ]
Jahr year [jɪə]
Jahrbuch yearbook ['jɪəbʊk]
Jahreszeit season ['siːzn]
Jahrgangsstufe year [jɪə]

German – English

Jahrhundert century ['sentʃri]
jährlich annual ['ænjuəl]; annually ['ænjuəli]
Jahrmarkt fair [feə]
Jahrtausend millennium [mɪ'leniəm]
Jahrzehnt decade ['dekeɪd]
Jammerlappen sissy ['sɪsi]
Jamsession jam [dʒæm]
Januar January ['dʒænjuəri]
Japaner/Japanerin Japanese [ˌdʒæpn'i:z]
japanisch Japanese [ˌdʒæpn'i:z]
Japanisch Japanese [ˌdʒæpn'i:z]
Jazz jazz [dʒæz]
je each [i:tʃ]
Jeans jeans *(pl)* [dʒi:nz]
jedenfalls anyway ['eniweɪ]
jeder/jede/jedes each [i:tʃ]; every ['evri]
jeder everybody ['evribɒdi]; everyone ['evriwʌn]
jeder (beliebige) anybody ['eniˌbɒdi]; anyone ['eniwʌn]
jedoch however [haʊ'evə]
jemals ever ['evə]
jemand somebody ['sʌmbədi]; someone ['sʌmwʌn]
jene those [ðəʊz]
jenes that [ðæt]
jetzt now [naʊ]
jetzt gleich right now [ˌraɪt 'naʊ]
jeweils each [i:tʃ]
Job job [dʒɒb]
joggen to jog [dʒɒg]
Jogger/Joggerin jogger ['dʒɒgə]
Joker wild card ['waɪld ˌkɑ:d]
Journalist/Journalistin journalist ['dʒɜ:nlɪst]
jucken to itch [ɪtʃ]
Jugend youth [ju:θ]
jugendlich teenage ['ti:neɪdʒ]
Jugendlicher/Jugendliche teenager ['ti:nˌeɪdʒə]; teen [ti:n]
Jugendtreffen rally ['ræli]
Juli July [dʒʊ'laɪ]
jung young [jʌŋ]
Junge boy [bɔɪ]; lad [læd]
der **Jüngere** junior ['dʒu:niə]
Jungfräulichkeit virginity [və'dʒɪnəti]
Juni June [dʒu:n]
Junior junior ['dʒu:niə]
Junior High School *(Vorstufe zur High School, meist 7.-9. Klasse)* junior high school [ˌdʒu:niə 'haɪ ˌsku:l]
Jurist/Juristin lawyer ['lɔɪə]
Justiz justice ['dʒʌstɪs]
Juwel jewel ['dʒu:əl]

K

Kabel cord *(AE)* [kɔ:d]
Kabinett cabinet ['kæbɪnət]
Käfer bug [bʌg]
Kaffee coffee ['kɒfi:]
Käfig cage [keɪdʒ]
kahl bald [bɔ:ld]
Kakadu cockatoo [ˌkɒkə'tu:]
Kakao cocoa ['kəʊkəʊ]
Kalender calendar ['kæləndə]
kalt cold [kəʊld]
Kamera camera ['kæmrə]
Kamerad/Kameradin buddy *(infml)* ['bʌdi]; mate [meɪt]
Kameramann cameraman, cameramen *(pl)* ['kæmrəmæn; 'kæmrəmen]
Kamin fireplace ['faɪəpleɪs]
Kaminfeuer fire [faɪə]
Kammer chamber ['tʃeɪmbə]
Kampagne campaign [kæm'peɪn]
Kampf battle ['bætl]; fight [faɪt]; fighting ['faɪtɪŋ]
Kampf (um) struggle (for sth) ['strʌgl]
Kampf- fighting ['faɪtɪŋ]
kämpfen to battle ['bætl]; to fight [faɪt]; to struggle ['strʌgl]
Kämpfer/Kämpferin fighter ['faɪtə]
Kampfrichter judge [dʒʌdʒ]
Kanadier/Kanadierin Canadian [kə'neɪdiən]
kanadisch Canadian [kə'neɪdiən]
Kanal canal [kə'næl]; channel ['tʃænl]
Kandidat/Kandidatin candidate ['kændɪdət]
Känguru kangaroo [ˌkæŋgr'u:]
Kaninchen rabbit ['ræbɪt]
Kante edge [edʒ]
Kantonese/Kantonesin Cantonese [ˌkɑntə'ni:z]
kantonesisch Cantonese [ˌkɑntə'ni:z]
Kanu fahren to canoe [kə'nu:]
Kapelle band [bænd]
Kapital- capital ['kæpɪtl]
Kapitalverbrechen capital crime [ˌkæpɪtl 'kraɪm]
Kapitän captain ['kæptɪn]
Kappe cap [kæp]; hood [hʊd]
Kapsel capsule ['kæpsju:l]
kaputt broken ['brəʊkn]
kaputtmachen to break [breɪk]
Kapuze hood [hʊd]
Karosserie body shell ['bɒdi ˌʃel]
Karotte carrot ['kærət]
Karriere career [kə'rɪə]
Karte card [kɑ:d]
Kartoffel potato, potatoes *(pl)* [pə'teɪtəʊ]
Kartoffelchip crisp [krɪsp]
Käse cheese [tʃi:z]
Kasten box, boxes *(pl)* [bɒks; 'bɒksɪz]; cabinet ['kæbɪnət]
Katastrophe disaster [dɪ'zɑ:stə]
Kategorie category ['kætəgri]
Kathedrale cathedral [kə'θi:drl]
Katze cat [kæt]
kaufen to buy [baɪ]
Kaufhaus department store [dɪ'pɑ:tmənt stɔ:]; store [stɔ:]
Kaufhausdetektiv/Kaufhausdetektivin store detective ['stɔ: dɪˌtektɪv]
kaum hardly ['hɑ:dli]
Kautschuk rubber ['rʌbə]
Kaviar caviar ['kæviɑ:]
kein/keine no [nəʊ]
keine Ahnung no idea [ˌnəʊ‿aɪ'dɪə]
keiner/keine none [nʌn]
Keks biscuit ['bɪskɪt]
Kelch cup [kʌp]
Kellergeschoss basement ['beɪsmənt]
Kellner waiter ['weɪtə]
kennen to know [nəʊ]
kennen lernen to get to know [ˌget tə 'nəʊ]
Kenntnisse knowledge ['nɒlɪdʒ]
Kerl bloke [bləʊk]; guy [gaɪ]
Kessel tank [tæŋk]
Kette chain [tʃeɪn]
Kick kick [kɪk]
Kickboard kickboard ['kɪkbɔ:d]
kicken to kick [kɪk]
kidnappen to kidnap ['kɪdnæp]
Kidnapper/Kidnapperin kidnapper ['kɪdnæpə]
Kidnapping kidnap(ping) ['kɪdnæp(ɪŋ)]
Kilo(gramm) kilo (kg) ['kɪləʊ]
Kilometer kilometre (km) ['kɪləʊˌmi:tə; kɪ'lɒmɪtə]
Kind child, children *(pl)* [tʃaɪld; 'tʃɪldrɪn]; kid [kɪd]
Kino cinema ['sɪnəmə]; movies *(AE)* ['mu:viz]; theater *(AE)* ['θɪətə]
kippen to tip [tɪp]
Kirche church [tʃɜ:tʃ]
Kirsche cherry ['tʃeri]
Kiste box, boxes *(pl)* [bɒks; 'bɒksɪz]
klagen to moan [məʊn]
Klamm gorge [gɔ:dʒ]
Klang sound [saʊnd]
Klappe shutter ['ʃʌtə]
klar clear [klɪə]
klären *(ein Problem)* to sort out [sɔ:t‿'aʊt]
klarkommen to get on [get‿'ɒn]
klasse neat *(AE)* [ni:t]
Klasse class [klɑ:s]; grade *(AE)* [greɪd]

Klassenarbeit test [test]
Klassenkamerad/Klassenkameradin classmate ['klɑ:smeɪt]
Klassenzimmer classroom ['klɑ:srʊm]
klassisch classic ['klæsɪk]
-Klässler/Klässlerin grader ['greɪdə]
Klatsch gossip ['gɒsɪp]
klatschen to clap [klæp]
kleben to stick [stɪk]
Kleid dress [dres]
Kleider clothes *(pl)* [kləʊθs]
Kleidergröße size [saɪz]
Kleiderschrank wardrobe ['wɔ:drəʊb]
Kleidung clothes *(pl)* [kləʊθs]; clothing ['kləʊðɪŋ]
klein little ['lɪtl]; small [smɔ:l]
klettern to climb ['klaɪm]
klicken to click [klɪk]
Klima climate ['klaɪmət]
Klingel bell [bel]
klingeln to ring [rɪŋ]
Es klingelt. The bell rings. [ðə 'bel rɪŋz]
klingen to sound [saʊnd]
Klippe cliff [klɪf]
klopfen to knock [nɒk]
fest klopfen to bang [bæŋ]
Klopfen knock [nɒk]
Kloster monastery ['mɒnəstri]
Klub club [klʌb]
klug intelligent [ɪn'telɪdʒnt]; smart [smɑ:t]
Klumpen clump [klʌmp]
Klunker bling bling *(slang)* [ˌblɪŋ 'blɪŋ]
knacken to crackle ['krækl]
knallen to pop [pɒp]
knallen lassen to pop [pɒp]
Knappheit shortage ['ʃɔ:tɪdʒ]
knarren to creak [kri:k]
Knäuel ball [bɔ:l]
Kneipe bar [bɑ:]
knicken to fold [fəʊld]
Knie knee [ni:]
knistern to crackle ['krækl]
Knopf button ['bʌtn]
Koala koala [kəʊ'ɑ:lə]
Kobold goblin ['gɒblɪn]
Koch/Köchin chef [ʃef]; cook [kʊk]
kochen to cook [kʊk]
Kochen cooking ['kʊkɪŋ]
Kofferraum trunk *(AE)* [trʌŋk]
Kohl cabbage ['kæbɪdʒ]
Kohle carbon ['kɑ:bn]; coal [kəʊl]
Kohlendioxid carbon dioxide (CO_2) [ˌkɑ:bn daɪ'ɒksaɪd; si:‿əʊ 'tu:]
Kohlenstoff carbon ['kɑ:bn]
Kollege/Kollegin colleague ['kɒli:g]
Kollegium staff [stɑ:f]
Kolonie colony ['kɒləni]
Koma coma ['kəʊmə]
ins Koma fallen to go into a coma ['kəʊmə]
kombinieren to combine [kəm'baɪn]
komfortabel comfortable ['kʌmpftəbl]
komisch funny ['fʌni]
kommen to come [kʌm]; to get [get]
Komm./Kommt. Come on. [kʌm‿'ɒn]
unter die Leute kommen to socialize ['səʊʃlaɪz]
Kommentar comment ['kɒment]
Kommunikation communication [kəˌmju:nɪ'keɪʃn]
kommunizieren to communicate [kə'mju:nɪkeɪt]
Komödie comedy ['kɒmədi]
Kompanie company ['kʌmpəni]
Komparativ comparative [kəm'pærətɪv]
komplex complex ['kɒmpleks]
kompliziert complex ['kɒmpleks]
Kondition condition [kən'dɪʃn]
konfrontiert werden mit to face [feɪs]
konfus confused [kən'fju:zd]
König king [kɪŋ]
Königin queen [kwi:n]
königlich royal ['rɔɪəl]
Konkurrent/Konkurrentin rival ['raɪvl]
können can [kæn]; to be able to (do sth) [bi:‿'eɪbl]
konnte/konnten could [kʊd]
könnte/könnten could [kʊd]; might [maɪt]
kann/könnte(n) vielleicht may [meɪ]
Konservierung conservation [ˌkɒnsə'veɪʃn]
Konstitution constitution [ˌkɒnstɪ'tju:ʃn]
konstruieren to construct [kən'strʌkt]
Konstruktion construction [kən'strʌkʃn]
kontaktfreudig outgoing ['aʊtgəʊɪŋ]
kontaktieren to contact ['kɒntækt]
Kontext context ['kɒntekst]
Kontinent continent ['kɒntɪnənt]
Konto account [ə'kaʊnt]
Kontrast contrast ['kɒntrɑ:st]
Kontrolle control [kən'trəʊl]
kontrollieren to check [tʃek]; to control [kən'trəʊl]
Kontrollturm tower ['taʊə]
Konversation conversation [ˌkɒnvə'seɪʃn]
konvertieren to convert ['kɒnvɜ:t]
konzentrieren to concentrate ['kɒntsntreɪt]
sich konzentrieren to concentrate ['kɒntsntreɪt]
sich konzentrieren (auf) to focus (on) ['fəʊkəs]
Konzert concert ['kɒnsət]
Kooperative co-operative [kəʊ'ɒprətɪv]
Kopf head [hed]
Kopfball header ['hedə]
Kopfhörer headphones *(pl)* ['hedfəʊnz]
Kopfsalat lettuce ['letɪs]
Kopftuch headscarf, headscarves *(pl)* ['hedskɑ:f; 'hedskɑ:vz]; scarf, scarves *(pl)* [skɑ:f; skɑ:vz]
Kopie copy ['kɒpi]
kopieren to copy ['kɒpi]
Koralle coral ['kɒrəl]
Korallen- coral ['kɒrəl]
Kordel cord *(AE)* [kɔ:d]; string [strɪŋ]
kornisch Cornish ['kɔ:nɪʃ]
Körper body ['bɒdi]
körperlich physical ['fɪzɪkl]
korrekt correct [kə'rekt]; right [raɪt]
Korridor corridor ['kɒrɪdɔ:]
Kosten cost [kɒst]
kostenlos free [fri:]
krabbeln to crawl [krɔ:l]
gegen etw. **krachen** to crash into [kræʃ]
Kraft energy ['enədʒi]; power ['paʊə]; strength [streŋθ]
Kraftstoff petrol ['petrl]
Krake octopus ['ɒktəpəs]
krank sick [sɪk]
Krankenhaus hospital ['hɒspɪtl]
Krankenpfleger nurse [nɜ:s]
Krankenschwester nurse [nɜ:s]
Krankenwagen ambulance ['æmbjələnts]
Krankheit disease [dɪ'zi:z]; illness ['ɪlnəs]
Krankmeldung sick note ['sɪk ˌnəʊt]
kräuseln to curl [kɜ:l]
sich kräuseln to curl [kɜ:l]
Kraut cabbage ['kæbɪdʒ]
kreativ creative [kri'eɪtɪv]
Kreatur creature ['kri:tʃə]
Kredit loan [ləʊn]
Kreis circle ['sɜ:kl]
kreuzen to cross [krɒs]
Kreuzfahrt cruise [kru:z]
Kricket cricket ['krɪkɪt]
kriechen to crawl [krɔ:l]
Krieg war [wɔ:]
einen Krieg führen to wage a war [ˌweɪdʒ‿ə 'wɔ:]
Krimi detective story [dɪ'tektɪv ˌstɔ:ri]
Kriminalität crime [kraɪm]
kriminell criminal ['krɪmɪnl]
Krimineller/Kriminelle criminal ['krɪmɪnl]
kristall- crystal ['krɪstl]
Kristall crystal ['krɪstl]

German – English

Kritiker/Kritikerin critic ['krɪtɪk]
kritisieren to criticise ['krɪtɪsaɪz]
Krokodil crocodile ['krɒkədaɪl]
Krone crown [kraʊn]
Krümmung bend [bend]
Küche kitchen ['kɪtʃɪn]
Kuchen cake [keɪk]
Küchenchef/-chefin chef [ʃef]
Küchenschrank cupboard ['kʌbəd]
Kugel bullet ['bʊlɪt]
kugelsicher bullet-proof ['bʊlɪtpru:f]
Kuh cow [kaʊ]
kühl cool [ku:l]
Kühlschrank fridge [frɪdʒ]; refrigerator [rɪ'frɪdʒreɪtə]
Kultur culture ['kʌltʃə]
kulturell cultural ['kʌltʃrl]
Kummerkastenonkel agony uncle ['ægəni ˌʌnkl]
Kummerkastentante agony aunt ['ægəni ˌɑ:nt]
sich **kümmern** to care [keə]; to take care [teɪk 'keə]
sich kümmern um to look after [lʊk‿'ɑ:ftə]
Kumpel buddy *(infml)* ['bʌdi]; homie *(slang)* ['həʊmi]; mate [meɪt]; pal [pæl]
Kunde/Kundin customer ['kʌstəmə]
Kundendienst after-sales service [ˌɑ:ftəseɪlz 'sɜ:vɪs]
kündigen to quit [kwɪt]
Kunst Art [ɑ:t]
Künstler/Künstlerin artist ['ɑ:tɪst]
Kunststoff(-) plastic ['plæstɪk]
Kurier courier ['kʊriə]
Kurs bearings *(pl)* ['beərɪŋz]; class [klɑ:s]; course [kɔ:s]
Kurve bend [bend]; curve [kɜ:v]
kurz short [ʃɔ:t]
zu kurz kommen (mit) to miss out (on) [mɪss‿'aʊt]
kürzlich recent ['ri:snt]; recently ['ri:sntli]
Kuss kiss [kɪs]
küssen to kiss [kɪs]
Küste coast [kəʊst]; seaside ['si:saɪd]
Küstenlinie coastline ['kəʊstlaɪn]

L

Labor lab(oratory) [læb; lə'bɒrətri]
lächeln to smile [smaɪl]
Lächeln smile [smaɪl]
lachen to laugh [lɑ:f]
lackieren to spray [spreɪ]
Laden shop [ʃɒp]; store [stɔ:]
Ladung load [ləʊd]
Lager camp [kæmp]
Lagerfeuer campfire ['kæmpfaɪə]
lagern to store [stɔ:]
lähmen to stun [stʌn]
Lamm lamb [læm]
Lammfleisch lamb [læm]
Lampe lamp [læmp]
Land country, countries *(pl)* ['kʌntri; 'kʌntriz]; land [lænd]; state [steɪt]; territory ['terɪtri]
landen to end up [ˌend‿'ʌp]; to land [lænd]
Landesverrat treason ['tri:zn]
landesweit national ['næʃnl]
Landhaus villa ['vɪlə]
Landkarte map [mæp]
Landschaft scenery ['si:nri]
Landstraße road [rəʊd]
Landwirt/Landwirtin farmer ['fɑ:mə]
Landwirtschaft agriculture ['ægrɪkʌltʃə]; farming [fɑ:mɪŋ]
lang long [lɒŋ]
Langbogen long bow ['lɒŋ bəʊ]
Länge length [leŋkθ]
langsam slow [sləʊ]
langsamer werden to slow down [ˌsləʊ 'daʊn]
langweilig boring ['bɔ:rɪŋ]
Laptop laptop ['læptɒp]
Lärm noise [nɔɪz]
lassen to leave [li:v]; to let [let]
jmdn. im Stich lassen to let sb down [let 'daʊn]
Lasst uns .... Let's .... [lets]
Lassi *(Jogurtgetränk)* lassi ['lasɪ]
Last load [ləʊd]
Lastwagen truck *(AE)* [trʌk]
Lastwagenfahrer/Lastwagenfahrerin truckie *(Aus)* ['trʌki]; trucker *(AE)* ['trʌkə]
lateinamerikanisch Hispanic [hɪ'spænɪk]
Laterne lantern ['læntən]
Latino Latino [lə'ti:nəʊ]
Latinomusik Latino [lə'ti:nəʊ]
Lauf run [rʌn]
Laufbahn career [kə'rɪə]
laufen to be on [bi:‿'ɒn]; to run [rʌn]; to walk [wɔ:k]
laufen gegen to run into [rʌn‿'ɪntə]
laufen mit *(Auto)* to run on ['rʌn‿ɒn]
Läufer/Läuferin runner ['rʌnə]
jmdm. den **Laufpass geben** to dump sb [dʌmp]
Laune mood [mu:d]
laut loud [laʊd]
laut according to [ə'kɔ:dɪŋ tə]
Es **lautete ....** It said .... [ɪt 'sed]
Leasing leasing ['li:sɪŋ]
leben to live [lɪv]
Leben life, lives *(pl)* [laɪf; laɪvz]
am Leben alive [ə'laɪv]
lebendig alive [ə'laɪv]
Lebens- vital ['vaɪtl]
Lebensart lifestyle ['laɪfstaɪl]
Lebenslauf curriculum vitae (CV) [kə'rɪkjələm 'vi:taɪ]
Lebensmittel food [fu:d]
lebenswichtig vital ['vaɪtl]
Lebenszeichen vital signs *(pl)* [ˌvaɪtl 'saɪnz]
Lebewesen creature ['kri:tʃə]
lecken to lick [lɪk]
Leder leather ['leðə]
leer dead [ded]; empty ['empti]
legal legal ['li:gl]
legen to put [pʊt]
sich legen to come down [kʌm 'daʊn]
lehnen to lean [li:n]
sich lehnen to lean [li:n]
Lehre apprenticeship [ə'prentɪʃɪp]
lehren to teach [ti:tʃ]
Lehrer/Lehrerin instructor [ɪn'strʌktə]; teacher ['ti:tʃə]
Lehrling apprentice [ə'prentɪs]
Lehrplan curriculum [kə'rɪkjələm]
Leibeigener/Leibeigene serf [sɜ:f]
leicht easy ['i:zi]; light [laɪt]
Tut mir **leid.** sorry ['sɒri]
leiden to suffer ['sʌfə]
Leidenschaft passion ['pæʃn]
leider I'm afraid ... [ˌaɪm‿ə'freɪd]
leihen to borrow ['bɒrəʊ]; to lend [lend]
Leinwand screen [skri:n]
leise quiet [kwaɪət]; soft [sɒft]
leistungsfähig powerful ['paʊəfl]
leiten to lead [li:d]
Leiter ladder ['lædə]
Leitungswasser tap water ['tæp ˌwɔ:tə]
Lektor/Lektorin editor ['edɪtə]
lernen to learn [lɜ:n]; to study ['stʌdi]; to train [treɪn]
Lernen study ['stʌdi]; studies *(pl)* ['stʌdiz]
Lernender/Lernende learner ['lɜ:nə]
lesen to read [ri:d]
Leser/Leserin reader ['ri:də]
letzter/letzte/letztes final ['faɪnl]; last [lɑ:st]; recent ['ri:snt]
Leuchte lamp [læmp]
leuchten to glow [gləʊ]
leuchtend bright [braɪt]; brilliant ['brɪljənt]
Leuchtfeuer flare [fleə]
Leukämie leukaemia [lju:'ki:miə]
Leute people ['pi:pl]; folks *(Anrede)* [fəʊks]

Level level ['levl]
Licht light [laɪt]
Lichtschein flare [fleə]
lieb dear [dɪə]
Liebe/Lieber ... *(Anrede in Briefen)* Dear [dɪə]
Liebe love [lʌv]
lieben to love [lʌv]
ich würde **lieber** I'd rather [aɪd 'rɑ:ðə]
Liebhaber lover ['lʌvə]
Liebling pet [pet]
Lieblings- favourite ['feɪvrɪt]
Lied song [sɒŋ]
liefern to deliver [dɪ'lɪvə]; to provide (sb with sth) [prə'vaɪd]; to supply [sə'plaɪ]
Lieferwagen van [væn]
liegen to lie [laɪ]
Lift lift *(BE)* [lɪft]
Liga union ['ju:njən]
lila purple ['pɜ:pl]
Limit limit ['lɪmɪt]
limitieren to limit ['lɪmɪt]
Limonade lemonade [ˌlemə'neɪd]
Limousine limousine [ˌlɪmə'zi:n]
Lineal ruler ['ru:lə]
Linie line [laɪn]
Link link [lɪŋk]
linker/linke/linkes left [left]
links left [left]; on the left [ɒn ðə 'left]
links abbiegen to turn left [tɜ:n 'left]
Lippenpflegestift lip balm ['lɪp bɑ:m]
Liste list [lɪst]
Liter litre ['li:tə]
live live [laɪv]
Lkw-Zug road train ['rəʊd ˌtreɪn]
Loch dump [dʌmp]
Lockenkopf curly ['kɜ:li]
lockig curly ['kɜ:li]
lodern to flare [fleə]
Löffel spoon [spu:n]
Logbuch logbook ['lɒgbʊk]
Logo logo ['ləʊgəʊ]
Lohn pay [peɪ]
lokal local ['ləʊkl]
löschen to erase [ɪ'reɪz]; *(Text)* to delete [dɪ'li:t]; *(Feuer)* to put out [pʊt‿'aʊt]
lösen to solve [sɒlv]
losgehen *(Alarm)* to go off [gəʊ‿'ɒf]
etw./jmdn. **loswerden** to get rid of sth/sb [get 'rɪd‿əv]
Löwe lion ['laɪən]
loyal loyal ['lɔɪəl]
Luft air [eə]
durch die Luft (schwebend) airborne ['eəbɔ:n]
Luftballon balloon [bə'lu:n]
Luftpumpe pump [pʌmp]
luftübertragen airborne ['eəbɔ:n]
Lüge lie [laɪ]
lügen to lie [laɪ]
Lunge lung [lʌŋ]
Lust desire [dɪ'zaɪə]
lustig funny ['fʌni]
sich lustig machen über to laugh at ['lɑ:f‿ət]
Lyrik poetry ['pəʊətri]

M

machen to do [du:]; to make [meɪk]
eine Diät machen to go on a diet [ˌgəʊ‿ɒn‿ə 'daɪət]
sich lustig machen über to laugh at ['lɑ:f‿ət]
Spaß machen to be fun [bi: 'fʌn]
Macht power ['paʊə]
mächtig powerful ['paʊəfl]
Mädchen girl [gɜ:l]
Magazin magazine [mægə'zi:n]
Magen stomach ['stʌmək]
Mahlzeit meal [mi:l]
Mai May [meɪ]
mailen to e-mail ['i:meɪl]; to mail [meɪl]
makellos pristine ['prɪsti:n]
Make-up make-up ['meɪkʌp]
Mal *(zeitlich)* time [taɪm]
malen to paint [peɪnt]
Mama mom *(AE)* [mɒm]; mum [mʌm]
man you [ju:; jə]; they [ðeɪ]
Management management ['mænɪdʒmənt]
Manager/Managerin manager ['mænɪdʒə]
manchmal sometimes ['sʌmtaɪmz]
Manga *(japanischer Comic)* manga ['mæŋgə]
Mangel shortage ['ʃɔ:tɪdʒ]
Mangel (an) lack (of) [læk]
manipulieren to fix [fɪks]
Mann man, men *(pl)* [mæn; men]
freier Mann freeman, freemen *(pl)* ['fri:mən, fri:men]
Männchen male [meɪl]
männlich male [meɪl]
Mannschaft crew [kru:]; team [ti:m]
Mantarochen manta ray ['mæntə ˌreɪ]
Mantel coat [kəʊt]
Mäppchen pencil case ['pensl ˌkeɪs]
Mappe folder ['fəʊldə]
Marihuana marijuana [ˌmærɪ'wɑ:nə]
Marketing marketing ['mɑ:kɪtɪŋ]
Markstein landmark ['lændmɑ:k]
Markt market ['mɑ:kɪt]
Marmelade jam [dʒæm]
Marsch march [mɑ:tʃ]
marschieren to march [mɑ:tʃ]
März March [mɑ:tʃ]
Maschine engine ['endʒɪn]; machine [mə'ʃi:n]
Maschinenbau engineering [ˌendʒɪ'nɪərɪŋ]
Maske mask [mɑ:sk]
Massage massage ['mæsɑ:ʒ]
Mast post [pəʊst]
Material material [mə'tɪəriəl]
Materie matter ['mætə]
Mathematik Maths [mæθs]
Mauer wall [wɔ:l]
Maus mouse, mice *(pl)* [maʊs; maɪs]
Mechaniker/Mechanikerin mechanic [mə'kænɪk]
Mechatroniker/Mechatronikerin mechatronic engineer [mɪkæˌtrɒnɪk endʒɪ'nɪə]
Medien media *(pl)* ['mi:diə]
Medikament drug [drʌg]
Meer sea [si:]
Meeresküste seaside ['si:saɪd]
mehr more [mɔ:]
mehrere several ['sevrl]
Mehrheit majority [mə'dʒɒrəti]
Mehrheiten- majority [mə'dʒɒrəti]
Mehrzahl plural ['plʊərəl]
meiden to avoid [ə'vɔɪd]
Meile *(brit. Längenmaß)* mile [maɪl]
meilenweit for miles [fə‿'maɪlz]
mein/meine my [maɪ]
Mein Gott! My God! [maɪ 'gɒd]
Meinung opinion [ə'pɪnjən]
einer Meinung sein to agree [ə'gri:]
das **meiste** most [məʊst]
die meisten most [məʊst]
melden to report [rɪ'pɔ:t]
sich melden to report [rɪ'pɔ:t]
sich melden (bei) to get back (to) [get 'bæk tə]
Meldung report [rɪ'pɔ:t]
Menagerie menagerie [mə'nædʒri]
Menge amount [ə'maʊnt]
eine Menge a lot of [ə 'lɒt‿əv]
Mensch human ['hju:mən]
Menschen people ['pi:pl]
Menschenmenge crowd [kraʊd]
menschlich human ['hju:mən]
Menü menu ['menju:]
sich **merken** to remember [rɪ'membə]
typisches **Merkmal** characteristic [ˌkærəktə'rɪstɪk]
merkwürdig strange [streɪndʒ]
Messe fair [feə]
Messer knife, knives *(pl)* [naɪf; naɪvz]

Metal *(Musikrichtung)* metal ['metl]
Metall metal ['metl]
Meter metre (m) ['mi:tə]
Methode technique [tek'ni:k]
Mexikaner/Mexikanerin Mexican ['meksɪkən]
mexikanisch Mexican ['meksɪkən]
mich me [mi:]
mich (selbst) myself [maɪ'self]
Miesmacher/Miesmacherin wet blanket [wet 'blæŋkɪt]
Miet- rental ['rentl]
Miete rent [rent]
mieten to rent [rent]
Mikrofon microphone ['maɪkrəfəʊn]
Mikrowelle microwave ['maɪkrəʊweɪv]
Milch milk [mɪlk]
Milchmann milkman, milkmen *(pl)* ['mɪlkmən; 'mɪlkmen]
Milchshake milkshake ['mɪlkʃeɪk]
militant militant ['mɪlɪtnt]
Militär armed forces [ˌɑ:md 'fɔ:sɪz]; military ['mɪlɪtri]
Milliarde *(tausend Millionen)* billion ['bɪljən]
Million million ['mɪlɪən]
minderjährig young [jʌŋ]
mindest- minimum ['mɪnɪməm]
mindestens at least [ət 'li:st]
Mineral- mineral ['mɪnərəl]
Minestrone minestrone [ˌmɪnɪ'strəʊni]
Minimum minimum ['mɪnɪməm]
Minister/Ministerin minister ['mɪnɪstə]
Minute minute ['mɪnɪt]
mir me [mi:]
Mischung cocktail ['kɒkteɪl]; mixture ['mɪkstʃə]
mit with [wɪð]
zufällig **mitanhören** to overhear [ˌəʊvə'hɪə]
Mitarbeiter/Mitarbeiterin employee [ɪm'plɔɪi:]
mitbringen to bring [brɪŋ]
miteinander together [tə'geðə]
Mitfahrgelegenheit ride [raɪd]
Mitglied member ['membə]
Mitglied des Parlaments Member of Parliament (MP) [ˌmembə‿əv 'pɑ:ləmənt]
Mitleid erregend pathetic [pə'θetɪk]
mitnehmen to take [teɪk]
zum Mitnehmen to go [tə‿'gəʊ]
Mitschüler/Mitschülerin classmate ['klɑ:smeɪt]
Mitspieler/Mitspielerin player ['pleɪə]
Mittagessen dinner ['dɪnə]; lunch [lʌntʃ]
Mittagszeit lunchtime ['lʌntʃtaɪm]
Mitte middle ['mɪdl]
mittel medium ['mi:diəm]
Mittel- middle ['mɪdl]
Mittelalter Middle Ages [ˌmɪdl‿'eɪdʒɪz]
Mittelpunkt centre ['sentə]; hub [hʌb]
Mittelschule *(weiterführende Schule in den USA, Mittelstufe)* middle school *(AE)* ['mɪdl ˌsku:l]
Mitternacht midnight ['mɪdnaɪt]
mittlerweile meanwhile [ˌmi:n'waɪl]
Mittwoch Wednesday ['wenzdeɪ]
Mixtur mixture ['mɪkstʃə]
Mobbing bullying ['bʊliɪŋ]
Möbel furniture ['fɜ:nɪtʃə]
mobil mobile ['məʊbaɪl]
Mobiltelefon cell phone *(AE)* ['sel fəʊn]; mobile ['məʊbaɪl]
möchte(n) gern would like [wʊd 'laɪk]
Mode fashion ['fæʃn]
Model model ['mɒdl]
Modell model ['mɒdl]
modern modern ['mɒdn]
modisch trendy ['trendi]
mögen to like [laɪk]
gern mögen to love [lʌv]
möglich possible ['pɒsəbl]
Möglichkeit chance [tʃɑ:nts]; opportunity [ˌɒpə'tju:nəti]
Mohrrübe carrot ['kærət]
Mole pier [pɪə]
Molkerei dairy ['deəri]
Moment moment ['məʊmənt]
Moment mal! Hang on! ['hæŋ‿ɒn]
momentan at the moment [æt ðə 'məʊmənt]
Monarch/Monarchin monarch ['mɒnək]
Monat month [mʌnθ]
Mond moon [mu:n]
Mongole/Mongolin Mongolian [mɒŋ'gəʊliən]
mongolisch Mongolian [mɒŋ'gəʊliən]
Monster monster ['mɒnstə]
Montag Monday ['mʌndeɪ]
montags on Mondays [ɒn 'mʌndeɪz]
moralisch ethical ['eθɪkl]
Mord murder ['mɜ:də]
Mörder/Mörderin killer ['kɪlə]
Mörder assassin [ə'sæsɪn]
morgen tomorrow [tə'mɒrəʊ]
Morgen morning ['mɔ:nɪŋ]
am Morgen in the morning [ˌɪn ðə 'mɔ:nɪŋ]
am nächsten Morgen the next morning [ðə ˌnekst 'mɔ:nɪŋ]
Guten Morgen! Good morning! [ˌgʊd 'mɔ:nɪŋ]
Morgenappell assembly [ə'sembli]
Morgendämmerung dawn [dɔ:n]
morgens in the morning [ˌɪn ðə 'mɔ:nɪŋ]
Motor engine ['endʒɪn]; motor ['məʊtəbaɪk]
Motor- motor ['məʊtəbaɪk]
Motorrad motorbike ['məʊtəbaɪk]
Motte moth [mɒθ]
Motto motto ['mɒtəʊ]
MP3 MP3 [ˌempi:'θri:]
MP3-Player MP3 player [ˌempi:'θri: ˌpleɪə]
müde tired ['taɪəd]
Müll rubbish ['rʌbɪʃ]
Mülleimer bin [bɪn]
Müllkippe dump [dʌmp]
Mülltonne bin [bɪn]
Müllverbrennungsanlage incinerator [ɪn'sɪnreɪtə]
multikulturell multicultural [ˌmʌlti'kʌltʃrl]
multinational multinational [ˌmʌlti'næʃnl]
Mund mouth [maʊθ]
Mund-zu-Mund-Beatmung mouth-to-mouth [ˌmaʊθtə'maʊθ]
mündlich orally ['ɔ:rli]
Mundschutz mask [mɑ:sk]
Muschel shell [ʃel]
Museum museum [mju:'zi:əm]
Musical musical ['mju:zɪkl]
Musik music ['mju:zɪk]
Musiker/Musikerin musician [mju:'zɪʃn]
Muss must [mʌst]
Muße leisure ['leʒə]
müssen must [mʌst]; to have to ['hæv tə]; to need [ni:d]
wieder guten **Mutes sein** to cheer up [tʃɪer‿'ʌp]
mutig brave [breɪv]
Mutter mother ['mʌðə]
Muttersprache mother tongue ['mʌðə ˌtʌŋ]
Mutti mom *(AE)* [mɒm]; mum [mʌm]
Mütze cap [kæp]
Mythos myth [mɪθ]

N

nach after ['ɑ:ftə]; *(Uhrzeit)* past [pɑ:st]; to [tʊ; tə]
nach draußen outside [aʊt'saɪd]
nach drinnen inside [ɪn'saɪd]
nach Hause home [həʊm]
nach Hause bringen to take home [ˌteɪk 'həʊm]
nach unten down [daʊn]
Nachbar/Nachbarin neighbour ['neɪbə]

Nachbarschaft neighborhood *(AE)* ['neɪbəhʊd]
nachdem after ['ɑ:ftə]
Nachhilfe coaching ['kəʊtʃɪŋ]
Nachmittag afternoon [ˌɑ:ftə'nu:n]
am Nachmittag in the afternoon [ˌɪn ði: ˌɑ:ftə'nu:n]
nachmittags in the afternoon [ˌɪn ði: ˌɑ:ftə'nu:n]
Nachmittagstee afternoon tea [ˌɑ:ftənu:n 'ti:]
Nachricht message ['mesɪdʒ]; news *(sg)* [nju:z]
Nachrichten news *(sg)* [nju:z]
neueste Nachrichten breaking news [ˌbreɪkɪŋ 'nju:z]
nachschlagen to look up [lʊk‿'ʌp]
nächster/nächste/nächstes next [nekst]
am nächsten Morgen the next morning [ðə ˌnekst 'mɔ:nɪŋ]
Nacht night [naɪt]
heute Nacht tonight [tə'naɪt]
nachts at night [ət 'naɪt]
Nachteil disadvantage [ˌdɪsəd'vɑ:ntɪdʒ]
Nachtisch dessert [dɪ'zɜ:t]; pudding ['pʊdɪŋ]
Nachtschwester night nurse ['naɪt nɜ:s]
nachweisen to prove [pru:v]
Nacktschnecke slug [slʌg]
nahe close [kləʊs]; near [nɪə]
in der **Nähe von** near [nɪə]
sich jmdm. von hinten **nähern** to come up behind sb [ˌkʌm ʌp bɪ'haɪnd]
Nahrung food [fu:d]
Name name [neɪm]
Nase nose [nəʊz]
die Nase voll haben to be fed up [bi: ˌfed‿'ʌp]
nass wet [wet]
Nation nation ['neɪʃn]
national national ['næʃnl]
Nationalpark national park [ˌnæʃnl 'pɑ:k]
Natur nature ['neɪtʃə]
freie Natur outdoors [ˌaʊt'dɔ:z]
in der freien Natur outdoors [ˌaʊt'dɔ:z]
Natur- natural ['nætʃrl]
natürlich natural ['nætʃrl]
natürlich of course [əv 'kɔ:s]
Naturschutz conservation [ˌkɒnsə'veɪʃn]
Naturwissenschaft Science ['saɪəns]
Nebel fog [fɒg]
neben along with [ə'lɒŋ wɪð]; beside [bɪ'saɪd]; by [baɪ]; next to ['nekst tə]
nebenan next door [ˌnekst 'dɔ:]
Nebenprodukt spin-off ['spɪn‿ɒf]
neblig foggy ['fɒgi]
Neffe nephew ['nefju:]
nehmen to take [teɪk]
Ich nehme .... I'm having .... [aɪm 'hævɪŋ]
sich in Acht nehmen vor to look out for [ˌlʊk‿'aʊt fə]
neidisch (auf) jealous (of) ['dʒeləs]
nein no [nəʊ]
nennen to call [kɔ:l]; to name [neɪm]
Das nenne ich .... That's what I call .... [ˌðæts wɒt‿'aɪ ˌkɔ:l]
neonfarben neon ['ni:ɒn]
Neoprenanzug wetsuit ['wetsu:t]
Nervensystem nervous system ['nɜ:vəs ˌsɪstəm]
nervös nervous ['nɜ:vəs]
nett friendly ['frendli]; kind [kaɪnd]; nice [naɪs]
Netz net [net]
neu new [nju:]; recent ['ri:snt]
auf dem neuesten Stand state-of-the-art [ˌsteɪtəvði'ɑ:t]
neuester/neueste/neuestes recent ['ri:snt]
Neuigkeit(en) news *(sg)* [nju:z]
neulich recently ['ri:sntli]
neutral neutral ['nju:trl]
nicht no [nəʊ]; not [nɒt]
auch nicht not ... either [ˌnɒt ... 'aɪðə]
nicht einmal not even [nɒt‿'i:vn]
noch nicht not ... yet [jet]
nichts nothing ['nʌθɪŋ]
Nickel *(Währung)* nickel ['nɪkl]
nie never ['nevə]
nieder down [daʊn]
Niederländer/Niederländerinnen Dutch [dʌtʃ]
niederländisch Dutch [dʌtʃ]
niederlegen to lie down [laɪ 'daʊn]
niedlich cute [kju:t]
niedrig low [ləʊ]
niemals never ['nevə]
niemand nobody ['nəʊbədi]; no one ['nəʊwʌn]
nirgendwo nowhere ['nəʊweə]
nirgendwohin nowhere ['nəʊweə]
Niveau level ['levl]
noch still [stɪl]
noch ein/noch eine another [ə'nʌðə]
noch nicht not ... yet [jet]
non-stop non-stop [ˌnɒn'stɒp]
Norden north [nɔ:θ]
normal normal ['nɔ:ml]; ordinary ['ɔ:dnri]
normalerweise normally ['nɔ:mli]; usually ['ju:ʒli]
Norweger/Norwegerin Norwegian [nɔ:'wi:dʒn]
norwegisch Norwegian [nɔ:'wi:dʒn]
Note grade *(AE)* [greɪd]; mark [mɑ:k]
Notfall emergency [ɪ'mɜ:dʒnsi]
Notiz note [nəʊt]; notice ['nəʊtɪs]
Notlage emergency [ɪ'mɜ:dʒnsi]
November November [nəʊ'vembə]
Nummer number ['nʌmbə]
nun now [naʊ]
nur only ['əʊnli]
Nutzen advantage [əd'vɑ:ntɪdʒ]; use [ju:s]
nützlich useful ['ju:sfl]
nutzlos useless ['ju:sləs]
Nutzung use [ju:s]

O

ob if [ɪf]
oben above [ə'bʌv]; at the top [ət ðə 'tɒp]; up [ʌp]; upstairs [ʌp'steəz]
oberer/obere/oberes upper ['ʌpə]
im oberen Teil at the top [ət ðə 'tɒp]
oberer Teil top [tɒp]
Oberfläche surface ['sɜ:fɪs]
oberhalb above [ə'bʌv]
oberster/oberste/oberstes supreme [su:'pri:m]
Oberstufe sixth form ['sɪksθ ˌfɔ:m]
Objekt object ['ɒbdʒɪkt]
obligatorisch compulsory [kəm'pʌlsri]
Observatorium observatory [əb'zɜ:vətri]
Obst fruit [fru:t]
obwohl although [ɔ:l'ðəʊ]; even though [ˌi:vn‿'ðəʊ]
oder or [ɔ:]
entweder ... oder ... either ... or ... ['aɪðə; 'i:ðə ... ɔ:]
offen open ['əʊpn]
öffentlich public ['pʌblɪk]
in der **Öffentlichkeit** in public [ɪn 'pʌblɪk]
Öffentlichkeitsarbeit public relations (PR) [ˌpʌblɪk rɪ'leɪʃnz]
offiziell official [ə'fɪʃl]
öffnen to open ['əʊpn]
sich öffnen to open ['əʊpn]
Öffnungszeiten hours *(pl)* ['aʊəz]
oft often ['ɒfn]
ohne without [wɪ'ðaʊt]
ohne ... auskommen to go without [ˌgəʊ wɪ'ðaʊt]
ohnmächtig werden to faint [feɪnt]
Ohr ear [ɪə]
o.k. OK [əʊ'keɪ]
Öko- eco ['i:kəʊ]
Oktober October [ɒk'təʊbə]

Oktopus octopus ['ɒktəpəs]
Öl oil [ɔɪl]
Olympiade the Olympics *(Olympic Games)* [əʊ'lɪmpɪks; əʊˌlɪmpɪk 'geɪmz]
Olympische Spiele the Olympics *(Olympic Games)* [əʊ'lɪmpɪks; əʊˌlɪmpɪk 'geɪmz]
Oma grandma ['grændmɑː]
Onkel uncle ['ʌŋkl]
online online [ˌɒn'laɪn]
Opa grandad ['grændæd]
Oper opera ['ɒprə]
operieren to operate ['ɒpəreɪt]
Opfer victim ['vɪktɪm]
Optimismus optimism ['ɒptɪmɪzm]
Option option ['ɒpʃn]
Orange orange ['ɒrɪndʒ]
ordentlich properly ['prɒpli]
Ordner folder ['fəʊldə]
in **Ordnung** all right [ɔːl 'raɪt]
Organisation organisation [ˌɔːgnaɪ'zeɪʃn]
Organisator/Organisatorin organizer ['ɔːgənaɪzə]
organisatorisch organizational [ˌɔːgnaɪ'zeɪʃnl]
organisch organic [ɔː'gænɪk]
organisieren to organize ['ɔːgənaɪz]
Orientierung bearings *(pl)* ['beərɪŋz]
Ort place [pleɪs]; site [saɪt]
örtlich local ['ləʊkl]
Ortsansässige/Ortsansässige resident ['rezɪdnt]
Osten east [iːst]
nach Osten east [iːst]
das **Outback** the Outback ['aʊtbæk]
outsourcen to outsource ['aʊtsɔːs]
Outsourcing *(Ausgliederung von Produktions- oder Dienstleistungen an externe Mitarbeiter)* outsourcing ['aʊtsɔːsɪŋ]
Ozean ocean ['əʊʃn]
Ozeandampfer ocean liner ['əʊʃn ˌlaɪnə]

P

ein **paar** a few [ə 'fjuː]
Paar couple ['kʌpl]
Pacht rent [rent]
pachten to rent [rent]
Päckchen packet ['pækɪt]
packen to pack [pæk]
Packmaterial packaging ['pækɪdʒɪŋ]
Paket packet ['pækɪt]
Palast palace ['pælɪs]
Palästinenser/Palästinenserin Palestinian [ˌpælə'stɪniən]
palästinensisch Palestinian [ˌpælə'stɪniən]
Palm- palm [pɑːm]
Palme palm [pɑːm]
panisch reagieren to panic ['pænɪk]
Panter panther ['pæntθə]
Panzer tank [tæŋk]
Papa dad [dæd]
Papier paper ['peɪpə]
Parade parade [pə'reɪd]
Paradies paradise ['pærəˌdaɪs]
Park park [pɑːk]
parken to park [pɑːk]
Parkplatz parking lot *(AE)* ['pɑːkɪŋ ˌlɒt]
Parlament parliament ['pɑːləmənt]
Partei party ['pɑːti]
Partikel particle ['pɑːtɪkl]
Partitur (music) score [skɔː]
Partner/Partnerin partner ['pɑːtnə]
Party party ['pɑːti]
eine Party feiern to have a party [ˌhæv‿ə 'pɑːti]
Pass passport ['pɑːspɔːt]
Passagier/Passagierin passenger ['pæsndʒə]
passen to fit [fɪt]; to suit [suːt]
passen zu to match [mætʃ]; to go (together) with ['gəʊ wɪð]; to suit [suːt]
passend suitable ['suːtəbl]
Passion passion ['pæʃn]
Passkontrolle passports *(pl)* ['pɑːspɔːts]
Pastrami pastrami [pəs'trɑːmi]
Patient/Patientin patient ['peɪʃnt]
Pause break [breɪk]; recess *(AE)* ['rɪses]
PC PC [ˌpiː'siː]
Pech bad luck [ˌbæd 'lʌk]
Pech haben to be unlucky [ˌbiː‿ʌn'lʌki]
Pedal pedal ['pedl]
Pegel level ['levl]
peinlich embarrassing [ɪm'bærəsɪŋ]
Pence *(Währung)* pence *(pl)* [pents]
perfekt perfect ['pɜːfɪkt]
Periode period *(AE)* ['pɪəriəd]
permanent permanent ['pɜːmnənt]
Person person ['pɜːsn]
Personal staff [stɑːf]
Personalabteilung human resources [ˌhjuːmən rɪ'zɔːsɪz]
persönlich personal ['pɜːsnl]
Persönlichkeit personality [ˌpɜːsn'æləti]
Perspektive prospect ['prɒspekt]
Perücke wig [wɪg]
Pest plague [pleɪg]
Pestizid pesticide ['pestɪsaɪd]
Petzer/Petze sneak [sniːk]
Pfad path [pɑːθ]
Pfannkuchen pancake ['pænkeɪk]
Pfeife pipe [paɪp]
pfeifen to whistle ['wɪsl]
Pfeil arrow ['ærəʊ]
Pferd horse [hɔːs]
Pfiff whistle ['wɪsl]
Pflanze plant [plɑːnt]
pflanzen to plant [plɑːnt]
pflegte(n) zu used to *(+ infinitive)* ['juːs‿tə]
Pflicht duty ['djuːti]
pflücken to pick [pɪk]
Pflücker/Pflückerin picker ['pɪkə]
pflügen to plough [plaʊ]
Pforte gate [geɪt]
Pfosten post [pəʊst]
Pfund *(Währung)* pound (£) [paʊnd]; *(Gewicht)* pound (lb) [paʊnd]
Physik Physics ['fɪzɪks]
physisch physical ['fɪzɪkl]
Pier pier [pɪə]
pikant spicy ['spaɪsi]
Pilot/Pilotin pilot ['paɪlət]
pink pink [pɪŋk]
Pionier/Pionierin pioneer [ˌpaɪə'nɪə]
Pizza pizza ['piːtsə]
Plage plague [pleɪg]
Plakat poster ['pəʊstə]
Plan plan [plæn]
planen to plan [plæn]
Planen planning ['plænɪŋ]
Planet planet ['plænɪt]
Planung planning ['plænɪŋ]
Plastik(-) plastic ['plæstɪk]
platt flat [flæt]
Platte panel ['pænl]
Plattform platform ['plætfɔːm]
Platz place [pleɪs]; room [ruːm; rʊm]; space [speɪs]
pleite broke [brəʊk]
plötzlich at once [ət 'wʌnts]; sudden ['sʌdn]; suddenly ['sʌdnli]
Plundergebäck Danish ['deɪnɪʃ]
Plural plural ['plʊərəl]
plus plus [plʌs]
Poet/Poetin poet ['pəʊɪt]
Poetry Slam *(Gedichtwettbewerb)* poetry slam ['pəʊətri ˌslæm]
Pokal cup [kʌp]
Politik policy ['pɒlɪsi]
politisch political [pə'lɪtɪkl]
politische Linie policy ['pɒlɪsi]
Polizei police [pə'liːs]
Polizist policeman, policemen *(pl)* [pə'liːsmən; pə'liːsmen]
Polizist/Polizistin cop *(AE)* [kɒp]
polnisch Polish ['pəʊlɪʃ]
Pommes frites French fries *(AE)* ['frentʃ ˌfraɪz]; chips *(pl)* [tʃɪps]

Pompon *(bunte Quaste der Cheerleader)* pompom ['pɒmpɒm]
Pony pony ['pəʊni]
Popmusik pop [pɒp]
populär popular ['pɒpjələ]
Portion share [ʃeə]
Porträt profile ['prəʊfaɪl]
posieren to pose [pəʊz]
Position bearings *(pl)* ['beərɪŋz]; position [pə'zɪʃn]
Post mail [meɪl]; post [pəʊst]
Post- postal ['pəʊstl]
postalisch postal ['pəʊstl]
Postamt post office ['pəʊst‿ɒfɪs]
posten *(im Internetforum)* to post [pəʊst]
Poster poster ['pəʊstə]
Postkarte postcard ['pəʊstkɑːd]
Prachtstraße boulevard ['buːləvɑːd]
prahlen to boast [bəʊst]
Praktikant/Praktikantin intern *(AE)* ['ɪntɜːn]
Praktikum internship *(AE)* ['ɪntɜːnʃɪp]; (work) placement ['pleɪsmənt]
praktisch practical ['præktɪkl]
praktizieren to practise ['præktɪs]
Präsentation presentation [ˌprezn'teɪʃn]
präsentieren to present [prɪ'zent]
Präsident/Präsidentin president ['prezɪdnt]
prasseln to crackle ['krækl]
Preis award [ə'wɔːd]; cost [kɒst]; price [praɪs]; prize [praɪz]; trophy ['trəʊfi]
zum halben Preis half-price [ˌhɑːf'praɪs]
Prellung bruise [bruːz]
Premierminister/Premierministerin Prime Minister (PM) [ˌpraɪm 'mɪnɪstə]
Presse press [pres]
pressen to press [pres]; to squash [skwɒʃ]
Pressesprecher/Pressesprecherin communications officer [kəmjuːnɪ'keɪʃnz ˌɒfɪsə]
prima brilliant ['brɪljənt]; cool [kuːl]
Prinz prince [prɪns]
privat private ['praɪvɪt]
Privatisierung privatisation [ˌpraɪvɪtaɪ'zeɪʃn]
Privatschule (GB) public school [ˌpʌblɪk 'skuːl]
pro per [pɜː]
Pro und Kontra pros and cons [ˌprəʊz‿ənd 'kɒnz]
proben to practise ['præktɪs]; *(ein Theaterstück)* to rehearse [rɪ'hɜːs]
probieren to try [traɪ]
Problem problem ['prɒbləm]
Produkt product ['prɒdʌkt]
Produktion production [prə'dʌkʃn]
produktiv prolific [prə'lɪfɪk]
Produzent/Produzentin producer [prə'djuːsə]
produzieren to manufacture [ˌmænjə'fæktʃə]; to produce [prə'djuːs]
professionell professional [prə'feʃnl]
Professor/Professorin professor [prə'fesə]
Profil profile ['prəʊfaɪl]
Programm channel ['tʃænl]; programme ['prəʊgræm]
Projekt project ['prɒdʒekt]
Prospekt leaflet ['liːflət]
Protest protest ['prəʊtest]
protestieren to protest [prə'test]
Prototyp prototype ['prəʊtətaɪp]
provozieren to provoke [prə'vəʊk]
Prozent per cent (%) [pə 'sent]
Prozentsatz percentage [pə'sentɪdʒ]
prozentualer Anteil percentage [pə'sentɪdʒ]
prüfen to test [test]
Prüfung exam [ɪg'zæm]; trial ['traɪəl]
Publikum audience ['ɔːdiəns]
publizieren to publish ['pʌblɪʃ]
Pudding pudding ['pʊdɪŋ]
Puder powder ['paʊdə]
Pulver powder ['paʊdə]
Pumpe pump [pʌmp]
Punjabi Punjabi [pʌn'dʒɑːbiː]
Punk punk [pʌŋk]
Punkt dot [dɒt]; point [pɔɪnt]
Pünktchen dot [dɒt]
punkten to score [skɔː]
Punktestand score [skɔː]
pünktlich on time [ɒn 'taɪm]
pur pure [pjʊə]
Pute turkey ['tɜːki]
putzen to brush [brʌʃ]
Putzerstation cleaning station ['kliːnɪŋ ˌsteɪʃn]
Putzkraft cleaner ['kliːnə]

Q

Quadrat(-) square [skweə]
Qual ordeal [ɔː'diːl]
Qualifikation qualification [ˌkwɒlɪfɪ'keɪʃn]
voll **qualifiziert** fully-qualified [ˌfʊli'kwɒlɪfaɪd]
Qualle jellyfish, jellyfish *(pl)* ['dʒelifɪʃ]
qualmen to smoulder ['sməʊldə]
Quartier quarters *(pl)* ['kwɔːtəz]
Quelle resource [rɪ'zɔːs]; spring fountain [ˌsprɪŋ 'faʊntɪn]
quer durch across [ə'krɒs]
quetschen to squash [skwɒʃ]
Quetschung bruise [bruːz]
quietschen to creak [kriːk]
Quote quota ['kwəʊtə]

R

Rad wheel [wiːl]
Rad fahren to cycle ['saɪkl]
Radiergummi rubber ['rʌbə]
Radio radio ['reɪdiəʊ]
Radiosender station ['steɪʃn]
Radiosendung radio show ['reɪdiəʊ ˌʃəʊ]
Radkranz rim [rɪm]
raffiniert streetwise ['striːtwaɪz]
Rafting rafting ['rɑːftɪŋ]
Rahmen frame [freɪm]
Rakete rocket ['rɒkɪt]
Rallye rally ['ræli]
Ranch ranch [ræntʃ]
Rand edge [edʒ]
Ranger/Rangerin ranger ['reɪndʒə]
rangieren to range [reɪndʒ]
Rap rap [ræp]
rapide rapid ['ræpɪd]
rappen to rap [ræp]
Rapper/Rapperin rapper ['ræpə]
Raps rape [reɪp]
rasch rapid ['ræpɪd]
Rasierwasser aftershave ['ɑːftəʃeɪv]
Rasse race [reɪs]
Rassen- racial ['reɪʃl]
Rassentrennung segregation [ˌsegrɪ'geɪʃn]
Rastplatz rest area ['rest ˌeəriə]
Rat advice [əd'vaɪs]
raten to advise [əd'vaɪz]; to guess [ges]
Ratschlag advice [əd'vaɪs]
Rätsel mystery ['mɪstri]
rau tough [tʌf]
rauben to rob [rɒb]
Räuber/Räuberin robber ['rɒbə]
Rauch smoke [sməʊk]
rauchen to smoke [sməʊk]; to smoulder ['sməʊldə]
Rauchen smoking ['sməʊkɪŋ]
Raum chamber ['tʃeɪmbə]; room [ruːm; rʊm]; space [speɪs]
Raumfähre shuttle ['ʃʌtl]
Raumpfleger/Raumpflegerin cleaner ['kliːnə]
Raumschiff spaceship ['speɪsʃɪp]
Razzia raid [reɪd]
R&B *(Musikrichtung)* R&B [ˌɑːr‿n'biː]

German – English

Reaktion reaction [ri'ækʃn]; response [rɪ'spɒns]
realisieren to realise ['rɪəlaɪz]
realistisch realistic [ˌrɪə'lɪstɪk]
Realität reality [ri'æləti]
Realityshow reality show [ri'æləti ˌʃəʊ]
Recherche research [rɪ'sɜ:tʃ]
Recht law [lɔ:]; right [raɪt]
  Recht haben to be right [bi: 'raɪt]
rechte/rechter/rechtes right [raɪt]
rechtlich legal ['li:gl]
rechts on the right [ɒn ðə 'raɪt]; right [raɪt]
  rechts abbiegen to turn right [tɜ:n 'raɪt]
Rechts- legal ['li:gl]
rechtswidrig illegal [ɪ'li:gl]
rechtzeitig in time [ɪn 'taɪm]
recyceln to recycle [ri:'saɪkl]
Redakteur/Redakteurin editor ['edɪtə]
Rede speech [spi:tʃ]; talk [tɔ:k]
  eine Rede halten to give a talk [ˌgɪv‿ə 'tɔ:k]
reden to talk [tɔ:k]
  reden mit to talk to ['tɔ:k tə]
Redensart idiom ['ɪdiəm]
Redewendung expression [ɪk'spreʃn]; idiom ['ɪdiəm]; phrase [freɪz]
reduzieren to reduce [rɪ'dju:s]
Referenz reference ['refrns]; *(Person)* referee [ˌrefr'i:]
Refrain chorus ['kɔ:rəs]
Regal shelf, shelves *(pl)* [ʃelf; ʃelvz]
Regalbrett shelf, shelves *(pl)* [ʃelf; ʃelvz]
Regel rule [ru:l]
regelmäßig regular ['regjələ]
regeln *(ein Problem)* to sort out [sɔ:t‿'aʊt]
Regen rain [reɪn]
  saurer Regen acid rain [ˌæsɪd 'reɪn]
Regenguss shower ['ʃaʊə]
Regenschirm umbrella [ʌm'brelə]
Reggae reggae ['regeɪ]
Regierung government ['gʌvnmənt]
Regisseur/Regisseurin director [dɪ'rektə]
registrieren to register ['redʒɪstə]
  sich registrieren to register ['redʒɪstə]
Registrierung registration [ˌredʒɪ'streɪʃn]
regnen to rain [reɪn]
regnerisch rainy ['reɪni]
regulär regular ['regjələ]
reich rich [rɪtʃ]
reichen to range [reɪndʒ]
reichlich abundant [ə'bʌndənt]
Reichtum fortune ['fɔ:tʃu:n]; wealth [welθ]
Reichweite range [reɪndʒ]
Reihe row [rəʊ]
Reihenfolge order ['ɔ:də]
rein pristine ['prɪsti:n]; pure [pjʊə]
reinigen to clean [kli:n]
Reis rice [raɪs]
Reise journey ['dʒɜ:ni]; tour [tʊə]; trip [trɪp]; travel ['trævl]
reisen to travel ['trævl]
Reisepass passport ['pɑ:spɔ:t]
reiten to ride [raɪd]
Religion religion [rɪ'lɪdʒn]
Religionsunterricht Religious Education (RE) [rɪˌlɪdʒəs‿edʒʊ'keɪʃn]
religiös religious [rɪ'lɪdʒəs]
Renn- racing ['reɪsɪŋ]
rennen to run [rʌn]
Rennen race [reɪs]
Reparatur repair [rɪ'peə]
reparieren to fix (to) [fɪks]; to repair [rɪ'peə]
Reporter/Reporterin reporter [rɪ'pɔ:tə]
Repräsentant/Repräsentantin representative [ˌreprɪ'zentətɪv]
Reservat reservation [ˌrezə'veɪʃn]
Reserve reserve [rɪ'zɜ:v]
Reservierung reservation [ˌrezə'veɪʃn]
Resonanz reaction [ri'ækʃn]
Respekt respect [rɪ'spekt]
Respektlosigkeit disrespect [ˌdɪsrɪ'spekt]
Ressource resource [rɪ'zɔ:s]
Rest remain [rɪ'meɪn]; rest [rest]
Restaurant restaurant ['restrɒnt]
  Restaurant mit Straßenverkauf takeaway ['teɪkəweɪ]
restaurieren to restore [rɪ'stɔ:]
Resultat result [rɪ'zʌlt]
retten to rescue ['reskju:]; to save [seɪv]
Rettung rescue ['reskju:]
Rettungsschwimmer/Rettungsschwimmerin lifeguard ['laɪfgɑ:d]
Rezept recipe ['resɪpi:]
Rezeption reception [rɪ'sepʃn]
Rhythmus rhythm ['rɪðm]
sich **richten an** to aim ['eɪm]
Richter judge [dʒʌdʒ]
richtig correct [kə'rekt]; properly ['prɒpli]; right [raɪt]
  richtig machen to get … right [get … 'raɪt]
Richtung direction [dɪ'rekʃn]
  in Richtung towards [tə'wɔ:dz]
riechen to smell [smel]
Riegel bar [bɑ:]
riesig enormous [ɪ'nɔ:məs]; huge [hju:dʒ]; large [lɑ:dʒ]; vast [vɑ:st]
Riff reef [ri:f]
Rind cattle ['kætl]
Rinder cattle ['kætl]
Rinderfarm cattle station ['kætl ˌsteɪʃn]
Rinderhirte cowboy ['kaʊbɔɪ]
Ring ring [rɪŋ]
ringen to struggle ['strʌgl]
Rinnsal trickle ['trɪkl]
Risiko risk [rɪsk]
riskieren to dare [deə]
  etw. riskieren to take your chance [ˌteɪk jɔ: 'tʃɑ:ns]
Ritt ride [raɪd]
Ritter knight [naɪt]
Rivale/Rivalin rival ['raɪvl]
Robbe seal [si:l]
Robe robe [rəʊb]
Roboter robot ['rəʊbɒt]
Robotertechnik robotics [rə'bɒtɪks]
Rock skirt [skɜ:t]
rocken to rock [rɒk]
Rockmusik rock [rɒk]
Rodeo rodeo [rəʊ'deɪəʊ; 'rəʊdiəʊ]
roh raw [rɔ:]
Rohr pipe [paɪp]
Rohrleitung pipe [paɪp]
Rohstoff resource [rɪ'zɔ:s]
Rolle part [pɑ:t]; role [rəʊl]
Roller kickboard ['kɪkbɔ:d]
Roman novel ['nɒvl]
romantisch romantic [rə'mæntɪk]
rosa pink [pɪŋk]
rot red [red]
  rot werden to go red [gəʊ 'red]
rotieren to rotate [rə'teɪt]
Rücken back [bæk]
rückenfrei backless ['bækləs]
rückgängig machen to reverse [rɪ'vɜ:s]
Rücklage reserve [rɪ'zɜ:v]
Rucksack rucksack ['rʌksæk]
Rucksacktourist/Rucksacktouristin backpacker ['bækpækə]
Rücksitz back seat ['bæk si:t]
rückwärtig back [bæk]
Ruf call [kɔ:l]
rufen to call [kɔ:l]; to cry [kraɪ]; to shout [ʃaʊt]; *(Eule)* to hoot [hu:t]
  rhythmisch rufen to chant [tʃɑ:nt]
Rugby rugby ['rʌgbi]
Rugbyschuh rugby boot ['rʌgbi bu:t]
Ruhe quiet [kwaɪət]; silence ['saɪlənts]
ruhig calm [kɑ:m]; quiet [kwaɪət]
rumhängen to hang around *(AE)* [ˌhæŋ‿ə'raʊnd]

Run run [rʌn]
Runde round [raʊnd]; run [rʌn]
Russe/Russin Russian ['rʌʃn]
russisch Russian ['rʌʃn]
Rüstung suit of armour [ˌsuːt‿əv 'ɑːmə]
rutschen to slip [slɪp]

S

Saal chamber ['tʃeɪmbə]; hall [hɔːl]
Saat seed [siːd]
Saatkorn seed [siːd]
Sach- non-fiction [ˌnɒn'fɪkʃn]
Sache thing [θɪŋ]
Sachliteratur non-fiction [ˌnɒn'fɪkʃn]
Safe safe [seɪf]
Saft juice [dʒuːs]
sagen to say [seɪ]; to tell [tel]
Sahne cream [kriːm]
Saison season ['siːzn]
Salat salad ['sæləd]
Salz salt [sɔːlt]
Samen seed [siːd]
sammeln to collect [kə'lekt]
Samstag Saturday ['sætədeɪ]
Sand sand [sænd]
sandig sandy ['sændɪ]
Sandwich sandwich ['sænwɪdʒ]
sanft soft [sɒft]
Sänger/Sängerin singer ['sɪŋə]
Satellit satellite ['sætlaɪt]
Satzung charter ['tʃɑːtə]
sauber clean [kliːn]
säubern to clean [kliːn]
sauer acid ['æsɪd]; sour ['saʊə]
saurer Regen acid rain [ˌæsɪd 'reɪn]
Sauerkraut sauerkraut ['saʊəkraʊt]
Sauerstoff oxygen ['ɒksɪdʒən]
Säugling baby, babies *(pl)* ['beɪbi; 'beɪbiz]
Säure acid ['æsɪd]
scannen to scan [skæn]
Schachtel box, boxes *(pl)* [bɒks; 'bɒksɪz]
Schaden damage ['dæmɪdʒ]; harm [hɑːm]
Schadensbemessung damage assessment [ˌdæmɪdʒ ə'sesmənt]
Schadensfeststellung damage assessment [ˌdæmɪdʒ ə'sesmənt]
Schaf sheep, sheep *(pl)* [ʃiːp]
schaffen to create [kri'eɪt]
es allein schaffen to go it alone [ˌgəʊ‿ɪt‿ə'ləʊn]
Schal scarf, scarves *(pl)* [skɑːf; skɑːvz]
Schallplatte record ['rekɔːd]
Schalter desk [desk]; switch [swɪtʃ]
scharf hot [hɒt]
Schatten shade [ʃeɪd]; shadow ['ʃædəʊ]
Schattierung shade [ʃeɪd]
Schatz *(Anrede)* dear [dɪə]
Schau show [ʃəʊ]
schauen to look [lʊk]
schaukeln to rock [rɒk]
Schauplatz scene [siːn]; site [saɪt]
Schauspieler actor ['æktə]
Schauspielerin actress ['æktrəs]
Scheibe slice [slaɪs]
Schein slip [slɪp]
scheinen to seem [siːm]
schenken to give [gɪv]
scherzen to joke [dʒəʊk]
Scheune barn [bɑːn]
Schicht shift [ʃɪft]
schicken to send [send]
per E-Mail schicken to e-mail ['iːmeɪl]
Textnachricht schicken to text [tekst]
Schicksal fortune ['fɔːtʃuːn]
schieben to push [pʊʃ]
Schiedsrichter/Schiedsrichterin umpire ['ʌmpaɪə]; referee [ˌrefə'riː]
schief gehen to go wrong [gəʊ 'rɒŋ]
schießen to shoot [ʃuːt]
ein Tor schießen to score [skɔː]
Schiff boat [bəʊt]
Schikanierung harassment [hə'ræsmənt]
Schild sign [saɪn]
Schimpfwörter bad language [bæd 'læŋgwɪdʒ]
Schinken ham [hæm]
Schinkenspeck bacon ['beɪkn]
Schlacht battle ['bætl]
Schlaf sleep [sliːp]
schlafen to be asleep [ˌbiː‿ə'sliːp]; to sleep [sliːp]
schläfrig sleepy ['sliːpi]
Schlafsack sleeping bag ['sliːpɪŋ ˌbæg]
Schlafzimmer bedroom ['bedrʊm]
Schlag knock [nɒk]; shot [ʃɒt]; stroke [strəʊk]
Schlaganfall stroke [strəʊk]
schlagen to bang [bæŋ]; to bat [bæt]; to beat [biːt]; to hit [hɪt]; to knock [nɒk]
k.o. schlagen to knock out [nɒk‿'aʊt]
Schläger bat [bæt]; thug [θʌg]
Schlagmann/Schlagfrau batter ['bætə]
Schlagzeug drums *(pl)* [drʌmz]
Schlagzeuger/Schlagzeugerin drummer ['drʌmə]
Schlange queue [kjuː]; snake [sneɪk]
schlau smart [smɑːt]
schlecht bad [bæd]
schlechter worse [wɜːs]
schlechtester/schlechteste/schlechtestes worst [wɜːst]
schleichen to crawl [krɔːl]
Schleiereule barn owl ['bɑːn‿əʊl]
schleppen to drag [dræg]
schließen to close [kləʊz]; to shut [ʃʌt]
Schließfach locker ['lɒkə]
schließlich eventually [ɪ'ventʃuəli]; finally ['faɪnli]; in the end [ɪn ðiː‿'end]
Schließung closing ['kləʊzɪŋ]
schlimmer worse [wɜːs]
schlimmster/schlimmste/schlimmstes worst [wɜːst]
Schlittschuhbahn ice rink ['aɪs rɪŋk]
Schloss castle ['kɑːsl]
Schlucht canyon ['kænjən]; gorge [gɔːdʒ]
schlurfen to shamble ['ʃæmbl]
schlürfen to sip [sɪp]
Schluss end [end]
mit jmdm. Schluss machen to chuck sb *(coll)* [tʃʌk]; to dump sb [dʌmp]
zum Schluss in the end [ɪn ðiː‿'end]
Schlüssel key [kiː]
schmackhaft tasty ['teɪsti]
schmal narrow ['nærəʊ]
schmecken to taste [teɪst]
Pizza schmeckt besser. Pizza is tastier. ['piːtsə ɪz ˌteɪstɪə]
schmelzen to melt [melt]
Schmerz pain [peɪn]
Schmetterling butterfly ['bʌtəflaɪ]
Schminke make-up ['meɪkʌp]
Schmuck jewellery ['dʒuːəlri]
Schmuggler/Schmugglerin smuggler ['smʌglə]
schmutzig dirty ['dɜːti]
Schnabeltier duck-billed platypus [ˌdʌkbɪld 'plætɪpəs]
schnappen to grab [græb]
Schnapperfisch red snapper [ˌred 'snæpə]
Schnappschuss snapshot ['snæpʃɒt]
Schnee snow [snəʊ]
schneiden to cut (off) [kʌt‿'ɒf]
schneien to snow [snəʊ]
schnell fast [fɑːst]; quick [kwɪk]; rapid ['ræpɪd]
schnorcheln to snorkel ['snɔːkl]
schnüffeln to sniff [snɪf]
schnuppern to sniff [snɪf]
Schnur cord *(AE)* [kɔːd]; string [strɪŋ]
schockiert shocked [ʃɒkt]
Schokolade chocolate ['tʃɒklət]
schön beautiful ['bjuːtɪfl]; fine [faɪn]; nice [naɪs]
schon already [ɔːl'redi]
schottisch Scottish ['skɒtɪʃ]
Schrank cabinet ['kæbɪnət]; cupboard ['kʌbəd]

einen **Schrecken einjagen** to scare ['skeə]
schrecklich awful ['ɔ:fl]; frightening ['fraɪtnɪŋ]; horrible ['hɒrəbl]; terrible ['terəbl]
Schrei cry [kraɪ]
schreiben to write [raɪt]
E-Mail schreiben to e-mail ['i:meɪl]
Schreibtisch desk [desk]
Schreibwaren stationery ['steɪʃnri]
schreien to cry [kraɪ]; to shout [ʃaʊt]; *(Eule)* to hoot [hu:t]
schriftlich in writing [ɪn 'raɪtɪŋ]
Schritt footstep ['fʊtstep]; move [mu:v]; step [step]
schrumpfen to shrink [ʃrɪŋk]
Schubkarre wheelbarrow ['wi:lˌbærəʊ]
schüchtern shy [ʃaɪ]
Schuh shoe [ʃu:]
Schuhkarton shoebox ['ʃu:bɒks]
den **Schulabschluss machen** to graduate ['grædjueɪt]
Schulbuch textbook ['teksbʊk]
schulden to owe [əʊ]
Schuldfähigkeit criminal responsibility [ˌkrɪmɪnl rɪsˌpɒnsə'bɪləti]
schuldig guilty ['gɪlti]
Schule school [sku:l]
Schule, in der in einer Fremdsprache unterrichtet wird immersion school [ɪ'mɜ:ʃn ˌsku:l]
staatliche Schule (USA) public school [ˌpʌblɪk 'sku:l]
weiterführende Schule secondary school ['sekəndri ˌsku:l]
Schüler/Schülerin pupil ['pju:pl]; student ['stju:dnt]
Schulfach subject ['sʌbdʒɪkt]
Schulhof playground ['pleɪgraʊnd]
Schulklasse class [klɑ:s]
eine **Schulnote nicht erreichen** to fail a grade [ˌfeɪl‿ə 'greɪd]
Schulranzen school bag ['sku:l bæg]
Schultasche school bag ['sku:l bæg]
Schulter shoulder ['ʃəʊldə]
mit den Schultern zucken to shrug (one's shoulders) [ʃrʌg]
Schuppen shed [ʃed]
Schuss gunshot ['gʌnʃɒt]; shot [ʃɒt]
Schüssel bowl [bəʊl]
Schusswaffe gun [gʌn]
schütteln to shake [ʃeɪk]
Schutz- protective [prə'tektɪv]
schützen to protect [prə'tekt]
schwach weak [wi:k]
schwach werden to go weak [gəʊ 'wi:k]
Schwäche weakness ['wi:knəs]
Schwamm sponge [spʌndʒ]
Schwangerschaft pregnancy ['pregnəntsi]
schwanken to vary ['veəri]
Schwanz tail [teɪl]
schwarz black [blæk]
Schwarzer/Schwarze Black [blæk]
schwatzen to gossip ['gɒsɪp]
Schwebebahn aerial monorail [ˌeəriəl 'mɒnəreɪl]
Schweif tail [teɪl]
Schweigen silence ['saɪlənts]
Schwein pig [pɪg]
Schweinefleisch pork [pɔ:k]
schwelen to smoulder ['sməʊldə]
schwenken to pivot ['pɪvət]; to wave [weɪv]
schwer heavy ['hevi]
Schwere gravity ['grævəti]
Schwerkraft gravity ['grævəti]
Schwester sister ['sɪstə]
schwierig difficult ['dɪfɪklt]; hard [hɑ:d]
Schwierigkeit problem ['prɒbləm]
Schwimmbad swimming pool ['swɪmɪŋ ˌpu:l]
Schwimmbecken pool [pu:l]; swimming pool ['swɪmɪŋ ˌpu:l]
schwimmen to swim [swɪm]
Schwimmer/Schwimmerin swimmer ['swɪmə]
Schwimmflosse fin [fɪn]
Schwimmreifen rubber ring [ˌrʌbə 'rɪŋ]
schwinden to shrink [ʃrɪŋk]
schwindlig dizzy ['dɪzi]
etw. in **Schwung bringen** to get sth going [ˌget 'gəʊɪŋ]
Sciencefiction science fiction [ˌsaɪəns 'fɪkʃn]
Scone *(Gebäck)* scone [skɒn]
Screenshot screen shot ['skri:n ˌʃɒt]
See lake [leɪk]
Seehund seal [si:l]
seekrank seasick ['si:sɪk]
Seele soul [səʊl]
Seelöwe sea lion ['si: ˌlaɪən]
Seetang seaweed ['si:wi:d]
Seetang seaweed ['si:wi:d]
Seewespe sea wasp ['si: ˌwɒsp]
segeln to sail [seɪl]
sehen to look [lʊk]; to see [si:]
Sehenswürdigkeit attraction [ə'trækʃn]; sight [saɪt]
sehr very ['veri]; highly ['haɪli]
Seife soap [səʊp]
Seifenoper soap [səʊp]
Seilbahn cable car ['keɪbl ˌkɑ:]
sein to be [bi:]
an der Reihe sein to be on [bi:‿'ɒn]
an sein to be on [bi:‿'ɒn]
sein/seine his [hɪz]; its [ɪts]
seit for [fɔ:; fə]; since [sɪnts]
seitdem since [sɪnts]
Seite aspect ['æspekt]; page [peɪdʒ]; side [saɪd]
Sekretär/Sekretärin secretary ['sekrətri]
Sektion section ['sekʃn]
Sektor sector ['sektə]
Sekunde second ['seknd]
selbst gemacht home-made [ˌhəʊm'meɪd]
Selbstachtung self-worth [ˌself'wɜ:θ]
selbstbewusst confident ['kɒnfɪdnt]
selbstsicher confident ['kɒnfɪdnt]
selbstständig self-employed [ˌselfɪm'plɔɪd]
Selbstständigkeit self-employment [ˌselfɪm'plɔɪmənt]
selbstverständlich of course [əv 'kɔ:s]
Selbstwertgefühl self-worth [ˌself'wɜ:θ]
selten rarely [reəli]; seldom ['seldəm]
seltsam strange [streɪndʒ]
senden to broadcast ['brɔ:dkɑ:st]
Sender station ['steɪʃn]
Sendung broadcast ['brɔ:dkɑ:st]; programme ['prəʊgræm]; show [ʃəʊ]
auf Sendung on the air [ˌɒn ðiˌ'eə]
separieren to separate ['sepreɪt]
September September [sep'tembə]
Serie series, series *(pl)* ['sɪəri:z]
Service service ['sɜ:vɪs]
servieren to serve [sɜ:v]
sich **setzen** to sit down [sɪt 'daʊn]
sich setzen zu to sit with ['sɪt wɪθ]
Seuche plague [pleɪg]
Sex sex [seks]
sexistisch sexist ['seksɪst]
Sexualität sex [seks]
Shorts shorts *(pl)* [ʃɔ:ts]
Show show [ʃəʊ]
sicher certain ['sɜ:tn]; certainly ['sɜ:tnli]; safe [seɪf]; sure [ʃʊə]
sichergehen to make sure [meɪk 'ʃʊə]
Sicherheit safety ['seɪfti]; security [sɪ'kjʊərəti]
sicherstellen to assure [ə'ʃʊə]; to guarantee [ˌgærn'ti:]
Sicherungskasten fuse-box ['fju:zbɒks]
Sicht sight [saɪt]; view [vju:]
sie she [ʃi:]; her [hɜ:]
sie *(Mehrzahl)* they [ðeɪ]; them [ðem]
sie (selbst) herself [hɜ:'self]; themselves [ðəm'selvz]
Sie *(Anrede)* mister ['mɪstə]
Siedler/Siedlerin settler ['setlə]
Siegel label ['leɪbl]
siegen to win [wɪn]
Sieger/Siegerin winner ['wɪnə]

Siegtreffer winning goal ['wɪnɪŋ gəʊl]
Signal signal ['sɪgnl]
signalisieren to signal ['sɪgnl]
simpel simple ['sɪmpl]
simsen to text [tekst]
singen to chant [tʃɑ:nt]; to sing [sɪŋ]
sinken *(beim Tauchen)* to drop [drɒp]
Sinn sense [sens]
Sinnbild symbol ['sɪmbl]
Sintflut flash flood ['flæʃ ˌflʌd]
Sirup syrup ['sɪrəp]
Situation situation [ˌsɪtju'eɪʃn]
Situationskomödie sitcom ['sɪtkɒm]
Sitz seat [si:t]
sitzen to sit [sɪt]
in der Falle sitzen to be trapped [bi: 'træpt]
Sitzplatz seat [si:t]
Sitzung session ['seʃn]
Skateboard skateboard ['skeɪtbɔ:d]
skaten to skate [skeɪt]
Skater/Skaterin skater ['skeɪtə]
Skelett skeleton ['skelɪtn]
Skifahren skiing ['ski:ɪŋ]
Sklaverei slavery ['sleɪvri]
Slang slang [slæŋ]
SMS text message ['tekst ˌmesɪdʒ]
Snack snack [snæk]
Snowboarden snowboarding ['snəʊbɔ:dɪŋ]
so so [səʊ]
so ... wie ... as ... as [æz ... æz; əz ... əz]
so (schlimm) that (bad) ['ðæt bæd]
so genannt so-called [ˌsəʊ'kɔ:ld]
so oder so either way [ˌaɪðə 'weɪ]
sobald as soon as [əz 'su:n‿əz]
Sofa couch [kaʊtʃ]; sofa ['səʊfə]
sofort at once [ət 'wʌnts]; immediately [ɪ'mi:diətli]; right away [raɪt‿ə'weɪ]
sogar even ['i:vn]
Sohn son [sʌn]
Soja(-) soy [sɔɪ]
solange as long as [əz 'lɒŋ‿əz]
solar solar ['səʊlə]
solch such [sʌtʃ]
Soldat/Soldatin soldier ['səʊldʒə]
solide solid ['sɒlɪd]
(etw. tun) **sollen** to be supposed to (do sth) [ˌbi sə'pəʊzd tə]
sollte/sollten should [ʃʊd]
solo solo ['səʊləʊ]
Solo- solo ['səʊləʊ]
Sommer summer ['sʌmə]
Sommerfest summer fair ['sʌmə ˌfeə]
Sonderausgabe special ['speʃl]
Sonderheft special ['speʃl]
Sonne sun [sʌn]
Sonnen- solar ['səʊlə]
Sonnenbräune suntan ['sʌntæn]
Sonnenkollektor solar panel [ˌsəʊlə 'pænl]
Sonnenschein sunshine ['sʌnʃaɪn]
Sonnenuntergang sunset ['sʌnset]
sonnig sunny ['sʌni]
Sonntag Sunday ['sʌndeɪ]
sonst else [els]
sich **Sorgen machen** to worry ['wʌri]
sorgfältig careful ['keəfl]
Sorte kind [kaɪnd]; sort [sɔ:t]; type [taɪp]
Soulmusik soul [səʊl]
Souvenir souvenir [ˌsu:və'nɪə]
sowieso anyway ['eniweɪ]
sowohl ... als auch ... both ... and ... ['bəʊθ ... ænd]
sozial social ['səʊʃl]
Sozialversicherungsnummer social security number [ˌsəʊʃl sɪ'kjʊərəti ˌnʌmbə]
Spa spa [spɑ:]
Spaghetti spaghetti [spə'geti]
Spam spam [spæm]
Spanglisch *(Mischung aus Spanisch und Englisch)* Spanglish ['spæŋglɪʃ]
spanisch Spanish ['spænɪʃ]
Spanisch Spanish ['spænɪʃ]
spannend exciting [ɪk'saɪtɪŋ]; fascinating ['fæsɪneɪtɪŋ]
Spannung suspense [sə'spens]; tension ['tenʃn]
sparen to save [seɪv]
Sparschwein piggy bank ['pɪgi bæŋk]
Spaß fun [fʌn]
Spaß verstehen take a joke [ˌteɪk‿ə 'dʒəʊk]
Spaß haben to have fun [ˌhæv 'fʌn]
Spaß machen to be fun [bi: 'fʌn]
Viel Spaß! Have fun! [ˌhæv 'fʌn]
spät late [leɪt]
zu spät late [leɪt]
spazieren gehen to go for a walk [ˌgəʊ fər‿ə 'wɔ:k]
Spaziergang walk [wɔ:k]
speichern to store [stɔ:]
Speisekarte menu ['menju:]
Speisesaal dining room ['daɪnɪŋ rʊm]
spektakulär spectacular [spek'tækjələ]
Spenden sammeln fund raising ['fʌnd ˌreɪzɪŋ]
Sperre ban [bæn]; barrier ['bæriə]
Spezialist/Spezialistin specialist ['speʃlɪst]
Spezialität special ['speʃl]
speziell special ['speʃl]; specific [spə'sɪfɪk]
Spezies species, species *(pl)* ['spi:ʃi:z]
spezifisch specific [spə'sɪfɪk]
Spiegel mirror ['mɪrə]
Spiegelei sunny side up [ˌsʌni saɪd‿'ʌp]
Spiel game [geɪm]; match [mætʃ]; play [pleɪ]
spielen to play [pleɪ]; *(Theater)* to act
Spieler/Spielerin player ['pleɪə]
Spielfeld court [kɔ:t]; pitch [pɪtʃ]
Spielplatz playground ['pleɪgraʊnd]
Spielstand score [skɔ:]
Spielzeug toy [tɔɪ]
Spinne spider ['spaɪdə]
Spirituose spirit ['spɪrɪt]
Spitze top [tɒp]
Spitzname nickname ['nɪkneɪm]
Sponsor/Sponsorin sponsor ['spɒntsə]
Sport sport [spɔ:t]; *(Schulfach)* Physical Education (PE) [ˌfɪzɪkl‿edʒʊ'keɪʃn]
Sport machen to exercise ['eksəsaɪz]
Sport treiben to do sports [du: 'spɔ:ts]
Sportfest sports day ['spɔ:ts deɪ]
Sportgeschäft sports shop ['spɔ:ts ʃɒp]
sportlich sporty ['spɔ:ti]
Sportplatz sports field ['spɔ:ts fi:ld]
Sportzeug PE kit [ˌpi:‿'i: kɪt]
Sprache language ['læŋgwɪdʒ]; speech [spi:tʃ]
sprechen to say [seɪ]; to speak [spi:k]; to talk [tɔ:k]
sprechen mit to talk to ['tɔ:k tə]
Sprechen speech [spi:tʃ]
Sprecher/Sprecherin speaker ['spi:kə]
Sprechgesang chant [tʃɑ:nt]
Springbrunnen fountain ['faʊntɪn]
springen to jump [dʒʌmp]
sprudelnd fizzy ['fɪzi]
sprühen to spray [spreɪ]; *(Funken)* to spark [spɑ:k]
spucken to spit [spɪt]
Spülbecken sink [sɪŋk]
Spur track [træk]
spüren to sense [sens]
Staat state [steɪt]
staatlich state [steɪt]
staatliche Schule (USA) public school [ˌpʌblɪk 'sku:l]
Staats- civil ['sɪvl]
Staatsbürger/Staatsbürgerin citizen ['sɪtɪzn]
Staatsoberhaupt head of state [ˌhed‿əv 'steɪt]
Staatsvertrag treaty ['tri:ti]
Stadion arena [ə'ri:nə]; stadium ['steɪdiəm]
Stadium stage [steɪdʒ]
Stadt city ['sɪti]; town [taʊn]
Stadtplan map [mæp]
Stadtteil borough ['bʌrə]

Stamm tribe [traɪb]
Stammkunde/Stammkundin regular ['regjələ]
Stand stall [stɔ:l]
Standbesitzer/Standbesitzerin stall holder ['stɔ:l ˌhəʊldə]
Standbild statue ['stætʃu:]
auf **Stand-by** standby ['stændbaɪ]
Standfoto still (picture) ['stɪl ˌpɪktʃə]
standhaft firmly ['fɜ:mli]
ständig always ['ɔ:lweɪz]
Stange bar [bɑ:]
Stangenbohne runner bean ['rʌnə ˌbi:n]
Stapel pile [paɪl]
Star star [stɑ:]
stark hard [hɑ:d]; powerful ['paʊəfl]; strong [strɒŋ]
Stärke power ['paʊə]; strength [streŋθ]
Start launch [lɔ:nʃ]; start [stɑ:t]
starten to launch [lɔ:nʃ]; to start [stɑ:t]; to take off [ˌteɪk‿'ɒf]
Station base [beɪs]; stage [steɪdʒ]; station ['steɪʃn]
statt instead of [ɪn'sted‿əv]
stattdessen instead [ɪn'sted]
stattfinden to take place [teɪk 'pleɪs]
Statue statue ['stætʃu:]
Stau traffic jam ['træfɪk ˌdʒæm]
Staub dust [dʌst]
stechen to sting [stɪŋ]
Steckbrief profile ['prəʊfaɪl]
Steckdose socket ['sɒkɪt]
stecken to stick [stɪk]
Stecker plug [plʌg]
Steelband *(Band, deren Instrumente aus leeren Ölfässern bestehen)* steel band [ˌsti:l 'bænd]
Steg walkway ['wɔ:kweɪ]
stehen to stand [stænd]
stehlen to steal [sti:l]
steigen to climb ['klaɪm]; to increase [ɪn'kri:s]; to rise [raɪz]; to step [step]
steigend increasing [ɪn'kri:sɪŋ]
Stein rock [rɒk]; stone [stəʊn]
Steinbruch quarry ['kwɒri]
Stelle patch [pætʃ]; place [pleɪs]
offene Stelle vacancy ['veɪknsi]
stellen to put [pʊt]; *(Uhr)* to set [set]
auf den Kopf gestellt upside down [ˌʌpsaɪd 'daʊn]
Stellenangebot vacancy ['veɪknsi]
stellvertretend deputy ['depjəti]
Stellvertreter/Stellvertreterin deputy ['depjəti]
sterben to die [daɪ]
Stern star [stɑ:]
Sternwarte observatory [əb'zɜ:vətri]
Steuer tax [tæks]; wheel [wi:l]
Steuerrad wheel [wi:l]
Stiefel boot [bu:t]
Stiefvater stepdad ['stepdæd]
Stil style [staɪl]
still quiet [kwaɪət]; still [stɪl]
Stille quiet [kwaɪət]; silence ['saɪlənts]
Stimme voice [vɔɪs]
stimmen für to vote (for) [vəʊt]
Stimmung atmosphere ['ætməsfɪə]; mood [mu:d]; spirit ['spɪrɪt]
stinken to stink [stɪŋk]
stinkend stinking ['stɪŋkɪŋ]
stinkig stinking ['stɪŋkɪŋ]
Stipendium scholarship ['skɒləʃɪp]
Stirn forehead ['fɔ:hed]
die Stirn runzeln to frown [fraʊn]
stöbern to trawl [trɔ:l]
Stock stick [stɪk]
im oberen Stock upstairs [ʌp'steəz]
im unteren Stock downstairs [ˌdaʊn'steəz]
Stoff material [mə'tɪəriəl]
Stollenschuh rugby boot ['rʌgbi bu:t]
stolz auf proud of ['praʊd‿əv]
Stolz pride [praɪd]
Stöpsel plug [plʌg]
stören to bother ['bɒðə]
Storyboard *(gezeichnete Version eines Drehbuchs)* storyboard ['stɔ:ribɔ:d]
stoßen to knock [nɒk]; to push [pʊʃ]
stoßen gegen to run into [rʌn‿'ɪntə]
Strafe penalty ['penlti]; punishment ['pʌnɪʃmənt]; sentence ['sentənts]
strafen to punish ['pʌnɪʃ]
Sträfling convict ['kɒnvɪkt]
strahlend bright [braɪt]
Strand beach [bi:tʃ]; sands *(pl)* [sændz]
Straße road [rəʊd]; street [stri:t]
Straßenrand roadside ['rəʊdsaɪd]
Strauch bush [bʊʃ]
Streich trick [trɪk]
streichen to paint [peɪnt]
Streit argument ['ɑ:gjəmənt]
streiten to argue ['ɑ:gju:]; to fight [faɪt]
sich streiten to have an argument [ˌhæv‿ən‿'ɑ:gjəmənt]
Streitkräfte armed forces [ˌɑ:md 'fɔ:sɪz]
streng strict [strɪkt]
Stress stress [stres]
strikt strict [strɪkt]
Stroh straw [strɔ:]
Strom current ['kʌrnt]; electricity [ˌelɪk'trɪsəti]
Stromausfall blackout *(AE)* ['blækaʊt]; power cut ['paʊə ˌkʌt]
Strömung current ['kʌrnt]
gegen die Strömung up current ['ʌp ˌkʌrnt]
Strophe verse [vɜ:s]
Stubenhocker couch potato ['kaʊtʃ pəˌteɪtəʊ]
Stück bar [bɑ:]; piece [pi:s]
Stückchen bit [bɪt]
Student student ['stju:dnt]
studieren to study ['stʌdi]
Studieren study ['stʌdi]
Studio studio ['stju:diəʊ]
Studium studies *(pl)* ['stʌdiz]; study ['stʌdi]
Stufe step [step]
Stuhl chair [tʃeə]
Stunde hour ['aʊə]; session ['seʃn]
eine halbe Stunde half an hour [ˌhɑ:f‿ən‿'aʊə]
stundenlang for hours [fər‿'aʊəz]
Stundenplan curriculum [kə'rɪkjələm]; timetable ['taɪmteɪbl]
Sturm storm [stɔ:m]
stürmisch stormy ['stɔ:mi]
stützen to support [sə'pɔ:t]
Subkontinent sub-continent [sʌb'kɒntɪnənt]
suchen (nach) to look for ['lʊk fə]
Sucht addiction [ə'dɪkʃn]
Südamerikaner/Südamerikanerin South American [ˌsaʊθ‿ə'merɪkən]
südamerikanisch South American [ˌsaʊθ‿ə'merɪkən]
Süden south [saʊθ]
nach Süden south [saʊθ]
Südwesten southwest [ˌsaʊθ'west]
Summe amount [ə'maʊnt]; total ['təʊtl]
summen to buzz [bʌz]
Superlativ superlative [su:'pɜ:lətɪv]
Supermarkt supermarket ['su:pəˌmɑ:kɪt]
Suppe soup [su:p]
surfen to surf [sɜ:f]
im Internet surfen to surf the Internet [ˌsɜ:f ði‿'ɪntənet]
Surfen surfing ['sɜ:fɪŋ]
süß cute [kju:t]; sweet [swi:t]
Süßigkeit sweet [swi:t]
Süßigkeiten candy *(AE)* ['kændi]
Süßwasser fresh water ['freʃ ˌwɔ:tə]
Sweatshirt sweatshirt ['swetʃɜ:t]
Symbol symbol ['sɪmbl]
Synonym synonym ['sɪnənɪm]
System system ['sɪstəm]
Szene scene [si:n]

T

Tabak tobacco [tə'bækəʊ]
Tabelle grid [grɪd]; table ['teɪbl]

Tafel bar [bɑ:]; board [bɔ:d]; panel ['pænl]
Tag day [deɪ]
Einen schönen Tag noch. Have a nice day. [ˌhæv‿ə naɪs 'deɪ]
eines Tages one day [wʌn 'deɪ]
jeden Tag any day ['enɪ deɪ]
Tagebuch diary ['daɪəri]
ein Tagebuch führen to keep a diary [ˌki:p‿ə 'daɪəri]
Tagesanbruch dawn [dɔ:n]
täglich daily ['deɪli]
tagträumen to daydream ['deɪdri:m]
Talent talent ['tælənt]
talentiert talented ['tæləntɪd]
Talkmaster host [həʊst]
Talkshow talk show ['tɔ:k ˌʃəʊ]
Tank tank [tæŋk]
Tanker tanker ['tæŋkə]
Tante aunt [ɑ:nt]
Tanz dance [dɑ:nts]
tanzen to dance [dɑ:nts]
Breakdance tanzen to break-dance ['breɪkdɑ:nts]
Tanzen dancing ['dɑ:ntsɪŋ]
Tanzfläche dance floor ['dɑ:nts flɔ:]
tapfer brave [breɪv]
Tarnkappenbomber stealth bomber ['stelθ ˌbɒmə]
Tasche bag [bæg]
Taschendieb/Taschendiebin pickpocket ['pɪkˌpɒkɪt]
Taschengeld pocket money ['pɒkɪt ˌmʌni]
Taschenlampe torch, torches *(pl)* [tɔ:tʃ; 'tɔ:tʃɪz]
Taschenmesser penknife, penknives *(pl)* ['pennaɪf; 'pennaɪvz]
Tasse cup [kʌp]
tasten nach to feel for ['fi:l fə]
in der **Tat** in fact [ɪn 'fækt]
Tätowierung tattoo [tæt'u:]
Tatsache fact [fækt]
tatsächlich actually ['æktʃuəli]
Tauch- dive [daɪv]; diving ['daɪvɪŋ]
Tauchbegleiter/Tauchbegleiterin buddy *(infml)* ['bʌdi]
tauchen to dive [daɪv]
Tauchen diving ['daɪvɪŋ]
Taucher/Taucherin diver ['daɪvə]
Taucheranzug wetsuit ['wetsu:t]
Tauchgang dive [daɪv]
Tauchzentrum dive centre ['daɪv ˌsentə]
Tausch exchange [ɪks'tʃeɪndʒ]; swap [swɒp]
tauschen to change [tʃeɪndʒ]; to exchange [ɪks'tʃeɪndʒ]; to swap [swɒp]
tausend thousand ['θaʊznd]
Taxi taxi ['tæksi]
Team team [ti:m]
Technik engineering [ˌendʒɪ'nɪərɪŋ]; technique [tek'ni:k]; Technology [tek'nɒlədʒi]
Techniker/Technikerin engineer [ˌendʒɪ'nɪə]
technisch technical ['teknɪkl]
Tee tea [ti:]
Teenager teenager ['ti:nˌeɪdʒə]
Teich pond [pɒnd]
Teil bit [bɪt]; branch [brɑ:ntʃ]; part [pɑ:t]
Teilchen particle ['pɑ:tɪkl]
teilen to share [ʃeə]
Teilhaber/Teilhaberin shareholder ['ʃeəˌhəʊldə]
teilnehmen an to take part in [teɪk 'pɑ:t‿ɪn]
Teilnehmer/Teilnehmerin participant [pɑ:'tɪsɪpənt]
Teilzeit- part-time (P/T) [ˌpɑ:t'taɪm]
Telefon phone [fəʊn]
telefonieren to phone [fəʊn]
Telefonnummer phone number ['fəʊn ˌnʌmbə]
Telefonzelle phone box ['fəʊn ˌbɒks]
Teller plate [pleɪt]
Temperatur temperature ['temprətʃə]
Temperaturregler thermostat ['θɜ:məstæt]
Tempo speed [spi:d]
temporär temporary ['temprəri]
Tennis tennis ['tenɪs]
Teppichboden carpet ['kɑ:pɪt]
Terminkalender diary ['daɪəri]
einen Terminkalender führen to keep a diary [ˌki:p‿ə 'daɪəri]
Territorium territory ['terɪtri]
Terrorismus terrorism ['terərɪsm]
Test test [test]; trial ['traɪəl]
testen to test [test]
teuer expensive [ɪk'spentsɪv]
textil textile ['tekstaɪl]
Textil(-) textile ['tekstaɪl]
Textnachricht schicken to text [tekst]
Theater theater *(AE)* ['θɪətə]
Theaterstück play [pleɪ]
Thema subject ['sʌbdʒɪkt]; topic ['tɒpɪk]
Thermostat thermostat ['θɜ:məstæt]
Thriller thriller ['θrɪlə]
Thron throne [θrəʊn]
Ticket ticket ['tɪkɪt]
tief deep [di:p]; low [ləʊ]
tief ausgeschnitten low-cut ['ləʊkʌt]
Tier animal ['ænɪml]
wild lebende Tiere wildlife ['waɪldlaɪf]
Tierpark zoo [zu:]
Tierpfleger/Tierpflegerin zookeeper ['zu:ˌki:pə]
Tiger tiger ['taɪgə]
Tipp tip [tɪp]
Tisch table ['teɪbl]
den Tisch decken to set the table [ˌset ðə 'teɪbl]
Tischtennis table-tennis ['teɪblˌtenɪs]
Titel title ['taɪtl]
Titelseite cover ['kʌvə]
Toast toast [təʊst]
Tochter daughter ['dɔ:tə]
tod- deadly ['dedli]
Tod death [deθ]
Todes- capital ['kæpɪtl]
Todesfall death [deθ]
Todestrakt death row [ˌdeθ 'rəʊ]
Todeszelle death watch cell ['deθ ˌwɒtʃ sell]
tödlich deadly ['dedli]; lethal ['li:θl]
Toilette restroom *(AE)* ['restrʊm]; toilet ['tɔɪlɪt]
toll awesome ['ɔ:səm]; brilliant ['brɪljənt]; great [greɪt]; hot [hɒt]
tollpatschig clumsy ['klʌmzi]
Tomate tomato, tomatoes *(pl)* [tə'mɑ:təʊ; tə'mɑ:təʊz]
Ton sound [saʊnd]; tone [təʊn]
Tonfall tone [təʊn]
Tonfilm talkie ['tɔ:ki]
Tonne (*Gewicht*) ton [tʌn]
Topf pot [pɒt]
Tor gate [geɪt]; goal [gəʊl]
ein Tor schießen to score [skɔ:]
Torpfosten goal post ['gəʊl pəʊst]
Tortur ordeal [ɔ:'di:l]
Torwart goalkeeper ['gəʊlˌki:pə]
tot dead [ded]
total total ['təʊtl]
töten to kill [kɪl]
Töten killing ['kɪlɪŋ]
Tötung killing ['kɪlɪŋ]
Tour tour [tʊə]
Tourismus tourism ['tʊərɪzm]
Tourist/Touristin tourist ['tʊərɪst]
Touristik tourism ['tʊərɪzm]
Tower tower ['taʊə]
toxisch toxic ['tɒksɪk]
Tradition tradition [trə'dɪʃn]
traditionell traditional [trə'dɪʃnl]
tragen to carry ['kæri]
Tragödie tragedy ['trædʒədi]
Trainer/Trainerin coach [kəʊtʃ]; trainer ['treɪnə]
trainieren to train [treɪn]
Training coaching ['kəʊtʃɪŋ]; practice ['præktɪs]; training ['treɪnɪŋ]

Traktor tractor ['træktə]
Träne tear [tɪə]
transferieren to transfer [trænts'fɜː]
Transport transport ['træntspɔːt]
transportieren to transport [træn'spɔːt]
Tratsch gossip ['gɒsɪp]
tratschen to gossip ['gɒsɪp]
Traum dream [driːm]
traurig sad [sæd]
treffen to hit [hɪt]; to meet [miːt]
sich treffen to meet [miːt]
Treffen meeting ['miːtɪŋ]
treiben to drift [drɪft]
Treibhausgas greenhouse gas [ˌgriːnhaʊs 'gæs]
Treibstoff fuel ['fjuːəl]
trennen to segregate ['segrɪgeɪt]; to separate ['sepreɪt]
Trennung segregation [ˌsegrɪ'geɪʃn]
Treppe stairs *(pl)* [steəz]
die Treppe hinaufrennen to run upstairs [ˌrʌn‿ʌp'steəz]
Tresor safe [seɪf]
treten to kick [kɪk]; to step [step]
treu loyal ['lɔɪəl]
Treue allegiance [ə'liːdʒns]
Tribüne platform ['plætfɔːm]; stand [stænd]
Trick trick [trɪk]
Trikot jersey ['dʒɜːzi]
Trillerpfeife whistle ['wɪsl]
Trimester *(Einteilung des englischen Schuljahrs)* term [tɜːm]
trinken to drink [drɪŋk]
schluckweise trinken to sip [sɪp]
Trinkgeld tip [tɪp]
Trinkwasser fresh water ['freʃ ˌwɔːtə]
trocken dry [draɪ]
trocknen to dry [draɪ]
Trödelstand white elephant stall [ˌwaɪt 'elɪfənt stɔːl]
tröpfeln to drip [drɪp]
tropfen to drip [drɪp]
tropfen lassen to drip [drɪp]
Tropfen drop [drɒp]
Trophäe trophy ['trəʊfi]
Trottel jerk *(slang)* [dʒɜːk]
trotten to shamble ['ʃæmbl]
trotzdem though [ðəʊ]
Truck truck *(AE)* [trʌk]
Trucker trucker *(AE)* ['trʌkə]
Trucker/Truckerin truckie *(Aus)* ['trʌki]
Truppen troops *(pl)* [truːps]
Truthahn turkey ['tɜːki]
tschüss bye [baɪ]
T-Shirt T-shirt ['tiːʃɜːt]
tun to do [duː]; to make [meɪk]
Tunnel tunnel ['tʌnl]
Tür door [dɔː]
Turbine turbine ['tɜːbaɪn]
türkisch Turkish ['tɜːkɪʃ]
Türklingel doorbell ['dɔːbel]
Turm tower ['taʊə]
Turnhalle gym [dʒɪm]
Turnier competition [ˌkɒmpə'tɪʃn]
Türstufe doorstep ['dɔːstep]
Tüte bag [bæg]
Typ bloke [bləʊk]; guy [gaɪ]; thug [θʌg]; type [taɪp]
tyrannisieren to bully ['bʊli]

U

U-Bahn underground ['ʌndəgraʊnd]
übel queasy ['kwiːsi]
Übelkeit verspüren to feel sick [fiːl 'sɪk]
üben to exercise ['eksəsaɪz]; to practise ['præktɪs]
über above [ə'bʌv]; across [ə'krɒs]; over ['əʊvə]; via [vaɪə]; about [ə'baʊt]
überall all over [ˌɔːl‿'əʊvə]; anywhere ['eniweə]; everywhere ['evriweə]
überall in throughout [θru'aʊt]
Übereinkunft deal [diːl]
Überfluss abundance [ə'bʌndəns]
überfluten to flood [flʌd]
übergeben to hand [hænd]
übergewichtig overweight [ˌəʊvə'weɪt]
überhaupt whatsoever [ˌwɒtsəʊ'evə]
überhaupt (nicht) (not …) at all [ˌnɒt … ət‿'ɔːl]
überholen to overtake [ˌəʊvə'teɪk]
Überholspur fast lane ['fɑːst ˌleɪn]
überleben to survive [sə'vaɪv]
Überleben survival [sə'vaɪvl]
Überlebender/Überlebende survivor [sə'vaɪvə]
überprüfen to check [tʃek]; to service ['sɜːvɪs]
überqueren to cross [krɒs]
überraschen to surprise [sə'praɪz]
überraschend surprising [sə'praɪzɪŋ]
überrascht surprised [sə'praɪzd]
Überrest remain [rɪ'meɪn]
Überschrift title ['taɪtl]
überschwemmen to flood [flʌd]
Überschwemmung flood [flʌd]
flutartige Überschwemmung flash flood ['flæʃ ˌflʌd]
in **Übersee** overseas [ˌəʊvə'siːz]
nach Übersee overseas [ˌəʊvə'siːz]
übersetzen to translate [trænz'leɪt]
übertragen to transfer [trænts'fɜː]
übertreiben to overdo [ˌəʊvə'duː]
übertrieben exaggerated [ɪg'zædʒreɪtɪd]
überwachen to monitor ['mɒnɪtə]
überwältigend overwhelming [ˌəʊvə'welmɪŋ]
überwiegend mostly ['məʊstli]
überzeugt confident ['kɒnfɪdnt]
üblich usual ['juːʒl]
übrig left [left]
übrigens by the way [ˌbaɪ ðə 'weɪ]
Übung exercise ['eksəsaɪz]
Übungsheft exercise book ['eksəsaɪz ˌbʊk]
Uhr clock [klɒk]; *(Zeitangabe)* o'clock [ə'klɒk]
Wie viel Uhr ist es, bitte? What's the time, please? [ˌwɒts ðə 'taɪm ˌpliːz]
ultra- ultra ['ʌltrə]
umdrehen to turn [tɜːn]; to turn over [ˌtɜːn‿'əʊvə]; to turn round [tɜːn 'raʊnd]
sich umdrehen to turn over [ˌtɜːn‿'əʊvə]; to turn round [tɜːn 'raʊnd]
umfassen to involve [ɪn'vɒlv]
Umfrage survey ['sɜːveɪ]
umgeben to surround [sə'raʊnd]
Umgebung environment [ɪn'vaɪərnmənt]
umgedreht upside down [ˌʌpsaɪd 'daʊn]
umgekehrt the other way round [ði ˌʌðə‿weɪ 'raʊnd]
umhauen to knock out [nɒk‿'aʊt]
umher around [ə'raʊnd]
umkehren to reverse [rɪ'vɜːs]; to turn back [tɜːn 'bæk]
Umsatz turnover ['tɜːnˌəʊvə]
Umschlag envelope ['envələʊp]
umschließen to surround [sə'raʊnd]
sich **umsehen** to look round [lʊk 'raʊnd]
umsonst free [friː]
umsteigen to change [tʃeɪndʒ]
umstoßen to upset [ʌp'set]
umtauschen to exchange [ɪks'tʃeɪndʒ]
umwandeln to convert ['kɒnvɜːt]
Umwelt environment [ɪn'vaɪərnmənt]
die Umwelt betreffend environmental [ɪnˌvaɪərn'mentl]
Umwelt- eco ['iːkəʊ]; environmental [ɪnˌvaɪərn'mentl]
umweltbedingt environmental [ɪnˌvaɪərn'mentl]
umweltbewusst werden to go green [ˌgəʊ 'griːn]
Umweltverschmutzung pollution [pə'luːʃn]
umziehen to move [muːv]
Umzug parade [pə'reɪd]

unabhängig independent [ˌɪndɪ'pendənt]
unbedeutend unimportant [ˌʌnɪm'pɔ:tnt]
unbeschädigt unharmed [ʌn'hɑ:md]
unbewegt still [stɪl]
uncool uncool [ʌn'ku:l]
und and [ænd]
undeutlich blurred [blɜ:d]
unerlässlich vital ['vaɪtl]
Unfähigkeit disability [ˌdɪsə'bɪləti]
Unfall accident ['æksɪdnt]; crash [kræʃ]
unfreundlich unfriendly [ʌn'frendli]
Unfug horseplay ['hɔ:spleɪ]
ungefähr about [ə'baʊt]; around [ə'raʊnd]
ungeschickt clumsy ['klʌmzi]
ungesund unhealthy [ʌn'helθi]
unglücklich unhappy [ʌn'hæpi]
unglücklich sein to be unlucky [ˌbi:‿ʌn'lʌki]
unheimlich scary ['skeəri]; spooky ['spu:ki]
unhöflich rude [ru:d]
Uniform uniform ['ju:nɪfɔ:m]
Union union ['ju:njən]
Universalsprache lingua franca [ˌlɪŋgwə 'fræŋkə]
Universität university [ˌju:nɪ'vɜ:səti]
Universum universe ['ju:nɪvɜ:s]
unrechtmäßig illegal [ɪ'li:gl]
Unruhe riot [raɪət]
uns us [ʌs]
uns selbst ourselves [aʊə'selvz]
unser/unsere our ['aʊə]
Unsinn rubbish ['rʌbɪʃ]
unten at the bottom [ət ðə 'bɒtəm]; below [bɪ'ləʊ]; downstairs [ˌdaʊn'steəz]
(nach) unten down [daʊn]
unterer Teil bottom ['bɒtəm]
unter under ['ʌndə]; *(zwischen)* among [ə'mʌŋ]
ohne **Unterbrechung** non-stop [ˌnɒn'stɒp]
Unterbringung accommodation [əˌkɒmə'deɪʃn]
mit Unterbringung live-in ['lɪvɪn]
Unterdrückung oppression [ə'preʃn]
unterer/untere/unteres lower ['ləʊə]
Unterführung tunnel ['tʌnl]
Untergeschoss basement ['beɪsmənt]
unterhalb below [bɪ'ləʊ]
sich **unterhalten** to chat [tʃæt]
Unterhaltung chat [tʃæt]; conversation [ˌkɒnvə'seɪʃn]
Unterkunft accommodation [əˌkɒmə'deɪʃn]; quarters *(pl)* ['kwɔ:təz]
Unternehmen organisation [ˌɔ:gnaɪ'zeɪʃn]
Unternehmensbereich sector ['sektə]
unternehmungslustig enterprising ['entəpraɪzɪŋ]
Unterricht class [klɑ:s]
unterrichten to teach [ti:tʃ]
Unterrichtsstunde period *(AE)* ['pɪəriəd]; lesson ['lesn]
Unterscheidung discrimination [dɪˌskrɪmɪ'neɪʃn]
Unterschied difference ['dɪfrnts]
unterschreiben to sign [saɪn]
unterstreichen to underline [ˌʌndə'laɪn]
unterstützen to encourage [ɪn'kʌrɪdʒ]; to support [sə'pɔ:t]
Unterstützung support [sə'pɔ:t]
untersuchen to check [tʃek]
Untersuchung research [rɪ'sɜ:tʃ]
Untertitel caption ['kæpʃn]
Unterwasser- underwater [ˌʌndə'wɔ:tə]
unvergesslich unforgettable [ˌʌnfə'getəbl]
unverletzt unharmed [ʌn'hɑ:md]
unverschämt rude [ru:d]
unverzichtbar essential [ɪ'sentʃl]
unwichtig unimportant [ˌʌnɪm'pɔ:tnt]
Update update ['ʌpdeɪt]
Ur- indigenous [ɪn'dɪdʒɪnəs]
Urdu Urdu ['ʊədu:]
Ureinwohner/Ureinwohnerin Amerikas Native American [ˌneɪtɪv‿ə'merɪkən]
Ureinwohner/Ureinwohnerin Australiens Aborigine [ˌæbə'rɪdʒni]
Urenkel great-grandson [ˌgreɪt'grænsʌn]
Urkunde certificate [sə'tɪfɪkət]; charter ['tʃɑ:tə]
Urlaub holiday(s) ['hɒlədeɪ(z)]; vacation *(AE)* [və'keɪʃn]
Ursprung origin ['ɒrɪdʒɪn]
Urteil sentence ['sentənts]
usw. etc. [ɪt'setrə]

V

Variation variation [ˌveərɪ'eɪʃn]
variieren to vary ['veəri]
Vater father ['fɑ:ðə]
Vati dad [dæd]
Vehikel vehicle ['vɪəkl]
sich **verabreden** to date [deɪt]
Verabredung date [deɪt]
verabschieden *(Gesetz)* to pass [pɑ:s]
Verachtung disrespect [ˌdɪsrɪ'spekt]
veränderlich mobile ['məʊbaɪl]
verändern to change [tʃeɪndʒ]
verängstigt scared [skeəd]
jmdn. **veranlassen, etw. zu tun** to make sb do sth [meɪk]
Veranstalter/Veranstalterin organizer ['ɔ:gənaɪzə]
Veranstaltung event [ɪ'vent]; session ['seʃn]
verantwortlich machen to blame [bleɪm]
Verantwortung responsibility [rɪsˌpɒnsə'bɪləti]
verärgert angry ['æŋgri]
verbannen to ban [bæn]
verbessern to improve [ɪm'pru:v]
sich verbessern to improve [ɪm'pru:v]
verbieten to ban [bæn]
verbinden to combine [kəm'baɪn]; to connect [kə'nekt]; to join [dʒɔɪn]
Verbindung fusion ['fju:ʒn]; link [lɪŋk]
in Verbindung stehen mit to be connected with [kə'nektɪd]
sich in Verbindung setzen mit to contact ['kɒntækt]
verbittert bitter ['bɪtə]
verbleiben to remain [rɪ'meɪn]
verblüffen to stun [stʌn]
verblüfft amazed [ə'meɪzd]; startled ['stɑ:tld]
Verbot ban [bæn]
Verbrechen crime [kraɪm]
Verbrecher/Verbrecherin criminal ['krɪmɪnl]; gangster ['gæŋkstə]
verbreiten to spread [spred]
sich verbreiten to spread [spred]
verbreitet common ['kɒmən]; widespread [waɪdspred]
verbrennen to burn [bɜ:n]
Verbrennungsanlage incinerator [ɪn'sɪnreɪtə]
Verbrennungsrückstände ashes *(pl)* ['æʃɪz]
verbringen to spend [spend]
mit **verbundenen Augen** blindfolded ['blaɪndfəʊldɪd]
verbunden sein mit to be connected with [kə'nektɪd]
Verdächtigter/Verdächtigte suspect ['sʌspekt]
verdammt damn [dæm]
verdampfen to evaporate [ɪ'væpreɪt]
verdanken to owe [əʊ]
verdeckt undercover [ˌʌndə'kʌvə]
verderben to spoil [spɔɪl]
verdienen to earn [ɜ:n]
Verdienst income ['ɪnkʌm]
verdunsten to evaporate [ɪ'væpreɪt]
Verein club [klʌb]; society [sə'saɪəti]
Vereinigung union ['ju:njən]
Verfassung constitution [ˌkɒnstɪ'tju:ʃn]

verfehlen to miss [mɪs]
verführerisch tempting ['temptɪŋ]
Vergangenheit past [pɑ:st]
vergeben to forgive [fə'gɪv]
etw. **vergeigen** to mess sth up [ˌmes‿'ʌp]
vergessen to forget [fə'get]
vergleichen to compare [kəm'peə]
vergrößern to increase [ɪn'kri:s]
verhaften to arrest [ə'rest]
Verhalten behaviour [bɪ'heɪvjə]
Verhaltenskodex code of behaviour [ˌkəʊd‿əv bɪ'heɪvjə]
verheiratet mit married to ['mærid tə]
sich **verirren** to get lost [get 'lɒst]
sich **verirrt haben** to be lost [bi: 'lɒst]
Verkauf sales *(pl)* [seɪlz]
verkaufen to sell [sel]
Verkäufer/Verkäuferin shop assistant ['ʃɒp‿əˌsɪstnt]
Verkaufsraum salesroom ['seɪlzrʊm]
Verkehr traffic ['træfɪk]
Verkehrsmittel transport ['træntspɔ:t]
Verkehrssprache lingua franca [ˌlɪŋgwə 'frænkə]
verklappen to dump [dʌmp]
sich in jmdn. **verknallen** to go soft on sb [ˌgəʊ 'sɒft]
Verknüpfung link [lɪŋk]
verkohlt charred [tʃɑ:d]
verkünden to declare [dɪ'kleə]
verlangen to demand [dɪ'mɑ:nd]
Verlangen desire [dɪ'zaɪə]
verlangsamen to slow down [ˌsləʊ 'daʊn]
verlassen to leave [li:v]
verlegen to transfer [trænts'fɜ:]
verlegen confused [kən'fju:zd]; embarrassed [ɪm'bærəst]
Verleih- rental ['rentl]
verleihen to loan [ləʊn]; to present [prɪ'zent]
verlesen to read out [ˌri:d‿'aʊt]
verletzen to hurt [hɜ:t]
verletzend hurtful ['hɜ:tfl]
verletzt hurt [hɜ:t]
Verletzung harm [hɑ:m]
verlieren to lose [lu:z]
verloren gehen to get lost [get 'lɒst]
verlockend tempting ['temptɪŋ]
vermarkten to market ['mɑ:kɪt]
Vermarktung marketing ['mɑ:kɪtɪŋ]
vermeiden to avoid [ə'vɔɪd]
vermindern to reduce [rɪ'dju:s]
vermissen to miss [mɪs]; to miss out (on) [mɪss‿'aʊt]
Vermögen fortune ['fɔ:tʃu:n]
vermuten to guess [ges]
vernünftig intelligent [ɪn'telɪdʒnt]; sensible ['sensɪbl]
veröffentlichen to publish ['pʌblɪʃ]
Verpackung packaging ['pækɪdʒɪŋ]
verpassen to miss [mɪs]
jmdn. **verpetzen** to sneak on sb [sni:k]
jmdn. **verpfeifen** to shop sb [ʃɒp]
Verpflegung catering ['keɪtrɪŋ]
jmdn. **verprügeln** to beat sb up [ˌbi:t‿'ʌp]
Verrat treason ['tri:zn]
jmdn. **verraten** to shop sb [ʃɒp]
verregnet rainy ['reɪni]
verrückt crazy ['kreɪzi]; mad [mæd]
verrückt machen to drive crazy [draɪv 'kreɪzi]
verrückt nach … sein to be nuts about [bi: ˌnʌts‿ə'baʊt]
verrückt werden to go bananas [ˌgəʊ bə'nɑ:nəz]
Vers verse [vɜ:s]
versagen to fail [feɪl]
Versammlung assembly [ə'sembli]; rally ['ræli]
verschieden different ['dɪfrnt]
Verschiedenartigkeit variation [ˌveərɪ'eɪʃn]
verschiedene several ['sevrl]
verschlafen sleepy ['sli:pi]
Verschluss shutter ['ʃʌtə]
Verschlüsselung code [kəʊd]
Verschmelzung fusion ['fju:ʒn]
verschmort charred [tʃɑ:d]
verschmutzen to pollute [pə'lu:t]
Verschmutzung pollution [pə'lu:ʃn]
verschneit snowy ['snəʊi]
verschwenden to waste [weɪst]
Verschwendung waste [weɪst]
verschwinden to disappear [ˌdɪsə'pɪə]
verschwommen blurred [blɜ:d]
versichern to assure [ə'ʃʊə]
Versicherung insurance [ɪn'ʃʊərns]
Version version ['vɜ:ʃn]
Versorgung supply [sə'plaɪ]
verspätet delayed [dɪ'leɪd]; late [leɪt]
versprechen to promise ['prɒmɪs]
Verstand brain(s) [breɪn(z)]; mind [maɪnd]
sich **verständigen** to communicate [kə'mju:nɪkeɪt]
Verständigung communication [kəˌmju:nɪ'keɪʃn]; understanding [ˌʌndə'stændɪŋ]
Verständnis understanding [ˌʌndə'stændɪŋ]
verstecken to hide [haɪd]
sich verstecken to hide [haɪd]
verstehen to understand [ˌʌndə'stænd]
sich verstehen to get along [ˌget‿ə'lɒŋ]
versteinert fossil ['fɒsl]
Versuch attempt [ə'tempt]; experiment [ɪk'sperɪmənt]
versuchen to try [traɪ]
verteilen to scatter ['skætə]
Vertrag contract ['kɒntrækt]; treaty ['tri:ti]
vertrauen to trust [trʌst]
Vertrauen trust [trʌst]
Vertrauenslehrer/Vertrauenslehrerin guidance teacher *(AE)* ['gaɪdənts ˌti:tʃə]
vertrauenswürdig reliable [rɪ'laɪəbl]; trustworthy ['trʌstwɜ:ði]
vertreiben to market ['mɑ:kɪt]
Vertreter/Vertreterin agent ['eɪdʒnt]; representative [ˌreprɪ'zentətɪv]
Vertrieb marketing ['mɑ:kɪtɪŋ]; sales *(pl)* [seɪlz]
verunreinigen to pollute [pə'lu:t]
verursachen to cause [kɔ:z]
Verurteilung sentence ['sentənts]
vervollständigen to complete [kəm'pli:t]
Verwaltung management ['mænɪdʒmənt]
Verweis reference ['refrns]
verwenden to use [ju:z]
Verwendung use [ju:s]
verwickelt sein in to be involved in [bi: ɪn'vɒlvd‿ɪn]
verwirrt confused [kən'fju:zd]
verwöhnen to spoil [spɔɪl]
verzeichnet on record [ɒn 'rekɔ:d]
verzeihen to forgive [fə'gɪv]
verzögert delayed [dɪ'leɪd]
verzweifelt desperate ['desprət]
Veto veto ['vi:təʊ]
V-förmig V-shaped ['vi:ˌʃeɪpt]
via via [vaɪə]
Video video ['vɪdiəʊ]
viel a lot [ə 'lɒt]; much [mʌtʃ]
viel versprechend promising ['prɒmɪsiŋ]
viel/viele a lot of [ə 'lɒt‿əv]; lots (of) ['lɒts‿əv]
Viel Glück! Good luck! [ˌgʊd 'lʌk]
viele loads of ['ləʊdz‿əv]; many ['meni]
vielleicht maybe ['meɪbi]; perhaps [pə'hæps]
vielsprachig multi-lingual [ˌmʌlti'lɪŋgwəl]
Viertel neighborhood *(AE)* ['neɪbəhʊd]; quarter ['kwɔ:tə]
Viertel nach quarter past ['kwɔ:tə pɑ:st]
Viertel vor quarter to ['kwɔ:tə tə]

Vierteldollar *(Währung)* quarter ['kwɔ:tə]
Villa villa ['vɪlə]
violett purple ['pɜ:pl]
virtuell virtual ['vɜ:tʃuəl]
Visum *(Plural: Visa)* visa, visas *(pl)* ['vi:zə]
Vogel bird [bɜ:d]
Vokabular vocabulary [vəʊ'kæbjəlri]
Volk nation ['neɪʃn]; people, peoples *(pl)* ['pi:pl]
Volksmusik folk [fəʊk]
Volksstamm tribe [traɪb]
voll (von) full (of) [fʊl]
Volleyball volleyball ['vɒlibɔ:l]
völlig absolutely [ˌæbsə'lu:tli]; completely [kəm'pli:tli]
vollkommen perfect ['pɜ:fɪkt]
vollständig completely [kəm'pli:tli]; total ['təʊtl]
Vollzeit- full-time (F/T) [ˌfʊl'taɪm]
von by [baɪ]; from [frɒm]; in [ɪn]; of [ɒv; əv]
vor before [bɪ'fɔ:]; in front of [ɪn 'frʌnt‿əv]; *(zeitlich)* ago [ə'gəʊ]
vor allem especially [ɪ'speʃli]
Vor- front [frʌnt]
vorbei over ['əʊvə]
vorbeigehen (an) to pass [pɑ:s]
vorbereiten to prepare [prɪ'peə]
sich vorbereiten to get ready [get 'redi]
Vorbild role model ['rəʊl ˌmɒdl]
vorbildlich ideal [aɪ'dɪəl]
Vorder- front [frʌnt]
Vordergrund foreground ['fɔ:graʊnd]
Vorderseite front [frʌnt]
Vorführung exhibition [ˌeksɪ'bɪʃn]
Vorgesetzter/Vorgesetzte supervisor ['su:pəvaɪzə]
Vorhang curtain ['kɜ:tn]
Vorhersage *(Wetter)* forecast ['fɔ:kɑ:st]
vorhersagen *(Wetter)* to forecast ['fɔ:kɑ:st]
vorlaut cheeky ['tʃi:ki]
laut **vorlesen** to read out [ˌri:d‿'aʊt]
Vormittag morning ['mɔ:nɪŋ]
vormittags in the morning [ˌɪn ðə 'mɔ:nɪŋ]; *(Uhrzeit)* a.m. [ˌeɪ'em]
vorne at the front [ət ðə 'frʌnt]
nach vorne forward ['fɔ:wəd]
Vorort suburb ['sʌbɜ:b]
Vorrat reserve [rɪ'zɜ:v]; supply [sə'plaɪ]
Vorschlag suggestion [sə'dʒestʃn]
vorschlagen to suggest [sə'dʒest]
Vorschrift rule [ru:l]
vorsichtig careful ['keəfl]
Vorsingen audition [ɔ:'dɪʃn]
Vorsitzender/Vorsitzende chief [tʃi:f]
Vorspeise starter ['stɑ:tə]
Vorsprechen audition [ɔ:'dɪʃn]
sich (etwas) **vorstellen** to imagine [ɪ'mædʒɪn]
Vorstellung image ['ɪmɪdʒ]; performance [pə'fɔ:məns]
Vortanzen audition [ɔ:'dɪʃn]
Vorteil advantage [əd'vɑ:ntɪdʒ]; asset ['æset]
Vor- und Nachteile pros and cons [ˌprəʊz‿ənd 'kɒnz]
Vortrag presentation [ˌprezn'teɪʃn]; talk [tɔ:k]
einen Vortrag halten to give a talk [ˌgɪv‿ə 'tɔ:k]
vorüber over ['əʊvə]
vorübergehend temporary ['temprəri]
vorwärts forward ['fɔ:wəd]
vorwärtskommen to get on [get‿'ɒn]
vorziehen to prefer [prɪ'fɜ:]
Vorzug asset ['æset]

W

Wache guard [gɑ:d]
wachsen to grow [grəʊ]; to rise [raɪz]
wachsen lassen to grow [grəʊ]
wachsend increasing [ɪn'kri:sɪŋ]
Wächter/Wächterin guard [gɑ:d]
Waffen arms *(pl)* [ɑ:mz]
eine Waffe auf jmdn. richten to point a gun at sb [ˌpɔɪnt‿ə 'gʌn‿ət]
wagen to dare [deə]
etw. wagen to take your chance [ˌteɪk jɔ: 'tʃɑ:ns]
Wahl election [ɪ'lekʃn]
landesweite Wahl general election [ˌdʒenrl‿ɪ'lekʃn]
Wahl choice [tʃɔɪs]
wählen to choose [tʃu:z]; to elect [ɪ'lekt]; to vote (for) [vəʊt]
wahr true [tru:]
wahr werden to come true [kʌm 'tru:]
während as [æz; əz]; while [waɪl]; *(+ Nomen)* during *(+ noun)* ['djʊərɪŋ]
wahrhaft truthful ['tru:θfl]
Wahrheit truth [tru:θ]
wahrscheinlich probably ['prɒbəbli]
Wahrzeichen landmark ['lændmɑ:k]
Wald forest ['fɒrɪst]; wood [wʊd]
Waliser/Waliserin Welsh [welʃ]
walisisch Welsh [welʃ]
Wand wall [wɔ:l]
wandeln to alter ['ɔ:ltə]; to convert ['kɒnvɜ:t]
Wandmalerei mural ['mjʊərl]
Wandtafel board [bɔ:d]
wann when [wen]
Wanze bug [bʌg]
Ware product ['prɒdʌkt]
Waren goods *(pl)* [gʊdz]
Warenautomat vending machine ['vendɪŋ məˌʃi:n]
warm warm [wɔ:m]
Warn- warning ['wɔ:nɪŋ]
Warnung warning ['wɔ:nɪŋ]
warten to service ['sɜ:vɪs]; to wait [weɪt]
Warte mal! Hang on! ['hæŋ‿ɒn]
warten auf to wait for ['weɪt fɔ:]
Wärter/Wärterin keeper ['ki:pə]; zookeeper ['zu:ˌki:pə]
Warteschlange line [laɪn]; queue [kju:]
warum why [waɪ]
was what [wɒt]
was auch immer whatever [wɒt'evə]; whatsoever [ˌwɒtsəʊ'evə]
Was ist los? What's up? [ˌwɒts‿'ʌp]
Was ist mit ...? What about ... ? [wɒt‿ə'baʊt]
Was steht da? What does it say? [ˌwɒt dʌz‿ɪt 'seɪ]
Waschbecken *(im Amerikanischen)* sink [sɪŋk]
Waschbrettbauch six-pack ['sɪkspæk]
waschen to wash [wɒʃ]
sich waschen to wash [wɒʃ]
Wäschetrockner tumble drier ['tʌmbl ˌdraɪə]
Waschmaschine washing machine ['wɒʃɪŋ məˌʃi:n]
Wasser water ['wɔ:tə]
Wasseraufbereitungsanlage water treatment plant ['wɔ:tə ˌtri:tmənt ˌplɑ:nt]
Wasserhahn faucet *(AE)* ['fɔ:sɪt]; tap [tæp]
Wasserstoff hydrogen ['haɪdrədʒən]
Webcam webcam ['webkæm]
Webseite site [saɪt]
Website website ['websaɪt]
Wechselgeld change [tʃeɪndʒ]
wechseln to change [tʃeɪndʒ]
wecken to wake [weɪk]
Wecker alarm clock [ə'lɑ:m ˌklɒk]
weg away [ə'weɪ]
Weg path [pɑ:θ]; walkway ['wɔ:kweɪ]; way [weɪ]
auf dem Weg sein zu/nach to be off to [bi:‿'ɒf tə]
sich auf den Weg machen to set off [set‿'ɒf]
Wegbereiter/Wegbereiterin pioneer [ˌpaɪə'nɪə]
wegbleiben to keep away [ˌki:p‿ə'weɪ]; to stay out [steɪ‿'aʊt]

wegbringen to take off [ˌteɪk‿ˈɒf]
wegen because of [bɪˈkɒz‿əv]; due to [ˈdjuː ˌtʊ/tə]
weggehen to leave [liːv]
wegkommen to get away [ˌget‿əˈweɪ]
wegnehmen to take [teɪk]
wegräumen von to get off [get‿ˈɒf]
wegrennen to run away [ˌrʌn‿əˈweɪ]
weh tun to hurt [hɜːt]
wehen to drift [drɪft]; to fly [flaɪ]
Weibchen female [ˈfiːmeɪl]
weiblich female [ˈfiːmeɪl]
weich soft [sɒft]
Weichei softy [ˈsɒfti]
sich **weigern** to refuse [rɪˈfjuːz]
Weihnachten Christmas [ˈkrɪsməs]
weil as [æz; əz]; because [bɪˈkɒz]
eine **Weile** a while [ə ˈwaɪl]
weinen to cry [kraɪ]
Weise way [weɪ]
auf diese Weise that way [ðæt ˈweɪ]
Weißwandtafel whiteboard [ˈwaɪtbɔːd]
weit far [fɑː]; wide [waɪd]
weiter farther [ˈfɑːðə]; further [ˈfɜːðə]
es weit bringen to go far [gəʊ ˈfɑː]
immer weiter farther and farther [ˈfɑːðə]
weit kommen to go far [gəʊ ˈfɑː]
weiten to widen [ˈwaɪdn]
weitergeben to pass [pɑːs]
weitergehen to continue [kənˈtɪnjuː]; to go on [gəʊ‿ˈɒn]
weiterkommen to get on [get‿ˈɒn]
weitermachen to continue [kənˈtɪnjuː]; to go on [gəʊ‿ˈɒn]
weitermachen mit to keep up [kiːp‿ˈʌp]
Weitsprung long jump [ˈlɒŋ ˌdʒʌmp]
weitverbreitet widespread [waɪdspred]
welche whatsoever [ˌwɒtsəʊˈevə]
welcher/welche/welches what [wɒt]; which [wɪtʃ]
Welle wave [weɪv]
Wellenreiten surfing [ˈsɜːfɪŋ]
Wellness-Center spa [spɑː]
Welt world [wɜːld]
Weltall outer space [ˌaʊtə ˈspeɪs]
Weltraum outer space [ˌaʊtə ˈspeɪs]; space [speɪs]; universe [ˈjuːnɪvɜːs]
Weltraumstation space station [ˈspeɪs ˌsteɪʃn]
weltweit worldwide [ˌwɜːldˈwaɪd]
wem who [huː]; whom [huːm]
wen who [huː]; whom [huːm]
wenig little [ˈlɪtl]
wenige few [fjuː]
weniger less [les]
wenigstens at least [ət ˈliːst]
wenn if [ɪf]; when [wen]
wenn nicht unless [ənˈles]
wer who [huː]
für etw./jmdn. **werben** to campaign [kæmˈpeɪn]
für etw. werben to promote sth [prəˈməʊt]
Werbespot advert [ˈædvɜːt]
werden to become [bɪˈkʌm]; to get [get]
werden (zu) to turn (to) [tɜːn]
werden/werden nicht *(futurisch)* will (ʼll), won't [wɪl; wəʊnt]
werfen to throw [θrəʊ]
Werfer/Werferin pitcher [ˈpɪtʃə]
Werk factory [ˈfæktri]; plant [plɑːnt]
Werkstatt workshop [ˈwɜːkʃɒp]
Werktag weekday [ˈwiːkdeɪ]
(es) **wert sein (zu)** to be worth *(+ gerund)* [biː ˈwɜːθ]
wertvoll valuable [ˈvæljuəbl]
wessen whose [huːz]
Westasiate/-asiatin West Asian [ˌwest ˈeɪʃn]
westasiatisch West Asian [ˌwest ˈeɪʃn]
Weste vest [vest]
Westen west [west]
Western Western [ˈwestən]
westlich Western [ˈwestən]
Wettbewerb competition [ˌkɒmpəˈtɪʃn]
wetten to bet [bet]
Wetter weather [ˈweðə]
Wettkampf match [mætʃ]
Wettlauf race [reɪs]
einen Wettlauf machen to run a race [ˌrʌn‿ə ˈreɪs]
Whiteboard whiteboard [ˈwaɪtbɔːd]
wichtig important [ɪmˈpɔːtnt]
widerhallen to echo [ˈekəʊ]
wie *(Vergleich)* as [æz; əz]; like [laɪk]; such as [ˈsʌtʃ‿æz]
wie how [haʊ]
Wie alt bist du? How old are you? [haʊ‿ˈəʊld‿ɑː juː]
Wie geht es dir/Ihnen/euch? How are you? [ˌhaʊ‿ˈɑː juː]
Wie heißt du? What's your name? [ˌwɒts jə ˈneɪm]
Wie spät ist es, bitte? What's the time, please? [ˌwɒts ðə ˈtaɪm ˌpliːz]
wie viele how many [haʊ ˈmeni]
Wie viel kosten … ? How much are … ? [ˌhaʊ ˈmʌtʃ‿ɑː]
Wie viel kostet … ? How much is … ? [ˌhaʊ ˈmʌtʃ‿ɪz]
Wie viel Uhr ist es, bitte? What's the time, please? [ˌwɒts ðə ˈtaɪm ˌpliːz]
Wie wäre es mit …? What about … ? [wɒt‿əˈbaʊt]
wieder again [əˈgen]
wieder erleben to relive [ˌriːˈlɪv]
wiederherstellen to restore [rɪˈstɔː]; to rebuild [ˌriːˈbɪld]
auf **Wiedersehen** goodbye [gʊdˈbaɪ]
wiederverwerten to recycle [riːˈsaɪkl]
wiegen to weigh [weɪ]
wild wild [waɪld]
wild lebende Tiere wildlife [ˈwaɪldlaɪf]
Wildcard wild card [ˈwaɪld ˌkɑːd]
Wildhüter/Wildhüterin ranger [ˈreɪndʒə]
Wildwasser whitewater [ˈwaɪtwɔːtə]
Willkommen (in) … Welcome (to) … [ˈwelkəm tə]
willkommen heißen to welcome [ˈwelkəm]
Wimpelfisch bannerfish [ˈbænəfɪʃ]
Wind wind [wɪnd]
windig windy [ˈwɪndi]
Windkraftanlage windmill [ˈwɪnmɪl]
Windmühle windmill [ˈwɪnmɪl]
Windrad windmill [ˈwɪnmɪl]
windsurfen to surf [sɜːf]; to windsurf [ˈwɪndsɜːf]
winken to wave [weɪv]
Winter winter [ˈwɪntə]
winzig tiny [ˈtaɪni]
wir we [wiː]
wir selbst ourselves [aʊəˈselvz]
Wirbel fuss [fʌs]
Wirbelsäule spine [spaɪn]
Wirbelsturm cyclone [ˈsaɪkləʊn]
wirken to seem [siːm]
wirklich real [rɪəl]; really [ˈrɪəli]
Wirklichkeit reality [riˈæləti]
Wirkung effect [ɪˈfekt]
wischen to wipe [waɪp]
wissen to know [nəʊ]
Wissen knowledge [ˈnɒlɪdʒ]
Wissenschaft Science [ˈsaɪəns]
Wissenschaftler/Wissenschaftlerin scientist [ˈsaɪəntɪst]
wissenschaftlich scientific [ˌsaɪənˈtɪfɪk]
Witz joke [dʒəʊk]
Du machst Witze. You're kidding. [ˌjə ˈkɪdɪŋ]
Witze machen to joke [dʒəʊk]
wo where [weə]
Woche week [wiːk]
in der Woche a week [ə ˈwiːk]
pro Woche a week [ə ˈwiːk]
Wochenende weekend [ˌwiːkˈend]
Wochentag weekday [ˈwiːkdeɪ]
wöchentlich weekly [ˈwiːkli]
wohin where [weə]
Wohlstand wealth [welθ]
Wohltätigkeit charity [ˈtʃærɪti]
Wohltätigkeitsverein charity [ˈtʃærɪti]

Wohn- residential [ˌrezɪ'dentʃl]
wohnen to live [lɪv]
wohnen bei to stay with ['steɪ wɪð]
am **Wohnsitz** residential [ˌrezɪ'dentʃl]
Wohnung apartment *(AE)* [ə'pɑ:tmənt]; flat [flæt]
Wohnzimmer living room ['lɪvɪŋ rʊm]
Wolf wolf, wolves *(pl)* [wʊlf; wʊlvz]
Wolke cloud [klaʊd]
Wolkenkratzer skyscraper ['skaɪˌskreɪpə]
wolkig cloudy ['klaʊdi]
Wolldecke blanket ['blæŋkɪt]
wollen to want (to) ['wɒnt tə]
Workshop workshop ['wɜ:kʃɒp]
Wort word [wɜ:d]
Wörterbuch dictionary ['dɪkʃnri]
Wortschatz vocabulary [vəʊ'kæbjəlri]
Wrack wreck [rek]
kein **Wunder, dass ...** no wonder [nəʊ 'wʌndə]
wunderschön beautiful ['bju:tɪfl]
Wunsch desire [dɪ'zaɪə]; request [rɪ'kwest]; wish [wɪʃ]
wünschen to wish [wɪʃ]
würde/würden would [wʊd]
Wurf throw [θrəʊ]
Wurst sausage ['sɒsɪdʒ]
Würstchen sausage ['sɒsɪdʒ]
würzig spicy ['spaɪsi]
Wüste desert ['dezət]
wütend furious ['fjʊəriəs]; mad [mæd]

Z

zäh tough [tʌf]
Zahl figure ['fɪgə]; number ['nʌmbə]
zählen to count (for sth) [kaʊnt]
zahlen to pay [peɪ]
Zahlung payment ['peɪmənt]
Zahn tooth, teeth *(pl)* [tu:θ; ti:θ]
Zahnarzt/Zahnärztin dentist ['dentɪst]
Zahnprothese false teeth [fɔ:ls 'ti:θ]
Zahnschmerzen toothache ['tu:θeɪk]
Zauberer wizard ['wɪzəd]
Zaun fence [fens]
Zeh toe [təʊ]
Zehncentstück *(Währung)* dime [daɪm]
Zeichen sign [saɪn]; signal ['sɪgnl]; symbol ['sɪmbl]
ein Zeichen geben to signal ['sɪgnl]
Zeichentrickfilm animation [ænɪ'meɪʃn]; cartoon [kɑ:'tu:n]
zeichnen to design [dɪ'zaɪn]; to draw [drɔ:]
Zeichnung drawing ['drɔ:ɪŋ]
zeigen to show [ʃəʊ]
zeigen (auf) to point (to) [pɔɪnt]
Zeile line [laɪn]
Zeit time [taɪm]
Du liebe Zeit! Good grief! [gʊd 'gri:f]
in letzter Zeit recently ['ri:sntli]
Zeitabschnitt period *(AE)* ['pɪəriəd]
Zeitalter age [eɪdʒ]
Zeitschrift magazine [mægə'zi:n]
Zeitschriftenhändler/ Zeitschriftenhändlerin newsagent ['nju:sˌeɪdʒənt]
Zeitung newspaper ['nju:sˌpeɪpə]; paper ['peɪpə]
Zelle cell [sell]
Zelt tent [tent]
Zelten camping ['kæmpɪŋ]
Zentimeter centimetre ['sentɪˌmi:tə]
Zentrum centre ['sentə]; hub [hʌb]
zerbrechen to break [breɪk]
zerbrochen broken ['brəʊkn]
zerbröseln to flake [fleɪk]
zerdrücken to squash [skwɑʃ]
Zeremonie ceremony ['serɪməni]
zerfallen to flake [fleɪk]
zerrissen torn [tɔ:n]
zerstören to destroy [dɪ'strɔɪ]; to spoil [spɔɪl]
zerstreuen to scatter ['skætə]
sich zerstreuen to scatter ['skætə]
Zertifikat certificate [sə'tɪfɪkət]
Zeug stuff [stʌf]
Zeugnis report [rɪ'pɔ:t]
ziehen to drag [dræg]; to pull [pʊl]
Ziehen tug [tʌg]
Ziel goal [gəʊl]; target ['tɑ:gɪt]
zielen auf to aim ['eɪm]
Zielscheibe target ['tɑ:gɪt]
ziemlich fairly ['feəli]; pretty ['prɪti]; quite [kwaɪt]
Ziffer figure ['fɪgə]
Zigarette cigarette [ˌsɪgr'et]
Zimmer chamber ['tʃeɪmbə]; room [ru:m; rʊm]
freies Zimmer vacancy ['veɪknsi]
zirka around [ə'raʊnd]
zischen to fizz [fɪz]; to spit [spɪt]
Zitrone lemon ['lemən]
Zitronen- lemon ['lemən]
zittern to shake [ʃeɪk]
zivil civil ['sɪvl]
zögern to hesitate ['hezɪteɪt]
Zoll customs *(pl)* ['kʌstəmz]; *(Längenmaß: 2,54 cm)* inch [ɪnʃ]
Zone zone [zəʊn]
Zoo zoo [zu:]
zu closed [kləʊzd]
zu to [tʊ; tə]
zuallererst first of all [ˌfɜ:st‿ɒf‿'ɔ:l]
zubereiten to prepare [prɪ'peə]
mit den Achseln **zucken** to shrug (one's shoulders) [ʃrʌg]
Zucker sugar ['ʃʊgə]
zuckerkrank diabetic [ˌdaɪə'betɪk]
Zuckerkrankheit diabetes [ˌdaɪə'bi:ti:z]
zuerst at first [ət 'fɜ:st]; first [fɜ:st]; first of all [ˌfɜ:st‿ɒf‿'ɔ:l]
zuflüstern to whisper ['wɪspə]
zufrieden sein mit to be pleased with [bi: 'pli:zd wɪð]
Zug train [treɪn]
Zugang access ['ækses]
zugehen auf to walk up to [wɔ:k‿'ʌp tə]
Zuhause home [həʊm]
zuhören to listen ['lɪsn]
Zukunft future ['fju:tʃə]
zukünftig future ['fju:tʃə]
zulassen to allow [ə'laʊ]
zulässig valid ['vælɪd]
Zulassung admission [əd'mɪʃn]
zuletzt last [lɑ:st]
Zulu Zulu ['zu:lu:]
zumachen to close [kləʊz]
zunächst at first [ət 'fɜ:st]; first of all [ˌfɜ:st‿ɒf‿'ɔ:l]
zunehmen to grow [grəʊ]; to increase [ɪn'kri:s]; to rise [raɪz]
Zunge tongue [tʌŋ]
zuordnen to match [mætʃ]
Zupfen tug [tʌg]
zurechtkommen to cope [kəʊp]; to get along [ˌget‿ə'lɒŋ]; to get on [get‿'ɒn]; to manage ['mænɪdʒ]
zurück back [bæk]
zurückdenken to reminisce [ˌremɪ'nɪs]
zurückgehen to return [rɪ'tɜ:n]; to turn back [tɜ:n 'bæk]
zurückkehren to return [rɪ'tɜ:n]
zurückkommen (zu/nach) to get back (to) [get 'bæk tə]
sich **zurücklehnen** to sit back [ˌsɪt 'bæk]
zusammen together [tə'geðə]
zusammen mit along with [ə'lɒŋ wɪð]
Zusammenbruch breakdown ['breɪkdaʊn]
zusammenfügen to match [mætʃ]
Zusammenhang context ['kɒntekst]
jmdn. **zusammenschlagen** to beat sb up [ˌbi:t‿'ʌp]
Zusatz extra ['ekstrə]
zusätzlich additional [ə'dɪʃnl]; extra ['ekstrə]
Zuschauer/Zuschauerin viewer ['vju:ə]
etw. **zusichern** to assure [ə'ʃʊə]
Zustand state [steɪt]
zustimmen to agree [ə'gri:]
Zustimmung consent [kən'sent]

German – English

zuverlässig reliable [rɪ'laɪəbl]
zuzüglich plus [plʌs]
zweifellos certainly ['sɜ:tnli]
Zweig branch [brɑ:ntʃ]; twig [twɪg]
Zweigstelle branch [brɑ:ntʃ]
zweimal twice [twaɪs]
zweisprachig bilingual [baɪ'lɪŋgwəl]
zweitens secondly ['sekndli]
Zwilling twin [twɪn]
Zwillings- twin [twɪn]
zwingen to force [fɔ:s]
zwingend compulsory [kəm'pʌlsri]
Zwirn thread [θred]
zwischen between [bɪ'twi:n]
in der **Zwischenzeit** meanwhile [ˌmi:n'waɪl]
Zyklon cyclone ['saɪkləʊn]

In the classroom

What you can say …

… if you meet people or say 'goodbye':	
I'm very pleased to meet you.	Freut mich sehr, Sie kennen zu lernen.
Nice to meet you!	Schön dich kennen zu lernen.
Goodbye./Bye. See you tomorrow/next … .	Auf Wiedersehen./Tschüss. Bis morgen/nächste/-n/-s … .

… if you need help:	
Can you give me a hand, please?	Kannst du/Können Sie mir bitte helfen?
I don't understand this.	Ich verstehe das nicht.
What's that in English/German?	Was heißt das auf Englisch/Deutsch?
Can I say: …?/What does … mean?	Kann ich … sagen?/Was bedeutet …?
How do you do/change/ … this?	Wie macht/ändert/ … man das?
Is this right? I'm not sure.	Ist das richtig? Ich bin mir nicht sicher.
Could you write it down, please?	Könntest du/Könnten Sie das bitte aufschreiben?
Could I ask you a question, please?	Könnte ich dir/Ihnen bitte eine Frage stellen?
Pardon?	Wie bitte?
Could you repeat that, please?	Könntest du/Könnten Sie das bitte wiederholen?
Could you show me that again, please?	Könntest du/Könnten Sie mir das bitte nochmal zeigen?
I'm sorry (to bother you), but could I please borrow your mobile/…?	Entschuldige, (dass ich dich störe,) aber kann ich bitte dein Handy/… ausleihen?

… if you have a discussion:	
In my opinion/I think/ … .	Meiner Meinung nach/ich denke/ … .
You are absolutely right/wrong.	Du hast/Sie haben völlig Recht/Unrecht/nicht Recht.
On the one hand … , on the other hand … .	Einerseits …, andererseits … .
I think we should read newspapers/watch …/… .	Ich denke, wir sollten Zeitungen lesen/… schauen/… .
The best news reports/… are in …/on … .	Die besten Nachrichten/… findet man in …/auf … .
The biggest problem we have today is … .	Unser größtes Problem heutzutage ist … .
I have the feeling/impression that … .	Ich habe das Gefühl/den Eindruck, dass … .
What we really need to do is … .	Wir müssen unbedingt … .
I'm really interested in working abroad/ … .	Ich möchte am liebsten im Ausland arbeiten … .
The most important thing in a job is money/ … .	Das Wichtigste bei einem Job ist Geld/ … .
I'd like a job where I can meet people/ … .	Ich möchte einen Job, in dem ich Menschen treffe/ … .

… if you give a talk/presentation:	
Today I'd like to/I am going to talk about/ give a (PowerPoint) presentation on … .	Heute möchte ich über … reden/eine (PowerPoint-) Präsentation zum Thema … halten.
The title of the talk/presentation is … .	Der Titel des Referats/der Präsentation lautet … .
It will last about … minutes.	Es/Sie wird etwa … Minuten dauern.
It would be good if you kept any questions until the end.	Es wäre gut, wenn ihr eure/Sie Ihre Fragen erst am Schluss stellen könntet/könnten.
I shall be happy to answer them after the … .	Ich beantworte sie gerne nach der/dem … .
Here/on the left/right you can see … .	Hier/auf der linken/rechten Seite seht ihr/sehen Sie … .
I hope you liked my talk/… .	Ich hoffe, euch/Ihnen hat mein Referat/… gefallen.

… if you want to talk about stories/poems/songs:	
I think this story/… is good/funny/brilliant/ … .	Ich finde diese Geschichte/… gut/witzig/toll/ ….
I think it's sad/a bit boring/ … because … .	Ich finde sie/es traurig/etwas langweilig/…, weil … .
I've read/heard/… better ones.	Ich habe schon bessere gelesen/gehört/… .
In my opinion …was better because … .	Meiner Meinung nach war … besser, weil … .
I think the ending/… is right/wrong/too … .	Ich denke, dass das Ende/… richtig/falsch/zu … ist.

... if you work with a partner:

Whose turn is it?	Wer ist dran?
What are we going to do first?	Was machen wir zuerst?
Let's write down our ideas.	Lasst uns unsere Ideen aufschreiben.
Let's act the story/play a game.	Lasst uns die Geschichte vorspielen/ein Spiel spielen.
You can be ... and I'll be	Du kannst ... spielen und ich spiele ... ..
I don't understand what you mean.	Ich verstehe nicht, was du meinst.
What did you find on the Internet?	Was hast du im Internet gefunden?
I really like your idea.	Mir gefällt deine Idee sehr gut.
What do you suggest?	Was schlägst du vor?
Where shall we start?	Wo sollen wir anfangen?
I think we need	Ich denke, wir brauchen ... .

... if you want to present results:

We did a survey on .../to find out/because we wanted to know	Wir haben eine Umfrage zu ... gemacht/um herauszufinden/weil wir wissen wollten ... .
We asked all the girls/boys in our group/class/ in class	Wir haben alle Mädchen/Jungen in unserer Gruppe/ Klasse/in Klasse ... gefragt ... .
There were ... girls/boys. The total number was	Es gab ... Mädchen/Jungen. Die Gesamtzahl war ... .
We'd like to explain/show you some figures.	Wir möchten euch/Ihnen einige Zahlen erläutern/zeigen.
The grid/flow chart/ ... shows	Die Tabelle/das Flussdiagramm/ ... zeigt ... .
A key to the symbols is at the side/	Ein Schlüssel zu den Symbolen ist an der Seite/ ... .
The red/ ... bar/the scale represents	Die rote/ ... Säule/die Skala stellt ... dar.
You can see that most/more than .../no pupils	Klar ist, dass die meisten/mehr als .../keine Schüler ... .
If we compare ... with ..., we can see that	Wenn wir ... mit ... vergleichen, sehen wir, dass ... .
We were surprised/disappointed/ ... to find that	Wir waren überrascht/enttäuscht/ ..., dass ... .
Thank you for listening.	Wir bedanken uns für eure/Ihre Aufmerksamkeit.
Are there any questions?/Does anyone have a question?	Gibt es Fragen?

What the teacher might say to you ...

... if he/she has a question:

What's the problem?/What's wrong?	Was ist das Problem?/Was ist los?
Describe what you can see/the people/ what's happening.	Beschreibe was du siehst/ihr seht/die Menschen/was passiert.
What do you think of ...?	Was haltet ihr von ...?
Have you got any other ideas/comments/...?	Habt ihr andere/sonstige Ideen/Anmerkungen/...?
What could be the message/the meaning of ...?	Was könnte die Aussage/Bedeutung von ... sein?

... if he/she gives you instructions:

Be careful with the word order/... .	Achtet auf die Satzstellung/... .
Make a grid/poster/... (like this).	Macht eine Tabelle/ein Poster/... (wie diese/s).
Match the questions/pictures with the answers/ sentences.	Ordnet den Fragen/Bildern die Antworten/Sätze zu.
Define these jobs/... .	Erklärt diese Berufe/... .
Present your topic/poster/... to the class.	Präsentiert der Klasse euer Topic/Poster/ ... .

List of irregular verbs

to **be** [bi:]	**was/were** [wɒz/wɜ:]	**been** [bi:n]	sein
to **beat** [bi:t]	**beat** [bi:t]	**beaten** ['bi:tn]	besiegen, schlagen
to **become** [bɪ'kʌm]	**became** [bɪ'keɪm]	**become** [bɪ'kʌm]	werden
to **begin** [bɪ'gɪn]	**began** [bɪ'gæn]	**begun** [bɪ'gʌn]	beginnen, anfangen
to **bet** [bet]	**bet** [bet]	**bet** [bet]	wetten
to **bite** [baɪt]	**bit** [bɪt]	**bitten** ['bɪtn]	beißen
to **build** [bɪld]	**built** [bɪlt]	**built** [bɪlt]	bauen
to **blow** [bləʊ]	**blew** [blu:]	**blown** [bləʊn]	blasen
to **break** [breɪk]	**broke** [brəʊk]	**broken** ['brəʊkn]	(zer)brechen; kaputtmachen
to **bring** [brɪŋ]	**brought** [brɔ:t]	**brought** [brɔ:t]	bringen, mitbringen
to **burn** [bɜ:n]	**burnt** [bɜ:nt]	**burnt** [bɜ:nt]	(ver)brennen
to **buy** [baɪ]	**bought** [bɔ:t]	**bought** [bɔ:t]	kaufen
to **catch** [kætʃ]	**caught** [kɔ:t]	**caught** [kɔ:t]	fangen
to **choose** [tʃu:z]	**chose** [tʃəʊz]	**chosen** ['tʃəʊzn]	wählen, auswählen
to **come** [kʌm]	**came** [keɪm]	**come** [kʌm]	kommen
to **cut** [kʌt]	**cut** [kʌt]	**cut** [kʌt]	schneiden
to **dig up** [dɪg‿'ʌp]	**dug up** [dʌg‿'ʌp]	**dug up** [dʌg‿'ʌp]	ausgraben
to **do** [du:]	**did** [dɪd]	**done** [dʌn]	machen, tun
to **draw** [drɔ:]	**drew** [dru:]	**drawn** [drɔ:n]	zeichnen
to **drink** [drɪŋk]	**drank** [dræŋk]	**drunk** [drʌŋk]	trinken
to **drive** [draɪv]	**drove** [drəʊv]	**driven** ['drɪvn]	fahren
to **eat** [i:t]	**ate** [et/eɪt]	**eaten** ['i:tn]	essen, fressen
to **fall** [fɔ:l]	**fell** [fel]	**fallen** ['fɔ:ln]	fallen, herunterfallen, hinfallen
to **feed** [fi:d]	**fed** [fed]	**fed** [fed]	füttern
to **feel** [fi:l]	**felt** [felt]	**felt** [felt]	fühlen, sich fühlen
to **fight** [faɪt]	**fought** [fɔ:t]	**fought** [fɔ:t]	kämpfen
to **find** [faɪnd]	**found** [faʊnd]	**found** [faʊnd]	finden
to **fly** [flaɪ]	**flew** [flu:]	**flown** [fləʊn]	fliegen
to **forecast** ['fɔ:kɑ:st]	**forecast** ['fɔ:kɑ:st]	**forecast** ['fɔ:kɑ:st]	vorhersagen *(Wetter)*
to **forget** [fə'get]	**forgot** [fə'gɒt]	**forgotten** [fə'gɒtn]	vergessen
to **forgive** [fə'gɪv]	**forgave** [fə'geɪv]	**forgiven** [fə'gɪvn]	vergeben, verzeihen
to **get** [get]	**got** [gɒt]	**got** [gɒt]	kommen, bekommen; werden
to **give** [gɪv]	**gave** [geɪv]	**given** ['gɪvn]	geben, schenken
to **go** [gəʊ]	**went** [went]	**gone** [gɒn]	gehen
to **grow up** ['grəʊ ʌp]	**grew up** ['gru: ʌp]	**grown up** ['grəʊn ʌp]	aufwachsen
to **hang out** [hæŋ‿'aʊt]	**hung out** [hʌŋ‿'aʊt]	**hung out** [hʌŋ‿'aʊt]	sich herumtreiben
to **have** [hæv]	**had** [hæd]	**had** [hæd]	haben
to **hear** [hɪə]	**heard** [hɜ:d]	**heard** [hɜ:d]	hören
to **hide** [haɪd]	**hid** [hɪd]	**hidden** ['hɪdn]	verstecken, sich verstecken
to **hit** [hɪt]	**hit** [hɪt]	**hit** [hɪt]	schlagen, treffen
to **hold** [həʊld]	**held** [held]	**held** [held]	halten
to **hurt** [hɜ:t]	**hurt** [hɜ:t]	**hurt** [hɜ:t]	verletzen, weh tun
to **keep** [ki:p]	**kept** [kept]	**kept** [kept]	(be)halten
to **know** [nəʊ]	**knew** [nju:]	**known** [nəʊn]	wissen, kennen
to **lay** [leɪ]	**laid** [leɪd]	**laid** [leɪd]	legen
to **lead** [li:d]	**led** [led]	**led** [led]	führen
to **lean** [li:n]	**leant** [lent]	**leant** [lent]	(sich)lehnen
to **learn** [lɜ:n]	**learnt** [lɜ:nt]	**learnt** [lɜ:nt]	lernen
to **leave** [li:v]	**left** [left]	**left** [left]	lassen, verlassen, abfahren
to **lend** [lend]	**lent** [lent]	**lent** [lent]	leihen

to **let** [let]	**let** [let]	**let** [let]	lassen
to **lie** [laɪ]	**lay** [leɪ]	**lain** [leɪn]	liegen
to **lose** [lu:z]	**lost** [lɒst]	**lost** [lɒst]	verlieren
to **make** [meɪk]	**made** [meɪd]	**made** [meɪd]	machen
to **mean** [mi:n]	**meant** [ment]	**meant** [ment]	bedeuten, meinen
to **meet** [mi:t]	**met** [met]	**met** [met]	treffen, sich treffen
to **overdo** [ˌəʊvə'du:]	**overdid** [ˌəʊvə'dɪd]	**overdone** [ˌəʊvə'dʌn]	übertreiben
to **pay** [peɪ]	**paid** [peɪd]	**paid** [peɪd]	(be)zahlen
to **put** [pʊt]	**put** [pʊt]	**put** [pʊt]	setzen, stellen, legen
to **read** [ri:d]	**read** [red]	**read** [red]	lesen
to **rebuild** [ˌri:'bɪld]	**rebuilt** [ˌri:'bɪlt]	**rebuilt** [ˌri:'bɪlt]	wieder aufbauen, wiederherstellen
to **ride** [raɪd]	**rode** [rəʊd]	**ridden** ['rɪdn]	fahren, reiten
to **ring** [rɪŋ]	**rang** [ræŋ]	**rung** [rʌŋ]	klingeln; anrufen
to **rise** [raɪz]	**rose** [rəʊz]	**risen** ['rɪzn]	steigen, wachsen, zunehmen
to **run** [rʌn]	**ran** [ræn]	**run** [rʌn]	rennen, laufen
to **say** [seɪ]	**said** [sed]	**said** [sed]	sagen, sprechen
to **see** [si:]	**saw** [sɔ:]	**seen** [si:n]	sehen; besuchen
to **sell** [sel]	**sold** [səʊld]	**sold** [səʊld]	verkaufen
to **send** [send]	**sent** [sent]	**sent** [sent]	schicken
to **set** [set]	**set** [set]	**set** [set]	stellen, einstellen
to **shake** [ʃeɪk]	**shook** [ʃʊk]	**shaken** ['ʃeɪkn]	schütteln, zittern
to **show** [ʃəʊ]	**showed** [ʃəʊd]	**shown** [ʃəʊn]	zeigen
to **shut out** ['ʃʌt aut]	**shut out** ['ʃʌt aut]	**shut out** ['ʃʌt aut]	ausschließen
to **sing** [sɪŋ]	**sang** [sæŋ]	**sung** [sʌŋ]	singen
to **sit** [sɪt]	**sat** [sæt]	**sat** [sæt]	sitzen
to **sleep** [sli:p]	**slept** [slept]	**slept** [slept]	schlafen
to **smell** [smel]	**smelt** [smelt]	**smelt** [smelt]	riechen
to **speak** [spi:k]	**spoke** [spəʊk]	**spoken** ['spəʊkn]	sprechen
to **spell** [spel]	**spelt** [spelt]	**spelt** [spelt]	buchstabieren
to **spend** [spend]	**spent** [spent]	**spent** [spent]	verbringen, ausgeben
to **spread** [spred]	**spread** [spred]	**spread** [spred]	(sich) ausbreiten, verbreiten
to **stand** [stænd]	**stood** [stʊd]	**stood** [stʊd]	stehen
to **steal** [sti:l]	**stole** [stəʊl]	**stolen** ['stəʊln]	stehlen
to **stick** [stɪk]	**stuck** [stʌk]	**stuck** [stʌk]	kleben, stecken
to **swim** [swɪm]	**swam** [swæm]	**swum** [swʌm]	schwimmen
to **take** [teɪk]	**took** [tʊk]	**taken** ['teɪkn]	nehmen, mitnehmen, bringen
to **teach** [ti:tʃ]	**taught** [tɔ:t]	**taught** [tɔ:t]	lehren
to **tell** [tel]	**told** [təʊld]	**told** [təʊld]	erzählen, sagen
to **think** [θɪŋk]	**thought** [θɔ:t]	**thought** [θɔ:t]	denken, glauben
to **throw** [θrəʊ]	**threw** [θru:]	**thrown** [θrəʊn]	werfen
to **understand** [ˌʌndə'stænd]	**understood** [ˌʌndə'stʊd]	**understood** [ˌʌndə'stʊd]	verstehen
to **unwind** [ʌn'waɪnd]	**unwound** [ʌn'waʊnd]	**unwound** [ʌn'waʊnd]	sich abwickeln
to **upset** [ʌp'set]	**upset** [ʌp'set]	**upset** [ʌp'set]	erschrecken, durcheinander bringen, umstoßen
to **wake** [weɪk]	**woke** [wəʊk]	**woken** ['wəʊkn]	(auf)wecken
to **wear** [weə]	**wore** [wɔ:]	**worn** [wɔ:n]	anhaben, tragen
to **win** [wɪn]	**won** [wɒn]	**won** [wɒn]	gewinnen, siegen
to **write** [raɪt]	**wrote** [rəʊt]	**written** ['rɪtn]	schreiben

Lösungen/Lösungsvorschläge Check-out

Topic 1, page 20 – 21

Option 1

1 Explain the role of English in the world.

a) – Multi-lingual means that you can speak three or more languages.
– Your mother tongue is the language that you learn to speak from the beginning of your life.
– An official language is a language which is used for all official activities and papers.
– If you are bilingual it means that you have grown up with two different languages.
– A foreign language is a language you didn't learn as your mother tongue.
– A world language is a language which is spoken internationally and which is learnt by many people as a second language.

b) – if someone asks me the way and doesn't speak German because he or she is a tourist
– in English lessons at school
– when I am doing research for a presentation, for example on English webpages

2 Talk about what you used to do.

My friends and I **used to** play in a field. We **used to** stay there until it got dark. We **used to** kick the ball into the river. We **used to** jump in to get the ball back and we got wet. My parents **used to** go crazy when I came home in wet clothes. They **used to** lock me in my bedroom. Then they **used to** take away my ball. So I **used to** hide my football. Then I **used to** climb out of the window. After that I **used to** play in the street with my friends.

3 Present facts and figures about the English language.

a) 1. Over 700 **million** people speak it as a foreign language.
2. Captain Cook was **an explorer**.
3. It shortest sentence is: **Go!**
4. It's the official language in **more than** 55 countries.
5. Its longest word has **45** letters.
6. International pilots **must/always** use it.

b) Australia, the US, Canada, India and Nigeria because these are former British colonies.

Option 2

1 Talk about languages spoken in Canada.

a) English and French. 67.5 % of Canadians speak only English. 85 % of all French speakers live in Quebec.

b) It is the official language in Nunavut. It is spoken by the Inuit people.

c) Canada's four non-official languages are Chinese, Italian, German and Punjabi.

2 Talk about past experiences in Canada.

Sean **used to live** in Ireland but now he lives in Canada. He **emigrated** with his parents when he **was** six. They **used to live** in Montreal but now they live in Vancouver. Sean **went** to a French school when he was six and he **used to speak/spoke** French there most of the time. When he **was** ten the family **moved** to Alberta. In Medicine Hat he **used to moan** that he **found** town life boring. He often **used to read/read** comics and he **used to spend** time at weekends drawing. Later he **got** the idea for a club from art books that he **used to read** after school.

3 Discuss mangas.

I know a manga called Musashi. It tells the story of a historical Japanese figure. It is longer than most mangas but it's really exciting. It's a thriller and a love story. I like it because it shows very well how people lived in Japan hundreds of years ago.

4 Write a profile.

Name:	Martin Müller
Education:	general qualification for university entrance
Job:	doctor
Interests:	cycling, reading
Strengths:	mobile, communicative
Weaknesses:	chaotic, not creative
Dream:	go on a journey around the world

5 Prepare for an interview.

1. Be polite.
2. Use the person's name in your first question.
3. Give a response to the answers.
4. Thank the person at the end.

Option 3

1 Describe new trends in English.

a) Spain, Germany, India

b) *mailen, chillen, jobben, shoppen, trampen, surfen, relaxen, downloaden, …*

2 Understand teenage chat.

a) mela – meeting, festival; mouse potato – a person who spends a lot of time using the computer; pukka – first-class, real; chuddies – pants; innit – isn't it; bling – jewellery; desi – local, real Asian; na – no; homie – close friend; thug – someone who beats people up; bhangra – Punjabi folk music/dance

b) 1. c; 2. b; 3. a

3 Explain a Hinglish menu.

Thali is different parts of a meal which are served in little metal bowls on a tray.
Chutney is a spicy, sweet and sour mixture made with fruit, tomatoes, etc.
Balti is curry which is served in a special pot.
Masala are spices.
Tikka and naan are Indian types of bread.

Option 4

1 Talk about rules at work.

1. I have to do night shifts every month. I'm not allowed to talk to my friends about my patients.
2. I have to be ready to drive the fire engine at all times. I'm not allowed to leave without my helmet.
3. I have to stay in school all day. I'm not allowed to smoke in the school.
4. I have to make sure that I write down the right measurements. I'm not allowed to drink alcohol while I'm working.

2 Report on what different people said about their jobs.

1. I think the teacher said that she had to work in the holidays and at weekends, but she added that she loved her job.
2. I think the builder asked if anyone would like to put on his helmet. He also asked why they thought he called it his 'life saver'.
3. I think the nurse/doctor said that her job was always interesting but that night shifts could be hard.
4. I think the fireman asked if we could imagine what a big fire was really like. He said that he was really scared first time.

3 Present yourself at a job interview.

a) Hello, my name is Anna Weber. I'm 17 years old. I went to secondary modern school and have worked in different hotels during the holidays. I live in Stuttgart. My mother is a baker and my father works as a builder. In my free time I like drawing and dancing.

b) I think I'm the right person for this job because I am a good organizer and I'm very creative. I like to do sports and communicate with other people. I'm a friendly and trustworthy person.

Topic 2, page 38–39

Option 1

1 Talk about the Middle Ages in England.

a) 1066–1485

b) the King ➜ bishops ➜ barons ➜ knights ➜ soldiers ➜ freemen ➜ servants ➜ serfs

2 Imagine situations that probably won't happen.

If I **had lived** in the Middle Ages, I **wouldn't have been** a knight or a lady. Probably I **would have been** a serf. That means I **would have belonged** to the land where I lived, and I **wouldn't have travelled** around the country. If I **had wanted** to marry, I **would have needed** to ask my owner for permission. If I **had married** without his permission, he probably **would have thrown** me into prison. If he **had done** this, **I wouldn't have had** a right to a fair trial before a judge. If I **had escaped** from the owner, and **had been able** to hide for one year and a day, I **would have been** a freeman. I don't think I **would have liked** life as a serf. I **would have tried** to escape.

3 Explain the beginnings of rights for citizens.

1. … Magna Carta.
2. … throw their servants into prison for no reason.
3. … the king had too much power.
4. … was above the law now.
5. … parts of the charter in it.
6. … those who drew up the Constitution of the United States.

Option 2

1 Recognize two different democratic systems.

a) US: Senate, president, state of the union, Supreme Court, veto
UK: monarch, PM, Armed Forces, House of Lords
The Senate is a part of the political system in the US.
The president is the head of state of a country like the US.
The US president gives a 'state of the union' speech to his people.
The Supreme Court is the highest court of law in the US.
If you put in a veto, you say 'no' to something.
A monarch can be a king or a queen.
The PM is the most powerful person in some countries like Great Britain.
The Armed Forces of a country fight to protect it.
The British parliament has two houses, one of which is the House of Lords.

b) US: elected: Senate, president; appointed: Supreme Court
UK: elected: PM; appointed: members of the House of Lords

2 Talk about the government in the UK and the US.

Treaties are drawn up by the Ministers and by Congress.
Laws are passed by Parliament and by Congress.
The Ministers are chosen by the Prime Minister.
Laws are checked by the Supreme Court.
Policy is made by the Ministers.
War is declared by Parliament and by Congress.
Meetings are led by the Prime Minister.

3 Describe the Queen's role as Head of State.

The Queen's duties are to open and close Parliament, to sign laws and treaties made by Parliament, to declare war if Parliament decides to, to appoint the PM and Ministers and other officials and to represent the UK abroad.
Her special right is that she cannot be brought to court, or put in prison for example for driving too fast or murdering her husband.

4 Explain the US President's powers.

He can refuse to sign a bill. He **can't** write new bills. If he refuses to sign a bill, it can **still** become law. He **can't** declare war **without Congress's permission**. He **can't** make treaties without the permission of the Senate. He **is allowed** to use his state of the union speech to explain his policy. **Not** all American citizens can become US President.

Option 3

1 Talk about a work placement.

a) 1. sex; 2. religion; 3. conversation; 4. well-informed; 5. interest

b) 1. At business: The supervisor is very important for an apprentice.
2. In action: The employees work on different tasks in their job.
3. Help: The law is responsible for the safety of all people.
4. Behaviour: When someone is rude and sexist, it is hurtful.
5. At work: Bullying and telling jokes show no respect.

2 Give advice on problems at work.

1. If a colleague had got too close to me, I would have told him that I didn't like it.
2. If some colleagues had taken off their protective clothing when the supervisor was away, I wouldn't have done the same.
3. If someone had made hurtful comments about my religion, I would have told them that they should stop saying things like this.
4. If my supervisor had given another young apprentice more ambitious projects than me, I would have talked to him about it.
5. If a lot of my colleagues had told rude and sexist jokes in the cafeteria, I would have asked my supervisor for advice.

3 Identify rights and duties at work.

a) to be treated with respect, to have a safe and healthy work environment, to get sick leave and holiday pay, to be treated fairly like any other employees and not to be treated badly because you're an apprentice or trainee, to join a union

b) to start work on time, to give an excuse if you are not able to come to work, to take a break during the day

Option 4

1 Talk about the risks journalists take.

1. A journalist could fall into the river and could not get out again.
2. A journalist could be hurt by a soldier.
3. A journalist could be hurt by a fire or in an explosion.
4. A journalist could be run over by a car.

2 Imagine what you would have done in a dangerous situation.

If I had been in situation number 1, I wouldn't have gone near the river and I would have put on a life vest.
If I had been in situation number 2, I would have tried to hide.
If I had been in situation number 3, I would have tried to run away.
If I had been in situation number 4, I wouldn't have walked in the middle of the street.

3 Decide how far journalists should go.

1. I think this is true. Many journalists risk their lives when they are working in dangerous areas or on dangerous topics.
2. That's true; there is also a law that protects this right.
3. Some things are dangerous but very important at the same time. I think the journalists should decide whether they want to risk their lives to report news to us. They can decide if they want to work in a dangerous region.

Topic 3, page 62–63

Option 1

1 Discuss living healthily.

a) Eat healthy food, do sports, take time off work and do something to help the environment, since good living conditions mean living more healthily

b) I don't have time, it is cheaper and it tastes better.

2 Summarize a text.

Global warming creates new jobs. Many areas of work which were seen as very boring some years ago are becoming more and more interesting now, because they help to save the environment.
Eco technology is big business and people like rangers or biologists are needed because they work for the environment. Other jobs like textile worker and farmer have also been influenced and have changed.

3 Talk about yourself, your friends and the environment.

My mum always makes **herself** a sandwich for breakfast and she tells **me** I should at least eat some fruit. But I never make **myself** breakfast. I often buy **myself** a bagel on the way to school. My friends and I don't always eat things that are healthy for **us**. After school we sometimes buy **ourselves** some chocolate. But we try to keep **ourselves** fit. One of my friends doesn't do anything to keep **himself** fit. We call **him** 'fossil'. He never comes swimming or skateboarding with **us**. And we try to help the environment, too. We all walk or cycle to school. We can't enjoy **ourselves** if we know that we are adding to greenhouse gases **ourselves**.

4 Write a stanza of a poem.

I give you trees
You give me wooden chairs
I give you fossil fuels
You give me CO2

I give you a colourful world
You give me chemical products
I give you everything you need
You give me new inventions

Option 2

1 Consider how important water is for you.

a) Drinking, watering plants, swimming, washing-up, cleaning

Drinking: Milk
Watering plants: Rain
Swimming: River
Washing up: Clean plates with paper
Cleaning: Vinegar

b) 1: pond, 2: river, 3: pump, 4: well
Other places: fountains, ocean, rain, … .

2 Recognize global water problems.

a) Problems: pollution, shortages, increasing population, growing need, old pipes, pesticides, salt water, cyclone, dry periods, bottled water
Solutions: dig wells, tanks, treatment plants, buy water, bottled water, solar power

b) Myanmar: water shortages after cyclone
Ghana: polluted water
Ethiopia: water shortages

3 Connect phrases using relative pronouns.

Salt water is water, **which** you can't drink because it is too salty.
Residents are people, **who** live in a certain area.
AVRL is a private organisation, **which** owns the water in Ghana.
Authors are people, **who** write books.
Goods are things, **which** you can buy or sell.
Survivors are people, **who** survive a catastrophe or an accident.
An expert is someone, **who** knows something very well

Option 3

1 Talk about carbon emissions.

a) to destroy – to create; tap water – bottled water; to add to – to reduce; to throw away – to recycle; high energy – low energy; to waste – to save; ordinary – special; below – above; very little – a lot

b) 1. We have to create new forests where we have destroyed trees.
2. Tap water is more environmentally friendly than bottled water.
3. Bottled water adds to pollution, so what can we do to reduce it?
4. When throwing away your rubbish you should think about how to recycle some of it.
5. High energy is bad for the environment; try to use as many low energy devices as possible.
6. It's important to save energy and not to waste it.
7. Throwing away all your stuff is very ordinary, thinking about recycling is special.
8. The family's carbon footprint wasn't below average it was above average.
9. They should use their car very little, instead of a lot.

2 Describe your activities over a length of time.

1. We have been learning about our carbon footprint: About what it is and what we can do, to make it smaller.
2. We have been reading about Justin Rowlatt and his family.
3. Eating food from abroad, driving a car and using the PC have been increasing my carbon footprint.
4. Yes. I have been trying to waste less water when I take a shower and I have been using my bike more often.

3 Understand the problems people have in 'going green'.

a) 1. We wouldn't be as flexible any more without a car.
2. We wouldn't be able to eat anything we liked.
3. We couldn't go on holiday anywhere we liked.
4. It would be expensive to insulate the house.
5. We couldn't use chemicals to clean things.

b) To save the world, to live more healthily, to improve your own environment

Option 4

1 Understand an ad for a job.

a) The duties, experience and skills you need, the pay, where the job would be and how to apply for it.

b) You can apply by post, on the Internet, by filling in an application form, by e-mail and by making a phone call. The traditional way is to apply by post, but I think the best way today is to apply on the Internet because it tells you exactly which documents you have to attach. It's also better for the environment if we don't use much paper.

2 Give details about eco jobs.

a) 1. conservation and education; 2. energy; 3. selling eco products; 4. campaigning

b) 1. He is talking to people and has a bird on his arm. He is probably telling the audience something about the animals. He takes care of the animals and feeds them.
2. He seems to be installing a solar panel. He probably also looks after other types of energy in houses.
3. The man is standing in a supermarket, wearing an apron and is sorting the tomatoes. He has to order new fruit and help the customers to pick the right vegetables and fruits.
4. He or she is holding a collecting box and is wearing a T-shirt which says for which organisation he or she is working. He or she collects money in the street and also informs people about the organisation.

3 Describe your 'dream' job.

a) A permanent contract is important to me because it gives me the feeling that my job is safe. Good pay is good, of course, because everything is expensive nowadays.
A friendly boss is helpful because the climate at work is nicer then and it is more fun to work there.
Working outdoors is important to me, because I like to be outside in the fresh air.
Being together with people is fun. I like meeting people.
Flexible hours are not so important to me.

b) A nice office is important to me because it is more comfortable to work there. Nice colleagues are good because it is easier to work with them. Working at a place close to my home is important to me because I don't have to get up early then.

Topic 4, page 80 – 81

Option 1

1 Discuss legal ages.

a) You can't drink beer. You can't ride a motorbike. You can't get married.

b) In the US you can't buy alcohol until you are 21. In some states in the US you can drive a car when you are 14. You can't get married until you are 18 in the US.

2 Recognize the 'age of consent' in different countries.

a) The age of consent is the age at which people can legally have sex.

b) 1. Germany/Poland; 2. Turkey/USA (in some states); 3. USA

3 Talk about decisions you have to make at 16.

Sean writes about six key decisions that teenagers **normally** have to make. The first is about staying or not staying at school. He says parents should talk **openly** to their kids about this. Choosing the right friends can also be **extremely** important. It is **absolutely** vital that parents don't give their kids more freedom without more responsibilities. Decisions about dating, sex and drugs should also be made **carefully**. Parents should **always** discuss risks and dangers with their kids. The most difficult decision is about self-worth. Parents can avoid problems here **largely** by listening and talking

Option 2

1 Talk about choices in the UK at 16.

a) They can continue in education or move into training and work.

b) 1. If they continue in education, they can go into a sixth form at their school, go to a sixth form college, go to a further education college or go to a specialist college.
2. If they don't continue in education, they can, for example, do an apprenticeship or a training programme, or choose self-employment.

2 Describe what happens in an automotive company.

a) drive, grandson, headquarters, internships

b) manufacturing, marketing and sales, customers, financial sector

c) 1. Longbow's design, develop and manufacture for a worldwide market.
2. They market directly to retailers and dealers.
3. Their customers include governments, rental companies and fleet customers.
4. Their financial sector offers loans, insurance and other financial products.

3 Talk about people in a company.

a) **An office specialist** works in a team. They organise meetings and explain equipment to others.
A mechanic makes body shells and vehicle frames and restores old cars.
A computer specialist designs systems and offers advice and support to other colleagues.

b) **An office specialist** needs good English. He/She must be able to use and explain modern communication equipment.
A mechanic needs good grades in Math and Physics. They must be interested in machines and be able to think in three dimensions.
A computer specialist needs computer skills and a good grade in Math.

c) To do an internship in a company is a good idea because it's good to find out about the 'real' world after ten years at school. You can find out what you enjoy doing. You can learn about things that you didn't learn in school.

Option 3

1 Understand how some ill people feel.

a) My grandad is seriously ill. He can't walk very fast and he sleeps a lot. Sometimes he gets angry if my younger brothers make too much noise.

b) I would advise other people to talk to the person about how he or she feels. They should try to listen to them and help them.

2 Decide what you are going to do in life.

a) I'm going shopping because I want to buy a new CD.
I'm making a cake because it's my brother's birthday.
I'm helping my dad in the garden because he asked me to help him.
I'm visiting my grandma because she's ill.

b) 1. I'm going to visit New York: My aunt could help me because she lives in the US.
2. I'm going to buy a car: My parents could give me some money.
3. I'm going to do bungee jumping: My cousin could help me. He has done it before.
4. I'm going to eat insects: My dad could help me. He's a cook.
5. I'm going to take part in a talent show: My youth club could help me.

c) It might be difficult to find a cheap hotel in New York because it is a very expensive city.
It could be difficult to save enough money for a car before I am 21.
It might be hard to jump because I might be frightened.
It might be a bad idea to eat insects because they might not taste very good.
It might take a long time to train for a talent show.

3 Use an English dictionary.

a)+b) 1. Trinkgeld, 2. Durcheinander, 3. kippen, 4. Tipp

4 Analyse an extract from a novel.

a) Picture 3 shows a scene from the extract. Adam was sitting next to Tessa in his garden. She was holding a drink in her hand. She was looking a bit pale. They were both looking at some things that were burning in a fire.

b) 1. Adam was burning some things in the garden when Tessa spoke to him.

2. Tessa was standing close to the fire when the garden suddenly turned bright.
3. Tessa and Adam were both watching the fire when a stupid moth danced towards the ashes.

c) The story is told by Tessa herself, from her point of view. The storyline tells us about how she meets Adam and how he helps her to burn things from her past.
d) Hi, Sophie! I must tell you about a great book that I am reading. It's called 'Before I die'. It's very sad but I really like it because it describes a situation from real life. I'll lend it to you. Love, … .

Lösungen/Lösungsvorschläge Test yourself!

Test yourself! 1, page 22–25

A Reading

1 block – Klotz, Block; arrogant – arrogant; version – Fassung, Version; inexact – ungenau; personality – Persönlichkeit; generation – Generation; colleague – Kollege; fixed – fest; dialect – Dialekt

2 a. In European languages each sentence is a string of beads but in Inuktitut the words are put together like Lego™ blocks.
b. She speaks English and Inuktitut. She can't translate Inuktitut into English and English into Inuktitut literally because it sounds strange and inexact.
c. The language has changed very little in the last century.
d. Languages spoken there are Inuktitut, English and French.

3 a. … wanted to apply for a job. b. … arrogant and cold. c. … strange and inexact. d. … the personality and the language. e. … Greenlanders and other people in the Arctic world.

B Language

Place/ country	Capital	People	Language
Nunavut	Iqaluit	Inuit	Inuktitut
Germany	Berlin	German	German
Britain	London	Briton	British
France	Paris	Frenchman/ woman	French

C Listening

1 b.

2 a. 3, b. 2, c. 1

3 a. brought bad weather, caused dangerous situations, damaged equipment, broke equipment
b. They could call up helpful spirits or fight the bad spirits by dancing and chanting. They could also give advice about what to do to make the spirit happy again.

D Speaking

1 a. In photo 1 a man is riding in a dog race and in photo 2 someone is driving a skidoo. I would prefer to ride in a dog race because I think it must be great fun to be in a race with dogs. I don't like skidoos. They make a lot of noise.
b. The house on the left is more modern and more comfortable than the igloo on the right. I would rather live in the modern house because it is bigger and doesn't look so cold.

2 Disadvantages: cold and dark in winter, far away from other countries, it is difficult to travel around, only a few jobs, no discos or swimming pools
Advantages: a lot of snow, you always have a white Christmas, a lot of nature around you, there isn't as much stress as there is in cities
Changes brought through technology: heating, Internet, TV, mobile phones …

3 You: Hello, I'm Anna, I live in Germany and I often spend time at the youth club. I'd like to know a few things about the activities that you do at your youth club in Iqaluit.
You: I go to our club to meet friends, too. And sometimes I go to a film night.
You: We don't have a summer camp. But a lot of youth clubs here arrange special summer events like music festivals or workshops.
You: That's interesting, what kind of festival is it? How long does it last?
You: Do you still live in igloos nowadays? I'd really like to learn how to build an igloo, it must be great!
You: Wow, that sounds cool! Do you have any photos of the race? Maybe we could stay in contact via e-mail? You can send me pictures and I can send you some pictures of our youth club, too.

E Mediation and communication

a. Ja, sie war die Meeresgöttin. So etwas wie eine göttliche Mutter für alle Meereskreaturen.
b. Sie lebte auf dem Meeresgrund. Ihr Vater war der Todesgott.
c. Sie war sehr groß und dick, aber auch sehr schön.
d. Ihr Vater wollte sie aus dem Kajak werfen, weil sie nicht heiraten wollte. Aber sie hat sich noch festgehalten und dann hat er ihr mit einem Messer die Finger abgeschnitten, die zu Fischen wurden und fortschwammen. Sie sank dann in die Unterwelt, Adlivun, und wurde zu Sanna, der Muttergöttin aller Meereslebewesen.
e. Wenn jemand Gesellschafts- oder Naturgesetze brechen würde, könnte sie als Strafe all ihre Meereskreaturen verschwinden lassen.
f. Sie könnten natürlich nicht mehr jagen und hätten nichts zu essen. Sie haben ihr Gebete und Tänze als Opfer dargebracht. Das hat Sanna besänftigt und sie hat ihnen vergeben und das Gleichgewicht der Natur wiederhergestellt.

F Writing

1 *Individuelle Schülerlösung*

2 Writing

Our youth club

A lot of young people come to our club. Some of them are from other countries, or their parents weren't born here, so you can learn about other cultures when you talk to them. Some boys only come here to play football and a few girls just hang out in the café and chat. But most of us like computer games. We have dancing classes, too and in summer there are special events like a 'Make a Difference Day' and a camping tour. If you want to know more, visit our website!

Test yourself! 2, page 40–43

A Reading

1 Lines 1–20 Commonwealth Day topic 2008 and events
Lines 21–44 What young people know about the Commonwealth
Lines 45–60 One person's experience of Commonwealth Day
Lines 61–72 Our common wealth
Lines 72–87 Commonwealth goals today
Lines 88–96 More information

2 a. Commonwealth Day topic for 2008: 'The environment – our future'
b. five activities/events in 2008: parades, concerts, talks, competitions, drama and dance events
c. four things the states share: English as official language, values, cultural wealth, the Queen as Head of State
d. number of Commonwealth states today: 53
e. the idea of the Commonwealth today (2 things): democracy and human rights
f. what its members fight against and one way they do this: poverty, intolerance and injustice. They build bridges between their peoples.

B Language

1 a. 2 b. 2 c. 3 d. 2 e. 2 f. 1 g. 1

2 a. subject b. worldwide c. population d. peers
e. in common f. recently

C Listening

1 a. 5 b. 7 c. 2 d. 8 e. 6 f. 1 g. 4 h. 3

2 a. The CYAs are quite young: between **15 and 29**.
b. They are involved at every level – even in **management**.
c. The group is involved in a '**Positive** Living Programme' in Chandigarh.
d. Vasanti and the others in her group are **trained** by a team of doctors.
e. Then **Vasanti and the others in her group** write the scripts or songs.

D Speaking

1 a. In photo 1 they are maybe in a poor country in Africa. They might be teaching children to write. I think they need to speak their language and have teaching skills for this job. In photo 2 it looks like they are building a house, it could be in America. Maybe they are in an area which was destroyed by a storm or an earthquake. For this job you need to be strong and shouldn't be afraid of heights.
b. I would like to work in Africa on a project for children without a home or parents because I can speak English very well and I like children.
c. Maybe it would be difficult because life in Africa is very different from life here. There are also other diseases there. Maybe I would feel home sick.

2 You: Hello, I'm Anna. I'm interested in working on a project in a foreign country.
You: I already helped on a building project last year. So I already know the work and have the necessary skills. I could imagine doing something like that again.
You: So what would my duties be on this project?
You: Oh, that's terrible! What happened there?
You: I like working with wood, but I will also help anywhere I am needed.
You: Could you e-mail me the forms and information? I will go to a doctor right away.
You: I will try to do everything as quickly as possible. Thank you for your help. You will hear from me soon. Bye.

E Mediation and communication

a. Es ist ein Museum über die Geschichte des Britischen Imperiums.
b. Weil das Britische Imperium 1840 begann.
c. Nein, es geht auch darum, wie das Britische Imperium endete und was heute daraus geworden ist.
d. Wie es entstand und sich entwickelte, auch wer in die neuen Kolonien ging, um diese aufzubauen, und welche Probleme es gab.
e. Der Kasten erklärt die interaktiven Angebote, die es im Museum gibt. Man kann seltene Objekte, Fotos und Filme sehen, Computerspiele spielen oder Puzzles machen und wahre Lebensgeschichten hören.

F Writing

1 *Individuelle Schülerlösung*

2 The Commonwealth

Today 53 independent states are members of the Commonwealth. That is almost a third of the world's population! An amazing number, don't you think? But it hasn't always been like that. Most of the countries are former British colonies but the Commonwealth only became multicultural when India joined it. Today its members organize a festival which helps to build bridges between the people from all the different countries. This is one way to fight against poverty, intolerance and injustice and help the principles of the Commonwealth to become true: democracy and human rights.

Test Yourself! 3, page 64 – 67

A Reading

1 bacteria – Bakterien
filter – Filter
disinfection – Desinfektion
plastic – Plastik
factor – Faktor
method – Methode
contaminated – kontaminiert, verseucht

2 *Individuelle Schülerlösungen*

3 b.

4 a. Over a billion people in the world have the problem that the water is polluted and there isn't enough of it.
b. One method of water purification is the use of a straw that kills bacteria as you drink.
c. The straw may not be suitable for people in poorer countries because it is still very expensive for them.
d. This technology is relatively cheap and it produces larger amounts of clean water.
e. You need a lot of sun and clean plastic bottles for the solar disinfection method.

B Language

a. alternatives b. life-saving c. disaster

C Listening

1 a. 1 b. 2 c. 1 d. 1 e. 3

2 reasons: a. feels she can help people, d. to give girls there the chance to go to school, e. has skills/experience needed on the project
problems: b. staying healthy, d. the old equipment there, e. the heat and the climate

D Speaking

1 a. The first picture shows a young African boy/girl who is holding a yellow gun in his/her right hand. It's a gun that you shoot water with. He/She is holding the gun towards his/her head. The picture is a poster from UNICEF.
The second picture shows a famous actress (Jennifer Aniston) who is smiling. She is holding a large bottle with water in it. You can read the words 'smart water' on it.
b. The first poster is from UNICEF. It is campaigning against contaminated water that kills people in Africa. I think this because the boy/girl is holding a gun which uses water at his/her head. The water is going to kill him/her.
The second poster is advertising water which you can buy in bottles. It is called 'smart water' because they want to say that people who buy it are 'smart' and it will make you beautiful and healthy, like the actress. I think this because they show beautiful Jennifer Aniston together with 'smart water'.
c. *Individuelle Schülerlösung*
d. I would support the campaign from UNICEF because the poster is very shocking and shows the truth. I wouldn't buy 'smart water' because I can't see what is so special about this water or what makes it better than water from the tap.

2 You: Which organisation are you collecting money for?
You: Thank you. I have heard the name already I think. I would like to know more about it.
You: Do you use the money to buy bottled water for them or do you build water treatment plants?
You: What does 'WaterAid' do in areas where there are water shortages?
You: I would like to/can't give you some/any money now. I think you do great work./I need to think about it. I'm going to read your leaflet. Do you need any trainees?
You: Thank you very much for all the information. I hope you will collect a lot of money for 'WaterAid'. Goodbye and good luck!

E Mediation and communication

a. It uses the UV-rays and the warmth of the sun to clean the water.
b. If you don't use clean PET bottles it can be dangerous.
c. You fill the bottles with the dirty water and put them in the sun for about 6 hours.
d. Yes. It is not very difficult to do and it isn't expensive.
e. You need a lot of sun and you can't use very cloudy water. You can't use all bottles for this method.

F Writing

1 *Individuelle Schülerlösungen*

2 The value of 'blue gold'!
Water is very valuable and that's why we call it 'blue gold'. A lot of people in our world don't have enough water or the water is polluted, so that it causes illness and death! Millions of people in poor countries don't have clean drinking water. They can't buy bottled water. They can't even buy something to clean the water. And we use too much water or waste it, because we don't know how valuable it is. We have to save water, because we all need it to survive and soon it will be as valuable as gold.

Test Yourself! 4, page 82 – 85

A Reading

1 b.

2 unspoken: no one says it; fit in: be suitable; potential: possible; flip-flops: open shoes that you wear, for example, on the beach; unexpected: sth you didn't expect; teleworker: sb whose workplace is far away from their company

3 *Individuelle Schülerlösungen*

4 a. Even in firms without written dress codes you can't just wear anything you like.
b. If there is no written code, it's a good idea to look at what your colleagues wear, and dress the way they do.
c. You should try to keep your own style but it shouldn't be too different from the style of your colleagues.
d. The difference between dressing for work and dressing for an interview is that you choose your clothes a bit more carefully than an employee normally would.

e. On dress down day you can dress more casually but it doesn't mean that you can wear just anything.

5 The text is about dress codes at work. A lot of firms expect employees to dress formally but many have a casual day when you can wear something more casual, but not your swimsuit, of course.

B Language

a. to be on the safe side b. ironed c. casual
d. a second chance

C Listening

1 A 2 B 4 C 6 D 5
2 The interviewer asks them about dress codes.
3 a. 1, b. 2, c. 1, d. 3

D Speaking

1 a. 1. The young woman in picture 1 has blond hair. She looks very clean and neat. She is wearing a white shirt and black trousers. Her shirt is ironed and she is not wearing any make-up or jewellery. I think she may be a model because she is very beautiful and has style.
2. The young man in picture 2 is wearing black trousers and a white T-shirt with the number 25 on it. He has a white cap on his head and he is wearing a watch. I think he might be a DJ because he looks like someone from the hip hop music world.
3. The young man in picture 3 is wearing a white shirt, a coloured tie and a black jacket. His hair is long and it isn't very neat. I think he might work in a sales department because he looks as if he is presenting something.
4. The young woman in picture 4 looks strange. Her clothes look a bit crazy and she is wearing jewellery and dark glasses. I think she is maybe a hairdresser because her hair looks very unusual.
b. 1. I think the girl in picture 1 is very well organised and confident because she is very neat and she has her hands in her pockets and is looking relaxed.
2. I think the young man in picture 2 is a bit crazy. I think he wants to draw attention to himself because of his clothes.
3. I think the young man in picture 3 is a bit big headed/too sure of himself because he isn't smiling at the camera and he is holding his tie with his hand.
4. I think the young woman in picture 4 is very confident and happy. She is laughing and looks relaxed.
c. *Individuelle Schülerlösung*

2 You: I have always been interested in fashion. I was quite good at Art in school. Last year I did work experience in a company that makes sports clothes.
You: During my work experience I took part in discussions about a new swimsuit that they were designing. I also spent two months in London. I had a holiday job in a big fashion store. I worked in the department for young fashions.
You: I love travelling. I speak French and a little bit of Russian.
You: I think that both things are important. If you make good quality things then you need to be able to sell them. You can only do this if your company presents itself well.
You: I think a dress code is really important. And I would be interested in taking part in a training course. I know, for example, that it is wrong to wear trainers at a business meeting.
You: When could I start if you offered me the job?
You: That wouldn't be a problem.
You: Thank you for the interview and goodbye.

E Mediation and communication

a. Nein. In manchen Ländern gibt man sich nicht die Hand.
b. In Indien, zum Beispiel, legt man die Hände zusammen wie beim Gebet, verbeugt sich und sagt 'Namasté'. In Japan verbeugt man sich auch.
c. Wenn man in Indien und arabischen Ländern in ein Haus oder eine religiöse Stätte geht.
d. Man darf Geschäftspartnern kein teures Geschenk machen.
e. alles, was von einer Kuh kommt
f. Fleisch, Pralinen und Alkohol

F Writing

1 *Individuelle Schülerlösungen*
2 How to get a job abroad
Before you go for an interview for a job in another country you should find out about that country, for example, what the weather there is like and what some important traditions are. You should try to imagine what the interviewer might ask you, and you should write down one or two questions which you would like to ask. You should smile when you meet the interviewer and should wear clean, suitable clothes. You shouldn't use a lot of make-up or put on a lot of jewellery. Your hair should be neat and clean and your shoes should be sensible.

Lösungen/Lösungsvorschläge Grammatik

Grammar practice, page 126–134

Ov 1 Pronouns

1 A report about summer camp

1. I hated my first few days at camp but I told **myself** it would not be forever.
2. In the mornings, for example, we all had to make our beds **ourselves**.
3. There are always people to help you, of course, but you have to do so much **yourself**.
4. They made our breakfast but then the kids **themselves** had to wash up.
5. But camp is also fun. We even learnt to make a fire and cook for **ourselves** on it.
6. Of course, our leader Mary-Lou checked the fire **herself** each time.
7. The best thing was rock climbing! I really surprised **myself**, because I hate heights.
8. Rock climbing **itself** isn't dangerous but you have to follow the safety rules!
9. One of the kids took off his helmet and hurt **himself** badly when he fell.
10. But the rest of us really enjoyed **ourselves** at the camp.
11. We all want to register **ourselves** for the same camp next year.

2 An e-mail home

Hi , you guys! Prepare **yourselves** for my first report on the camp! I'm not going to tell you everything – that would just take **me** too long. The first thing you need to know is that we're enjoying **ourselves**. Really! This place is fun. Nicole thinks so, too. Remember when you warned **us** about the other kids – that we would have to speak English with **them**? Well, you were right! At first I was really mad at **myself,** because **I** hadn't tried harder in English class. But after a week I surprised **myself** and the coaches! One of the girls hurt **herself**, when a ball hit **her** in the face. The coaches were on the other side of the field and I had to get help from one of **them**. I had to speak English with **him** because he didn't speak German. I was quite proud of **myself**, because he seemed to understand **me** . But I made a real idiot of **myself**, when I told **him** what was wrong with **her** . "She has hurt her nose leg," I said. He thought she had broken her leg! In English, you see, they say 'bridge of the nose'.

Ov 2 'be' in different tenses

1 Get it right, Ronaldo!

1. These **are/aren't** my boots. And this **is/isn't** my T-shirt.
2. **Are** these my new T-shirts? I thought they **were** yours.
3. What **is** the name of that French player? His boots **were** gold.
4. I **wasn't** very good today. My game **was** terrible.
5. I think it **was** a good idea to come to the camp.
6. I **was** frightened at first that I wouldn't find any friends.
7. But this **is** the best camp that I **have ever been** at.

Ov 3 Verbs in past tenses

1 A chain of events

a) First he **woke up** at 8:30. Then he **jogged** at 9 o'clock. Then at 10:15 he **had** a shower. Then he **cooked** a meal at 10:30. After that, at 11 o'clock, he **worked** at his computer. Finally at 12 o'clock he **phoned** his girlfriend.

b) Nick woke up at 8:30. After he **had woken up**, he jogged at 9 o'clock. After he **had jogged**, he had a shower at 10:15. After he **had had** a shower, he cooked a meal at 10:30. After he **had cooked** a meal, he worked at his computer at 11 o'clock. After he **had worked** at his computer he phoned his girlfriend at 12 o'clock.

2 Before and after

a) They **had fed their** cat. They **had packed their** maps. They **had given their** keys to the neighbour. They **had left** a message on the answerphone. But they **hadn't thrown their** rubbish in the bins. They **hadn't locked their** flat. They **hadn't posted their** letters. They **hadn't taken their** bottles back to the shop.

b) After I **had thrown** your rubbish in the bins, I **locked** your flat./After I **had locked** your flat, I posted your letters. After I **had posted** your letters, I took your bottles back to the shop.

Ov 4 Reported speech

1 Jane's quiet evening

Jane was sitting at home checking **her** e-mails. **She was** a bit worried. **She could** hear funny noises from the flat upstairs. Someone **was running** around the flat. It **had started** at about eight o'clock. First they **had been** running around the kitchen. **Then** they **were throwing** things around the living-room. They **had** just **broken** a window! **She didn't know** what to do! The Wilsons **weren't** at home. **She had seen** them leaving the flat. They **had been** away **then** for about two hours. Maybe their son **had come** back while **she had been** in the bathroom. She **didn't know**. **She hadn't seen** him. **She thought** maybe it **was** a burglar. But **she didn't want** to bother the police. So, **she was wondering** what **she should** do.

2 Mack's accident

a) *Individuelle Schülerlösungen*

b) The teenager **said** that his name **was** Mack Simpson. He also **told** me that he **lived** around the corner, in number 51 Green Street. He **said** that he **was** 16 years old. He **told** me that his parents **weren't** at home. But he **said** that he **had** a number in his mobile to ring to let them know.

3 How the accident happened

a) *Individuelle Schülerlösungen*

b) 1. The patient said that he **had hit** a streetlamp.
2. He told me that he **had been riding** on his skateboard.
3. He said that he **had been going** to his mate's house.
4. He explained that he **had needed** some snacks for a DVD evening.
5. ..., he said that a guy **had shouted** his name.
6. He explained that he **had turned** his head to look.
7. He said that he **hadn't recognized** the guy.

Ov 5 Verbs in present tenses

A group of young people from Berlin **is visiting** South England on a language exchange. They **have been** here for a week already. They **have been staying** with local families and **have seen** lots of interesting things. In their language school they **have not just been improving** their spoken English. They also **have been finding out** about the people and the culture. It's Tuesday afternoon and Hussein and his girlfriend, Alina, **are waiting** at a bus stop. Suddenly they **hear** some young British people. They **are speaking** a strange language. It **sounds** like a muddle between Turkish and English. Hussein **tells** Alina that it's just like back home: He and his mates often **mix** German and Turkish. Then they **get** on the bus and **go** home.
A few hours later the same thing **happens** again. Alina **hears** a couple in a shop – and this time the people **are speaking** English and Russian. When she **is eating** supper, Alina **tells** her guest family. They all **laugh**. "That's pukka English!" **explains** the daughter, Nasreen. "Mix and match – anything you like!"

Ov 6 Future forms

1. Unfortunately tomorrow **will be** cloudy but it **won't rain** in the afternoon.
2. You lucky girl, you **will** probably **meet** a stranger and you **will be** very happy.
3. Attention please, the train **will be leaving** in 2 minutes.
4. Oh, dear, I **am going to miss** you very much.
5. Don't worry! We **are coming** back tomorrow.
6. I'm very sorry, but she **is not coming** this evening.

Ov 7+8 Modals, auxiliaries and modal substitutes

1 Some hotel rules

a) You **must** carry your passport with you at all times.
You **mustn't** buy train tickets from people in the street.
You **mustn't** use the lift after 10 p.m., or if there is a fire.
You **can/may** have breakfast after 7 a.m.
You **must** leave your keys at the reception desk when you leave the hotel.
You **can/may** get another blanket if you are cold.
You **needn't** make your bed every day – we will do it for you.
You **must** always turn off the lights when you leave your room.
You **mustn't** smoke in your room. This is a no-smoking hotel!
You **can/may** borrow a bike if you want to cycle round the island.

b) I **will have to** carry my passport with me at all times.
I **won't be allowed to** buy train tickets from people in the street.
I **won't be allowed to** use the lift after 10 p.m., or if there is a fire.
I **will be able to** have breakfast after 7 a.m.
I **will have to** leave my keys at the reception desk when I leave the hotel.
I **will be able to** get another blanket if I am cold.
I **won't have to** make my bed every day – they will do it for me.
I **will** always **have to** turn off the lights when I leave my room.
I **won't be allowed to** smoke in my room. This is a no-smoking hotel!
I **will be able to** borrow a bike if I want to cycle round the island.

c) I **had to** turn off the lights. I **didn't have to** make my own breakfast.
I **was able to** have breakfast after 7 a.m. I **wasn't able to** have it before 7 a.m.
I **was allowed to** buy train tickets from the hotel. I **wasn't allowed to** buy them from people in the street.

2 A holiday by the sea

1. When I was really young my mum and I **used to live** in Birmingham.
2. I **would dream** every summer about spending a holiday near the sea in Devon.
3. I **used to tell** her this but my mum **would** always **say**, "That **does sound** like a good idea."
4. But then she **would** just **go** back to what she was doing.
5. I **used to go** to our travel agent every summer holidays.
6. The girl there always **used to give** me catalogues and leaflets about holidays in Devon.
7. I **would take** them home and my bedroom **would be** full of them for the next few weeks.
8. There **used to be** competitions in them. I don't really like them but one year I **did do** one and I won!
9. When I showed my mum the prize, she was amazed. "Oh," she said, "It **does look** quite nice there".

Ov 9 Active and passive voice

1 Talking about television

a) 1. Television **wasn't invented** by a woman, it **was invented** by two men called Zworykin and Farnsworth.
2. It **wasn't called** that because they liked the name, it **was called** that because the word means 'far sight'.
3. The first programmes **weren't shown** in colour, they **were shown** in black and white only.
4. In fact colour TV **wasn't introduced** into Europe in the early 60s, it **was introduced** much later in 1967.

5. TV satellites **weren't launched** into space in the 1950s, they **were launched** in the 1960s.
6. The biggest choice of channels **wasn't offered** in Germany, it **was offered** in the US.
7. Bigger screens **weren't developed** immediately, they **were developed** many years later.
8. In the 1980s television **wasn't linked** to the Internet, it **was linked** in the 1990s.

b) 1. Do you think a touch screen **will be invented**?
2. What do you think it **will be called**?
3. Do you think the first programmes **will be shown** in colour?
4. When do you think the first colour screens **will be introduced**?
5. How many channels do you think **will be offered**?
6. When **will** bigger screens **be developed**?
7. **Will** the screens **be linked** to other forms of communication?

c) *Individuelle Schülerlösungen*

2 Nico's dream

In the first scene I was sitting in a spaceship with you and Ted. – I knew that we **were being transported** to some distant planet. My hands **were not tied** behind my back. But I **was not allowed** to see anything. A kind of hood **had been pulled** down over my head before I had entered the spaceship. When we landed the hood **was removed** and we **were taken** to a strange building. It was really huge and it **was covered** in silver and gold. Then we **were left** alone. We **were not told** what to do. Suddenly a door **was opened** by two green creatures and we **were pushed** through it. Then the scene changed: I was in a dark room alone and I **was being spoken** to by someone. I couldn't see his face because it **was hidden** behind a curtain. Suddenly I **was woken** up by my dad. He was knocking on my door, saying, "Time to get up, Nico!"

Ov 10 Relative clauses

1 The only film that made me ...

a) 1. The Pink Panther 2 is the only DVD **that/which** made me laugh till I cried.
2. The main character is a detective **who/that** is called Clouseau.
3. He tries to find a burglar **whose** name is 'the Tornado'.
4. So he works with a team of detectives **who/that** come from different countries.
5. They all think 'the Tornado' is the man **who/that** they need to find.
6. It's only Clouseau **who** believes that he was not the burglar.

b) 'Dragon Tears' is the only film **that/which** made me cry last month. And I know someone **whose** dad acted in the film! Yes, his name's Danny and it was he **who** lent me the DVD. His dad is the character in the film **who/that** attacks the dragon. It's really exciting but I think the best scene is one **which/that** is near the end. Lyreena, the young girl **who** is the heroine, becomes the dragon's friend.
The story tells us that dragons can look terrible and make fire but they are really sad creatures **which/that** are very lonely. It's only the dragon **whose** tears can put out its own fire. And it's these tears **which/that** flood the village where Lyreena lives near the end of the story.
It's a great story **which/that** was taken from an old Chinese myth and it's a film **that/which** everyone should see!

c) *Individuelle Schülerlösungen*

2 Talking about films

'Star Wars' was the first science fiction film I ever watched. It was also the first film **that** ever really scared me. I knew it was very popular. My older brother said it was the funniest film he had ever seen. So one afternoon I borrowed his DVD and watched in on the TV **that** was in my bedroom. But after an hour I suddenly decided it was too frightening for me. I ran out of my room and fell into an empty box **that** was outside my door. My brother saw me, and he laughed and said, 'I told you it was a funny film!' But only he was laughing.

Ov 11 Conditional clauses

1 If I met the US President, I'd ...

a) 1. If I met the US President, **I'd ask** him about his hobbies.
2. If I won a lot of money in a TV quiz show, **I'd spend** it on a holiday in Australia.
3. If Superman flew through my window, **I'd be** very excited.
4. If a friend was angry with me, **I'd ask** him or her why.
5. If my mobile phone was stolen, **I'd report** it to the police.
6. If a firm offered me a job abroad for a year, **I'd be** happy.
7. If I saw a pickpocket on the job, **I'd call** the police.

b) 1. If I met the US President, **I certainly wouldn't speak** to him in German.
2. If I won a lot of money in a TV quiz show, **I certainly wouldn't buy** a big car.
3. If Superman flew through my window, **I certainly wouldn't scream** at him.
4. If a friend was angry with me, **I certainly wouldn't forget** the friend.
5. If my mobile phone was stolen, **I certainly wouldn't ask** my parents for money.
6. If a firm offered me a job abroad for a year, **I certainly wouldn't say** 'no' to the firm.
7. If I saw a pickpocket on the job, **I certainly wouldn't say** anything to him or her.

2 Historical events

a) 1. If I had lived in 1492, I **might have crossed** the Atlantic with Columbus.
2. If I had lived in 1558, I **might have made** dresses for Queen Elizabeth the First.
3. If I had lived in 1642, I **might have fought** in the English Civil War.
4. If I had lived in 1789, I **might have become** the first president of the USA.
5. If I had lived in 1846, I **might have emigrated** to the USA because of famine.

6. If I had lived in 1963, I **might have heard** a speech by Martin Luther King.

b) *Individuelle Schülerlösungen*

3 Just imagine

1. If I hadn't lived in this century, I **would have liked to have lived** in the twentieth century.
2. I **would probably have lived** in the USA.
3. I **would have spoken** American English.
4. I **would have travelled** to California and **I would have seen** Hollywood.
5. I **would have** met Elvis. **I would have said** to him, "You were great!"

Ov 12 Adverbs: Summary

1 Very important words

a) completely, terribly, extremely, really, especially, equally

b) a bit, almost, quite, super, very, very much, ultra, absolutely, greatly

c) 1. The trip up the mountain was **really** exciting.
2. The view from the top of mountain was **very** beautiful.
3. But the climbers had to be **quite** careful when they climbed down again.
4. This was because they were **ultra**-high up.
5. They were all **especially** proud of the long climb they had just done.
6. But they were all thirsty – and their water bottles were **completely** empty!
7. So they were all **equally** happy when they reached their camp.
8. By evening they were **terribly** tired and **extremely** hungry!

Ov 13 Word order

1 When and where

1. last week:	(1)There was a trade fair in West London (2).
2. to the fair:	On Saturday a group of us went (1) in the afternoon after school.
3. at two o'clock:	(1)We took the train to London (2).
4. at the station:	The train arrived (1) at three o'clock.
5. by 3:20 p.m.:	(1)We were in Hall 2 (2).
6. in Hall 2:	(1) At three o'clock (2) there was a product presentation (3).
7. a moment later:	(1) A man walked onto a stage in the middle of the hall (2).
8. suddenly	(1) He called out some numbers (2), but I didn't hear them.
9. on the stage:	I was more interested in the box (1). But one of my mates checked my ticket.
10. in the end	(1) I was surprised to find out (2) that I had won the box!
11. at five o'clock:	It was huge! So (1) I rang my dad where he worked in London (2).

2 How often?

1. Shops have **often** got too many products.
2. So I can **never** find what I need.
3. On the other hand I **sometimes** see three products which are all OK.
4. If that happens, then I **always** buy the cheapest product.
5. But then they're **usually** quite expensive.

	GB 	IRELAND 
15th century	**1455–1485:** The 'Battle of the Roses' is fought and Henry VII becomes king.	**1494:** The Irish parliament meets with permission of the English King.
16th century	**1534:** Henry VIII becomes head of the Church of England. **1542:** Mary Stuart becomes Queen of Scotland. **1558–1603:** Under Elisabeth I England becomes a great power in Europe.	**1569–1583:** The rebellion against Elisabeth I fails. **1595:** A new rebellion starts.
17th century	**1642–1646:** There is civil war between soldiers of the king and soldiers of Parliament. **1649:** King Charles I is executed. The monarchy is abolished and a republic called the "Commonwealth" is created under Cromwell. **1660:** Charles II becomes king.	**1649–1650:** England sends Oliver Cromwell to end rebellions in Ireland. He defeats the Irish with 120,000 soldiers. During this time nearly half of the Irish population dies.
18th century	**1775:** Great Britain wants their American colonies to pay taxes. **1783:** Britain accepts the United States of America as an independent country. **1793:** The war between France and Great Britain starts.	**1703:** Catholics are oppressed and many emigrate to the USA. **1720:** The British parliament declares its right to rule Ireland. **1798:** Rebellion of United Irishmen.
19th century	**1801:** Great Britain and Ireland become the United Kingdom. **1805:** At Trafalgar the British defeat Napoleon. **1815:** At Waterloo England defeats the French again and the war is over. **1877:** Queen Victoria becomes Empress of India.	**1823:** Daniel O'Connell starts a movement to fight for freedom from Britain. **1843:** The first railway in Ireland is built. **1846–1851:** During the "Great Famine" over 1.5 million Irish die and over 1 million emigrate.
20th century	**1914–1918:** World War I **1939–1945:** World War II **1947:** India becomes independent. The British empire begins to break up. **1968:** Britain sends troops to Northern Ireland. **1994:** The Channel Tunnel opens.	**1916:** The Easter Rising: Irish republicans try to end British rule in Ireland. **1921:** The Irish Free State is created. **1955:** Ireland joins the United Nations. **1956:** The IRA (Irish Republican Army) starts its attacks in Northern Ireland.
21st century	**2001:** Britain supports the plans of US president Bush to attack Iraq. **2005:** London's Underground and buses are attacked by Islamic terrorists. **2009:** The last British soldiers leave Iraq.	**2001:** The IRA agrees to lay down their weapons and apologizes for the murder of hundreds of civilians. **2005:** The EU recognises Irish as a working language.

USA 	Australia 	
1492: The American continent is discovered by Christopher Columbus.		15th century
1565: The first colony is founded by the Spanish in St. Augustine.		16th century
1620: The Mayflower arrives in Massachusetts. **1626:** The Dutch buy Manhattan from a Native American tribe.	**1606:** On February 26th a Dutchman, Willem Janszoon, landed on Australian soil in what is now called Queensland. **1642:** Abel Tasman made a map of the coast of North Australia.	17th century
1775: The war against Britain starts. **July 4, 1776:** Declaration of Independence **1789:** George Washington becomes the first president. **1791:** The Bill of Rights is passed.	**1770:** Captain James Cook discovered Australia and claimed the land for England. **1788:** On January 26th first convicts arrived at Sydney Cove. Many had escaped the death sentence in England. This day later became Australia Day.	18th century
1854: First struggles against slavery **1861:** The Civil War begins. **1865:** The war ends and slaves are freed. **1890:** A massacre at Wounded Knee ends the war against Native Americans.	**1842:** The city of Sydney was founded at the Sydney Cove Colony. **1851:** Gold was found in Victoria and the Australian Gold Rush began. **1869:** Aboriginal children were first taken away from their families by government officials. **1879:** The Royal National Park (2nd in the world) was opened south of Sydney.	19th century
1917–1918: About 116,000 US soldiers die in World War I. **1920–1933:** Prohibition: Alcohol is forbidden all over the US. **1931:** The Empire State Building is completed. **1941:** Japan attacks Pearl Harbour and Germany declares war on the US. **1963:** Martin Luther King gives his famous speech "I have a dream". **1968:** King is shot in Memphis.	**1908:** The capital, Canberra, was founded. **1915–1918:** Australia sent many thousands of soldiers to Europe to fight for Britain. Over 60,000 died and more than 160,000 were wounded. **1919:** Australia became independent of Britain. **1942:** The first modern road train was used. **1948–1975:** Two million immigrants arrived in Australia. **1951:** The School of the Air started. **1970:** Aboriginal children were removed from their families for the last time. **1975:** The Great Barrier Reef Marine Park opened.	20th century
2001: On September 11th the Pentagon and the World Trade Center in New York are attacked. 3000 people die. **2003:** The US starts a war against Iraq. **2009:** Barack Obama becomes the first Black president.	**2000:** The Summer Olympics took place. **2008:** On February 13th the Australian Prime Minister apologised to Aborigines for the 'Stolen Generations'.	21st century

The British system = A parliamentary democracy

The United Kingdom has two branches of government. Parliament controls the Monarchy.

The Monarchy (King or queen) *hereditary*

Duties
- open and close Parliament
- sign laws + treaties made by parliament
- declare war if parliament decides it
- must follow the wishes of Parliament
- cannot enter the House of Commons

Rights
- cannot be put in prison
- doesn't need a driving licence

Head of State *hereditary*

Duties
- represent[1] the state
- appoint the PM, Cabinet Ministers[2] and other officials (e.g. judges, officers in the army[3], …)
- must follow instructions from PM / government

Rights
- must be informed about Cabinet decisions[4]

Parliament

elected by people

Parties[5]*=* *Labour, Conservative, Liberal, Democrats, …*

House of Commons (646 members)

House of Lords (about 740 members) *hereditary or appointed by government*

Duties
- debate policy, laws and treaties

Rights
- can make or reject laws and treaties
- can decide to go to war
- can reject PM

Government

elected by majority[6] *party*

Head of Government Prime Minister

Duties
- choose Cabinet Ministers
- lead the Cabinet (PM + Ministers) meetings
- control the Civil Service[7]
- inform and instruct the Queen

Rights
- can dismiss Cabinet ministers

Cabinet Ministers *appointed by PM*

Duties
- make policy
- draw up treaties and bills
- control ministries[8]

The American system = A constitutional democracy

The United States of America has three branches of government. Each controls the other two.

Congress

Senate (100 Senators: 2 from each state)

House of Representatives (435 Congressmen/women)

- can impeach[9] and remove the President.
- may ignore[10] the President's veto.
- The Senate approves the appointment[11] of members of Supreme Court.
- The Senate approves treaties made by President.

The President
- controls foreign policy and makes treaties.
- may veto laws made by Congress.
- can recommend laws.
- appoints members of the Supreme Court.

The Supreme Court
- watches over the Constitution and interprets the laws.
- can call laws made by Congress unconstitutional.
- can call the President's decisions unconstitutional.

The people
- elect a President for four years.
- elect Senators for six years.
- elect one third of Representatives every two years.

Do you agree with these statements? Give reasons for your answer.

1. *All British people love the Queen.*
2. *The American President is the most powerful man in the world.*

[1]to represent [ˌreprɪ'zent] – *repräsentieren,* [2]Minister ['mɪnɪstər] – *Minster/-in,* [3]army ['ɑ:mi] – *Armee,* [4]decision [dɪ'sɪʒən] – *Entscheidung,* [5]party [pɑ:ti] – *Partei,* [6]majority [mə'dʒɒrəti] – *Mehrheit,* [7]Civil Service ['sɪvəl'sɜ:vɪs] – *Staatsdienst,* [8]ministry ['mɪnɪstri] – *Ministerium,* [9]to impeach so. [ɪm'pi:tʃ] – *jdn. seines Amtes entheben,* [10]to ignore [ɪg'nɔ:r] – *ignorieren,* [11]to approve the appointment [ə'pru:v ˌði: ə'pɔɪntmənt] – *eine Ernennung anerkennen*

Textquellennachweis

S. 22: Our Language, Ourselves © Alexina Kublu, Mick Mallon. Any changes/additions/adjustments made to be vetted and approved by the authors prior to reprinting.
S. 36–37: BBC MMVIII © http://news.bbc.co.uk/2/hi/programmes/from_our_own_correspondent/7048652.stm
S. 34–35: TUC 1997, 2001, 2003, 2006 © http://excellence.qia.org.uk/media/doc/YoungApprentice.doc
S. 44–49: On the rocks from the novel "Snakehead" © Snakehead, ISBN: 978-1-4063-1039-9, Text © 2007, 2008 Stormbreaker Productions Ltd
S. 55: Roger McGough © taken from Feeling the Pressure, the Poetry & Science of Climate Change, to be published by the British Council in 2008
S. 56: © IRIN
S. 56: Lucy Hooker © BBC MMIX
S. 56: © Guardian News and Media, http://www.guardian.co.uk/environment/2008/sep/02/alternativeenergy.solarpower
S. 58: © BBC MMVIII
S. 59: © ESRC Research Group on Lifestyles, Values and Environment (RESOLVE), University of Surrey
S. 59: © 2008 Associated Newspapers Ltd
S. 60: © Tourism Queensland, 2009
S. 61: © The Guardian 2006
S. 71: © Crown copyright
S. 72: © Sean Covey: Adapted from The 6 Most Important Decisions You'll Ever Make by Sean Covey, Simon & Schuster, 2006
S. 76–79: Before I Die: Jenny Downham © Random House Group Company (ISBN 978-0-552-77462-8)
S. 88-89: adapted from Larry Fondation "Deportation at Breakfast" © 1991 Larry Fondation, Leaping Dog Press/Asylum Arts
S. 104: Slumdog Millionär © www.kinocritics.com/film_review
S. 105: Barack Obama´s election victory brings a new dawn of leadership - Jonathan Freedland in Chicago © http://www.guardian.co.uk/world/2008/nov/05/obama-victory-chicago-new-era

Bildquellennachweis

Cover 1 Avenue Images GmbH (Digital Vision), Hamburg; **4.1** iStockphoto (Lise Gagne), Calgary, Alberta; **4.2** Imago, Berlin; **4.3** shutterstock (Martine Oger), New York, NY; **4.5** Alamy Images (SCOTT WOLFE), Abingdon, Oxon; **4.6; 4.12** Avenue Images GmbH RF (Corbis RF), Hamburg; **4.8** iStockphoto (FotoVoyager), Calgary, Alberta; **4.9** Geoatlas, Hendaye; **4.10** iStockphoto (Eliza Snow), Calgary, Alberta; **4.11** iStockphoto (Kiyyah), Calgary, Alberta; **4.13** iStockphoto (Deejpilot), Calgary, Alberta; **4.14** shutterstock (Debra James), New York, NY; **4.15** iStockphoto (Dalton00), Calgary, Alberta; **4.16** iStockphoto (Digital planet design), Calgary, Alberta; **4.18** iStockphoto (Annarki), Calgary, Alberta; **4.19** iStockphoto (Claylib), Calgary, Alberta; **4.20** iStockphoto (Bodhi hill illustration), Calgary, Alberta; **8.1** Getty Images, München; **9.1** Das Fotoarchiv, Essen; **9.2** Getty Images (Gallo Images/Getty Images), München; **9.3** Alamy Images (Martin Berry/Alamy), Abingdon, Oxon; **9.4** Imago, Berlin; **10.1** Corbis (Stephanie Weiler/zefa), Düsseldorf; **10.2** Fotosearch Stock Photography (Stockbyte), Waukesha, WI; **10.3** Harper Collins Publishers (2006, B K Mahal), New York, N. Y. 10022-5299; **11.1** Corbis (Christopher Morris), Düsseldorf; **11.2** laif (B.&C. Alexander/Arcticphoto), Köln; **11.3** Klett-Archiv (Hamida Aziz), Stuttgart; **11.4** Koterba, Jeff, Omaha, NE; **12.1** iStockphoto (Alexander Hafemann), Calgary, Alberta; **12.2** iStockphoto (Jane norton), Calgary, Alberta; **12.3** iStockphoto (Lise Gagne), Calgary, Alberta; **12.4** iStockphoto (Huchen Lu), Calgary, Alberta; **12.5** iStockphoto (Marko Radunovic), Calgary, Alberta; **13.1** shutterstock (Robert F. Balazik), New York, NY; **14.1** Alamy Images (Steve Skjold), Abingdon, Oxon; **14.2** iStockphoto (Richard Baird), Calgary, Alberta; **16.1** Getty Images, München; **16.2** Corbis (Granger Wootz/Blend Images), Düsseldorf; **17.1** Corbis (Sophie Elbaz/Sygma/Corbis), Düsseldorf; **17.2** Alamy Images (SCOTT WOLFE), Abingdon, Oxon; **18.2** iStockphoto (Huchen Lu), Calgary, Alberta; **18.3** JupiterImages photos.com, Tucson, AZ; **19.1** JupiterImages photos.com, Tucson, AZ; **20.1** iStockphoto (Matthew Pullicino), Calgary, Alberta; **21.1** iStockphoto (Jacob Wackerhausen), Calgary, Alberta; **21.2** iStockphoto (Jeffrey Smith), Calgary, Alberta; **21.3** shutterstock (WizData, inc.), New York, NY; **21.4** iStockphoto (Sean Locke), Calgary, Alberta; **22.1** Corbis (Marilyn Angel Wynn/Nativestock Pictures/Corbi), Düsseldorf; **22.2** shutterstock (Martine Oger), New York, NY; **24.1** shutterstock (Marcel Jancovic), New York, NY; **24.2** iStockphoto (Wsmahar), Calgary, Alberta; **24.3** shutterstock (Inger Anne Hulbækdal), New York, NY; **24.4** creativ collection Verlag GmbH, Freiburg; **25.1** iStockphoto (CENTAURIA), Calgary, Alberta; **26.1** Das Fotoarchiv, Essen; **26.2; 26.5** JupiterImages photos.com, Tucson, AZ; **26.3** iStockphoto (Marianna Bettini), Calgary, Alberta; **26.4** iStockphoto (Eliza Snow), Calgary, Alberta; **26.6** Avenue Images GmbH RF (Corbis RF), Hamburg; **27.1** Getty Images (Rob Griffith-POOL/Getty Images), München; **27.2** Corbis (Les Stone/Sygma/Corbis), Düsseldorf; **27.3** Alamy Images (TNT Magazine/Alamy), Abingdon, Oxon; **27.4** Alamy Images (Eddie Gerald), Abingdon, Oxon; **28.1** JupiterImages photos.com (RF/photos.com), Tucson, AZ; **28.2** Bridgeman Art Library Ltd. (Roy 2 B VII f.78 Reaping corn harvest in August, from the Queen Mary Psalter, c.1310-20 (vellum) by English School (14th century) British Library, London, UK/© British Library Board. All Rights Reserved), Berlin; **29.1** Getty Images (BBC via Getty Images), München; **29.2** www.cartoonstock.com (Jerry King), Bath; **29.2** iStockphoto (FotoVoyager), Calgary, Alberta; **29.3** www.cartoonstock.com (Mike Baldwin/Cornered), Bath; **32.1** Ullstein Bild GmbH (iT), Berlin; **33.1; 33.2** Wikimedia Foundation Inc., St. Petersburg FL; **33.3** Corbis (Brooks Kraft), Düsseldorf; **34.1** iStockphoto (O'Luk), Calgary, Alberta; **34.2** Corbis (Ariel Skelley/CORBIS), Düsseldorf; **34.5** JupiterImages photos.com, Tucson, AZ; **34.6** iStockphoto (Mosquito), Calgary, Alberta; **34.8; 34.3_1; 34.4_1; 34.4_2** iStockphoto (Zak), Calgary, Alberta; **34.8** iStockphoto (appleuzr), Calgary, Alberta; **34.2_1** iStockphoto (Andres), Calgary, Alberta; **34.2_2** iStockphoto (Monolinea), Calgary, Alberta; **34.3_2** iStockphoto (David Safanda), Calgary, Alberta; **34.7_1** iStockphoto (Marko Radunovic), Calgary, Alberta; **36.1** Getty Images (Getty Image), München; **36.2** Geoatlas, Hendaye; **37.1** Getty Images (Abid Katib/Getty Images), München; **38.1** iStockphoto (dumayne), Calgary, Alberta; **38.2** iStockphoto (RF), Calgary, Alberta; **39.1** iStockphoto (Cstar Enterprises LLC), Calgary, Alberta; **39.2** iStockphoto (Ryan J. Lane), Calgary, Alberta; **39.3** iStockphoto (Adventure Photo), Calgary, Alberta; **39.4** iStockphoto (Tillsonburg), Calgary, Alberta; **40.1** Ullstein Bild GmbH (Lineair), Berlin; **42.1** Corbis (Andy Aitchison), Düsseldorf; **43** Alamy Images (somewhere else), Abingdon, Oxon; **44.1** Cover design © 2007 Walker Books Ltd., Boy with torch Logo & Alex Rider & © 2007 Stormbreaker Productions Ltd., Reproduced by permission of Walker Books Ltd, London SE11 5HJ; **44.2** iStockphoto (PeteC77), Calgary, Alberta; **50.1** Corbis (Inspirestock/Corbis), Düsseldorf; **50.2** Alamy Images (Ashley Cooper), Abingdon, Oxon; **51.3** Alamy Images (Janine Wiedel), Abingdon, Oxon; **51.4** iStockphoto (Klaas Lingbeek-van Kranen), Calgary, Alberta; **51.5** Alamy Images (Chad Ehlers/Alamy), Abingdon, Oxon; **51.6** Alamy Images (Keith Morris), Abingdon, Oxon; **52.1** iStockphoto (Eliandric), Calgary, Alberta; **52.2** www.cartoonstock.com (Grizelda), Bath; **53.1** JupiterImages photos.com, Tucson, AZ; **53.2** MEV Verlag GmbH, Augsburg; **53.3** iStockphoto (YinYang), Calgary, Alberta; **53.4** Alamy Images (Foodfolio), Abingdon, Oxon; **53.5** iStockphoto (Roman Chmiel), Calgary, Alberta; **53.6** iStockphoto (Redmal), Calgary, Alberta; **53.7** iStockphoto (Airyelf), Calgary, Alberta; **54.1** iStockphoto (Monolinea), Calgary, Alberta; **54.2** iStockphoto (Ivanmateev), Calgary, Alberta; **54.2** iStockphoto (kemie), Calgary, Alberta; **55.1** iStockphoto (Blueclue), Calgary, Alberta; **55.2** iStockphoto (Konradlew), Calgary, Alberta; **55.3** iStockphoto (Sven & Manuela), Calgary, Alberta; **55.4** iStockphoto (Kiyyah), Calgary, Alberta; **55.5** iStockphoto (InkkStudios), Calgary, Alberta; **55.6** iStockphoto (Dalton00), Calgary, Alberta; **56.2** Corbis (Louise Gubb/Corbis), Düsseldorf; **56.5** Corbis (Stringer/ Reuters/Corbis), Düsseldorf; **57.1** The New Press (first published 2002, Empire Design Studio NYC: The Fight to Stop the Corporate Theft of the World¿s Water by Maude Barlow and Tony Clarke), New York; **58** iStockphoto (Deejpilot), Calgary, Alberta; **58** A1PIX (DUC), Taufkirchen; **58.3** JupiterImages photos.com, Tucson, AZ; **60.1** iStockphoto (HooRoo Graphics), Calgary, Alberta; **60.2** shutterstock (Debra James), New York, NY; **60.3** shutterstock (Ian Scott), New York, NY; **60.4** iStockphoto (Christian Nasca), Calgary, Alberta; **60.5** iStockphoto (Rainforest Agencies), Calgary, Alberta; **61.1** Alamy

Images (Rainer Unkel/vario images), Abingdon, Oxon; **62.1** JupiterImages photos.com, Tucson, AZ; **62.2** BigStockPhoto.com (jackierae1), Davis, CA; **62.3** iStockphoto (Sean Warren), Calgary, Alberta; **62.4** iStockphoto (Peeter Viisimaa), Calgary, Alberta; **63.1** Alamy Images (Arco Images/Delpho, M.), Abingdon, Oxon; **63.2** shutterstock (John Keith), New York, NY; **63.4** Alamy Images (Paul Doyle), Abingdon, Oxon; **64.1** Vestergaard Frandsen SA, Lausanne; **64.2** Eawag Water and Sanitation in Developing Countries, Dübendorf; **66.1** Unicef/Jung von Matt, Schweden; **66.2** SmartWater Technology Limited (Mario Testino), Shropshire; **67.3** Eawag Water and Sanitation in Developing Countries, Dübendorf; **68.1** Corbis (Walter Lockwood/Corbis), Düsseldorf; **68.2** Alamy Images (UK Stock Images Ltd), Abingdon, Oxon; **69.1** Getty Images (Punchstock), München; **69.3** Alamy Images (Mike Goldwater), Abingdon, Oxon; **69.4** Alamy Images (Janine Wiedel), Abingdon, Oxon; **70** iStockphoto (Bodhi hill illustration), Calgary, Alberta; **70.1** The Random House Group Limited, London; **71.1** iStockphoto (Resonants), Calgary, Alberta; **71.2** iStockphoto (Mark Stay), Calgary, Alberta; **71.3** iStockphoto (Images Unlimited), Calgary, Alberta; **71.4** iStockphoto (Annarki), Calgary, Alberta; **74.1** iStockphoto (Wide Angle), Calgary, Alberta; **74.2** iStockphoto (Claylib), Calgary, Alberta; **74.3** iStockphoto (EasyBuy4u), Calgary, Alberta; **75.1** iStockphoto (Digital planet design), Calgary, Alberta; **76.1** iStockphoto (Biliana), Calgary, Alberta; **76.2** iStockphoto (Eyecrave LLC), Calgary, Alberta; **77.1** iStockphoto (Jeridu), Calgary, Alberta; **77.2** iStockphoto (Zande Basenjis), Calgary, Alberta; **77.3** iStockphoto (Fluxfoto), Calgary, Alberta; **79.1** Okapia (Hans Reinhard), Frankfurt; **79.2** iStockphoto (Pailoolom), Calgary, Alberta; **79.3** Reinhard-Tierfoto, Heiligkreuzsteinach; **82.1** iStockphoto (Jordi Delgado), Calgary, Alberta; **82.2** www.cartoonstock.com (Fran), Bath; **84.1** Alamy Images (imagebroker/Alamy), Abingdon, Oxon; **84.2** iStockphoto (Nikita Buida), Calgary, Alberta; **84.3** shutterstock (Serg Zastavkin), New York, NY; **84.4** shutterstock (Serhiy Kyrychenko), New York, NY; **85.1** iStockphoto (Btrenkel), Calgary, Alberta; **86.1** Corbis RF (Corbis), Düsseldorf; **86.2** Corbis (Richard Cummins/CORBIS), Düsseldorf; **86.3** iStockphoto (Bryan Faust Photography), Calgary, Alberta; **86.4** Alamy Images (Pictures Colour Library), Abingdon, Oxon; **87.1** Photographic service of the Council of the EU © Eu, Bruxelles; **87.2** Photographic service of the Council of the EU © European Communities; **89.1** Alamy Images (Janine Wiedel Photolibrary), Abingdon, Oxon; **89.2** Fotosearch Stock Photography (Image Source RF), Waukesha, WI; **89.3** Corbis (Lowell Georgia), Düsseldorf; **104.1** Alamy Images (Archives du 7eme Art), Abingdon, Oxon; **106.1** Kessler-Medien, Saarbrücken; **106.2** iStockphoto (Kryczka), Calgary, Alberta; **123** iStockphoto (Klikk), Calgary, Alberta; **124.1** shutterstock (Henrik Andersen), New York, NY; **124.2** iStockphoto (Birgitte Magnus), Calgary, Alberta; **124.3** shutterstock (Vladimir Daragan), New York, NY; **124.4** iStockphoto (tomazl.sopca.com), Calgary, Alberta; **124.5** shutterstock (Supertrooper), New York, NY; **124.6** shutterstock (Jason Stitt), New York, NY; **125.1** iStockphoto (Jacus), Calgary, Alberta; **126.1** shutterstock (Galina Barskaya), New York, NY; **126.2** Avenue Images GmbH RF (Brand X Pictures), Hamburg; **126.3** iStockphoto (Pidjoe), Calgary, Alberta; **126.4** iStockphoto (Olaf Bender), Calgary, Alberta; **126.5** iStockphoto (PeskyMonkey), Calgary, Alberta; **126.6** iStockphoto (Abalcazar), Calgary, Alberta; **126.7** iStockphoto (Alex Nikada), Calgary, Alberta; **127.1** iStockphoto (Pkfawcett), Calgary, Alberta; **128.1** Bananastock, Watlington/Oxon; **129.1** iStockphoto (Videowok), Calgary, Alberta; **129.1** iStockphoto (Constance McGuire), Calgary, Alberta; **129.2** iStockphoto (Duncan1890), Calgary, Alberta; **129.3** Alamy Images (Mary Evans Picture Library), Abingdon, Oxon; **129.4** iStockphoto (Joel Blit), Calgary, Alberta; **129.5** iStockphoto (HultonArchive), Calgary, Alberta; **129.6** Corbis (Bettmann/CORBIS), Düsseldorf; **131.1** iStockphoto (RichVintage), Calgary, Alberta; **137.Vokbox 1.1** shutterstock (Robert F. Balazik), New York, NY; **146.Vokbox 2.1** Ingram Publishing, Tattenhall Chester; **156.Vokbox 3.1** iStockphoto (Dieter Hawlan), Calgary, Alberta; **165.Vokbox 4.1** Fotolia LLC (RF/Yuri Arcurs), New York 282.1; **282.2; 283.1; 283.2** Dream Maker Software (RF), Colorado; **284.1** Fotosearch Stock Photography (Brand X Pictures), Waukesha, WI; **284.2; 284.3** MEV Verlag GmbH, Augsburg; **284.4** Getty Images RF (Photodisc), München; **hinterer Vorsatz.1** Perthes World Atlas, 2nd Printing 2009, Revised, p. 78-79, Gotha 2006

Sollte es in einem Einzelfall nicht gelungen sein, den korrekten Rechteinhaber ausfindig zu machen, so werden berechtigte Ansprüche selbstverständlich im Rahmen der üblichen Regelungen abgegolten.

Canada: Political